Blurbs and reviews of the
1996 precursor text to
New Moon: A Coming of Age Tale

"At once a memoir, an account of psychoanalysis, and a both savage and loving account of New York in the '50s, *New Moon* is a work with many layers and a unique tone, reminiscent of Robert Musil's *A Man Without Qualities* in its blend of analytical realism, melancholia, and acute psychoanalytic and philosophical penetration."

—Andrew Harvey, author of *The Divine Feminine: Exploring the Feminine Face of God Throughout the World*

"A strange and remarkable self-evaluation in the form of a novel—illuminating, tender, moving, evocative … any number of adjectives of praise would be appropriate."

—George Plimpton, author of *Out of My League*

"A fascinating self-portrait of the youth of one of our most profound and rebellious thinkers, told with a deceptive simplicity that is capable of shifting at any moment into the haunted resonance of a fairy tale, and in a language so nakedly honest it is never more than one step away from tenderness."

—Gerald Rosen, author of *The Carmen Miranda Memorial Flagpole*

"Indeed, some readers are going to rank this memoir of baseball, summer camp, Latin classes, domestic terrors, and enchanted moments at Grossinger's as a spiritual quest in the tradition of Blake, Emerson, and … James Agee...."

—Mike Harris, *Los Angeles Times*

"Richard Grossinger tells me who he is, so he shows me who I am."

—Joy Manné, author of *Soul Therapy*

"... skillfully evokes the world of '50s New York and Grossinger's Catskills as well as the counterculture of the '60s...."

—*Publishers Weekly*

"*New Moon* is something new under the sun, a real psychoanalytic autobiography."

—*Psychoanalytic Books: A Quarterly Journal of Reviews*

New Moon

—A Coming-of-Age Tale—

RICHARD GROSSINGER

North Atlantic Books
Berkeley, California

Published by
North Atlantic Books
Berkeley, California

Cover art by James Rauchman
Cover and book design by Jasmine Hromjak
Printed in the United States of America

New Moon: A Coming-of-Age Tale, is sponsored and published by the Society for the Study of Native Arts and Sciences (dba North Atlantic Books), an educational nonprofit based in Berkeley, California, that collaborates with partners to develop cross-cultural perspectives, nurture holistic views of art, science, the humanities, and healing, and seed personal and global transformation by publishing work on the relationship of body, spirit, and nature.

North Atlantic Books' publications are available through most bookstores. For further information, visit our website at www.northatlanticbooks.com or call 800-733-3000.

The Library of Congress has catalogued the first edition as follows:

Library of Congress Cataloging-in-Publication Data
Grossinger, Richard, 1944–
New moon : a memoir / Richard Grossinger.
p. cm.
ISBN-13: 978–1–58394–985–6
ISBN 1–883319–44–7
1. Grossinger, Richard, 1944– —Homes and haunts—New York (N.Y.)
2. Authors, American—20th century—Family relationships. 3. Grossinger, Richard, 1944– —Childhood and youth. 4. New York (N.Y.)—Social life and customs. 5. Grossinger, Richard, 1944– —Family. 6. Resorts—New York (State)—Ferndale. 7. The Grossinger, Ferndale, N.Y. I. Title.
PS3557.R66Z468 1966
813'.54—dc20   96-2106
CIP

1 2 3 4 5 6 7 8 9 UNITED 21 20 19 18 17 16

Printed on recycled paper

This book is for my daughter Miranda

Dedicated in 1987 when she was thirteen

CONTENTS

SEA WALL

Life is as fathomless at its alpha point as in mementos of yesterday. We seem to ourselves much like the universe: originless, sealed by walls of gravity, light, and space-time, or by the innate warp of beingness. Reality is a construct, but of what? We matriculate from an egg, a chrysalis, on a planet lassoed to a star in a void of inexplicable nature and proportions. Even that is circumstantial. Our existence could be any number of things.

For a place of so much light, for such a glistening, intaglioed husk, this world is a hoax. Only its appearance is bright, its surfaces and subsurfaces. Otherwise, we live among shadows on a darkling plain.

Memories define us because they lie along the thread that recognizes us as ourselves. At the same time, we sense the background of everything we *don't* remember and in most cases never experienced, which is many times greater and constitutes the fabric of existence.

I can even vaguely remember a time before any of this existed or had to exist.

We fall too against a screen which, although no longer explicitly astrological and feudal, is just as hierarchic and zodiacal.

Other than a thread spun by heart-lung machines, time is timeless: we are inoculated, like a ghost through a cone, into a mirage. There everything seems to take hours, days, decades; in fact, it's over in a blink: an instantaneity experienced as an eternity. An aquatic mayfly enjoys thirty exquisite minutes in a pond, a creosote bush converts sunlight in a desert for 11,000 years—these are at par. However many times a creature falls asleep and wakes, it lives but a single day, a Great Day rotating about a Great Sun.

As we age, the dot of location erodes. Prior decades fission, wrapping around each other like waterbugs on decaying insects.

Each moment is already eternal. Each moment reverberates forever. Each moment is already obliterated.

PART ONE

THE CHILD IN THE CITY
1944–1956

I

The Beginning Of Time

My oldest memory is of seeing an Easter egg in a bush where branches met at the trunk. I had already found that one, but the man had rehidden it.

I came back clutching it as he laughed.

That chalky blue is anterior to my life. I can touch it still, radiant and unscathed.

But who was that man? Where was there a yard with such a bush?

On the first morning of time Nanny stood in the alcove, grinding oranges. She poured them into a glass decorated with flowers. Orange flooded my mind.

I crawled on a carpet among stuffed chairs. At its end stood bureaus with ivory figurines, flat goblets of colored oil. Golden frames held etchings of long-whiskered dancing men. There I played with rubber farm animals, stuffed clowns and donkey dolls, metal buses, and pearly white schmooes, one inside another inside another. Yarn of treasure balls unravelled into trinkets of tiny plastic airplanes and jeweled rings. My mind was a quandary of voices. I was no one in particular. The adults kept saying, *"Open the door... Riiich-ard!"*

Photographs of the time show sedans on streets, people in shaggy coats. I can't believe I was young so long ago. Those were the Christmas trees and frosted bulbs of the 1940s. Every toy was a rough amulet, every button, colored thread, and bundled sweet an art and craft. Snow was a wild thing.

Nanny slept in a corner of my room. She dressed me, made my food, put me down for nap, bathed me. She was a witch who loved me but a witch all the same.

In the afternoon I lay in my crib, waiting for her to come fetch me. I explored the contours of my chest and legs. Knees, feet, and elbows thrashed, snagged at sheets.

Along the crack between ceiling and wall I glimpsed the portal, the juncture between life and everything else. I still see that line: the same mis-assignment of coordinates, the same impervious crevice to another couloir. String theory approaches the possibility: universes tucked inside fibers, one in another in another. A child feels only enormity, immanence, danger.

I chased my balls in their lining. I rubbed sore the light in my eyes.

The animals on my quilt were loyal—Zebra and Tiger and Bear. My hands underneath moved them. I caused them to tussle, then make nice, as I tossed up the covers around me, pressing them into each other in friendship, until I rolled into sleep.

… awoke babbling … the room drained to purple, the opera singer practicing in the courtyard, her trills echoing throughout my mind.

I imagined her later as the lady on the cover of a record whose name began with the impossible letters "Xt….," a songstress with hands held upward as if trying to stop something horrible from happening—gold shells on her forehead and dangling from her face and body, eyes staring blindly outward; a stone god breathing on her from above, another behind her. ("Voice of Xtaby" was the Capital Release of Peruvian soprano Yma Sumac, made famous by her vocal range. But throughout Mesoamerica "Xtaby" meant "Female Ensnarer," a demon who seduced and killed.)

After nap I helped Nanny make dinner, pulling limas from their spongy shells, plunking the beans into a pot, delighting in the pings. Scent of turnips, carrots, and pot roast enveloped the kitchen.

After dinner, after playtime Nanny cuddled me in bed. Then I slipped into my own shadows. Then another morning began another day.

Daddy wore brown suits and beat-up felt hats, smoked a cigarette and chanted in Hebrew, *Anakhnu modim ....*" and *"Shama Yisra-el."* He also sang, *"Old Man River, that Old Man River.... "*

I remember waiting the whole afternoon to see him again, breaking loose of Nanny, who regarded him with suspicion and held me back ... running down the hall and throwing my arms around him as he came through the front door. It was the longest I had stayed on my feet without toppling, and I tumbled into his embrace. In great surprise he exclaimed and hoisted me in the air. At least he smelled of other worlds and not our charnel home.

One evening with the help of his taxi man Daddy carried a large box. He unpacked it, pulled off papers and tossed them on the floor. It was a victrola. He took a large black disk from an envelope. He set it on the machine's spinning platform and lowered a metal arm into sound: *"Oh where have you gone Billy boy, Billy boy?"* Then ... *"Cruising down the river / on a Sunday afternoon ..."*

Those melodies join this world to another; all you need do is change their syllables to a language of Toliman or the Pleiades, which are not so different as you might think.

In retrospect I don't see (nor did I then) any ordinary river but, from a 45 degree angle, a cobblestone canal, its banks swarming with adults at carnival. Through a gap in notes of the song swims a giant turtle.

Billy emerged from the mists of a bog forest, suspenders holding up his farmer's pants: *"Oh where have you gone, charming Billy?"* In the minor chord between "charming" and "Billy" lay a blankness, a hiatus where hearts beat but minds could not go.

"It was a horrible experience," my mother recounted. "It almost killed me. You were black and blue. I was covered with blood. He used forceps." The word itself conjured implacable machinery, as if the doctor had plied a pillory and heretic's fork to get me out of her. "You were screaming so—I thought you were dying."

That was *her* story. I have had (all my life) a recurrent dream: an elevator in a hospital, very old, long ago. Unseen, I visit her in her room and wait, expectant in darkness as in a theater. (In later years my wife is there instead, about to have our son. These epochal events merge and I am witness to both as one.)

I have no name for this dream; it is just "the feeling." Words give pale approximations: "homesick" ... *"déjà vu"* ... "alien" ... "acrid." The sense of premonition is inescapable: footsteps approaching ... I feel I cannot prevent calamity.

And yet I have waited beyond time for this being's appearance, long after my children were born and had grown into adults.

Even now I wander in a labyrinth of births of children and old men dying.

At other times I have discovered, in that same room, a jungle of orchids, a fountain bursting through the floor, exotic species of water blossoms and long-extinct sea animals quivering in shells—in short, an interstellar laboratory.

I have dreamed that it was not my mother in the room at all. A replica lay in bed in her place, just as tall as her, just as red lips and black hair. She had Martha's appearance and gestures. She spoke exactly as my mother spoke. She knew everything about me my mother did.

Then a doctor came from nowhere and attacked me with his knife. I felt his hard, grimy body, stinking of medicines. I fought him off but awoke with the scar of his strike just above my Adam's apple. And glimpses of a fleeing intruder.

Other times I cannot find my mother's room, so keep returning to crowded elevators; I take them up higher and higher, hundreds of storeys through decorated corridors and ballrooms, each filled with weddings and celebrations.

Our apartment was at 1220 Park Avenue on the corner of 95th, a block before the train shot out of the ground, turning the landscape squalid. Buildings became blackened caves. On our side of 96th doormen guarded entrances to castles that grew more magnificent and fancier as they progressed downtown.

Sometimes wind along the Avenue rattled our windows behind closed drapes, but never so fiercely as during the hurricane. Mommy was giddy in preparation, making phone calls, ordering food, warning me to keep back from the glass.

Sky blackened. Rain splattered the pavement. Daddy put on an overcoat and scarf, the door slamming behind him. He ran down the street to pick up groceries. As he worked his way back he held onto lampposts to keep from being blown away.

Despite Mommy's admonitions, I peeked. I saw a man stuck at the corner, his umbrella turned inside out. Sheets of paper danced through air; boreal spirits rapped harder and harder on the glass, but it didn't break.

I kept to the center of the room, filling my scrapbook with cars and trucks from magazines, cutting around tires and bumpers and sticking them two to a page from a jar of white glue.

Mommy was a perfume demon with dark piercing eyes. At bedtime I pulled back from her Noxzema kisses, but she grabbed me, forcing affection, eyes trapping, red nails sharp on my arms till I made a kiss back. "Don't you love me?" she insisted.

How could I not?

I took her hand down 96th Street. In an indoor garden, orchid mist scented the air. It was a fairy tale: many-colored blossoms, fragrant dew. She commanded the proprietor in a strong but persuasive voice until he brought single blooms from his refrigerator. These he tied in a bunch and wrapped in colored tissue. At home she arranged them with brusque hands in a purple (almost black) vase.

Sometimes Mommy screamed, pounded at walls, and ran from room to room. I heard her whimpers, doors slamming, then muffled sobs. Daddy tried to cajole her, but his appeals brought only ghostlike howls.

She shrieked a demonic word. "Don't get hysterical, Martha," he pleaded.

Cancer wasn't just a malignancy, a monster that turned you into a cadaver; the very sound of it released dreaded meanings. When I learned to read, I found it secretly lurking behind "candy" and "canary" and "Canada" until I could see the rest of their letters.

Dr. Hitzig was called—a fat goblin in a black suit. In her nightclothes Mommy ran down the hall to meet him. With a magisterial hand he patted her shoulders and settled her shudders. "You don't

have anything," he said, "but an unstable constitution and an over-
active imagination." He turned to Daddy, "Codliver oil and honey.
No heavy meals. Four times a week chicken soup."

It wasn't death we feared but a spookier thing that went by its
name. What made it so horrible was that no one knew what it was,
when it was coming, or what would happen to us when it did. We
were on constant alert.

Mommy knew that we were in danger. She sniffed stuff in cans
and jars for venoms meant to get us. She found fungus on mar-
malade, though it was a fleck of butter from the knife. She kept
scrubbing tabletops, sinks, toilet seats. Everything was suspect, ripening with something else.

Most people were our enemies. It didn't matter that we pretended
to like them. Even Dr. Hitzig was bad.

I was playing submarine in my bath when dark rust spurted out its
seams. I could feel the contamination spreading, touching me. I pushed
it away and leaped from the tub. I ran naked down the hall. Nanny
caught me, wrapped me in towels, held me till my shaking stopped.

One morning Mommy was gone. She stayed away a long time. Nanny
told me she would return with a baby. When I realized another of
us was coming I saved a favorite stuffed animal, a bear for him, and
was hurt that he didn't take it from me when I held it up as he was
rushed past in his blanket. His name was Jonathan; he was placed on
the other side of my room, a china bug whimpering and bawling.

Everything was proceeding according to plan.

I planned to hide this brother behind a chair, teach him my words,
and surprise everyone with a talking baby at dinner.

Pushing the carriage with my brother, Nanny took me to the playground. I mastered the little slide and gradually got up courage for
the big one. I climbed the stairs and sat at the top. A line of kids
collected behind me. They shouted Go! I flew down the chute. I
came to my feet and ran into Nanny's arms.

She put me in the sandbox, telling me to be careful of other kids'
peeing. I rolled in granules, pressing my cheeks against the moist

fuzziness. They were a cake, not quite baking. I dug marbles out of dirt, tiny planets emblazoned with smoke. I was burrowing with my nails, making a cave-world when Nanny stood me up and brushed me off.

We walked through the park. I followed squirrels stopping and starting along the bushes, running up and down bark. When I saw the wagon man, I begged Nanny to buy nuts. She agreed, as long as I didn't sneak any for myself. "Peanuts are poison," she said.

A sweet odor rose from a small heated bag, elephants drawn on its sides, top pleated and tucked. Unwrapping its folds, I tiptoed through the grove, coaxing fluffytails from afar, tossing a treat at a time as they took the shells in their paws, transferred them to their mouths, scooted away to eat or bury them. I would hold different squirrels in my mind, tracking their progress, regretting their departure if they hadn't gotten any. When the bag was empty I tried without success to get them interested in spiny brown balls that lay under trees. Then Nanny summoned me on.

As we passed the Museum, I wandered in a garden of white stones, hundreds of smooth ones all around, an unguarded treasure. Clouds roared overhead like pirate ships. Mica sparkled silver. A witch in a black coat spread bread and corn pellets from her purse, yellow and orange gems, crumbs and bits of old rolls. Pigeons flocked, so many wings she seemed to be growing them from her coat. I tugged on Nanny to go.

We walked along Madison. Its streets were filled with characters, their perfumes mingling with vapors of shops, fruits and vegetables set on boxes, air conditioners dripping, hot grills blown by fans. Each store had its signature—a bubblegum of toys, a frosty cavern of roses, a cookie circus with amulets of sparkling sugar and chocolate rings, a restaurant puffing charcoal from a grate.

Nanny asked my help in pressing Jonathan's carriage up the steps through the door. I hurried to be good.

I used to get lost. These episodes have a quality of wandering beyond the world. In the original such adventure I strayed from Nanny,

who was reading a book as her foot rocked the carriage, to a spot I
later recognized as 99th Street by Fifth Avenue. As I proceeded in
my trance, I was astonished suddenly to find the sidewalk rippled.
I had assumed all pavement was smooth.

I came to an atrium of tulips about a silver orb, the reflection of
a child passing through an asterisk of light. Flowers stretched above
me like trees.

This was the lost garden, its goblets of watercolors.

I waited there, outside the flow of time.

Then Nanny came with a policeman.

The summer of 1949, our Oldsmobile piled with suitcases, Daddy
took us to a house in Westport and returned to the city to work.
Everywhere trees surrounded houses.

I lay in grass and the purple flowers. I stared at swooping birds.
Wind stampeded branches against a blue canopy, each leafy ripple
singing "Cruising Down the River."

I tracked fuzzy caterpillars on twigs and watched processions of
ant armies into and out of their castles. I played trucks and cars on
the pavement, found buried marbles, peeled and sharpened sticks
into white arrows and made bows with twigs and string. I drew fat
boys and girls on the sidewalk with colored chalk sticks.

It was a summer of lime and strawberry jellos, packages of pineapple charms and peppermint rings with holes, bells of the Good
Humor truck, black raspberry coated in thin, cold chocolate. I
watched a lemon and cherry world through lollipop wrappers and
collected prizes and cartoons from the bottom of boxes of wrapped
candy and Cracker Jacks.

With a shovel I dug lines for seeds, then set them in, one by one,
like on the farm in my Little Golden Book. I graded the dirt, and
Nanny and I stamped on it.

One morning, barely visible sprigs had emerged from our furrows.

With his tools a workman in overalls put together a Donald Duck bike
with training wheels. I tore along concrete making up adventures.

"Is Judy there?" I asked her mother standing in front.

The big girls were allowed to take me to the playground and candy store.

"She went to the lake today," her mother said. "Is it important?"

I nodded.

I rode around the block again … and again. Each circuit I checked.

"Judy's still not home."

I pedalled to the corner. I turned and looked down the block, its canopy of trees eerie and portentous. I travelled along its tunnel. I turned the corner again and passed my own house.

Judy was standing in her yard. Her presence startled me; I had not expected her so soon. I tore past on my Donald racer, wolves in pursuit. I heard Judy's mother calling in bewilderment, trying to tell me that Judy was home.

Nanny taught me to pull up weeds in my garden. I felt sorry for the discarded plants, their roots smelling of trolls and dragons. Carrots from the farmer's stand had the same sweet aroma and they weren't poison. I could swallow their rust.

My garden rows had grown into little stalks with nips of fuzzy beans, and I was lying on the ground, face up close, my nose touching, when I heard Mommy's voice.

"Dinner time!"

"It's still sunny," I complained. The world was bathed in pale saffron light.

She poured me a cup from a brown bottle. "The days are getting longer."

I knew that wasn't the answer. I looked suspiciously at the gold apple bubbles, drank them in a gulp. Trees rustled on the horizon. The moon was too large.

I lay in bed. Fading umber prowled the perimeters. I pushed against it with my mind, refusing its luminosity.

I woke to the whine of Nanny making juice, wet PJs matted to my skin.

Daddy came for the weekend. Before I knew he was back, he had mowed my whole bean patch. It was hard to tell there was anything but grass. Mommy had one of her laughing fits. "He's a city boy," she said. "He doesn't know a tomato from an artichoke." Then Daddy got angry at me for crying.

"It's only goddamned string beans. You know how many string beans there are in the world? You want more string beans, I'll buy string beans."

He did in fact return from the store with a huge bagful and dumped them on the table.

At summer's end we went to a Punch and Judy show. Chains of purple lollipops were distributed at the ticket counter, big children directing the crowd. I was sucking my grape when a witch puppet burst in, cackling. My baby brother started crying. Mommy hushed him, but he only got louder, so we ran down the aisle, into a night of more twinkles than I had ever seen. *The stars above, the one I love, / waiting for the moon...."*

Mommy took me and the cousins in an armada of taxis to view one of her favorite alter egos, Mary Martin (as Peter Pan). This was the zenith of the Mommy realm: flying actors, dancing crocodiles, Tinkerbell above a pirate galley. We all cheered for her failing light to be relit.

Another time, Mommy led me silently on the longest walk ever, traipsing determinedly in her chunky black coat into the Park, along paths, through tunnels, past lakes with toy boats.

I had never seen any of these places.

We came to an amazing land—castles, moats, rocky precipices. Its creatures played in cages: porcupines, tortoises, elephants, snakes, flamingos; lions sleeping and snoring, their orange fur going up and down. Bears prowled pale boulders, then splashed in a grotto.

Mommy sat on a bench and read while I watched seals climb onto rocks. I scanned the black eagerly, hoping to spot flutters as they surfaced with comical snorts. Then—she finally said okay—I entered a brick castle by myself. In a screeching room, monkeys dashed about, hung from single arms, made funny faces. I called for her to come. She shook her head and said the smell made her nauseous. I liked its jungleness, so I walked through again, mesmerized by the antics of little beings. When I arrived at the other end, she was waiting in daylight. I reached for her hand.

Sometimes she would seize me on her lap and sing in another language:
    Frère Jaques, Frère Jaques,
    Dormez vous, dormez vous.
"Are you sleeping, are you sleeping?" she insisted of me in a bemused voice.
    Brother Jon, brother Jon.
She pulled my face into hers and rubbed our noses together. Then she swung me scarily outward, letting me drop until my head tilted backwards:
    Bateau, bateau yey,
    O bateau ve san-francez.
I knew what was coming next. Our boat was in a storm. We were going to sink. Were we going to drown?
"Are you going to fall; are you going to fall?" shaking me an extra time and tickling my belly.
Then she shouted, "No!," pulled me back with a rough jerk, and hugged me.
Rescued again!

They held my fifth birthday at our apartment. Mommy insisted we wear silly hats and carry wands of rainbow maché. At each doorbell aunts and uncles arrived with cousins. Jostled among large kids, I tore open wrapping paper to find stuffed animals, trucks, and puzzles.
In a last tiny box (about which Mommy showed unusual interest) was cotton around a barbell-shaped rattle. She said it was real gold and given to me by someone named Irving Berlin. He was a famous man from her world. I ran my fingers across the bumps his name left on the metal.
They brought the dining-room chairs into the living room and set them in a row facing different ways. I couldn't guess the purpose.

Then impish music began. Unexpectedly it stopped. The game was to sit in the chairs first because they took one away each time while the music played. Everyone pushed and shoved hard.

I lost my place and sat by the side while Mommy delighted in her role at the victrola, setting down and raising the needle. A man in a clown suit pulled strings of pastel handkerchiefs out of a tube, and my Uncle Eddie blew balloons and twisted them into animal shapes so rapidly that the room was filled with floating creatures as I ran, slapping them in the air.

Nanny placed a cake with blue frosting and candles in front of me. Mommy held a shining sword. With her weight we came down together through the frosting. Then I filled myself with yellow.

At first I might have seemed to my mother like a generic child. She left my care to Nanny as she passed me in her distractions. Gradually we developed a true antipathy.

A boy inside me was inattentive, stumbling, late. I was never grateful enough. I spilled my plate. I dropped my glass on the floor and it smashed. I fumbled my toothbrush into the toilet.

Mommy punished me with quick, sharp slaps, calling out my blame so shrilly my ears hurt. She grabbed my toys and threw them. She sent me to bed without dinner. She made me sit on a stool facing the wall. Yet I continued to misbehave: toothpaste on my jammies, crayon drawings on the wall, pee in my bedsheets, water on the floor.

Too late I felt the trickle down my legs: the reddest flower germinating in my core, engulfing me like a second skin.

Later it turned into a cold wire fence.

Nanny pulled down my pants and pointed to reddened thighs. "You're going to make yourself sick!"

One morning, playing on Park Avenue, I decided I would ride my fire truck through the bronze plug. I kicked off and rolled its way, then ... a rush of sparkles and pain ... standing outside the door in another body that was screaming, my hand against my head soaked with blood. They called Aunt Dotty, and she came with us to the hospital for stitches, nine of them—ouch! ouch! ouch!

Another time, I decided to leave a surprise when Mommy left her bath running to answer the phone. I got books off her shelves and turned them into boats, setting them one by one on the surface of the water. I was gleeful, proud of myself as I watched them float and sink. I ran away before she could return.

She screamed and called for me. I told her I was washing them for her. Trembling and wild, she whacked me with a hairbrush. "Mischief, mischief," she said. "You're nothing but a big mischief."

She thought I had a disease. She squeezed my chest, felt my neck. When my knee got puffy and swollen, she had me walk back and forth. She detected a limp. She asked Dr. Hitzig about polio, a word I had never heard. He shook his head: "The boy is fine." We both knew that he was lying.

She took me to his friend Dr. Hunt, a brusque, humorless man who handled my body mechanically, drawing on my skin with his crayon, shining a cold tool in my ears and eyes, listening to my chest and tummy through his probe, finally putting me naked on a metal stand and turning out the lights. I huddled there shivering while he made pictures of my insides. Then she and Nanny talked with him in his private room.

As I watched her behind the soundproof window, imploring him, I thought of Santa: *"He's gonna find out if you're naughty or nice...."* I propelled a small wooden train around the floor, wondering if Dr. Hunt had glimpsed the terrible thing inside me. The way Mommy looked at me afterwards I knew it was bad. It had to do with wetting. I had a disease they couldn't see. That's why they were making pictures of my bones.

Daddy sold his yellow Olds and got a green Mercury. Mommy told him to put it in the garage till we had to go somewhere, but he said, "Let me show it off, Martha!" He took us on a ride into the country, but he went too fast and curvy. He and Mommy were yelling at each other. In auto smell and cigarette smoke I tasted orange juice and began to cry. "He's carsick, Bob." I clutched the seat. Everywhere I turned was dizziness. I began to whimper.

Daddy didn't want to stop. His lips were pressed, and he smacked the dashboard. Mommy smiled and teased him.

I stood by the roadside. At my feet in clover was a bee, spreading lavender grains. I didn't care if he was a stinger; his undulating fur and humming filled my mind. Far off in the field, bugs and butterflies floated; orange-black susans shone like elfin pots. I smelled honey. Then car-tasting liquid poured out of me into the dust.

The haunting was the worst, tendrils of poison spreading along my throat and belly, colder than ice. I felt the reverberation of an earlier, more catastrophic thing. But what could that have been?

Then one afternoon Nanny left her radio on in the kitchen and a voice said: "Yet another one fell down the stairs, into the dungeon … forever!"

"… *forever* …!"

I heard it and was stunned that it dared come so close, a child's simple consideration of what a telling meant: *This is real.* And I am in it, *forever.* I felt my mind balk, then the universe come apart, an abyss beyond artifice—obscure, hostile, spreading.

My life sank into infinity against the other. It wouldn't listen. It had never listened. Frosty the Snowman *"… alive as he could be …"* was a mere jingle against the resonance of existence.

Most children would have mocked the voice as dramaturgy of little consequence. A different kid might have thought, "Wow, that was scary!" and writhed in delight. Not me. It wasn't the dungeon per se, which resembled trite threats on television and at the theater: evil vicars, cutthroat pirates, Ming the Merciless. Those were make-believe. But there was a prerogative behind the voice that neither its hack author nor sinister narrator recognized. It expressed something I had always known, a prophecy eking into a vague room in an obscure city, a witch cooking poisons while her chattle waited.

I could pretend to be safe in a family, but camouflage didn't hide me. The smudge on the far horizon wasn't just an inkling; it was *exactly what it looked like.* "They" could come for me at any time, put an end to such paltry protection. They could do anything they wanted, for there was no one to stop them. It was futile to imagine

outrunning them by being alive. Even policemen were cartoon dolls.
"... into the dungeon ... forever!"

Since I couldn't escape or hide, I ran into the hallway and, finding nowhere else to go, writhed in terror, screaming, shivering, stamping in place, socking at anyone who dared console me, tearing away as the vertigo went deeper. It turned into sensations I didn't know even existed.

I didn't understand the sound coming out of me—I was keening.

The adults, not guessing the cause of my jig—not that it would have made any difference if they had—tried to convince and inveigle me. They shouted for me to stop. But they were rote and irrelevant, their yells and histrionics a farce.

They had no idea what I was confronting. My mother, however Xtaby-like, was just a lady. The real danger wasn't a poison or disease. It was *much* worse.

I believe the haunting was primordial and did not occur in language.

Its vigilance is forever.

Its other side was enchantment—green sprinkled cookies and bagpipe parades on Saint Patrick's Day, solid chocolate eggs and coated yellow marshmallow Peeps at Easter, orange and black gingerbread men of Halloween with their raisin buttons. Each of those tastes and colors was a land on a sacred calendar through which I was led in rapture and to which I returned aeons later in the journey of the sun.

My records were yellow circles: shepherds in Bethlehem, a beguiling caterpillar on his mushroom, tinder-box dogs with saucer eyes, loquacious rabbits and frogs—charmed creatures in a medley of songs. In my mind Tweedledum and Tweedledee were chubby decorated ones to whom "God rest ye merry gentlemen" was addressed.

I played among colors of my singing top, fright clown of jack-in-the-box, shaggy mane of rocking horse; making buzzing noises for trucks and trains, blowing a yellow whistle in a sink filled with water so it warbled like the bird perched on it. I set rubber knights on tops of houses amid plastic trees, wedged Indians and soldiers onto horses, and planted them on carpet in forays of battle. I tumbled them, twisting and bumping their forms. I opened packages of game cards and spread them on the floor, rooster and elephant and mouse.

Pulling our sled by a string, Daddy took me on the Avenue. Sunshine sparkled so that I could barely keep my eyes open. The world was etched in exquisite detail, my breath making cartoon puffs. Pigeons purred, their feathers clean as pins, gray and white, an occasional black one. Awnings were heaped with the aftermath of snow, doormen trying to beat it down with brooms. Smoke rose from a chestnut vendor at the entrance to the park, roasting stones in his pot.

We climbed a hill. Inside mittens my fingers glided along a railing, slapping poles. Daddy climbed over and I ducked under. People were whizzing—one to a sled, two, three, and four to a sled, tumbling in their heavy coats.

Daddy kneeled on the flyer boards and then lay down, instructing me to get on his back. I hesitated but finally crawled onto his rough camel's hair and balanced myself there. He told me to put my arms around his neck. Stale tobacco from his coat enforced an unusual intimacy.

He began slowly, then accelerated as I gripped tight. He hollered exultation, ice crystals splattering my skin as he pumped his body and urged our frame a little further, a little further.

On the walk home, sounds of bells and metal runners evoked gaiety, store windows peopled with puppet villages, music everywhere: "Winter Wonderland," "Frosty," "Santa Claus Is Coming to Town." I sat on the living room floor, moving Uncle Wiggily's yellow and blue chalkmen across their kingdom of squares.

I got sick for real and was put in Mommy's bed. I felt strangely protected by its power. Dr. Hitzig viewed me there, running fingers down my cheeks and neck and along my back. He wrote something on a sheet of paper, told a joke in Yiddish, said "Mazel tov" to Daddy, and left.

I was fed spoonfuls of horrible-tasting medicine, "Myocin," like dead mice ground up. I went to the hospital, "to have your tonsils

out. They will give you something to drink ... and you will go
to sleep.... "

The serum was sweet bubbles. I tried to fight, but those in white
surrounded me. It seemed as though it might already be the end of
life I had been here so long.

I awakened abruptly with a sore throat, gargling and spitting.
The nurse insisted I drink a tiny cup of pineapple. It hurt so much
I could barely swallow.

In the summer of 1950 I was sent to a camp in Pennsylvania called
Swago. I lived in a cabin with ten other boys and Bob, our counselor. He would wake "bad" kids in the middle of the night and
paddle us with a slipper—the number of blows dependent on our
crimes. "Violations" included talking during silent time, spilling
food at a meal, being late for activity, leaving clothes on our beds,
and wetting. I was pulled from sleep again and again, swatted and
dragged back. Night became a labyrinth in which I forgot how often
I woke and whether I was summoned or dreamed I was.

Bob warned me to say nothing to my parents. He hung close to
us on visiting day. Still I whispered it to my mother.

"That couldn't be true," she snapped, "but I'll speak to the director." Afterwards she told me it was my imagination.

She brought a glider with a propeller wound by a rubber band,
slices of balsa wood for the wings, and a green plastic nose. The
plane could go higher than the propeller-less gliders we threw. It
travelled beyond imagination, chugging gracefully through sky,
landing far away. No one had seen a prop-driven glider before, and
even big kids came to watch it sail over fields.

At twilight we took turns throwing our planes in the air and
chasing them. One swooped back into our group, its wing crushed
under our feet. Bob strode into our midst pointing at me. "You
broke it," he yelled. "You give him your plane." Sorrowfully I
went back to the bunk, took it from my cubby, and handed it over.

That evening I began coughing and coughing and couldn't
stop. I was brought to the infirmary and put to bed. I lay there
for days. They said it was whooping cough. Plates of hospital

food came and went. Sun shone in the bushes beyond. I heard the shouts of games.

Then Daddy came in his car and got me and took me to the Nevele Hotel, his advertising account. I was filled with joy and relief when I saw them all again. I couldn't believe they were real—Nanny kissing me, Jon such a big boy.

I have one other memory from Swago: the frog. In coins of dispersed sunlight at the bottom of a pool.... "Catch him," I pleaded. An older boy dove down through the water. I saw his fingers reach out as the frog sprang. He grabbed its legs in his hand. He set it in a coffee tin and handed it to me. I looked at it resting there in bright silver in undulating ribs of light ... and I am still looking at it, alive and green, legs extended, the water unimaginably clear.

That fall I began school at a strict French academy on Fifth Avenue, but I wet in class, so I was switched to P.S. 6 on Madison. There we painted from jars of colors onto easels, built block villages, and scuffled in circle games at recess. Balls from the bigger kids' games rolling into our midst were booted back.

When a bell rang, we lined up quickly and proceeded in rows onto the street. This was fire drill.

There was also an air-raid siren. We crawled under our desks and covered our heads with our arms, the teacher warning of invisible radioactivity and broken glass flying across the room.

Nanny met me after school. We shopped for groceries at Novack's Market. While she read her list I followed Mr. Novack around. With a long stick ending in a "hand" he plucked boxes of cereal and crackers, cans of vegetables, juices, and soups from higher shelves. These would be delivered to our apartment.

One Saturday afternoon our family drove across the Hudson to Palisades Amusement Park. I was placed in a chair on a carousel. It began to go fast and zigzag. I got dizzy. I struggled out of the clamp but was thrown to the ground. Amid shouts the ride stopped and they led me off.

I had heard a wordless directive: no way am I going to be tricked into marching down the aisle and putting my neck on the executioner's stone again.

In the spring P.S. 6 held a fair. Colored paper hung from the walls, and booths of cookies and toys filled the recess room. I knew I couldn't visit them all, so I hurried from thing to thing, rolling marbles into holes, betting coupons on paper horses, aiming balls through rubber-band mazes around nails in plywood. With a dollar I bought a book called *The Dragons of Blueland*. On its cover a boy in a red and white striped shirt hugged a blue and yellow striped creature above its tiny yellow wings. The dragon had a tiny red horn and was soft and pudgy and hugged back. All about them five-pointed yellow stars filled midnight blue.

I carried this prize everywhere. I loved to stare at its map—the train headed to Nevergreen Village, a church with a steeple, tiny cottages, the lighthouse offshore, a snake elevating himself onto a cactus, cows sleeping on either side of a squiggly river that wound into mountainous cones, dragons perched on their peaks, a single one blimp-like in flight.

Nanny read me the story at bedtime—how Boris the baby dragon found his family trapped in a cave, enlisted Elmer, and flew him on his back over the Spiky Mountain Range. My favorite picture showed the family of dragons: spotted, calico, banded, and decorated; tumbling, leaping, peeking at their tails through their legs, hopping over one another, rolling onto their backs, and prancing human-like on two legs. In a two-page illustration crossing the fold, all the dragons burst from the cave, bounding and taking flight. The bad guys scattered. A few ended up in the water amid floating hats.

I adored the dragons of Blueland, and I wouldn't let Nanny say a word against them or deny their likelihood (as she was wont to). Blueland was immutable. Lying in bed, I imagined the wind against my body as I flew on my dragon's back.

The morning after we moved to our summer cottage in Long Beach, I got lost again. Mommy wanted to see the ocean, so we pushed my brother until pavement turned to sand. Waves uncurled and crashed into bubbles in sand.

The stroller stuck. After yanking so hard that she fell down, Mommy sent me to fetch Nanny. "It's only two blocks," she pointed back. "Don't get lost."

I had never been sent on my own before.

Men trimming our hedges made the house look unfamiliar, so I walked past it, street after street. The scenery became city-like. I began to cry.

I stopped where workmen in uniforms were cleaning up. I wasn't supposed to talk to strangers, but I didn't know what else to do. One of them offered to take me in his truck. I climbed into the high seat.

We drove up and down streets, searching for where I lived. "Does this look familiar?" he kept asking. But it was all new.

Then I saw it—two police cars parked outside, Mommy on the porch. As I got out, she was yelling at them to arrest the man.

I had the feeling of reentering my life again from the outside.

Day after day, I played by the ocean as it crashed in. I sat in the foam with my toys, raking sand into a sieve, collecting and washing broken shells in a Bugs Bunny pail, digging channels and holes for the water to swirl into. I made sand castles and waterways and watched real vessels cross the horizon. I turned my back and let the crash surprise and knock me down. As I lay in the suction of retreating water, yummy salt filled my nose and mind.

My wind-up plane buzzed on tin pontoons. I would let it go, then rush through the tide to recapture it.

On the way home we went into a beach-house and showered off the sand among naked men. I was overwhelmed by the stale aroma of their flesh. The horror was that they were so wrinkled they were almost dead, the drain collecting their skin and hair.

I vowed I would never get that old.

Then Daddy visited his college friends Moe and Nook. Beside a rotating sprinkler Nook's wife, Aunt Alice, served us lemonade. As they laughed and teased, I stared into the jewel-sparkled grass, greener than any I had seen. Uncle Moe pretended to punch Daddy in the arm, then said, "You're quite the man about town with your dame."

Daddy laughed and answered with something that sounded like "your hazz-a-rye."

"You make a dashing couple," Aunt Alice declared. "Your pizzazz and her high carriage. She's a drink of water, your Frenchie."

"She's got a simmer of Rita Hayworth," remarked Moe, "a bit of Ava Gardner too." They were talking about Mommy, but their meaning didn't come into focus until years later.

"Of course this here schnook's no louse," bellowed Nook. He didn't seem aware that "schnook" rhymed with his name. "He cuts the figure of Cary Grant, got the moves of Astaire, voice of Jolson. You blue-eyed Jew, you cur you, Towers!"

"I know the shtick," Daddy said. He began to dance back and forth in place. "Give'm a little this, a little that, a little this, a little that."

"Go, Turetsky," shouted Aunt Alice, "go!" I knew the circusy sticklike word used to be Daddy's last name.

We climbed the steps to the boardwalk and walked along the row of amusement stands. Ignoring shooting galleries, balloons and darts, and turtle races (because Daddy said there was "only one real game here"), we spent our time at Skee-ball alleys, their shelves packed with different-sized stuffed animals and porcelain objects to be garnered by coupons over many visits, the higher the row the greater the number of points needed for them. Daddy helped me roll wooden balls toward pockets with numbers. Targets were rimmed circles inside of larger rimmed circles; the smaller ones made the most points: forty and fifty.

The balls were rough and solid, well worth the attention. We got ten at a time. At the insertion of a coin and yank of a lever they came clanking down a tunnel.

I loved their clatter, the release of new ones, the snugness of their plunk into the center hole, the near misses into adjacent ledges.

The moon huge over trees, I pulled sticky paper off a popsicle and sucked its sweet ice, *"The old accordions playing, a sentimental tune.... / Cruising down the river, on a Sunday afternoon."*

These events seem no further from me now than a month ago or fifty years ago. The agenda has not changed.

The rusty submarine, the dungeon, the ride at Palisades Park recall the horror. Toys and records recall the enchantment, Christmas lights and snowy hills the wonder. Life was as gentle and speechless as the squirrels who came from behind bushes to take nutted shells in their paws. I was vague as the vastness of the City, its edifices turning to silhouettes against twilight.

What is missing is a quality that lies beneath these details, the cauldron of reality at their core.

When I approach this realm now, I find the barest mists of sensation, its ambiance vast but diffused. There is no relief or scale by which to identify what actually happened.

I sense a white miasma. It is gaunt as snow, or cream on my mother's face. Ghosts surrounding my hospital bed are the white miasma. They glisten and shift in particles. I emerge amid snowy canyons in a place far from home. Villages appear, then whip past so that I cannot enter them. These vistas could be a movie or an illustration from a children's book. But they are the shroud upon another whiteness that seethes and snaps in unlocalized time and space. It forms the icicle of panic, the world blanching in a pang.

Then there is a yellow miasma. It pours out of my gut, a field of daisies and insects, an ocean so thick I cannot swallow it, a spinning chamber, a tan Daddy driving the lining of a dizzy car, my own pee.

The miasma is Mott's apple juice, a too-early moon, buttercup-do-like-butter? It is buzzing, but I can't see a bee.

In the yellow dream I am trapped in industrial basements, toilets overflowing. I wade through wastewater and urine. Even standing in the shower I am knee-deep in it. The drain is clogged. Shreds of paper and crud cake about my legs. It is impossible to rinse them because the water itself is filthy.

The blue miasma is medicinal and bitter: the glow of my mother's bedroom, Xtaby singing. But it's also the background against which Christmas lights sparkled. Nanny called me to watch as men in trucks hoisted trees by ropes along the center strip.

They moved slowly along the avenue, mall by mall, redirecting cabs and cars.

At dusk these giants ignited in unison, all the way to the

clocktower. Their red, blue, yellow, orange were the most radiant colors I had ever seen. Stationary amid traffic signals and streams of lights, at nightfall they reminded me of who I was.

In the red miasma Dr. Hitzig arrives with his leather bag to examine Mommy. She wants him to look at me too. For all the years I have been truant I must have grown a fatal disease. She points to my head and there is a scar. The all-seeing Hitzig parts my hair and examines my scalp. I think, "It's from riding my bike into that fireplug, but it's healed." He says that we have let a malignancy form through our inattention. A thing is rising in my skull, merging with flesh, infesting my cap and spreading downward. I pull away, but he holds me in his metallic grip. He is going to operate and dismember me.

Dreams take me back to that old ground-floor flat at 1220. I knock at the door. The present occupants let me in. I see the living room stretching like countryside to my right, the land of bureaus and statues. The hallway to my bedroom curls off beyond, blank now and invisible. Crumbling walls form foyers like rooms in a museum, their lengths draped in hieroglyphic tapestries, gold ornamental ceilings merging with sky.

These zones are in decay, hidden from current inhabitants. Yet I see through them into other habitations as well as vacant rooms without end.

I tell the people that something happened to me there once. I want to go back and find it. They direct me to the oldest sector (which they never use). I start down the hallway. I intend to see where the spell was cast.

I tell myself it's just a dream. I push against its sides, twist, and propel my body backward through grains of fog. Finally I tumble into the room I shared with my brother long ago. It is an eddying, shapeless black.

Once, grotesque dolls with muttering wooden heads drove me out. More often the interdict is implicit ... there is nothing at all, just space abandoned, its sterility and disuse marking quarantined dimensions, the closure of a zone of consciousness.

On at least two occasions gentle magi have intervened to lead me up the elevator onto the roof where they demonstrated windmills of the future, drawing power from light.

Once, I forced myself down the hallway, expecting to meet the apparition, but all I saw at its end was Nanny and me on a couch reading together. The scene was bountiful and sunny and betrayed all my suspicions ... until I turned and looked the other way and found myself staring into the black light from beyond existence.

Looking back at my earlier years I am seeing my substance at its far girth. There it is denser, brighter, its separate threads less accessible: truly a milky whey.

Life begins with an explosion much like the one we postulate for the origin of the universe. Everything is blown out of an original moment atomistically and settles in the tensility of space. I can see now at the beginning I was locked to my mother like a small satellite sun in a twin star system. It was not her exogenous presence that compelled me but her gravitation in the region of space from which I emerged. It was imprinted on everything I did. I was always shrinking from her, even when she was not present.

She watched my every move and pried into my thoughts. She was so close to me, so repellent, she wasn't a person at all.

Although her life was removed from mine by a discontinuity of scale and kind, I understood our grim kinship. She was the exact mother to punish and correct me. I felt her bleak intimacy and was drawn to her—unerringly. I knew that her qualities in me made me repugnant too, a negativity passed through the blood: her skitteriness and treachery, her alarms and false smiles. It didn't matter that I hated her, that she was beautiful.

As people often said, I was my mother's "picture image." So there was never the possibility of a clean escape.

I was afraid, not as it might have seemed, of her anger or spankings. I accepted that I was inordinately bad. I was afraid of who she was—*who she really was*. Her room was a catacomb of shrouds, homunculi amidst garments on the floor, hints of a pigeon knocked dead by a car, a dried-up goblin. When I was taken to visit her propped in her bed in her chamber I saw the haggard but adorned ruler of a nation at war, and I was proud to be associated with her.

2

P.S. 6 and Bill-Dave

In the fall of 1951 I was sent to P.S. 6 at a new building on 81st Street between Madison and Park. Each morning Nanny laid out my clothes and made breakfast. While I ate, she prepared carrots, celery, quartered tomatoes, and a sandwich, wrapped them in wax paper and arranged the wads in my Howdy Doody lunchbox. Then she took me outside to wait for the van, a vehicle they called the "wagon." As I got in, a place was made for me in one of the rows. Then the driver collected other kids at their awnings, packing us in like sardines (he said), so that we had to negotiate each other's elbows, legs, lunch boxes, and smells. Then he drove to P.S. 6 and dispatched our rumpus into the yard.

At the sound of the bell we hurried in and found places, our chatter stilled by a loud buzz. My classroom was on the first floor facing the street. From her position beside the flag Miss Tighe led us in the Pledge of Allegiance. Standing in aisles, our hands on our hearts, we recited the words automatically in singsong, "One nation, indivisible, with liberty and justice...."

I sat in my combination desk and chair watching words spelled and simple sentences sounded out. Our picture book was about Dick and Jane, their dog Spot, a cat Puff. We made the sounds of the letters as a group: "This is Jane. See Puff jump." After recess in the yard, addition and subtraction were demonstrated on the blackboard.

I became restless. My mind was occupied with adventures in which I hunted for treasures and escaped from enemies. I drifted between daydreams and drones of planes changing pitch, shadows of window casements as they bent from near rectangles to rhomboids and diamonds and crept across the room, pigeons against far rooftops.

I drew penguins playing trumpets with musical q's rising into double-u birds. I wound two pencils in a rubber band and then into a knot so that they danced weirdly to come undone. Kids at desks around me giggled. I looked at unintelligible combinations of letters in the back of the reader, trying to guess from the pictures what they were.

I was delighted when the single-letter word "a" appeared on an upcoming page. I had been looking ahead to it, wondering what it meant, Miss Tighe not forewarning us. A faint image of that "a" has stood before untranslated text ever since.

During that year our family moved across 96th Street to 1235 on the northeast corner. There, on the sixth floor overlooking a narrow alley, my brother and I shared a room again, our beds contiguous along one wall, Nanny at the opposite corner.

Relatives gave Jonny and me a black globe with a light in it to put stars on the ceiling and a wood-burning kit that released industrial smells as it heated up. We sat on the rug, etching lines on blocks while Nanny warned us about nipping ourselves with the coil.

We got a painted turtle in a plastic bowl, a track for him to walk on, a parasol at its center. Somehow Timothy escaped. We found him only after pulling up carpets and lifting cushions. He had made his way to a corner where his legs plowed against the wall as his head twisted. We returned him to his bowl and poured in dehydrated insects, almost suffocating him. But he left again, and after three weeks Nanny found him dried up under the radiator.

A three-year-old in cahoots with a first-grader, Jonny and I launched more escapades than our nurse could handle. We hid in closets and behind beds and played pranks on her, rearranging her clothes, putting plates and silverware in her dresser, and hiding her medicines. She yelled at us, took our toys and cap guns away, and made us drink our dinner disgustingly in our milk as punishment. She told our mother we were the worst kids she had ever minded.

One morning my brother and I decided to save our BMs as a joke. We stored them under his bed. After just a few days the room stank, but the bed was low-slung, disguising the source.

Our mother collared Mr. Borrig, the superintendent, and he appeared with a plumber in tow. After checking the toilet, the handyman worked his way into the bedroom, yanked the bed forward, and announced, "There's your problem, lady."

She stared at me in disbelieving horror. I shook my head in denial.

"It was him," Jon insisted. "It was his idea."

My brother was Mommy's favorite. She boasted to relatives how handsome and spunky he was. Compared to such a boy I was not worth mentioning.

As Jonny got larger he became a real nuisance, strutting and boasting in front of me, appropriating my things, claiming my trucks and boats were his. He had an ornery energy about him, a chippiness, plus a sour, powdery smell that I associated with his banditry. We would shout names and then begin hitting.

"Dumb brat!" I yelled as he showed off his boxing style, dancing from atop his bed to mine.

"Pee face!" he retorted wickedly. His mouth sprayed spit.

It seemed as though he always made his elbows jab, his knees butt on purpose. He never gave ground or let an advantage by me go by, no matter how meager. If I got a step ahead of him in our progress to the door, he had to restrain me by a hard push and get back in front. If I danced around a piece of furniture, he had to dance around it too. So I teased him, leading him in pied-piper chases. By indicating he was a baby or stupid, I riled his quick temper. He charged me and initiated fisticuffs.

Screams and thuds brought Nanny or our parents. They pulled us apart.

"A born instigator," Daddy said, glaring.

"He put my trucks with his toys! He stuck out his leg and made me trip. *On purpose!*" I was the picture of righteous indignation. But I knew my dark motives. I wanted to pummel him.

Jonny shook his head and grinned. To this day I can picture

him, forcing tears, telling on me, innocent as a lamb.

"You're older," Mommy said, "and should know better."

During one tussle Jonny and I wrestled to a stalemate. I refused to let go, and I couldn't budge his death grip. Suddenly his fingers caught hold of my ear; he tugged without mercy. I shrieked in pain and bit his forearm as hard and deep as I could. Howling, he reached for a pair of scissors. "I'm going to get you for that," he shouted, voice quavering. "I'm going to kill you."

I dove at him, tried to grab away the scissors. By the time our parents arrived he was bleeding from a cut on his cheek. We were both crying. The weapon lay beside us.

I wanted to tell my side of the story, but Mommy socked me on the head—a hard, painful club. Then she smacked with her fists, crouching over and kicking me as I squirmed along the floor. Daddy joined her yelling: "He's an idiot. Let him crawl into his hole."

I pulled away, slithering into the closet under the coats.

"You're the lowest form of creature alive," Daddy called in, "picking on a harmless child."

I sat there in a forest of wool and flannel, fascinated by the cadence of my sobs, staring into the patterns inside my eyes, calling for my Nanny. Inside me a strange, dry voice heaved all by itself.

I learned to cry long and deep and sing my own symphony.

Mommy thought if she spanked me and sent me to my room often enough I might change. She didn't mince words either; she called me "Hitler's boy" and "the devil incarnate." I deflected these slanders into nonsense syllables: "Dev-ill, in-car-nate." Even though I understood (more or less) what the words meant, how unthinkably vicious for a mother to say to a child, I didn't relate to them; it was more random noise aimed at me.

I may have tuned out her disparagements, but I breathed their field of attraction. The identity of a "knave" blended into my life: I became ugly Richard, diabolic Richard, prankster Richard, conniving Richard, Richard the rogue. "R" was the foulest, sneakiest letter, while "ch" scrunched up my cheekbones into a quailing mask. To this day ancient voices compel me to don it.

Grandpa Harry, a tiny man with a foreign voice, showed up on occasional Sunday mornings with his chauffeur, Joe. His accent and rapid garble made him unintelligible and he always was in a hurry. His sole purpose was depositing boxes of cookies, lox for Daddy, and the same set of fancy chocolate silverware in a flat box covered with cellophane. This included not only knives, forks, and spoons of different sizes, but pushers with sharply bent chocolate ends. Having presented his gifts, he was waving goodbye despite Daddy's protests that he should stop, break bread, and say a Sabbath blessing.

It was a major victory if he took off his hat and progressed out of the hallway to the nearest chair and occupied it briefly.

At the most unlikely times Uncle Paul, a fat, jolly man, would appear at our front door, exchange greetings with Daddy, and sometimes give Nanny a hug. Best of all, he took me out alone. No one said why, but I assumed it was because I was older.

At F.A.O. Schwartz, the toy emporium downtown, he stood alongside while I picked a wriggling fish from the pool of battery-operated toys. "How about that?" he pointed to the rear of the store. I could scarcely take my attention from the fish; then I did.

Two trains in motion wound through villages on opposite sides of a giant table, past people in cottages. Roving waitresses delivered food to autos, as miniature logs were loaded onto flatbeds. There was a sudden puff of smoke, a light through a tunnel, the engine entering, caboose last. I watched enthralled until, at Uncle Paul's prod, we returned our attention to the pond where he plucked the electric fish and bought it for me.

At the Penny Arcade we played Skee-ball and got fortune cards from a glass-enclosed gypsy doll. With cork rifles we knocked down prizes and collected our booty in my uncle's bulging pockets—gum drops, tiny boxes of Oriental cards, puzzle rings, packages of miniature books.

To win coupons, we slid a metal puck down a saw-dusted surface beneath bowling pins that lit up scores on an overhanging screen as they collapsed upward with the passage of the puck. Then, together in a recording booth, out of harmony and tune, we sang my children's songs into a microphone imbedded in the wall—me and Uncle Paul doing "Frosty the Snowman" and "The Thanksgiving Squirrel." I alone knew the words, so he slurred syllables to catch up.

Afterwards, we got to hear ourselves through a scratchy speaker; then a record with our voices dropped out a slot for me to take home.

Uncle Paul always concluded our visits by buying me a new game or a boat. He heralded the moment by asking me questions that implied our decision was a serious matter: "How many tugs you got? How many barges? how many canoes? any in drydock? any rafts? any ferryboats?"

One time, he honored my pleas to buy a hard plastic man with answers to questions floating in liquid inside him and visible through a plastic window. Another time, he picked out a game with presidents' faces on gold coins like real money. The most special present, though, was when he purchased a red motorboat with batteries at F.A.O. Schwartz. I was beside myself with how jealous Jonny would be, that I got it and he didn't.

After each visit I asked Mommy when Uncle Paul was coming next, but she didn't want to be bothered by questions about him and, if pressed, got angry. His appearances were so far enough apart that I almost forgot about him each time. He had become a vague memory of something wonderful when suddenly he was back at the door to claim me.

At P.S. 6 Miss Tighe set aside a period each day to practice with me while the other kids were doing lessons. I wanted to stay good and reward her kindness, but, back at my desk, daydreams took over. Then a trickle ran down my legs. Kids smirked, giggled, and hooted, holding their noses when they passed me.

At lunch a boy purposely spilled his juice on me, then yelled, "Wet pants!" I shoved him. He socked me. Soon I was the center of a circle, everyone pointing and teasing.

"Just get up and take this," Miss Tighe said, pointing to the bathroom key on the wall. "You don't even have to raise your hand." What she didn't realize was that I had no sensation of pee starting, so day after day I disappointed both of us.

One morning, without notice, Mommy packed our suitcases. We were going to Texas, she said, to visit Grandma Sally. In the train Jonny and I kneeled on seats by a window, watching buildings sweep by. Soon it was countryside … then lights in the dark.

We spent the whole night and next day on the train and, when we awoke in Dallas, everything seemed old-fashioned and warm like summer. We had strapped on our holsters and guns but spotted no cowboys in the streets.

Grandma and Uncle Tom's home was two storeys; it had a yard with a small brambly jungle leading to other yards. Using string, boards, and sticks I arranged a fort from which I spied on activity in all directions. I befriended a stray kitten I named Katey after my Little Golden Book, but she scratched me and I kept my distance after that.

"She feels as bad as you do about it," Grandma said, and she urged me to make up. I tried, but Katey didn't want to.

On his way to work, Uncle Tom drove me and Jonny to a school for little kids. No more numbers and letters, it was back to building block villages and painting on easels. At naptime the class lay on fold-out cots, and the teacher read to us from *The Wizard of Oz*.

Late-afternoon yolk flickered on the wall, as a Lion, a Scarecrow, and a Tin Woodman travelled an enchanted forest: a Scarecrow who had been made only yesterday, a Woodman whose joints creaked because he needed oil, a sad, meek Lion. I adored these characters and was so concerned for the outcome of their quest I could barely wait between installments. Since I was older the teacher took me outside during naptime and read to me under a tree: the jabbering field mice, the winged monkeys and—"Richard, today we meet the Wizard himself!"

One evening Grandma put a surprise at our place settings: look-and-see straws so we could watch our milk spin in spirals around Goofy and Donald Duck. For days Jonny and I found juices, sodas, and punches to sip and watch their colors swirl. Then we sucked Kool-Aid out of a pitcher and began spraying each other. Uncle Tom reclaimed the straws on the pretext they harbored germs.

He took us to a rodeo where cowboys and horses pranced to loud music; men wrestled steers to the ground. He kept asking us if it was exciting enough. Jonny thought so and clapped, but I was sullen and silent, leading him to tease me about being a city boy.

With no more warning than when we came, we got on a train and went through cities into winter. Only when I was older did I learn my mother had left Daddy, then changed her mind a month later and came back.

When I reentered Miss Tighe's class, everyone had gotten far ahead. I stared at gibberish. I couldn't do the numbers or read most of the longer words, so I was given separate pages to work on while the others moved ahead.

At the three o'clock bell, we ran down halls into the yard and sorted in clumps for "group"—that was the name for our after-school program: a boys-only day camp. Wagons along the curb represented different companies: mine was Bill-Dave, the same fleet of drivers who picked me up in the morning—a rival group was Leo Mayer's Champions. Bill was our fat, friendly ringmaster; Dave was the name of a man fighting in Korea.

On the curb we were counted and culled into wagons. I was put in the younger batch with seven- and eight-year olds. From there we were driven to Central Park. A counselor found an empty field where he organized games. These included "Capture the Flag," bombardment, volleyball, and soccer.

In Capture the Flag, shirts or sweaters were set at the back of enemy territory. We had to run the gauntlet of the opposing team, grab the "flag," and return with it to our own base without being tagged. If caught, we were put in jail near the flag, but any member of either team could release all his team's inmates by dashing toward the prison, eluding pursuers by swerves, tagging a prisoner, and shouting some part of the mantra "Ringoleavio! Ally Ally, All Free."

In bombardment a scratch in the dirt made by a stick separated teams. A fat, blubbery ball was heaved back and forth by those on the other side. If a player was hit, he was "out," but if the ball was caught, the one who threw it was "out." The best strategy was to charge the line and make a target of one's self so as to be in position for a catch. Since a throw had to be from the point of getting the ball—no stepping up to aim!—a close-in dare also allowed a well-targeted return.

I delighted in the smack of rubber in the chests of kids who caught it, the suspense of a sudden toss back among scattering opponents. I wriggled my body, jumping up and down. Sometimes the ball came my way and, once, I surprised myself by snagging it in my stomach and holding on. "Throw it!" they shouted. But I was slow to let my prize go.

More often I imagined that by whirling around I could avoid getting hit. The actual thump always startled me.

Soon after I began Bill-Dave Mommy wanted me to go on Saturday too. She said it would be good for me to be with boys my age. "And anyway all you and Jonny do is fight."

I had to get up early to meet the wagon downstairs. I felt my innards tingling with their special Saturday weakness as if I were stringy and hollow inside. I wanted to stay home, but the day beckoned too with majesty and depth. I ran among other kids in soccer and football, a chill wind stealing the last ornaments from branches as, to the frustration of Bill, we abandoned plays to try to catch them mid-air.

Some Saturdays Bill held treasure hunts. Sent among fields and copses, we collected colored strings, leaves, clovers, bubble-gum comics, and candy wrappers, to complete a schedule of items. Stray amulets were precious when happened upon, but one had to be cautious in the brush, for we also came upon mushed pinions of pigeon slabs and dead rats: lady's hats and dolls that weren't hats or dolls.

My favorite activity was "Hares and Hounds." In this adventure, a team called the Hares set out across Central Park, drawing chalk arrows on the pavement to signify their real direction, other arrows as camouflage—occasionally sending scouts to leave long false trails ending with suddenly no more arrows. After giving the Hares a fifteen-minute head start, confirmed by a counselor with a wristwatch, the Hounds had to track and catch up to them and, if there was time, become Hares and hide.

As Hares we crossed the park in haste, racing through tunnels and playgrounds, creating labyrinths, dispatching scouts—"Let me! Let me!"—to lead the Hounds to dead ends, waiting till they returned with proud tales of dupery: multidirectional arrows, spoors down remote paths.

As Hounds we followed the Hares' markings on pavement, dispatching our own scouts to check out forks and see if one was actually the main trail, hurrying to make up ground.

Our counselors took these hunts seriously and discussed strategy with the older kids. They were concerned never to be done in by fellow counselors who had tricked them before. "Remember the time those pricks crossed that meadow with no arrows?" counselor Freddie said to counselor Wally.

"Remember? I'm going to put those jackasses in a corral and throw away the key. They break the fartin' rules every time."

Once we spent a whole day looking for the Hares while our counselor cursed and kicked the dust. Every trail, it seemed, was false, the most promising one ending in taunting crisscrosses pointing every which way.

They had hidden in the weather castle on the lake, a path we had discounted as an obvious false trail. The custodian, not realizing they were Hares, invited them in for a tour of the facility. We were hunted down later by howling Hares.

"Not fair!" we shouted when they led us to their hiding place. "The rules say you can't go indoors."

But we visited the necromancers' chamber together. With its spinning globes and glowing dials, in my imagination this castle *made* the winds; its keepers, standing over maps and drums, decided when to send rain and snow through the City.

In late afternoons counselors acted out stories about "the olden days." Bill-Dave Group was supposedly founded by a hero named Ranger, but almost from the beginning he was sabotaged and duped by the Bully. Throughout each episode, as Ranger turned the tables and got revenge, we shouted and cheered his feats. The Bully sniggered away, but he'd be back.

These were lazy, priceless times, as I lay with the others in our make-believe fort of rock outcroppings, eyes on horizons of buildings. Raptly following the action, we laughed at imitation voices and clapped or moaned at each turn of fate.

On the way back to the wagon on Fifth, we stopped at the drinking fountain, lining up for our chances. A spout was initiated and cobblestones moistened by pushing in a hard metal knob. I eagerly awaited my time at the oasis, to lean and put lips and palate and tongue into the flow, take cold greedy sips and quench thirst forever.

At the end of the day a short, round counselor named Bert drove people home in a familiar order while teasing and heckling us and giving disgusting accounts of war mutilations: severed arms and penises and other deformities. "You want to talk blood and guts," he serenaded. "I'll give ya blood and guts." He described Japanese and Korean torturers, how they drove stakes through victims' eyes, cut off hands, and held noses under dripping faucets.

Other times we convinced him to turn the radio to "Tom Corbett: Space Cadet" and "Planet Man." As our vehicle swerved through traffic, eerie sounds sent rockets zooming to other worlds. One by one, to hoots and distortions of our names, we hopped out at our apartment buildings.

Before dinner I watched television. For the puppet show *Kukla, Fran, and Ollie* Jonny and I sat alongside each other, charmed by the squawky rumpus of marionettes. Daddy knew Fran, so he brought home a rubber Ollie-dragon glove and Kukla finger-clown after which my brother and I staged our own performances from behind a living-room table.

Although *Flash Gordon* terrified me, I never missed a show. Night after night I followed his escapades, as his rocket took him to covens of regal and rhinoceroid creatures. One time Flash got imprisoned on an enemy world in an acid shower and was pounding on the door, screaming to get out. I turned the TV off. I didn't want to watch.

In a similar story on *The Cisco Kid* Indians wrapped his sidekick in poisoned blankets. The coverlets were killing him, as he shook spasmodically.

My blankets could be doused too. How would I know? Some nights I kicked them clear down the sheets, unable to get the squirming man out of my mind.

Other times as I lay in bed before sleep, my hands changed shape and size on their own, my feet dwindling to beyond my torso. As fingers and lips swelled into fat trees, my legs shot out in the distance, so far beyond that my toes were as remote as a city seen from clouds. Inside my lips and up my arms I felt thick water pulled by a magnet.

I was frightened but curious, so tried staying there long enough to fill with electricity. In ensuing paralysis I struggled to move even a finger. Finally I willed myself to wiggle my left pinky, and the spell snapped as if it had never happened.

Nanny and Mommy didn't know about these matters and, though I have no idea what they were, I think of them now as migranoid/hypnagogic trances. But they could have been anything. In the mystery that gives us a mind and a body, there are countless unknowns.

Mean kids and bullies at group enforced their authority with sticks and fists, stings from rubber bands and pea-shooters. The only alternative to a fight was being harassed and goaded, called a spastic—"you spazz!"—or worse. My wet pants qualified me as a full-fledged schmendrick, so I was shoved against the side of the wagon or someone stuck gum on my shirt. A kid elbowed me and then turned away, pretending not to notice: "Geez, who would have done that!"

Amused by such antics as if watching chimps at the zoo, our counselors rarely intervened.

My mother presumed that I provoked other kids, but bullies didn't need provocation.

A wish to retaliate smoldered in me. One time I did swing back. "Oh, the baby wants to fight!" my tormentor goaded as others went, "Woo-woo, nincompoop." He put up his boxing stance and socked my chest hard, stunning me. They laughed, made faces, and sang:

> Richie is a friend of mine.
> He resembles Frankenstein.

"You think that's funny!" I spat, delirious with rage. I punched back.

"Harty-har-har!" he countered, slapping my fist away and knocking me in the face as they finished their rhyme:

When he does the Irish jig,
he resembles Porky Pig.

During winter, dusk came early, and Bill-Dave kids were beans in sweaters and overcoats. Our wagon skidded on snowy streets as we squealed and threw our bodies into one another.

On sunny days we stayed outdoors, sledding, building forts, staging snowball wars that seemed to last a lifetime. I felt like a soldier in an ancient battle of ice. We had to fight our way sector by sector around the rear of an opposing army, gain high ground on boulders and rock ledges, store enough ammunition (piles of hard snowballs), and charge their positions, heaving bullets down on them as they scattered.

We were sometimes surprised from another flank. Snow was stuffed down our collars and backs. We sought shelter behind any bush or tree.

Finally the glow of evening ended the battle. We trooped through the Park, our mittens caked with ice, our bodies throbbing, frost in our pants … past the Museum, past the chestnut man, into the wagons, then home.

On rainy afternoons, Bill-Dave went indoors to a variety of places: a drafty downtown gym where we heaved a basketball at hanging chains; the Metropolitan Museum of Art with its suits of armor, mummies, and stone tombs; the Planetarium where we could read our weights on the Moon (light as a sparrow) or Jupiter (heavier than a whale); the Penny Arcade (handed $2 each in a package of dimes); and a roller rink. I remember working my way around the circle of the dreary ballroom, dodging other skaters, going fast then slow, fast then slow, lumbering toward openings, passing through hot and cold drafts, collecting unexplained ball bearings from the hardwood as piped music played yet another same polka … waiting for the endless day to end.

At the Museum we chased through catacombs, making werewolf faces and moans, while long-dead kings, queens, and their runes watched impassively.

Next door at Hayden Planetarium we took seats in a round theater, a huge legless robot mounted in its center. Celestial music sounded as the ceiling darkened into the New York skyline followed by a starry night at which we let out a collective "oooo." Soaring into the heavens, we landed on a Martian desert, as the narrator described the world's bitter cold and tiny red sun; then we watched the planet's two tiny moons rising and setting . After taking off, we shot farther out as the sun dwindled rapidly in the ceiling. Suddenly we plunged through Saturn's rings to frigid Mimas. After a tour of its snowy crags we levitated out of our galaxy into violet-tinged nebulae, birthplaces of stars and the whole universe.

We spent many inclement afternoons at the 92nd Street Y. Rows of nuts and nougats sat in windows by magazines in the foyer, their indescribable smells cascading into the room. ... Mounds, Oh Henry!, Spearmint Leaves, Butterfinger, Mallow Cup, Clark Bar, Hershey's Krackle, Goobers, Cherry and Grape gums, Jujyfruits, Chunky, Snickers. These arrays were replicas of eternal events. Each bore some essence of hunger and was capable of filling me with its gist. All afternoon I longed to bite into morsels of their confection, but my allowance, a dime raised gradually to fifteen cents and then a quarter, was long ago spent.

Mallow Cups had a sweet, sticky vanilla cream in hard rippled chocolate. Mounds were pulpy with sugary coconut. Almond Joys were Mounds with nuts imbedded in their chocolate glaze. Butterfingers were a crunchy nougat of chocolate-covered caramel. Mars Bars had a mocha nutty goo. Chunkies were raisins and roasted peanuts in a hard cube of chocolate. Three Musketeers ensconced a whipped fluff, moist and porous to the bite.

Mommy told me to buy only raisins, never candy. That's what I said I did, but she was uncanny at guessing the truth. She announced one night at dinner that I was destroying my insides with junk.

I sat there, imagining my guts rotting away, plus a twinge of regret at her picturing innocent raisins while I was betraying her.

Yet I went on devouring these chemical bricks as if they were manna, the epitome of culinary pleasure as well as a true resolution to my hunger. Years later I realized that each bar not only had a distinctive flavor but a vibration which activated subtle energies percolating through its congealed sucrose and corn syrup like a stream through a sweet aquifer. The bars may have been dietary frauds, mirages to fill the coffers of sugar pushers, but I was *thinking* their nourishment too and that made them healthier in the imagination than ingested molecularly.

Large vending machines flanked the Y's atrium, some with candy bars, some with apples, some with ice-cream cups, some with sandwiches. The alcove was scented with chlorine from a pool we never saw, though we heard distant splashes.

From the atrium we trooped upstairs to our assigned room and piled coats on a table—tight quarters for hyperactive lads. With shouted commands, our counselors ended freelance melees and organized us into games highlighted by Telephone and Snatch the Club.

Turkish carpets decorated the walls; pigeons cooed against a rain-streaked, dust-soiled window, soot dripping and blowing about the alley. We sniggered as nonsense syllables and curse words came out the end of our whispered chains. Then we were divided into teams, bunched at opposite ends, and an Indian club was set in the middle for rounds of pluck and tag.

Light of chandeliers, clatter of play, and gloomy vapors kerned an endemic spell, as I fantasized chocolate-covered peanuts, coated marshmallow bars, black-cherry popsicles. Hunger and sadness ran in a stream together because hunger was so deep it could never be filled and sadness was so vast I could never envelop it.

One snowy day we went for a tour of the Tastee Bread factory. At its end everyone was given a silken white package of bread, warm from the vats of dough. By the time we got home I had consumed the entire loaf, amazed that it fit in me.

Fear remained my close companion. It was the dungeon stairs, poisoned blankets, Dr. Hitzig—and something else: the color of light, the persistence of morning, afternoon, and dusk; the same streets, shop windows, rooms, scenery, day after day, hour by hour, relentless, inexhaustible—these people, this family, their carpets and furniture, plates and cups, meal after meal, the sound of Nanny pushing the carpet sweeper back and forth. No single thing was particularly disturbing, but all these things together, unbroken and unending, were like a death march. I stood alone in the watchtower.

I woke in the dark, terrified and shivering, usually wet, and staggered into their room, willing to ask even them for help. Their husks heaped in murk, Daddy was snoring. As I hovered there whimpering, Mommy separated, jumped out of bed, put on a bathrobe, and herded me down the hall, turning on lights as we went.

She opened a wooden cabinet. Out of a bottle she poured a shot glass of brandy. I didn't want adult liquor inside me, but she moved my hand and the warm bitter gave such a buzz that I stopped shaking and sat down. The spook was gone; the medicine had worked.

She was so relieved she began laughing. She laughed so hard tears ran down her face.

I wanted to stay with her there in the light forever.

There was another evening when I turned the handle for my bath and watched water surge out of the faucet against the luster of the tub.

Suddenly it came.

Not the gush—its force, if anything, was elating. It was the sheer fact of being there at all, naked, in relief against white stone.

I couldn't bear it, so I let out a wail.

Mommy and Nanny came running. They looked about in bewilderment. I felt filaments of ice expanding from my throat and belly as if I was about to be blown apart.

"What happened?" my mother shouted.

"I don't know! I don't know!" A word commanded my mind. It was the only one strong enough. "I have cancer," I said. I didn't want any association with the name, but I needed them to know how bad it was.

I had broken her most inviolable taboo.

"Stoppit!" she screamed. "Stoppit this instant and tell me what's wrong! If you think I'm going to tolerate this nonsense any longer you've got another thing coming."

They put me in my bed and … slowly it faded.

Mommy surveyed me lying there. I said I would never be okay again.

"Did you ever hear such nonsense?" she asked, turning to Daddy.

"Talk some sense into him," he insisted.

"If you were poor," she said, "you'd have something to be scared of. If you didn't know where your next meal was coming from, if you didn't know where you were going to live the next day. … You do a million and one things any child would give his right arm for and you're too selfish to appreciate it. How can anyone be so self-centered?"

I tried to say something about how it was difficult at Bill-Dave and P.S. 6. I knew that wasn't it, but I had to stop the inquisition.

"Why don't you run away if you hate it so much here? We pay good money for Bill-Dave."

I said nothing.

"Well, I'll tell you why: You want attention. You enjoy upsetting me."

"No."

"Don't call me a liar."

Later I heard it on the victrola—Eddie Fisher singing, *"Oh my Papa. …"*

I recognized this dirge from long ago: *"To me he was so wonderful, / To me he was so good."*

"Wonderful"? "Good"? That's what the words said, but the melody was maudlin and bottomless.

Nanny left, just like that, without ceremony or forewarning. I heard Mommy saying that she was a traitor—she had opened our mail and spied through the keyhole. I missed her, but I felt relief too because Jonny and I no longer had to share our room with a witch.

After my return to first grade I joined a few boys from my class who were also in Bill-Dave. At lunchtime we met in the yard and hiked three blocks up Madison to "Jessie's Jip Joint" (we knew how to spell "gyp" but we liked the triple "J's"). There we spent our allowances on M&M's, chocolate wafers, Hershey bars, and other candies plus occasional packs of cards.

The kids in our gang collected Flash Gordon cards, a nickel pack a day, torn open, viewed, and sorted. We kept our stashes in rubber-banded stacks. I loved to shuffle through mine and check what I had.

Inside Jessie's disarray of commerce we goofed off axiomatically, a form of worship. We were delighted by the motley parlor of bubble gum, comics, old rubber balls, waxed syrups, tiny prizes in cellophane stapled to cardboard plaudits. Toy- and puzzle-packed shelves and cabinets erased corners at every level.

Our allowances were hardly adequate to such a cornucopia, so our gang stole from other kids in class. I took six quarters and a fifty-cent piece out of a bankbook in a girl's desk and, with this pirate silver, bought a magical bulb that needed only a copper penny at its base to turn it on. I presented it the next day at "Show and Tell," but it wouldn't light, which prompted Miss Tighe to call Jessie and demand he stop cheating the children.

In the tribe at Jessie's I attached myself to a red-haired, freckled kid named Phil Wohlstetter who was livelier and goofier than anyone else. He could dart around, stop short, and twist the other way so fast that no one could catch him. Phil didn't fight much, but when he did, he was surprisingly effective, his quickness making up for heft and muscle. He was great at faking punches one way and then sneaking one in under an opponent's guard. "Made you look!" was his war cry.

By hanging around with Phil, I became a member of his special clique. In fact, I was his sidekick, like Tonto on *The Lone Ranger*.

Phil called us The Throw Your Lunch in the Garbage Can Club. We'd come tearing out of class at the noon bell, head for the nearest city trash container, open our metal boxes, and artfully dump their contents into the can. We each had similar combinations of white bread and cheese, or peanut butter and jelly, a raw vegetable, maybe a few cookies worth salvaging (since my mother thought peanuts were poison, I got cream cheese and jelly). Phil took particular pleasure in smashing a ripe tomato against the container, some of it invariably splattering the concrete. Once he tossed his cheese high in the air and called out, "Velveeta!" as it burst apart on the sidewalk.

My daydreams at P.S. 6 flowed into a single complicated fantasy. It began when friendly aliens came to the bedroom window and beckoned me into the courtyard. From there, they flew me to a field where they brought down a spaceship big as city blocks. Once they taught me how to use it, they gave it to me. I pressed a button and it shot into the sky. Earth dwindled against the stars.

I zoomed to Mars. After that, I changed to longer needle-like engines and blasted out of the Solar System, rocking my desk gently to simulate acceleration.

With this ship I could go anywhere in the universe. Travelling at speeds well beyond Flash Gordon's, I kept mental records of the landscapes and creatures I saw, along with the leagues of outer space crossed to reach them. My vehicle moved rapidly but not instantaneously. I could always imagine more territory and stars, so sometimes I would spend five minutes or more supplying the energy in my head, propelling myself, observing minute details of suns and comets as I manufactured them.

My annals of other worlds were comforting and compelling in a way that nothing else was, so I continued to expand and extend their chronicle. That way I had a storyline to return to whenever necessary—during a lesson, in the school wagon, or lying in bed at night waiting to fall asleep.

I took along imagined cohorts, though never Phil and my actual friends. That would have felt ridiculous. I picked other chums to fill out my crew: Joyce who drew a perfect Donald Duck with eyelashes, Andy Pfeiffer because he had a cute smile and I liked his name, Joey because I found myself wishing he was my friend during a game at his birthday party when we chose papers from a hat and, from their instructions, ran each other through gauntlets. My attachment to him was instantaneously erotic, as he slapped my behind on drawing such a lot.

In fact, all my shipmates were kids to whom I was attracted but never turned into real-life friends. Instead, I invented their characters and our relationships.

After escaping atomic war we searched for another habitable planet. We visited worlds with green and blue rain, quadruple and quintuple moons: spiderweb villages, dragon-filled cocoons, yellow oceans, forests of talking birds and hedgehogs, underground tunnels and caves. I tried to drag out each phase of exploration as long as possible, returning to former venues to fill in missing details. We finally chose a home planet, built houses there, and befriended local animals and made up rules for our society. This activity spawned a continuous virgin papyrus for me to emboss and then commit to memory—just keeping track of the names of make-believe animals: Snellems, Hop-Hogs, Mugwums, and the like.

As life on our new world lapsed into squeamish intimacy, I created interlopers with their own plots and machines. I always stayed a step ahead of the story with predicaments for which I had no solutions. Dreaming up perils kept the daydream urgent and pure and gave my mind crises to solve. Just when our plight seemed most hopeless we would discover new regions of our world—deeper forests, further tunnels, abandoned forts—or sometimes fresh powers in our vehicle. Eventually we were forced to flee and go deeper into the universe, so I had to create a new home planet.

The "tale" was with me for all the years of my childhood. In some part of my mind I held the up-to-the-minute situation and map of our universe with a backlog of worlds we had visited and lived on. At any time I could either pick up where I had left off or replenish an old episode.

I especially liked to revert to the setting in which the visitors contacted me and made a gift of their ship. To refine it reinforced its authenticity and essential nature. I never had my benefactors return. I didn't want that option. They were almighty and inchoate. *I* needed to be the driving force behind my fantasy, to generate adventures and resolve them from my own deeds. To have gods rescuing us would have obviated the whole basis of the story.

I regularly reenacted our last-minute escape from Earth, mushroom clouds spreading, parts of buildings flying apart, maneuvering the spaceship to get to and save each member of my would-be crew—then our fiery blast-off ... tearing through the atmosphere toward the stars—each iteration as suspenseful and gratifying as the original.

The story touched something in me that admitted no other form.

It was my chance to fight back against terror, to become a likable boy at last, to make friends with kids whose allure intimidated me. But there was another element, a mystery hard to diagnose.

Rain whipped through a valley of phosphorescent trees. Hedgehogs bounced alongside our gang—they were our telepathic allies. I called to Andy and Jill to help. They brought wood from the ribbony forest. Joey had taken the ship and gone back to rescue Jimmy. The Snellems were searching for us on the other side of the great ocean and soon their warships would be drawing near. A music-like theme built in my mind, a sense of fascination like trance. I was checking star-maps in case we had to escape.

It was heady to look around the classroom and see unaware people accompanying me across the stars.

At night I dug deep into the covers as I kindled my universe into being. Daddy had taught me to say, *"Baruch atah Adonai elohaynu melech ha'olam,"* so I obediently mimicked the jingle each night as my head dropped onto the pillow. And, though he told me the words meant "Blessed Art Thou, O Lord and God, King of the Universe," I didn't know what *that* meant except someone like my ethereal benefactors. The story bridged the gap between *melech ha'olam* and sleep. It made there be a King and a Universe and placed me in it too. My spaceship couldn't be as sacred and important as *"Baruch atah Adonai …,"* but it was.

At a hint of warm weather in March, Phil brought out a Spaldeen rubber ball and tossed it toward me down 92nd Street. I stabbed at his throw, but it hit my hands and bounced off; I picked it up and heaved it back as best I could. We repeated this ritual wordlessly, as he raced ahead, making leaping grabs.

"Like this," he said, demonstrating how not to throw like a girl. Then he gestured for me to loft the ball opposite where he was. I tried, but it went sideways, rolling down the street.

He tore after it, stopped it on the run and, after faking a side-arm throw, brought it back. "Up high," he pointed.

I aimed it away from him; he sped down the sidewalk, leaped, caught it, and threw himself onto the hood of a parked car.

I wanted to be able to do this, yet I flubbed even the easier flips he lobbed my way.

Phil was Bill-Dave's star athlete and leader of our club that included Freddie, Herbie, Davey, Ronnie, me, and Al. We eyed him for instructions. If the Bill-Dave was marching home in its orderly column he would signal a detour and we would surge behind him through bushes onto dirt, rejoining the main party on the other side of the loop. In tunnels we would answer his howls with our own, kids pretending to be Indians pretending to be animals. We bowed flamboyantly on each pass of Cleopatra's needle, imitating Phil's voodoo-sounding gibberish. Most of the other kids ignored us, but a few were provoked to rebut, a quick charge and shove or calling out "Dummies!" as we bowed.

Herbie brought a magnifying glass to school and used it to incinerate ants in the yard—a thrilling demonstration of the power of curved glass to pull the sun's fire onto Earth. When Phil handed the death ray to me, everyone shouted to get the spider. I held the magnifier over it. Ambling along, it scurried, curled, and melted, squirming in a stream of smoke while my friends cheered. Then Billy burned the wings off a fly. I realized, in sudden consternation, we were imitating Bert's Korean tortures.

For weeks afterwards I pictured that poor creature just going about his business, reduced to fragments and ash. It is a regret I still have, an unsquared issue between him and me, a stone in my heart. Yet boys do mindless things even as a cat claws apart the wings of a struggling bird.

When a bunch of us visited Phil's apartment on 93rd Street he sassed his parents (mostly under his breath). His mother called out, "Hello." Phil said, "Hello, ma'am," and then, in a whisper to us, "... idiotbrain."

One afternoon, as we poured from the elevator into the apartment, Phil's father intercepted him for introductions to adult company. "Good to meet you," he said with exaggerated politeness, courteously shaking each hand. Then, in front of the grown-ups, he began shaking our hands too: "Good to meet you, Herbie. Good to meet you, Al. Good to meet you, Richie. Haven't I seen you somewhere before?" At the conclusion of the charade we galloped into his room for games and comics.

Phil had a peerless collection of Bugs Bunny, Porky Pig, Mickey Mouse, Tubby and Little Lulu, piles of Donald Ducks and Uncle Scrooges. I would grab a stack and shuffle through them, looking for ones I hadn't read: Bugs and Elmer wrapped to a post with Indians around them, Bugs slicing carrots into a piggy bank, Mickey giving a bath to a yelping Pluto while water splashed all about.

It was an afternoon's treat to lie akimbo against the furniture, silently zoning out, periodically exchanging fascicles, as we gorged on Wohlstetter cookies and ice cream. There was something about the images and blurbs that made them irresistible, especially when ingested with good food. They were so clean, simple, and bright. The trees were bushy, the carrot wedges tangerine orange, the lightning jagged gold, Donald's eyes so wide, his aura so yellow, the snow so creamy.

Stories sprang up instantly: an old map with a bit of shoreline, a ship at sea, an iceberg, Crash!, black sky, green waves. Donald's dream bubble had him sitting on the throne, "King of North America: The Viking Kid," Olaf the Blue's gold helmet resting snugly on his head. Lawyer Sharky—a dog dressed as a sleazy man with bifocals—was after the helmet too; he represented Azure Blue, eldest descendant of Olaf, and was claiming North America under a 792 law of Charlemagne. Phil looked over.

"Weirdo Charlemagne," I said.

"Char-lee-mane," Phil repeated deliberately. "Charleemane and Shoeless Joe and Minnie Minoso."

"I'd give the State of California for a hamburger," a famished Donald told Lawyer Sharky.

"I'd give the state of my underpants for your elixir," Phil intoned, grabbing Al's butter pecan.

"Hey," snapped Al, grabbing the dish back.

Phil had a collection of water guns and rifles. We'd choose our weapons—the rifles contended for because they had greater range and capacity—and then conduct wholesale war, dashing about the apartment. Nothing close to that could ever happen at my home—hot hisses against light bulbs, soaked pillows as shields, everyone shoving for refills at the sink, snacks whenever you wanted.

Phil said that since Jessie, the stubby, growling proprietor of our candy shop who looked like Iggy from *Little Lulu,* was a crook, it was okay to steal from him. In the commotion around the counter Phil had no trouble making off with several packs from under Jessie's overtaxed eye.

We watched our friend, not wanting to miss his sly feint while "Iggy" was distracted: up his ladder, counting change, or barking at some kid—he was barely tall enough to see above his own cash register. It was easy as punch, but only Phil had the panache.

One day our leader announced he was going to steal a whole box, an unprecedented ante. We waited outside for him, expecting it to be a bluff, also not wanting to be implicated in a major felony. After a suspenseful span Phil appeared like Bugs Bunny with a mother lode of carrots, the treasure clutched under his shirt: dozens of unopened packs straight from the manufacturer. We spent lunch period tearing open our booty, divvying it up. Of course, Phil got to keep the best ones—and I still don't know how he did it.

In spring of '52 wrapped baseball bundles replaced Flash Gordon packs. As usual Phil led the way—he already knew the names of most of the players on the Major League teams. At first, ordinary men seemed a letdown after outer-space landscapes and court interiors, but the insignias, a Tiger or Cub or Cardinal birds in the corner of a card, and the solid colored backgrounds—yellows, oranges, and blues—transcended the athletes. They had the bubblegum dust and lost aroma of newly minted amulets, as they recalled game boards and museum crests.

Every day we competed for prizes from each others' stashes in duels and tourneys. Kids crowded around the action, shouting, bumping in communion. We mainly "flipped"—the first person putting down a random pattern of heads and tails by floating his cards from a waist-level position, and the second trying to match the combination on the ground—the cards themselves at stake.

It was a suspenseful business, watching a lemon Gene Woodling or red-orange Turk Lown flutter in the air, front and back alternating, one of which would land upright. Four tails was a hard combination to match. Three tails and a head gave a bit of room for error. Two of each was ideal but no guarantee against an unlikely streak of one's own. If I got to within a card of matching, a pin cushion of nerves watched the final spin. If it showed the right face, I felt a jolt of delight as I reached down and scooped up the jackpot, gathering and neatening the cards, fitting them into my handy cube and wrapping it back under its rubber band.

Flipping was mostly luck, but there must have been skill involved—card angle and height of drop, pressure of hold, jimmy and trajectory of release—because the same kids regularly won. Or perhaps they had mastered Gyro Gearloose's telekinesis and could send brainwaves to alter spin.

In another contest, with flicks of the wrist we sailed cards up to and against a wall in rotations of two or more players. Anyone who landed a card on any part of another got his own back plus the one he "covered." This *was* a game of finesse like tiddlywinks or pick-up-sticks. As card after card travelled with our distinctive spin rates over a landscape left by prior cards, we stared intently, trying to put mental english on the flight. A perfect shot covered an indisputable portion of a card on the ground. Others were too tantalizing to judge from afar, so we kneeled on the ground in serious adjudication, trying to figure out if certain cards were actually touching or just close.

In the spring of 1952 Phil debuted punchball at lunchtime in the schoolyard. With his fist he whacked the Spaldeen high off the fence above the wall, scattering pigeons: it was a home run, circle the bases unchallenged. I swung at the pinky and set it skipping along the ground. Phil shoved me so hard toward the wall (first base) I stumbled, but the ball rolled away, and I got all the way to the pile of coats at second, just ahead of the tag. "Way to go, Towers!"

That Saturday Daddy responded to my tales of the week with a taxi ride downtown. At his advertising account, a store called Miller's Sporting Goods, he bought Jonny and me gloves, a bat, and hardballs. The next morning, he took us to Central Park where we found an open area. After setting his hat down for home plate, he pivoted my arms with the bat to demonstrate correct form, then lobbed pitches to me.

Gradually I smacked the ball sharper and farther, as my brother ran after my hits and brought them back. Then Jon took a turn with the bat. After that, Daddy set both of us at a distance and floated the ball in the air, calling out my name. I turned and somehow it landed in my glove. "You're a natural!" he shouted.

As soon as Daddy said those words, I had magical abilities. I imagined that I could run down everything, so I did. I grabbed the next ball in the tip of the webbing while tumbling, clutching it high over my head. "A real natural!" he announced with a delighted grin. "You've got the coordination of a pro." It was as if I had been anointed by a baseball jinni. Only three days earlier I had been lunging and missing. Now I *was Phil.*

Thereafter I embraced the knitted spheroid and its vectors of flight and ricochet. I played as often as I could—in the schoolyard, at group, on weekends. Nothing before had been as much fun or as real. I loved running at full speed, snaring a hit or toss. When no one was around to play, I lobbed a hardball or Spaldeen as high as I could in the air and caught it where it came back down, or I bounced it off a wall and snared its caroms.

That year Mommy became pregnant again and stayed in bed all spring. One morning I straggled into the kitchen in my PJs and was startled to find Nanny squeezing half-oranges into a pitcher from the whirling juice-maker. I had been told I would never see her again. I ran up and threw my arms around her.

Soon after Nanny's return we moved to a bigger apartment across the hall. Daddy had to hold Mommy up and walk her a step at a time. Now we lived in 6B overlooking 96th Street's boulevard. Jon and I still shared a room and there was a nursery behind the kitchen for the baby.

Late one night Mommy left for the hospital and came back several days later with a sister named Deborah. Nanny kissed us goodbye shortly afterwards and never returned. Her macabre landscape faded; *in absentia* she became a numinous being, vast and sepulchral as life itself.

One afternoon we strolled to the corner of 96th and Central Park where we met a young pretty lady named Bridey. The famous Fifth Avenue wind whipped at our jackets and blew newspapers past like missiles. Bridey held a little hat on with her hand, and Jon and I bounced a ball while she answered my mother's questions in a brogue. A month later she moved in as our new nurse.

From the day I picked Gil McDougald as my favorite player from a card of a friendly pixie face gazing at far-off sky, I became a Yankee fan and joined Phil in a pact of loyalty.

When I told Uncle Paul about this new thing, he bought me a Yankee history in which I acquainted myself with prior seasons. That opened a legacy as primeval as the Egyptian tombs and labyrinthine as Jessie's cave. I started at the beginning when they were the Highlanders, then went through eras of Babe Ruth, Herb Pennock, Bill Dickey, Waite Hoyt, Joe Gordon, Joe DiMaggio, and Old Reliable, Tommy Henrich. None of those players were still around, but their photos were pinstriped heirlooms out of which the 1952 squad took the field. Allie Reynolds and Vic Raschi pitched; Yogi Berra was their catcher, Charlie Silvera his alternate; Joe Collins played first, spelled by Johnny Mize; Billy Martin was at second, Phil Rizzuto at short, McDougald at third backed by Bobby Brown. Gene Woodling, Mickey Mantle, and Hank Bauer started in the outfield, Irv Noren and Bob Cerv filling in.

These were my ikons, their names indelible. They were fighting Cleveland for first place, the same Indians they had been battling for years. Casey Stengel was the manager. A savvy old-timer who had not been successful with other teams, he surprised the baseball world by leading the Yanks to the pennant in 1949 as they beat the Red Sox in the last two meetings of the season to prevail by a single game. They edged out Detroit, Cleveland, and Boston in 1950. Then in 1951 they ran away from the Indians, and Rookie of the Year Gil McDougald hit a grand slam against the crosstown Giants in the World Series. That was all before my time, the prologue to 1952.

Daddy pulled his old Philco from the back of a closet, a red plastic box with a big square battery. I carried it around the house and on walks, trying not to miss an inning. Now I had a daily narrative of games, a pennant race, to keep me company. Mel Allen's voice called me into a parallel world: "That ball is going, going, gone!"—pure consummation, the home run that ended discourse in speechless sound, the player who hit it elevated to temporary adulation.

I hurried upstairs from the Bill-Dave wagon, heart beating, to catch the endings of games, though sometimes Bert put the Yankees on the wagon radio. (In the early 1950s only rare Yankee games were on Channel 11, but these were monumental affairs, from pregame home-run contests to postgame interviews.)

A victory by the Yanks would wash out all other sadnesses and disappointments. Like a fairy's wand it would enhance and color the day, giving it a rhapsodic spark. I would become happier, friend-lier, more cooperative, even more attentive in class. Likewise, if the Yanks lost, everything would become glummer and drearier; I would turn sullen and inward. This dance of Yankee highs and lows was a reliable mood-barometer throughout my childhood.

Jonny declared himself a Yankee fan too and picked his own favorite player. So Daddy took us back to Miller's and bought Yankee caps and pinstriped uniforms. We proudly donned these for our Sunday outings, number 12, Gil McDougald, and number 7, Mickey Mantle, the switch-hitting star.

For years my brother and I routinely carried a Spaldeen and threw it over and under obstacles on the street, widening our range as we hit Central Park. Bridey said we had "ball-itis" because a round object was all that was needed to instigate this behavior. She may not have understood the impulse, but she knew its outcome. Spheroids, however large or small, generated energy fields that ran us around like marionettes. A marble or rounded gob of Silly Putty cast pretty much the same spell.

The way to our hearts was through baseball, so Bridey would tease us by calling me "Richard McTowers" and Jonny "Whitey T."—she had a particular fondness for the name Whitey Ford and used it on unlikely occasions. Jon appreciated his nickname and, at its summons, snapped imaginary curve balls for her. We tried to get her more involved, telling her scores about which she cared little. "It's not an Irish game," she insisted. "And my kinfolk wouldn't want me rooting for such as Yankees anyway."

To her mind, we honored the players like priests, and it was sinful to put so much emphasis on mere mortals. If we waxed too euphoric about a Yankee win, she said things like, "Hush now with your idolatry."

Sometimes Daddy peered in when we were listening and commented on the game, though he was a Giants fan. He had stock lines, like when Eddie Lopat was having a rough outing: "He's not fooling anyone today, boys." We laughed, as though he were Casey Stengel remarking to his bullpen coaches.

One afternoon, Uncle Moe made an appearance, kneeled down right beside us, and requested an immediate update. I told him that Johnny Mize had just missed a pinch homer. Jim Delsing dove into the stands to take it away.

"Did he buy a ticket?" Uncle Moe asked.

I stared back at him without smiling. This was not a trivial matter, and I was hardly over my disappointment.

"Why, he can't go into the stands without a ticket!"

At home I made up my own games. I would divide cards into nine-man teams, set one into fielding positions on the carpet, the other into a batting order, make one of my "doubles" the "ball," and play nine innings, with the team of cards at bat taking turns swatting the "ball," card-face against finger-teed card-edge. An out was when the "ball" landed on another card or near an infielder (from where I could flip it onto a part of the first baseman card—or fail for an error). Players took on distinct personalities, as regions of rug became sectors of a diamond. Jon's and my bureaus were the bleachers: home-run territory. Few pleasures exceeded the feeling of a seemingly solid hit floating across my room and landing smack on an outfielder's card—or grazing the bureau for a Ballantine blast.

During spare moments at Bill-Dave (or whispered at school) Phil and I played the "Initials" game: L.D., outfielder, Indians?; P.S., second-base, Athletics?; A.S., pitcher, Yankees? (We would never miss a Yankee no matter how obscure.) J.O., infielder, Pirates? Though not a Yankee, Johnny O'Brien was Phil's favorite, the player he imagined and announced himself as, going into the hole at shortstop, making the throw to get the force play with his brother Eddie at second. It was the "O-apostrophe" of their names, not their abilities, that captivated Phil, for neither O'Brien could hold a candle to Bill-Dave's all-star shortstop.

En route home Phil and I would sit together in the back of the wagon pretending we were Mel Allen and Jim Woods announcing innings, complete with introductions, disclaimers, and Ballantine beer ads. We would go pitch by pitch: "Reynolds winds, checks second; now he comes to the plate ... swung on.... "

We also had a rendition of Lou Gehrig's legendary speech. I'd speak it, and Phil would do the echoes:

"I consider myself—"

"... consider myself—"

"... the luckiest man—"

"... iest man—"

"... on the face of the earth—"

"... face of the earth."

Then we applauded wildly, other kids joining in like the 1939 crowd. It seemed strange that, when he spoke those happy words to a full house at Yankee Stadium five years before we were born, Gehrig was dying of a fatal disease—strange too that we replicated them so lightly, taking on the role of the doomed hero. Yet as I performed them, I felt a sense of honor and reverence—a chill down my spine. More than Abraham Lincoln's "Fourscore and seven years ago ...," it was the most important speech in the universe or at least the most important that I knew.

3

UNCLE PAUL

I arrived at Miss Hazel's second grade still behind. I could read, but I couldn't make all the letters in script and didn't know how to carry over columns in addition and subtraction. I left puddles on the floor, so the teacher sat me apart with newspapers under my desk. I plucked Landmark books off nearby shelves and read them while others worked: the Louisiana purchase, Ethan Allen and the Green Mountain Boys, the Lewis and Clark Expedition, the Wright Brothers, the Panama Canal, the Winter at Valley Forge, Pocahontas and John Smith. These myths became my alternate education as well as my basic map of America to which all later ones had to conform. It is still my phenomenological America, sealed by the Pony Express and a last golden spike joining transcontinental railroad lines from the east and west in Utah Territory.

On the day of the seventh game of the 1952 World Series I felt dizzy, so I was taken to the nurse's office and sent home. Bridey helped me change into PJs. As cartoon figures danced with oversized letters in my brain, I dozed in and out of sleep.

I awoke with a start in the seventh inning. The Yankees were up 4-2, but the bases were loaded with Dodgers. Bob Kuzava was coming in from the bullpen in relief of Vic Raschi. Eddie Lopat and Allie Reynolds had preceded him: the Yankees' three main starters all used. I took out Kuzava's card and reviewed his career. The whole season was on the line, and a journeyman southpaw was about to face mighty Duke Snider and Jackie Robinson.

Then Billy Martin, racing out of nowhere as the other infielders stood paralyzed, made a lunging catch of Robinson's infield fly near the mound, a second pop-up in a row induced by the unlikely hero. I cheered out loud. "A great hunch by Casey," Mel Allen declared. "I was sure it would backfire."

"Home sick, are you?" laughed Bridey. Ramon, the elevator man, had told her I was playing "World Series hookey." (He spelled his name R-a-m-o-n, but it was pronounced "Ramone.")

But if I wasn't sick, why did I fall into such a whirligig trance and miss most of the game?

One afternoon the principal of P.S. 6 called Mommy in for a conference. He said that I was either brain-damaged or mentally ill. He required a medical affidavit if I was to continue.

What I remember is a day of no school and a trip downtown in a taxi, sportive but ominous. My mother took my arm as we turned the street corner into a hospital-like structure. There a doctor led me down a hall, but, to my relief, he didn't ask me to take off my clothes or even have an examining table. Instead we sat on opposite sides of a counter where he set before me a series of mazes and puzzles. When I finished solving these he reached into his drawer for a box and, one by one, put down large cards with pictures that I had to interpret for him. I looked at drawings of people peeking around doors, of weird cloud-like houses and groups of men and women doing unexplained things and, as requested, made up stories for them. I viewed rows of faces of strange characters, some with large warts, moustaches, or eyeglasses, and said which ones I'd go out with or wouldn't. Then he pulled out a page of twisted shapes and asked me to sort them.

Finally I studied a necklace of different colors and shapes of beads, memorized their positions and restrung them. "Perfect," the doctor acclaimed. "Hardly anyone gets them all." I emerged triumphant and reported my success to Mommy.

In the session after lunch, there were no games. I was asked to lie on a cot. A nurse taped wires to my head, my life apparently revealed in a code that a needle translated onto a drum. I shielded my mind so that my spaceship and travels would not be discovered.

Years later I learned that the tests showed I was normal but emotionally disturbed. At the time Mommy said only that I would be seeing another doctor. At first I complained because she had scheduled it on my birthday and it didn't sound like much fun. "Sure it will be fun. Remember how much you enjoyed the puzzles and beads."

She brought me there on November 3rd, 1952. We took a bus further downtown than I had ever gone. Then we walked along old-fashioned streets, turned into a doorway, and found ourselves in a foyer with fancy chairs. *New Yorker* magazines were piled on a table, so I turned through the cartoons, occasionally asking Mommy to explain one. Finally a door opened; the doctor gestured me in. Mommy kissed me on both cheeks and left.

It was a ground-floor flat, bookshelves up to its ceilings. A window faced Seventh Street. I saw a girl skipping rope, a man strapped to a building washing windows.

His name was Abraham Fabian. He was tall and resembled Abraham Lincoln. I sat in a chair across from him, answered his questions, and gradually warmed to tell him about school, Bill-Dave, and my family. He was cordial and attentive, so I confided the thing that excited me most: my Uncle Paul was taking me out afterwards. When I exited the office, sure enough, Uncle Paul was there, large as life, reading a magazine. "Richard my boy!" he exclaimed. He threw out his arms and invited me into a bear hug. Then he shook hands with Dr. Fabian as though they were old buddies.

"Have a good birthday," the doctor called as we left.

Outside, we hailed a cab. In a river of green lights the driver tore uptown, then swerved onto a side street and screeched to a stop: Al Schacht's Restaurant. A doorman led us into a baseball palace—its staircase railings were made of lacquered bats and balls, and all the choices on the menu were puns on players' names: Dizzy Trout, Ty Corn on the Cobb, and Yogi Berries. I ordered a fruit cocktail on ice and was picking out the sweet cherries when two tall men in suits joined our table. In answer to Uncle Paul's question, I insisted that I didn't know these fellows. "Sure, you do," he kept saying as I shook my head.

Then he threw up his arms and declared with chagrin, "Why, I was told you knew all the New York Yankees. This is first-baseman Joe Collins and catcher Charlie Silvera." My heart skipped, and I stared again. They were real, the faces from the cards, dressed in suits and ties. No one I knew had ever had *dinner* with one of them.

The room was a bustle of activity and yummy smells. I sat watching balancing feats of waiters, meals sailing out of the kitchen. Uncle Paul ordered everyone steaks and French fries and, while we ate, people came up to shake hands with him and his Yankee friends.

The players were large, like cowboys, and they and Uncle Paul talked adult stuff to each other, never once mentioning baseball. Al Schacht, an old man who was once a pitcher, pulled up a chair and told jokes. After a while the Yankees began to laugh. Then Mr. Schacht rose to greet a cake of baseball decorations and candles. He led the singing of "Happy Birthday," which even Charlie Silvera and Joe Collins participated in, gazing at me with big grins. I couldn't wait to get to school the next day to tell Phil.

After my first time at Dr. Fabian's I was brought there twice a week by a graduate student from Columbia named Neil. Grateful to be rescued from the after-school melee at the Bill-Dave wagon, I pranced alongside my new companion, anticipating our next escapade in the subway. Neil bought me comics, shared his nickels in candy machines, and played "Geography" (the last letters of places providing the first letters of other places you had to supply). If we were early, he took me to a nearby cafeteria, ordered treats, and bought me a puzzle book. We would sit on adjacent stools connecting numbered dots and solving things like "One of these objects is not like the others" and "What's wrong with this picture?" "Well, the clock has three hands, the table is missing a leg, the dog has the back legs of a rabbit, and the lamp isn't reflected in the mirror."

He liked to tease me about baseball being so important. In challenge of that, he invented a game in which he said words that supposedly had nothing to do with baseball and I tried to make up a baseball sentence about each of them. His first two were stumpers:

"paradise" and "florist," so I said, "The baseball player went to paradise" and "The baseball player bought flowers at the florist."

He called that cheating but said that it taught us an important lesson. I couldn't guess, so he told me, "It's that human beings can't make up anything that isn't human."

Neil would sit in the waiting room while I went inside. Afterwards, if there was time, he asked Dr. Fabian questions about his own studies. Then he took me on the subway home.

Dr. Fabian never said precisely who he was or what his job comprised, but I understood that he was my special ally. He got in on everything, reviewing and correcting my arithmetic and spelling and teaching me stuff I hadn't understood in class. Sympathetic about hectoring at school and miffed on my behalf about being blamed for everything at home, he mainly wanted to hear about Nanny. Unfortunately, I could remember little except how she reminded me of the cackling witch in *Tubby and Little Lulu*.

"But you loved her too," he submitted.

I considered the notion, then nodded.

From the long line of volumes on his shelf I understood that Dr. Fabian was a spokesman for a man whose name I misread as Dr. Freund because there was a brass plate with that name on the outside of our apartment building. "He lives downstairs from us," I told him.

"Dr. Freud does?"

I nodded.

He didn't correct me.

With a deck of cards we played War and Casino and then Hangman, a paper-and-pencil word-guessing game, with stages toward a completed figure on a noose tabbed by lines representing wrong guesses. He also taught me Battleship—a duel of hiding and "shooting" ships by placing them in grids we drew on blank pages and then guessing each other's coordinates (a foreshadowing of algebraic axes)—then how to fold and tear pieces of paper many times over into boats and little flat diamonds that blew up in balls with a single puff.

Our routine was to use part of each session for me to tell him about what had happened since I last saw him. He always inquired how often I had wet my pants and bed that week, but he didn't stop there. "What do you think at the moment you are wetting? What do you feel when your mother takes Jonny's side?" No one had ever asked such stuff before, and I was usually stumped, so he drew responses by asking me to say the first thing I thought of, no matter what it was or how unrelated ... then the thing after that ... and so on. These chains of thoughts, like the game of Telephone, led us in unlikely directions, through comic book characters, fairy tales, baseball players, puns, jokes, advertising rhymes, and plain nonsense. Yet they always astonishingly got to something that made sense and gave a hidden explanation for my behavior. It was by far the neatest game I had ever played.

After a few sessions Dr. Fabian explained that we were trying to get into my unconscious mind where the true causes of my fears and wetting were disguised in a code. "Things you can't tell yourself directly you let dreams and unconscious actions speak for you. Once you learn what these are, they can no longer control or harm you."

This was unexpected, bizarre information. To me, danger was, as Flash Gordon knew ... danger. When someone threw you in a scalding shower or said, "Down the dungeon stairs with you, into the dark forever," he meant it. Cancer was cancer, the worst of killers and calamities. Polio was the name of another terrible disease. You could hear it in the very word, pretending to be "polo," then tricking you with that evil "i."

"No," Dr. Fabian insisted, "those are cover stories, ruses you've made up to hide other things you don't want to know, things you can't face." He promised that by our interpreting my dreams and free-connecting my thoughts, we would be led to what he called the promised land. We'd undo Nanny's hexes and repair the damage she had done. "Your fears will evaporate," he declared with a beatific smile, "just like that!"

I thought of my record "What Makes Rain," in which gleeful little droplets are converted by the sun into clouds and sing happily as they fall back onto the earth into thirsty flowers, rivers, and seas.

Could I turn my own pangs of terror into harmless vapors as easily?

I asked Dr. Fabian where I hid things. After all, there was only me and I knew about myself.

"In wet pants," he replied, "in daydreams, and in fears. Richard's unconscious self makes decisions for him too."

It seemed absurd that some person inside me would cause me to wet my pants and conceal stuff to my detriment. Why would I sabotage myself? Finding a way through this subterfuge was our next order of business.

In the first dream we studied, I was arranging a chemistry set. The flask suddenly cracked in my hands and I was running down the hall to throw it in the toilet bowl, but I was too late. A burning liquid spilled through my fingers onto my legs. That, Dr. Fabian told me, was a symbol; it combined urine and poison. Nanny's warnings about infecting myself with my own pee had turned it into an acid that I failed to dispose of in time. "This dream by itself doesn't answer the big question," he explained, "but it tells us many important things; for instance that there's a relationship between your wetting and your fears."

I was delighted by his clever deciphering and I tested it in my mind over and over again. It fit as perfectly as a solution in the back of a puzzle book. "What figures go together? Which one doesn't match? What's the only path through the maze?" Peeing was not peeing, poison was not poison; even fear was not fear. Bedwetting was an unconscious deed, committed in the darkness of sleep, but it left a rebus, a chain as incremental and traceable as those in the game of Telephone.

Week by week a dream landscape unfolded. Bob, the mean counselor from Swago, represented Daddy—he had the same first name. My mother was a giant wounded bird. My brother was a scruffy, black dog who clamped his teeth onto my arm so that I couldn't pull it away. Dr. Fabian was flattered to find himself a magician, then General Manager of the Yankees.

The most surprising interpretation involved St. Louis Cardinal outfielder Enos Slaughter, who appeared as a Bill-Dave counselor. After free connection Dr. Fabian concluded that his name referred to Dr. Hitzig and he was trying to tell us about the dungeon stairs. "How'd you like to have a name like that?" he ad-libbed, disappointed that I hadn't caught onto the bloodshed at once. To me Enos Slaughter was just another player on a card until Dr. Fabian decoded him.

Symbols gradually made fissures in a reality that had seemed till then impassive and beyond appeal. The unconscious was everywhere, so it transformed the world. My mother was no longer either a monster and tyrant or a decent woman under attack by ungrateful children; she was trapped by her own fears and problems, more sphinx than harpy. Bullies at school and in group, though they pretended to be kings of the universe, controlled nothing; they didn't even know who they were or why they were doing stuff.

Years before I was capable of understanding symbolic thought, let alone information theory, I had its rudiments installed in me by psychiatric transference. Through Dr. Fabian's affection for me, his intention to rescue a troubled child, he handed over the key to the arbitrary link between two unconscious messages that generate each other. Of course, he couldn't teach me something that subtle, so he imbued it by his sheer desire that I know. I didn't grasp its myriad nuances, but I got its simple, raw essence. In fact, I got it so profoundly that a part of my life thereafter became interpreting events, using symbols as clues.

Yes, I was behind in class and a misfit, but I was solving real puzzles. Plus to everyone's surprise, my daytime wetting stopped, confirming Dr. Fabian's method.

I was still in the watchtower, but I was acquiring the tools of a wizard.

My mother tried to reestablish her authority over the psychiatrist, sending away for a booklet advertised in the *Daily News:* "How to Conquer Your Fears." It was a stapled pamphlet with cartoons illustrating individual fears. Each had a number of points. Starting with the lowest-rated one, you strove to achieve a better score over weeks by making your mind master a fear at a time. The highest was "Fear of Failure," fifty points' worth. I didn't have that one. By comparison, fear of disease was only five. That was a ridiculously low grade, a tipoff to the ignorance of the author! There were also fears I had never heard of; for instance, fear of being buried alive. That recalled the Cisco Kid's poisoned blankets (not on the list) and led me to obsess about coffins.

I told my mother that the pamphlet only gave me new fears and that I knew from Dr. Fabian using your will and keeping score wasn't the way you got rid of fears. "The reasons they are there are unconscious," I explained to her. "You can't just tell them to go away."

She was infuriated. "It helps thousands of people but not him," she shouted to no one in particular. "After all, he's not like the rest of us; he's special."

She was in the majority. In truth, no one else seemed to act as though Dr. Fabian's symbols existed—not my teacher, not Bill-Dave counselors, none of my uncles or aunts.

I wore my Yankee pinstripes into the winter at Bill-Dave, an over-coat on top, refusing to play soccer or football, carrying a glove and a hardball, ready to have a catch with anyone who dared join me in the snow. Well into February I portered these items, more as totems than useful props since no one was willing. Even if someone had wanted to play and could tolerate the sting of a hardball in freezing temperatures, it was just too weird. My schoolmates worshipped conformity; in the fifties it was our state religion. "Don't be a dope," everyone said without having to say it. "No one plays baseball in the snow." *I* did.

Despite the entreaties of Bill and the other counselors, I never conceded a scrap of loyalty to the other sports. I refused to play imposter games with their leathery blimpballs and bumptious thuds. Baseball was my alias. When no one played with me, I threw the ball in the air and caught it, over and over.

A dope I was—an obstinacy I regretted years later because I would love to have bounced a basketball to an open teammate or stepped in front of an opponent to intercept a pass, skills and moves I for-feited forever. I didn't dare look at what was going on around me, risk seeing my place in it. I was cutting an ugly, trenchant shape, yet one I had to have.

It was never about fun or success; it was about survival. Before my selfhood was assured, I had to fight a life-and-death struggle for every morsel of it, within an oppressive society, in a jealous family, in aggressive schools and camps. I had to safeguard my psyche by the strictness of my intent.

I got something untellable by showing up with a glove and ball out of season, for I was engaged in a ritual far more ancient and serious than baseball.

In fact, the official American League amulet with its red-zippered coat proved a disappointment when Jonny and I completed our dissection of a cowhide that got scuffed and was coming apart anyway. After we cut and removed the glossy white veil, we found only yarn around cork: a puny little paddle-ball. Yet an untarnished baseball was an inviolable symbol, a touchstone that opened an enchanted realm. Though we had split a real one, we hadn't touched the thing it stood for.

Baseball was a voice that never stopped talking to me. I was lost without box scores, daily averages and standings, without Mel Allen to remind me who we all were and where this was taking place. His mantra, rising and falling in swaths of revelation as the game progressed, was a broadcast from the homeland to a child in exile, issuing a password through the great dark, when there was no other.

I remember as if yesterday Daddy, Jonny, and me sitting on a park bench in high suspense, waiting for Irv Noren to take his turn as a pinch-hitter—two on, two out in the eighth, two runs down. When he doubled into the corner, the three of us jumped up and down, hugging each other, as Mel Allen crooned the hymn of redemption.

A child's parable, a phonograph record called "Little Johnny Strikeout," told my story through a glass darkly. In this fairy tale Joe DiMaggio, without revealing his identity, approached a kid my age after a game he happened to observe while strolling in Central Park. To the jeers of his friends Johnny had just struck out for the third straight time while DiMaggio stopped to watch ("Little Johnny Strikeout," the chorus sang, "he can't hit the ball!"). The despondent boy was on his way home alone when DiMaggio got his attention and convinced him to stay a bit longer and take a lesson from him. After some whiffs, a bit of instruction, and a few hopeful foul tips—suddenly, smack! You can imagine the scene the next day when Joe showed up again as a passing spectator, and, after the usual taunting chorus, Johnny hit a home run to win the game. Afterwards ("Say, who is that friend of yours, Johnny?"), the Yankee Clipper disclosed his identity to the ovations of the kids.

One day Dr. Fabian asked me an ordinary question about Daddy. When I answered, he startled me by his response. "No, I mean your real father."

I considered this for a while. Was it a trick, another kind of symbol?

No, not the way he posed it. I grinned playfully and said, "Daddy is Daddy. Don't you know, Bob Towers?" He had never met Daddy, so anything was possible; yet it hardly seemed like a confusion he would have.

"Not Bob Towers. Don't you know Bob Towers isn't your father?"

I shook my head. This game made me goofy, but something about it rang true. I thought, "Martha Towers, Richard Towers, Jonathan Towers, Deborah Towers. Not my father?" It was a riddle, but it was more than the riddle. It was a changing stage set in a darkened theater. What would I see when the lights came on?

"I think you know who your father is."

I sorted back through memories until I was arrived at the Easter egg in the bush. I looked at the face of the one who had rehid it. I felt a shock of recognition. He couldn't be just an uncle—this man who sang with me at the Penny Arcade, who knew the Yankees in person. "Uncle Paul?"

"Right. Paul is your father. I asked you because I wanted to see if you knew."

I pondered this for a moment. Did I really know, or was it the only plausible guess?

"It was there all along," Dr. Fabian said, "in your unconscious mind."

As the universe wobbled to let Uncle Paul shift denomination, he seemed oddly overdressed in his new role, too sartorial to be my Dad. I tried to hold him there, but he slipped away because there was nothing to connect me to him in the way I was joined irrefutably to my mother. Why had I guessed it? I didn't look or act like him: he was large, fat, and gregarious, a walking fortress. I was small and sinewy and shy. I hadn't earned such a grand, noble father, and he didn't deserve such a wee, inadequate son.

"Is that why he comes to our house?" I finally asked.

"Yes, you are his child. Bob is Jonny's father," he continued. "That's why Uncle Paul takes you out alone. Your mother tried to keep him out of your life. But he loved you so much he kept coming, even against her wishes." The world was turning boundaryless. "He's the reason you see me," Dr. Fabian continued. "He found me and pays for me. Your mother would never permit it."

Then he explained how, after the tests at the hospital showed that I wasn't brain-damaged but emotionally disturbed, she decided to get Uncle Paul involved. "Before she learned you were sick she was very jealous of your father. She wanted you for herself. But once you were damaged goods she didn't mind if he shared you. She thought it might be costly, that you might need medical care and a special school. She knew he would pay for it."

Revelation upon revelation! But I was willingly borne along.

Dr. Fabian had unmasked my father partly because he wanted me to spend more time with him. From then on, Uncle Paul planned an evening together every month. His phone call announcing the occasion was more glorious than a birthday. "Richard," he would say in his big voice, as if he had just discovered me, "how'd you like to get together?"

"Yay!"

My mother would put me in my best clothes and send me in a cab to the Plaza where my father stayed. With newfound confidence I marched down lobbies of chandeliers into quiet elevators that opened onto grand hallways. Uncle Paul's room number was the key to happiness.

He met me at the door to his suite. Then we went out on the town, returning most often to the Penny Arcade where I progressed to air hockey (rotating guns blowing a ping-pong-like ball back and forth into slots for goals) and racing each other in imitation cars against landscapes that rolled by on drums.

Once, he took me to the Silver Skates at Madison Square Garden. At the start of the longest-distance race he told me to keep my eyes on a contestant he sponsored named Ray Blum. Wearing a blue and white jersey with the name "Grossinger's" diagonally across it, his skater dropped behind and stayed in last, even as the contestants entered the final few laps. I felt sorry for him. "You watch," Uncle Paul promised. "Ray always saves his run till it counts. He's conserving his energy."

I was sure he was wrong; yet, moments after he said that, Blum began to pick up speed. He caught the other skaters one by one. We cheered together as he ate up ground in great strides, streaking past the leaders as they were standing still.

Sometimes we ordered dinner by room service. I could choose anything from the menu. I usually ordered steak or liver with onion rings, pie with ice cream for dessert. *"A la mode,"* Uncle Paul called it.

I had a real father now, but Daddy had been my father for so long that the setup didn't take. Daddy acted like a Daddy. He helped me with my homework and taught me to play baseball. Uncle Paul was more like a king who left his castle now and then.

The effect of Uncle Paul becoming my father was the nullification of the word itself. He didn't seem like my father, so I could never call him Daddy. As hard as I tried, I couldn't get the name out. I always encountered a pause mid-word, a lapse of intonation. So I didn't call him anything.

Yet I couldn't call Daddy Daddy anymore and I also couldn't call him Uncle Bob—so I called him nothing too. For the remainder of my childhood I maneuvered between raindrops, timing my cadences, offsetting my phrasing in advance so as never to stumble into the word: "Daddy."

Usually my outings with my father were planned in advance, but on three occasions he surprised me by showing up at P.S. 6 after school. The first time we took a cab and met the governor at a cocktail party, then went across the Bridge to Newark Airport where we watched planes take off and land. Great roars preceded the transition to flight, soft touchdowns and promenades in the other direction. We continued to look through a picture window during dinner while they served a dazzling dessert: coconut-covered ice-cream balls carried across the darkened room with sparklers.

After that excursion, I searched every day for Uncle Paul beside the Bill-Dave wagon. Twice I rushed toward him in the crowds, only to find another fat man.

Then on an afternoon when I had forgotten to look, there he was, talking to Bill by the wagon. He hugged me and shouted at a cab. We went straight from P.S. 6 to a rehearsal with Eddie Fisher and later dined at a restaurant called Stockholm that had large figures of carved ice around a buffet.

Paul Grossinger was an enigma. Grand and important, smelling of perfume and outfitted in the fanciest suits (PG on his pockets and shirt cuffs), he moved awkwardly, bumping into people, and was often tongue-tied. Though he had both his eyes, I was astonished to learn that he had lost total sight in one. "A kid shot me with a beebee," he said with surprising irritation over something that had happened when he was younger than me.

In the course of our visits he quizzed me about schoolwork and asked repeatedly if my behavior was improving. "That's not what I hear from your mother!" he would retort with a wave of a finger. But then he'd chuckle.

He usually had inside scoops from Yankee players and executives, but if I pressed him too much on these, he acted as though he were guarding top-secret information and changed the subject. He preferred to describe his hotel: swimming pool, eighteen holes of golf, ice-skating, and a dining room that could hold five Plaza dining rooms. He mentioned his wife, Aunt Bunny, and my brothers, Michael and James. "You three will raise some hell!"

I didn't plan on that, but I was dying to meet them.

Though he addressed me in baby language and barely listened to what I said, he was sententiously reassuring, promising that between him and Dr. Fabian all my problems, including my fears, would soon be gone. With his huge belly and soft, round face he reminded me of Babe Ruth, and he had such a warmth and generosity that I wanted to be with him always. I was teary in the cab going home, though he handed me too much money for the fare and told me to keep the change. I would return to icy stares from everyone, even Bridey. It was as though I had been consorting with a convict. My seeming willingness to "be bought" was further proof to them of my selfishness and disloyalty.

On holiday weekends Daddy got his Mercury from the garage and took the whole family, Bridey included, into the countryside three hours to the Nevele. Our room was old-fashioned, with metal beds, fancy quilts, and a singing radiator. In the morning we accompanied our parents to the dining room where folded cloth napkins made goblets into tall birds alongside baskets of hot breakfast rolls and stacks of pancakes.

Daddy's first order of business was to lead us into the back room to pay our respects to Uncle Ben and Aunt Marian, the owners. Their space was smoky and crowded, people crouching over ledgers. Like the operator of a saloon Aunt Marian rose to greet us with strong handshakes. She gave Mommy a long, concerned hug: "How are you, Martha dear?" Her husky Ethel Merman voice carried innuendos of both rivalry and solicitude. Marian Slutsky was a powerful statuesque lady—Daddy's boss, Mommy's confidante, a formidable rival to Uncle Paul. In her presence Mommy acted meek and seemed about to cry.

"She treats me like a dog," she complained later to Bridey. "You'd think I was some sort of charity case. I used to be Martha Grossinger."

"She acts like Queen Elizabeth," Bridey concurred. "Someone ought to knock her off her high horse."

Released to our designs, Jonny and I played in reeds where minnows darted past, occasional sunnies tantalized—fish too swift to touch. We staged apple fights, climbed small trees, and collected horse chestnuts and rubber molds of cartoon characters from outside the pottery studio. Then we hiked with our parents through the forest to Nevele Falls. Eleven schoolteachers had discovered this site—the hotel's name honoring their number spelled backwards. I loved to watch the water gather speed, spool white, and roar down rocks and explode in whirl-pools. My brother and I threw sticks and bark into its stream.

When I look now at an old snapshot of us standing beside Nevele Falls, I wonder what became of our rubber boots and the toy gun lying on the ground. Jonny was asked to drop it for the photograph and tossed it aside unhappily because he wanted a cowboy look. They have almost certainly turned to pixels of gunk and rust and reentered nature untracked. They could be anywhere now—in the iron of someone's blood or carbon dioxide in the atmosphere or the soil of Mars. But they still exist. Someday the photograph will undergo degradation too and return to the common pool.

At Ivy's Store in the hotel lobby we bought puzzle books, baseball newspapers, and magazines and lay on couches reading comics and solving picture games while Daddy took forever in his business meeting with Aunt Marian. In a tall red chair under a mirror Bridey wrote to her family in fountain-pen script.

She told us she came from a land where there was fighting and that's why she was with us. We accepted such history as another game board like our one of the Civil War with its bearded faces. It was sad, her having to be away from her beloved sisters and neph-ews, Margaret and Siobhan, Patrick and Jimmy. She awaited their letters, aerograms with foreign stamps, and, after perusing them slowly and sometimes tearily, told us about their achievements in the much stricter schools in Belfast.

Yet Bridey was delighted to be in America, and steak dinners and vacation trips made up a bit for her exile in our mayhem. She wore floral scents, and on Saturday nights policemen rang our doorbell to take her to dances in the Bronx. Jon and I pranced around her, teased her, loved her like a second mother, and included her in our prayers at night: "God bless Mom, Dad, Jonny, Deb, Bridey.... " Gradually, she became part of us, this stranger from *"the place where the dark morn sweeps down to the sea."* She learned our secrets and was sucked into our cabal.

The third time Uncle Paul showed up after school he grabbed me from behind, calling out, "Richard the lion-hearted." I was ecstatic, though I was anything but a lion.

He told the cabbie to make a U-turn and head uptown. We attended a brief business meeting, then caught another cab at rush hour. I thought he was sending me home but, to my astonishment, he said, "Yankee Stadium!" I had seen the Stadium only in the distance from a car. Now the colossus grew larger and larger until it towered before us, banks of lights gleaming against a violet sky. We passed the unlit Polo Grounds and crossed the Harlem River. Then we were in the crowd, entering through turnstiles, swathed in aromas of tobacco and fries.

We ate dinner at a restaurant in the ballpark where the manager knew Uncle Paul, addressing him as "PG." After that we went to the souvenir stand where my father asked me to pick out anything I wanted. There was so much with "Yankees" on it I didn't know where to begin. First I got a scorecard and a yearbook. Then I saw a pen-and-pencil set of wooden bats, the pencil the type that you put thin sticks of lead into, so I pointed to that. After Uncle Paul pulled dollars out of a wad in his wallet and set them down on the counter, I noticed black-and-white glossies of many of the Yankees—Yogi Berra, Mickey Mantle, Gil McDougald, Allie Reynolds. It turned out that twelve came in an envelope—I wanted one of those too. Uncle Paul asked the man to throw in an autographed ball and an ice-cream cup. I carried my sack of treasures as he showed our tickets to an usher. We were led to our seats in the very first row behind the home-team dugout.

Floodbanks illuminated the green field and baselines. This was baseball's real site and it was much vaster and more complicated than it seemed on radio or TV. You could look everywhere and see things happening. Players were warming up so close I sat transfixed. Then, to my horror, Uncle Paul stood and began calling out to them. I didn't think they would answer, but Eddie Lopat jogged over. "What do you think of this weather?" he asked Uncle Paul.

"Colder than a witch's tit," my father responded.

I was mortified.

Uncle Paul next coaxed the name of my favorite player—just to hear me say it—for he knew.

I mumbled the answer.

"Well, let's get Gil over here."

"No," I protested, tugging at his sleeve to pull him away, but he was already calling. Finally he got his attention. McDougald jogged from his warm-up, glove in hand, and stood there with us by the railing. My heart was thumping as he asked Paul about his golf game and they talked about difficult holes and recent shots. This man had both everything and nothing to do with me and he didn't even know it. I wanted him sent away before it was too late. I didn't like mixing worlds, converting a baseball card into just another person. The longer I stood there and the more expressions of his I saw, the less he looked like Gil McDougald. Without the pinstriped uniform he could have been a Bill-Dave counselor.

Then I was introduced. "You play golf too?" McDougald asked.

"Gosh, no," I thought, but I could hardly mumble an answer. It seemed inappropriate to tell him I played baseball.

Later some friends of Uncle Paul's joined us in the row behind. "Sorry I couldn't get you any closer," he teased. They laughed and slapped his back. Then the three of them made bets on the game, Paul alone picking the Yankees.

In the eleventh inning Gene Woodling hit one high and far into the lights. I watched the ball disappear against the crowd. It was a meteor more than a cowhide I could hold in my hand or mind. Most of Yankee Stadium stood, and the roar grew and grew. I felt excitement all up and down me. There was no Mel Allen or Jim Woods, no words at all, just the actual din!

The men opened their wallets, and each gave a bunch of dollar bills to Uncle Paul. He folded them into a stack and handed it to me. "Your team won for me," he said. I was as flabbergasted as gratified. This was my father—my hero.

I was put in a cab. Through swift darkness of the city I stared at streams of lights leading me home.

"The show-off," my mother jeered the next morning. I knew I had been indulged, so it was almost a relief to have her put things in perspective. "Throwing money around, annoying ballplayers at the park where they have to play. What a big shot he is! Let him have to live with you. Disgust him with your antics. Pee in his bed. Leave him some dripping wet sheets. Then see how much he adores you."

"The man's a sloth," Bob chimed in. "Everything was given to him. He doesn't know how to work for a living. If he weren't handing out free vacations, the players would have him evicted from the park."

"Don't try to talk sense to this kid. He's so gullible he'll believe anything. Just let him be seduced."

"I know, Martha. There's no point in reasoning. He sees what he wants to see."

When I heard this I flushed in anger and shame. I felt naked before them, as though they read my mind. I knew I had betrayed family solidarity. I had valorized an outsider and accepted unwarranted gifts.

"Try the school of hard-knocks for a change," Daddy said, "like the rest of us. No one's out to do you a favor."

"Paul Grossinger was born with a silver spoon," Mommy added. She called him "a lazy bum, flaunting his parents' wealth."

Then Daddy compared him to the degenerate kings of England, adding that Aunt Marian had built the Nevele from her own sweat and blood. "No one gave her and Ben anything. The man is in the best business of all," he concluded with a flourish, "the inheritance business."

Uncle Paul's friend Dr. Fabian likewise was a "no-good son-of-a-bitch who can't hold down a job, a parasite living off other people's money. What an excuse for a human being!"

This was our household patter with predictable strophes and refrains. We kept performing encores as if we hadn't sung and danced it identically dozens of times already. It centered around exposing Uncle Paul and Dr. Fabian as collaborators to whom I was selling Towers secrets, spies and enemy agents (like keyhole-peeping Nanny who, it turned out, was paid for by Uncle Paul too). By contrast they were laboring, devoted parents struggling to cover our bills and teach us about the world. This litany never seemed to grow old for them.

Part of me saw my parents' side: I *was* out for myself at their expense. Their household was real; Uncle Paul was a cartoon.

Mommy and Daddy grew so self-righteous about their opinion that they made an appointment with Dr. Fabian. I couldn't imagine what would happen, but I hoped he would convince them of the value of what he did—after all, he was the acme of good sense. Apparently, they never gave him a chance; the whole time they were there they lambasted him for encouraging insolence in children. While gesturing angrily, Daddy smashed a lamp by accident. "I told Fabian to send me the bill," he recounted later. "The sonofabitch!— he could afford it. The man cowered before me like a mouse."

Dr. Fabian reported this event somewhat differently (in his version he hardly cowered). Still, I was astonished. How could they have been exposed so blatantly without anything changing?

I withdrew even more. For hours I sat by the window staring into the flow of activity along 96th Street. There was a melody to the thoroughfare: teenagers dashing, Puerto Rican women strolling, baby carriages, old men trekking from horizon to horizon, trucks and taxis, horns, every now and then a train bursting up from the tunnel. It held me in a kind of static contemplation beyond time or self.

4

CAMP CHIPINAW

The summer after we met as father and son, Uncle Paul decided that I should go to a camp near him, a place called Chipinaw. I told him my woes at Swago, but he assured me that no such things would happen. "I'm going to have a bear watching out for you. If you don't have a great summer," he swore, "he'll spit in the owner's eye."

I smiled stoically.

"And then after camp you'll come and stay with me at my hotel. It's the biggest, fanciest place in the country. It's better than a circus, a toy store, and a country club put together. What do you think of that?"

The bear was hardly convincing, so we dreamed up a code to evade any counselor spying on our phone calls: if I started telling him the names of moons of planets he would know something was wrong and come fetch me at once.

Bridey took me to Rappaport's, an official campers' outlet, on the West Side to be measured for the entire red and gray Chipinaw outfit: pants, T-shirts, sweat-clothes. It was the most exhaustive fitting I had ever undergone. Shirts and shorts piled up on our counter in mounds. The performing salesman kept directing me back onto the stool with jokes at my expense at which I refused to laugh.

"Why do you have to be so crabby?" Bridey snapped as we walked to the bus stop. "He was such a cheerful chap."

But what did she know about these matters except that she thought he was handsome? It was too much activity, too much focus on my body, too much putting on and taking off for no

purpose. I felt anemic, about to dissolve, my eyes locked in their
"I'm not here" position.

A week after second grade ended, Mommy brought me downtown
in a taxi to the Port Authority (I heard it as "Port of Authority")
where the Chipinaw-bound bus was loading. In a bustle of departing
children I kissed her cheek and burrowed aboard into the first empty
seat by a window. As mean as she was, she was known territory;
she *had to* take care of me. The owners and counselors were under
no such obligation. Despite her repeated assurances (on top of those
proffered by Uncle Paul), I knew, from firsthand experience as well
as her glib tone, that she had no idea what went on at camp.

As a series of war whoops spread throughout the vehicle, the driver
made a U-turn and headed back uptown. In the pandemonium I
mainly tried not to get carsick. I watched unknown parts of the
city turn shabby, then into countryside. I didn't take the peanut-
butter-and-jelly they handed out because I had never eaten such
a thing, so I dozed off, imagining how the grape and nut cream
might have tasted.

I was awakened by everyone singing. At first I didn't understand.
They went: *"Ninety-eight bottles of beer on the wall, / ninety-eight bottles
of beer. / If one of those bottles should happen to fall, / ninety-seven bottles
of beer on the wall."* Eventually I caught on and, as countryside and
towns zipped by, I was one of the few who lasted till *"zero bottles of
beer on the wall, / zero bottles of beer.... "*

It was late afternoon when our tires crunched into a gravel-filled
lot and motion ceased. "Last stop, Chipinaw," shouted a rising
counselor. "We're taking no prisoners, so everyone, alley oop!"
We filed into air ripe with buzzing things. The smell was pungent
and sticky, redolent of hay and manure.

I was in the youngest group, the Midgets—that was our name
by contrast with Freshmen, the next youngest (I have no idea how
long it survived into more politically correct eras). From the lot we
were marched across the road downhill to one of four adjoining
rooms located in the quadrants of a large cabin. Our individual beds
jutted out from its walls. At their heads, cubby-shelves stretched
above our reach. Already convened there was a noisy klatch of

parents who had toted their kids to camp by car and were helping them put away their stuff. I was pulled aside by a rotund, heavily perfumed woman who told me she was my Aunt Ruthie. "Here he is," she called out. "I found Richie." She clamped onto my hand and towed me to her son.

Jay had been coached because, after a surprisingly intimate hug, he took me under his wing, leading me from camper to camper: "Artie, this is my cousin Richie." I shook hands. "Barry, I want you to meet my cousin Richie." Then to me, "Barry's my best friend, so you're in with us."

"Hey, Schwartzie, you see this kid here. Well, lay off 'cause he's my cousin, and Barry and I'll kill ya."

Jay had a commanding presence and a reassuring rubbery fragrance. The largest kid my age I had ever seen, he acted like an adult, initiating clinches of greeting with other campers.

Our counselor, Larry Abelman, helped us make our beds, empty our trunks, and arrange our cubbies. Then he coined an identity—we were more than just Bunk 4 of the Midgets: we were the "Famous Five," and we got private nicknames—mine was Sparky because the first night at dinner I told Larry the story on my favorite record, how Sparky heard the train engine talking through the clatter, complaining that its right rear wheel was coming loose—then persuaded the conductor to stop seconds before they would have crashed. "Well, then that's *your* name," he declared. "You can warn us about hidden dangers the rest of us don't see."

Every day, at the second bugle (the first being dream-curdling reveille), the whole of Chipinaw lined up for personal inspection and then flag-raising to the blast of a third clarion.

As we hiked to the mess hall in fog, wet grass clung to our sneakers, frigid dew finding its way through our socks. A few yards from the rickety door, oatmeal-cocoa steam wafted over us.

Camper-waiters brought out bowls filled with sections of orange, jugs of milk, and platters of pancakes and eggs. I surprised my bunkmates by consuming Rice Krispies straight from the box.

"Gad, he eats them dry." I did; I considered soggy cold cereal yucky.

"That's okay," Larry joked. "Sparky's a horse."

I skipped the scrambled eggs but consumed half of the rye-bread basket, chewing the middles and then the crusts because they were different tastes.

After breakfast we were ordered to clean our bunk for inspection. I held the dustpan while Jay swept, but he was too rambunctious, so plenty of dirt and fluff landed in my face. "Hey," I cried out, "quit it!"

"Ooops!" He wasn't even looking, he was swinging for home runs.

As the Midgets' head counselor scrutinized the room, he pointed out subpar regions for improvement; then we were led to the day's first activity.

The venue varied. Some mornings we went to the crafts shop, where we threaded and tied thin colored plastic strips into lanyards, belts, and wallets. I liked selecting and cutting yellow, orange, blue, and red lengths from long rolls, and knitting various box, diamond, and cobra stitches into different-patterned snakes.

Sometimes we molded cups and statuettes out of clay, mud figures that turned to stone in the shop's oven.

Other days we were assigned to archery, softball, nature, volleyball, and boating.

Chipinaw remains an indelible mandala: its mess hall on the hilltop beside the flagpole and O.D. shack. The letters, I later learned, stood for "On Duty." The tiny cottage was an office for older kids who helped out around the camp.

At the bottom of the slope, twin rows of bunks ran along the forest. At a right angle to them was our Midgets' hut followed by ten or so large tents on platforms for the Seniors and Waiters, a queue that turned the corner and ran briefly parallel to the bunks at hilltop. The infirmary stood behind the tents near the Midgets' house. Beyond that was a fence separating Chipinaw from Camp Ge-Wah-Na across the woods.

We lined up every Friday in front of the infirmary for Aunt Mary, the nurse, to wash our hair. As we stepped forward one by one in turn, she poured green antiseptic from a jug and then ran a quick icy nozzle against us, grasshoppers and sow bugs scurrying, my eyes riveted shut against a venom that might render me blind.

I had seen the skull-and-crossbones on the back of the container from which she poured her potion, had felt its sharp sting the first time it got into my eyes. In fact, I experienced the longest blind spell ever, unable to open them to see if they still worked or had been burned out by acid. My fright dissolved as a bleary focus came back, but adults were blunderers and could not be trusted.

The forest primeval was Chipinaw's backdrop. Everywhere mowed fields ended, woods began with their denizens: cushions of green moss with tiny club-moss copses, beetles of different sizes, shapes, and speeds, clustering ferns, pale lichens on stone and bark, salamanders under rocks, centipedes and snakes that traversed the brush, their movements ending in camouflage. We explored this realm with the nature counselor.

His shack was a mournful, spooky place. It had the medicinal aroma of the infirmary but with gamy animal musk and an undertow of mineral slime. Frogs were gassed and, still throbbing, turned over on their backbones, their bellies slit to reveal iridescent innards and throbbing guts. Snakes caught by campers summers ago lay dormant in cages or as dried-out skins hung on walls among relics that included stuffed skunks, minks, and squirrels, pinned butterflies, fish skeletons, a fox skull, and a bear claw. Next to the shack was a cistern of standing water so green and dirty it seemed to drain to the bottom of the earth.

After late-afternoon flag-lowering and dinner, we engaged in freewheeling games, Snatch the Club and Color Tag, a twilight gambol in which a blindfolded counselor would call out a color and everyone wearing it would have to run between poles without being caught by the other team. We played into early darkness.

Without sounds of traffic, it was hard to fall asleep, but when the crickets converged, I fell into their directionless call.

Across a narrow road along which flitted a rare car or truck were ballfields, archery targets, tennis courts, stables, and a rifle range.

The meadows fanned out to more forest and Chipinaw's farther boundary with Ge-Wah-Na.

In the opposite direction at the end of a cobbly dirt path down a slope was a huge lake. We hiked there single file—moccasins and bathrobes required—towels about our necks.

It is a journey I still take in dreams. The woods are denser now, no longer uninhabited. As I leave the trail to scout, I discover its indigenous peoples: *tai chi* masters warming up next to builders of solar yurts, dowsers with willow twigs beside slabs of glowing quartz, ginseng- and shiitake-collectors in Mongolian robes. Their dwellings are wind and rain phenomena, rough facsimiles of huts and cabins. Deeper in are caves to antediluvian worlds, passes over cliffs to captured asteroids, massive amethysts in clusters. None of this did I glimpse in childhood, only pale intimations from which they later took form. I saw only pine cones amid leaves and dry needles, blueberry bushes and, once, a perfect navel orange said to have been left by the Cropsey Maniac, the mythical madman loose in those woods.

Toward the foot of the hill was our first outpost, the swimming counselors' tent. Then came a wooden bathhouse overlooking a cat-tail marsh and a dock area demarcated into boats at anchor and swimming zones from shallow to medium to deep, formed by barriers of wooden "eggs" strung together (called lemon lines). We were expected to get into our still-damp bathing suits and gather in rows in our assigned spots. My bare flesh crawled, and my lips felt as though daubed in the powdery white paint that rubbed off the bathhouse if glanced against, the mere thought of which gave me goose bumps.

Midgets populated the shallows where we were taught to swim. Beyond, splashes of competitive water sports blended with medleys of shouts and squeals from older boys and lifeguard whistles.

I was the only one among the Midgets who failed to progress. I thrashed about in the water, picking up stones with my toes, making bubbles with my arms and legs. I didn't consider swimming. I was satisfied to pretend while the more precocious of my bunkmates graduated to the intermediate and then into the deep end. It didn't bother me, for I wasn't a swimmer; I was a puddle creature.

There was plenty else to do on shore. I collected various sizes of rocks and stones and hurled them at trees, announcing strikes and balls depending on whether or not I hit the target. I often pitched a whole game of twenty-seven batters that way—all strikeouts and walks.

I skipped flat stones, counting their bounces: one, two, three, four.... Some of them made so many short skips at the end it was like a dotted line. I was thrilled to get those and tried to figure out which stones and angles made them. Then I tossed rocks of different sizes and shapes into the lake to hear their distinct plunks and hollow gulps as if the water were an ogre swallowing them. Some hit other stones and made a pleasurable tick or series of clacks. I floated sticks and bark and watched them travel beyond my reach. Edging along shoreline, I cracked open mussels and threw their goo into the shallows so that small fish gathered and tore it apart. Then I rinsed my hands.

I saw the rest of Chipinaw cavorting in blue water while I honored these drier rituals of my invention.

The view was mesmerizing. Crows travelled from tree to tree along the shoreline; darning needles buzzed over lily pads; frogs hopped from camouflage. Four other camps were visible. Ranger was as close as a stage set, its landscapes dotted with tiny figurines engaged in activities paralleling ours. Camp Ma-Ho-Ge and a more distant one whose name I never knew were panoramas of faint sounds and silhouettes, the farthest a mere vignette in a locket. Their universes were audible as faint recoils of near and far bugles and loudspeakers and an occasional staticky din of voices like an atmospheric displacement.

The Sea was called Silver Lake, but its name was equivocal; we called it alternately White Lake, Swan Lake, and Moon Lake. It was mostly just "the lake," or Chipinaw Lake. At sea in rowboats we looked down through opacity and saw sunnies hanging, an occasional fleeting turtle or tadpole. It was a spooky darkness, portending the immensity in which one would drop if he fell overboard. Yet it was pregnant with possibilities of life: mysterious splashes, giant submerged logs like dragons. If we passed a vessel from another camp, we stared at its occupants in awe as if they spoke a different language. The counselors, like Indian scouts, might greet one another.

Pine Cove was an uninhabited stretch of shore to which we travelled by canoe for an overnight. Debarking one by one, we waded ashore and stood in the clearing. Chipinaw's waterfront was now one of the vignettes on the horizon. A frog plunged beneath lily pads, stirring up mud at my feet. He was perturbed by the arrival of so many noisy animals. The Lake smelled as if a giant watermelon had been cut open, one so vast it included sun and sky and trees.

The nature counselor, leading the way with his hatchet, cleared a trail while raising the canopy. After we arrived at the campsite, he instructed us to collect wood and twigs—anything of size that was once alive and now dead and flammable. As twigs and timber were deposited beside him, he stacked them around the log he had hewn. Then he poured liquid from a can and ignited the teepee. Flames shot up, and we watched little stick forma-tions we called igloos collapse into red-orange ingots. Then we roasted hot dogs and corn in cans. The forest changed from sight to sound, and small animals could be heard running along pine needles and leaves.

Huddled around whining embers, we heard accounts of the Cropsey Maniac. Cut up real bad in a mill accident, his body had been sewn back together by incompetent doctors. Now he prowled the forest, seeking revenge. He kidnapped young campers and per-secuted them—none yet from Chipinaw, we were told, but he had his eye on us.

As sparks rushed upward into the black, I invoked the habitable worlds I knew and imagined my ship hurtling at terrific speed toward them. The fusion of wind through trees, starting mysteri-ously, then ceasing, and a brilliant Milky Way, made it seem that the breeze was rustling the stars, though I knew it was only the woods of my home planet. Mostly the bigness overwhelmed me, and I bowed to the omneity of light. Under the Dipper and Orion, marshmallows bubbling crisp black on peeled sticks, I was happy just to be alive and didn't care who or where I was.

By sleeptime the last coals were disintegrating into whitened ash.

I remember our columns of pre-breakfast "spread-eagles" trekking along hillsides in soaked sneakers, collecting stray wrappers, bottle caps, and bits of foil into garbage bags (the required weekly campus clean-up) ... punching the pocket of my glove and backing up as the batter swung (a stretch of flowering weeds separating outfield from forest) ... lines at the one cold drinking fountain along the maintenance hut (by contrast the spigot at the stable was fed by a hose from the barn and repugnantly lukewarm and smelly) ... waiters streaming through swinging doors with food for the famished ... the Midgets' march from the mess hall back to the cabin.

Thunderstorms passed close by as we lay in a blackened canopy. No formal activities—just Chinese checkers, comics, Rafter Ball, All-Star Baseball—a delirious litany of indoor fun. I alternated with an opponent, flipping a Spaldeen onto the central beam in the bunk and counting the bounces for single, double, triple, home run, playing nine innings. It took a fine touch (and luck) to get anything more than one bounce on the narrow board, though once it actually rolled to a stop for an alternate version of a homer.

All-Star Baseball's board had a spinner over which we fit individual player disks with different-size zones for home runs, singles, doubles, strikeouts, and the rest of the plays based on career stats of each. I lay on my belly with the others, spinning for long-retired Charlie Keller or Aaron Robinson, trying to hit a home run by landing the arrow at the top on the sector marked 1—fat on Ted Williams and Mickey Mantle, a mere sliver for Pee Wee Reese and Billy Martin. There was an irresistible draw to the game's circlets of thin cardboard, the spinning pointer, and the numbers 1, 2, 3, etc., assigned scientifically to achieve real game effects.

From out the windows came brief dazzles of light, which sent bowling pins, clearly of great size, toppling across Chipinaw. We giggled and threw ourselves onto one another, feigning terror.

In the damp undergrowth afterwards, we collected salamanders, plucking soft, wriggling bodies from moss and upturned stones and dropping them into coffee cans. We transported these to the nature shack, where they were set in a glass terrarium.

I liked to run through fields by the stables, trying to catch grasshoppers before they flew up. If they jumped, I chased to where they landed, held their rickety beings in a cupped palm for an instant, then let them go.

This was the fabled countryside I had visited briefly at Swago and the Nevele. Now I lived there every day on the edge of unexplored wilderness.

Beside horses and straw, a hose siphoned into a rusty barrel. In puddles formed by its overflow, I rescued flies and other insects by floating leaves to them. Once these creatures started to crawl onto dry ground I bolted from their revivals. They were too wounded and precarious to watch, like miniature cropsies.

Fragrances of new-mown grass and flowering trees worked their spell. My toes wriggling in anonymous dirt and dead moths, the gurgle of a warm shower on my back, something foreign spread throughout my being. I was no longer Martha's son or Jonny's brother. I was a pagan thing.

My cousin Jay, his best friend Barry, and I forged an unlikely trio—the charismatic slugger; the pudgy mother's boy; and the day-dreaming pip with whom they bickered and bonded. Jay was our king, power broker, and athlete supreme. Barry was his crony, another large butterball but a highbrow sourpuss too and a fitful student of the trumpet. I was our group's jester and lone wolf.

Despite our dichotomies we melded realities, becoming close buddies and incorrigible needlers. Insofar as they were both Dodger fans and abhorred the Yankees, their preferred teasing was to grab each other in ballroom posture and wriggle around in a dance they called "the Gil McDougald." "Stop!" I would protest, but that only made them pretend to kiss like birds.

I was the confederate to whom Jay confided his fear of the dark, for someone had to go ahead and flip the switch. The flashlight didn't reassure him, and if I held it below my face aimed upward and made horror masks, he hated that despite its obvious frivolity. At nightfall we kept a mutual eye out for the Cropsey Maniac as well as sources of unexplained plunks and snaps in the dark. Perhaps the Maniac lurked nearby or had sneaked into our cabin. Meanwhile we spooked each other with flashlit visages and squeals of "Eek, a freak."

Jay told the rest of the bunk that teasing over my wet bed would not be tolerated. "He can't help it," he said. "How would you like it if it was you?"

My cousin's protection was necessary, for mayhem was always imminent and some kids apparently existed only to deliver little hurts and pain. The means were as varied as they were ingenious, ranging from good-natured horseplay to recreational sadism. A damp towel could be lethal if snapped by letting it fall alongside someone's legs or balls and then pulling it suddenly back, leaving a nasty sting. It seemed that the boys who delivered these surprisingly acute bites were themselves as lean and stringy as their towels. There were also nougies, subterfuge knuckle blows to the shoulder or head, delivered without warning or provocation. Part of one's being was always alert and on guard against such intrusions, a way of life at Chipinaw.

We had rope-burn specialists too among us. I don't know how mastery was gained, but aficionados would, almost any time that you were vulnerable, grab an arm or leg and, by a quick twist, one hand going one way, the other the opposite, leave a sensation of fire. Successful rope burns were these kids' greatest amusement, so they collected coups like scalps; the fiends would say stuff like "Ready for my Indian rope burn?"

Of course we all tried this stuff, but we were not as effective or persistent as the pros.

Other kids specialized in the bending back of arms, a local favorite with all sorts of personalized signatures: an extra coil or jiggle, an off angle. The way some boys put a signature on their arm-twisting technique was unconsciously presexual—the precise seductive obverse of seduction, a flirtatious prod that jerked one into the allure of their craft and ravishment.

Fatsoes preferred the cobra grip; they would clutch you to their rank, porky bellies and hug as hard as they could while affecting a German accent that was supposed to sound reptile or Dracula-like: "I'm going to squeeze the life out of you." Under such attacks, I felt my nature change. All I wanted was to claw or kick or bite my way out.

By comparison to such recreant bullies, Jay was virtue plus brute force. His presence kept trouble at bay.

One afternoon Jerry, the head instructor, asked me to stay after General Swim. The rest of the Midgets hiked up the hill. I stood by the grandstand, curious to see what would happen next.

Jerry led me into the water and tried to coax me into swimming. I swung my arms in place.

Taking a loose egg from the lemon-line, he tossed it over my head and called, "It's hit to the outfield. C'mon … bring it in. Get him at home." I half-ran, half-paddled to the piece of wood and tossed it to him. He made the tag … but the runner was safe.

We continued that way several times a week, alone in the shallows—no talk about swimming but catches in deeper and deeper water, plays off the outfield wall … and gradually I was gliding along the water to corral the floating wood. He had this unspoken pact with me that I would pass the test and go into intermediate water.

On the chosen day I had to jump into the lake and sink beneath my head. I stood on the edge of the dock, hugging myself, feeling like an insubstantial wisp compared to the sleek tanks around me. But I shut off my mind and leaped. Plummeting into bubbles and green light, I felt the shock of cold and glimpsed the muddy bottom for an instant. I saw my terror clearly—that I'd become so dizzy I'd disappear, that I'd turn into a drowned body, floating like the cardboard I saw once, or thought I saw, along the surf at Long Beach: a dead lady. These semblances passed in a gasp as I shot to the surface, water clogging my nose and throat.

I swam to the far dock.

It was not difficult at all. In one part of me I knew why everyone else simply did it. In another sense I was a company of fragmented beings borne along together. Yes, swimming was important, but it was also a distraction. Or perhaps it was that I had to be distracted from fantasies in order to do anything real. Like baseball—I didn't learn to swim; it was inside me and I found it.

Saturdays were official visiting days, and we wore our Chipinaw whites. All morning we sat, restless, anticipative, through compulsory Hebrew services—the boys' camp on one side of the armory, the girls on the other, counselors stationed along the aisles, trying to keep brothers and sisters, boyfriends and girlfriends, apart.

In relief at the nearing conclusion we raucously mangled the words of the final prayers *("Dy-Dy-ASSHOLE!"* instead of *"Dy-Dy-Aynu!").* Parents flooding the campus were already impatiently peering into the armory.

Then we were set free, and all hell broke loose—kids running to their Mommies and Daddies, presents and treats, no activities at all, do whatever you want.

This was a bittersweet interlude for me. The world was frayed, rife with possibility, but since neither Mommy and Daddy nor Uncle Paul came, I spent the time with Jay's and Barry's families. This meant dozens of new aunts and uncles and their cohorts from Uncle Paul's hotel. Most of them weren't *real* aunts and uncles, but they comprised a large clan and I appreciated being welcomed into it. The odd thing was, I didn't like them individually—they were ostentatious and crude and talked too loud about stupid, made-up stuff. Almost every comment they made—it didn't matter if it was an "uncle" or "aunt" speaking—was a joke that wasn't funny or a flagrant boast. Being part of a prominent community eclipsed the embarrassment, so I attached myself to the periphery of the action and ignored its nonsense. "Richie is so shy," people said, which excused my diffidence and concealed my disdain.

Aunt Ruthie and Barry's mother, who was her best friend and whose name was also Ruth, flagrantly disregarded visiting rules. Ignoring Chipinaw's limits as if they didn't pertain to them, they dropped in at odd hours during the week to observe archery, baseball, arts and crafts—sometimes early enough in the day to help us clean our bunk for inspection. The Ruths were predictably back every weekend, carvanning from Grossinger's in chauffeured cars.

They arrived with giant sacks of fruit and freshly made white boxes of cookies and cakes, the largest bakery size. Though they didn't bring quite enough to feed the whole camp, they came surprisingly close. Five sacks would be all peaches. You tore open a different carton of sacks to find grapes, apples, cherries, and honeydews. I remember the sweet redness of plums, our pilfered mess-hall knives splitting watermelons, cutting strings on boxes of chocolate chip cookies and chocolate-frosted trees, honey and marble cakes. That was Grossinger's before I ever saw it.

Mommy and Daddy did show up once that first summer, in the middle, and by then I had a deep longing for them. The very sight of Martha Towers was heartbreakingly special, a lank handsome figure in a dark dress suddenly there in the line of parents streaming from the parking lot on visitor's day, like no one else who ever was. I recognized her like Yankee pinstripes or the blue sky. Her smile was open and yearning, and she seemed delighted for once to see me. This was the woman whom Jonny and I called Mummsy Wine. There was an ashen sharpness to her, a quality I might call cynicism now—mocking the other parents, making cracks about their pretentiousness, their ugly clothes, their Cadillacs—but it was comforting because I agreed with that voice and heard it inside me all the time.

There wasn't much to do with them except walk around aimlessly, though Daddy viewed the facilities with gusto, wishing he could dive into the lake or play a set of tennis. Mommy was on the look-out for notable people from her Grossinger days whom she enjoyed meeting again and introducing to her son. Deep down it was as though she really appreciated Uncle Paul and the fact she was once married to him. Grossinger's made her special, and she shared that allegiance with me no matter how meager a son I was otherwise.

Then, as suddenly as it came, the cult of the parents left. The campus returned to ordinary time and the bugle took back our days.

One afternoon in mid-August we had the best, most special adventure: the four bunks of Midgets hiked together into the woods to pick blueberries. The deeper into the wilderness we went, the more bushes there seemed to be, thick with fruit. Our last one stood in a shaft of sun in a clearing so prolific its blue filled the remaining space in our containers. That night the cooks made us our own private pies to the envy of the rest of the camp.

Swago had come and gone in an eternal moment—Chipinaw was abiding and whole.

5

GROSSINGER'S

At the end of that summer I didn't go back to the City. After the other campers left on the bus, a large black Cadillac came for me. "Ready for Grossinger's?" asked my grandfather's driver, Joe, as he pulled up at the bunk. After he wedged my trunk and duffel bag into the car, I sat quietly next to him as he steered unevenly up the hill on which we had so recently conducted flag-raising and spread eagles. Then we bumped along farm roads, past small lakes and bungalows. It was Uncle Wiggily Land, though the cartoon rabbit was transcended by a game board without end.

We glided up a short hill into a cluster of gingerbread castles. GROSSINGER'S HAS EVERYTHING! proclaimed a large notched sign. I saw small jeeps marked S & H Grossinger, some double-parked, others darting about. Amid ornate brown and yellow villas, crowds in beach clothes filled thoroughfares, oblivious to traffic. It was like the Nevele but on a giant scale and with a combined feeling of Times Square and a village fair. Apart from anything perceptible, I had a sense of having entered a new zone of the universe, like Yankee Stadium or the Plaza.

I stood in a marble alcove. Light poured through white curtains onto an orange rug. A Creole singsong summoned "Mr. Richard" to a palatial kitchen where a portly lady named Beulah handed me a bowl. Shiny pots and utensils hung on the walls, plants covered the window sill. There were two vases of flowers, several rows of spice jars, egg-shaped statues for salt and pepper, and a yellow ceramic stove with an overhanging oven—a scullery from a fairy tale.

Bearing strawberry ice cream and a plate of cookies, I sat on a sofa in the living room a bit dazed, taking stock. *This was Uncle Paul's house.* Suddenly a blond kid a bit younger than Jonny burst in the front door and greeted me with a yodel-like call and a finger pointing to stairs up which he sailed. That was my new brother Michael.

I found him on the second floor down a short hall where he demonstrated a closet filled with toys, stuffed animals, and dozens of games, though in total disarray: boards, tokens, cards, dice, and spinners on the loose and scrambled; different seasons of baseball cards randomly strewn, electric planes, electric boats, miniature football fields with knights and cows on them, the flattened court of ping-pong basketball in among children's books. As Michael pulled out these items willy-nilly to show me, I got into the spirit. Soon we had most everything in the room and we were riding jumbo toy elephants and tossing clothing and cushions in the air, my mood having changed from trepidation to madhouse.

Our bedlam was interrupted by a stern but bemused voice. I looked up and knew at once this was Aunt Bunny. "Okay, you guys. If you want to play together, behave. Clean up now. Right away." Afterwards, she led me away into her room, "to get acquainted," she said.

She looked a little like my mother—dark hair, deep eyes, a large-featured strong face but with an indescribable aura of empathy like the first baseball card of Gil McDougald. She asked me about camp, so I described cookouts, salamander hunts, blueberry pie, and learning to swim. Instead of expecting me to tell her everything was great, she made faces at most of the activities and said I deserved a badge of honor for surviving such a joint.

I smiled bashfully. There was such an obvious buoyancy and kindness to her.

Then she planted herself, chin in hands, on the edge of the bed and asked to my surprise how I liked Doctor Fabian.

"A lot!"

"Is he good on the fears?"

I nodded.

"You and I share that. I don't know if it makes us special people or just unlucky."

"Are you afraid of diseases too?" I asked.

"Every one in the book. Cancer, leukemia, MS; I'm even afraid of ones people only inherit. Howd'ya like to see your Aunt Bunny a sudden dwarf, or a giant?"

I laughed at her exaggeration of mock horror, then warmed to the topic, "Sometimes I hear about new ones that make me scared. When I see an ad on the subway for something like 'nephereetis' or MS, I think about having that disease."

She raised her eyebrows and nodded enthusiastically. "It's on sale. You can't even pronounce the name, but you know what it feels like to be dying from it just from looking at the picture."

"Yup!"

That evening after dinner, sitting alone with Aunt Bunny in her room again, I betrayed the Towers household a dozen times before bedtime snacks. Descriptions of my life there just poured out of me. At hearing criticism of someone else my mother would have flashed a gleam of triumph, but Aunt Bunny seemed honestly pained and said that my mother was one of the frightened people in the world too but too proud to admit it.

She and Uncle Paul had a baby Debby's age named James. He was cute as a chipmunk, and I carried him around and set him on the floor beside his toys where he made faces and squealed. Michael brought in a record-player and put the needle on *"Jimbo, Jimbo, / whatcha gonna doeeoo?"*

After Aunt Bunny read Michael and me a story about Br'er Rabbit and the briar patch in her funny dialect, I was led to my room on the third floor, a realm I shared with Beulah. There was a smaller empty guest room down the hall. My one was a large, spooky chamber with two closets, one to the left and one to the right of a quilted double bed with posts. Under the far window was a radio cabinet with a knob for AM, FM, and short-wave bands. It drew in late-summer ballgames from distant cities; these mixed with songs and voices that waxed and waned in the country night. When I moved the stiff knob one click to short wave and turned the dial, it made squealy, squeaky sounds as foreign languages rolled across each other. After I finished playing with the radio, I explored the closets.

They were empty but had ominous second closets inside. I *had* to know what was in them before I got into bed. Their doors squeaked spookily as I pulled on the handles. They were as tight as if they had never been opened.

A musty odor enveloped me, and I felt wobbly and homesick, though I was not homesick for the Towers family and could recall no other home.

I stared at old paintings, bottles, lamps, and furniture covered in sheets and dust, locked trunks, portraits of strange people, jacketless hardcover books, bottles, jars. Everything was covered with cobwebs, dead insects, grime that stuck to my touch like mud.

Who were these people? Why I had been brought to this place?

I didn't belong here, in an assigned room in a strange family's huge bed, now mine—two new brothers, a different father, a stepmother.

It was a stark capsule into which to place a nine-year-old already on a strange walkabout.

But I climbed into the sheets in exhaustion—for the day had begun at Chipinaw—and fell asleep.

In the morning Beulah had a picnic ready for us. After pancakes and bacon, Aunt Bunny, Michael, and I carted her basket onto a small blue bus. It wound among hills of golfers, down a glen, and then pulled up at a smaller version of Chipinaw Lake.

"This is my favorite spot in the whole hotel," Aunt Bunny announced as we strode across gravel onto a beach.

From a wee cabin a custodian selected fishing rods and prepared a can of wet leaves and worms. As we finished collecting our gear, Michael pranced ahead to the dock. We got into the bright green rowboat he had chosen. With Aunt Bunny on one oar, me on the other, we made our way out to deep water and cast our lines. After a few minutes I felt a tug and pulled my first small fish wriggling and flipping into the bottom of the boat—such a sad thing bleeding on the hook but its yellow fins luminous in my hand as Aunt Bunny undid it. By lunchtime we had six of them.

That whole day my mind was as empty of fantasy and fear as it had ever been. I was delighted by every tinge and nuance ...

racing in my sneakers across the beach to get a pail of water for our catch, setting it beside me on the bus, and handing it triumphantly to Beulah.

Uncle Paul made quite a fuss about our success when cooked versions appeared on our dinner plates. "Well, I married a fisherwoman." He turned to me. "I bet you didn't know when you came here you were going to have to catch your supper?"

I shook my head. It was inane but good-humored.

After dinner, Aunt Bunny made popcorn in expanding silver bags that filled to the brim and began to split, hot white kernels popping through. She dumped it in a bowl, then shook salt over it, poured melted butter on top, and stirred it with a wooden spoon. I didn't know that such an operation existed.

Then she and I set up a board for Monopoly. Michael watched and tried to claim properties and plop down hotels before he knew the rules. Eventually he was satisfied to let me make the moves and just be on my side. Aunt Bunny had grown up in Atlantic City on which the game board was based, so she had stories about real Baltic and Ventnor. As we landed on each property, she told us what it was like to visit them as a little girl. Some of her tales were funny, like her mother stepping in a puddle on Marvin Gardens and splashing her father's new pants or fleeing an aggressive beggar on Oriental.

"Park Place," she announced upon my reaching it and pulling out the correct bills to buy it. "That's where all the expensive properties and high rents still are. You're a big-time landlord now."

I grinned despite myself. That she had played in a park by Pacific and St. James Place and gone to dinner on the Boardwalk turned the board's yellows, reds, and blues into bucolic gardens, flags of a more peregrine world; it wasn't Monopoly anymore, it was a map of Aunt Bunny's Oz.

The next day my stepmother led me down the road to the Hotel itself. We entered at a row of indoor shops, like at the Nevele except more in all directions. One was a barber, another a clothing store, another a jeweler, another a lady's hair salon. Lobbies were packed with people, many of them in fancy clothes and pool gear, greeting or waving to each other.

On nearby walls hung pictures of baseball players and movie stars posing with Uncle Paul and other family members. As we passed offices, people waved and shouted hellos to us. Pointing at me, Aunt Bunny repeated, "This is Richard, Paul's son." Acknowledgments and handshakes went on room after room, floor by floor.

Upstairs where the flow and bustle were headed, we came to a dining room so large I couldn't see the other end from the entrance. Tables stretched in all directions. As the crowd surged in, wait-ers glided past, bearing trays stacked with metal-covered plates. It smelled like a restaurant but looked like a busy city.

Uncle Abe, the tiny cherubic maître d' wearing a carnation in his lapel and lots of cologne, hugged me and had me kiss him on the forehead, then led us to the section where, he explained, family members and celebrities sat. At a cluster of three tables every boy and girl was a new cousin, every adult an aunt or an uncle. I was introduced to each, though a few of them I had met on Saturdays at Chipinaw.

After lunch Aunt Bunny and I came home by a different route, past flower gardens around a flagpole, along the edge of a baseball field where men were choosing up a game. I stopped a moment to watch a bobbling catch by a fat guy who lost his glasses while trying to hold on to the ball. Then she led me to her garden behind the house.

I weeded and trimmed with her, picking strawberries, snapping off pods swollen with peas, helping her assess the ripeness of tomatoes of different shades of green, pink, and red, as we put our pickings in baskets and colanders. I could walk in my mind through gate-ways the smell of tomato leaves opened as plants brushed against my cheeks and hair and their essence oozed into the summer air. Their piny resins, though mildly poisonous (Aunt Bunny said), were piquant and suspenseful, made of moss and peppermint both. They told me everything I needed to know about this place.

The family had a collie named Boy, and he became the first animal I got to know up close. Initially I was cautious, but Boy wasn't. He came right up, drummed his paws, and jumped up on me. It wasn't long before I was wedded to this creature, taking him on expeditions as we traversed the Hotel grounds. He ran alongside me and chased crabapples and sticks I threw, his eyes meeting mine in expectation of action.

I thought how amazed Jonny and my mother would be. To us dogs were alien, hostile creatures whose very existence on sidewalks we viewed with contempt, concern if they growled. We always sidled away from the man who walked his bulldog. Here I was wrestling with a collie like Lassie while he barked and pawed. I buried my nose in his pungent belly and again allowed myself to be an unrepentant turncoat. ... because this was, maybe, paradise. But did I merit it, a boy who still wet his bed and made trouble? Would they discover who I was and kick me out, send me back to the Towers den?

The next morning I walked to the Hotel myself. Now that I knew the protocol, I headed straight for the family section. Jay was sitting beside Aunt Ruthie and his older brother Siggy. My father's sister, Aunt Elaine, a tall blonde woman, arrived soon after with her kids Susan and Mark.

After dessert and permission from his mother, Jay led me into the kitchen, which was as busy as a factory: chefs in tall hats, soups and cakes, melon balls and juices crashing onto counters from their hands. "We go where we want here," he said. "It's not like camp where they order you around." I huddled close to him.

With my cousin introducing me at every station, cooks and bakers treated our incursion as an honor. The high point was getting served chocolate-chip cookies on a wooden paddle straight out of an industrial oven.

We found our way down a back staircase, past the bar, which was dark except for a pink glow. We continued through a closed nightclub behind it, out a stage door into bright sunlight, then along flagstone to a pool crammed with swimmers and people sunning on towels, the surrounding patios colorful with umbrellas. The water was too bright and twinkling to look at.

From the edge of the pool Jay led us into crowds around piles of folded towels, past a basketball game, to the edge of a golf course, down along tennis courts and the sand-covered pipes of an ice rink, onto a road beside greenhouses and handball courts. We passed groups of men and women and caddies carrying bags of clubs. Everywhere, I saw riotous arrangements of pansies, zinnias, gardenias, petunias, and other flowers, as well as fountains, gazebos, and wishing wells, trimmed lawns and bushes shaped in smoothly rounded designs around cottages. I bathed in intoxicating wafts of geraniums and roses.

Our expedition took us to the riding stables to see the horses; from there we ran up and down the ski slope, goofing off in improvised skits as we headed to Jay's bungalow.

In the morning my cousin called me on the house phone and invited me back. With mitts, bat, and ball, we trooped to the playing field. As we swatted fungos to each other I was amazed at how many grown men showed up with gloves and joined us kids. One guy remarked that Jay smacked the ball like a major leaguer. He did. I loved to spot his whacks in the sky, mark their zenith, and stalk the arc of their descent.

I stayed a week the first time at Grossinger's. I didn't see much of Uncle Paul, who was hardly ever home, or Jay, who returned to the City the next day but, once I realized I was free to go where I wanted, I explored the grounds: a boy with a dog named Boy. Up beyond our house, I collected old license plates along dirt slopes at the edge of parking lots. Once Boy knew what I was looking for he found some great ones, sniffing Mississippi and Georgia out of garbage. Then we took the bus to the Lake and followed a brook to a small waterfall. There we waded among fish and tiny frogs, turtles of varying sizes sunning on rocks so that I could reach down and lift their shells, my pants pulled up over my knees, the collie muddy and splashing.

That night, surveying my caked clothes, Aunt Bunny summoned me into a bathtub with Michael. I was astonished when we were handed two cans of shaving cream. It was part of the ritual—constructing our own floating castles, shooting lather all over each other. When we left, there were three fizzed-out canisters and foam running down the walls. Now that was a real bath!

Each day for lunch I returned to the family section among my new relatives. As they encouraged me to sample the menu, I became more courageous. In the course of a week I overcame my squeamishness and tried all manner of mixed and "touching" foods: mushrooms and noodles, lima beans and groats, fruit with beef, ice-cream cakes with lime and bing cherry sections separated by chocolate bread, raspberry parfaits, fluffy cheesecakes. We ate nothing like this stuff at home

As I walked the lobbies, everyone seemed to know who I was. Strangers greeted me by name and expected enthusiastic responses. I watched a comedian named Lou Goldstein play Simon Says with guests. As he tricked his victims into doing things to which Simon didn't first say okay, he made jokes in Yiddish and English, embarrassing them further, and to increasing gales of laughter fooled them yet again while their guard was down because they thought the dupery was over. In the next lobby, people sat at tables playing Scrabble with stacks of dollars in little piles beside them. Someone I didn't know called me over and asked me if I could make any words from his rack. His opponents grumbled and laughed.

"Currying favors with the boss!" a bejeweled lady said.

I told him that "gaze" would get his "Z" on a triple letter score.

"That's my buddy for you."

One afternoon Aunt Bunny took Michael and me in her car off the grounds to a miniature golf course with animal statues, windmills, and tunnels, each to putt a colored ball through. Then she bought cotton candy for us. I had never seen a toy golf course or eaten fluff from a silver drum. That night I had my first pizza and saw my first drive-in movie. Life in paradise was becoming more and more real.

Perhaps I *could* get away with a whole different identity.

The next day the director of the nightclub found me at lunch and made a promise; then he kept it by showing up at Uncle Paul's after dinner. He took my hand and led me back to the Hotel, through a tiny door near the kitchen into a dark space, then into a room of levers and costumes. From there I could watch the show backstage.

I stood alongside the curtain, while dancers, a singer, and then a comedian passed me going to and from their acts. Wreaths of bluish smoke rose into the spotlight from an invisible audience that periodically burst into applause. Everything was so extravagant and close, the adult performers vivid and intense, the stagehands purposeful and alert, the tap dancers sweating in their tuxedos, the lady singer in a giant pink poofy dress, her face a painted doll, her voice bigger than her body. I had never been to Broadway, but here it was, before my eyes. I didn't have to identify or understand this adult world. I was allowed to be part of it.

Departing in an uproar of laughter, a comedian named Joey Bishop gave me a pat on the fanny and asked me to remember him to my father: "Tell him I brought down the house. Don't forget!" Then he kissed my cheek and twisted my ear.

Two nights later I got taken to a booth where a technician taught me to turn the translucent rings over the spotlight. While dancers were performing onstage, I changed their landscape from blue to purple to lemon yellow.

In New York I was the bad guy; here I was a virtual prince.

During the week Aunt Bunny never said anything sarcastic. She got angry sometimes, but it was a word or glance, then on to the next thing—no threat of punishment on the horizon, no subterfuge, no comeuppance anywhere.

After breakfast one morning, as I was setting out with Boy on an adventure, a publicity man in a suit arrived at our door and announced that he was taking me to visit my Grandma Jennie. I put Boy back inside and stood ready. As we paced briskly, he described what a wonderful, generous woman my grandmother was. "She can't wait to meet you."

Jennie Grossinger lived in Joy Cottage, a deluxe bungalow down the hill from my father's. Passing alongside a small garden, I was directed through a glass door, My guide departed, but a maid was waiting and led me from the foyer down a series of hallways. I encountered an obscure apothecary aroma. It reminded me of soap balls and vitamin stores selling Tiger's Milk. She opened the last door on the right. Grandma Jennie sat in a gold bed in a rose-colored room. "Richard!" she exclaimed, throwing open her arms, her face breaking into a bountiful smile. "Welcome home."

Home? I searched my memory as though I should remember this—and in a way I did.

Grandma was an older blonde woman with a strong, intelligent face. I knew that she was famous. Even Bob Towers spoke well of her. I was flattered that she was my relative and, at her invitation, returned to see her on my own the next day. As I sat on the corner of her bed, she initiated a serious, wide-ranging discussion, wanting to know everything about me. I felt like someone who had been rescued from another planet or awakened from a long amnesia.

Grandma not only wanted to find out what I was learning in school but had patience for me to demonstrate arithmetic and recite tales of the thirteen colonies. Unlike most others at the Hotel who regarded me only as Paul's son without a past, she had an interest in my other family, including Jonny and Debby. "I want to hear how everyone's doing," she declared. When presented my mildest version in deference to her age and stature she urged me to have sympathy for my mother. "Her father was taken ill when she was very young and she was left alone in a boarding school in Paris. Her mother treated her very badly. She is married to a difficult man. I'm so sorry she takes this out on you, but you must be forgiving and rise above it." I promised to try.

On the day I left for home she sent me to the canteen to buy the most luxurious presents I could find for my brother and sister—"and I mean the finest," she said. "Price is no object"—so I picked out games, dolls, and stuffed animals. She also arranged for smoked salmon and honey cakes to go back with me for my mother and Daddy. "This way," she remarked drily, "they'll treat you better."

In a sober end to a summer's ramble that began with uneaten peanut butter and jelly and "99 Bottles of Beer," Joe drove me back to New York. As I watched country turn into outskirts of tenements, I grew morose and teary. Strange neighborhoods became familiar blocks, and streets that had once been second nature looked derelict and dreary. I was returning to a city no longer home.

In the elevator at 1235 I found it hard to greet Ramon or look him in the eye. The contrast between his surliness and the affability of the Grossinger's staff was too painful. My mind raced as I girded myself for my arrival upstairs. My mother was waiting to retrieve what was left of my soul.

I expected her to be furious, so I tried to camouflage my mood. But she still had her Chipinaw smile and seemed unusually gay and glad to have me back. In fact, she stayed up late in the living room and told me tales of her own time at Grossinger's, how slim and handsome Paul was then, how she fell in love with him, how much they wanted a boy like me. She described the jobs she had held, recounting in a childlike voice how she stood behind the front desk as Mrs. Grossinger and, just like Aunt Marian, welcomed guests. She asked me about staff people who were still there from her time. Most of them I had met, and I was able to report that they remembered her and sent their regards.

During those initial weeks back I talked openly from habit of being at Grossinger's, as I considered that in my fresh outlook my mother might be an ally too. I told her about my problems at school, my frustration with Jonny and, when that seemed to go well, my adventures with Michael, James, and Boy. She heard it all with a show of great empathy. "I know how you feel at Grossinger's," she said to me. "I was overwhelmed the first few times. It was like fairyland. I never wanted to leave."

Then one evening as a family quarrel intensified, I tried to act both sympathetic and blameless, to appease our mother's rising anger while keeping my poise, a ruse I had never tried. I was now "Richard from Grossinger's," not "Richard the Rogue." Mommy caught the drift at once and blurted out, "Save that crap for your Uncle Paul. It doesn't work here." Her abrupt reversion startled me.

A day later, rushing to intercept Jonny and me in argument, she seized the opening she had been waiting for: "Get away from him, Jon. He's got other favorite brothers he plays with now." I burned with shame and guilt. Then she began to bait in a mocking, sing-song voice, "Now go tell on us to your Auntie Bunny." Jonny and Daddy stared darts, while Bridey stood suitably stolid beside them.

For months, in fact years, afterward, if I appeared too cheerful, she snapped, "Where do you think you are, Grossinger's?"

She had lured me into confession and then used my admissions as proof of my disloyalty. Dr. Fabian had warned me about just such a trick.

I turned myself into a hardened outsider, giving them nothing. Mommy had the appropriate taunt for that too: "He's only a boarder here, so he'll be treated like a boarder now."

One day when Dr. Fabian took a phone call, I pulled down a fat volume that had tantalized me from a distance, *The Interpretation of Dreams*. On his return he was pleased with my interest so, at our next session, he made me a gift of the Modern Library edition and showed me how you could find single dreams in it in italics and then go to Freud's interpretations of them. The slant of the dream letters acknowledged the power of symbols. Viennese ballrooms and museums of antiquities were transformed by the master's interpretations. Umbrellas and pianos—and a particular straw hat of a peculiar shape (its middle piece bent upward, its side pieces downward, one hanging lower than the other)—became penises; laboratories revealed the situation of treatment; animals represented people or were transformed by puns into events. There were symbolic "puddings," "dumplings," "trellises," "chapels," "donkeys," "Turkish embroidery," "horse-drawn cabs," and "Kings of Italy."

I struggled with this book for years, never flagging in my goal to understand it, especially difficult parts like "The Dream-Work" and "The Psychology of the Dream-Processes." Initially these were blocks of impenetrable text.

Mommy succeeded in reducing my time with Dr. Fabian by appropriating one of his two days for Hebrew School. Now I only went to the Village on Friday afternoons with Neil's replacement, a tall, thin lady with a wart on her forehead named Jo. On Wednesdays I had to attend a ghastly joint called Ramaz. Uncle Paul was no help on the matter. Since he ran a kosher hotel, he agreed that his son should attend a Jewish institute.

Men in yarmulkes taught the Hebrew alphabet and language and lectured us on the new state of Israel. We read a primer about a pioneer family on a kibbutz and were regaled with recitals from the lives of Jewish patriots, tales of their prowess against their enemies—language lessons imbricated. My teachers boasted shamelessly. I heard how Jews made the deserts bloom, brought civilization to the Holy Land, that Arabs were dummies or criminals.

It was supposed to be religious training and, during spells of sanctimony, God *was* invoked under His Hebrew name Yahweh. Yet Yahweh was more an afterthought than our focus—someone who had to be acknowledged to legitimize the enterprise. What would Hebrew School be without God?

Every so often our teacher would glance skyward or toward the horizon as he paid tribute to ... what? A Zionist archangel, a magical person, who once created the universe out of nothing and later appeared in Moses's burning bush? Yahweh was a Superman-like mover of stars, and he could be alternately a strict biblical king or an incredibly nice guy; but his masculine persona was essential because you had to get along with him, be on his good side, form a personal relationship with him. You couldn't concede him to thunder and wind or creative intelligence.

He became a tyrant I could dismiss even though I was Jewish.

I continued to imagine my own God somewhat along the lines of the aliens who gave me my spaceship—a supernatural chaperone who watched over me, heard my prayers, and helped me when he could. My guardian wasn't as imposing or brusque as Ramaz's Yahweh; yet he was dignified and forgiving. I found intimations of him in the starry night, the crashing waves of Long Beach, or even Mel Allen going crazy during an eighth-inning rally—that inimitable fusion of epiphany, wonder, and awe. He was in the room with the double closets, promising me implicitly that important things remained unchanged and he would abide like the Yankees and the Milky Way. While I didn't presume to conflate him with Yahweh, a Being just as ineffable and omniscient held my universe together. I see his vague shape over my childhood even now.

I was bashful and silent at P.S. 6, cowed by teacher prerogative.

But Ramaz with its comic-book deity peeking out from behind clouds seemed fake and overblown, more like a parody of pedagogy. Hebrew seemed less like a real language than a punishment couched in letters and words. I found it humiliating to have to be learning them instead of interpreting dreams with Dr. Fabian, and it brought out the rebellious side of me. I openly acted the buffoon, disrupting class. I folded my yarmulke into an origami-like boat. I challenged Bible stories. I asked where the cavemen were in the Garden of Eden.

Though the word with its negative connotation wouldn't come into vogue for another half century, Ramaz was a madrasa, albeit an upper-middle-class burlesque of religious zealotry.

One afternoon in the gym before classes began, without realizing what I was doing—I thought I was trying to run faster than I had ever run before—I put my head down and crashed full speed into the wall, knocking myself out. I remember sitting on the floor, dazed, crying from pain. That was my last day at Ramaz.

I enjoyed a minor break from Hebrew School before they enrolled me in the Park Avenue Synagogue. The setting was more grandiose, but it was the same conspiracy of elders. Once again, I intentionally botched translations and mispronounced lessons, throwing in the names of baseball players. I translated a Hebrew phrase that vaguely sounded like a Yankee shortstop as "Willy Miranda," another as "Bill Skowron," the new first baseman. The teacher said that I was committing sacrilege in the House of God. I said, "Yankee Stadium is the House of God."

"God punishes blasphemers like you."

During Purim fair, our class made a Gamal Nasser dart board. As the child artist finished her caricature to giggles and claps, I whispered that this was wrong, that Arabs were people too—first, to Elisha (who told on me); then, when summoned to the front of the room, to the teacher. I was ordered downstairs to the principal's office. "Good," I announced. "I like him. He's a nice guy." The room erupted in laughter.

The principal, Mr. Liechtling, summoned the rabbi and, on request, I repeated my comment to him. He gasped and said, "No, they're not, they're animals."

I couldn't take this duo seriously; they were too much like a comedy routine, Abbot and Costello. I shook my head and repeated the offensive sentiment, "You shouldn't throw darts at human beings."

"You're an anti-Semite," Liechtling said. I had never heard the word so, at his invitation I looked it up in the dictionary on his stand.

"So, *are you* an anti-Semite?"

The definition said: "… hostile to the people and language of Israel."

"Yep."

I was expelled from the Park Avenue Synagogue. I couldn't believe such a lucky punishment.

After that I was required only to attend Saturday services. I hated those too—having to hold the prayer book open, stand and sit with crowds of fancy dressed people, pretending to read along. I despised the stink of lotions and sweat, the unacknowledged mood of an ethnic gathering, the pretentious march of loyal students bearing the Torah. I played games based on page numbers, flipping up corners impartially to see which digit was in the last position. Odds and evens fell on both sides in the Haftorah, which made a fair match of integers. I used divisibility and indivisibility into twelve—Gil McDougald's number—as my means of drafting two teams: 1, 2, 3, 4, and 6 versus 0, 5, 7, 8, and 9. There were great streaks by each squad, but I have forgotten them all by now, just that they occurred, defying the odds and making time pass more quickly.

Yet I readily accompanied Daddy to his orthodox schul across Lexington because it was old and smelled like Jessie's Jip Joint. There was a science-fiction quality to the gold-encrusted Torah and rough-throated ram's horn, its sound making pungent ozone in my marrow. The cantors' impassioned chanting got hysterical and zany, and Daddy, who had been raised to be a cantor before he fled to CCNY and then the Catskills, was called to the pulpit many times per service to help with *davening*. I liked to observe him, a man among men, a ringer among devotees, a showman always.

My mother, who had no religious interests, accused me of phony superiority and blamed psychiatry for my bad attitude.

During baseball season, there was a special treat after schul, for Daddy regularly stopped at a garage below Lex to bet on Sunday's games. He'd offer me a Chiclet from his yellow pack, then another, as he sat going over the day's line with the attendant, occasionally asking my opinion of a starting pitcher. I kept his faith and never told.

I went willingly with Bridey to her church on the Spanish side of 96th Street too. There I felt the enchantment of forbidden territory, the hauntingness of hymns, the pitch of a solemn ceremony, tone of an alien crowd. I could somehow feel the choir and organ telling me where the dungeon stairs were located, for they raised a merciful deity and cast a salient spell.

I realized that liking church was blasphemy for a Jewish boy, but antithetical forces battled inside me. I had been called the devil incarnate by my own mother and needed to redeem that hex somewhere, certainly not in a synagogue. The real demon was far worse than Satan and quailed before the nomenclature of Catholic prayers—I knew as much from Bridey. So I wanted to cross 96th Street and confront his shadow, join soldiers who were Irish like her, Puerto Rican like Ramon. Most of all, I was following my intuition, and it told me that if I was going to be a Hebrew School truant, I better make my peace with God elsewhere. Bridey's church was that place.

As at Dr. Fabian's, I was touching the wan edges of exorcism without recognition.

I dreamed of going beneath into grottos where I saw a deactivated dungeon. Half decayed, it was once stately, even beautiful.

Though I was glad for the mitigation, these dreams didn't fix me—dereliction was never an antidote to terror. The form that gave rise to the dungeon was illimitable, so it could stage other ambushes, machinations more macabre and hideous.

Somehow between between Towers household spooks and Grossinger's version of paradise, my terror of the void and my spunk in standing up against the rabbis—between the Park Avenue Synagogue and the nether side of 96th Street—I found a viable *minyan*.

At Christmas that year I got the only present I cared about—to return to Grossinger's. Uncle Paul invited Larry Abelman, my counselor, and his new bride Jackie to take care of me there the first few days.

On the much awaited afternoon my mother remained in her bedroom; she would not come out to say goodbye, so I went down in the elevator with my suitcase to wait on the sidewalk. Joe had already picked up my counselor, so Larry and Jackie were in the back seat when he pulled up. What a strange transposition this was: my counselor and his wife in my grandfather's car! We inched along crowded streets across the George Washington Bridge onto the highway north. Until major roads reached the Catskills it was a three-hour journey, most of it on old Route 52. I passed the time by racing Larry and Jackie to find letters in the shifting landscape in order from A to Z, hunting for "Antiques," "Exit," and "Pizza" at prime moments. We dashed through the alphabet three times, each of us winning once. Joe pulled over at the approximate mid-point, the Red Apple Rest, a sprawling truck stop upgraded to a restaurant, and treated us to cherry pie.

In the mountains the world was bright with crystals and dunes of snow.

Arriving at dusk, we were directed to our rooms on the third floor of my father's house. In the morning we ate breakfast at the Hotel and then hiked across the snow-covered golf course all the way to the Lake where people sat on chairs, fishing through holes in the ice.

There was extra excitement that afternoon because Whitey Ford was rumored to be at the skating rink with his wife. I hastened Larry and Jackie through lunch so we could go see. At the rink, Selma, who was in charge of the skate shop, stepped out of her office to fit us. As I rose in the strange footwear, I found it a chore to balance on its narrow blades while making my way along the carpeted floor, down the stairs to a rubber pad. Once on the ice, I stumbled beside the railing while Jackie held my hand.

Holding my arm, Irving Jaffee, the pro, gave me a brief lesson in gliding, which concluded with his presenting me, Paul's son, to Whitey Ford. We shook hands with mittens. Then I edged alongside the blond Yankee, amazed to be looking up and seeing his visage in an overcoat rather than pinstripes, having him right me when I fell, though he was having a hard time keeping his own balance. "Casey's gonna kill me," he announced, "if I break my left arm." Back at P.S. 6 I told that to an astonished Phil. Afterwards Whitey conducted a baseball clinic around the fireplace, and I impressed everyone by asking questions about Yankee farmhands.

The next day Larry got his movie camera, and we went to the toboggan, a frozen track on the hillside behind the rink. There he directed a short film in which we were the actors. He called it "The Human Cannonball." First, he stood at the bottom and filmed Jackie and me going up the hill alongside other guests on a rope-drawn trolley. Then he followed behind as we ascended a ramp into an elevated hut warmed by a fire in a metal barrel. There a gruff dwarf in an overcoat, ear-muffs, and a scarf that made him seem to have no neck packed people onto long flat sleds and sent them flying out the chute. My boots were lugged forward into Jackie's lap as she gripped them. I held on so tight I could barely see. With the dwarf's shove we shot out the opening and, in exhilaration (a pinch of fright too), we seemed to fly, as the friction of wood on ice made a satisfying hum. I kept my head buried in Jackie's coat, air nipping my cheeks and ears. We were slowing on the straightaway when we crashed into bales of hay. Larry ran toward us with the camera and filmed as we got to our feet, brushing off stalks.

On the next trip he sat in the front of the toboggan, braving the cold as he held the lens out.

My hands were numb by the time we headed to the canteen for milk shakes and cookies. The place was a hubbub, filled with cigarette smoke and chatter. On the way home we passed Grandpa Harry. He stood by a construction site, observing men putting up scaffolding, yelling orders to them, the collar of his overcoat pulled up tight around his chin. "You keepin' warm?" he asked me. "Look at those gloves. They aren't warm enough! Are your feet dry? Those boots are no good." He turned to Larry. "Get him others. Charge 'em to me."

Later I visited him in his room, the door on the left at the rear of Grandma's house, where he sat in stiff dignity in a blue shirt, underpants, and suspenders, watching a boxing match on TV. In his heavily accented Elmer Fudd voice he asked me, how's my mother, how's Bobtowers, does he miss Grossinger's, do I remember when he and Joe used to come by with lollipops and chocolate spoons?

I did.

"Your mother nearly bit my head off, that's what!"

Day after day in Uncle Paul's living room, presents piled up for Michael and James, countless boxes left by guests and clients. On Christmas morning Michael got exhausted opening them, then surly, as machines didn't work right or came without batteries. "Junk!" he cried, throwing stuff against the walls. Aunt Bunny put an end to this tantrum, saying, "Enough of them there apples." She took us outside to build a snowlady, providing some of her own clothes for realism. Then, to my astonishment, she started a snowball fight with Michael and me. She got right into the thick of it and hit me three times with solid shots.

My visits to Grossinger's were a treachery for which my mother never forgave me. She had uncommon discipline to look at me for the remainder of my childhood as if I were Benedict Arnold and Judas combined.

When I reported my ice-skating with Whitey Ford, she subtly baited Daddy to draw him in. "You hear that? He needs to be told the facts."

"Who do you imagine brought ballplayers to Grossinger's in the first place?" he asked. I acknowledged that it must have been him. "They live off the success of Bob Towers," he said. "And they parade around second-rate idiots like Lou Goldstein in my place. They're going to destroy their reputation in one generation."

"He thinks everything's going to be handed to him, just the way it is at Grossinger's," she rejoined. "Well, it's not. It's dog-eat-dog out there."

"Amen," declared my stepfather.

When I told Uncle Paul about these comments, he heard them

unperturbedly, a tinge of annoyance but mostly amusement and disdain. He said my mother and Daddy were jealous. He was particularly provoked by the idea that Bob had made Grossinger's and could do a better job running it. "You tell my old buddy Bob Towers," he chuckled, "that any time he wants to set up his own hotel and go into competition with us, I'll be glad to meet him on even terms." He seemed delighted by the challenge. "Richard, you should know that people like Bob are second-rate grumblers. They can't be big enough on their own so they complain about others' success. There's no reason for you to believe him. You're a Grossinger yourself and that's something he can never be." I stared at his gold PG cuff links. He cut such a giant figure with governors, movie stars, and ballplayers that I wondered if I could ever attain his level of prestige. "Your mother never wanted to leave," he finally added. "Me, yes! The Hotel, no! She and Bob would love to have remained at Grossinger's, but actions come with a price. Sour grapes. That's all it is."

Sour grapes? I had an image of little blue barrels of candy, but I sensed that Uncle Paul didn't appreciate the degree of oppression I was under. I pleaded to live at his house, but he told me that wasn't possible. "Of course, I want you to, but the law says otherwise, and you and I have to obey the law."

During the next attack on Uncle Paul I argued back and defended him. Mommy's and Daddy's screaming got louder and louder until their clamor in close quarters began to crack my brain. I ran down all six flights of stairs out onto the street and continued around the block, fantasizing that I'd see the Hotel car and it would pick me up. Every doorway and alley attracted me, but in the end, of course, I returned.

"How could you scare me like that?" Mommy shrieked.

"Do you know what you're doing to your mother?" Daddy added, turning his back and walking away. "You're killing her."

I was the Prince of Darkness in that household, a representative of a hostile foreign country. "The devil," Jonny said in retrospect after we were both grown up. "You were the devil. Everything you did was wrong because you were, like, from hell. All your friends were demons or thieves. You were crazy because you had to go to that doctor all the time. Only it wasn't a real doctor; it was like learning to be more evil. You were always undermining Mom and Dad's authority, explaining why they really did things. You had a way to get at them because you knew all this stuff from the outside. And you had this other family of rich bad guys."

The third time I went to Grossinger's, during Easter vacation, I was sent with Gail, Daddy's oldest niece, plus a kid my age also named Richard, the son of one of my mother's friends.

Uncle Paul and Aunt Bunny were travelling in the Caribbean with Michael and James, yet my mother wanted me to go partly because they *weren't* there but also because she had promised a free trip to Grossinger's to the parents of both my alleged companions. When I balked, she rebuked me with "Would you deprive your cousin of a chance to find a husband?"

Upon arrival Gail got a social calendar and went off looking for men, so I was left alone with Richard, one of the worst kids I had ever met. He had a "torture kit," as he called it, a tiny leather pouch of pins and blades. He would regularly threaten to "punish" me if I did not show him the proper deference. Actually, except for the occasional stab of a pin, he resorted to his full array of tools only once, when I was beating him in Monopoly. Suddenly he reached across the board and grabbed my $500s, $100s, and property cards.

When I protested, he took out the kit, unzipped it, and began scratching my arm, muttering in a theatrically sinister voice, "You want to argue with me knife?" I called for help, but Gail, who was reading a magazine, told us to settle it ourselves. Then he twisted my arm behind my back until I agreed, in increasing agony, that he had won fair and square. That was the last time I let my mother cast my trips to Grossinger's.

As for Richard, I knew only that his mother died from cancer a few years later after giving birth to a girl, an event that sent *my* mother into a tailspin of panics. I forgot about them until thirty years later when a college acquaintance became the piano teacher of Richard's grown-up little sister and discovered that her brother had once been my "friend." "Not quite," I wrote to him, explaining why Richard was not a fond childhood memory.

"Your letter gave me the chills," he responded. "Do you know what became of your tormentor? He's now in the upper echelon of counterintelligence for the Army. Obviously, he started young!"

6

Riddles and Clues

During the spring of fourth grade Phil and I began reading Hardy Boys mysteries together. The series began with hidden loot of *The Tower Treasure*, a first edition of which I found covered with dust in Aunt Marian's library at the Nevele like a collector's cherished stamp. "It's yours now," she declared. It ended thirty-four volumes later with *The Hooded Hawk Mystery* in which the two teen detectives use a tamed bird to break a crime ring.

Each Hardy Boys cover was a panel of mystery, a portal that dissolved into the landscape of Bayport with a cliff-hanger, the rustic scenery as compelling as the plot. There was something simultaneously old-fashioned and modern, dreamlike and real about the stories: covert houses, hidden chests, underwater rocks, abandoned islands, smuggling rings, racehorse kidnappers.

When we got through all of the available Hardy Boys to date we moved on to Rick Brant, Tom Swift, Tom Quest, Ken Holt, even Nancy Drew—other young sleuths brooking mysterious landscapes.

When a perspicacious lad (or girl) discovered an unused bus ticket, a piece of suspicious cargo, a trinket, a tribal mask, or a torn map, it was both a marker and rune, the start of a suspenseful chain that led to haunted bridges, leaning chimneys, boats buried among bushes, amulets of grinning tigers, and humming gypsy dolls (that weren't dolls). I would save my money and wait outside the bookstore across Madison from P.S. 6 for the silver-haired lady to appear around the corner five minutes before the school bell—like a comet she showed up at that precise time every day. After she unlocked the door, I followed her into the papyrus-scented alcove, picked the next volume from its shelf, gave her my dollar, and ran to class.

Phil and I sank so deeply into the genre that we began writing and illustrating our own versions combining characters from different series. Phil dreamed up one ingenious plot in which Rick Brant, Ken Holt, Tom Swift, and the others got recruited into the same case but were unwittingly helping the crooks. Event after event was scribbled on our yellow pads, an occasional full-page illustration with a caption like "They had vanished without a trace."

Then the two of us went searching for clues at lunchtime. On one such occasion we found a silver watch on a chain with a small plastic skull attached to it on the street—a remarkable object under the circumstances—and, by deduction, attributed it to a nearby apartment building where we tried to decode the engraving on the watch by matching it to names of tenants on mailboxes. It would have worked for Frank and Joe Hardy, but it didn't for us. We must have gotten in too deep because a policeman arrived at the lobby, listened to our tale, and told us that we could collect the watch from the City lost-and-found if no one claimed it within a month.

Riddles and clues were my forte, whether in detective novels, puzzle books, or *Interpretation of Dreams*. My case with Dr. Fabian was the best and most suspenseful mystery of all, for he was searching for the clue that would unlock the secret of me. I knew by then that he was a highly regarded psychiatrist with famous patients and that he considered me a first-rate enigma. In fact, I came to see myself as his toughest challenge ever because the dungeon stairs felt as indecipherable and unfathomable to him as they did to me. I was the equivalent of a secret panel or flashing lighthouse and we were hundreds of pages in without a verdict in sight.

My trails of clues were more furtive and baffling than those followed by the Hardy Boys, for they led *inside* the world. I imagined their "source" as being like a pot of gold in a fairy tale: a cache of symbolic coins from the early days of Nanny, a rebus-like glass of apple juice at sunset, a primal egg in a bush, or something forgotten long ago. Since I had no idea what clues Dr. Fabian needed

I volunteered as much as I could. I rattled off my weekly tales, updating him on my mother, P.S. 6, Bill-Dave, Grossinger's, while providing strings of hopeful symbols and Hardy Boys–like traces and tips, from vagrant shapes on ceilings and brick walls to patterns seen in bubbles of urine while peeing. Detective novels had shown me how subtle and indirect an indication might be.

I could not see through my own veils to any sort of clarity or resolution, no hint of a shape or even a promising shadow. So I kept delivering fresh intelligence. I hoped that Dr. Fabian, with his greater powers of discernment, was on the case and making progress, that one day he would leap from behind his desk like a scientist in a comic book and shout "Eureka! I've got it." Then my mystery would be solved and I would be reconciled and happy.

My life became a story I told—a more primitive version of the one I am telling now. The members of my family were its characters. I was the main character (as well as the narrator): a troubled boy talking to a wise doctor.

My fears were invoked so regularly they became characters too, invariable abstractions with personalities. "I'm afraid of being poisoned," I said. "I'm afraid of being kidnapped. I'm afraid of getting cancer." I played along but I was fatalistic. That any of these could be cured by a medicine made of words seemed ridiculous, for I continued to sense how trenchantly my symptoms were rooted. What abracadabra would rip them out, what elixir dissolve them?

My splurges of thoroughness and candor changed nothing. I wet my bed just as much. I still had impromptu panics, bottomless in their scope and range of representation. I didn't keen or do jigs in the hall anymore, though I felt the same stampede of desperation.

It was better if Mommy and Daddy *didn't* know; they only made uninformed and exasperated comments or, even worse, blamed Dr. Fabian for his incompetence. I carried my terror silently like a gremlin I dare not disclose. Sometimes I curled up around it on my bed, girdling and containing its throb with my whole being.

More profound than any of the threats, I experienced a lesion, a place with no content at all.

"You are afraid that something terrible is going to happen to you!" Dr. Fabian finally declared. That was his firm professional conclusion. He announced it one day triumphantly like the long-awaited eureka. Then he repeated the refrain so many times over the years that it became like a proverb or maxim, the lyrics to a tuneless song. Its oracular ring held the gist and upshot of my whole situation, almost biblical in tenor, but what did it actually mean?

Not long after his revelation our quest took an unexpected turn. At the start of a session Dr. Fabian gave me a rare treat: a vanilla ice-cream cup. I was digging at the hard cream with the flat wooden spoon when I suddenly worried that the black specks were poison. It seemed ridiculous to have such a confusion, let alone in his presence. I knew that vanilla made black specks in ice cream, but I couldn't stem my surge of terror.

Pleased with the opportunity to work on a panic directly, Dr. Fabian tried in vain to get inside my thinking. Then he suggested we do free connection on the specks. Okay: "seed," "tree," "apple," "orchid," "baby," aha! He surmised that I was worried about eating seeds and getting pregnant. Folllowing his hunch, he drew detailed diagrams on a sheet of paper, explaining the process of conception—the role of the penis and the vagina, the fertilization and growth of the egg. This was to establish that boys were in no danger of being inseminated by specks in ice cream.

I listened dutifully, but I had already heard this stuff from kids at school. Dr. Fabian may have been satisfied that he had solved the mystery of the ice-cream cup, but I knew better. I preferred to play dumb, not acknowledge the error even to myself. I needed him to be perfect. After all, I relied on him for proof of who I was. If he didn't know what was going on, I was in big trouble indeed, alone with stuff like dismemberment of my body and the dungeon stairs—a kid in a canoe without a paddle, headed for Niagara Falls.

We could only get so far with "You afraid that something terrible is going to happen to you" because, however weighty and portentous it sounded when he intoned it, all it added to the fears was a myste-rious hovering specter. Then a few months later, Dr. Fabian solved that guise too, settling on a surprisingly tame origin for such an elemental augur: the terrible thing had already happened—it was the divorce of my parents.

That didn't seem sufficient either, nowhere near the gravitas I felt, but he was so convinced that he pushed it with all his authority. Since I trusted him, I became reconciled to my parents' divorce as the main culprit in a "crime" committed hundreds of pages back that gave rise to all my twists of plot. It was apparently formidable enough to launch full-blown panics, for it bound a mysterious intrinsic power belying its relative blandness. To my mind a divorce was paltry and overt, cherry-pie by comparison to a "coiled cobra," "crisscross shadow," or "sinister signpost." Plus, by Dr. Fabian's logic, its deposition should have caused my fears and bedwetting to stop.

They didn't. Nothing changed.

Dr. Fabian never got past this signature revelation. Once framed, he made it our singular philosophy and sovereign agenda. He applied it not only to bed-wetting and panics but to dreams and relationships, and he always made it fit. Session by session as I continued to tell my story, he found ways to reshape it along the authorized line—that my troubles arose from a Martha-Paul sundering that split not only my family but my identity.

I abided by Dr. Fabian's verdict for years, spouting his mythology to Aunt Bunny and anyone else worthy of hearing. Only later did I realize how slack his interpretation, how random its applications. He was oddly making the same mistake that Phil and I had with our watch and skull!

There was nothing in my root feeling that came close to validating this explanation. What about semblances at the window? What about dungeon stairs? They couldn't be reduced to a mere maxim. What about atom bombs? What about death itself? Where did they fit into the divorce? How could any of this be made normal, okay—ever?

But then who was I to argue with the master of symbols and dreams?

Meanwhile I withheld from him my real secrets (as I withheld from myself that I was withholding them): ungenerous emotions toward friends and family, erotic episodes during interplanetary daydreams, frustration with his solutions, irritation that he showed up with his wife at Grossinger's for Christmas and joined Aunt Bunny and Uncle Paul for drinks by the fireplace. I *didn't want to be angered by that*—it was a celebratory affair merging my two most important worlds—but I was, and I didn't want to discuss it when he brought it up, wondering if it bothered me seeing him there. "No," I replied cheerfully, "I wasn't upset." But I had not liked seeing him a regular man in conversation with adults. I did not want him to have an ordinary-looking wife. I did not appreciate his putting the Hotel's largesse ahead of me, taking advantage of his position as my doctor. I didn't tell him any of this because I thought it was ungenerous and petty of me. I didn't want to be a run-of-the-mill Towers-family grouch.

We each missed the crux of my case. I was portraying only a part of Richard and in a way that was comfortable—self-flattering. Having made myself Dr. Fabian's star pupil, I could not abandon the aggrandized role or my gallant martyrdom. He went along with the charade; yet he was marking time, probably waiting for me to mature and provide a hook or gem he could recognize.

I never told him that while I was free-associating specks in my ice cream, I was lying. My *real* first connection was that he was trying to poison me with the vanilla cup. Like an evil magician, he had been saving a black powder for years. He had sprinkled it in the ice cream, made it look undisturbed, then fit the top back on as if it had not been tampered with. That's why the specks in the creamy white changed context in his presence, intimating something *that vanilla never had before.* I knew that the fear was irrational, that I wasn't really afraid, but *I was unable to stop scaring myself.* Once I had dug in with my spoon, I found it impossible to remember whether the surface had been perfectly smooth or ruffled.

I couldn't tell him any of that, yet it was *exactly what he needed to know and what I needed him to know.* I never considered confessing. His job was to make me a hero, his protégé, not a suspicious, ungrateful wretch. So we ended up with how babies are made instead of my fury at him or guilt for that anger, for suspecting such a turncoat deed from my benefactor and friend. We were staring at an obsessive-compulsive loop and missed it.

It never occurred to me that I would rather hold onto my secrets and fantasies than shatter their reverie. Nor did I let myself suspect, while I led him on a merry chase all those years, that Dr. Fabian himself was baffled by the increasing intricacy of my associations. I had figured out his game pretty well by then and perfected my resistance. While I dutifully provided ever more complex and bizarre material—after all, I was a reader of both Freud and the Hardy Boys—he kept searching for some classic etiology, finally settling on the divorce, out of either frustration or desperation.

I didn't think to look out for him; I figured he was smart enough to look out for himself.

It never occurred to him that to tell a child, "You are afraid that something terrible is going to happen to you" is tantamount to saying *something terrible is going to happen to you*—that to make a pathological mother a piñata of clues, an oracle needing deciphering, was to inflate and empower her above mortal ken, the last thing his young charge needed. And to produce a vanilla ice-cream cup out of the blue was to suggest seduction, an inappropriate adult interest.

A better strategy would have been to produce gloves and a ball and propose having a catch in the neighborhood park. The unfraught camaraderie of a toss, acknowledging my baseball skills while setting us at a neutral distance, would have been ideal and more beneficial than our psychoanalytic burlesque—except that's what we *did,* the best part of it. His sheer presence across the table, the origami boats and balls, his authentic interest in my life, his unconditional love for me were the therapeutic equivalent of having a weekly catch with Gil McDougald. It was more salutary than all his symbols and interpretations put together.

The ice-cream cup was a mistake only in that he lost track of where we were: my fear of poisons, my need to know where every-thing came from, his own unconscious ambivalences, about his feelings for a child, about crossing a professional line with a treat. He couldn't help but serve all that with the vanilla, so I got it unconsciously too. Together we projected enough onto that cup to convert its specks from purity to danger. The ice cream became

like the Cropsey's orange at Chipinaw. Billy Cabot tricked me into
eating it by pulling it from a bag and pretending it was a different
one, before claiming that he picked it from the woods. Dr. Fabian
wasn't pretending, but he didn't realize how horrible it was to think
I ate the Cropey's fruit, how long it stayed with me even though I
didn't believe that the cut-up maniac was real.

At rare moments I was able to get across, if barely, that there
was something else, something bigger and different. I was afraid—
really and truly and irreconcilably afraid, and enchanted too, even
redeemed—in an ambiguous way he didn't understand. He thought
that I was describing affect rather than core—he didn't understand
how I could follow the Yankees or enjoy Grossinger's so much and
be torn apart by terror. He didn't perceive how dichotomy and
ambivalence were generic to my wound, how obsessive compulsion
was my mirror—so I settled for narrations from Grossinger's lobbies,
Towers family spats, and hoopla at Chipinaw and Bill-Dave.

I *was* afraid of something terrible, and it *had* already happened,
but it wasn't my parents' divorce. It was more like starry night or
cavemen contemplating snow and wind with no hope of obviation
or succor, without knowledge of what *it* was or who *they* were.
Pulsations of panic evoked the Crusades, the Nazi death camps—an
irreparable breach between fantasy and reality, a sphinx without
gods or language.

Sometimes the haunting in me softened into sadness, a sense of
being lost and forlorn (like Heidi's grandfather searching frantically
for her through wintry villages). It was more than a sadness. It was a
shadowing of limitless depth, of layers parting to reveal other layers
themselves parting like the leaves of maples in a breeze, like the rich,
intoxicating solitude of autumn. In this form sadness was not only
not sorrow; it was paradoxically the most joyful thing I knew. Not
joyful like Grossinger's but joyful like absurd reparation, like abject
terror suddenly and inexplicably turning into bliss. I never understood the seesaw between those two halves of me: was I fortune's
most irrepressibly charmed kid who got to go to Grossinger's and
play with Boy or the world's loneliest, most doomed pariah, the devil
incarnate, sentenced to perdition forever? How could I be both? It

was like "Did the Yankees win or lose?" but to the zillionth power.

The songs of the play *Finian's Rainbow* (as performed by the older kids at Chipinaw) bore shards of the elusive dichotomy. I tried singing but couldn't keep a tune. Upon request (and with a little help from me on the lyrics) Bridey reproduced them in her brogue: *"How are things in Glocca Morra ... / Does that leapin' brook still.... "* Words and melody put their spell over me; the world itself seemed to drop a chord into slow motion and swim by in solemn, stately fashion. Yes, it was sad and fearful, but it was beautiful—shockingly, unprecedentedly beautiful. Then she sang, *"Look, look, look to the rainbow.... "* I had no words to match it, but I leaned into the song like a sunflower into sun.

Jonny and I would run along the Nevele solarium, building little piles of snow on the railings in an effort to thaw some of the winter away in March while Debby splattered in her red rubber boots among puddles at our feet. Mommy sat on a lawn chair, her eyes closed, a silver reflector about her neck capturing the nearest star. Clump after clump of puffy cold was placed on rusty ledges as Jon and I called to each other to check the progress of the melting at either end. This industriousness would arouse a sense of the profoundest well-being in me. I'd be thinking about where I was in my latest science-fiction book and how later I'd lie toasty by the radiator and read it—then we'd eat dinner; afterwards, we'd have a plate of chocolate horseshoe cookies ... and suddenly the song would seep through my existence: *"Follow it over the hi-ill and stream.... "* I twisted the vowels in "follow" and "hill" and "stream" until they were barely English in the back of my mouth. There was a tenuous point, before they became garble, at which they held the whole mystery, the fairy tale, Bridey's Ireland.

It was a book I read, maybe; a dream I had; or it was something else entirely, vast and incomprehensible. All the time, this mood dogged me, conveying feints and masks—and also that strangely immense joy *("... so I ask each weeping willow, / and each brook along the way ...").* Jon and I would buy candy bars and comics at Ivy's Store, go pinball bowling, and then sit in the lobby engrossed in Almond Joy and Porky Pig while languid crowds swept past. Smell, color, and mood combined in a wonder and delight that we existed at all. Gradually the mood would fade, or it might call to me from the faint center of a dream. Suddenly I was more than the recipient of a make-believe saucer, I was ward and guardian of the universe itself!

Its nether side was blind terror. The less there was to explain it, the more powerful its claim. It happened one night, as I came into the dining room for supper. I just looked at everyone seated there at the table—Mommy, Daddy, Jonny, Debby. Bridey was serving halved grapefruits for a starter. I adored sectioned grapefruits with a light coating of sugar, but the ambient shade of the walls was too pale. I thought, "This is it, forever—no!" I couldn't relent to it, so I ran into my bedroom, hurled myself onto its blankets, and clutched them tight enough in my fingers and palms to make a hole in reality if such was possible. A beam of black light shot through my forehead—an apparition far graver yet more aware of who I was.

I could tell later, from their judging looks, they thought it was that I'd rather be at Grossinger's, but it was more a feeling of having come into the wrong century, the wrong existence altogether.

7

CAMARADERIE

Across the landscape of our shared childhood my brother and I commanded a repertoire of games, concurrently chummy and cutthroat. The two of us were trapped inescapably in combat and collaboration. That our relationship was a competition was taken for granted, for we were born onto opposite teams—dogged opponents from the get-go like the Union and Confederacy. Our battles activated grudges from just beneath the surface, as we fought with tokens and cards, with rubber bands and words, and in currying parental favor.

Neither Jon nor I understood how our parents played us off against each other or used our enmity to defeat Grossinger's and get their long-sought revenge. Ironically it wasn't Bob who most perfunctorily scapegoated me, it was Martha. He was a dupe for her exotic legends and paranoid fantasies, and all too easily goaded. He respected her ferocity and intelligence, plus he didn't want to be left behind by a woman on the march. In their gaze Jon and I could never exhibit too much affinity. If we did, they would find a way to spur us to combat like prize roosters. So, my brother and I had to find each other in secret, unacknowledged ways.

Our fraternization was imbedded in the diplomacy needed to conduct an open-ended clash. We would not have carried out such a ritual if we hadn't hated each other, but likewise we could not have carried it out unless we were in simpatico. We had to concur on ethics and rules. The statutes of war, while not always obvious, invariably became so without undue dispute. Yet our surface rage blinded us to how we shared a mindset and an agenda—how we read the terms of engagement identically.

Much of our childhood was spent deciding in which competition to engage next and then enacting the chosen match, for there were long hours to fill. We would go from board and card games to baseball derivatives and other improvised contests of skill, strategy, and luck.

After setting up cowboys and Indians along the end of the hall, we aimed a marble back and forth, trying to knock over each other's plastic figures. A perfect shot might ricochet and topple two or more of them. As the field became emptier of targets, hits became more difficult. We rolled back and forth, targeting the last standing men, often chasing the errant pellet down the hall and around the corner. Sometimes we included farm animals and knights and gave extra points for getting the marble up the ramp into the castle.

In another contest we set trash cans at opposite walls and tried to bounce a Spaldeen into it, either directly (for one point) or off the wall and back in (for two points) or off the wall and upon a second bounce (for three points). We played a related game on the sidewalk with a Spaldeen and a dime; only there we stood farther apart and tried to hit and spin up the coin on a fly.

A plop in a cylinder, the spin and clink of a dime, the recoil of a falling horse into two upright figures brought an ineffable jubilation every time.

Among our regular games were Chutes and Ladders, Quizkids, and Uncle Wiggily's rainbow maze, the boards as intimate to us as our own lives. A meandering numbered path led from Wiggily's ramshackle bungalow in the lower lefthand corner—the rheumatoid rabbit setting out with cane and bag—to Dr. Possum sticking his snouty head out the stone house with its patchwork gray chimney at square 151 (upper right). In between lay the Skillery-Scallery Alligator with open jaws, the dreaded Rabbit Hole under the rotted trunk and ferns (back to square 13), the Wibble Wobble Pond (which was either good or bad depending on how far before or after square 60 you had gotten when you drew its yellow card), and the Bad Pipsisewah and Fox Den (where a player lost turns).

We played in order to reexperience the board's radiant landscape and to renew our eternal rivalry. The cards, both white and colored, were familiar, but their sequences made them novel, disclosing unforeseeable outcomes—and those were infinite. Since our personal battle was never resolved, each new match presented a fresh opportunity to query fate.

I remember the excitement at drawing a 10 or 15, the sinking sensation when Jonny got one, the pleasure when he was sent back to the Bushytail Squirrel Tree after he was almost to Dr. Possum's. No amount of repetition diminished the novelty of those moments. It was always a delight to see Jonny slide down the major chute at 87 all the way back to 24—or land on Skeezicks' mouth. That never lost its unique thrill.

The boldly black-scripted cards of Sorry! with their numerical scriptures occupied another domain of our minds, as we raced to get four pawns of our color (red, yellow, green, or blue) around a track of periodically slide-enhanced squares. The plastic round-based, beadlet-topped tokens were clean and evocative—primary hues. Ones and twos released pawns into activity. Twelves conferred leaps forward, but an opportune four (backwards only) could dispose of the whole circuit around the board and put a token on the edge of the Safety Zone, an inopportune four set you back as well as waste a draw. Sevens were divisible in any combination between two pieces. Elevens allowed changing places with an opponent, a potential double whammy. A ten could be played as one-backwards in a gamble that required a quick second ten (or a four) to save a loss of the move and a longer journey around the board anyway.

I usually took the yellow, him the red—blue and green went unplayed. We so identified with yellow or red that their draws and strategies swept our minds clean of everything except completing the circuit and tucking all four pawns into the safety zone. I knew his red so well I was reminded of it when I saw a bright red toy or picture. I flinched a bit inside: red was the enemy, a show-off's color. I felt sordid pleasure in knocking off a red token with an assassin Sorry! card just short of it gaining immunity, likewise in bringing home two delicious canary yellows with a seven.

I responded just as exigently to an icon of a rope or candlestick, a golden $500 Monopoly bill, the ten of diamonds in Casino, or a yellow Marvin Gardens card. I lived for the bliss of Park Place and Boardwalk under my ownership, a red hotel on either awaiting Jonny's next toss of the dice. These moments, and the strategies generating them, temporarily replaced reality, as they explicated our brotherhood—telling us who this Jonathan, this Richard were. Without them we were in free fall, for there were no other safe boundaries or wayposts in the Towers realm, no fallback life-jackets or life-jacket-like roles.

Baseball variants were our favorites, and our mainstay was sockball. With a tennis racquet as our bat, socks tightly wound as our ball, one of us lobbed in a pitch. The batter did not so much whack as aim for spots in our room—a bid at finesse.

Singles were drives that bounced uncaught off a hollow canopy around the ceiling. They had to be smacked hard and aimed well or they'd be caught in the small room. Doubles landed on Jon's or my bed. Almost always rebounds off walls, they came to a state of rest on either coverlet.

A catch, even a rebound, resulted in a double play, though a catch off the high canopy simply negated a single into an out.

A waste-paper can placed before the radiator was a triple. One never aimed for triples. They were accidents. To see a sock bounce off the wall delicately into the can was as exhilarating as a golfer getting a hole-in-one. Likewise, a sock rolling on a chair, about to rest there or topple, was spellbinding, as was any rolling orb between outcomes, where it would stop: fair or foul, a score or nothing.

Positioning on a grid was a way of seeing the world, an innate phenomenology of weights, shapes, and objects. Jonny and I could play from any angle at any scale, whether tiddly-winks in the hall, shuffleboard on a Nevele court, or flipping cards. When there wasn't a game in progress, we set instantaneous measures anyway. Watching a stray ball roll from a game of other kids across a sidewalk in the Park, a spiny horse chestnut plunk from a tree, we knew instinctively the boundary, the odds, and when to cheer for a placement and score, like the time a falling acorn bounced once before landing in a park water fountain. "Triple!" we called out spontaneously.

The bedroom left field window at 6B had a glass guard set against it at a forty-five-degree angle. Inside it was a home run, either on a soft lob or a carom off a wall. A lob might be defended by a leap, with the sock sometimes accidentally batted down into a double for the opponent. However, there was a perfect arc, just over the pitcher, gentle enough so it didn't bounce off the window back past the guard. A home run was the most delicate shot of all.

Our mother detested sockball and came to recognize its sounds from afar. Even when we played in a disciplined hush, we couldn't hide the game's cadence. She charged in, grabbing the racquet away. She thought baseball belonged outdoors, but, more notably, she believed socks were for wearing, not batting, and she was convinced ours went out the window, even though it was shut tight.

Hers, though, was a self-fulfilling prophecy because, after she suggested the idea to us, we opened the window a little bit behind the guard to add drama to home runs. There was a garbage can on 96th Street and, if one of us put it in that, you got credit for winning ten games. Needless to say, it never happened, though my friend Phil took up the challenge and landed one so close we were astonished. It was thrilling anyway to run to the window and watch a home run sail out of sight and then spot it down on the street below. Sometimes a pedestrian looked up in astonishment—a sock from the sky! We would interrupt the inning and take the elevator to the street to collect it.

Ramon the elevator man was not amused by the extra summonses and trips, but contrary to our mother's belief, no one wanted our socks, and we never lost a single one at sockball. They disappeared for other reasons, an issue of general cosmology not resolved to this day.

At other times we staged epic rubber-band fights, ducking behind furniture and firing with our favorite weapons. Mine was a porcelain statue of a stalking tiger I won at Skee-ball. I strung my "bullets" around its mouth and aimed usually at Jon's butt. It was a great pajamas sport, rolling on the rug, pulling our bottoms back up amid hurried attempts to zing bare bohunkus. When our stockpiles ran out, we collected shots from all over the room, different colors and sizes of rubber bands that had come to rest on, under, and behind objects, and returned them to our ammunition bags.

Though we didn't keep a cumulative score, Jonny and I had an unerring feel for who had won more life-to-date. I held an edge at age nine, but as he got older and bigger, he gained the upper hand, and the all-time tally fell into doubt, so it needed to be adjudicated again and again. We certainly knew who was winning lately, and it mattered a great deal; it determined the mood between us, our relative prestige and power in the apartment. And though we played countless rounds with varying outcomes, we seemed to know that only one of us would finally win.

I tried to disguise my pleasure in victories, but I didn't fool Jon. He liked to lord his successes over me. If I lost, I'd often bargain at once for a new game, all the while trying to maintain an older sibling's air of superiority. He preferred to savor his triumphs. It often took teasing or a bribe to get him to play again. "If you win this next one," I'd say, "it counts double," as if I could sell such a blatant ploy.

"I don't care," he'd retort. "I'm champion." That would sting despite my determination to stay above such fatuous boastfulness.

We spent so much time together that our competition blended almost indiscernibly into camaraderie. Our antipathy would soften, reconcile, and become its antithesis: fellowship, intimacy, something resembling love. The shifts were obscure, unaccountable, and disconcerting—and usually begrudging. Because we were uncomfortable with each other, we were less embarrassed by stalemates of inured hostility than lapses of affection. We didn't acknowledge good will as readily as mutual hatred. I couldn't stand having such a hoodlum get a close-up look at me or witness my gaffes and fears, my wet sheets. His condescending smirk needed no words and took no holidays.

He couldn't bear me watching him either but, whereas I flinched with shame, he lashed out in wounded pride and defiance.

Roommates and companions of necessity, we lay in bed at night watching the Knickerbocker Beer sign blink on and off in the northern distance over Harlem, pretending it was a signal to Martian ships or smugglers on the Hudson. Whispering across the room, we filled the interval before sleepiness with games—Animal-Vegetable-Mineral, Initials, Geography—hushed undertones so as not to arouse the Cyclops.

For numberless hours we would perch beside our record-player, laying our favorite disks on the rubber wheel and setting the needle down, using pins from Mommy's pin cushion when we ran out: *"There's a little white duck sitting on the water,"* and *"... among the leaves so green-o."* Blending with buttered toast and vegetable soup, these tunes spun webs of afternoons, a symphony of lives played by pipers in an upholstered box. When a narrator signaled us, we turned pages to follow Bozo the Clown on his travels through Europe and Asia, from the Leaning Tower of Pisa and the Eiffel Tower to the lair of the Wild Man of Borneo with the ring on his nose. In *Bozo Under the Sea* the clown in diving gear visited sea horses, fish with lights, even a great whale. We stuck our faces in a sink of water and mimicked his bubble-filled voice exclaiming, "What could that creature be?" (It was an octopus.)

Mr. Borrig, the super, was Jon's and my chief nemesis, continually coming to the front door with complaints from the apartment beneath. That would lead to prompt punishments—a confiscation of the tennis racquet, an early bedtime, sometimes a whipping. Overly exuberant tumbling catches and dives to block the socks from landing on a bed were often followed by a ringing doorbell. Once, in revenge, we lowered a red water-balloon on the end of a string slowly down six storeys and, as Borrig sat on his customary stool by the service entrance on 96th Street, set it softly on his bald pate before ducking back inside. I don't know how we got away with that one—who else would have done it?—but there were no repercussions.

I remember a Monopoly match in which I was beating Jon so badly he was on the verge of tears. I had most of the red, green, and blue properties, and they were packed with hotels. I had thousands and five hundreds in abundance. With only a few hundred dollars and no houses on his properties he fought on, occasionally biting his lip. It was as though no prior game counted, no future game would ever be played. In a moment of inspiration (that stands out over our whole childhood together) I invited him over to my side of the board to play against that bum Borrig. We slaughtered him. We took all his money. We forced him to mortgage his properties. We jumped up and down with excitement calling him names.

When our family rented its cottage in Long Beach, Jon and I transposed sockball to the front yard, the farthest bushes serving as home runs, sections of grass as singles and doubles, the ornamental bucket a triple. We also invented a beach game called Ocean Ball, based on home run derbies on TV. We swung with a broomstick at a Spaldeen from a "batting box" line of seaweed. Home runs were shots that landed in water of any depth, even retreating surf.

As defenders we guarded the shifting boundary-line of wetness trying to nab long drives while running through tide. Making or missing circus catches, we tumbled gloriously into waves. Our Philco sat on a blanket in the sand, awaiting the jingle that inaugurated the day—*"Oh that Ballantine! / ale with brewer's gold.... "* After the rousing bars, Mel Allen announced the Yankees' starting line-up. Exhausted salt-and-sand outfielders, we strode along the beach mimicking the lines. "Make the three-ring sign!" I shouted.

"Purity, body, and flavor": Jon's well-rehearsed response.

Baseball provided much of the glue between us, a ritual beyond our ramshackle lives. The Yanks were the one clan in which we could be true brothers. Dale Mitchell, Don Bollweg, Bill Renna, Phil Rizzuto, Ewell Blackwell, Johnny Sain were our uncles, Casey Stengel our grandfather. Many an afternoon we sat in our room with our radio, rooting together, filling time.

How it fanned our imagination (and bedroom chatter) that November when the Yankees and Orioles traded eighteen players, and both Don Larsen and Bob Turley came to our team!

To my chagrin my brother became the warrior-hero of P.S. 6, elected first-grade president, recipient of the highest marks in the class. He was king of the punchball court too, regularly swatting the Spaldeen over the fence with his fist. Cultivating a tough-guy swagger, he dared the toughest yard bullies to fight him. Surrounded by cheering supporters, he won a number of after-school brawls in the alley, though I never viewed them (except at a distance once and quickly looked away). To have to do with him was unthinkable, so I kept a wary eye out for where he was, shifting accordingly to be somewhere else. At home he was a relentless, sweaty chunk that I could, at best, wrestle to a standstill, then hold onto for dear life.

There was a secret rite too. In lost watches of the night I would see him standing in the center of our room, punching the darkness, spitting out curse words, mouthing unintelligible rasps. When I asked him what he was doing, he told me he was fighting ghosts. I looked for shapes, Casper-like figures, but I saw nothing. It was chilling to watch, a wake-up call from my deepest dreams. I don't know how often it happened, but he made the matter plain: "Every night." The schoolyard champion never stopped fighting, even in sleep.

The ghosts were guises of his adversaries, notably a bully named Roy or Harry Pin. Jon knew that he had to fight him or be declared a coward forever. I never figured out if Harry Pin was a real kid or a made-up witch who stabbed him with a pin and then became a sorcerer who held him in thrall. There was no Harry Pin at P.S. 6 or Bill-Dave, and Jon did once tell me of such a dream.

"He's not real," I offered in my best psychiatric tone. "He's a symbol for something else inside you."

"You don't understand. He *is* real; he's not from P.S. 6, you don't know him. He comes to Central Park. He challenges me. He calls me names. He won't stop baiting me until I come after him. I can't stand having him mock me like that, thinking he's better than me, that he can get away with anything he wants."

A dull clank or thud would wake me. Half-asleep, I would recognize him swinging at the air, dropping into a boxer's stance, bobbing, jabbing, tossing a sudden overhand haymaker. It usually ended with him dropping to the ground and sobbing. It wasn't because Harry hit back; it was, Jon said, because he had vanished; he evaporated before the matter could be resolved.

I didn't realize at the time how my brother's phantom combat was an exquisite representation of our plight. It was far too close to my life for me to recognize either its pathos or brilliance. It had nothing to do with me even as it had *everything* to do with me—it was his personal stamp on our shared terror, the only way he could admit it.

He knew that I was afraid because he was *just as afraid,* but he had turned the matter inside-out and, in so doing, thought to win, not just our make-believe games but the real one. It wasn't a gimmick; he truly believed the answer was to take it to the enemy, to retaliate like a champion. He was saying, not all at once and not in these exact words, "Don't cower before demons; don't tell on them to some stupid adult, a faggot psychiatrist. Have some pride. Fight your own battles in the schoolyard. Confront them the way a soldier would. Be the Cisco Kid and smash them before they turn you into a bum."

If he had heard the dungeon voice, he would not have become a passive dupe like me. He wouldn't have keened in terror or given the phantom an edge, allowed it to suspect it could scare him. He would have socked his way to the source of its illusion, given it human form, and pounded till it pleaded for mercy. He would have tried to pulverize those stone stairs with the hardest punches and kicks he could muster, to prove his superiority—his invulnerability.

He loved to serenade at full volume, *"From the halls of Montezuma, to the shores of Tripoli,"* a catchy tune I shunned because the last thing I was was a Marine. But *Jon* was. Or he aspired to it so assiduously, to being Roy Rogers, Mickey Mantle, Sugar Ray Robinson, that he *felt* like them to me, grown men who didn't even know him. Whenever I saw one of them on television, I noticed his uncanny resemblance to Jon.

I couldn't escape Jonny-ness. By contrast, I was a yellow-bellied chicken.

When I told my parents about my brother's nocturnal fisticuffs, they were furious.

"Look who's talking!" scoffed my mother, "Mr. Know-It-All."

"You spend too much time," chimed in Daddy, "with that mouse Fabian. So now you're a psychiatrist too! Well, you can look forward to a lucrative life, you lazy *gonif.*"

They thought I—rogue Richard—was trying to slander my brother, either making it all up or exaggerating wildly. How could anyone who threw touchdown passes and owned the Honor Roll punch at figments in the middle of the night? That would mean he was demented. Yet everyone knew he was sane, I was the crazy one. Case closed.

So vehemently did they accuse me of bad faith that I lost any sense of why I was bearing the news. I thought that I was trying to be helpful, but did I secretly relish his obligation in the dark? Was I unconsciously gloating by reporting it?

At heart I stood guilty before them. When I made a stand, it was not as a good guy unjustly accused but with steeled tenacity of an outlaw. That's what I knew they saw, but that's also what it felt like inside me. They didn't see Jon as a swaggering ruffian, a brawling street rat; they saw young King David, the first Jewish president in the making. They saw me as a hooligan in cahoots with outsiders. All Richard's victories were at the charity of their altriusm: inroads of a quisling.

It was never clear what my real crime was. They tried repeatedly to pass it off as connivance with Dr. Fabian, treachery and sedition at Grossinger's, yet their judgment long preceded the psychiatrist or the conversion of Uncle Paul into my father. It was more like a Superman comic, as if I were the born adversary of my mother and Jon back on Krypton and now we lived on Earth.

One afternoon when I was about 11, Jonny 8, and Debby 4, we were walking with our mother down 96th toward the Park. Jon must have asked about his virtues because she was reciting them aloud: "You're handsome ... brave ... courteous ... strong ... intelligent ... and you have this special quality of leadership."

Debby immediately chirped, "What am I?"

She was "beautiful, loving, and have a stage presence many actresses on Broadway would kill for. You're another Shirley Temple."

I refused to be part of this charade, but Jon was curious, as no doubt was I. "What about Richard?" he asked.

"Richard is.... " She paused for a moment and then offered,

with a curious smile, "Richard is loyal."

We continued walking, past the playground to the reservoir. I didn't ask for elaboration nor did they.

It was such a strange answer, given that I was famously disloyal. Was she being sarcastic? Or did she mean that I was loyal to Grossinger's and even in the service of the enemy it was an admirable trait?

Why was it my only virtue?

Looking back I wonder if maybe she knew who would be telling this tale today.

8

ANTIPODES

I went to Grossinger's every major holiday and for the week before and after Chipinaw. My clearest memory is of the arrival, Richard Towers converted to his alter ego on the spot. I bounded from the car and raced down the road. Every tree and sign, even the dust I kicked up was special—it was Grossinger's! My sneakers tore along the dirt twice as fast as anywhere else. I looked for Aunt Bunny at the house. If she wasn't there, I sought her at the pool and beauty salon. When I glimpsed her, I felt waves of hope and well-being. The mere fact of her existence comforted me. She had such good spirit and an instinct for fun while, at the same time, she was the most serious and insightful adult I knew.

She liked to tell me silly things that happened when I was away, like a commotion she caused at a dinner party: "I shouted, 'Throw Mr. Cats in the basement, or he'll fight with the dog.'"

That was our cat's name but, unknown to her, she had a guest that evening named Katz.

"He was standing there holding his drink. He said, 'Please, don't send me to the basement. I won't fight with the dog.'" She did an imitation of him cringing, hands on her hips.

I remember once she came into a gathering with an aerosol can and I thought she was after bugs, but she began spraying pine air-freshener directly at Uncle Paul's butt because he was farting silently. "I might as well," she told her startled guests, "go to the source."

I loved to monopolize her for conversations as she moved across her busy life. I kept her company in the kitchen, at the hairdresser, in the garden, even at the bar while she drank gin-and-tonics. She listened to whatever I had to say: Hardy Boys plots, my dreams, Dr. Fabian's comments, my fears, stuff from school and camp. She not only heard it all but shared her life with an intimacy that would have been unthinkable from my mother. She was more than a parent; she was my best friend.

I continued my exploration of the Hotel's lobbies and underground passageways, every bungalow, office, plaza, tunnel, and path, until I knew the entire iconography. It was more than being impressed by famous scenery. I *was* Grossinger's.

One evening Aunt Bunny invited Yankee pitchers Johnny Kucks and Tom Sturdivant and their wives to sit with us at our table in the Terrace Room. At the show's conclusion a crowd was blocking the door. The players were in a hurry to get back to their baby-sitter, so I led us out a fire exit, up onto the roof, and across buildings on platform steps.

"Great route, kid," Kucks said.

"I live here," Aunt Bunny remarked, "and I didn't even know these stairs existed."

An ordinary day began in the dining room with waiter Jack Gallagher, the old Marine vet with the Popeye face who, in season, would go over each last Yankee game, adding his complaints about managerial strategy (as if Casey Stengel were a madman or in cahoots with crooks and gamblers). He also growled good-naturedly about the mess left by any of us kids from the last meal, usually deposited after he had cleaned up and retired to his room for siesta.

On the way to Jack's station I would pick up all four morning papers. Usually I arrived so early that they were tied in steel bands by the service desk: *Daily News, Daily Mirror, New York Times, Herald Tribune.* I turned the bundles over in the lobby in high suspense to trace line scores as far as the innings went in rural editions, extracting single copies by a series of tugs. If there was a leftover *New York Post, World Telegram,* or *Journal American*, I grabbed that too. Hard to believe, but there were seven New York dailies then, four morning, three evening. When necessary, Jack provided the final score with a recap. He would be in street clothes and suspenders, enjoying his own breakfast, so I'd wait on myself.

In the walk-in pantry refrigerator I'd mix boysenberries, raspberries, blueberries, peaches—whatever was available in the serving vats—and put them on Rice Krispies, Corn Kix, All Bran, or Cheerios. Dozens of each brand were stacked in single-serving boxes in the far corner of the dairy section, waiters converging there at hit-and-run speeds. Sometimes a new kind appeared like Frosted Flakes or Special K.

Then I'd petition waffles at the grill and occasionally sample a lunch dessert while waving hi to the bakers. My sense of entitlement was implicit, but I tried not to be a brat; I was diligently courteous and respectful. In summer I'd cut a giant slab of watermelon and, after the meal, walk alongside pansy-and-geranium beds, spraying seeds and smelling the scented air. This was my territory! A voice inside continually reminded me how incredible it all was, to get to be Richie Grossinger, blasting it at evocations from Bill-Dave and P.S. 6 who knew me as Richie Towers: "Look at this, Freddie Meyers, Andy Pfeiffer, Phil Wohlstetter!"

Some days I would take the house bus to my father's bowling alley in town and stay there for hours, rolling game after game, trying to beat my successive tallies. It was yummy and peaceful compared to playing against Jon. I liked the giant score-sheet pads with their rows of clean fat squares for one's accumulating sum, codes for spares and strikes—the former (a slant) if you knocked all of them over with two shots, usually by a fortuitous ricochet; the latter (an "x") if you got them down on one roll, that rare pin-exploding concussion.

I made individual trips to visit relatives in their separate cottages: Aunt Lottie and Uncle Louie, Jay's grandparents; my father's sister Aunt Elaine, her husband Uncle David, and their children, Susan and Mark; deaf Uncle Harry and Aunt Flo who ran an antique shop next door to us and shouted fitful syllables as they pantomimed a butter dish or china platter they were giving me for free to bring to my mother.

Doing my rounds of family and friends was the heart of my Grossinger's ritual. The dour troublemaking kid from New York proved an amiable, cheerful sprite as he marched through lobbies smiling and waving. I prided myself on knowing everyone's names—clerks in shops, veteran waiters and waitresses, bus drivers and members of the maintenance crew, Uncle Eli and his tennis pros, Uncle Abe and the athletic staff, all the lifeguards, chefs, bakers, even janitors and dishwashers. These were my people.

My main conversational buddy was Nat Fleischer, the staff hypnotist, a man who knew a great deal about symbols and dreams. In fact, he lectured on Sigmund Freud to assembled guests in the lobby. I'd watch him put volunteers into trances and instruct them to blurt out stupid remarks and kiss strangers. At meals he and I talked about psychotherapy and the strange case of Bridey Murphy who, in a hypnotic trance, had recalled a prior life in Ireland.

Nat liked to mimic Morey Bernstein's technique. "He was an amateur, but he had the perfect cadence, the perfect style of repetition, just the right tone: 'I will talk to you again. I will talk to you again in a little while. I will talk to you again in a little while. Meanwhile your mind will be going back, back, and back until it picks up a scene, until, oddly enough, you find yourself in some other scene, in some other place, in some other time, and when I talk to you again you will tell me about it. You will be able to talk to me about it and answer my questions. And now just rest and relax while these scenes come into your mind....' What a routine! What a goddamn brilliant routine! The guy was an artist, a genius. No wonder something happened, but what the hell was it?"

The *Mirror* ran daily accounts of their scribe's search through nineteenth-century Ireland for traces of the original Bridey Murphy, but they were unsuccessful, each day a fresh letdown or setback. By then I wondered if the link Dr. Fabian couldn't find in me, the terrible thing that had happened, occurred in another place, another time too. I wanted the reporter to succeed, to prove that we had been other people once, had lived prior lifetimes that were unconscious now. It was such a spooky thing, much more mysterious and haunting than the secret in the attic or the sign of the twisted candles.

But Dr. Fabian had laughed off Bridey Murphy, and Nat shared his view. "I didn't expect them to find her," he confessed one morning as he offered me some of his lox on poppyseed rolls, "but then what did she see, Richard?" While he seemed unwilling to admit it could have been a past life, at least he knew it was *something*. He agreed with me that stuff like reincarnation was more interesting than the stunts in his show, but he said the guests would revolt if he talked about it: "I'd wake them from their dazed stupors for which they are paying good money. Your father would fire me. This is a Jewish resort hotel, not CCNY or Milton Erickson's clinic."

The director of daytime activities was Daddy's much-maligned successor, Lou Goldstein; he ran not only Simon Says shows but general participation comedy in the lobby. I'd try to observe him surreptitiously for, if he glimpsed me spying, he'd always embarrass me. "There goes the owner," he'd say, and everyone would turn around and look at me. "Don't let him fool you. He's a midget."

I wrestled and ran with Boy, spent hours brushing and feeding him. Then one visit during fourth grade, I arrived with Joe to hear he was lost, had been missing for over a month. I went out searching the far reaches of the grounds, even into neighboring forest. Frank Hardy and Rick Brant wouldn't fail at this. But, in the farthest parking lot at the bottom of a hill with garbage, I found only another dead dog, and the horror of that ended my hunt.

Miltys Stackel was my best adult friend. He was perhaps six-foot-ten and two-hundred-and-seventy-five pounds. He had come to the mountains as a barnstorming basketball star and settled at Grossinger's as proprietor of the combination drugstore/coffee shop we called the canteen—a miniature Jessie's Jip Joint with soda fountains, ice-cream bins, and an adjacent TV room.

Milty was a pushover—the source of candy bars, toys, games, sports magazines, comics, and sundry beguiling items. It was all free; family members just put their signature on a dollar-size charge slip that Milty tore from a pad. Michael and I used to joke that he drank two milkshakes for every one he sold—and these were not ordinary shakes; he would fling scoops of butter pecan, vanilla, coffee, strawberry, peach, and whatever else we requested into a silver canister before locking it onto the beater. Even Bluto couldn't have sucked that mortar through a straw.

Not only did Milty not object to our raiding his larder, he encouraged us to dig into fresh stacks of every imaginable comic while he was still unpacking them from manufacturers' cartons. He saved dozens of *Heckle and Jeckle* for his personal stash because he adored those daffy crows, black birds with wide eyes and gigantic beaks. A flip through his archive showed them as dentist and patient, hot-dog vendor and customer, twin waiters (one holding the other up by the feet as he took the order), bookends with sombreros, golfers playing with brooms and placing an 18th-hole marker over a garbage can.

Upon petition for a half hour at a time Milty would leave his post and toss me fly balls on the lawn. Back and forth I'd go, diving on the grass, asking him to put them just over my head, to the left, to the right, high in the air. My side ached, my heart thumped, my legs were wobbly, but I kept pushing—one more catch—one more ... my mind and body primed for either a fling to the side or a dash and plummet backward. I missed plenty and had to chase balls into bushes and across the road, but the great plays more than made up for those—a treasure in the tip of the webbing as I dove or jumped, then tumbled and held on. It was ecstasy, just me and that white stitched pellet, the tug of interrupted zing, proof of a perfectly timed leap or plunge on a planet of grass and sky.

"Don't you ever quit?" he'd say. *"You're* running and I'm beat." Finally, I'd give myself permission to collapse into the sweet throb of my own heart, the cool shade.

After I got a box camera I badgered Milty for free film and developing. Then I trooped the Hotel grounds looking for compositions to shoot: bluish shelves of fungi, sky through leaves, reflections on puddles. For one whole roll I set coconut-covered marshmallow puffs next to hydrangeas that resembled them in color and shape—I wanted to show my stepfather I could make ads too.

In the winter, snow piled up atop wrinkled red berries on bushes, turning them into cherry ice-cream sundaes, so I shot different angles of those. Then I took pictures of dripping icicles against the blue. When a roll was done, twelve exposures, I'd tighten and glue the strip at the end so stray light didn't get in; then I'd bring the spool to the canteen. Milty would drop it into an envelope on which he scribbled my name, then set the packet in a stack of others like it for the lab's delivery man.

I eagerly awaited the return of the fat package with its glossy relics of my compositions. It was always a surprise—what shots came out just as I expected (or even better), which ones lost pizzazz in transposition to a flat surface, which showed an inadvertent blur or light leak. One unintentionally blurred garden view made such a nice rainbow that it was my favorite on the roll. After that, I began lying on my belly, lens up against a dandelion or buttercup so that the bloated orange or yellow transferred its flavor to a meadow of wild flowers beyond.

I even photographed big Milty from down low, aiming straight up into a distortion of his basset-hound face.

In fifth grade I made a Mars scrapbook and wanted to get my own picture of the planet, however faint and blurry, so I went out on a December night when the red dot sparked as bright as I had ever seen it. Milty came along with the longest flashlight he could find (five batteries). Although I told him it wouldn't help, he insisted on shining it up in the sky while I held lens open on time exposure. "A little more light" he said, "couldn't hurt."

A couple of times a winter Irv Jaffee, a former Olympic speed skater, put on a fox costume and whizzed along the ice with dollar bills, fives, tens, and twenties pinned to his fur. Kids had to chase him around the rink and try to get near enough pull off a president as he feinted and swirled. I never nabbed a single one, as the gold medalist zigzagged and spun through our grasps, though I came tantalizingly close, fingers glancing off paper.

The fox was followed by a Lou Goldstein–narrated ice show culminating with championship barrel-jumping—a speed skater building up momentum and then leaping over fifteen or sixteen cylinders in a row, landing with a screech and spray of snow to great applause. I was wide-eyed and proud.

Often I stopped at Joy Cottage for an hour or so to keep Grandma company. I was an attentive audience for tales of her odyssey: how she came to America a poor girl, studied hard, learned English, and became God's custodian of the land. She taught her life as if a proverb of a Biblical character rising above hardship. It was tedious and redundant, but I liked listening politely. I remembered that it was an honor just to be there, and a rare chance to represent my mother well.

Although the contrast between our upbringings couldn't have been more definitive, Grandma Jennie imbued me with a sense of deeper affinity, as if we were two unique members of the Grossinger family. "Our success should have bred vision and generosity among our own," she lamented; "instead it has bred envy and greed. You have suffered like me, so you understand this."

Near the end of each stay she splurged anew on gifts for me, Jonny, and Debby. I got a blue and white Magnavox record-player with sequins on the case, then a tape recorder. Jonny got a set of battery-operated motor cars. Debby got the thing she wanted most—a full cowboy suit with a hat, a holster, and two pistols. Even Bridey was rewarded with a set of jeweled brooches.

"If they try to hurt you," Grandma proclaimed, "we will still shower them with kindness."

During one visit my offhand comment about the Yankees led Grandma to recall a treasure she had kept for years and she summoned the maid to go to her safe for it. Wrapped in a piece of pink velvet in a box, it was a baseball autographed by dozens of famous old-time players, including Ty Cobb and Babe Ruth. She displayed it, rewrapped it, and then handed it to me. "Save this for your children. They can remember me by it."

I returned to New York with these wonders, time and again surpassing everyone's hopes, which should have made my homecomings welcome events. It didn't. Though appreciated, the largess was regarded with suspicion, my mother adopting a familiar wryly querying tone as if to say, "What's all this?" when surely she knew.

They could never quite acknowledge me as their benefactor because they believed *they* deserved what *I* seemed to have acquired without earning, not only the merchandise but the prestige that went with it—Daddy and Mommy because they had made Grossinger's what it was (and Grandma was only using me as their messenger), Jonny because he was the real champion.

In New York I became Richard Towers again. His life was beads strung on a thread: bittersweet days at P.S. 6, Phil and our gang at Bill-Dave, sessions with Dr. Fabian, hardball with Jonny and Bob in the Park. It was walks around the reservoir, me pushing Debby in a stroller; dinners at Grandma Sally's apartment after she and Uncle Tom moved back to New York—Grandma demanding strict manners and polite speech, Jon and I enraging her (and embarrassing our mother) by goofing off, Grandma calling us "insolent" and "impudent," so we made up an insolent, impudent ballad about her. It was seders on the Lower East Side with Daddy's sisters and their husbands and cousins during which our mother, as much an outsider as us, flashed Jonny and me snickers of contempt for the clannish performance, as we were compelled to recitations of *Ma nisthtana ha-laila ha-zel …"* and then had to find the dumb matzoh. It was daydream planets and outer-space adventures (I never enacted the spaceship fantasy at Grossinger's. It didn't belong there). It was epic battles between Jon and me followed by brittle reconciliations; long Monopoly afternoons while rain beat on the window … buying the light blue of Connecticut and red of Kentucky and putting houses and hotels on them.

Stormy days were especially cozy with their myriad lush layers, drips and splashy tires leaving wet aliases on the sidewalk—the City double with melting colors, as my forehead pressed foggy spots on cold window glass. And time oozed past, molecule by molecule.

Phil's father took us to a batting cage in Long Island. A mechanical arm slowly climbed to the top of its arc, then snapped forward, flinging a zip of a pitch. We had chosen "slow," but only fastballs hissed by, the pellet sailing above my bat every time. Then, like Little Johnny Strikeout, I got the knack. We batted toward long nets with hits marked on them. Saying that we should go for swatting one out of Yankee Stadium, a feat never accomplished even by Mickey Mantle, Phil launched shots into the "home run" twice. I hit a double.

At Palisades Park with Bill-Dave I spent an hour one Saturday diagnosing a machine, a claw inside a glass case that, upon the insertion of a quarter, passed over watches, tiny cameras, rings, and other prizes. I longed to have one of those cute cameras so I tried it, but the metal snapped on air, then nothing came through the slot. Afterwards, I went inside a booth and, parting with my last dime, put my eyes in a goggle-cup and watched Woody Woodpecker flash by on cartoon cards. The process of animation was so compelling and accessible that I made my own show at home. As I flipped oblong cards, musical notes seemed to rise and fall from penguins playing trumpets. It was convincing enough for Bridey to ask for an encore.

In the winter we drove to the Nevele, my brother and sister wrapped in blankets beside me in the back seat, asleep. Signs across the Hudson shimmered at night like portals to fairy-tale duchies. The grandest one blinked remorselessly, "Spry for Frying, Spry for Baking"; others shone Maxwell House and Colgate; Pepsi Cola and Nabisco if we left by the East River—yellow, blue, and red beacons. Then the greater unknown....

I stared out into the Martian darkness, picturing the alien towns we passed, the tall, slender skaters on the Red Planet's canals. As I bundled myself deeper and deeper, I turned us into a saucer and sailed beside Wynken, Blynken, and Nod.

I remember outings on the Staten Island Ferry: the rumble of its motor, exploding foam under us, our retinue of gulls, Manhattan becoming an island in the distance, Mommy sitting with her eyes closed, her silver cardboard reflector open, trying to capture every last ember of sacred warmth.

I remember Daddy leading us in prayers as we lit the Hanukah candles: "Vitzyvanoo, lihadlik nair. ..." Then he told the story of the Maccabees and their magic lantern that kept burning after it ran out of oil. We spun dreidels with letters of the Hebrew alphabet and were read stories in which those letters came to life. Till bedtime

Jonny and I lay on the floor, watching wax collect in colored piles on the menorah as we bet on which candle would go out last.

On special Sundays we ate at one of Daddy's restaurant accounts where the owner invariably came and interrupted our meal for a bout of corny hoopla. Between courses we were encouraged to tell stories from our week. Mine tended to be ironical and downbeat (Daddy called me droll). Jon was always triumphant, or outraged if anything went less than perfectly. Debby was a goofy comedienne. Daddy would entertain us with his rendition of the menu, sometimes offering insightful comments on our choices. One of his cues was the delivery of the rolls. "Martha, the way those three attack a bread basket you'd think they were just let out of prison. Hey, guys, this fella here loves a saltstick too. Save a couple."

To our astonishment, we saw Mel Allen once at McGinnis' bar after a Yankee loss. He looked sad, old, and a bit daft compared to how he appeared on TV. "He's feeling no pain," commented Daddy. To him that meant he was in his cups, but to us it meant that he was more than just a commentator of the Yankee games, he cared about their outcomes as much as we did and was drinking off a ninth-inning rally that fell one base hit short.

Sunday nights the family watched *Roy Rogers*. Pat Brady kicked his jeep. Jon and I chuckled, and Daddy let out a loud laugh: "They know how to entertain, son of a gun!" Then came *The Ed Sullivan Show.* Eddie Fisher sang, and Mommy was transfixed in rapture, as Daddy joined in, sometimes crooning the words one beat ahead, sometimes humming only the melody as if it were a synagogue service.

Later, during my bath, I would gather six or seven boats from the hamper and set them in the water with me. As I pulled my body away, the displacement set them moving. There was a tugboat and a motorless motorboat, a submarine that half-floated, half-sank, an ocean liner and its lifeboat, which raced separately, and my favorite, an old sailboat missing its sail, which I called *The African Queen* after a movie Aunt Bunny took me to.

In the opening heat the first one to reach the other end of the bathtub was the winner. Boats would "stick" together and separate; some would move forward for a bit and then drift back. I was not supposed to affect the outcome; yet, as I slid around under them, their whole arrangement shifted, for I was a geography of islands, tides, and winds.

Light shone in soapy water as I began the fourth heat, the one in which the winning boat had to touch the drain and then return to start. Only craft that had contacted the metal circle were in the running and needed to be kept track of.

Over the months, new entrants came and went—canoes and houseboats and barges—but *The African Queen,* paintless and rotted, stayed and held all the bathtub records.

The annals of my childhood embraced this dichotomy—Grossinger's and New York. Jonny, Debby, Martha and Bob represented one jurisdiction; Aunt Bunny, Uncle Paul, Michael, and James the other—and never the twain did meet. It wasn't that Grossinger's was utopia and New York was hell. The City was my background planet, enthralling and tenacious in ways that the Hotel wasn't: its dawns of stone shadows, its eves of glitter and clatter, the epic of the Yankees playing on its marquee.

Sometimes my two worlds strangely collided; for instance when maître d' Abe Friedman's nephew, a New York cabbie, recognized me on the street and screeched to a stop to say hello. He gave me and a startled Bridey a ride home with the grocery bags, refusing her offer of payment. I thought, as my heart outraced feelings that had no outlet in Towers Land, "See, Bridey, it's more than brooches from Grandma Jennie. It's real, *and it's benign."*

One afternoon I came home from school to find that Yogi Berra had written me on the back of a postcard of the Grossinger's ski slope, telling me to behave myself and do my homework! "We should get Yogi Berra here," Bridey proclaimed, his name odd in her brogue. As my brother and I danced about, holding the card in the air, she said, "Maybe he could introduce some law and order before you wear your mother and me to death."

The years in New York settle into a directionless flux, timeless tangles of convergent themes: pennant races with the Cleveland

Indians, World Series games against the Dodgers, Grandma Sally's ashtrays full of hopjes candies that tasted like coffee, dinners with Uncle Paul, check-ups at Dr. Hunt, verbal cipher hunts with Dr. Fabian, bus rides up and down avenues, haircuts from my mother's French barber on Madison, Bridey singing while she cooked. I would be feeling an outcast, longing for my other home when the world suddenly sank into its New York mood, not as banishment but with a kind of bone-chilling awe. Suddenly, from the kitchen would come the lilting soprano of Bridget McCann: *"It's that old devil moon / That you stole from the skies. / It's that old devil moon in your eyes."* Then the sheer depth and texture of existence filled me.

New York defined the "me" who got to go to Grossinger's. My brother Michael had always lived in paradise, so he didn't understand it. I was willing to be sullen and brooding in my other life as long as I could return to my true abode. As Grandma Jennie said, "Welcome home."

I kept her autographed ball in its box at the end of one of my bookshelves. I didn't think about it much, so I didn't notice at first when it was missing. Presuming Bridey had moved it while cleaning, I went to her. She shook her head and didn't want to discuss it. Then Jonny said, "Ask Daddy."

That evening, unaware of what I was about to invoke, I wondered if maybe Daddy borrowed it to show to a client.

"What do you mean, *your* baseball?" he exploded. "I brought those players to Grossinger's. Without Bob Towers, you don't have a baseball."

"But where is it?"

"He doesn't have to answer to you," my mother said, giving me her most authoritatively threatening scowl. Jon and Debby stared grimly. "You are insolent!"

"One Sunday we didn't have a ball," Bob shrugged. "Babe Ruth and Ty Cobb signed a thousand of those, or every clubhouse boy in America signed them for them. What did you think? You had something special? Richard, that ball was a big nothing."

I couldn't believe what they were saying. They had played with it, the last time I was at Grossinger's. Now it was just one more dirty hardball.

"It serves you right," my mother said.

It was never clear what she meant. Either it served me right for being at Grossinger's or it served me right because it was never really my ball. Then Bridey arrived with our dinner plates, and no one mentioned it again.

That "old debbil moon" was everything we were and weren't and, although Bridget McCann couldn't have known, a Gaelic leprechaun inside her told us what was happening: *"Does that laddie with a twinkling eye / Come whistling by. / And does he walk away, / Sad and dreamy there / Not to see me there …,"* her brogue putting the pauses right where they belonged, where the shadow was, where light crept through. Rhyming outside, then in. Impossible hopes leaping from the abyss. Mysterious and profound. Melody and dirge.

Right! I was there, but they never saw me. I loved them and was loyal even in my betrayals. But they excluded me from their creed.

9

SORCERY

The high crime of treason might have been reserved for me, but at another level, Jonny and I were egalitarian truants our mother reviled as an indivisible pair. We would be lying in bed, talking to each other against the rules, and suddenly she would burst in with a belt and start whipping us through the covers. "Do you realize what time it is?" We were supposed to be asleep.

An automatic alert was set in our minds for the sound of her approach. When we played sockball, we had a drill for hiding the paraphernalia instantly if we heard an ascending scale of footsteps.

In Victorian novels women are always fainting away, rushing to their chambers from emotional shock or constitutional excitement, a restorative at hand. My mother didn't swoon, but her nerves and hysteria were a legendary factor that had to be reckoned with. We continually worried about vexing or upsetting her, inciting tremors and rages. There was no restorative against her rampages—pills and bitters didn't go that deep.

Either preparing for a crisis or having just overcome one, she took to her bed for such long hours that we forgot she even lived there. Then from her room she would unaccountably subpoena me or Jonny or both of us for an interrogation or charge out on a foray, looking for misconduct: a toy left on the floor, unfinished dinner on someone's plate. "You don't have to like it, just eat it" was a common rejoinder to a familiar complaint. Putting uneaten meals into our milk was an infliction that originated with her.

In her untied bathrobe, hair askew, creams dabbed irregularly on her face, Martha Towers would paw through the garbage looking for wasted food, crawl along the rug in her bathrobe, collecting evidence—telltale candy wrappers, crumbs, baseball cards, even dustballs. "There's going to be a pogrom in this house," she'd announce. Then, with swipes and shoves, as forceful as they were uncoordinated, she'd help pull games and cards out of closets and drawers and start "cleaning up," which meant throwing out perfectly good stuff.

We were maddening to her, just about everything we did. Yet it was a paradox: I was bad and Jon was good, but we were *both* bad. Though he was a saint by comparison, together we were a debacle. Half the time I was singled out for blame and Jon was exonerated, but the other half—and it was much more than half—she bemoaned that she had been given two such beasts for children: "What did I do, Bridey, to deserve this?"

Beyond her idealization of Prince Jonny—either because he was the son of a man she claimed to love or because she regularly singled out individuals to valorize or defame for abstruse and perverse reasons of her own—she had no more use for him than she did for me, and no interest at all in who either of us was.

One rainy day Jonny and I were behaving so sillily in Novack's Market that, as we were about to enter the fish store next door, Mommy stuck out an arm and insisted that we remain on the street while she shopped in peace. In our slickers and galoshes we leaned against the plate-glass window, staring at stacks of what used to be living creatures and lobsters crawling on crushed ice beneath the taxidermy of a giant turtle. Suddenly she burst back out at a tremendous clip, not even acknowledging us. She sure was angry. The drizzle had become a downpour, but it was impossible to catch up even to share her umbrella.

We followed her from Madison to Park, then up along Park in increasing sheets of rain. She had never let us get wet before, but she didn't break stride. She turned into a strange building on Phil's block of 93rd. We made the elevator just before its door closed. Only when she took off her rain-hat did we realize we had followed the wrong lady home.

Though we weren't allowed to cross streets on our own, we had no choice but to hurry three blocks to 96th and stand outside the door waiting for Ramon to deliver our nemesis. She spanked us both, starting right at the elevator, but the worst part was afterwards when she just lay in her room crying. We didn't know how to fix who we were or undo what we had done.

Once Jonny started kindergarten at P.S. 6, we were dispatched to school together in the Bill-Dave wagon. Usually we got off to a sluggish start and had to pick-up momentum through breakfast to make our transportation. Bridey was often shoving us out the door just as van was turning the corner of Park at 96th. "Hurry, you two," she'd urge. "I know it must have left by now." The cranky elevator would whine to a stop, sometimes as Bert was pulling up. Jon and I stood by its metal gate ready to dash, Ramon invoking his authority and ordering us back until he had officially opened the door. He usually introduced a slight pause, probably wanting to assert regency over those pesky kids or eavesdrop on another exotic punishment.

One morning the wagon didn't come. Jon and I stood there in disbelief as the day grew old and we watched a stream of business-men heading off to work, a sure sign we had blown it. We dragged ourselves back to the apartment to Ramon's jests. "See, your mamma right! She told you, you gonna miss! She gonna beat you!"

She was getting dressed and startled to see us again. Saying not a word, still adjusting her collar with one hand, she herded us into her room and swatted with the nearest implement, an umbrella. We were grabbing each other and trying to get away under the bed, but she followed, slamming harder and harder.

During this improvisational beating, the phone rang and Bridey broke in.

"I'm sorry to interrupt, Mrs. Towers, but that was Bill-Dave to say the bus had a flat tire; it's on its way."

Mommy was undeterred. "The way they dawdle at breakfast they would have missed it a hundred times if it came when it was supposed to." And she continued smacking.

Jonny and I relied on Daddy for fun and activity, to get us out of the apartment. He was mostly good-natured and participated in household frays mainly to defend his pride, for Mommy liked to needle him. He put a special effort into our escaping on Sundays, for that was the day on which she was most volatile. Dr. Fabian called it a "Sunday complex," saying that Freud himself had diagnosed the symptoms.

Most Sunday mornings in the spring and fall, Daddy took us to Central Park. We picked home plate by a tree, and he pitched while we alternated turns of ten swings. It felt almost major league to be stinging his overhand tosses or snagging the line drives of Jonny's bat. As I ran across the grass and cut off a grounder, Daddy exclaimed, "Gil McDougald couldn't have done it any better!"

Sometimes he orchestrated games, inviting Puerto Rican kids our age from their own fungo matches. These hoods with bright-colored Spanish T-shirts and early bling were dubious at first, like "Are you saying like what I think you're saying, sir?" but an adult-chaperoned match with real positions and rules was a chance to shine they couldn't turn down.

Daddy was always the pitcher, balancing the teams by playing harder for the losing side, applauding everyone's plays as he umpired.

This was totally out of character for our family. We never talked to anyone; we crossed the street not only for large dogs but to avoid walking near the kinds of youths he was summoning over and telling, "Son, with that raw ability you're going to be in the outfield next to Mickey Mantle in a few years." On the way home, sweaty and content, we stopped at the drugstore for lemonade on crushed ice. I loved sucking the sweet citrus into my body, so cold it gave me a headache.

Other weekends we went on outings to Daddy's advertising accounts downtown, stopping first at the Lower East Side apartment where his mother and father still dwelled, tiny brittle creatures like the spiders that Coyote found spinning cloth when he climbed the topless tree into the world of the ancestors. They were apparently friendly but almost motionless, and spoke to us in cautions and prayers. "You see what I came from," Daddy would tell us in the car. "I made it on pure spirit and guts."

Our favorite client was a kosher delicatessen near their place. Abe Gellis, the owner, a short. stout man who looked like the ringmaster at a circus, would reach into every pocket of his floppy jacket and pants for stacks of flat cardboard which, when dropped in water, turned into colored sponges with ads for his meats. We came home with twenty or thirty of these and played with them for weeks—their magical expansion never losing its amusement value.

In our booth we were served roast beef sandwiches made of the pinkest, softest slices layered in the world's largest, crispest kaiser rolls thick with poppy seeds, separate plates of fat, crispy french fries, bottles of Dr. Brown's orange ("Do they make a sandwich here, Ricardo, Jonno, what do you say ...?"), while the men smoked and talked business—Daddy's booming voice a blend of charm and outrage as he serenaded all in earshot with tales of uptown ("The no-good sons of bitches! Abe, are you listening ...?"), and made the Gellises millionaires times over with his promotional plans. Then he drove through the City singing Jolson and cursing the lazy good-for-nothings he had just courted.

Soon after my sister Debby was born, Mommy took a job running the New York office of the Fontainebleau Hotel, which was starting up in Miami Beach. The position was offered to her from old Grossinger connections, though it helped that she could say the name in flawless French from her childhood in Paris. She answered the reservation line downtown in an office all day, then from an extension at home up to bedtime. Her representation of the resort became her life's calling, as she made the booking of rooms into a thespian art, entertaining guests with gossip and intrigue, the sounds of which filled our apartment.

In her office at Fifth Avenue and 57th Street she thrived on the flurry of paperwork and ringing lines, rushing between file cabinets and a patron on "hold." Her voice commanded a five-person suite. By comparison with the second-rate males demoted from Florida, she was witty and vivacious—in charge, though I realized years later, paid a third of what they were. I watched their baffled looks as she exchanged insights and ironies or twinkles of the eye with her brassy blonde assistant Helen.

Over the years the Fontainebleau office was my favorite place to visit her, for she was convivial and almost normal there, a different woman, more likely to order me a hamburger from downstairs than to harangue me over some truancy. Yet I recognized the brittleness and instability of this mood and never let down my guard.

Back at home, she reverted to a one-woman totalitarian regime. We were an odd blend of a superstitious shtetl clan addicted to shouting, browbeating, and rampages, and a household from Dickens in which every slight or insult was weighed meticulously, then leveraged back, its ante adjusted for fullest effect, petty honor more important than charitable conduct or even common sense.

There was something in my mother's nature that kept permanent tally of wrongs done to her. Transgressions and encroachments on her dignity were the most important things in the world—they held the mythic significance of the Ten Commandments and trials of Job. She was the embodiment of tribunal, revenge, and retribution, despite fancy proclamations to the contrary, so we were quarantined from anyone disloyal to her. When I first heard the phrase "iron curtain," I imagined that it originated with us and was applied to the Soviet Union later.

She and Daddy lived at a breakneck pace, catching their shared cab downtown in the morning, arriving home for dinner exhausted, often conspiring a mile a minute against some "total idiot" or bickering with each other.

Their arguments were endemic, for they bore an unsettlable vendetta between them too. As children we had no notion of the issues but read its prodrome: irreversible throbs of resentment and exploratory salvos cascading into full fusillades. Like brushfires, the irritant might smolder a while, then germinate anon from tense, suppressed voices in their room. Mommy would escalate from hollering to screeching to paroxysmic fits beyond delineation. Daddy would come running out of the room, her chasing after him with a purpose. She threw books, ashtrays, and other objects. If the skirmish spilled into the kitchen, she might pick up dishes, silverware, even kitchen knives, once actually wounding him with one. Yet, as Jonny and I would joke, it was lucky she didn't have much of an arm. He would go right to the elevator and disappear, either for hours or days.

The time he was injured he locked himself in the bathroom and wept. She brought iodine and bandages to the door and seemed genuinely distraught at the damage she had caused, though she resumed yelling as soon as he emerged.

I wished we could somehow just be friendly, trust each other, that I could feel safe and happy. But things were too complicated for that. I couldn't trust my own feelings, let alone those of the others. I didn't love my brother, so why would any of them love me?

Living in such a milieu was not just piddling harassment by a neurotic scold or hysterical Jewish-American Princess. If she had been shallow or superficial, everything would have been easier. We would have laughed behind her back, humored and ignored her. But she had much bigger plans for us. From her bottomless web she conducted a dirge for the annihilation of happiness forever, like the whole of nature struggling to be born after a thousand years of winter. And no certainty it would.

Episodes like following the wrong lady out of the fish market or missing a school wagon that never came stand out as myths, yarns to be retold and savored years later, because they were hilarious and absurd. If anything, they were comic relief to a macabre regime— fey outcroppings of moods with minor reprisals. The real anguish formed beneath the vaudeville, a sense of gloom and impending disaster, a constant reminder to stop acting bad when we knew we couldn't.

Relics of an unspeakable crime occupied every nook and cranny, reminding us of sins that could neither be uttered nor expiated. Their bleak profundity and ritual mourning imbued every gesture. They fed the ambient light, the seams between rooms, the dishwa- ter, the taste of Sugar Pops and Frosted Flakes, the sound of "Some Enchanted Evening" in the living room: *"Once you have found her, never let her go"*—another song that meant not only exactly what it said but something it couldn't say.

At unpredictable times Mommy seemed inundated by feelings of tenderness for us; she would address us with giddy appreciation. She'd tell funny stories and display an uncanny memory of all the good things we ever did. Where had our Mummsy Wine been hiding? Why did we not know that she was keeping track of our virtues too.

But even as she eulogized, she was challenging us to doubt her, pleading with us not to make a false move because then we would be responsible for the return of winter. Her cheerfulness was so fragile that we never completed an episode without an onset of suspicion. "What's wrong? Why won't you tell me?" We knew it couldn't last.

No description of my mother does her justice because her reality contained so many other layers and anomalies. She wasn't unhappy as much as she was inconsolable. She met us with a fierceness and vengeance that had no object, merely a longing to set things right in a condition in which something incredible was expected of all of us that we could never enact ... and then at times she could be so gay we followed her like the pied piper, this woman who turned men's heads on the street. She must have held in her mind a magnificent object, a requiem big as the sky, a kaleidoscope of all the songs Irving Berlin ever wrote, one *"Easter bonnet/girl that I marry/ white Christmas,"* but no way to meet her there, no way to get into her imaginary paradise.

Sometimes it will all come back in a flash of déjà vu: the walk to the barbershop, the color of light against a particular building at a time of day, Michel with his scissors, the hair all around us on the floor ... how I woke in the middle of a winter night, shivering, trying to hold the lost tendril of a dream, wet bedsheets clinging to goose bumps in lost watches of the night. I lay in damp warm islands diminishing slowly to ice. Getting toasty was my whole existence as I shivered against the clammy flannel.

Finally, I roused myself, spread my sheets and blankets on radiator pipes, and lay atop them in imaginary summer, aromatically steaming them dry, until sun itself rose through city stone—first light blending with vapors from my own body.

I will feel the melancholy of then, suspended in a sorrow I will always have. I did not minimize the pain later. I simply engorged it. I changed it into something else, as I changed—into a numb, flattened ache so that now I remember mainly how desolate it was. Nothing will ever feel that old way again because, back then, I imagined that my range of feelings and possibilities *was* the world. I had no reason to suspect it would ever be different, that I would be paroled. And I adhered to it like a penitent because it also held mystery, depth, and wonder of my own being.

The things I did during childhood do not seem as important to me as the overall mystery of it. I went from one event to another, as the Buddhists say, like a drunken monkey. Toys, games, comics, candy bars—these are what we are raised on in the West, and in much of the world they are considered the acme, worth rewriting history for.

Years later I look back on that childhood with dismay. What did I learn compared to peasant children in China who worked the farms and raised food for villages? What about the self-sufficient offspring of the Eskimo and other northern tribes? From the beginning they are taught where they are, the habitats of plants and animals, and how to find their way home in a blizzard. If they have spooks, the tribal elders gather for a ceremony to honor and release them. Alien forces are named and addressed respectfully; they are not allowed free rein in a child's mind. A boy is given his own totems, the wind to ride.

In 1950s New York City we were raised in an arcade without a sense that our survival was provisional. In place of spirit release, we had doctors, churches, synagogues—stand-ins for the power of the cosmos, its capacity to transform and heal.

Behind the scattered memes and memories of childhood, a vast incomprehensible fog envelops my life. I can create names for that fog, but they are intellectual constructs. The original sadness was an ocean. It wasn't only sad; it was sensual and rich, and I swam in its eternity—a planet of waters as large, in scale, as the lake into which *The African Queen* plunged in the movie. It too had lightning and demon cruisers. There was no opposite shore to that lake, but childhood was the process of sailing there anyway. Fear was my guardian, but fear was the same as timelessness—unrelinquishable, impenetrable.

Games kept me busy—toys, comic books, movies, water guns—so that a yellow plastic Sorry! token or a green Pennsylvania Avenue card brings back the whole enchantment.

10

Color War

During fifth and sixth grades I remained a member of Bill-Dave Group and loyal friend and foil of Phil Wohlstetter. A list of our adventures would fill five volumes. Good old Phil—switch-hitting shortstop, platoon leader, Tom Quest himself. We shared the Yankees, the Hardy Boys, and a litany of cards, comics, and capers.

Most adults admired Phil's spunk and irreverence and laughed at his antics, but to my mother he was a juvenile delinquent on the brink of big-time trouble—another in my legion of errors in character judgment starring Dr. Fabian and Aunt Bunny. Phil had been caught by Jessie in the act of stealing. He had talked me into throwing my undershirt out the window to win a bet with Jonny Wouk. He had led us on nutty detective ventures that brought the police.

Yet by fifth grade Phil was being tutored for prep school as if a newly discovered scholastic genius. Prior to that, he had been as much of an anarchist and goof-off as me, albeit with better grades. Now he lorded his status over me, quoting algebraic formulas to prove his ascension to seventh- and then eighth-grade math, spicing his sassy slang with new vocabulary. Miss Fitzgerald, our teacher, infuriated my mother by saying she wished some of my friend's spark would rub off on me: "He's just so energetic and creative."

"If you follow her advice," Daddy said, "you'll end up in jail."

"Daydream" was the word most often written on my report cards. That didn't require much perspicacity from my teachers. But they thought I just didn't pay attention; they had no idea what I was imagining. Beside such sagas, school hardly moved the needle.

I spent my summers at Chipinaw, ascending the row of bunks with Jay, Barry, and whatever three or four miscellaneous kids were assigned to our cabin. Some years we had "good" counselors who threw in with us. In Bunk 9 Sam Rosenberg spent what seemed like half his salary on food and prizes for his boys—he also gave up time-off during rest periods to serve as commissioner for our All-Star Baseball tournaments, arranging brackets and umpiring the matches. When we began fighting over Yankee, Dodger, and Giant farm clubs for our team names, he resolved the matter by making us pick other minor-league towns in Colorado, Kansas, and Nebraska.

Bunk 12 saw us in constant strife with authority, punished for poor inspections and bad attitudes. As Jay, Barry, and I made improvisational horseplay and insubordination a way of life, we were deemed bad influences on our bunkmates. But it was our métier, for we were pretty much what the constabulary told us we were: goof-offs, lazy slobs.

Because I had a growing reputation as a prankster, Jay and Barry liked to egg me into providing entertainment: water traps over doorways, sometimes with dangling strings to tempt; unmaking beds and short-sheeting them so that the victim would be unable to get his feet down; conducting all sorts of unlikely movements of unlikely objects.

I could ill explain some of my demonic streaks. In the middle of one night, I collected a few baseballs, bars of soap, and loose moccasins from people's cubbies, tiptoed through the bathroom, and tossed them over the divider into the next bunk, causing an impressive clatter of thuds and clunks, especially for the hour. I hadn't known that I was going to this; the deed furnished its own impetus. Tearing back to my bed, I pretended to be asleep.

I repeated this bizarre disturbance twice more over the next week. The kids in the adjoining cabin were fired up to identify their nemesis and get revenge.

Jay, Barry, and I had a bunkmate that year even sloppier and more eccentric than me. His first name was also Richard, and he corrected mispronunciations of his last name Oranger so prissily that we contrived garbles of it. On my return to bed from the third enactment of my stunt, I pushed Oranger, covers and all, onto the floor before diving under my sheets. The lights went on, and soon our bunk was filled with O.D.'s and kids from next door (remember, O.D.'s were older campers with paid jobs, one of which was to oversee bunks after Taps).

"Well, if you don't remember doing it, dammit," said a frustrated O.D., "you must have sleepwalked."

To my horror Oranger agreed.

Years later Jay and Barry were still telling the story. "And that's why," Barry would conclude ceremoniously, "you don't see the Orangeman today."

But I rued the cruel-hearted imp who incriminated a meek boy when he should have been his ally and friend. I had no more planned to push him on the floor than commit the crime in the first place; *I just did it.*

My pranks represented gaps in myself, when I felt more poignancy than I could bear and there were no other outlets. I vaguely recall that when I tossed the items over the wall the first time, I was responding to an evocative smell of toothpaste and soap near the sinks. Feeling equal parts attraction and repulsion, I acted rashly and resolved the matter.

At Chipinaw, nonconformity was my safety valve, mutiny my artform. I rebelled instinctively, going truant from activities like a dog slipping his leash. Not only didn't I swim, I skipped other activities.

I played seasons of solitaire Roofball. In this game a Spaldeen was tossed onto a bunk roof, and it was either caught by me on the rebound for an out or it landed and then bounced (single ... double ... triple ... home run ... depending on how long it took me to chase it down). An irregular roof with peaks and vales was far more challenging than a stone wall. I learned the bumps, elbows, and slopes of the various bunks and used them as different home fields. The ball could be angled high so that it ricocheted back as a long fly ball, or I could attempt to fool myself (or an imaginary opponent) with spins, recoils off pipes sticking through the roof, rolls along seams, or even innocent sequences of bounces that either just hit or just missed the front lip. I cultivated these techniques as well for matches with friends during free play.

Counselors would announce our required activity, but I would be camouflaged between the back of a bunk and the woods. The grass was unmown there, the weeds often wet from dew. "McDougald into the hole … fields … throws … gets him!" I would toss the rubber pinky as high as I could, then back up like an outfielder against a wall, coil, and leap at the edge of the forest to meet the apogee of the ball's arc off the roof, stealing a home run and falling into moist foliage. "There's a long drive … Mitchell back … that ball is going … going.… "

Sometimes they forgot to look for me, and I played through a whole period. More often I was herded to where I belonged, the daily regimen of games, hikes, lessons, and drills—softball, hardball, tennis, lanyards, volleyball, soccer, track, boxing, nature cabin, swimming, rowboats, canoes. These were relentlessly imposed, with meals, rest period, and meager slots of free time.

The worst were archery and riflery. I could barely hold the arrow straight while pulling on the giant bow or point it anywhere near large straw-stuffed bulls-eyes. I didn't want anything to do with the rifle range's gunpowder and empty shells, which we were warned not to touch because they could give us lockjaw, such a terrifying prospect that I kept moving my mouth and tongue while I routinely missed the entire paper target despite aligning the sights. These weapons were powerful and scary. Steel-tipped sticks and metal slugs that moved too fast to be seen but made ominous hisses, clanks, and holes didn't belong in our unpredictable paws. I pictured arrows through chests and gunned-down young cowboys.

In retrospect, I estimate that my life at Chipinaw was twenty percent successful escapes, eighty percent conscription, but my extemporizations were richer and more memorable. It wasn't that the regular activities were always awful and unpleasant, but counselors' continual sanctimony and coercion made them feel like punishment rather than fun. There was zero recognition of the need to dawdle, laze, imagine, just stare. For me, playing hooky was intrinsic and visceral.

I made up another private game in which I would stand at the downhill edge of a long hangar-like building called "the armory" (which housed the crafts shop and theater) and fungo a hardball as far as I could, converting the adjacent landscape into a baseball zone with designated hits. I revised and nuanced this event over many a summer, as it settled into my most ambitious and reliable diversion.

Over the hedge in front of the girls' dining room was a homer; before the hedge was a triple. Up to the end of the armory was a double. Past the midpoint of the stairs was a single. Everything else was an out.

There was an ambrosial sensation to tossing a ball up, swatting it, then seeing where its flight landed it, in what patch or rough, near and far, as I narrated the play silently (à la Mel Allen). I took my time, savoring the sun's warmth and occasional breezes over my sweaty brow, stopping to watch the flights of bugs, to blow dandelion heads.

Reaching the hedge on a fly was an epiphany—a soaring bird, a squirrel hiding its farthest nut, a spaceship dropping an Easter egg—and the memory of those rare synchronies of bat and ball, the torque of my swing, is ineradicable.

After each round or inning (the number of batters dependent on how many balls I had) I would retrieve my shots from all over the field as I continued to announce the game. I filled the home-team line-up with Yankee subs and farmhands whom I wanted in the major leagues and played people in odd or former positions (Don Bollweg at first, Pedro Gonzalez at second, Mickey Mantle at short, Kal Segrist at third). That alone made it special. "Gil McDougald leading off. Early Wynn winds and fires. It's a drive down the left field line. He turns at first and holds. Now catcher Gus Triandos." In the distance I could hear the echoes of camp events, remote like a half-forgotten dream.

After completing five innings, batter by batter, I'd collapse beneath a pine and review the action like a sportswriter, cozily AWOL. Eventually a counselor would come to fetch me back to whatever activity I had deserted.

At nap-time after lunch we got to stay in the bunk and play games, write postcards, get mail delivery, and follow baseball on the radio. Eager for the Yankee score, I galloped downhill from the mess hall, almost outpacing my own legs, thinking of how, in just another moment, I would crash onto those coarse green blankets, warmed by the sun, turn on the game in the second or third inning, and lie there listening.

This was a time of boundless nostalgia, reading letters from Mommy and Daddy, aunts and uncles, leisure in which to send them each back a Chipinaw postcard and tell them what I was doing. As I narrated my life, I imagined myself a character in a story, a forerunner of this text.

Radios were strictly forbidden in the mess hall or at any of our activities, but I began setting the Yankees in the outfield of softball games and beyond the fence of the tennis court, racing from activities to pick up a pitch or two and hopefully the score.

At Sunday evening barbecues, which were held on blankets hauled from our bunks, radios *were* allowed. Beside a plate of hamburger, beans, and potato chips, a slice of watermelon, I sank into the luxury of the second game of a doubleheader with its assortment of utility players. That was heaven.

On game nights I maintained my Yankee vigil in bed as stations crossed and interfered, the radio on softly so that O.D.s couldn't hear. Mel Allen's voice waned and came back through the darkness, and I pieced together missing action until I clicked the knob just before sleep. In the morning I turned to WINS 1010 for the final score.

Chipinaw was the liquored scent of its infirmary, the cracked paint of its bathrooms, the smell of old pipes and cleansers. It was rabbits that appeared at twilight and darted away at my approach. They had no intent to be part of the kingdom, but they dwelled in its environs.

I remember our bodies crammed together—in the bath-house at the lake, the bunk latrine while we brushed our teeth, along the armory wall in games of charades, on the floor in rough-housing and pillow fights—our clammy, clabbery aroma, childlike and dank.

Mealtimes at Chipinaw were loathsome but sensuous. The mess hall was a clatter of trays passing through swinging doors on waiters' shoulders, cheers when one was dropped, giant ladle-bearing platters and basins of saltpeter- and MSG-spiced pottage (this intelligence awaited our more mature tenures), jugs of purple and orange Kool-Aid for our thirst. No one removed the live and dead flies that lodged above sugar level in the large shakers. A prank that never grew old was surreptitiously to pour sugar into the salt-shaker or, better yet, salt into the sugar urn. The dessert that brought the loudest cheers was single-serving ice-cream cups, vanilla, strawberry, chocolate, and chocolate chip, off the lids of which a thin paper layer could be peeled revealing a round baseball card with the face of a player.

The intricately eroded resin of table surfaces were like maps of other planets. In tedium before and between courses, we played a game across their width with salt and pepper, propelling the small glass shakers back and forth between contestants on opposite sides in an attempt to land part—even a fraction of the glass rim—over the edge so that a flat hand pressed against the table lip and then raised would jiggle or dislodge it. We sprinkled salt on the mottled maroon for better sliding and mastered a quick upward swipe (with an attendant grimace of "drats" or smirk of "no cigar," depending on whether the shaker moved even a feather's breadth). Usually the shaker stopped far short or went flying off the end and had to be caught by the facing player.

They fed us noodles and cheese onto which we poured a warm fruit-salad sauce; tasteless chow mein on soggy, cracker-like noodles; and egg and egg-salad gunks, vittles from which I willingly went hungry, awaiting rations from Grossinger's or town.

In exchange for passes to the Hotel, we bribed counselors to drive into Monticello after Taps and bring back roast-beef sandwiches and potato knishes. Awakened past 1 a.m. for goodies wrapped in paper, sleepily we munched away, hearing our mentors rhapsodize about movie stars and babes in swimsuits by the G. pool. The smell of warm dough with its spud filling, the resilience of soft rye through its wrapper, harboring pickles and sliced pink meat, were dream-like assuagements of hunger.

I remember the delivery of laundry every Friday: fat bundles wrapped in crisp brown paper, heaved from the back of a rickety truck onto the center of the campus. Each bore a rude number in black crayon. We hunted among the digits for ours. They weren't Christmas presents, but there was a merry quality to such pudgy, amorphous wads. The smaller cubes could be lugged back by a single person, but the largest took two or three of us, often busting as we carried them, leaving trails of socks and underpants. Occasional mispacked bras and girls' underwear led to further slapstick and merriment.

Stashes of comics piled in campers' cubbies, beatitudes beckoning a stray glance: a rocket blasting out its innards as an astronaut floats above Saturn in his space suit; a man and a woman submerged in test tubes attended to by tentacled monsters with two tiers of vertical eyes each; men beside their vehicle on the surface of a Martian moon under the giant Red Planet crisscrossed with canals; alien creatures with crinkled green heads like external brains, emerging from a spaceship while in the background flying saucers stream out of a larger saucer silhouetted against a yellow moon.

As we lay on our beds for rest period, wasps whined at screens and the scent of grass mowers perfumed the air beyond. We were in a diaspora we could hardly gauge, seamless and bottomless in all directions.

For tear-out camp money (a booklet of different-colored pennies, nickels, dimes, and quarters), monitors from the O.D.'s shack sold us candy—Almond Joy, Spearmint Leaves, or Mallow Cups—from manufacturers' boxes. We ate and read to the narrative buzz of the ballgame. Our respite ended when the bugle blared, calling us to the next activity.

On stormy nights we converged on the armory for movies. Boys and girls bustled in through separate doors in yellow or orange gear, looking alike until the girls took off their round hats and shook loose their hair. Rain-wear, moisture, and gender gave the room a plasticky sachet recalling other storms. O.D.s passed around candy bars; then the lights went out and on the screen flashed the credits for some black-and-white spy movie or, on a number of occasions, *It Came from Outer Space* (the camp owned a recycled repertoire). Events on the screen notwithstanding, the room was a bedlam of whispers, whistles, and shouts. As the first pretty actress appeared, a bunch of girls hollered in unison, "Judy," and broke into giggles, then "Barry and Ellen," and, from the boys' side, "Tom in the shower" ...whistles and hoots.

Dave Hecht, the unpopular owner, was regularly evoked. A surly, plump tyrant, he invaded camp events like a cartoon mogul. A prominent attorney during the rest of the year, he seemed to enjoy firing counselors for momentary indiscretions, often with a flamboyant gesture like an umpire banishing an offending player. During the major theatrical production one year, his daughter Lynn, acknowledgedly stunning, kissed an actor on the mouth. Dave came up on stage and interrupted the play; there he reduced her to tears. The maiden appearance of the space monster always brought the same collective outcry of his name.

As campers performed skits, short plays, and vaudeville in the armory, Dave was routinely portrayed by an actor with a painted mustache and a pillow stuffed under his pajama top.

During talent shows, my bunkmate Barry put on blackface. Every muscle straining, he blew Louie Armstrong out his trumpet. Later in the program a tiny girl with a winsome voice sang a cappella: *"When you walk through a storm, / keep your head up high, / and don't be afraid of the dark."* The boys around me guffawed, but I felt transported.

At the end of each day's activities we were summoned to a trade-mark Chipinaw ritual. In the armory (moths rattling in ceiling lamps), on an outdoor field at twilight (stars beginning to appear), a counselor would announce it was time for "Friends" followed by "Taps." A few kids would groan, but we put our arms around each other, forming a long chain of all of us, and then swung back and forth in place, our voices in and out of unison:

"Friends, friends, friends, / we will always be."

Ridiculous but irrefutable. No matter what we did to one another during the day, how much we razzed and tormented, how grimly we competed and fought, something about this comical, affectionate ritual locked our hearts together.

The camp was pure blatancy, avoidance of anything inward or mysterious, denial of loneliness and sorrow. But joined in a chain against each other's boninesses and individual weights, we were obliged to acknowledge how awkward and vulnerable our situation really was. There was no avoiding one another: boys bumping into each other's bodies and moods. The most competitive, aggressive athletes had to give up some of their bluff and join the others in a prayer that said that none of the rest mattered ... that we were all one. It may have been lip service, like good sportsmanship, but I experienced it as if we were all on a spaceship, hurtling together through the big dark:

"Whether in fair or in foul stormy weather, / Camp Chipinaw will keep us together."

Decorum never held up. People would pull too hard and parts of the line collapsed in heaps—or someone stopped swaying and we'd crunch and fall into each other's laps. I was yanked to one side and, with no return tug from the other, toppled back clownishly.

Then we stood and sang the other song that made me think of a planet in space:

"Day is done. / Gone the sun, / from the earth, from the sky..."

We marched back to our bunks, got undressed, into PJs, and lay in bed telling stories across the room; "Taps"—the bugle—would sound, from camp to camp across Silver Lake. Mothwings flapped around bulbs until counselors doused the lights and hushed us.

"All is well. / Safely rest. God is nigh."

Cozy in bed I broadcast my position to the gods and warned them—you sent me here, now watch over me. This playful blasphemy (in place of the rabbi's prayer) eased my body and tucked me in.

In my third summer Jonny began as a Midget. Homesick, he sought me out during free play and I taught him Rafterball and my armory game. It was strange that he should suddenly be so close to Grossinger's—a place that had everything to do with me and nothing with him—but my mother and stepfather identified with its world as much as they vilified it. They never considered another camp for

Jon. He joined me for the dispensation of Grossinger's food, an assumption of privilege that made me furious because he refused to acknowledge their source. I meanwhile pretended to be generous, but he saw through my magnanimity, that I was rubbing his nose in how posh my other family was. Soon he was rebuffing "your rotten illegal food." That was okay with me. Jon was a stuck-up goody-goody, and any connection between him and Grossinger's weirded me out. Let him remain a Nevele acolyte—I was a scion of the Big G, pinnacle of the Catskills.

Its prestige was corroborated one day when I got a call from Uncle Paul. He told me he had a big surprise in store. I knew what it was because it was All-Star break, but I pretended not to be able to guess. Then he said he was going to visit with two New York Yankees.

Word of this event turned Chipinaw upside-down, making me an instant celebrity. Kids put on facetious shows of friendship: "I was always Richie's buddy, right? Remember when ..." and then they'd invent something.

On the anticipated afternoon, activities were cancelled; all Chipinaw mobilized on the hill. I ran past the camp's boundary, an act strictly verboten at a less mythic time, and stared down the road in the direction of Grossinger's. It seemed so unreal that I was worried it couldn't happen.

They were forty-five minutes late, an hour and a half late, when finally a black limo came crashing out of the horizon, suspending time. Uncle Paul emerged with an ear-to-ear smile; behind him were pitchers Mickey McDermott and Don Larsen.

"Are you in charge here?" Larsen teased as I paraded around, announcing the arrival through a megaphone.

They stood by the flagpole where they demonstrated plays and answered campers' questions.

Jonny was astonished. It was proof of the power of villains, that they had access even to the Yankees. I had told him about Whitey Ford and he had seen Yogi Berra's postcard, but Uncle Paul standing there in public with me, McDermott, and Larsen was a reversal of fortune he found hard to swallow. Then Uncle Paul invited him to join us. No one but me saw his glare, cavalier swagger, and look of wounded pride and resignation.

Unexamined modes of discipline and competition permeated Chipinaw. It was as though we were on a forced march under commanding officers, no particular reason, just a state of reality. Many of my preceptors were a type I encountered nowhere else during my childhood. They blended Park Avenue Synagogue's piety with a drill-sergeant obduracy as if we were all in boot camp—a style likely borrowed from TV sitcoms and war movies since none of them had been in the service. They spouted regular disdain for Arabs, fags, and "colored people," a faux hysterical patter of taunts, imitation dialects, and unabashed bigotry.

When almost four decades later a Jewish settler gunned down Palestinian parishioners in a mosque, I imagined that I had served under the guy in the summers of my youth—not the same zealot, of course, but his forerunners, boasting about turning rifles on Arabs (or niggers) while aiming their imaginary weapons at us. I can't begin to do justice to the blend of sanctimony and sadism. Yet no one could express disapproval or rebel for risk of reprisal, i.e., getting smashed.

The head counselor and ultimate authority of Chipinaw boy's camp, Abbey West, was a model of rectitude and decorum. A high-school principal and semi-pro basketball referee from New Jersey, he was a stern, towering foreman with a smattering of gray hair. Older than the rest of the counselors, Abbey lived beyond the infirmary in a four-room cabin with his wife Dorey and son and daughter. On my father's urging, he extended an open invitation to me back in my Midget days, and I continued to call at his dwelling, year after year, even after it was clear that it was the lair of the lion. *No one* ventured there unless summoned for interrogation.

Yet Abbey's cabin was Chipinaw's secret treasure. It provided sanctuary in the midst of hazing—plus, the best way to deflect the lion's ire was to confess openly and entertain him with my truancies. I would periodically stop by the hut and show him and Dorey my current book or explain the rules of an invented pastime, trying to earn tacit consent, even praise for my devotion. I found him usually (but not always) receptive and willing to overlook my absence from wherever I was supposed to be. He might be astonished, but I could tell not only that was he fond of me but amused by the creativity of my rebellion. Though he never explicitly condoned my actions, counselors seeing me drop by the court and leave unscathed were loath to interfere further.

As Dorey poured lemonade and offered cookies, I recounted local happenings and offered interpretations. Dr. Fabian's apprentice gabbed precociously with adults in ways that other kids and counselors didn't—it wasn't exactly an era of inner probing or naming projections.

By mirroring the psychoanalyst, I touched a compassionate chord in men who otherwise practiced rigorous stringency, so I occasionally turned the most unlikely tyrants into allies. A stern magistrate to most, to me Abbey was a salvagable despot, albeit one unimpressed by my reports of hectoring and bigotry, offering only a "what else is new?" shrug.

Chipinaw rules set off a couple of hours after lunch and nap each weekday for "Optional Period." We could pick anything we wanted but were permitted no more than three consecutive days for any one activity. Choices ranged from swimming and archery to theater, arts and crafts, nature cabin, etc.—pretty much anything under adult supervision. I took to filling out my morning's card for "baseball" every time. Counselors told me that a third repeat wasn't allowed, but they couldn't figure out how to stop me. Even when our group leader crossed out my entry and wrote in an alternative, I showed up at baseball anyway—and the guy in charge always included me in the game.

The perplexity was: I didn't like baseball that much. The long innings of batters and fielders turned monotonous and banal: players shouting, running the bases and chasing balls as if the outcome mattered after so many iterations. I hankered for the relief of arts and crafts or nature, even volleyball and tennis. But as a practice beyond pleasure, baseball chaperoned me through Chipinaw (and

Bill–Dave) like a magical cloak.

I seemed to have to be both special and in peril to be anything and, though baseball wasn't really dangerous, my involvement in it reflected the degree of jeopardy I felt.

The beauty of the situation—and my smokescreen—was that baseball's rituals were so commonplace and legitimate in fifties America that it was the perfect subterfuge. I could conduct another ceremony in their guise and be totally screened, to would-be authorities and enforcers, to naysayers of all ilks, to myself as well. My mother had declared I was loyal and so I was.

But my compliance was mutiny, my dedication blasphemy. My version of baseball was an unconscious parody of their own luke-warm commitment to *everything:* everything they espoused, baseball included.

We weren't allowed to follow our infatuations to their conclusion, cultivate real courage, seek actual initiations. We never got close. Everything then was a joke or a contest; incipient mantras, visions, and divine riddles were ignored or mocked. If someone had managed to smuggle yoga or *t'ai chi ch'uan* into Chipinaw circa 1955, we would have laughed, goofed off, and turned it into the heebie-jeebies.

Until I could recognize sacraments in other forms, baseball was my compass—and even after I developed more refined skills and asanas, it was in my blood too deeply to purge. With its daily gematria, devotional precepts, and metaphysical subtexts, it kept my mind occupied and provided prayer beads against obsessive thoughts. Baseball was just as obsessive, *but that made it the antidote.*

My mother mocked me by saying I "loved" baseball, implying (as I approached teen years) that I loved it more than girls, hence was some kind of nebbish. But it wasn't that at all. Baseball was the cachet through which an innocence of love was preserved, transposed to beyond her intervention.

And love it was. When Bob Kuzava got those two Dodgers to pop out in the seventh game of the 1952 World Series, that was a talisman I kept alive long enough to put at the beginning of a poem to my college girlfriend!

So I continued to sign up for hardball at optional period and, when left field lost its luster, I became a submarine pitcher like Ewell Blackwell.

Just past the mid-point of every summer Chipinaw was divided into Red and Gray teams that competed against each other for points during a one-week competition called Color War. Athletic contests were only part of this festival. All of waking life, and to some degree sleep, were coopted by it. The moment war was declared, the Reds and Grays—those assigned to either team—became mandatory enemies. Despite prior friendships opponents barely spoke to one another for the week. Bunks were rearranged, with the beds of teammates grouped together, the mess hall divided into team tables. We were expected to eat silently, any spoken word charged against the team on whose side it was uttered.

I dreaded Color War, for I knew its precise plunge of despondency. We now might be judged for points at any moment. The incompetence of my bed-making and state of my cubby could lower my team's score. Every clean-up job at inspection, every line-up held a potential for demerits. Even legendary slobs like Jay and Barry scrubbed and swept like fiends.

All summer I could be an eccentric nonentity, as I strolled in and out of venues with my books and radio. During Color War my acts of rebellion fell under a microscope. A Yankee game on the radio cost points, as did Roofball or Armory Ball. In wartime these were acts of desertion approaching treason. My bedwetting became a public nuisance, team members unhappily having to help me with my sheets in order to prepare for inspection.

Not only were campers all distributed to either the Red or the Gray, counselors were too. The sole noncombatants were the nurse and the doctor, the owners and administrators, and the elderly maintenance men who lived in tents between the armory and the woods and were dubbed "the zombies." The five head counselors served as judges, Abbey the commissioner. He sat at the center table in the mess hall with Nurse Mary, the doctor, and the judges and, if I went to his house for solace or conversation, Dorey turned me away so no one would think she was favoring one side.

In Bunk 9 at the beginning of July, I went around announcing that I was going to be neutral this year. I made sure every potential captain and judge heard me. But no one took me seriously, and for good reason. One August night the team rosters were on our dinner tables, and right away we were instructed to find new places. Where could I go? My name was on the Red team list. There were no neutral tables. Likewise back at the bunk, symmetry required that my bed be moved into the Red zone.

One never knew when War would "break." In theory it could come at any time, though it never occurred during the early weeks of summer. As we approached the July-August cusp, campers were on pins and needles, in continuous expectation and speculation.

A dramatic event always heralded Color War's launching. A bunch of costumed figures would burst onto the campus and throw around fliers listing the Red and Gray teams. Or the bugle would suddenly blast out a jagged fire call or mid-day reveille and everyone would run to the O.D. shack to find team lists tacked on the bulletin board. The most spectacular inaugural was a crop-dusting plane flying low over the camp dropping parachutes with the team lists. Back and forth it rumbled, filling the air with them: birds materializing into mandates, a spectacle both magnificent and ominous.

With the peremptory division into teams the prior schedule of activities was terminated. We were summoned by our captains to solidarity meetings and strategy sessions.

In the first days following the onset of War the captains and counselors of Red and Gray stayed up late and wrote songs: marches, alma maters, and novelty verses. Then the rest of us had to memorize their words and melodies and render them in chorus: *"The trees that wreathe our Chip'naw, / the bunks along the hill, / Abbey and Nurse Mary / the games our hearts do fill ..."* and then *"The old gray mare / she ain't what she used to be...,"* a Red-team rag refreshed each year by a new set of lyrics.

Whoever wasn't engaged in matches was rounded up into the armory or mess hall for rehearsals—top secret. If I was playing Roofball or reading, someone found me and dragged me to our team's drill. I remember a bossy senior smashing me across the face with his megaphone every few seconds because he said I wasn't mouthing the words, and then putting his ear next to my lips, giving me a knuckle sandwich to the shoulder whenever he thought my voice had gotten too faint.

Red and Gray captains carried around the unofficial tally on clipboards and, receiving messengers from far-flung fields and courts, added in estimated points and came up with the informal standings, but their tallies were guesswork. The official score, the sum points for each side, was read by the judges to hushed silence at the end of each dinner: "The Red team: three hundred and ... sixty-five; the Gray team ... three hundred and ... sixty ... NINE!" The Grays went crazy. Paraphrasing football coach Vince Lombardi—this wasn't life and death, it was *more* important.

Athletic overachievers, the more militant counselors their enablers, had free rein to keep everyone else in line, the accusation being, "You prick, those points you're losin' I sweated for on the playin' field."

Chipinaw was *supposed to* be competitive, in fact hardcore; that was its publicized merit, preparing *nouveau riche* princes for the rat race. Behind the scenes we were inventing lives and foreshadowing iconoclastic careers. The camp was filled with incipient Jewish power brokers: my cousins Jay and Siggy were en route to becoming Wall Street financiers, partners with arbitrageurs Ivan Boesky and Michael Milken; our bunk-mate Barry was a world-class hematologist in the making; other Chipinaw brats were nascent surgeons, judges, politicians, orchestra conductors and, of course, corporate attorneys (a few judges and Civil Rights lawyers too). Such embryonic prodigies were barely held in check by the authorities, though I was the only one skedaddling. Most would-be insurgents managed to get themselves out of Chipinaw altogether—paroled or dishonorably discharged—but they had more amenable parents than mine.

During a packed week of competition, intensity climbed to a frenzy as campers not engaged in a match gathered in throngs to watch and cheer for their team. It was meant to be Major League, but it felt more like Alice in the court of playing cards. Nights were spectral and mute, as the moon became a spy in the enemy camp. Then the sun met reveille with a combat-zone hue.

One of Color War's main contests was a several-hour tag-team relay around the entire campus, requiring 100-percent camper participation—a hefty chunk of points at stake. Older kids and waiters sprinted the longest distances, for instance, from the O.D. shack to the lake; younger kids like us ran from bunk to bunk or from the armory to the flagpole. A baton was passed from runner to runner, as the course of the race wound back and forth across the campus, building to a crescendo near the finish line at the mess hall almost an hour later.

Those who had completed their laps paced along, urging others to go faster, to receive the baton while in motion. The race periodically disappeared into the woods and reappeared from different spots, sometimes with dramatic lead changes, single runners making up ground somewhere in the forest, even taking the lead to a startled burst of cheers as they emerged. Fat kids strained at every muscle while seniors and waiters shadowed them, shouting for them to move their asses. Sprinters of the final laps were often hard to spot, as waves of spectators surrounded single points of energy travelling with batons. As the last carrier crossed the line, the victorious team danced, hugged, and slapped palms.

Despite myself, I felt elation when my team won the relay, for I had run a lap somewhere in that maze, a small but essential patch of our victory. I could not deny the power of a campus-wide race inducting everyone, fast and slow. It was Lewis and Clark ... the Louisiana Purchase ... a voyage to Saturn.

At age eleven, Bunk 12, I was openly defiant. I didn't show up at any of my activities, and I didn't clean my area. Some of the judges were quite gung-ho about their roles and, to force the matter, points were deducted from the Reds in unprecedented clumps. This created a furor. Seniors and waiters made pilgrimages to my bunk to coax and pester me, but I held firm: I wasn't for either side, I hoped they had a good War.

They confiscated my radio. They woke me up in the middle of the night, marched me to the lake, and dunked me in my pajamas. They put me in wrestling holds. But I wouldn't give in. I experienced in myself a stubbornness so firm and invulnerable it was astonishing even to me. I felt that I was right and, though the entire camp stood against me, I wasn't going to back down. "Kill me!" I screamed, as they shook me awake in bed a third night in a row.

The morning after the dunking I borrowed Sunday's sports pages from a counselor's bed, grabbed comics from various cubbies along with my current book, then pocketed some bread at breakfast, and took an unfamiliar path into the woods. I spent the morning in a clearing, sitting on a log reading. I was bored and a bit scared, but my obstinacy sustained me, along with the small dramas of nature: anthills, crows, butterflies, garter snakes.

That afternoon Dave Hecht, leading hounds on leashes, found me. He stood at leash length, staring with utmost disapproval. "Dickie," he said, which almost no one called me, "you have violated the basic rule of camping. In my twenty years in this business you're the first person I've had to go looking for."

Crying, I stood up. I offered to come back if I didn't have to be in Color War.

"I'm not asking you," he pontificated, "I'm telling you. We're making no deals. Campers don't just walk off."

I was hungry anyway, and I wasn't going to argue with a two-hundred-fifty pound lawyer with three dogs. I had to go through the motions for the rest of Color War, and even won a tennis match and was half of a victorious duo in a rowboat race. I was also a throw-in (to even up the numbers) in a contest involving mess-hall plates and bowls tossed into the deep water. Each team tried to fetch more than the other in three minutes. The captain knew I was unskilled at going underwater, but our team had a star diver so they could afford a concession, as opposed to gambling on me in the breast-stroke or butterfly competitions.

Though I didn't plunge headfirst, I sank beneath the surface. The scattered porcelain on the lake bottom, spotted through fluctuations of light and mass, cast an alabaster glitter like gold doubloons. I captured a cereal bowl with my feet, transferred it to my hands, and added it to our pile.

When I visited Abbey the following week, he tried to explain: Color War couldn't be optional or it wouldn't happen. It was a big part of the camp, and many parents felt it was the single most important event in their children's lives.

After Color War ended, summer drew to a close. I put a handmade calendar over my bed beginning with fifteen days left and crossed them off until eventually everyone got the spirit:

Five more days of vacation,
Then we go to the station,
Back to civilization,
Oh how I want to go home.

Cubbies were emptied, trunks were packed, and finally Joe came for me. Jay, Barry, and I met next at the lunch buffet amid platters of roast beef, melons filled with fruit salad, and trays of chocolate cakes and fruit tarts. It was rapture, just to walk by the sparkle of the pool among the chattering crowds, to look up into the sky and watch the white cumulus exploding forever.

II

THE CLUE IN THE EMBERS

In 1955 I started sixth grade with Mrs. Lewis, a zealous old-timer near the end of her career. She was notorious throughout P.S. 6 for a flask of strong-smelling liquid masquerading on her desk as a water jug (the student who refilled her glass from it was known to us as the "whiskey monitor"). She was an activist, though we barely understood the concept. Her specialty, labor unions, was not in the curriculum, but that didn't stop her from diagramming their history for two whole weeks, as she let us in on the historic merger between the AF of L and CIO. She reminded us—every day in fact—that it was a privilege for eleven-year-olds to get such a close-up view of a current event. A skilled storyteller, she made the rivalry of industrial versus craft shops as cloak-and-dagger as any adult fairy tale could be. We had no idea that, if the bureaucracy found out, she would have been fired.

My mother set her heart on my going to Horace Mann or Riverdale, difficult prep schools in the upper Bronx near Westchester County. She had especially admired kids in maroon Horace Mann jackets. In her mind despite indications to the contrary, her sons were scholars, intellectuals in the French tradition, like her brother Lionel who had run away from home during World War II as a teenager and become a renowned professor of history in Pittsburgh. However, the outlook for my going to either academy was dim to nil. Not only were my grades poor, but Uncle Paul was opposed to private school. He said it was a waste of money because it didn't prepare you for the real world.

But I could tell that he and my mother were hatching some sort of deal because at World Series time he brought me to Grossinger's for the weekend as a treat. There Milty and I sat with Al Rosen and a bunch of other Cleveland Indians beside the canteen watching the Dodgers play the Yankees in the 1955 World Series. The Indians had overtaken New York the previous year, winning 111 games, the most by a team ever, but the winter's eighteen-player trade had revived the Yanks, and Casey's upgraded crew finished with a three-game edge over Cleveland, albeit losing thirteen of twenty-two meetings head-to-head. Rosen did not let Milty or me forget: "Early Wynn, Herb Score, Bob Lemon, Mike Garcia, Larry Doby, Al Smith, we won 111 games last year and would have crushed the Dodgers. The Yankees can barely handle them."

I was back in New York by the time Johnny Podres shut out my team to bring a championship to Brooklyn. In the sixth inning Sandy Amoros made a game-saving catch on an opposite-field drive by Yogi Berra; it was headed for the corner with two runners aboard. Not only did the Yankees lose, but Gil McDougald, who got three of their eight hits that day, was doubled off first on the play, a pretext for weeks of ribbing by my friends. I so identified with my favorite player that everyone acted as though *I* had been the base-runner who miscalculated.

Then one evening at dinner my mother startled us all by announcing, "Richard's father agrees to send him to Horace Mann or Riverdale in the unlikely event he gets accepted."

"What's the catch, Martha?" asked Bob.

She smiled conspiratorially. "Just that his name be changed to Grossinger."

"What, Towers isn't good enough for him!"

"Well, Turetsky wasn't good enough for you."

"You needler," he retorted. "I'll be Turetsky again when I make enough money to afford it."

As a first step toward putting me into prep school she made a rare phone call to Phil's mother and ended up hiring the young woman from Riverdale who had tutored him. Elisabeth Youmans showed up two days later, a hoity-toity marm in a dark blue dress, primping and distracted at our front door as if under duress. She told my mother right away that Phil was the smartest child she ever met. Then she sat me down for an hour of tests, assessed my results, and informed my parents I wasn't "Riverdale material." Handing back her advance payment, she would not be my tutor.

Undeterred, my mother called Columbia and got an older graduate student of history named Abraham Hilowitz. He arrived one night in a brown raincoat, handed his hat to Bob who put it in the closet, and then shook my hand.

"Educate this lad," my stepfather announced as we headed down the hallway.

"Your father has a sense of humor," Mr. Hilowitz remarked once we were in my room.

After an exploratory session he took a deep breath and said, "You've missed a lot of basics, so let's go back to the beginning."

From then on we spent two hours together three nights a week, redoing my education. It was all dimly familiar because I had watched it through a veil. Now I wanted to see how it actually worked: numbers carried over, parts of speech becoming grammatical units. He was a charming teacher and, under his aegis, I swept away encumbrances that had stymied me for years. As long as I got it he kept speeding up the pace. In a matter of months I had reached sixth grade again. Nobody quite knew what happened—not the astonished Mrs. Lewis, not my mother, not even me. I had been so involved in daydreaming that I didn't realize how accessible the real world was.

I honor Mr. Hilowitz most for the day I had a panic. I was setting up a Sorry! game with Jon. As I stared at the yellow and red tokens at Start, I felt the disease. "I have it! I have it!" I screamed. Ice formed along my spine and neck and seeped into my chest. I was too wobbly to stand. My mother tucked me into bed, filled my nose with bitter drops, and smeared Vick's Vaporub over my chest. An hour later my tutor arrived.

I lay there, staring at the window, ashamed to be so revealed, trying to keep grim thoughts at bay. It was obvious I would do no work tonight. But he sat on the edge of the covers and told stories for the whole two hours, creating voices for historical figures as he went—Christopher Columbus, John Cabot, Roanoke and the mystery of Virginia Dare, Marquette and Joliet along the Mississippi, the French and Indian War, the Spaniards' unsuccessful search for gold. He lured me back into the world of things and made existence normal again.

That was my last full-fledged panic for almost ten years.

The admissions interviews were intimidating and I clammed up, answering only as I was asked. At Horace Mann the teacher read from a list of questions that included: "What are your hobbies?" None came to mind.

"Then what do you do in your spare time?"

"Watch TV, listen to ballgames."

"Couldn't you at least have told him you have a scrapbook on Mars?" my mother asked in the cab home.

"I forgot." It would have been a gold-star answer, but I didn't begin to know how to distinguish my virtues from my vices.

I failed the exam for Riverdale but got into Horace Mann. Phil was unimpressed. "That's mostly for Jews and colored kids," he said, "and even worse, it's only boys. You won't find Nancy Drew or Annie Welch there."

We all considered blonde tomboy Annie the cutest girl in Mrs. Lewis' class.

"I'm glad *I'm* not going," he finally scoffed.

I stopped talking to Phil after that. In fact, I interacted with him only one more time in childhood. During the fall of our first year at our new schools he called me to procure three out-of-print Tom Quest books I had bought at a used bookstore near Grossinger's; he couldn't find them anywhere and wanted to complete his set. I had stopped collecting the series by then, so we met on the east side of Park Avenue halfway between our 1235 and 1175 awnings where I sold him the copies. We didn't even bother to catch up on each other's lives at the new schools.

All that time I was doing something different with the sinister signpost and hooded hawk. Now I was done with the mystery story forever. In fact, I was done with Richard Towers.

I didn't buy *The Clue in the Embers,* the Hardy Boys volume that appeared my last month of sixth grade. Because I never read the real version, the title came to stand for all emergent signs and mysteries. I had found the melted coins, opened the secret panel, learned the identity of the figure in hiding. The "lost tunnel," "hidden harbor," "green flame," "whispering box," et al., each had settled into latency, but they were indispensable, for they gave shape to my inner life and would appear over the years in other guises. "The clue in the embers," though, remained my ultimate sphinx—beyond Fabian, beyond Freud. Unread, it couldn't be known, so it made all other knowledge possible.

Near the end of sixth grade I felt wild and unbounded. I wanted to bust out of the boy whose name I was surrendering for good.

I had been collecting a cumulative set of Yankee cards but was missing three rare ones. A kid showed up on my next-to-last day of Bill-Dave with the coveted trio but would flip only if I put my precious Yankees at stake. There would never be another chance to acquire them, so I agreed to match his cards with prized ones of my own. He landed three tails and cheered aloud, pumping his fist. My heart in my throat, I flipped a second, then a third tail!

But something else was happening, exploding from a place unknown into something I adored, had always adored but couldn't get at. *I was somehow being absolved.* Dr. Fabian hadn't found the link, but there had only been symbols to work with, symbols to lead the way. Now there were only actions—life itself.

The next day I brought my cherished collection of cartoon, Flash Gordon, and other non-baseball cards to school and tossed them in the air, free for all takers. They blew about the P.S. 6 yard, causing a commotion.

"The kid's a madman!"

"Totally nutso!"

I loved it.

And it was spring and cherry blossoms in Central Park, and something still bigger, bigger than even that, was called for. On the last day of group I brought my box of baseball cards and dispersed them too, an unexplained trail through the Park with the entirety of Bill-Dave following and fighting for possession a few hundred yards behind me as I ducked in and out of bushes—an anonymous Robin Hood—saving my Yankees for last, and finally at a kid's request, a gag he didn't expect me to take seriously, dropping those too, picture after picture, just days after winning the final three, even my years of every hard-earned card of Gil McDougald. I had no idea why. I had planned to keep those talismans forever. I only knew that I watched gleefully from a million miles away. "It's Towers again," they shouted, for the pictures gave away the identity of a person who no longer existed.

I was free.

One afternoon Mrs. Lewis asked me to stay after school for a conference. As I approached her desk, she congratulated me on my improved work and admission to Horace Mann. "You're going to have to work even harder there. I want to get you off to a good start, so try to be more alert in class." Then she extolled my new last name, which had been added to her records. "You must be related to Jennie Grossinger."

I nodded.

"What a marvelous woman. She does so much for charity."

When Mrs. Lewis taught us about apples a few weeks later, she asked for extra-credit papers on one or another variety, so I raised the ante by writing on all three of them: the pippin, the winesap, and the MacIntosh, the separate colors and tastes of which still have a sort of runic depth for me—they mark the moment of transition.

In the last weeks of school a few boys and girls began to go out with each other. A kid named Jimmy McCracken gave a studded dog collar to Annie Welch. She wore it around her calf above her ankle. That Annie Welch had travelled with me to other worlds was something I would tell no one, not even Dr. Fabian, as much as he might have wanted to know. Though Phil had proclaimed his intention to find a girlfriend like her, it was mainly boasting.

He wasn't any more ready than me.

Then one night I dreamed that I had been hoodwinked in my pajamas, the very sheets and blankets still wrapped around me, back to the classroom. Only the girls were there, and three of them took my clothes off. They moved in a circle about me, silently, in a dance of animals. The room was thick with perfume and flowers.

And then it became … walking in a forest, emerald moss beneath my feet. Long, light vines hung from the branches, exuding musty dew. I could actually feel their moisture and smell them. *This dream was real!*

I came to a log shack—the true one, the prototype of the place that Joey, Andy, and I had built on another planet.

Annie Welch was sitting there with two other girls. It was as though *she was waiting for me.* "I'm not Jimmy," I tried to warn her, but she didn't seem to care. She stood and approached me, set her hands on my shoulders and sat me down on a rock. Then she put a blindfold on me. One by one they kissed me on the face. I felt their lips in intoxicating sequence. Girls, that's what they were! They could as easily have been a circle of wolves.

I began spinning. Then the whole world around me was tumbling. I awoke in great joy with my penis hard. I lay in bed in a kind of ecstasy. I did not understand what was happening to me, and yet I had experienced such a complicated texture once before, in Westport when I was playing in the attic and *the same hypnotic waves* came over me from the aroma of an old leathery trunk.

My dream now bore the resolution of this childhood experience, not so much the intimation of sexuality as the power of being enfolded within a sensuous and opulent space. It was not just an image or landscape; it was everything I was before Richard Towers and everything I would be after.

Against that sensation my outer-space daydreams were faded postcards. It was one thing to fantasize settling on other worlds and another *actually to be there.*

The memory of that dream gave me solace for years—the fact that someone kissed me, the richness of the green, the scented moisture, the way I merged with everything as it spun instead of becoming dizzy and separate, how the throbbing filled me from inside out.

I couldn't believe this had been there all along and neither I nor Dr. Fabian had noticed it. *I* was that forest. Its familiarity was the sweet caverns of my own being. I didn't know it yet, but I had discovered that I was intact, that my body and spirit could still be recovered whole.

When I fell back asleep, though, I found myself in the vacant classroom at night. I ran down the hallway in fear of what might come out of such an emptiness, ran all the way to the auditorium where—in pitch black, just what I feared—a rude billowing voice arose from behind the stage and roared through the room like a beast. I turned and fled out the door. I raced for blocks, but the sound pursued me, persistent against the sky.

PART TWO

THE KID FROM GROSSINGER'S

1956–1960

I

Horace Mann

The summer of '56 I went, as usual, to Chipinaw, this time as a prep-school-student-to-be. We were expected to have read at least four books of our choice from a Horace Mann assigned list, so I arrived with instructions from my mother that I be given time off for the task, the precise exemption I had long sought. Taking advantage, I packed not only the required *David Copperfield* but two other Dickens novels, *Martin Chuzzlewit* and *Our Mutual Friend,* and bought the complete Sherlock Holmes rather than the recommended *Casebook.*

I lived that summer in fog along the Thames, unravelling John Rokesmith's multiple identities and accompanying Martin Chuzzlewit from America to England. Whole nineteenth-century realms passed through me as I lay in the grass, beyond the stridency of games.

Bunk 14's regular counselor, Bernstein, had to leave for an undisclosed emergency mid-August—or maybe it was that we ran him ragged. He was a legendary disciplinarian who had sought the glory of whipping us into shape. But Bernstein was no match for our *chutzpah,* wits, and arrays of water traps and disappearing and reappearing objects. We left him apoplectic.

An older guy was hired from off campus and put in charge of Bunk 14. Rumor was that he was an escaped convict and they had found him hitchhiking. Probably not, but it fit his m.o. He carried a mean-looking knife, drank straight from a bottle of hard liquor, and cursed us with four-letter words. He didn't care about our keeping things neat—a tip-off that he was not Chipinaw stock—though he liked to order us around like slaves. He raided our secret food caches and, at meals, ate many of our portions too. He also invited kids to reach in his pocket while he lounged on his bed and feel a special treat he had there if anyone was hungry.

Nothing close to this redneck had ever happened at Chipinaw. In retrospect, I can't imagine how the anally fastidious management slipped up or recall why we didn't report the dude's malfeasances: I mean, a weapon, alcohol, pedophilia. I guess we thought we had lost all credibility by then.

At breakfast one morning after our usual allotment (when French toast was on the menu) of eight pieces was deposited on the table, Ralph grabbed the platter and, in a deft scoop of his fork, stabbed four, leaving the rest for us to divide. I didn't care much for Chipinaw French toast—and I had stayed mostly out of Ralph's way—but this was an over-the-top psycho and I was incensed that he should have been put in charge of us. When the platter reached me, there was one piece left and one more person to go after me. I handed it back to Ralph and said, "Here. Maybe you didn't get enough." There was a hush as he surveyed me with wild eyes.

"Stand up!" he screamed. That was the supreme embarrassment in the Chipinaw dining room—public reprimand. I sat there. *"Stand up!"* He rose and pointed at me. The cavernous room had turned silent. Jay and Barry were staring in horror.

"Stand. Up!"

I complied more in fury than obedience and, with a quick swat of my hand, turned over the pot of hot coffee on him. He let out a howl and dove across the table at me. Three other counselors wrestled him to the ground. "I'm going to kill him," he screamed. "The little bastard, I'm going to kill him."

Despite the incident they left him in our bunk. I got only sporadic sleep after that, waking in starts, staring across the murk at his quiescent hulk, wondering if he was asleep or just pretending, and where the knife was (if not tucked under the covers with him). But I made it through the final week to the banquet alive (in some alternate reality I was murdered and Chipinaw was front-page headlines). All that last day we packed our clothes in trunks. I felt so much frenzied energy I could barely contain it: I didn't have to sleep there another night—our beds were stripped, our cubbies bare. Deliverance!

Near the end of the after-dinner awards ceremony, cars arrived to collect us: me, Jay, Siggy, Jay's cousins from the girls' camp, and Barry. No imagined escape by flying saucer was more thrilling or exotic. We were lights moving along back roads toward the Emerald City. Everything was charged, intricate, weird—billboards gateways to welcoming universes.

I had dreams of Horace Mann before I went there. Hiking up marble steps, I passed between pillars fronting a Greek temple. As I entered, it turned into a large industrial building. Once inside, I could find no classrooms, only hallways through which crowds of people rushed. I saw no kids either, just preoccupied adults carrying papers and books.

My mother took me to Saks Fifth Avenue and had me fitted for an entire wardrobe of sports jackets, ties, slacks, and shoes. As at Chipinaw accouterings, I was only an incidental mannequin to the deliberations of a woman and a salesman, as though they were deciding how some abstract child might look if he were properly attired. I could barely imagine attending a boys' academy where jackets and ties were required and the teachers had to be addressed as "Sir," so I felt like an impostor in these expensive duds.

On the evening before the first day of Horace Mann my mother and Bob marked the occasion by taking me out to dinner at Tavern on the Green in Central Park. He spoke with his familiar adman flamboyance: "I hope you appreciate where you're going. This is your chance to join the archons of our society."

"I don't think he realizes how much work it will be," my mother inserted.

I was silent; I already feared the worst. "This is his last free night," she continued, staring at me, "for six years!"

"Don't be ghoulish," Bob chided.

Lying in bed on the eve of a new life, I tried to grasp what was happening. Why had they even admitted a boy who barely made it through P.S. 6?

Awakened by Bridey's cheery 6 a.m. summons—"New school for the lad, rise and shine"—groggily I pulled pins and tissue paper out of a shirt and, before the bathroom mirror, knotted a red-and-brown striped tie. Trepidation warred with suspense, layers of sleepiness stirring remembrances in nausea-like aftertastes of breakfast: the dragons of Blueland, Flash Gordon at the Martian court. My mind kept supplying guises of stern, unsmiling masters like the signers of the Declaration.

I glanced at the harlequin child in the mirror. Six years! I didn't think I could do this for a week.

By phoning the school my mother had gotten the names of two older students who lived in our neighborhood and arranged for them to teach me the route. I left Jon waiting for the Bill-Dave wagon at the 1235 canopy and proudly strode west across Park, then north across 96th Street to where a group of Horace Manners had gathered at the bus stop. My chaperones quickly identified themselves.

Boarding, we dropped coins into the driver's box, then found seats along the rear window. There they taught me a game played with serial numbers on the transfers we had requested (but didn't need). We raced each other to be the first to make our consecutive digits end up at ten by trying out sequences of addition, subtraction, division, multiplication, and squares until we landed on the decimal ten at the end (for instance, 71435 could hit the target as 7 squared minus 1 divided by 4 plus 3 minus 5). It would be months before we tired of this exercise (it now seems apropos that my first contact with Horace Mann was a cerebral math game). Meanwhile, Madison and Fifth flew by as we zipped into the Park through its tunnels to the less familiar West Side. After Central Park West came Columbus and Amsterdam, foreboding side streets before the years of gentrification. We disembarked next at commercial Broadway and plunged into the tenebrous IRT (Interborough Rapid Transit).

Purchasing fifteen-cent tokens from the lady at the booth, we bombed through the turnstiles to catch a pausing train. In later weeks I would simply flash my student pass at the agent as I opened the gate.

Barely beating the thud of metallic doors, we sat in contemplative silence as—stop by stop—the car filled with attendees of different schools, most of the further uptown arrivals having to stand. Then the train rattled out of the underworld onto stilts and wound above the northern city, emptying by portions onto streets in the 200s.

Horace Mann shared the last station with Manhattan College: 242nd Street—all off—the train emptying in a bustle verging on pandemonium. From there we hiked four blocks up a hill to 246th. (Unaccompanied on my second day, I overrated the age of Horace Mann upperclassmen, joined the wrong crowd, and ended up at an edifice resembling the temple of my dream.)

I was expected to report to Pforzheimer Hall, its sleek modern box hugging a slope below ivy-covered classrooms. Designated expressly for the Lower School, it was like an elongated space station with entry ports. We were its baptizers, which postponed the start of classes for a ceremonial ribbon-cutting. I was grateful for a few extra hours before any action was required other than getting my schedule from an alphabetical stack—no way to mess up yet. On the other hand, I had a full calendar card of classes in separate rooms—not one teacher for everything like at P.S. 6—and a new last name. This was getting serious!

We were each assigned a locker on the ground floor of Pforzheimer and given the combination to the lock on it. Mine was 22-36-10. I had no idea how to rotate the nob onto those numbers in such a way that the pins would drop. Arnie Goldman, alphabetically one locker to my left, taught me that you had to make a full circle and then, after lining up the black notches of each digit, reverse direction. Like a parent he put his hand over mine and turned it with me until I got the flair.

My first day as Richard Grossinger seemed an eternity among mobs of First Formers scurrying with and against traffic. Each teacher, though amiable, without fail warned that his course would take at least an hour's homework every night and that we had better pay scrupulous attention to his lessons. "Every pearl of wisdom that comes from my ruby-red lips," advised Mr. Allison in American History when asked by an earnest lad, "What are we responsible for, sir?" Maybe this *was* the end of freedom. But for one precious day I was snug and anonymous among the masses, no different from any other plebe. The second morning, lectures began in earnest.

Almost immediately I realized that I couldn't maintain a folio of interplanetary adventures and stay alert. That had been true, of course, at P.S. 6, but I didn't take the matter seriously there. The spaceship I launched in Miss Tighe's class had an irresistible appeal. Here I was a new person, caught up: I didn't want to slide back into truancy and forsake this exciting new world.

In a series of elaborately plotted installments I concluded my odyssey among the stars. That was no mean feat, for, though imaginary, the ship was an intricately conceived machine, each detail of its manufacture and function committed to memory. I couldn't just expel such an object from myself. I had to unravel its history with the same care and credibility with which I had invented it.

To dismiss the craft and its adventures fliply—easy come, easy go—would have broken faith with my samaritans as well as the characters I had adopted over the years. They had been faithful companions and I would miss them.

I extricated myself by making the end of the narrative as meticulous and definitive as its beginning. While falling sleep those first nights of Horace Mann, I flew back to Earth and returned everyone to their lives. I needed the logic and maturity of a twelve-year-old to break a seven-year-old's spell.

Sometimes the great vehicle crashed; sometimes it was returned to its makers; sometimes it was hurtled out of the Galaxy and swallowed into infinity; but it had to be put irretrievably beyond reach. Without a clean break, I risked relapse. Although I reclaimed the vessel briefly in later years, it would never again be real.

In jacket and tie, scrawling till my hand ached, I tried to capture the gist of recitations and blackboard demonstrations—arithmetic formulas, families of languages, parts of speech, the Preamble to the Declaration of Independence. All around me in jackets and ties were fellow scholars, scribbling away. No one knew that Richard Grossinger had never been a scholar, that he was dressed like a gentleman for the first time, that he was really Richard Towers.

I was mostly cheerful, for I felt a respite from both the family hothouse and the premonition of a Horace Mann beyond reach. The math turned out to be no harder than what Mr. Hilowitz had taught me. General Language, English, and history were straight-forward exercises in the roots of common words, sentence structure, and the laws of the Constitution. I regurgitated from heart the rules of parliamentary order. I learned how to diagram sentences: subject, verb, object in a horizontal row; vertical lines with hooks for adverbs, adjectives, and prepositions. I solved equations that had letters as well as numbers.

In Music I learned to identify composers and their symphonies. I loved hearing the anthems and guns hidden in Tchaikovsky's *1812 Overture,* the aroused skeletons of Saint Saëns' bewitching-hour graveyard. Here again were symbols wrapped in façades. I even had Daddy get me *Danse Macabre,* my first-ever classical disk in its fancy cardboard wrapper.

Twice a day a random cull of us rotated into study hall, a silent period during which the rest of our classmates were at a lesson. There we were expected to start our night's homework.

Yanking me out of the academic spell were two hours of gym that capped each afternoon. At two o'clock the whole First Form straggled from separate classrooms in Pforzheimer to the campus walkway and around it into the basement of a gray fortress on the far side of the playing fields. There we were assigned a second set of lockers and ordered to get into sweat clothes pronto.

The gazes of our coaches, credentialed deliverers of male author-ity, bore right through cowed young scholars. Calling us by last name only, often preceded by a scornfully prolonged "Mister," they explained that we would be issued instructions "just once, faggots, so you better get it on the first try." After imparting each drill, they stood back with folded arms and squinched eyes to observe our renditions.

For weeks we strove to produce unachievable numbers of barbell lifts, sit-ups, and push-ups. Then we sparred with gloves and grap-pled on a mat. Our ensigns used each of these vocations to expose our bodies and attack our isolation, barking and calling us girlies or queers if we were timid or klutzy. Ducking behind more massive classmates, I prayed not to be noticed, not to have to wrestle, not to have my ragged sit-ups evaluated. But everyone took his turn and suffered an appraisal and unforgiving score.

I quavered through appearances in the spotlight, straining and kicking my legs to pull my frame up on jungle bars, warding off punches, jabbing out a glove in return, trying to get my arms around the surreal neck and legs of a huskier kid as we rolled in embrace on the mat, amazed I came out the other end of each gauntlet without some major breakdown or shame.

I showered, bought a snack from the subway cluster at the foot of the hill, and rode homeward on the El with my new friends.

After a month our P.E. group moved on to soccer, charging down an immense slope into Van Cortlandt Park where we squared off—vestiges of Bill-Dave in the autumn air as I dribbled and then kicked at the goal, volleys of oranged and reddened leaves gusting amid whistles from games near and far. My discarded past and unknown future balanced on a razor's edge as Jeff Jones hit me in the clear, a brilliant pass across the field. "Go!" he shouted. "Go!" One of the two black kids in the class and a super athlete, he had inexplicably adopted me.

Nights and weekends were packed with homework. In terms of study habits I was crossing light years in months. I routinely started math and English in study hall or on the subway, getting basic stuff out of the way, building up a margin for protracted readings in history and General Language. Most nights I didn't quit working until just before I dropped into bed.

I handed in assignments and weathered spot quizzes and tests. When Uncle Paul sent tickets for Daddy to take me to the two weekend games of the 1956 World Series it was a revisitation of a childhood abandoned long ago, but I went with him and Uncle Moe and we saw Whitey Ford and Tom Sturdivant pitch the Yankees back to even after they had lost the first two games at Ebbets Field. The next day while I was in class, my Chipinaw buddy Don Larsen tossed a perfect game. To miss such an event would have been unthinkable once, but now Yankee interdiction was as mandatory as discarding my spaceship. Horace Mann superseded everything that preceded it.

To my mind I did okay. I got plenty of things wrong, but I didn't daydream and I basically understood the material. When the first report card came, however, it showed all C's, except for a D in math accompanied by a probation report.

My mother was frantic; she thought I was close to expulsion and blamed herself for not paying enough attention to my study habits. She began scrutinizing me like a hawk. Her injunction to study merged with and gradually replaced her general outrage at me and gave her fresh ammunition for reprimanding me continually.

She had no idea of the actual scope of the homework or my progress. Yet she was sure that I was way behind and that the situation could be handled only by tight reins and constant threats. Becoming a caricature of an oblivious martinet, she judged me by one standard alone. As long as she saw me at my desk she was appeased. For years I was fixed in her brain as the single command to "get back to work"—no matter the time of day or circumstance. Horace Mann became my single identity to her. She forgot P.S. 6 and Bill-Dave as though they never existed. Even my apostasy at Grossinger's and Dr. Fabian's became peripheral matters.

I remember the famished rush from the last morning class to the cafeteria line; I can still taste those mushy piles of spaghetti in meat sauce (yummier than any version before or since), the filet of sole with a lemon slice on Friday, crisp, tangy, and delicious; a block of ice cream or scoop of jello for dessert—we were starving! After lunch we gathered at the bookstore to buy marshmallow bars kept in ice-cream lockers—so hard that chunks of them fractured like stone in our teeth, blends of chocolate frost and whipped mallow melting in my mouth together.

Before afternoon classes that late October a bunch of us stood in the path between buildings, trying to catch leaves off maples. Frigid squalls issuing from the sky dropped our prizes, singly and in swarms. Clad in requisite jackets and ties, we twisted and grabbed at fluttering golden and rouge figments, colliding with one another, stumbling and giggling as our apparel flew open and shirts got untucked. I played with a vengeance and, like a knuckleball catcher, was making one darting catch after another when a group of upperclassmen stopped to look.

I heard a whisper of "Fags!" A super-cool-looking guy, thin as a rail with pomaded wavy hair and lots of cologne, grabbed the arm of the kid next to me and pronounced through curled lips, "I just *hate* little queers." No one played again.

One morning I awoke to see snow falling in the courtyard. I opened the window and put my fingertips in feathery fluff on the windowsill. Bridey had the radio on. They were reading a list of schools closed in the New York area. The names went on and on, Catholic schools and academies and colleges in Brooklyn, Queens, Manhattan. I wanted a snow day, a vestige from another time. "Adelphi, Hofstra, Horace Mann …"

I cheered aloud, as Bridey gave me a funny look, part amusement, part censure.

Central Park was an ancient village, snow falling so rapidly I could barely see. As I clopped perfect footprints, I stared at figures materializing through veils. Fifth Avenue was bare of cars. A few people skied down the thoroughfare while others made snow statues and chased after the occasional lonely bus like a wooly mammoth. I wished I had a sled or companions for a fort and snowball fight, but I wasn't that kid anymore.

The next day the sun shone on a new white world, and I rejoined my comrades on the subway, returning to Horace Mann as if from time travel to prehistoric Wales.

Naked in gym that winter we stood by the unheated pool while Mr. Mathaner demonstrated the butterfly and sidestroke. I sought radiator pipes along the wall, trying to avoid bumping into other bare bodies or scalding metal, my arms hugging my chest.

Mathaner blew his whistle, and we dove in a collective chlorine splash, thrashed to the other end, then got out, and jockeyed for positions near new radiators. "Mr. Grossinger!" Invariably he found me and re-demonstrated the stroke.

I jumped back in alone and strained to imitate his spiralling arms and muscled chest.

"Better! Now work on it."

Through the entire period I longed for the steamy shower room ... until at last I stood mesmerized in hot spray, spinning my body, letting the waterfall sweep down, cloud over my shoulders, touch every part of me. Ecstasy!

Nakedness was a rite in which we observed our own bodies changing in the mirrors of one another. Beneath the mask of our shouting and ribaldry we spied on classmates' physiology, degrees of pubic hair and different-shaped penises. So many of them were already men, their basso voices booming, and yet I was becoming more of a man than I could admit.

In threadbare towels we raced across the stone of the locker-room, got somewhat dry (except hair), restored jackets and ties, gathered our books and papers, and headed down the hill to the ride home.

The subway bonded those of us who commuted from Manhattan— other classmates came by bus and car from Westchester and New Jersey suburbs. The train imposed a tempo and I learned its musical score. The symphony began with the harbinger of a massive metal object, a faint tremor followed by the deafening clangor of machinery wheezing to a stop. Our boarding stirred the adagio of transport: an opening clack and thump as the doors slammed shut, then the screeching sway of tracks between stations; how the snake lurched at each bend, where its drumroll quickened, where its bass ceased, where the string section whined, where the lights went out (once I caught on, I no longer got alarmed). Ultimately my group came to prefer the long express stops and breakneck speed of the older, sootier IND, which we called Renegade Insane Transit instead of Independent Subway System. We routinely switched from the IRT via the elevator at 168th Street, as some of my colleagues worked out exotic routes for evading a bus fare, including one that took us to the East Bronx where we stared down from the platform at Yankee Stadium, snow on its fallow field. From there we rode the Lexington Avenue express to midtown.

For a whole month we held a contest of "subway basketball," shooting for the grimy vents above the windows with crumpled-up notebook paper. We got two points when the "ball" was sucked out into the tunnel. It felt a little funny making our shots in front of an incredibly tall schoolboy across the aisle because he was supposed to be a famous player. It was young Lew Alcindor in his Power Academy jacket, but I doubt he realized the game we were playing was basketball.

When I got home I consumed whatever was available. I made toast and then layered on gobs of apricot and grape jam, gnawed down half a pack of cream cheese from peeled-back aluminum, then devoured a combination of bananas, oranges, devil's food cookies, chocolate-glazed or coconut-sprinkled Malomars, and two or three tiny boxes of Rice Krispies or Frosted Flakes. Later I got a light golden tan on slices of bread and coated them with melting butter. I alternated Arnold's "vanilla" and Pepperidge Farm Whole Wheat. One night I ate seven bananas; another time I went through a loaf of Thomas' raisin bread with Philadelphia cream cheese. I would sit at my desk, stuffing in vittles for my reward while I worked.

At quarter term, Woodshop supplanted Music, so I made a rough facsimile of a stool for Bridey and a birdhouse for Aunt Bunny. Impressed that the elderly teacher was missing three fingers, I was careful not to slip as I band-sawed along my pencil markings on a piece of plywood set in a vise. After two months, Woodshop students moved on to Theater Arts where we cast and put on a play about a talking caterpillar.

Because we would be expected to type all our papers in Second Form, I was put into class where I struggled to learn QWERTY and acquire nimble enough fingers not to keep hitting "Y" for "T" and "B" for "V." Our machines were huge manual robots that took purposeful pounding to get text. I was the only one who didn't have access to a typewriter for practicing at night so, after I got a D on my first exam, my mother brought home a monstrosity from work.

Twice a week the whole school gathered in the auditorium for Chapel at which we sang hymns and college songs. Words on a light tan background were projected onto a screen: *"A mighty fortress is our God"* and *"Stand and drink a toast to dear old Maine."* Every so often Mr. Allison led us in a rousing version of *"Give me ten men who are stout-hearted men…. "* The room resonated with male voices. I liked being in the midst of such robustness and I brought the songs home to the shower: *"We gather together to ask the Lord's blessing"* and *"To the Earth, to the stars, / to the girls who will love us someday!"*

For the first time in my life I was free to come and go as I wished. No one knew where I was between the end of school and dinner, the subway having replaced the Bill-Dave wagon. Staying on the Broadway train three extra stops after school and getting off at 59th Street was a favorite alternative to going straight home. All three parental offices lay within four long blocks on 57th: the Fountainbleau at Fifth, the Grossinger's New York agency between Avenue of the Americas and Seventh, and Robert Towers Advertising between Broadway and Eighth.

On days that homework allowed, I liked to visit PZ, a longtime Grossinger's employee who preferred to work in the City to be near his ailing mother. PZ (never Paul Zousmer) was a short Danny Kaye lookalike, a miscast journalist and unappreciated house historian who handled details of Hotel archiving in a cubicle stuffed with piles of old photographs and yellowed newspaper clippings.

PZ's face always lit up when I arrived. I was not only a devotee of Grossinger memorabilia; I was a Grossinger myself and appeared in dozens of glossies and press clippings from the week of November 3, 1944, as a newborn, my mother and Uncle Paul both young and wide-eyed, holding me between them—the caption: "His Majesty, The King": proof of my authentic origin.

A fiery CCNY grad named Bob Towers was another mainstay of the 1940s lexicon, pictured with golfers, ballplayers, and stage stars, often microphone in hand, a stage smile. In one, Uncle Paul and he walked arm-in-arm.

On the next block was a store called Photographic Fair where PZ went for film, equipment, and conversation. Our buddy there was a thin, balding clerk named Charlie de Luise who handed us

expensive cameras from behind locked glass and helped me adjust
their finely tuned dials for light and shutter speed. I wanted to be able
to shoot close-ups and action photos, impossible with a fixed-lens
box, and I particularly admired a Minolta with a two-thousandths-
of-a-second shutter speed. PZ promised to hire me after school was
out so I could earn the hundred dollars necessary to purchase it.

He also told me that Grossinger's had accounts at Womrath's
(next door to Photographic Fair) and Colony Records (a few blocks
southwest), so I would bring lists of desired items—science-fiction
novels, astronomy and dinosaur books for the bookstore; 45s of
the Kalin Twins, the Ames Brothers, and Paul Anka for the record
shop—and charge them like at Milty's canteen. Going to these stores
conferred the Hotel's aura and magic momentarily in the City, as
I brought home a tangible smidgen of it in my hands.

Just before Christmas our routine at Horace Mann was halted by
final exams, scheduled one or two a day in the gym. Their accrued
tension was greater than a close game in late innings. All the way
to 242nd Street we quizzed one another, intimidated by how much
our comrades knew, trying to digest a few last facts right up to
the door. Cartons were sliced open and bluebooks poured out.
The basketball court was coopted by desks window to window.

Hearts thumping, we picked our tests from the correct stacks
and took any seat along the sawdust-sprinkled floor. All grade
levels were mixed, as students of different ages sat side by side in
solitary contemplation of their quandaries. I scanned my printed
pages with their finality of truth-telling runes, relieved by the
familiar, chilled by inevitable surprises. Then, heart in throat, I
began scribbling for dear life.

After exams Joe drove me to Grossinger's. I arrived wanting
to tell Aunt Bunny all about my new school but, to my surprise,
found my brothers alone in their house. Our parents were vaca-
tioning in the Caribbean. The living room was a mess—liquor
bottles and newspapers strewn on the floor. Michael filled me in:
Beulah had gone to see a sick aunt, and Housekeeping had sent
over a substitute maid who barely spoke English. "But she knows

what *that* is," he declared, pointing to the liquor cabinet. He led me on tour: "Empties in every room!" He threw up his arms in theatrical disgust.

When I encountered the lady, she was brandishing a mop and chased me out of the third floor, flinging a bottle at my retreat. It bounced crazily against walls and landed without breaking. This was great stuff, but it got even better! Soon she began throwing ashtrays and clothing down the stairs. I called the head of House-keeping, but that was Grandpa's sister, Aunt Rose, a tiny dynamo of spittle who had no use for children and was barely more sober than our guardian. She would scold Michael and me as if on cue whenever we passed her: "You goddamned kids, whatcha doing now? No good I betcha!" We'd purposely steer within view to elicit such a greeting.

This time she barked something unintelligible and hung up.

The three of us plotted. While the maid was at the liquor cabinet, we took a human-sized stuffed monkey, dressed it in Uncle Paul's suit jacket and tie, and put him to bed in my room on the third floor. We spilled ketchup on his white shirt, knocked over some lamps, and led a string of knotted sheets from the bedpost out the window. Then we taped groans on the tape recorder and slid it under the overhang of the counterpane.

The odd noises engaged her curiosity. She edged her way up the stairs and across the hall, looked in the room, screamed, and went running back down and out the front door. We had gotten rid of her just the way Bugs Bunny would have!

Two days before Christmas our parents returned, and the next evening Michael's teacher came to talk to Aunt Bunny about his problems in school. All that afternoon, in preparation for the visit, my brothers and I rehearsed *Curley the Talking Caterpillar.* As the two women sipped tea in the living room we appeared suddenly in costume and put on a semblance of the script. In one totally ad-libbed scene Michael ran around in a mustache and black derby, carrying a doctor's bag, yelling, on respective circuits, "If you think I'm Groucho Marx, I'm not.... If you think I'm Walter Winchell, I'm not.... "

This latter-day brother and I were connoisseurs of daffiness in general: leaving cryptic notes for a baffled Milty, hiding surprises in Jack Gallagher's silverware drawers, doing parodies of fat, tongue-tied Uncle Paul, parading to the dinner table chanting, *"The big baboon by the light of the moon ... / And what became of the monk, the monk, the monk ...?"* Volatile friends, we were inseparable for days—building snowmen, racing sleds, riding Hotel buses into town to explore shops—but the Monk was unpredictably moody and, when he got furious at me, the worst insult he could think of was to call me by the name with which I had arrived years earlier as an outsider: "Go back where you came me from, Towers." Yet how clean that was compared to layers of proxy warfare with Jonny!

My father was a Jekyll and Hyde character. In the City he was my gregarious, permissive savior, but at the Hotel he was strict and irascible, always checking to see if we were violating rules. He hated to spot us cutting through the kitchen or serving ourselves at the pantry: "You are *never never* to go in there again! We could lose our insurance!"

I was surprised how many of the staff were terrified of him: from old men who washed floors to directors of departments; even Irv Jaffee, speedskating champion; even huge Milty who would cringe if he were summoned to PG's office. "Your father wants me, Richie," he would say. "You suppose this is the end?" I assured him that Paul was a good guy and I would put in a word for him if necessary.

I tried not to notice my father's threatening side, for on me, generally, shone his protective face and I was contained in his beneficent orbit.

Aunt Bunny told me one day, to my astonishment, that Michael and James were adopted; they came from non-Jewish families in Hartford, Michael was Italian, and James was lots of things, including American Indian. "Your father and I couldn't have children," she explained, "so our friend Dr. Krall arranged for us to get two very special boys. Paul didn't want girls because he didn't think he could deal with their teenage years, dating and all that. Pretty silly, but that's your father."

That I adored my non-blood brothers so much more than my blood one was an anomaly I took at face value. I didn't need to know why.

As James got older he joined Michael and me in improvised adventures, some of them quite heedless. The three of us spent one entire morning rolling old automobile tires down the main hill, chasing alongside them—cars and pedestrians beware! It was equally reckless to collect golf balls from the road and woods around the course and then fungo them with a baseball bat into the unseen distance over the parking lot.

For afternoons across the grounds and in underground passageways we played hide-and-seek. The rule was, the mark had to keep moving. It would have been impossible to find a person who dallied in any of the thousands of closets, alleys, or guest rooms.

Inspired by a Baby Huey comic, we set out a lemonade and soda stand, mixing concoctions from kitchen storerooms and the canteen to sell to passing guests. Any fruit in seltzer was a soda. Any fruit mixed with sugar and water was an ade. We offered exotica like watermelon soda and boysenberry ade. Uncle Paul ended that venture quickly, but not before we had made almost twenty bucks.

Then we collected sections of picket fence, truck tires, pipes, and other junk from the various warehouses, garages, and maintenance shops and constructed our own miniature golf course in the backyard, digging tunnels and burying plumbing in them for the tiny ball to rattle through. Our four-holed citadel sat in the landscape for days. We had turned old fences into slotted conduits, elbow joints into underground changes of direction and level, dais decorations into obstacles.

You had to stand and admire it. PG didn't. He made us tear it down at once, refusing to play even a hole. To him, just about anything we thought up was seditious in principle. On occasions like that he squared with my mother and I understood their primeval marriage. Passing me in the living room one day, he gave me a hard swat on the backside.

"What did I do?" I asked.

"I don't know, but you must have done something!"

As often as Aunt Bunny and I talked about psychology, our lives, books we read, and characters at the Hotel, we rarely mentioned Uncle Paul. In fact, one odd aspect of my stepmother was how little she seemed to have to do with my father. They slept in the same bed, but I rarely saw them together in public, and I couldn't imagine what they found to talk about. She tended to go to the nightclub alone and drink and dance. Once, Michael and I (with James in tow) sneaked over to see what she was up to. There she was, in red dress and jewelry, the center of much male attention, hoofing up a storm to a Latin band. We were sure she was drunk. "You kids go home," she shouted. "Your mother's entitled to party without being spied on."

Grandma Jennie seemed to be running her own hotel. Because there was rancor in the family about it, my brothers were not encouraged to visit her and rarely did. Even Aunt Bunny had little to do with the world at Joy Cottage. It seemed peculiarly to have more to do with my other family.

Every night Grandma would work her way through the dining room, table by table, greeting each group of guests as if they were the dearest of friends. Because she was a celebrity they had seen on bread packages and television, grown men and women were thrown into a tizzy by her mere presence. Sometimes she would summon me to accompany her and be introduced. I would stand at her side trying to look appropriate, as she told them about Horace Mann. Grandma's capacity for strangers was indefatigable.

My father ignored this hoopla around his mother as if it was happening in a dimension invisible to him, but I could tell he wasn't happy. One night I heard him say in response to her doting attentions to a particular group, "Mother, they're crooks; they've robbed us blind!"

And she answered, without irony or self-conscious sanctimonious-ness, "Then we'll turn the other cheek." Pretty much the sort of thing she said to me about my mother and stepfather.

I sat on her bed, correcting diagrams of sentences her tutor had given her, telling her what I knew about prehistory and landscapes on Mars. It was pretentious but guileless. She urged me not to limit my vision to the Hotel but to move beyond it. "Your father is narrow. He doesn't realize that our good fortune has come because of the way we've treated people and the largeness of our vision. We have been blessed, but we must continue to earn our blessings with good deeds."

I could tell that she thought of Grossinger's as a cultural institution more than a business. That gave my role as heir apparent a legitimacy, for I doubted I could conduct commerce like Uncle Paul.

Grandpa Harry was alienated from Grandma too. As the Hotel's architect and contractor, he had his crew build a separate doorway onto his room so he could come and go without contact. In all my time there I never saw them together. He was usually out on the grounds at dawn and went to bed early. Visited in the late afternoon, he sat hunched before his TV, often watching boxing. Piles of birdseed lay around the stone slabs marking his entrance, bright jujubees in which a confab of sparrows, wrens, pigeons, and blue jays nibbled furiously. For years I thought Grandpa had spread them because he liked birds; it was the main civilizing aspect in my portrait of him. Then a chance remark led a bellhop to inform me that a room-service waiter did the honors and, though Harry G. had bawled him out for all the birdshit, the vested old-timer refused to stop.

Still, I liked Grandpa Harry. He made much of me and gave me fifty-dollar bills, a fortune back then—almost ten times the purchasing power of the same tender today—plus he talked so much like Elmer Fudd that in his company I felt transported inside a comic book.

In Grandma's part of the house—all of it except that one room—I met the cliques of hangers-on my father stewed about: has-been singers, once-famous agents without clients, "doctors" (at least they were called "doc"), athletes in retirement, authors of religious books, cooks with foreign accents. I remember one-time boxer Barney Ross throwing his great arms around me like a mother and hugging me much too hard while singing a lullaby in Yiddish. Ostensibly he did public relations, but he seemed to reside solely in my grandmother's house and PZ's office.

To Grandma these were not freeloaders; they were gentlemen
and ladies under her protection. Stray women with academic pre-
tensions became her tutors, the only ones who actually lived in her
house; the others stayed at the Hotel—for a weekend, a week, or
months, depending on their situations. Collectively they made up
Grandma's salon, complete with two snapping Pekinese dogs and
a mynah bird that shouted, "Ship ahoy!" and let out wolf whistles
in the middle of parties.

Because Grandma invited so many diplomats, clergy, entertainers,
and politicians to stay gratis, there were frequent cocktail parties at
her house. I was usually the only child, once at a gathering for an
ambassador from Israel, another time for Cardinal Spellman, then
for the Lord Mayor of Dublin whose autograph I got for Bridey,
along with a promise to reunify Ireland for her.

Aunt Bunny didn't object to my introducing Michael to this
scene. "Your grandmother's quite the empress," she said, "but she
never accepted us the way she did your mother. You might as well
be our Lewis and Clark."

Soon Michael and I were making regular forays to Joy Cottage,
goofing off at Grandma's parties while collecting unexpected gifts
and expressions of affection. The Monk would characterize these
missions as "a quick twenty," which is often what we got. Grandma
was delighted by visits of the two of us, though it was strange that *I*
should be my brother's chaperone given that he lived so close to her.

I understood even then that the world at Joy Cottage was a
mirage, Grandma's admirers the leftovers of a previous generation,
my mother's era, which is why I was automatically embraced and
granted stature there. Grandma's graciousness and generosity, even
if self-serving, were appealing. She upheld something I knew to be
true—no matter how successful Grossinger's was, the world was
filled with sorrow and poverty, and that was far more important.
She told me that she made certain that a portion of Hotel prof-
its went to local orphanages—the car taking me home routinely
stopped at one of them in New Jersey, bringing surplus food from
the kitchen.

In New York I carried around coins for cups of beggars and cigar boxes of amputees on crate stools selling shoelaces. I even took up a collection at my family's various offices for the amputee outside Carnegie Hall on 57th Street and brought a wad of bills and fistful of coins to where he lay among overcoats. As he looked up in astonishment, I froze and fled. He was muttering gratitudes and accolades, but I was running to the corner, then racing across the street at the first break in traffic. Something about this was terrible. He shouldn't be thanking me. I shouldn't be fleeing him. Yet I continued to feel ungrateful and insincere.

"God bless you," shouted the blind man on Broadway as my money clanked in a battered tin cup he was shaking. I felt the same flush of confusion, the same urgency to get out of earshot. It was like when I rescued insects from puddles but didn't wait to see them dry themselves and regain flight. I couldn't bear the intimacy of a tramp's gratitude.

Yet I never understood why my mother and Bob as well as Uncle Paul opposed me so adamantly in this charity. For my mother, giving away money apparently showed infidelity to the family because these people were strangers. "You don't treat us half as well," she complained, "as you do bums on the street."

As for my father, once I was walking with him along Central Park South when a blind man with a muzzled dog approached us and I put some change in his cup. "You were just taken in," he proclaimed, "by one of the oldest rackets in the world." I silently bit at my lip, which disappointed him, so he continued, "I betcha he's not even blind."

"So what?" I told him.

"Isn't that why you gave him money?"

I shook my head. "I gave him money because he's sad."

"When you grow up you'll see that the world is full of crooks. You can't make everyone rich and everyone happy and, if you've got, those that don't are going to be looking for ways to take it from you. Remember that."

But I saw only chestnut vendors in rags, beggars crouched in alleys.

I befriended a dishwasher at the Hotel canteen, a gentle old Hungarian named Ziggy whose shoes were so ripped that his feet were more out than in. I asked him about them, and he said his toes hurt so he had cut them open. I told Grandma Jennie.

"I can't allow someone in my employ to be in that condition," she exclaimed.

She had her driver take him to a podiatrist. When I met him next, he was wearing white therapeutic clogs. His eyes twinkled as he pointed down at them. Grandma was so proud of me that she told my father, but he wasn't of like mind. He called me into his office and informed me gently but firmly that I should stay out of things I didn't understand. He meant it as a joke, but it had a sinister air to it: "I can't have you coming here if you're going to tell Grandma about every employee who needs shoes. Because if you do we're going to go bankrupt. She'll reclothe the whole hotel and send everyone to the podiatrist." He chortled. "That's Mother for you."

It wasn't a joke to me: people were fired, and when I complained to my father, he was belligerent—it was none of my business. One day he would dispose of Big Milty too.

After the first term at Horace Mann it was not my mother who drove me. The competitive milieu of the school became my habitat. The fact that I nearly flunked all six years of grade school had lost all relevance: Richard Towers was a fiction and I no longer acknowledged his defects or disgrace.

I imposed an attractively spartan existence on myself, and the rest of the family was compelled to respect it. No one was allowed to interrupt my studying—and I was always studying. Finally I could ignore Jonny with impudence. I didn't have to be a captive audience for his latest victories in the schoolyard or re-election as class president. I just excused myself from dinner early.

I had beaten my mother at her own game and won a haughty privacy.

Jonny was infuriated by this gambit. He tried to retaliate by ignoring me too, but I was a camel. I could go days, even weeks, without acknowledging his existence. No matter how loud he shouted or how often he imposed his body in front of mine I acted as though

I neither saw nor heard him. Even if we came face to face I would step around him and continue on my way—a preoccupied student. Eventually he would attack, or tell on me, but I would pretend that he had been disturbing my homework. For once he became the recipient of parental scolding: "Don't distract your brother when he's studying."

"I'll get you for this," he said. He continued to report every slight in detail as if a truant officer logging my demerits. Gradually our mother became suspicious of my devotion to schoolwork. Jon was ever her sweet baby while I was the incorrigible saboteur from the other family. Suit and tie (and HM maroon) notwithstanding, she knew I couldn't have been turned so suddenly into a gentleman scholar. Finally she clawed her way through my ruses.

"He can't stand that child being happy and successful," she proclaimed. "He's jealous and wants to squash the joy out of him."

Bob glowered at me as though his eyes had just been opened. "Mental cruelty," he said. "Is that what you specialize in, you silent instigator, you no good. ... You're a real needler aren't you, a real tormentor behind our backs."

They were right of course, but I couldn't back off. Jonny was just too virtuous and boastful. I couldn't accept his kinship. My revulsion for him—his style and mien—was an unyielding compass of my existence.

At P.S. 6 I had been a loner, but at Horace Mann I seemed to be friends to some degree with just about everyone in my Form. One group of intellectuals, more articulate and world-wise than me, held an informal symposium during lunch and between classes. I joined them as they bunched up in halls and the cafeteria, trying to be part of their confabs which favored Marxism, classical music, and abstract mathematics. The only topic on which I could offer expertise was symbols and dreams. Once I got up my courage and spoke, I was surprised I held their interest.

Thereafter I established myself as an authority on hidden meanings and produced them on cue, finding them in assigned books from *My Ántonia* to *Martian Chronicles*. I descried them as well in daily words and acts, in popular songs and beer ads, and I interpreted classmates' dreams on request. No one thought that psychoanalysis was as substantial as Red China, set theory, or Bach—in fact, I was accused of capitalist sophism—still, it gave me a foothold among the intelligentsia.

I felt more comfortable with my buddies on the train. We gossiped about school and talked baseball, television shows, and subway routes. I was well into my second year before I realized that my friendships with these kids were suppositious. Boys in the train crowd maintained significant contact with one another on the outside, while I never engaged with any of them except en route to and from Horace Mann. I was still a child in that regard, participating in my family's activities, their walks in Central Park and dinners out—and then I went to Grossinger's every vacation.

I never thought of calling up my friends to see what they were doing, and it was inconceivable that I would invite any of them to our household, for we never had guests. During the whole of Horace Mann I think my mother's brother Paul came to dinner twice, her legendary brother Lionel once (en route from Paris to Pittsburgh), my grandmother Sally maybe three times, my mother's assistant from work (Helen) once, Bob's pal Moe three or four times.... That was it except for a friend of Bridey's picking her up. Our apartment was taboo, a sanctum where the privacies of the Towers family were carried out: the nuanced sarcasms, my mother's facial packs, her early bedtimes, her "palpitations" (as she called her panics), our unabating derision of outsiders.

Not only would I have been ashamed to have anyone over, there was nothing to do at our place; our dramas occupied all the space. An outsider would not have gotten it. Even worse, we would not have known how to play our parts with strangers observing. There was no transition between private and public in 6B; it was *all* proscribed.

The Manhattan kids' favorite hangouts were East Side coffee shops and movie theaters, carryovers from P.S. 6 and other grade schools. They talked on the subway about cute girls who frequented them, neighborhood parties on the weekends.

My mother was little help on the topic. In retrospect I see that she was relieved I showed no outward interest in girls. What caught her attention, though, were the mailings from Horace Mann about formal dances. She wanted me to have the right social connections and decided that my next step was to learn to dance. Against my wishes (though I secretly appreciated the opportunity), I was signed up for Saturday classes at Miss Viola Wolfe's on Madison Avenue, to which I had to wear not only a full suit like at Horace Mann but white gloves. The elderly Miss Wolfe taught us the steps first by far-too-swift examples to mimic except clumsily. Then she clicked her metal cricket, an assistant dropped the needle onto a record, and we each had to pick a partner and execute a fox trot or waltz, later the lindy and cha-cha.

The moment of choosing a partner was excruciating. I would set my imagination on a pretty girl or a friendly face and try to end up beside her. But I never seemed to move fast enough—musical chairs again.

Each time, with unimportant variations, the dancing was the same. We stood facing each other but not really looking, and then put our hands on the indicated spots of the other's waist and shoulders (an assistant checked us pair by pair). The music began, and we attempted to carry out the proposed choreography for its duration, as the assistant and Miss Wolfe walked around, correcting us.

Usually we alternated partners in a sequence, so I even got to dance with the ones I wanted, but it made no difference. I was a poor dancer and the wrong boy, to boot. Anyway, at Viola Wolfe's the other person didn't exist; there were only rules and steps. The partner was an accessory to the lesson. And yet the partner was everything—the look on her face, her scent, the cloth or velvety feel of her dress, the stiffness or grace of her body in the dance.

I was Pip at Miss Havisham's mansion, with the bare longing of regret.

2

DR. FRIEND

Now that I attended Horace Mann, summers at Chipinaw felt even more incongruous and degrading. My classmates went to arts camps like Buck's Rock in Pennsylvania. I was the only one, so far as I knew, dispatched like clockwork to a militaristic establishment. After all my studying successes, I protested, how could I still be required to go to a place full of anti-intellectuals and self-anointed drill sergeants? My mother sympathized, but my father was intransigent. Chipinaw was filled with Grossinger's loyalists and patrons, plus he thought that it was better training for the real world than Horace Mann.

The summer after starting prep school I found a new escape: I volunteered for *The Chipinaw Chirp*. The camp newspaper—a one-page mimeographed collection of stories, jokes, and drawings—was put out weekly by a counselor as part of his job. Though I thought of the rag as useless, the *Chirp*'s new overseer, a journalism student named Alan Schecter, made me his assistant editor. I was the only candidate—the activity was too much like school for the average Chipinaw acolyte.

I was the ideal recruit. Trained in writing at Horace Mann, I also knew how to run a mimeo from working at the Grossinger's New York office. Right off, Alan was determined to do something livelier than in previous years: "Let's leave out the silly jokes and dumbo stories. We can cover camp events instead. Plus, we'll load it with human-interest items."

Since Alan also had six rambunctious imps to attend to, he was happy to let me take over the writing and production. For each issue

I featured a counselor's biography and personal opinions. I included a question-and-answer column for which I went around the bunks and tents asking people: What is your favorite activity and why? What meal do you like best? What was your most exciting moment ever at Chipinaw?

I sat in the O.D. shack for hours, writing articles, cutting the stencil with a typewriter, brushing on purple correction fluid when necessary, relishing its iodine-like aroma. Then I carried the finished product to the administration building, a cluster of offices at the edge of the girls' campus, otherwise off-limits to boys. There I hand-cranked several hundred fresh-smelling sheets.

I loved being back in the normal world, watching *Chirps* collect at the other end as the rolling cylinder hit a stack of 8 ½ by 14 paper, transforming type, artwork, and correction wax into flawless pages.

I spent increasingly less time on my camp activities and more and more on the *Chirp*, and no one seemed to mind.

The improved newspaper was a hit. I made the question column idiosyncratic, asking things like: What is your favorite water fountain (of the three on campus—by the workshed, alongside the tennis courts, or at the stables)? What is the best stoop for Stoopball? The best roof for Roofball? Should Dave Hecht fire counselors publicly? And most dangerously, what do you think of Color War? I posed these questions to not only campers and counselors but anyone I could find—Abbey, Nurse Mary, and some of the zombies. I even did interviews with the zombies about their maintenance jobs—an asocial act that no one seemed to understand. "Why?" counselors asked in bafflement, as though these laborers in our midst weren't real. Chipinaw's class hubris had turned them into robots as well as zombies.

My high point was composing arty descriptions of our environs. My first was a portrayal of a thunderstorm: I recreated the colors and movements of the clouds, rain on roofs, rivulets behind the tents, different moods during and after. A number of counselors complimented me on my style, so I wrote another about sunset. After that, I depicted Silver Lake, then the night sky, using plenty of adjectives while relying on the office copy of Roget's *Thesaurus*.

I always closed with a statement about the great beauty of our camp. Soon the secretaries were requesting hundreds of extras to include in the office's promotional mailings. What had begun as delinquent behavior had me in the service of management!

When Color War broke I was ready. An editorial declared the *Chirp* and its editor neutral. I printed lists of both teams (without my name) and announced that, for the first time, the newspaper would not suspend operations but instead publish an enlarged edition, reporting on *all* activities and keeping an up-to-date tally. Ignoring my assigned competitions, I ran around with a clipboard, gathering results and interviewing participants. My product was meant to read like *The Daily Mirror*. Even captains and pro-war counselors encouraged me—they loved the publicity.

I had no reason to think that the judges would approve of my defection, let alone show me the official scoresheet. "Ask Abbey," shrugged Arnie, the chief arbiter, so I approached the head counselor in his cabin. He didn't turn me away but, since he had not pronounced judgment on my neutrality, he was silent for a spell, then said that he'd consider the request. I darted back to my bunk before he could order me into battle.

That afternoon, without comment, Arnie handed me a copy of the day's scores and point totals. I took it from him in awe, the first camper in my time at Chipinaw to view the sacred document.

By dinner my coup was complete: I was invited to eat (for the duration of the week) with Abbey, Nurse Mary, the doctor, and the judges at the center table. I sat there, a child on Olympus.

I had finally achieved neutrality.

After the final reading of the official score Abbey asked for a standing ovation for the editor of the *Chirp*. Both teams rose, clapped, and whistled.

Only with the passage of time did I understand my real accomplishment. I had transformed an intransigent reality not, as I once presumed, by willful rebellion, but by forging a role for myself within it—one that my rivals accepted because I valorized and affirmed rather than derided or dismissed them. At the same time, using the clichés of big-time reporting I parodied not only Color

War and its overblown rhetoric, but my own charade of superiority. I got other people to see themselves as competing … for what? … the Red and the Gray!—and thus brought irony and self-reflection to the gambit. And I was exposed along with the rest of them—the imperious renegade and self-anointed scribe.

In Second Form (otherwise known as eighth grade) I had courses on Ancient and Mediaeval History; an Earth Science class featuring astronomy, geology and meteorology; requisite English and Math; and Beginning Latin taught by Mr. Jurka, a fellow from Albania who warned, "If you do not study it will be too too bad for you— not for me, but for you."

Our sunny yellow reader had an irresistible flavor and charm, as though I were entering the rebus of an extinct outer-space people. I was enchanted by strings of endings for nouns and verbs and vocabulary that bore English words in prior forms. It was by far the vastest cipher I had undertaken, plus these were not rank puzzles or juvenile games, they were codes at the scale of the Earth.

I memorized *agricola, agricolae …, porto, portas, portat …,* and the wonderful *hic, haec, hoc; huius, huius, huius …*. I translated sentences like "The man carried the water" and "The soldiers attacked the village." When Daddy quizzed me, we sang out the *"arum"* and *"orum"* of the genitive plural together with gusto (those were his favorites too at CCNY).

In Earth Science I learned taxonomy of sedimentary, igneous, and metamorphic rocks and started a collection. After charging an illustrated field guide at Womrath's, I bought a white scratch stone and magnifying glass at a hobby store. My best specimens were a piece of rose quartz from Central Park, a granite gneiss from a trip with Daddy to the Goldman (his main account in New Jersey), an amethyst cluster from Grandma Jennie, and chunks of dolomite that a school friend found at a quarry in Yonkers.

Rocks I couldn't identify with confidence—most of them—I piled in a bag and hauled to a room marked "Private" next to the geology exhibits at the Museum of Natural History. With trepidation I knocked on the door. The guy who opened it was genial enough to stop what he was doing, judge and correct my attempts at taxonomy, and show me how he arrived at the right names. Every few weeks I returned with a new batch for deciphering.

Meanwhile science class moved from rocks to clouds: stratus, cumulus, cirrus, and their crisscrosses: cirrostratus, cirrocumulus, and stratocumulus. With insider knowledge, the sky became paradoxically both more codified and more dreamlike, as I stared into its pantheon of dynamic billows and vistas. I took photos of each type, or my best hunches, and made a collection of skyscapes in a three-ring binder.

After our teacher, Mr. Kelly, told us that we could order daily weather maps for a small fee from a government address, I began a subscription that I retained for years, as I tried to predict local weather from front lines and temperature differentials, for any relatives who would listen (as well as all the following summer in the *Chipinaw Chirp*).

My mother was left speechless when a gigantic folded weather map began arriving every day in the mail. She disliked watching me examine the full-length instrument on the floor, so I hammed it up, running my fingers along rows of glyphs, as I decoded the various triangles, whorls, and other symbols, sometimes announcing my meteorological deductions to passing family members.

As with Dr. Fabian, she imagined I could be exposed to knowledge and gentrified without disrupting the status quo. I was only her moppet and clone. You would have thought that the maps contained plots against her, but then she never liked uninvited guests she couldn't control.

When we studied planets of the Solar System and stars, Mr. Kelly showed us a movie about cosmic rays—energy, he proclaimed (with the reverence of a rabbi), that comes from the beginning of the universe and penetrates the Earth, passing invisibly through our bodies every day. Cosmic rays were responsible, he added, for the color of our hair and the freckles on a girl's nose.

One day he brought in an old wire recording of actual particles howling. Our class sat in awe before the spooky warble—the stuff of outer-space comics coming off a thin strand of rapidly spinning steel. The crackle and pop sounded like an alien dragon trying to speak. Its soundtrack evoked not just the origin of galaxies and stars but my oldest daydreams, for the source of my ship lay somewhere in that cryptic chatter.

Pasting Kodacolors and wads of cotton on a piece of cardboard, I assembled a cloud taxonomy for my first-term project. After carting the cumbersome object to school on the subway, I watched a more ambitious classmate arrive in a station wagon with his physicist father and the two of them tote a large wooden box up to Mr. Kelly's room; it contained cotton strung on wires to make a 3D diorama of cloud shapes, showing how they developed by increments of wind, altitude, and humidity, each parameter labelled on a background grid.

An even more talented science buff launched a three-stage rocket and landed a satellite with a parachute on the baseball field. I can still picture how the missile shot out of its holder and vanished in less than a second, then the minute-long wait during which no one was sure what would happen. I had lost many less complicated plastic water rockets to covert landing sites and upper branches of trees. Finally a black dot materialized out of the empty blue and floated gently down, swinging its payload—a *tour de force*.

At the other end of Pforzheimer's second floor we entered the jurisdiction of Egyptians, Assyrians, and Persians, a classroom covered wall-to-wall with maps and photographs of antiquities. For homework I memorized names and dates of dynasties and battles and who invented what. I wrote my term paper on the Phoenicians: alphabet, trade routes, shellfish dye, and how their descendants in Africa were the Carthaginians of my Latin texts.

Mr. Hathaway added one full point to our final grades for every outside topical book we could prove we had read, so I checked out volumes on Picts, Anatolians, Medes, and Cretans, and, one by one, consumed them with the zeal of a science-fiction fan—these were archives of far-off planets with exotic customs and artifacts. After I passed oral tests on each ancient tribe and empire, respectively, my teacher took out his ledger and made a red check after my name. Soon I had five points, the difference between a B+ and an A-.

When we reached *Life on a Mediaeval Barony,* Mr. Hathaway told us to put our thinking caps on and come up with a project based on the book, so I hiked down Broadway, scavenging items from toy and hobby shops. I finally constructed a castle of balsa wood with a moat, knights and horses, little rubber farm animals, and ducks for its "mirror" lake. Like my cloud display, my barony fell short of some of the ingenious fabrications of my classmates, which included flowing water, battery-operated serfs and drawbridges, and tiers of ducks, some in midair with wings spread, others landing with feathers tucked in.

At winter midterms in the gym we would be asked to describe the birth of Christianity and the War of the Roses. Inspired by the oxymoron of a fracas of flowers, I had memorized intricate details of fifteenth-century campaigns between the House of Plantagenet and the Houses of Lancaster and York, the lives of Richard III and Henry Tudor, and the Battle of Bosworth Field. I got a clean A.

In fact, I spent much of that year memorizing. It was my trademark: at the window sill overlooking 96th Street with its ever-changing stream of traffic, alone on park benches, riding the subway, at restaurants while we waited for our food (filtering out family chatter). I kept it up while we trekked around the reservoir, a finger marking my spot in a book as I tagged behind them, reviewing my progress through conjugations and dynasties, expanding mnemonic chains item by item inside my mind.

I committed to heart the planets of the Solar System, their sizes, distances from the Sun, irregular verbs, verbs that govern the dative, the third and fourth declensions, ablatives of place and time, and chronologies of Old World civilizations. Each of these topics spun its own imaginal web, as I wove myself into their spells and embraced their grandeur. It was amazing my brain had that much space, but then I had once dreamed up and memorized an entire universe. The more I assimilated, the more I personified my topics. I began to sound like a bona-fide Roman historian and meteorologist.

Daddy marvelled at my increasingly sophisticated vocabulary at dinner, telling Jonny, "I hope you follow in your brother's footsteps." The worm was turning, just a bit.

But something else was happening too. From the car taking me to
Grossinger's for Thanksgiving, staring out at the moving landscape
I imagined a long, invisible sword extending from the near wheel,
shearing away fences, trees, telephone poles, bird baths, and houses.

What was *I* transforming with my scythe?

When Uncle Paul insisted I renew Hebrew classes that fall in order to
be bar-mitzvahed I protested on the basis of too much homework.
My mother ridiculed his fake holiness but told me to go through
with it so as not to endanger his paying for Horace Mann and also
because I would get expensive gifts from his clients. Pure bribery!

I was mortified at having to return to the Park Avenue Synagogue—I imagined I had outgrown it—but I took perverse delight
in hiding my Latin grammar inside the Hebrew prayer book and
memorizing declensions and conjuations while other kids chanted
Haftorah selections. I eventually got caught, which led to a sermon
forthwith about the barbarian Romans. When I rebutted from
my knowledge of the ancient world, my teacher rolled his eyes
away from the prep-school wise guy and directed his comments
to the class, "This is what people mean when they speak of Jewish
self-hatred. Some of the worse anti-Semites are our own Hebrew
brethren."

I am reminded of a story my half-Jewish grade-school friend
Phil Wohlstetter—his mother was a Ziegfeld showgirl courted by a
Jewish stockbroker—told me forty years later when we reconnected.
After he spoke on behalf of the Palestinian cause at a public event
in Seattle, a woman called him a self-hating Jew. "Only half of me
is a self-hating Jew," he retorted, "the other half is an anti-Semite."

Well, back in 1957 there was a faction at the Park Avenue Synagogue who still believed I was an anti-Semite, or at least an infidel,
and shouldn't be bar-mitzvahed. "A miserable excuse for a Jew,"
declared Mr. Liechtling, still the principal. Yet the fact of being
Jennie Grossinger's grandson outweighed being me. From the way
that Liechtling went on, you would have thought that she was
single-handedly responsible for turning the Negev into an orchard.
His compromise was that I learned my Haftorah at home from the

cantor's recording, assisted by a tutor from Yeshiva.

I could sound out Hebrew letters so, for a month and a half, I memorized my section of the service by singing it over and over with the prayer book in front of me. A bearded young student came three nights a week to correct my errors. He was relentlessly efficient, never once cracking a smile.

I couldn't carry a tune nor was I a flawless phonetic reader of Hebrew, so I barely met the synagogue's low bar. Then a week before the event, I composed a bland essay on the teachings of the prophet Isaiah, which was approved by a delighted Liechtling. "You came around," he declared. "I'm impressed." But I was just a Horace Mann student slumming, saddened to have given him false hope.

My bar mitzvah was the first among my contemporaries. On November 9th the Saturday morning after my thirteenth birthday, I arrived at 7 a.m. at the Park Avenue Synagogue to await the grand occasion in a state equal parts dread and relief. Gradually, the figures of my world streamed through the temple doors, each bearing a gift—a passage-of-life ritual belied by an extravagant commercial display. Envelopes with bonds, shares of stock, watches, leather-bound dictionaries and prayer books, even checks and cash piled up with Bridey beside the coatroom. Despite her calls of amazement I kept my distance, refusing to come look.

Once the service began, I sat on the dais in a throne-like object between Rabbi Nadich and the cantor. In a dark gray suit I felt less like a prospective man than a few sparkles stuck together in the semblance of a human doll, frangible enough to go flying in opposite directions. On cue Rabbi Nadich turned to me. I looked out over a congregation packed with relatives and friends and strode to the podium, a spy in the House of the Lord. There I stood beside the cantor, swaying nervously, as I *davened* from memory and phonetics.

It was a moment of truth before a substantial assemblage, so I regretted not being able to chant something meaningful like the history of the New York Yankees or the interpretation of dreams, even the planets and their distances from the sun. Instead, I droned an impersonation of Hebrew characters whose shapes matriculated before my eyes. After so many rehearsals, the fabled performance was at hand, the assignment completed, tossed into the void. I imagined myself expunging this deed forever.

After my recital on Isaiah, Judah Nadich seized the moment—his presentation of the implements of Jewish life to a bar mitzvah boy—for a canned sermon about their meaning and uses. Cringing inwardly, I held his solemn gaze—we were on stage.

Yarmulkes and *tallits* never felt to me like the sacred objects they are, power suits of magicians and shamans. They seemed more like clown costumes wherein others could ostracize us—yokes to the neuroticism of my Park Avenue culture and the entire grotesque Manhattan scene. For me, those straps of fancy leather and wooden blocks were baubles from the schul, a house that already assailed with waves of garish oils and aphrodisiac scents, with unspeakably dark desires and their just-as-unspeakable repressions. I wanted to throw them away with the fury of a horse bucking its gaucho. Our Hebrew names condemned us likewise to a strain of kinky exclusivity—mine had been Reuven at Ramaz, Selig for my bar mitzvah (my father preferred me to take an old family name—which was my middle name too—in place of the Hebrew approximation for Richard).

The elders never taught us that totem objects used properly confer a special view of the universe, its hidden planes and cycles, the very things I most sought; they never spoke of an Alcheringa or *sefirot,* Hebrew or otherwise. Instead, they prattled on about duties and pieties and their partisan Zionist Yahweh. Like counselors, teachers, and other assorted mentors of my childhood, they never said anything, about anything. Being Jewish was an honor and an obligation, quite enough for them.

I *was* a self-hating Jew. I never wrapped my body or head with the *tfilim* (I hid them in the back of the closet until they conveniently disappeared). By my defection I waived not only my initiation into my own Hebrew lodge but manhood in any kiva—as I would later realize—Hopi and Aranda lodges too.

After my bar mitzvah people gathered for a reception downstairs in the synagogue. Figures of my life milled with one another out of context—schoolmates, family, family friends. It was the first time I experienced all my worlds together. Bridey, Jonny, and Debby had never laid eyes on Aunt Bunny, or Michael and James (and vice versa). I pointed them out to one another and presided over bashful introductions. All these people did not belong together; yet there was a banquet in progress, and I rushed from table to table, accepting congratulations.

It was utterly bizarre, for I had been two people: Richard Towers and Richard Grossinger. Now these figures and their retinues encountered each other across a quarantine of lives; but the time was too brief and thin to contain such a powerful manifestation. Meetings between strangers passed in a moment. No one but me had anything at stake.

Dr. Fabian attended; he gave me a box of half a dozen books on topics ranging from the great explorers and Greek antiquities to the quest for identity, an attached note saying that I was setting out on my own epic voyage. I acknowledged him throughout the day with glances and smiles, as he beamed his approval. But even Fabian could not initiate me into a sacred lodge.

To give the appearance of orthodoxy my father had purposely not hired musicians. Instead the Yiddish comedian Emil Cohen told jokes for an hour. Bridey, having drunk too much champagne, laughed uncontrollably, finally tumbling off her chair. Then Grandma Sally's brother Mooney did a vaudeville routine he once performed professionally (as a fake stumbling busboy behind the startled actual waiters). "There he goes," shouted Daddy, rising to his feet, "the old Moonbeam is back, in finest form!"

To add to my awkwardness among my friends, not only was there no band, there were no girls. Actually, there was one. My mother insisted on that; she wrangled Vicki Berle, the daughter of the comedian, to join a dozen boys on the dais. The presence of a celebrity did not make up for the lack of a real party and, once Emil Cohen began his patter, my classmates, having made their polite appearances, fled the disaster.

I felt the deepest pangs of loneliness, the one time everyone was there.

The subsequent bar mitzvahs of my friends were grandiose balls with bands, bars, and charismatic adults—handsome men, fashionable ladies, dancing couples. None were in synagogue basements; they were held in suites in midtown hotels or country clubs in Westchester. I either took the train or went in a carpool. There were numberless pretty girls my age and a bit younger (and older), crowds of chic, cocksure boys, surges of pop music as if the orchestra kept suddenly recalling a new tune and burst into commemorative acclaim. I remember walking down a hallway of mirrors, the sound fading into the distance as my mind supplied its lyrics: *"Non Dimenticar, though you've travelled far, / my darling.… "* Nat King Cole's ballad was profound beyond words, and the feelings it aroused in me were chilling and tender—snow on pine trees, liners crossing oceans.

Given the nightclub settings of these bar mitzvahs, I assumed that my glumness came from intimations of Grossinger's and my wish to be there instead of in exile, to have grown up a real boy like the rest. All the way through P.S. 6, Chipinaw, and the early years of Horace Mann I met only one other kid with divorced parents. That was the fifties in a nutshell.

Dr. Fabian continued to push this interpretation, his theme of the tragedy of Martha and Paul's disunion. It remained his preferred explanation for all my problems: other kids' families were whole whereas I was a pariah in my own household; that's why I felt so alienated and scared. Superficially it fit; it made logical sense— broken family, estrangement, separation, loneliness—but I resisted shoehorning into its script.

My bedwetting had pretty much stopped. Occasional relapses— awaking to an icy tang of wet sheets—were atavisms of an otherwise cured condition. Yet the thing was, I hadn't a clue as to how I did it—or why. Dr. Fabian was sure he knew: he had touched the unconscious source and released its trauma. If so, it happened by hypnotic suggestion—a watchword wherein he bypassed me entirely. I knew that he didn't just say, "Stop peeing at night!" That wouldn't have impressed the keepers of my unconscious. But what exactly *did* he say or do? He had interpreted some dreams and made observations about my parents' divorce; how did that stop me from wetting my bed? If it was that easy, Nat Fleischer could have accomplished it in the Grossinger's lobby.

So as not to risk subconscious saboteurs, I kept my doubts to myself, though I had long ago ditched the interpretation. Paul and Martha together would have been hellions. The mere thought of it gave me the creeps. I didn't want that, even if it meant having always lived at Grossinger's. There would have been no Aunt Bunny, no Dr. Fabian either. Grossinger's wouldn't have been Grossinger's, not with Martha Grossinger ruling it.

My yearnfulness was remote and ineffable, as I watched kids from school dancing with unknown girls in a giant ballroom while the band played *"Somewhere, beyond the sea, / somewhere waiting for me...."*

I came home late at night, let myself in, found my bed and sleep almost simultaneously, got up the next morning and did my assignments. I even translated the Bobby Darin song into Latin, complete with gerund. The clue in the embers was real, its guardians real—they had always been real, reaching out from incomprehensibly far away. And it wasn't a clue at all; it was some other enigmatic thing:

"My lover stands on golden sands, / and watches the ships, / that go sailing...." (Mea amens in harena aurea stat, spectatque naves per mare cedentes.)

I stared out through darkening twilight over water towers atop buildings, the blown dust that was no longer organic let alone human: *"It's far beyond a star; / it's near beyond the moon."*

Not a salient trace, nary a semi-intelligible murmur.... Only those invisible cosmic rays.

It was a mistake, clearly, all of this. But at last I was calm, unafraid.

At school I fantasized that this kid Jeffrey, who commuted from Yonkers, would adopt me and I would come to HM with him every morning. His family, I heard, was having trouble paying the bills, so I imagined that the money from taking me in as a boarder would allow him to stay. I could share a room with him instead of that ruffian Jon. I was jolted each time I saw him in the flesh: his long thin face, black straight hair, odd tan coloring. It was him whom I missed and longed for, not some original unity of my parents. It wasn't that I wanted to be him, but I wanted to stand in relation to him. I longed to hold out a hand and set my fingers on his forehead. His very existence was the feeling I wanted inside myself.

These were not things I could tell to Dr. Fabian, but he sensed their existence. "You have to tell me what you're thinking," he would protest; "it's the only way I'm going to able to help you." I would agree in principle but never in deed. I merely pretended to be summoning deeper, truer thoughts—snippets of erotic fantasies, never their painful heart. Seeing him at my bar mitzvah after his appearance as a guest at Grossinger's, I realized he was not special; just a man with a wife at a party, shaking hands, smiling, drinking stupid wine.

Before and after sessions I observed his other patients more closely and recognized myself as one in a line of patrons, each with his or her stories and symbols. I was nobody special, just another customer. One time, I forgot my coat and came back in off the street for it. A woman lying on his couch leaped to her feet in embarrassment. Dr. Fabian insisted that my return was from curiosity and my coat was not left by accident. But viewing another patient in his presence drove me deeper into my pod and I denied everything.

The last time I saw him he was strangely irritable, like a cop unable to budge his prime suspect during an umpteenth interrogation. He asked me if I had had any sexual fantasies. I bristled at the explicitness of his invasion and dismissed its insinuation by shaking my head. He kept at me as he never had before, as though somehow he knew this was his last chance to solve my case. "You must have had some," he insisted, but I was tight-lipped.

Then he missed the next two sessions because he was called unexpectedly out of town. It was midterms of my second year at Horace Mann, and I didn't pay much attention to the interruption. I was obsessed with studying, the moment of truth in the gym. I memorized so hard that by Sunday night I began to forget things. I told my mother I was going to fail, and she ordered me to bed.

"You know there's such a thing as overstudying," Daddy chimed in. "You want to be in fighting condition tomorrow, not all worn out from too much sparring."

During each allotted two-hour span during the next week I drew on days of review and cramming, making a record of my partial mastery: the War of the Roses; cloud types; Latin to English, English to Latin; pristine integers extracted from quadratic jumbles. I pushed a pen until my fingers cramped. At the approach of the hour I rifled back to problems or questions I hadn't be able to get and gave them a last desperate shot.

Abruptly a command halted us: "Put down your writing implements at once!" I felt a surge of relief, then headed home to study for the next one.

Two weeks later my grades came in the mail; they were all A's except for a B in math. My mother was stupefied. She had no premonition of this happening and acted as though I had achieved the impossible. She was slaphappy on the phone, spreading the word to Grandma Sally and other relatives. She even got my father on the line, asking first, "Guess what Richard did?" in a tone sure to solicit, "What now?"

When he finally spoke to me he asked, "What happened in math?" That was meant to be funny too, but I didn't laugh.

As a reward, my mother invited me to her office for a special meal after school on Friday.

I took the subway to 57th Street and walked to the East Side. I sensed her unsteady mood as she phoned downstairs for a sandwich and then led me by the hand into the conference room. "Something I have to tell you. Dr. Fabian died." She planned this quick strike to avoid any clumsy dawdling. It was how she would have wanted to be told and I appreciated her diligence.

I felt a shock of surprise. It was hard to register such a big reality or its meaning. Then I thought confusedly back over the last weeks. "Was it on his trip?" I wondered.

"He never went on a trip. He died the evening of the last day you saw him. He had a sudden stroke. I didn't tell you because I didn't want to disturb your studying."

Now I adjusted to the fact that he had been dead for three weeks. Morbidly I thought back to our session and felt a flurry of guilt. I didn't imagine that I had caused his stroke by my intransigence, but I knew I had failed him nonetheless. I had failed the person who meant the most to me. And now I was alone.

On the way home in the back of a cab with my mother, my tears faded into an uncomfortably impassive breeziness that said: no more prying into fantasies, no more subway treks downtown, plenty of extra time for homework. *Maybe even no more fears.*

I had the illusion I could make it on my own, and I told myself a dark, shameful secret—that I wouldn't miss him. Then I locked it inside my heart. I went bowling with Eddie Schultz the next day, accepting a rare social date because my mother said it would be good to put my mind on something else. I pulled off my best round ever, my friend a witness. Life was improving!

When I started to go to sleep that night I had nightmares. I saw figures tumbling off a tower atop a faraway mountain, disappearing into a chasm. Dr. Fabian was one of them, unable to help himself, falling, screaming too.

At another juncture of the dream his bodiless head came to the window of my bedroom; I cried out silently. His voice was everywhere. "See," it said, "I can't save anyone. I never could. None of it ever really mattered. Not even the symbols. Now I'm one of the dead too."

Then I saw something else. His bones were in a garbage can. He was pale and rotted. He lay in a pond face down. Fragments of his body rippled like cloth, wrapped around telephone poles. Something terrible *had* happened to him.

I woke, looked around the room, remembered where I was, and tried to go back to sleep. Every time I closed my eyes I saw the same tower, the figures closer and more human. Yet I felt that as long as they didn't see me looking at them I was safe.

For years previous I had had a recurring dream of going to see another doctor, a dull, grouchy man whose ineptitude made a travesty of the session. It was always a relief to awake and remember good old Dr. Fabian. Now I encountered a live enactment of the dream. Two weeks after my mother broke the news, I took the elevator to a penthouse apartment overlooking Central Park West at 86th Street. Its occupant was a psychiatrist named Maurice Friend whose specialty was teenagers. He had agreed to take Dr. Fabian's one patient in his age range. The final decision, however, was to be mine.

This small, heavy-set man with a typical adult look seemed an unlikely replacement for my larger-than-life savior, not as banal and gross as in the dreams but a step in that direction. He didn't seem anything like a wizard, let alone Honest Abe.

Yet there we were, the two of us in chairs, facing each other, talking about a relationship like some sort of business deal. I couldn't focus on the issue at hand or take him seriously. All through the trial session—as he explained his method of working and opened his shirt to show me on his chest a scar from an operation (he was also vulnerable to death, he was saying)—I sat there contemptuous, imagining I would find someone more special. But then Dr. Fabian had stopped being a wizard long ago and, when the hour was over, the only answer I could think of was "Yes."

At first Dr. Friend was able to squeeze me into his schedule only at six o'clock in the evening. I took the subway straight from school to his building and sat in the waiting room doing homework for two hours, sometimes (if I caught the early train) longer, while other patients, mostly surly, suspicious teenagers, came and went. At a table by the window I solved math problems, summarized history readings, and translated Latin sentences while the sky darkened behind the reservoir and lights kindled across town on the East Side, scenery as picturesque as it was allaying. It was as though I were in a mirador or castle, elevated and grand—at least not my cloying apartment. I felt superior to the delinquents and slobs who preceded me. They *looked like* dysfunctional dolts, mental patients from central casting—*I* was a well-dressed Horace Mann student who had actually read Freud.

I might have been in a library carrel too, for Dr. Friend and I maintained a code of silence. I wasn't supposed to be there, so I wasn't. He might sneak me the slightest glint of recognition while greeting the next patient; yet at my turn he welcomed me enthusiastically.

From the beginning he insisted I lie on the couch while talking to him. I balked at being forced into the psychiatric stereotype. I

had imagined Fabian and me as engaged in something more dis-
criminating. Since in all our years he didn't once ask me to use the
couch, I had never considered its possible value. Lying down made
Dr. Friend disappear into an omnipresence behind me. For weeks
I dawdled there, re-narrating my stories as if on an empty stage, his
voice inserting minor queries and redirects. I told him my dreams
of the tower and the other incompetent doctors without letting
on that I held him in their company. Then I ran off the version of
my crisis that Dr. Fabian and I had collaborated on over the years.

When Dr. Friend finally chose to intervene at length his comments were unexpected: "You're not as crazy as you like to make
yourself sound. You've been in psychoanalysis from such a young
age that you now think of yourself only in terms of your problems."
I turned to face him in the overstuffed chair by the horse-statue
lamp. He smiled cheerfully as he picked up steam. "Dr. Fabian was
obviously a great support and helped you through difficult years,
but I think he underestimated you. He made you into a sick child,
a helpless boy who needed that support all the time. You may have
been that once, but you're not anymore. I think it's an interesting
coincidence that right after he died—even though you didn't know
it—you got almost all A's. Now you *can't* go back to the excuse that
you're an invalid and nothing should be expected of you. You are
going to have to perform at your level."

He had little interest in my recollections and recitals of Nanny,
Fabian's fallback scoundrel. "She no doubt had an effect on you, but
she's not active in the present. I can't do anything about the remote
past or your mother's behavior, but I can teach you how to react in
the present in ways that don't do you as much harm."

As our sessions deepened he routinely cut off my stories. "You
tell me about being afraid, but I don't see you afraid. You tell me
about your sadness, but you don't act sad or cry. I want to know
what's happening inside you when you're here, *now*. I see you day
after day studying in the waiting room, seemingly with tremendous
patience, but you are not a patient person. How do you control
yourself? How do you create these rigid masks?"

He insisted on hearing my fantasies and daydreams. When I balked and tried to substitute my usual expurgations he wasn't fooled. "Richard, I can't do anything unless you're here too. You're wasting my time, your time, and your father's money. I'm not prying because I'm nosy. I need to know what's going on with you, not what you choose to edit out for me. I'm not going to be a second Dr. Fabian. I'm no friendly uncle."

Yes, Dr. Fabian had been an ally, a buddy, and a magus, appearing at the brink of the dungeon stairs, leading me away from danger, then teaching me like a sorcerer's apprentice. Dr. Friend was the doctor of my teenage years: hard-nosed, demanding, incisive. Much of the time I would lie there irritated and mum, staring up at photographs of shell-like Grecian artifacts. "What do you feel?" he would ask tiredly. The last patient of his day, I could smell the cooking odors of his dinner drifting in from another quarter of the apartment, forcing me to withhold that I considered him repulsive too.

His name was ironical. It was because Dr. Fabian was too good a friend that I became unable to confide in him. Dr. Friend I found harsh, almost antipathetic, yet I eventually told him the truth, all the ignominious and sordid things I had long withheld, the yearnings and enmities that put my innocence and integrity in doubt. In all the time at Dr. Fabian's I never really looked at that stubborn boy with his outer-space adventures, pranks, and infatuations; now I did.

3

Please Don't Leave the Party Yet

The spring of Second Form, I went out for baseball, but the fastballs petrified me and I had never seen a curve before, so didn't know how to do more than lurch at them. I made occasional running catches, but I didn't have an arm for the outfield. When tried at second, I booted grounders. I started only one game (against Riverdale when someone else was sick) and, facing a guy who threw faster than a batting machine, by luck I hit a line drive to the shortstop, a real coup when twenty-five of our twenty-seven batters struck out. I can still feel the electricity of my bat turned wand.

Most of the other players were from the suburbs so I rode the subway home alone or, sometimes, with one other kid. It was the first time that I experienced the divide between the athletes—jocks—and the so-called brains. Bill-Dave and Chipinaw had bred an ineradicable competitive spirit, and baseball was my game, but none of the intellectuals in my circle even thought about going out for teams. They operated in another universe entirely. My fellow players talked drinking and parties and I felt like a child beside them.

I had to admit, I wasn't a real player, I didn't belong there. But if I was no longer a left fielder or spaceship recipient, what was I?

Dr. Friend was right. It was hard to know what I felt because I almost didn't feel it anymore. An ancient wistfulness hung over those years, protecting them like soft rain. I wasn't harried by terror; I didn't panic or feel the old amalgam of dread and hopelessness. I didn't obsess about poisons or terminal diseases. I wasn't phobic or hypervigilant. I wasn't happy or sad. I was in a limbo of suspended animation. And I didn't probe too deeply, for I found only layers of recalcitrance and discontent.

En route home, I gazed out the window of the El before entering the tunnel at 200th Street. The world seemed to have grown even more vast and mysterious in my absence, all that time studying and memorizing. I watched a young mother, kids chasing a ball until a building blocked them, a cluster of men at a corner store, women hanging from windows shouting, wind dissipating through leaves ... sun glinting off surfaces ... a dark alley ... a hobo with a dog ... a Puerto Rican girl in a bright yellow shirt, long black hair, a face I couldn't quite catch. Then the screech of wheels buried their images forever beyond swerving track. I yearned for something lodged inside the very depth and substance of the world. But intimations flipped by, not even like dreams.

Finals that year were my moment of truth, the only clear ultimatum on Earth. All May and June I studied into early morning hours every night. Latin was the most hopeful subject because I could at least translate the texts and explain their grammatical architecture. But Science and European History were bottomless, Algebra always on the edge of obscurity. I was not a math natural like most of my high-achieving peers; no matter how many problems I wrested to solution, I stared into the next bundle of numbers and letters like a Gordian knot.

For weeks beforehand I had the same nightmare in which I looked at my test and could decipher nothing, as though I hadn't even attended the course. I still have such dreams. Chuck Stein, a classmate then who's now a practicing Buddhist, tells me that fifty years of Zen and Tibetan meditation have not brought to an end his traumatic flashbacks of the showdown in the HM gym.

During those days Dr. Friend heard perfunctory dreams and petty frustrations. I not only lost all emotion, I forgot I existed. Course books and note binders subsumed my world, as I force-fed reams of minutiae into my brain. I was determined to learn *everything*. Grades had become their own vindication.

"A" was an ace in a deck of cards, a letter stolen from a sacred alphabet. I wanted to be defined by immaculate "A," to feel at its appearance a release of tension in my gut … its deliciously sovereign coils of anointing. All of us shared that ambition to some degree—Chuck Stein, Erwin Morton, James Polachek, Andrew Schloss, Bob Karlin. We clustered before and after exams, alternately competitive and empathic, compelled to the ceremony. We had accepted blind invitations into an arcane guild when there was no other—no other invitation, no other guild.

After finals I returned awkwardly to who I was, a person with vague aches and yens, not quite the performer in whose behalf I imagined I was toiling. Formulas and facts crumbled into aimless static as though the knowledge itself didn't matter, its grade already in the unseen book. Only the imminent report card counted, a week to ten days down the road, an oversize envelope with the HM return address. I sat at my desk, listlessly crumpling obsolete notes and shooting for the far trash basket, collecting my misses and shooting again.

Arriving in a stack of mundane mail on the 6B doormat, the holy epistle coopted every prior essence. I could barely tear open the envelope, my arms felt so weak.

It was all A's and high B's—vindication! I was not only exonerated but free. Yet the sense of being on trial remained. Somewhere once I had committed a crime, perhaps a murder. It wasn't the crime my mother held against me—it was much, much worse—something from another life. Nothing I did could atone for it, and now a judge in a wig was about to pronounce my sentence, to send me to prison for the rest of my natural life. I knew that incarceration because I had already lived its eternity in a stone cell, died there a madman. Who cared about "A" when once long ago I had failed the final exam of character and motive?

But where was it taking place? Where dwelled this cryptic court that arose in a dream beyond memory like some dank Romanian visitation?

A premonition hid in my background—an obscure, unnamed malignancy. Was I like Bridey Murphy?

I went to my annual check-up with Dr. Levine. I sat in his office, watching little kids build block cities on the floor. They were young and protected; nothing had happened to them yet. I knew better. The muteness of that room masked a cataclysm, a white noise in which everyone went about their business as though we were invulnerable to what was at stake. Traffic roared by on the streets. One by one, the nurses called them in. Then me.

Was my heartbeat okay? Why did he listen so closely? Did he sense something Dr. Hunt had missed all these years? Why was he squeezing my belly again? Did he feel a lump? I watched his face for a clue. If he lingered anywhere too long, it was bad. If he passed too quickly it was bad too because it meant he already knew and was pondering how to tell me. But nothing came of it, nothing at all.

I strode into a boiling-hot city, vindicated again, almost light-hearted, disbelieving my luck. When had summer exploded, had so many flowers and branches bloomed so exorbitantly? I felt dropped into a future time and its elusive joy. The subway roared under grates, releasing a sultry stench and recalling my unknown destiny. This was an overripe Eden. But who was I now that doom was in remission and I had an option to live?

Not really. The Chinese were suddenly threatening to invade Quemoy and Matsu. President Eisenhower vowed to defend the islands with everything America had. The world was on fire. I was sure I would never make it to Grossinger's alive.

Bridey customarily turned on the news every hour, from 7 a.m. till bedtime. Now I attended to its chimes, the chant of the global announcer: Quemoy and Matsu, Red China and Taiwan, an inevasible collision. As I glanced nervously at newsstand headlines, every screeching sound and whine of machinery startled me: back on red alert—something terrible, worse than terrible, was about to happen. It was blatant, screaming from newspaper headlines, all of us at stake.

The testing of air-raid sirens sent me searching for a clock face to confirm it was noon. Give or take a minute or two for imperfect gears, it was always reassuringly twelvish. Whew! My heart gradually stopped pounding.

I couldn't understand why no one else was concerned—but then no one else had ever been concerned.

One day the sirens went off in the late afternoon. I thought—fire engines, no! Noon, no! Then this was it!

I stood there in the apartment listening to their unabated drone. Would I hear the bombs first or see the light? Would the buildings ignite and crumble? My heart was beating so hard I could almost not bear its weight. But another part of me seemed to be laughing, as if to say, "This is all crazy. This makes no sense at all, none of it."

I tore to the radio and turned it on. I expected to hear the warning tone, but there was music, station after station … music and voices.

Now I listened to the sirens with a different attitude, one of mockery and defiance … even though somewhere the bombs were still mounted, their missiles ready….The keepers of doom were imperfect, hysterical. And this time *they were wrong.*

For two weeks that June I worked for Paul Zousmer at the Grossinger New York office. I typed his press releases, sorted and cleaned his collapsing files back into the 1920s, and ran errands. Each day at lunch the gang of us went to a nearby luncheonette and ordered soup and slices of the meat special with fries and the vegetable of the day.

I finally earned $150. In a festive mood PZ accompanied me to Photo Fair. Charlie was waiting. He brought out a sealed box, cut it open, and took the camera from its foam shell and handed it to me. I held the cold, sleek-smelling metal to my eye and focused on people outside the storefront. No longer confined to a fixed lens, I tested the delicate registers of its dials, watching fog crystallize into moving faces and bodies. Across the counter, de Luise pointed out singer Phil Everly with his black pompadour. He was examining, then buying a Yashika with his brother. I pretended to take a picture of him, depressing the button at the highest speed and listening to the fine ping of the shutter. Kids at the Horace Mann camera club had said a two-thousandth of a second was pointless, a waste, but it made my Minolta special, like Bob Turley's fastball. When I took out my wad of bills, Charlie laughed. "No charge," he said.

I didn't understand.

"Your grandfather already paid for it. Harry Grossinger. He

wanted it to be a gift from him."

Now PZ was laughing too. "He found out you were working in the office, so he decided to surprise you."

I was astonished. Grandpa Harry, while generous, had never been interested in anything I did or said; he was a cartoon figure, acting out a benignly irascible role. Now I saw him in a new light: a cagey old coyote not missing a beat, not letting on—and he had chosen to sponsor my photography!

I spent half of my cash on a light meter and then hurried home with my treasures, testing the viewfinder on lights in the subway tunnel, people walking dogs along the park, silhouettes of water towers, cherry blossoms, an altocumulus sky ... the whole superb world.

A week later, Grandpa's new driver, Ray, picked me up for the summer, first Grossinger's, then Chipinaw. But instead of going directly to the Mountains, he stopped in the Bronx because he had tickets from Ingemar Johansson for his second heavyweight bout with Floyd Patterson. Johansson had trained at the Hotel, and Ray had become pals with him in the course of ferrying him back and forth to the City.

I wanted to get out of the nuclear target zone, so attending this fight was just one more obstacle. What if the attack came while we were dallying at a needless affair? But I was also involved in wanting the Grossinger's fighter to smash my brother's ballyhooed guy. I knew he rooted for Patterson only because I had befriended Johansson at the Hotel. He wanted to see *me* lose.

In Spanish Harlem on our way to Yankee Stadium, the Caddy broke down and, while I stood in the street alongside the open hood—Ray working feverishly underneath—an old man approached me and offered to start our vehicle by pouring liquor into its gas tank. He reached for the cap before Ray dissuaded him. A crowd began to gather.

I wasn't afraid. World War III was scary; the judge in his wig was scary. This was an interlude in a strange place about which I was curious. What did it feel like to stand in streets beyond the El, breathe their soot, their pizza-popcorn air, be among their ripples of activity, gaze at the habitants up close? Twilight fell.

Suddenly Ray got the engine running. He was dripping sweat as we gunned out of there. I was laughing to myself at what a great story this would be. "Liquor for the engine!" Michael would roar. And then he'd dance about, making it into a song.

I missed all the political nuances. I was too young and credulous; everything noteworthy or odd was either a tall tale or a prank.

PZ occupied the seat next to us. We had barely settled when he shouted, "No!" Patterson had sent the Swedish champion sprawling across the canvass. I was shocked. Jonny had won. But we found our way to the car and headed north to the Catskills. I was alive, en route back to paradise. Time would go on, a while more.

At lunch the next day a pleasant man at the family tables introduced himself as Steve Lawrence; he said that he was singing that night in the Terrace Room. When I realized who he was, I told him how much I liked his version of "The Banana Boat Song." He was pleased that I had heard of him. "I never turn down praise," he added, "but don't you think Harry Bellafonte has the real claim on that one?"

"I like yours too. You make it a different song."

"Well, I did my homework. I researched the roots. 'Hill and gully rider' is my own touch. Gonna come and hear me tonight?"

"Yep!"

Then he began humming, *"Comes the light / And I wanna go home."*

We were in a discussion about the song's meaning and symbols in general when he cut me off, "Gotta go do a sound check, but let's continue tomorrow, same time, same station, buddy. Breakfast?" And so we did.

That summer at Chipinaw, Jay, Barry, and I graduated to the tents; we were Seniors. Our habitats were large wooden decks on which beds were set. Flaps of canvas arranged on ropes and supported by poles formed a pyramidal canopy above each provisional floor. When I was younger I was relieved to be in a safe and spacious bunk, but a tent was a box kite of shifting breezes, sunlight, and flaps, a vagabond perk for recently admitted adults—we had earned our flaps like a sea captain his sails.

I loved the nearness of the starry vault, the whisper of rain on cloth. I considered it one of the all-time highlights of Chipinaw when we were visited by three skunks in the middle of the night. Everyone in the tent froze while the creatures poked about, raising themselves on front paws to look into garbage cans and trunks, knocking over bottles, disappearing into piles of clothes and under beds. On the whispered count of three we rolled across our blankets and scattered into the night. Then we ran around yelping and giggling, waking our neighbors.

That was the summer of 1958 when kids first began to talk about girls and "making out." But we were fourteen years old, and it mostly rumor and hearsay. I experienced my incipient sexuality only in fantasies and allusions.

Bearing an especial aura of seductiveness was a rock 'n' roll tune (single guitar plinks in the background) that went, *"Don't go home, my little darling, / please don't leave the party yet.... "* I would picture a girl in a slinky dress, wrapping her arms around me, keeping me there.... That had an allure like nothing else, or at least since the spell cast by Annie Welch.

I had never heard the term "getting laid" before the summer, so it conjured all sorts of beguilingly intimate (and impossible) acts around the topology and logistics of an egg before I learned that it simply meant sex, as in fucking.

Horace Mann kids on the subway would report on girls who had made out with them, swapping lurid details. Trying to picture the deeds boasted of, whether hyperbolic or real—though always presented as real—was excruciating: chimeras as succulent and irresistible as they were beyond imagination. Surrogate sensations wafted over me, and then the song.... *"Can't you see I came to the party, / 'cause I knew that you'd be here.... "*

But who was she? I tried to picture her; she was a different girl each time, waiting at the party that never happened for the boy who never came, who dared not even kiss make-believe Annie Welch on another world. It was a wave that would not break, that was made out of everything that was me becoming everything that was not me—and it was suddenly what I wanted more than anything.

Chipinaw Seniors had regular socials with the girls' camp. Trooping with Jay and Barry to the first one, I hoped that Viola Wolfe's lessons might be of some use, but as soon as we arrived at the armory older kids were dancing with all the girls and we were left standing along the benches trading wisecracks. Only one guy in our tent had any success—a red-haired sweet-talker named Alan who was new that summer. A clumsy athlete with an affected air, he took up with a tall dirty blonde named Joan Snyder, pert face, friendly eyes. I didn't remember when I became infatuated with her, but soon her image filled my life. I would sit by the side watching her dance with Alan, daydreaming as if I were back at P.S. 6.

In my main fantasy Joan was being persecuted by her counselor, so I snuck over to her bunk at night and called to her. She heard me and climbed out the window. "Who are you?" she wondered, but she was glad for the chance to escape.

We dashed for the woods. Angry counselors close behind us, we scrambled into the brush and lost them in a series of thickets and briars. Then we found our way through grottos and glens, alternately running and hiding. Through various twists of plot (including a return of my spaceship) I transported us to the jungle where we made our way past waterfalls, along canyons, and over mountains to the Amazon. There we built an *"African Queen"* and fled down a tributary.

Every detail of this fantasy was luminous to me, a trance made real by the meticulousness with which I evoked and fed its reverie. As I reenacted it each night, the grass became damp again, pools glowed in moonlight. Our flight through the brush became ever more serpentine, full of swerves and narrow escapes. The more vividly I rendered each object and event, the more spellbinding its effect until I was drawn into an enchantment more palpable and ecstatic than life.

Later in the summer, seniors went on a co-ed field trip to Ausable Chasm. At the souvenir shop after the boat tour, daring myself to do it, I bought a stuffed terrier and walked right up to Joan outside the bus where she was standing with other girls, Alan having left her to board the boys' bus. I silently handed it to her. It was brash and foolish. We had never spoken a word, but I had recreated her from effigy so often I couldn't believe I didn't know her. She took it in surprise, thanked me, and hurried onto the bus in a cluster of yakkity friends.

In another version of the daydream we fled the girls' camp in a motorboat and then outraced pursuers to a raft camouflaged by my allies on the far side of the lake. There we followed tributaries of a previously unknown stream until we made it all the way to Grossinger Lake, a mere seven miles. I saw the Hotel's buildings through her eyes as if for the first time.

I would lie in bed after Taps in a rapture of dramaturgy, cozy in pajamas, a wind in the forest matching internal sound effects, Mars red-tinged among glittering whites, the portentous notes of Taps fading, voices of counselors passing in the dark, the rescue about to get underway ... as fresh and new as if it had never happened.

After I gave her the dog I arrived apprehensively at the next social. She danced with Alan as usual. Then suddenly she was heading my way. I was dumbstruck. I tried to look elsewhere, but her eyes were directly on me. She came right up and coolly asked, "You want to dance?"

I nodded. It was awkward putting my hands on her actual shoulder and waist as the record began, struggling to remember steps. None of the dancing at Chipinaw was particularly intimate, for Dave Hecht came around periodically with a tape measure and checked the distances of partners. Six inches was the minimum.

She didn't evaporate; she was there and smiling at me, not the girl from my fantasies, but a girl. She told me that I was very nice but she was going with Alan, so she wouldn't dance with me again after this time. I returned to my seat in a daze.

And in my mind Johnny Cash sang: *"I don't like it, / but I guess things happen that way."*

At midweek movies I'd spot Joan Snyder across the armory, her presence transforming me, the adventure untold. A titillating aroma of Chipinaw girls in the room, I'd forget the film and sink into my fairy tale, leaving camp, starting again from the beginning ... that very night, racing through the woods, an owl whistling, moths fluttering at her screen.

And, yes, Phil Everly: *"Only trouble is, gee whiz, / I'm dreaming my life away."*

Two nights later some guys in the next tent claimed to have made it to the girls' camp on what they called a "raid," returning with lewd tales and a girl's panties as proof. Their testimony beckoned vicariously, even if it was apocryphal. It was quite a poke through those woods, after all, and the girls' bunks had monitors at night. But to go on even an imaginary raid you needed a girlfriend, so I stuck to my make-believe escapades.

Toward the end of the summer was an evening carnival at the girls' camp. I was holding my camera with its fancy Honeywell strobe, and Joan Snyder came up to me as if out of nowhere, laughing, and said, "Goodbye," and, "Guess what, I'm leaving early and going to Grossinger's." And then "Aren't you going to take my picture?"

Yes ... and that snapshot, utter blackness behind her, was all I ever saw again. She never came back to Chipinaw ... and by the time I got to Grossinger's she was gone. I had that picture of her—head thrown back, wide-eyed, quixotic, laughing then forever—until I left for college and my mother threw my scrapbooks away. Now I have only a memory of the picture.

In later years, though, I had a recurring dream of returning to New York City and looking through old phone books for "Joan Snyder." She lived in a strange part of town. I finally had a date with her if I could find her. Depending on which version I dreamed, I would get off the subway at some deserted station uptown ... buildings crumbling, their numbers missing. I wandered through parks with small chapels, crawled over rock piles, and walked up stairs of abandoned apartments to see only hag women cackling at me. I slunk invisibly through skid-row streets packed with hoodlums, armed gangs everywhere. It was like every place in the City I had been warned never to go, and had never gone; now their latencies were in full bloom, aroused and truculent.

I was in grave danger if a gang member spotted me, but before that happened I flagged the last bus out.

Even in my dreams about Joan Snyder, she never appeared.

4

ADOLESCENCE

In Third Form, the first year of high school, our classes moved to the gray edifice opposite the gym, Tillinghast Hall. I was placed in almost all Honors sections, my competence no longer a question. Horace Mann was my life—its classrooms where I earned my grades, its corridors where I met my friends, its auditorium where we sang hymns and heard senior speeches, its cafeteria where we gathered in groups to talk sports, philosophy, and politics over the daily fare, its teachers ("Sir!") now familiar elders to petition and charm.

I advanced to Caesar in Latin, Tennyson and Sinclair Lewis, Geometry, and Biology with its white formaldehyde rats. We each had to slice open a wet furry body and pull out and identify its intestines, liver, kidney, heart, and vaguer organs. This was far more tangible a demonstration of reality than I was ready for, plus I didn't like to think about how we came by so many rats.

During respites in the day a group of us took to heaving a baseball back and forth across the central campus. My main partner was a classmate named Steve, a flippant kid with a childlike face and freckles, one of the wise-guy jocks. I knew him mainly from Latin where he was struggling, his butchered translations earning Mr. Metcalf's taunts and antics. Our teacher regularly slammed a paperweight on his desk to keep us alert and occasionally threw chalk or hardballs at the unprepared—he had a drawer of different-sized baseballs for this purpose and laggards had to duck whenever a side-armed toss went careening across a desk. Steve was his favorite target.

One afternoon, my classmate trailed me from the field and, out of the blue, invited me to his house in Scarsdale overnight for a party. It was the first such offer I had ever gotten—the risk of bedwetting a long-time deterrent—so the whole rest of that week seemed charged and buoyant.

On Saturday morning I took the train from Grand Central, past Harlem, into the countryside. Steve and his mother met me with a station wagon and drove us back to their house. From there he and I trekked to a neighborhood field and joined local kids in skying a hardball across the meadow.

Everyone was jiving, launching shots, making plays, hitting the cut-off man. I was in perfect rhythm, attentive to the moment, its impermanence making its auspiciousness more dear. I gave the ball everything I had that day, racing to intercept its pellet flight, rolling as I trapped it, jumping up and flinging it back in, acting as if I belonged. My life was somehow on the line in that ragtag game, if only I could time my breath, the arc of flight, the infinity of blue.... As usual I felt hopelessly complicated and obscure—Pinocchio's dilemma: "I want to be a real boy!"

Dr. Friend would lecture on about alienation, trying to get me to acknowledge feelings of depression and anger as if these were now the clue in the embers. One day while I was talking about Joan Snyder, he startled me by asking if I had masturbated. I knew the word, but I didn't know what it meant. He explained.

I couldn't imagine more than my penis getting hard. He said that semen could spurt out too.

"Fantasies are imaginary," I responded. "They're not real enough to make something like that happen."

"Oh yes they are," he rejoined. "And you, of all people, should know that."

He didn't pursue it.

He wanted to wake me up, melt Pinocchio's numbness and turn him into a real boy, and I wanted that too. But something was missing, some basic fact of life.

"Whither is fled the visionary gleam? / Where is it now, the glory and the dream?" That was it in a nutshell, clear as day, one unlikely afternoon

in Alfred Baruth's English room, sending a chill down my spine. It needed no scholarly exposition, no psychiatric unravelling. Could Wordsworth have known something that Dr. Friend didn't, born as he was more than a century before Freud?

Anyway, I would be dispatched at day's end, back to the Towers apartment, and I sensed that it would take me half a lifetime to return to this dandelion field.

After dinner Steve led me upstairs to his room and we took places, me on the couch, him slouched on his bed, as we rehearsed translations for next week's test. I knew he was failing the class, so I adopted the role of enthusiastic tutor, throwing my ballfield rhythm into Caesar's Gallic campaigns, line by line, mimicking Metcalf's renditions of onomatopoeia and the uses of the dative and ablative, hamming it up with the master's husky metronome-like intonations. I was quite willing to give my friend everything I could in exchange for the gift of this day. Suddenly I noticed it was getting dark, "Hey what time is the party?"

"I forgot to tell you. It was cancelled."

It meant nothing to him, but my heart sank at those words.

A moment later, with a mischievous smile he pulled a tape recorder from under the bed. He had made a copy of my performance and was going to use it for his homework. For the rest of our time at Horace Mann he thought that's why he lost me as a friend.

Wordsworth's "Ode on Intimations of Immortality" was my baptism, the awakening bell. Throughout the autumn of '58 I made kinship with an autonomous literary voice, a timeless hit parade with compass to inspire across centuries beyond life and death. Its chart-toppers included John Donne's blood-mingling flea, Walter de la Mare's *"silver fruit on silver trees,"* Matthew Arnold's *"naked shingles of the world,"* the wolf dog of Jack London's *Call of the Wild,* the suicidal sleigh ride on which Edith Wharton sent Ethan Frome. It resonated in Willa Cather's "precious, incommunicable past" and Emily Dickinson's *"blue and gold mistake"*—a sixth sense for recovering cardinal runes and dissolving surface mirages. Such was the power of art to grant a fourteen-year-old safe passage, anywhere.

I was reading not just for graded study now but catharsis, for I intuited in myself the same mystery that drove Baruth's authors to eloquences of revelation. Freud's symbolic universe loomed large, but it was a façade. A more abstruse reality seeped from every courtyard light, Indian-summer tree and rooftop water tower, from flocks of birds crossing the last luminations of urban twilight. There was a realm of untapped wonderment, as big as the sky, and it conjured me through my turbulence and gloom.

I spent hours in the Museum of Natural History, passing from mural to mural, gazing at animals in dioramas of the Rockies ... Africa ... Alaska ... the South American forest, the pygmy drawing his bow by a broken ostrich egg. Their stark, magnificent specificity reflected my mood. The Siberian tiger in his golden striped flesh against violet-dimmed winter was a force, though stuffed and mounted in artificial scenery, a force I acknowledged but could not name. His majesty—and that of mountain sheep and antelopes and snow leopard—held the key to the trance I was in.

"Twas brillig, and the slithy toves" said it all by saying nothing. Alice in Nonsense-land, the world *did "gyre and gimble in the wabe."* My vernacular Top Twenty was full of it's inscrutable rapture. It was the Platters, *"tears I cannot hide,"* Ricky Nelson, *"and the only price you pay,"* Little Anthony, *"I'd gladly take you back / and tempt the hands of fate."* What else was there but those hands of fate, that stranger across a crowded room? *"Who can explain it, who can tell you why? / Fools give you reasons, wise men never try."*

I opened most weekends with a Friday night concert before our parents got home. Alone with my Magnavox I put on one 45 after another and lay there suffused in the worlds of feeling they invoked. It was not so much their lyrics—although those uncannily paralleled my sentiments. No, it was that each tune-word combination was idiomatic and complete, a trace of something ineffable.

My song for those months was Cathy Carr's "First Anniversary." Her happy/sad tomboy voice spoke for Joan Snyder and my unlived self:

> *Look at you. Look at me.*
> *See the way we glow*

You'd believe that we just met
One week a-go-o-o-o.

Though such sweet, perky simplicity seemed beyond me, it was everything I worshipped and wanted to be, wanted to find in the world. I would sprawl on the floor against my bed, in touch with a reverence, an incipient joy that, though not as familiar to me as languor or fear, seemed equally to lie at my core. It was, as Bobby Darin proposed, *"Every night I hope and pray"*—a prayer—and: *"Dream lover, until then, / I'll go to sleep and dream again.... "*

Then those Photo Fair, gee-whiz-dreaming Everly Brothers; Paul Anka summoning three syllables of a teen goddess *"Di-an-a";* Neil Sedaka, "Happy Birthday, Sweet Sixteen" *("It's just that you've grown up / before my very eyes);* Dion & the Belmonts: *"Now if you want to make me cry, / that won't be so hard to do.* But the promise always, from Wordsworth to "Dover Beach" to Thornton Wilder: " ... the bridge is love, the only survival, the only meaning"; so Dion on cue: *"And if you should say goodbye / I'll still go on loving you...."*

How could lyrics be any more exquisite, more perfect? I melted my heart and voice into theirs, participating in a spontaneous force that supported and carried me along, as if melody were rich enough to hold Creation. Even the uncued silences between words resonated with undisclosed meanings.

"Each night I ask, the stars up above ..."—my echo drawling out the "s" and "r" and "v" even more than Dion, in total agreement: that it was sad but that it was also wonderful ... that someday I would get to the bottom of this.

There was one song in which the deceptively simple words had no discernible connection to their power over for me:

I've a-laid around / and played around / this old town too long,
Summer's almost gone, / winter's comin' on.

Which winter? What town?

I saw a village out west. I heard the distant echo of "Winter Wonderland," my mother in her black velvet overcoat, walking on new-fallen snow of Central Park in a landscape that seemed before even Lenape longhouses and canoes, a panorama of childhood in a divining jar through whose opacity crystals fell.

But it was more than that. Just the word "winter" was evocative—the feeling of cold flakes on my skin, sleigh rides with Daddy, steering around the Park's titanic outcroppings, colored lights street after street.

Dr. Friend would review the song with me by stanza:

Papa writes to Johnny, / but Johnny can't come home. / Johnny can't come home, / no Johnny can't come home.

"It's your brother, of course," he noted cursorily, an obvious association for which I took his word.

Papa writes to Johnny, / but Johnny can't come home. / 'Cause he's been on the chain gang too long.

Yes, Jonny it must be. So obvious. Yet it didn't ring true. Right name, wrong tone. The "Johnny" in the song was some sort of bandit hero. He was an offshoot of *"Oh, my papa,"* Eddie Fisher singing his requiem, *"To me he was so wonderful …,"* the sword of cancer shadowing those very words … "another place/another time" (Bridey Murphy). Everything so convoluted, so inextricable!

"What about the chain gang, Richard? Do you picture your family in New York as a prison in which your brother is trapped? Your own father can call you home but not your brother who can't leave his family."

Maybe. Then, does that mean I feel sorry for Jon? Is there some other Jonny hidden inside my brother who would be my friend in better circumstances? Are we westerly bound bandits in another place, another time? Does the song call for him from behind its yearnful drone and jaunty cowboy voice?

Not enough! Still not enough! This was Planet Mars big, big as the ocean sending waves across itself, cosmic-ray big, big as all the cities on all the stars in the universe. Or, maybe it was just the prophecy of escape, that someday I was going to walk out of this place into my destiny. A dark November day bearing the amulet of my birth sign.…

And I feel like I gotta travel on.

Soon after getting my Minolta, I became friends with the president of the Horace Mann camera club. His name was Billy; he was short with a big owl-like face, and I liked him because he was kind and well-spoken as we ranged over topics on our subway route home. He didn't talk about sports or girls and parties—a relief. As we sat in facing seats, I blabbed on about my mother and stepfather, the family at Grossinger's, the scene at the Hotel.

The first time we got together outside of school or the IRT was a Saturday gathering of the camera club—a trek through Greenwich Village, each of us stocked with recycled canisters of bulk film from 35-millimeter rolls—less than a penny a shot. We loaded them ourselves inside black boxes we all owned—a giant reel in one compartment, a spool, tin capsule, and clip-top assembled in a tiny adjoining one after attaching the exposed leader with scotch tape to the spindle and rotating the crank.

Moving as a group, we photographed derelicts, kids at play, and generic urban landscapes, occasionally isolating car tail-lights into funny faces, racing to be the first to find and frame a qualifying vehicle. Afterwards Billy and I went to his apartment where his stepfather orchestrated a wide-ranging dinner debate on world events.

I couldn't imagine reciprocating at my apartment, so I came up with a more audacious plan: I asked Aunt Bunny if I could invite Billy to Grossinger's.

"Of course. I think you're old enough to have a guest along." While conceding that my father would probably object, she brushed it off, "He'd just be scared that Billy would trip over a rock and his parents would sue us—that's all."

My promise such a thing wouldn't happen caused her to laugh out loud.

Ray picked me up after school on the Friday of spring vacation and headed downtown to collect my stepmother at her psychiatrist. As she emerged from the canopy I ran from the car to greet her. She was whistling and didn't stop, nodding hello in lieu of words. She asked if I could guess why. I couldn't, so she told me: Dr. Corman was leaving the building at the same moment, and she was letting him know I was her son too, a version of *"Yessir, that's my baby."*

I felt an unexpected surge of tears.

Then she remembered about Billy and began to list the exciting things we could do together. Right then and there I knew I had made a mistake.

I had five days of breathing room before my friend's arrival, so I made the most of them, throwing myself into an old-fashioned Grossinger's spree. The first morning in the country Michael, Jimmy, and I took sleds to the golf course and raced one another down hills. We were daredevil clowns, flying over bumps and tumbling into drifts. Then, noisy enough to be hushed by Uncle Abe, we hit the dining room at the peak of lunch, hair covered with ice balls. After gobbling down potato pancakes and pineapple blintzes, we ordered all four desserts (cookies, lime sherbet, strawberry shortcake, and date-nut slices) and went back out for a snowball fight.

All day long I was the kid from Grossinger's, the native son, carefree and reckless—I had heard the call of the wild. At night I reverted to the scion of Horace Mann, an equally sublime role.

"Richard's doing his Egyptian hieroglyphs," Michael announced. Aunt Bunny smiled and half-heartedly told him to get back to his own homework. But you couldn't change the spots on the leopard or turn Grossinger's into the Sorbonne. It was near impossible to disengage from the Hotel's mood of dalliance and return to my lettered allotments. No one there paid more than lip service to schoolwork or grades. Toys, desserts, TV shows, and whims of recreation ruled. Michael and James at best raced through an abridged version of a spurned ritual. The mere solving of a page of math problems or translation of a Latin chapter—assignments on which I spent hours per night and entire weekends in New York—seemed as alien here as decoding a document from a Phoenician shipwreck.

I'd be in my hardcore study mode, bearing down, driven by monastic pride, as from the background came decibels of *77 Sunset Strip* or *What's My Line?,* the whole family watching, a rite I adored too, particularly our last call for milk shakes, cookies, and ice-cream sodas from the canteen. For that I took a break and crossed over.

Later in the week the air turned warm, and the snow melted. It was suddenly spring. Upon hearing that I was studying biology, Milty found an old microscope somewhere in his domain and presented it to me. The next morning I collected water from the lake; then Michael and I kneeled on the floor of his room, directing sunlight from the machine's mirror through a slide. It illuminated paramecia and other tumbling creatures: a miraculous spectacle—a world inside a world, shut off and immune, invisible except for the curve of a tiny round glass.

Michael was amazed to see such beings, astonished that they looked like real animals, swimming about with a purpose. I told him that we were like Alice at the bottom of the rabbit hole after swallowing the EAT ME cake, too large to make ourselves known.

The next morning I brought the metal scope to a different pool, the golf-course water-hole. Kneeling on its edge, I used a dropper to fetch a bead of elixir, put it on a slide, and found an unexpected treasure: a bumper crop of one of the secondary phyla Mr. Moody had cursorily scooted over—dozens of whiskered rotifers whirling about and caroming off each other.

After dipping an empty honey jar and filling it with the pond's broth, I carted my sample and the microscope around and demonstrated the animalcule circus, first to a flabbergasted Milty, then to an applauding Grandma Jennie, finally to Aunt Bunny and Michael and James. Cute rotifers collided and veered among the diatoms and plankton like a cartoon of tiny cats, unaware that they had been in a pond and were no longer there. "What a delightful discovery you have made," Aunt Bunny declared. "And not a golfer would suspect it; he would only be concerned with his lost strokes."

Before dinner I returned the unviewed remainder to their home.

That Friday the event I had set into motion came to its inescapable denouement. Ray pulled up at the house. I prayed for PG's car to be empty. It wasn't. My friend got out and stood in the road, yawning. I observed him from the upstairs window: a diffident, self-conscious boy I barely knew, in a suit jacket and tie with a beat-up suitcase. He didn't belong here.

I wanted to run away, to never have been wiled by him or shared intimacies on the subway. I hated the part of myself that had been needy enough to befriend him. Michael grunted in slapstick, declaring, "Your friend looks like Iggy." He didn't, but this was no joke and I refused to meet his flippancy.

"Aren't you going to show me the Hotel?" Billy asked excitedly as I led him upstairs. I had talked about it enough; now it was at hand. I managed a nod. As my mother liked to say, "You made your bed; now you can lie in it."

For the next two days I took Billy on a tour of my alternate reality while trying to regain camaraderie. Yet habits and gestures of his that once attracted me to him now seemed pretentious and affected. As he stumbled around the rink, I pretended not to know him. Later that day I left him in a beginner's group at the ski slope while I took the rope to the top and sped down past. What an asshole I was! But I couldn't help myself. The next morning I avoided getting packed into a toboggan with him, squirrelling my way into a different group, leaving him to ride alone with a couple and their child.

Without the charisma I had projected onto him, Billy was a priggish adversary who resented my indifference and demanded courtesies I withheld. But he was also a decent kid who lost his way in the hullabaloo of Grossinger's. He didn't know how to act or what was expected of him. How could he? That was my job, his host, to make him comfortable enough to shine. Trouble was, I didn't like him anymore. So I made things hard for him much in the way I learned to do with my brother Jon—sneakily and irreproachably. I lavished more attention on Michael—on Milty, Irv Jaffee, and Jack the waiter. This was my preserve—no intruders allowed, certainly not uncool chumps or jackasses. All along I maintained a supercilious, chatty front. He kept asking, "What's wrong. Did I do something?"

"Nothing," I snapped.

It seemed that, once upon a time, through an improbable act of fate, I had escaped the Towers household and been given an unwarranted dowry like Dickens' Pip. I should have been grateful, forever humble, but I had been practicing anything but humility. Through the years of coming, as if self-effacingly, to my father's preserve I had turned into a tyrant too. Even as I gallantly pretended to disavow Richie Rich, I played him to the hilt, the owner's son. I enacted my mother's false pride, exclusivity, and misanthropy, her condescension and cruelty toward others.

New York Richard was a shy, accommodating chap, modest and deferential, nose to the grindstone. He kept a low profile and turned the other cheek. Grossinger's Richard was a careless, slaphappy miscreant, lacking, when the chips were down, even minimal decency. Handed everything, he extended and bestowed nothing. The two selves denied, even shunned each other. Together they had conspired to fool Dr. Fabian; now they kept their scheme from Dr. Friend.

I had told myself for years that Jonny was the bad guy in our household, a bully and punk; I was his hapless victim. Now I found myself just as much a bully, in fact more so. For I was not only treating a harmless friend worse than my brother ever treated me, I was proving that this behavior of mine didn't need a valid excuse; it was in my character: I was an irascible trickster, Martha's son through and through. Olivia de Havilland—as Catherine in *The Heiress*—spoke my lines when I spurned Billy exactly as she would have: "Yes, I can be very cruel. I have been taught by masters."

I didn't realize this as much as forebear its tawdry implications and unconscious guilt. I felt like a centipede exposed by its rock being turned over, scurrying to dig back into the dirt.

After three days Billy and I had run out of ruses. Our silence marked the demise of our friendship. But this time I was an undisputed jerk. I had been provoked by little more than embarrassment over a boy's ugly suitcase and provincialism.

Perhaps that's why I nursed the story of Billy and me so long, drawing it out until even Dr. Friend was exasperated: it held an unpleasant truth which I could neither admit nor stop picking at. I couldn't tolerate intimacy. I couldn't permit my two identities, Horace Mann and Grossinger's, to share a friend or, more precisely, have that friend watch me squirming between them while pretending it was business as usual. I couldn't integrate my two selves: the docile, intellectual schoolboy and the slaphappy, arrogant prince regent. Each was the other's worst nightmare.

"What are you really thinking?" Dr. Friend would ask tiredly, again and again. "You're a human being, you have flaws, you don't always behave well. Welcome to the club."

He was right, but my split selves, even as they hid behind each other, refused to come clean, to become reconciled enough to answer.

The end of P.S. 6 for my brother marked our departure from Park Avenue. Debby was attending the private bilingual Lycée Français, so there was no longer any reason to hang on at the boundary of the Upper East Side school district. We could get more space for less money on the West Side.

Placards advertising "apartments available" on façades of stone buildings had been invisible mainstays of New York, background art in an illustrated Gotham. Now as I saw them with fresh eyes, I imagined life inside each unknown monolith with six or seven cryptic rooms to let: kitchen, living room, dining room, bedchambers. Every time we were given a key and shown around, it was like briefly being another family, filling those spaces with our meals and melodramas.

After a six-week search, my mother and Bob settled on an affordable unit in a huge twin-towered building on the Park at 90th, the Eldorado Towers; we became denizens of 8C, 300 Central Park West. Bare of furniture, the space was evocative, an uninterpreted dream. A small cubicle with its own bathroom adjoined the room deeded to Jon and me. It was pronounced my study in order to allow me to work at night after he went to bed.

"How do you like it?" my mother asked.

I surveyed the gloomy nook overlooking a dark courtyard and answered without thinking, that it looked a bit cramped. That sounded ungrateful, so she slammed the door, adding a few seconds later from down the hall, "You'll learn to like it. At least you better."

Before the move she took me downtown to buy furniture for both my study and the "boys' bedroom," though she far exceeded their combined capacity—throwing in a desk and bureau for Debby, some chairs for the living room, and assorted tables. Then she charged it all to Grossinger's by having me sign the slip. We had performed this ritual numerous times—the previous summer the Hotel paid for Jonny's as well as my Chipinaw clothes. My autograph was gold.

"They can afford it," she said, "and they owe me this."

I played a prank on Jon soon after we moved in. I attached a ball of string to the cord of the ceiling light in my study and ran it under the door into our bedroom. I took the remaining core into bed with me and, after an interval of feigned sleep, tugged the string to turn on the light. Jon propped himself up. "Who's in there?" he whispered.

"I don't know. Maybe someone's gotten in the back door."

I shook the string to create a rattling noise. Then I jerked it twice in succession to turn the light off and on again.

He jumped out of bed. "I'm getting Mommy."

"No, wait." I hadn't meant for it to get that far.

I heard him waking them up, so I pulled on the string to turn out the light, but it snagged. I pulled harder and harder.

They were walking down the hall. They were opening the study door. I gave one last frantic yank! The light went out, the string came loose, and there was a crash of things falling off my desk— shades of Richard Oranger.

I pulled and pulled on that string until finally I got to the knot at its end, which I gripped to my belly like life itself. When they burst into the bedroom, I was frozen in perfect mime of sleep.

Jon and I didn't fight physically anymore. We had begun to find language for our quarrel. Before sleep we lay in bed, dickering philosophies across the room. In our customary debate he took the viewpoint that the main goal in life was to have fun. "You have to agree to that, Richard!" he insisted. "How could you not admit something so obvious?" He thought I was denying it only to provoke him.

I, in turn, argued that the point of life was to figure out who we were.

"You think you're such a bigshot," he rejoined, "with that doctor telling you stuff. You don't know anything. What you're saying is so stupid and fake! Even the rabbi calls you an infidel, but you try and get away with being superior and holy."

That was household orthodoxy: on top of my other vices Jonny was a good Jew and I was the quintessential anti-Semite. Furthermore, anything colored by psychoanalysis was discredited perforce, as if obvious to anyone with half a brain, anyone except indoctrinated fools like Richard Grossinger.

We had no subtexts, no sublimations, no shadows. Paradoxes were prohibited within ten yards of discourse. The Towers family meant to go the distance by declamations, fake moralities, and righteous indignation. They were interested in things, not their effects.

For the rest of my sojourn in 8C Jon challenged me on this point—meaningfulness over fun—not considering I might really believe what I was saying, that it wasn't a ploy to get his goat, though I could see he wasn't having much fun. In fact, he was miserable, fighting ghosts, performing other compulsive rituals.

He would put a hand on the light bulb of his desk lamp and dare himself to keep it there. When that became unbearable, he cried out in pain and asked me to remove it because he would be a coward if *he* did it. He would read the same page again and again, reaching the end and then going back to the beginning. Desperate to break the spell, he would transfer the responsibility, summoning me from across the room or my study to turn his page, to dispatch the demon so he could read his book.

He was not unaware of these self-imposed torments, but he believed he was enjoying himself nevertheless because fun was his priority. These episodes were not anti-fun, they were just a different path to gratification.

His lack of curiosity about his own nature consigned him to blind misery.

Eventually we agreed to have Bridey judge our respective positions: whether the meaning of life was having fun or solving its mystery. After we presented our briefs to her (like the golden apple at the Judgment of Paris), for a moment she stared at us in stunned disbelief. Then she snapped: "Get out of here with your tomfoolery, the both of you!"

Debby and our nurse shared a room at the rear corner of our apartment. On Bridey's nights off, she went home to the Bronx where she kept a small flat. Our sister would rap softly on the wall, which was Jon's and my room, and whimper softly, "Rich or Jonny, come." She didn't like being alone, but we were forbidden to visit her. She was ostensibly being trained to lose her fears so she wouldn't end up like me.

I would tiptoe down the hall, slowly turn the handle and open the door. I'd kneel by her bed, make jokes, cuddle her, hold her sweaty hand, and tell her stories. These were what she and I called "rescue missions." Often I'd enact shadow cartoons on the ceiling, making animal shapes with my fist and fingers—rabbits and foxes in the dim light of the courtyard. This was Squizzle Drip, the baby I once tumbled with in the park and pulled on a sled, the lone innocent in our cabal.

In the midst of my puppet show one night—my whispering having inadvertently gotten too loud—my mother was on me like a rabid dog, mauling my back through my PJ top. With hysterical shrieks, she chased me back to my room.

Her appearance was supernatural and hideous, blows on my shoulders while I imagined her still asleep. By then Daddy was awake and chose to bombard me with epithets until the walls shook. This was overkill even by Towers family standards, but they actually believed I was making her *more* susceptible to fear by comforting her.

In my attempts to win over my siblings, I was undiscourageable. Inexplicable surges of good will put magic in the air, as something leprechaun-like flowed into 8C's leaden chamber, an autonomous power and glee penetrating even its bastille. I imagined I could set everything right, reverse our troubles in one fell swoop. I knew, of course, that that was impossible; everyday I experienced the actual depth and entanglement of our situation. Yet I found myself bubbling with empathy and gratitude, and I wanted to turn the mood into something lasting.

When both our parents were off the premises and neither Jonny nor Debby was watching, I laid out treasure hunts: successive clues scribbled on pieces of paper and stuffed into hiding places (the metal rim of a lamp shade, a keyhole, the top of a table leg, the crook of a statue), each providing a hint to the next, and so on, until the grand prize, a present I bought for the winner.

My most beneficent lark was a surprise party. At Cushman's Bakery I'd buy serrated cupcakes with lemon or chocolate frosting plus a container of ice cream and smuggle these into the house. Then I arranged them on the table with simulated elegance, a paraody of a party converging with the party itself.

"Happy no one's birthday!" I shouted euphorically.

They dropped whatever they were doing. Debby would prance in delight and, as we gobbled our treats, Jon and I would tell her outré stories of the past, like the time we followed the wrong woman home from the fish market. Our sister was astonished: "God, Mom was even worse. You guys got to see all the good stuff!"

We were recklessly blasphemous, calling her the "Wicked Witch of Central Park West" and the "Ice Queen," Debby's precociously brilliant sobriquet. Afterwards, we did the dishes together, tossing plastic plates and cups acrobatically from sink to wiper to putter-away.

We were such great friends then, and there was such promise in our togetherness that a shred of it might have stuck, but our roles were as subterfuge and interchangeable as Colonel Mustard and Mrs. Peacock in the game of Clue, our true alliances undisclosed even to ourselves. Under pressure they would tell on me, every last thing I said during our powwows. They never intended to; they always swore loyalty to our trio, but Mom was an enchantress and she could wring or entice a confession as she wanted. It was decades before I learned the full extent of their betrayal.

From our new location on the West Side Dr. Friend was only four blocks away, so I began seeing him at odd hours, usually seven at night. Taking a break from homework, I grabbed a jacket and slid away, making as soft an exit as possible.

In a cross-breeze of cherry-blossom petals, I traipsed along Central Park West. The moon was above the City and I was on Fabian's incomparable quest. Even if Dr. Friend was a mercenary, I was a worthy cipher and we were engaged in a mission that transcended his fee. In a few moments life would loosen its grip and became its own daffy topic. I would throw off strangleholds, break out of ruts, roam unencumbered among the week's events, witnessing them as something else—actions of my hapless self.

Dr. Fabian had originally characterized psychoanalysis as "a method of learning why one had certain feelings and behaved in particular ways." We were, he said, bound in habits by forgotten events.

I pictured Sigmund Freud then as an immense arcane system, towering above me like the Parthenon in which I pictured Horace Mann before I went. The founder embodied the infinity and wonder I felt emanating from my own existence. ("You had such an advantage," a Horace Mann teacher told me. "You got to see the psychiatrist as magician at the only time such a thing could happen—the beginning of your life.")

The demons I had brought to the office in the West Village overwhelmed me with their omnipotence and fathomlessness. Then through Fabian's intercession, they had taken on denomination. They were still shadow figures in an abyss—just as grim and treacherous—but I had confidence he knew (or at least suspected) the manner of thing they were. Ultimately, if I reached a crossroads of desperation and implored him, he would break his pact with the oracle and spill the beans.

Dr. Friend made it clear he didn't know and never would. There was no pot of gold; there was in fact no rainbow. The spooks and phobias were my own, as stubborn and insoluble as I was, as life itself. "You expect to leave here someday with the solution," he said one day, "but, in this business, cure is called termination. When you feel able to end this relationship, that's when you're well."

On my way home from baseball practice one afternoon, I told a teammate, who also had trouble hitting, that my problem was psychological. "I'm afraid of what the ball represents."

"What do you think it is with me?" he retorted. "Just because you go to a psychiatrist doesn't make you any more psychological than anyone else." My peers had finally caught up to me.

I realized something else too: it was time to take leave of the baseball jinni. At this level, my calling was the *mythology* of line drives, not their athletic accomplishment.

Rodney had entered Horace Mann the previous year, and I got to know him in the camera club. He was its most elite and vocal member. He subscribed to the two major photography magazines and brought current issues to meetings where he analyzed elements of prize-winning photos, turning the rest of us into pretenders and novices. He wanted to strike gold with his Rolliflex, so he stayed abreast of contests and deadlines and regularly proved the mettle of his Franke & Heidecke lens by resolving random stone walls on fine-grained Pan X film. Then he printed them for every morsel of contrast and grain. Neither a member of the intelligensia nor a major jock (though he did run track), Rodney held his status by oratorical authority and a James Dean look, a persona he played to the hilt by cultivating a sneer and slouch and greasing his hair straight back from a broad forehead. He had a dense solid body with penetrating, occasionally wild eyes. At Horace Mann he was an anomaly: the embodiment of nasty charm.

I don't remember when I become infatuated with Rodney, for I knew he was special the moment I saw him. Thereafter I insinuated myself into his company at every opportunity. I used our shared history seminar with Mr. Clinton as an excuse for discussing assignments. We gradually became good enough friends for him to risk candor. My dressing, he confided, was abominable. "It's because your mother buys your clothes. You look like someone dressed by a mother." He was right. I had long suspected that she went out of her way to make me look dippy.

Thereafter Rodney tried to upgrade my fashion as well as educate me in the ways of the world. He was doing me a favor, he said, teaching me to act cool, not be a twerp.

Inspired by his wardrobe critique, I visited Saks on my own and came home with black-and-white checked jackets and powder-blue shirts of soft cotton like his. I imitated his dabs of Brylcreem and slicked down my hair. My mother was as amused as she was aghast. I had touched her 1940s funny bone—sarcasm was her main mode of humor. "You think that's handsome? You're making a spectacle of yourself, drowning in lard. What are you, some kind of greaseball now? Gonna rob a bank? And look at how you're dressed! Checkered tie and striped jacket! Gray slacks and brown socks! No one in the world wears gray and brown together."

I was on my way out the door to catch the subway to school as Bob came to observe the latest dust-up. He commented dryly, "Some of the best dressed men in the world wear gray with brown, Martha."

"He's not one of the best dressed men in the world!"

One Friday afternoon Rodney invited me home, straight on the bus from Riverdale to Yonkers—no parental prearrangements, no PJs or change of clothes. I was old enough for that kind of prerogative: fifteen. I immediately called Dr. Friend to cancel my appointment. I expected that he would share my delight, but he only reminded me that my father would still be billed. "I'm at Rodney's!" I enthused.

"I'll see you on Tuesday," he said drily—no acknowledgment of my pluck.

As Rodney and I studied together in his room that afternoon, I felt like a character in my own fantasy. We ate dinner with his parents, then walked to a movie like real teenagers. This was an intimacy I had dreamed of with Jeffrey, dabbled in with Steve for a day. We lay in beds on opposite sides of his room and talked past midnight—teachers, girls, summer camps, pranks. Just as I thought we were about to doze off, he lowered his voice for a segue of intimacy and confessed his string of sexual successes with an older woman who found him attractive. This was a caliber of derring-do no one in my circle had claimed; it was also unprecedented candor from another guy. I felt a tumult of conflicting emotions: awe, envy, gratitude, pride at our friendship, shame at my deficiencies. I was like an eighteen-year-old's little brother, not daring to identify with him because his station was so elevated.

Rodney's matter-of-fact tone implied that he wasn't bragging, just being straight because I had earned his trust. When he finally yawned, "Hey wow, goodnight," I sank into sleep and awoke to country morning: the smell of bacon and birds chirping in the trees.

As we were getting dressed, me in the slacks and shirt I had worn the day before, Rod made an out-of-the-blue promise that if I came to camp with him next summer, I would meet a lot of girls and have a good time. The implication was obvious, but he voiced it anyway: "We don't just steal panties there. We have *real* raids."

Camp Wakonda in the outer reaches of the Adirondacks was owned by the parents with whom I had just supped. The rest of the year his father was a high-school principal in Brooklyn and his mother taught grade school in Rye.

A month later, I came back home with Rodney, this time having packed a toothbrush and change of clothes. His parents were ready with a slide show. It took only a few shots to see that Wakonda was Chipinaw's antipode. It had minimal athletic facilities; instead, a bistro-like hall featured a variety of social events, each of them enticingly depicted. It wasn't an arts camp like Buck's Rock either; it was a teen country club. By the end of their pitch I couldn't imagine going back to my follies with Jay and Barry. Rod's parents might have produced a dog-and-pony show, but I would have followed their son to the North Pole.

My mother preferred to keep her flock together, and she pointed out that my father wouldn't allow such a switch anyway—the camp wasn't kosher and also he didn't know the owners. When I raised the matter with him she turned out to be correct.

"But *you're* not kosher," I protested. "We eat bacon and shrimp."

"That doesn't matter. It's in our private home. The appearance is what counts."

However, Aunt Bunny thought it was a wonderful idea for me to strike out on my own. Since she was sending Michael and James to a non-Jewish camp in Maine, she didn't see why I had to be held to a higher standard.

"What is it, Paul? Is he the only Grossinger in this family, so he alone gets to suffer?"

Not only did he give in but, when the time came, he drove me to the Adirondacks himself, stopping at a couple of resorts along the way to schmooze and talk shop. It was our first father-son junket, and I loved arriving with Paul Grossinger, owner of the Big G., president of the New York State Hotel Association. We were greeted by proprietors of lesser establishments and given tours of their grounds. I got to listen in on regional trade plans, how to stop unions, and other gossip. Then, back in the car, PG encouraged questions (and compliments) and responded with lengthy discourses on the future of the Catskills.

One look at Wakonda made me wonder if I had seen pictures of a different camp. The bunks were bare-bones shacks, playing fields nonexistent or in disrepair. Weeds grew up through the tennis court's clay, and part of its net was torn, the hem hanging loose. On the ballfield, second and third base were missing— pentagonal patches where they had once been—and the backstop had basketball-size gaps in its wire. Color War would have been ludicrous here.

On a hill near the dining room sat the fancy nightclub with its Coke machine and jukebox. Full of anticipatory razzing, our bunk made the trek the very first night. Girls clustered along the far wall, as the juke box blared away. I stayed by the side, telling myself that I was getting my bearings. Four or five songs played while I stood mesmerized.

Rodney strode across the room. "Hey, man," he called out ahead of himself, "this isn't the way it works. Nothing's going to happen if you park yourself. You've got to find a likely candidate and dance with her."

"I don't," I demurred, "see any likely candidates."

He looked around, then pointed at a crowd, "How about her? That bird over there."

At first I couldn't tell whom he meant, but when my eyes fell on the chosen girl, she was raised to instant charisma by his regard.

"Look at those tits."

I grimaced but maintained contact with his bravado.

"Now, go ahead." Mission accomplished, he returned to chatting up the raven-haired beauty he had selected.

The music played "Dream Lover" and then the music played "The Battle of New Orleans"; still no other guy approached the one Rod had pointed out. She was wearing a tight sweater, swaying to the music. Now that he had highlighted it, I couldn't keep my mind off her obvious bustiness. I wondered why *he* had passed on her, designating her my speed. She seemed way over my head. Plus, girls were too serious a matter for charity—well, maybe she was too stout.

I waited until waiting was unendurable and then, on the next slow song, I walked over and asked her to dance. She nodded, smiled, and we walked to the center of the room. I placed my arms around her, and we seesawed in a square while exchanging talk like "Where do you go to school?" and "Oh, so you're Rod's friend.... "

Her name was Phyllis, and she came from the Bronx where she went to public school. She was amazed when I told her about Grossinger's. After the record was over she returned to her group, and I sat down on my side. Rod, whom I had observed watching me the whole time, came across the room and played mentor to the hilt.

"I told you I was going to teach you how to act if you came to Wakonda. Now here's your first lesson. You've got to hold your partner really close. Girls don't think you like them unless they can feel you up against them, your hand full, like this—" he flashed a quick open palm "—and going up and down their back like this. Then, after the dance, you sit down with her. It's not tag team."

I found him crude and boastful, and I wasn't used to translating desires into strategies. Yet I couldn't articulate a credible alternative. What *did* I want to happen and what was I willing to do to accomplish it? I hadn't had success doing things my way—that led only to fantasies and daydreams—so I waited out two fast dances for the next slow one: *"I'm Mr. Blue-oo-oo-uh-oo / when you say you love me.... "*

Melding with Rodney's gumption, I got myself back to Phyllis' spot. I approached her, our eyes met. I asked, she nodded. As we walked to an open area of the floor, I put my arm hesitantly on her waist.

I had never danced close—neither Viola Wolfe nor Dave Hecht permitted it—but I saw everyone else doing it and I realized it would happen if I just moved my hand to a different place on her back. By that elementary gesture I fell into total intimacy. Her breasts grazed my chest, a friction I had never felt before. My penis grew hard, as a charge ran up and down my whole being. *What if she could feel me?* Holding her close was my only assurance *no one else* would. This time we said nothing at all. I could hear my heart beating. My throat was dry and becoming sore.

Now she moved her hand along my back the way Rod had instructed. Yikes! This was it! In my mind I reprised Mel Allen's voice: "That ball is going, going.... " I tried to picture Mickey Mantle's homers, one after another into the stands, deep into the bleachers, far back, against a pale sun; Bob Turley's fastballs, launched again and again out of his big easy pitching motion: a combination of play-by-play with deepening baseball images. These represented the old rhythm, the familiar grace of a childhood suddenly gone.

For the next several nights I danced with Phyllis and sat by the side talking with her. She told me about her school life, her parents, past summers at Wakonda. The real event was the dancing, and I learned from other guys to wear a large sweater to hide excitement.

After a few days I wasn't the only one asking Phyllis to dance. My rival was Bobby Sackett. He was my loudmouth bunkmate, so I knew that he wanted to be a dentist like his father because he thought it would make him rich; his only other ambitions in life were to own a motorboat and a sports car. He regularly beat me to the club to get a jump on the dance card. If he was late, he promptly cut in on me and then monopolized Phyllis. In order to recapture her company I had to walk over to where they were sitting and invite her to dance from scratch. When I questioned her about this arrangement, she told me that we were both her friends, she didn't favor either of us—which I couldn't understand. I had little personal confidence, but Bobby Sackett had the visage of a crocodile and was an obnoxious ass as well. Back in the bunk he talked about Phyllis boorishly, in fact only her breasts, usually the nipples, and always in the most vulgar language.

But how clean was I? Though I said nothing I would lie in bed imagining reaching inside her sweater and touching her, or having her pull her sweater over my head and letting me lick those nipples. I would feel my erection pushing to the end of possible space.

On his home court Rodney grew ever more despotic, never

deigning to join us in board games or softball, compulsively primping with a comb before the mirror as if he were Kookie Byrnes
on *77 Sunset Strip.* It was almost diabolic the way he combed and
recombed his black strands with Brylcreem, putting on layers of
aftershave lotion and doing fake karate leaps half-naked, landing
with his hand around his jock and a *kiai*-like shout—purpose, even
tone, unclear. What did he think a man was? What kind of man
did he want to be, did he think any of us should be?

On the pretense of helping his father do maintenance he prowled
the girls' camp with self-appointed authority, plucking sweethearts
effortlessly. He used the darkroom for his trysts, mainly with Harriet,
the first night's damsel, an Indian-complexioned girl from Montreal
with a sad, profound face. He didn't talk about much else—it was
girls or Pan X enlargements.

Our rapport had evaporated, our good times a million miles away.
I couldn't imagine what I had seen in him, he was obviously a lunk-
head. I had invented and aggrandized him even as I had demoted and
discarded Billy. Commuting heroes and cads, I was my mother's son.

Rodney and I had one serious confrontation that August. He
heard that a dog had treed a cat in the woods and ran to get his
Rolliflex to catch the action. Moments later I heard too and came
right behind him. He carried a tripod and set it at the base of the
tree. As I arrived he exploded at me. "This is a prize-winning
shot, you asshole. Get outa here. I've had enough of your fucking
stealing my ideas."

I ignored him for the rest of the summer. He was easy to give up;
he had become the enemy.

It was now Harriet who beguiled me. In my fantasies she was the
one I rescued, as I reclaimed my spaceship and set the old opera in
motion. She and I built a house and sat out at night on our farm in
another solar system, the Earth's sun a star in our sky.

From dozing I was awakened by a creak of doors and whispers.
This was the fabled raid. A bunch of girls had made it past the lax
guards, and they quickly matched up with guys. I could hear them
making out, giggling. I had no idea whether Phyllis was there, but
the sounds of making out were disturbing. For all the gossip, I had

never been in a room where "it" was happening. I pulled the covers over my head and burrowed deep in my romantic innocence.

The proximity of attainable sex should have emboldened me, but I was chastened by people my age making animal-like sounds. Plus I didn't relish competing with a pompous creep for Phyllis' affections. Bobby was too showboaty and gregarious. I wanted out of his idiot crosshairs. I hated how he pretended to savor our rivalry as much as her company, posing dumb challenges to keep it going. Every time I danced with Phyllis he went through a charade of allowing me a certain quota of time before cutting in. Back at the bunk he liked to tally how much he was winning by, but he'd always add, as if genteelly, "Of course, we'll let her have final say."

By then I didn't know if I cared about Phyllis that much or saw her as a person beyond the force of my desire, which at times seemed so overwhelming it would dissolve me. The trouble was, I was also offended by her presence, by the debauchery of my attraction to her more than anything in her personality or style. She was pleasant and ordinary enough, maybe a bit gross. But I didn't like her flaky temperament and contrived ethicalness, her severe countenance when viewed at a certain angle, as if she were already an old lady. In an involuntary twist one night when I was fantasizing making out with her, she turned into a wrinkled crone like the sneezing baby of Wonderland who became a pig in Alice's arms. Phyllis was as repugnant as she was alluring—now young and erotic, now a harridan and hag.

I couldn't help it. I was tending my own changeling shadow. Because I didn't dote on Phyllis like Joan Snyder, she became, in lieu of a muse, the exemplar of my kinkiness and guilt. Half the time I couldn't bear to meet her eyes as we danced and gabbed, to risk having her read my thoughts, to watch her watching me watch her and guess my motives and real opinion. I preferred my chaste daydreams and idealized trysts with Harriet.

One night, I grew irritated enough to ask Phyllis to promise to finish our dance.

"Not if Bobby cuts in."

"Well, would you rather dance with him? That's okay with me."

"Why don't you cut in on him?"

I shook my head at the stupidity of this game. When she responded to his tap a moment later, I turned and left the hall. It was Bobby who went on the next raid. He returned boasting of total triumph. I didn't believe him, but I also didn't care.

Near the end of the summer Rodney surprisingly asked another girl, not Harriet, to the Wakonda prom. It was Karen, whom we collectively had come to regard as the sexiest woman at camp. Not a girl—a dame. Tall and lissome, she wore skimpy blouses, talked like a starlet, and strolled casually with her whole body in motion. She seemed quite aware of how sexy she looked and wanted everyone to know it. "What a bod," I overhead a counselor say. "Now that's one fine piece of ass." Her face was pale and Cleopatra-like, and she smelled of spice. Although a camper, she dated counselors, and gossip had her sleeping with more than one.

She reminded me of Jayne Mansfield, whom I had met recently in the family section of Grossinger's. Accompanied by her agent George Bennett, a former Grossinger's publicist, she enthused about riding on an elephant in New York the day before—then admitted how little she liked it "but Georgey set me up so I had to follow through." Then, patting me on the head, she said, "What a cute little boy!" Back at Horace Mann, guys asked exactly which strands of hair. They wanted her direct transmission. ("I'm not surprised," a friend remarked years later. "It's not every day that one gets *Shaktipot* from Jayne Mansfield.")

Karen was dark-haired, sleek, certainly not buxom—not at all like Jayne in looks or presence—but she exuded the same bombshell energy.

"And she's fast," Rodney announced to his fans in the bunk. "She gives."

The moment when I could have appeared out of the blue and asked Harriet to the prom passed in a twinkle. A caustic, runty kid nicknamed The Bug must have had his eyes on her too because he found her at once, invited her, and won her pledge to go with him. I was astonished. He didn't come up to her shoulders and hadn't been to the social hall all summer, but he kept saying he was going to get inside her pants. By challenging such comments, I ended up in a fistfight with him. We wrestled on the ground until counselors pulled us apart.

Back at the Hotel I sat in the den and told Aunt Bunny my tales of the summer. "I feel badly for you," she said, "but you certainly make it into a great story."

She had her own news: she had hired a teacher from the Liberty public school to live in the smaller guest room because Uncle Paul wasn't around enough to serve as a father. "Your brothers need more male discipline and companionship," she explained. "In this permissive environment they are getting out of hand."

Jerry MacDonald was a former semi-pro shortstop, and ten minutes after I met him I thought he was the greatest guy ever. A marginally chubby young man with the sweetest of classic Irish faces, he continued to slay me with his playful disposition and cheerful laugh on top of feigned bafflement at local characters and high jinks. He knew how to be simultaneously fun-loving, courtly, and modest at Grossinger's, not an easy trifecta.

We spent our first afternoon together on the ballfield, hitting fungos. I had never played with anyone that good before, who hit the ball so high and far and put such zing on his throws. "You're not too bad yourself," he volunteered generously.

"Yeah, but you came down from a higher league."

"Pretty funny, but I'll take it."

Afterwards I led him on a tour of the grounds.

"This is some kind of place for an old Celtic ballplayer to end up," he said with a grin. "When do I get to wake up?"

At Christmastime Wakonda held its winter reunion at a studio in downtown Manhattan. I took a break from Saturday homework and rode the IRT down Broadway; from there I walked to the address on the invitation. It was an indifferent social hall midtown, the sort of joint I regularly strolled past without notice. I spent an hour in the crowd, munching cookies, drinking sodas, bored. After reminiscing with a few acquaintances, I was on my way out when

I got tapped on the shoulder. I looked around ... it was Karen. She was wearing a Wakonda T-shirt and had on very red lipstick. "Richie," she said, speaking my name though I had never spoken to her, "guess what? I'm going to Grossinger's on Washington's Birthday. Are you going to be there?"

"Yes," I managed. There was no other answer possible. But I had never gone there that weekend. It was my mother's birthday.

"Good. Then I'll see you."

What to do? I pleaded with Aunt Bunny. I told her I couldn't explain why but I had to come. A week later she let me know that a driver would be there to pick me up on Friday.

As for my mother, she had written me off and, to my relief, was paying no attention.

For two whole months I wove fantasies. I tried to resurrect the scent of Karen's perfume in my mind, the slink of her torso, her red lips. In reverie I would hold her, undress her. There was no way to contact or release the sensation—it was as unerring as it was unendurable.

When I told Dr. Friend, he asked again if I had masturbated.

"I don't know how to."

"There's nothing to know. You get hard. You keep rubbing. You ejaculate." His candor and lack of sentiment were unsettling.

"But I don't," I protested. "Nothing happens. It gets hard; then it gets soft." I turned to face him and cast a pleading look.

He smiled enigmatically. He wasn't going to tell.

But he made me curious, so I would lie against the back of the bathtub with the door locked, chin just above water, think of Karen, get an erection, and then rub harder. I would try to imagine her more exquisitely, invoke more intimate postures and activities, give her seductive words.

Clearly I was missing something.

When the car left me off at Grossinger's, I went straight to the reservation desk to check the guest list.

Unbelievable! She was there!

I dressed up and headed over to the Main Building. The dining room was packed. In recent years I had stayed away from night activities because I hated the dressy formality and ramped-up gala atmosphere. It was a stage for extroverts and, since I was automatically a public figure, I drew all too much attention from waiters, relatives, and pesty guests who knew who I was and wanted to greet me. Tonight I moved quickly and pretended I wasn't me, not acknowledging callouts of my name. At the spinning rack of names I located her table.

"Hey, what! Looking for girls?" snapped the assistant maître d' all too presciently.

"Nope." And I wasn't looking for girls anyway. I was looking for this one person ... and she wasn't at the table she was assigned to ... . and I was too bashful to ask the adults if any were her parents.

After dinner I searched the lobbies again, hoping I would see Karen, hoping I wouldn't so that I could go home and talk baseball with Jerry. Too late! I caught sight of her in a long white dress, standing by the dining-room entrance. I felt a dizzying rush. Each step in her direction increased a roar in my brain so that I hardly knew what I would do when I got there.

She greeted me enthusiastically but said that we should make a date for the morning because she had to meet her cousin. She stood there, taller than me, smiling bewitchingly. I turned and sprinted back to the house. Outside in moonlight, I fired stones at a telephone pole. My hits echoed like line drives.

In the morning I went straight to her table. Getting up from breakfast, she said, "Lead the way." We circled the downstairs lobby to the indoor-pool building where, through its giant observation window, we watched an underwater landscape of swimmers, some comically flailing, some diving in trails of bubbles like seals, most of them headless bodies thrashing in billows of swim wear. I showed her how to see a full rainbow by looking straight up through the glass. That was a hit. Then, at her request, we got paddles and played ping-pong at one of the tables by the pool window, not keeping score. I chased an elusive puff to the wall and had it bounce back past me—the volley itself was a blur.

After ping-pong we went to the ice rink, where she struggled along the rail while I sailed through the crowds, waving or smiling each time I passed. Though my trajectory was caused this time by attraction, my orbit was the same as with Billy. I knew that it was wrong but, as much as I wanted to, I couldn't bring myself to take her arm. Not only did I lack the poise and audacity, I couldn't handle the pulse of my own energy. We went from the rink to the toboggan, then the ski slope.

As ordinary activities gradually filled hours together, my fantasies came to feel absurd. Karen wasn't Rodney's living centerfold; she was just a mature teenager. There was a younger part of her with whom I could be pals, as we cruised my home turf and I led her and her cousins through secret passages to the kitchens where we begged cookie samples. I doubted that she had slept with Rodney, let alone counselors.

We watched the afternoon's ice show together … and then she was gone, off to dinner and the nightclub with her family. I trudged back to the house.

"What's up, Richard?" asked Jerry.

"Girls," I said, shaking my head. "Don't even ask."

"I know. Don't I ever know!"

In the morning Karen was magically transformed, a coquette again: aloof, preening, red lipstick, slinking as she walked. I was instantly hooked, thrown back into salacious desire *("Don't go home, my little darling; / please don't leave the party yet …,"* always the song for these moments). Her pose seemed so obviously intentional. Had she changed her mien or was it my wild imagination? I had lost all bearings. I couldn't read her demeanor and didn't begin to understand our yo-yo.

"Richie, I missed you last night after dinner. We had such a good time in the Terrace Room!" What was she saying? What did she mean? She told me she wanted to try swimming in the indoor pool. "Don't you think I'd look wiggly through the window?"

I said I'd go with her. *("I have waited long for the party, / 'cause I knew we'd finally meet …"* The tune drifted in my mind like a striptease: *Dun, Dun-Dun-Na / Dun, Dun-Dun-Na.…* ")

"Good. I was hoping we could have some time alone together.

I have to go upstairs and get my bathing suit. Come." She turned and glided toward the elevator, sashaying two fingers my way.

"This is it," I told myself, and the phrase echoed in my mind: "... is it ... is it ... is it"—like Mel Allen's description of a home run, building in tension to something beyond imagination, wordless and final. I paced dutifully behind her, Pip again, all fated long ago. I had been in that lobby a thousand times, but now it was astonishingly luminous and immaterial ... I felt it all might float away. I was weak; I had nothing left at core. In her tight pants she swung back and forth. She was too old for me. I wanted to hold her for even a second.

In the upper lobby Nat Fleischer was conducting his hypnotism show and it caught her attention: people in farcical stupors, the audience erupting in laughter. "Oh, look at that!" she cried out, stopping. I felt my tension snap and snag. I stood by her side in bored frustration, watching a person pretend to row a boat in the air, another take bites of a pretend apple. Why had I never noticed how dumb it was, the same gags and stunts, year after year? Nat, do something different; help me! As he held a match under a woman's hand I tried to think up a way to get Karen propelled toward her room.

Mine was such an unlikely scenario anyway—it had too many moving parts, needed too many fanciful things to go right—but I had locked onto its design and was committed beyond rationality or abjuration. Suddenly her cousin appeared and asked if she wanted to watch a beauty show that was just beginning in the lower lobby. Part of me assumed that Karen was playing out my seduction fantasy; after all, she was Rodney's alter ego. That part expected her to say no, but she looked at me almost routinely as she shrugged, "I guess we can go swimming later."

The letdown was worse than any embarrassment. Desperation was leading me nowhere as I somehow induced her to a corner of the lobby. I had not the slightest idea what I would say. She looked at me curiously.

"Can I kiss you ... sometime?" I couldn't believe the thing I had just spoken, that those words had come out me, that my flustered brain had landed on that petition, the summation of all the hope I had invested in her.

She seemed dumbfounded, unable to answer. I left my words there for a second, maybe another, but her face was still a mask, an inkling of confusion, maybe. Then I said, "I've never kissed a girl."

"Ask Rodney. I can't explain it. I'm a girl." I didn't get what she meant, but I knew it was checkmate.

She smiled and turned, leaving the troubling inappropriateness of her response in my mind. I ran full-speed back to the house, tearing my nails into the back of my hand so that there were four red bleeding lines when I arrived. Even with that gesture I couldn't reach deep enough inside or relieve the tension.

Then one night that spring in the New York apartment I lay in the bathtub imagining the moment in the lobby again, that she had said, "Well, come upstairs to my room, and I'll show you." And then.... And then.... I had this hard penis in my hand. I had a slidey bar of soap that I rubbed it against, back and forth. I was thinking ... and then the thoughts took over, casting an episode. There were three girls walking toward me ... Phyllis and Harriet too. They were shimmying toward me, in fact singing the song *Shimmy shimmy coco bop / shimmy shimmy bop* ... now silently, diagonally, then straight, with terrible and terrific motion, in precise rhythm, oddly expressionless, two steps, then one, two steps, then one, putting me in a trance.... *"Don't go home...."* Then there was only Phyllis and her full body and breasts against me... and then she reached me ... but she didn't stop.

PART THREE

TEENAGER IN LOVE

1960–1962

I

WITNESSING

The next summer I went back to the tents at Chipinaw. I was fifteen. Jay and Barry had graduated to being waiters, not a job I aspired to, so I signed up to live with the camper-counselors who ran the O.D. shack, taking shifts with them—sorting mail, depositing laundry, answering the phone. Now *I* was the one carting candy bars to bunks, playing the recording of the bugle for activity changes, enforcing Taps.

I had a new fervor for the Yankees. I listened to every game and, during my shifts, posted Major League ball scores on the O.D. shack (along with homers and winning and losing pitchers). Back when girls had dominated, baseball didn't seem as real. Now I found it where I had left it, bright and innocent, an alternate version of life itself.

The 1959 team that I had pretty much jilted was the Yankees' worst since I had been following them; they didn't even compete for the pennant. After the disastrous season, a changing of the guard was underway. Mickey Mantle, Whitey Ford, and Yogi Berra were still in their primes but approaching what PG called "the back nine," while Gil McDougald delivered an unlikely spate of early-July home runs, a portent that marked my return from the Underworld. It was as if he had been saving this singular display of power for late in his career, to reclaim me from the scourge of female infatuation. New arrivals right fielder Roger Maris, shortstop Tony Kubek, and Luis Arroyo, a National Leaguer revived by a dazzling screwball, played major roles in a revival, and Jerry's friend Bill Stafford was called up mid-summer. Just six years ago, they had been playing semi-pro together on Quebec diamonds where they got scouted by the Yankees, so it was as though Jerry himself were now on the team. Baseball was in place and special again, though something was asunder that had no fix.

I became Chipinaw's pied piper of truant and homesick kids. I arranged croquet matches with a forsaken set of mallets and balls from the equipment shed, set up treasure hunts with folded paper clues, and oversaw hide-and-seek among the trees and bushes. I rough-housed with them, made up stories with heroic characters, and played Fabian to their fears. On some O.D. shifts I had a whole troupe of Midgets with me. They helped me put mail in slots, placed the needle on the fast-spinning 78 of bugle calls (not without an occasional campus-startling screech), and slid the eyelets of painted wood activity tags over the hooks on the bulletin board. Passing our hubbub one day, Abbey flashed a rare smile, then patted me on the back.

It was a quiet, aimless summer. I wasn't alienated; I wasn't home-sick; I wasn't overly yearning. I just had no place else to go. My tent-mates cultivated a style akin to Rodney and his Wakonda crew, though in a lighter, more self-satirical vein. They talked cars, beer, pranks, and sex ad nauseam. These topics trailed back and forth through each other in a ritual of swearing, jibes, and put-downs (called "ranking," as in "Oh did I rank you!"). We were like a troop of randy chimps in pecking order, almost nothing else in play. It was jokes, sexual fantasies, boasts, and ranks.

In one popular activity, a few guys, with much banter, would select a centerfold, form an impromptu circle, and compete to masturbate onto her, all the time shouting taunts like "Man, your dick's got the pick-up of Pat Brady's jeep!" I was far too bashful to join, my own fantasies private and dear. It was the only time in my life (never before and never after) when I could intrude upon three guys with their pants open racing one another to splatter a pin-up. I had gone from the evanescence of Dr. Friend's proposition to full-out blatancy.

Insensible to the displacement and irony of their performances, my bunkmates bought the era's mirage hook, line, and sinker; they searched no further. Five tortuous years remained before the Stones would break the daze with *"I Can't Get No Satisfaction,"* would see a red door and want it painted black. People would start to realize that the appearance wasn't the reality, that they were in a trance.

My O. D. crew thought that they could *get* satisfaction from their kodacolor incubi and aphrodisiac fantasies. They viewed themselves as suave hedonists confirmed by their can't-miss colognes, collections of *Playboy,* wardrobes bunched on hangers along our tent's center pole—their personae of Jewish wise guys pretending to be Italian hoods.

A tall F. Scott Fitzgerald–looking kid named Bud, whose hair was impeccably parted at all hours, put us under his spell that July and August by relating his sexual encounters with almost eerie detachment, like how the kids at his school had paid a girl to beat them off, describing the satiny feel of her hand on his cock, the smell of the lubricant she had used. In the background Johnny Mathis sang "Chances Are," then "The Twelfth of Never."

"Unadulterated pleasure," Bud said, lolling on his blanket in a small patch of sun. But I think that he was referring to the song.

Then there was the night an older girl from Camp Ge-Wa-Na slipped through the barbed wire and, in a flouncy chemise dress, was looking for a Chipinaw counselor she knew, a planned assignation no doubt. That kind of incursion never happened—Ge-Wa-Na was effectively as quarantined as Mars—so it had a strange-love *Twilight Zone* quality, like the aftermath of a UFO landing. We watched from a distance as the alien stopped Kenny in his PJs en route back from the latrine, toothbrush and tin cup in hand. She seemed to hold him next to her as she whispered in his ear, then was gone. "She was looking for Davey Kaplan," he explained, with a far-off wistful look, "so I told her the way. She was so scared she was shaking. Man, she gave me a hard-on."

He was still talking about it a month later, ever more longingly—her perfume, the fabric of her light, loose blouse, the graze of her touch—so that we all felt, or wished, that we had been the one returning from the latrine and, far-fetched as it might have been, that she *hadn't* been looking for someone else.

One afternoon I lifted the main flap and ducked into our tent. There was Elliot with his watch off; he was clocking a contest. The target was a Betty and Veronica comic. "It's Kenny, Joe, and Bud," he told me, "and all of them are going for Archie's record."

"You guys are sick," I said. "Betty and Veronica aren't even real."

"Not real?" Elliot screamed, as they all turned to glare at me. "Did you ever look at Betty? That long yellow hair. That pair of boobs. How'd you like to feel that red lipstick coming off on your dick?"

"I'm a Veronica man myself," added Kenny. "Elliot and I have different targets. I'm taking that white sweater right over the tits. Oooh, man!"

I looked at their inspiration. There was Archie with his combed pompadour, Betty wearing a red, busty sweater, Veronica trying to entice him away with Bambi eyes, Reggie lurking in the background in a sports car. On the adjacent page both girls lolled in bikinis at the beach, and Jughead, with his "X" eyes, overdressed (including his dumb crown), was carrying their lunch basket.

"What do you think Jughead's going to do when he gets home?" Elliot asked me.

"I can't guess."

"He's gonna beat the meat because neither Betty nor Veronica got the hots for crowns."

Suddenly Bud scored. Splat, a dark spot.

In a blast of warped exuberance Kenny exclaimed, "The hairy wazoo! The big schlong!"

"No way," Elliott shouted. "Wrong target." He had splotched the "geiger counter for girls" in another comic.

It was all perfect. Archie and Jughead were who they—the ones who drew the comics—thought we were, or perhaps who they *thought* we thought we were. It *was* like an alien woman passing in the dark. We didn't know that we could feel sex any other way.

When I returned to Grossinger's at the end of summer, the fantasy bacchanal continued. I was surrounded by teenagers in bikinis and shorts—younger than me, older than me. The Hotel had become a palestra of forbidden acts and prurient desires. Glances and gestures bred throwaway nuances, equivocal arabesques, innuendos of allure exuding from tinctures of Chanel and other fragrances, designs of swimwear, even motions of shadows in cabana dressing rooms. It was a bottomless labyrinth of glamor, no satisfaction anywhere.

My own body felt gawky and exposed as I wandered through sun-worshipping crowds in my bathing suit. I was no longer a child, but was far from ready to be a man, let alone one of them. I didn't know the way into their lair. I felt its ambient power and call, but its objects were forever someone else's property. My sense of lust remained solitary and furtive, perverse and licentious too, I was sure.

The "dames" from my father's mystery novels lurked in the cabana where he had left them. I sat in a tin toilet stall, summoning my erection with visualization, spit, and soap. A mood grew: trancelike, sorrowing, hungering, blending rapacity with tenderness, compulsion and regret, always indescribably profound. I was lured by the teaser on a back cover: "Wearing nothing but too much perfume, she threw her arms around me ... and I acquiesced.... "

Behind my closed eyes the image dilated, intensified, became palpable, and then, from within a musky rose-iris whiff of Dove soap, flooded me into a strange, irresistible montage. I too acquiesced, despite my wish to remain stolid and immune.

I would go to the Nightwatch, the new teen room overlooking the indoor pool, and hang out there. I thought maybe being a celebrity would help, but it never made any difference. There were unlimited Rodneys and Buds cruising about, older and sleeker. It was all a light-speed stream of jive and double-entendre, guys and girls coming and going, gathering in groups, plotting strategy. The teen world was insouciant, vain, defiant.

Girls would be amazed when they heard my last name: "No, really? You're kidding. Wow, I'm going to tell my parents. Would you sign an autograph?" But that didn't make me desirable. Autograph? What about ... ? I could barely name it even to myself. And I didn't know what it was for *them*. It came, to my best comprehension, solely from inside me.

I would see many of them again throughout the Hotel and attach myself to their periphery, but I was at best a novelty—Pinocchio again, not one of the real boys. Then they checked out, and others replaced them. I would have taken Betty or Veronica in an instant.

In their stead I relished the Yankees' battle with Milt Pappas, Chuck Estrada, and the upstart Orioles, the so-called Kiddie Corps. A lemonade with a porcelain-lemon-tipped glass straw, sun streaming in the window ... I stretched on the couch and floated in the residue of innings. We were being transported into a new era: Eli Grba, Ryne Duren, Kent Hadley, Johnny Blanchard, Clete Boyer, Jesse Gonder. Bill Stafford pitching to Ted Williams felt like me facing Joe DiMaggio in a time machine, as Jerry called out, "How you chuck, Billy boy, how you chuck!"—echoes of Canadian infields. Billy was our alter ego, so each called strike or foul was miraculous, as if *we* had somehow popped up the Kid, the Splendid Splinter, The Greatest Hitter Who Ever Lived. I had never identified so closely with a pitcher or the projectiles he threw; they had always been preternatural events. Now as if by sympathetic magic Billy had become my baseball alias.

After taking a pair of pivotal contests, the Yankees pulled away even as the Orioles claimed veterans Del Rice and Dave Philley from the National League, too late. Yankee killer Bill Hoeft was past his prime, though Gus Triandos, the slugging catcher, remained a thorn in the Yanks' side, my Armory Ball farmhand sent packing six years earlier in the eighteen-player trade.

Existence was a tumult of nostalgia and obscure qualms. I didn't know what I felt. I was tragic and buoyant both, certain that I could not survive the wave and yet riding it in wonder. The Hotel was still a paradise of cherry-tart and chocolate-tree desserts, gardens filled with every color of pansy into whose aromas I poked my Minolta, lobbies buzzing in excitement, a cloud of cigars and cigarette smoke and wizened sharks gambling—and I was still the child Richie, getting their handshakes and greetings, summoning maestro Milty for a butter-pecan/peach malt, culling tomatoes with Aunt Bunny from among the minty leaves of yore. While everything else inside me ached, the sheer habit and density of existence bore me along.

One afternoon I sat with staff hypnotist Nat Fleischer, under a tree by the Lake, trying to explain my tangled emotions. He was charmed by my adolescent restiveness but refused to acknowledge its cosmic edge. To his mind I had yearnings and intimations because I was feeling unfamiliar hormones, that was all. "You'll always want to remember this time," he added, "because love will never be so innocent again."

I would watch him romancing guests, women not particularly attractive to me (but then he told me I had no notion of what real erotic power was). I startled us both when I came upon him a few days later beneath that same oak with an ugly but naked lady. He had the presence to pull a towel around himself, a blanket over her, get up, and politely introduce us. He was continuing to inform me, "No big deal."

Back at Horace Mann I entered Fifth Form. I was a high-school junior, sixteen. I had Cicero in Latin class, American History and Government, Advanced Literature, Chemistry, and French.

I loved trying to solve for unmarked compounds provided in test tubes: the clue in the embers. We used litmus paper, Bunsen burners, water, and known substances as filters, then wrote our guesses on slips of paper we signed before handing them in. Was it potassium or sodium carbonate (or chloride)? In one test, acidifying the unknown solution with dilute nitric acid and adding drops of lead precipitated yellow, proving iodide. Poisons as puzzles were venoms no more—they were symbols and gems, yellow as a fairy-tale crown or false sky, faithfully unpeeling their hues from within.

I played an epic prank just before class one day. I placed a patch of rubber vomit from a novelty store on the lab's polished stone counter. Doc Kroner, our absent-minded professor who had recently retired from a college in New Jersey, apparently mistook it for the real thing. He muttered, "Very funny, very funny," then (as he scrubbed), "Who didn't digest his lunch?" He finally tried to liquidate it with an acid inimical to rubber and raised a cloud of black smoke.

"The greatest prank ever at Horace Mann!" shouted Stricker, our class bookie, but I had no certainty that Kroner wasn't playing *us* instead.

Strick had made a fortune on his daily pool for how many times Doc half-lisped, half-belched during class, a disruptive spectator sport. I was sure that our teacher never caught on to *that one,* as the class went wild during the last pass of the second hand—would he belch again before it hit the twelve?—thirty dollars or more at stake!

At the start of the term my English teacher and advisor, Mr. McCardell, spoke to me about being one of the enrollees in a new creative writing program. Since the course was not for credit and there was so much graded schoolwork, few students had volunteered; now he was recruiting in earnest.

"But I don't write," I protested.

"You don't have to. That's what the class is for, to teach you."

"I have too many courses already."

"It's not a time-consuming subject, and you have a study hall when it meets. You're one of the few people here who has done any creative writing. You put out a whole camp newspaper, plus you're a science-fiction addict like me."

Persuaded by magisterial flattery, I agreed at least to try the seminar, which turned out to be composed of mostly highly skilled seniors with one foot already in college. It was taught by Kingsley Ervin, a tall, thin Harvard newcomer considered the best English master in the school. He met us relaxedly once a week at the end of the school day, weather permitting under reddening maples. The mood was more coffeehouse than Horace Mann, as classmates read from recent work aloud. I looked forward to literary aspirants offering the next installments from their binders, Mr. Ervin commenting insightfully like Dr. Friend.

What I heard was truly dazzling: a science-fiction tale about Armageddon as seen by an absent-minded God, a description of a circus and a whorehouse through the mind of a midget, a Civil War veteran recalling old battles on his deathbed. I was back in the stone forts of Central Park, spellbound by Ranger and the Bully.

Chuck Stein, my one fellow Fifth Former in the class, read elliptical, complicated poems I didn't fully understand but adored: *"August came / and September / through the grass / her / blondness was / unap-proachable in / the sand boxes / I / remember her because / she had a sandy / name."* He could have been Andrew Marvell, or e e cummings!

By the end of the first month everyone else had read from their own work twice and I hadn't presented a thing. I seemed to have forgotten I was there on the same basis as the rest and owed a story or a poem. Since the course was ungraded, I hoped that I could coast as a spectator. But Mr. Ervin scheduled me for a conference. There he prodded me with friendly enthusiasm. He told me to write anything at all, to take a chance on my own words.

When I couldn't provide apt ideas on my own, he assigned me an exercise, to do an imitation of Tennyson's poem "The Eagle." At the next class, feeling rather foolish, I recited my effort aloud:

> *He grips the ground with grasping claws*
> *Deep in lush weeds of tawny lawns....*

No one had any comment except, "Glad you at least put your toes in the water." They were being gentle.

I felt the ancient call of narrative. It was an old blend of longing and awe—an echo of Willa Cather and John Keats, the mood of walking to Dr. Friend's at twilight. But I was skittish and shy. I told myself I needed a fairyland setting to convey the strangeness and presentiment I felt. After trying out numerous landscapes I decided to set my account in a family of moles (I was only vaguely aware that a classic such tale already existed). I spent hours that weekend laying its groundwork, describing the exotic scenery around the moles' village: the fields in which they hunted, their outlying croc-odile swamp, the serpentine stream bubbling past their hut. I even drew a map of the habitat. By then I had lost my original impetus and was involved in laborious depiction of a shrew village, adjec-tive by adjective. At its conclusion I added, as little more than an afterthought, some passages of dialogue among the moles to show where my story might lead. I planned to work my mother and other family members (as moles, of course) into the next installment.

On Tuesday I raised my hand and was called upon at once. I began with gusto but within two sentences was mortified and wanted to stop—I had produced mud. Words I had chosen so painstakingly from the thesaurus had lost even their ordinary meanings because no art or logic held them together. It was not a story; it was a crossword puzzle. Everyone agreed that the mole dialogue was promising but a dead end. "Contrived" was the consensus word for my effort.

"You all share Mr. Grossinger's fault to a degree," Mr. Ervin said. "You are trying too hard to be sophisticated or cute and are not writing from your own experiences."

For weeks I backed off, but I was *thinking about it*. Something in me wanted to tell the story, the big one, but I didn't know how or what exactly it was. It was exploding silently in me like rock 'n' roll. I wanted to convert Buddy Holly and Little Anthony into Wordsworth and Faulkner. It was a tune I could almost grasp, palpable yet far away. The world was mysterious, was terrifying, was vast, beautiful, seductive, downright bizarre. How did I say these things? How did I find their theme and voice?

The Yankees met underdog Pittsburgh that year in what became an epic World Series. In game one, the Pirates eked out a win behind Vernon Law and Elroy Face; then the Bombers of yore crushed them in games two and three—only to have the Pirates pull out the following contest 3-2 behind Law again. Art Ditmar flopped a second time in game five, having to be relieved by Luis Arroyo in the second inning; meanwhile shifty Harvey Haddix kept the Yankees off-balance all day. Then Whitey Ford shut out the Pirates 12-0, leading to a decisive seventh game.

I sat in Latin, suppressing wild curiosity, my ears straining for any trace of an announcer. When I heard a roar out the window I tried to guess for which team—we were in New York, but Yankee haters abounded. Dozens of radios blared in semi-synchrony in the hallways and, as we passed between classrooms, I pleaded with anyone for a recap. Finally I raced from an exam on *Moby Dick* to the gym TV for the climax. The school had provided this outlet for upperclassmen with a study hall or their day's activities completed.

Kids were crammed onto benches in contemplation of the screen. Forget *The Brothers K.* and "Call Me Ishmael"; forget algebra—this was reality. The Yankees had come from 4-0 down to take a 5-4 lead, then increased it to 7-4. Former Philadelphia A's star, tiny lefty Bobby Shantz, the best pitcher in the American League the year I began following baseball, now in the twilight of his career, was coasting along in relief like it was 1952 when a ground ball skipped off an infield pebble and hit Tony Kubek in the Adam's apple, putting a runner on first and driving the shortstop out of the game. When Jim Coates came in to relieve, the "Damn Yankees" contingent hooted in glee. I was sure the gaunt righty, a redemptive 13 and 3 during the season, would show them, but the stringbean klutz almost collided with Bill Skowron as he failed to cover first in a timely fashion after inducing a two-strike infield chopper by speedy Roberto Clemente, an abrupt reversal of fate. What followed was shocking: a home run, two runners aboard, by unheralded catcher Hal Smith to put the Pirates ahead 9-7.

The Yankees made a valiant comeback to tie the game in their last at-bat—Bobby Richardson delivering a single and recent Pirate Dale Long following with another as a pinch-hitter. Then Mickey Mantle singled to right, making it 9-8 and sending Long to third, only one out. When Yogi Berra's smash down the first-base line was fielded by Rocky Nelson, Mantle dove safely back into first base, preventing a season-ending double play while allowing the tying run to cross the plate, a stroke of spontaneous genius and moxie that left Nelson baffled as he held the ball. A weirdness momentum was building and it wouldn't be stopped. Then, as simple as that, Bill Mazeroski cleared the left field wall off Ralph Terry in the bottom of the inning. I rode home on the subway stunned.

Friday afternoon of the following week was my turning point. I felt not just the hollowness of the lost Series but irretrievable seasons of yore. Indian summer tore at ocher leaves against a bottomless blue. 242nd Street was a paradise I could not barter—luminous trees, subtle breezes, a group from Manhattan College doo-wopping outside the station, a newly arrived train parked for its return downtown. I ran for it.

Forget them all, / But for goodness sake, / For-get me not.

I was headed home to the pit—a doleful weekend at hand. But

this time I vowed I wouldn't let the spirit die or pass unheeded. I
nursed it on the subway, kept it alive in views of the world beyond
the train, a funk I wanted to capture. I reached our apartment with
a spark of it inside me. It was the original feeling of my friendship
with Rodney, the excitement of arriving at Grossinger's ... and,
long before that, dragonflies, squirrels, toy boats, dragons, Skee-
ball, cherry blossoms in Central Park, frogs in the summer lake. It
was a hundred other elusive things. Now it sought a self-organizing
form—I needed to claim it as my own.

My illusion had been that my intellect alone could craft literary
text, that I needed moles as foils. I still didn't take the mystery, the
epiphany or the terror, seriously, as actual things, as currency for
other than psychoanalysis. I tended to view my alienation and afflic-
tions as flaws in me, mistakes: symptoms of a disease that needed
a cure. I had overlooked their sheer texture. They were the cloth
from which art was cut. What I once thought I needed to escape I
now needed to go toward, to meet head-on.

I recalled my day of baseball at Steve's, my betrayal of Billy, my
crush on Joan Snyder, my first dance with Phyllis, taking my oracle
of a "kiss" to Karen. I perceived an emergent shape in my childhood melancholy. It wasn't unequivocal or boundaryless or even
unhappy. If seen from another angle, it was rich and fissury. I had
always known that.

I had finally come to where Wordsworth and John Donne, Willa
Cather and Emily Dickinson, shared a playing field with Bobby
Darin and Dion & the Belmonts. I didn't need to pitch to Ted
Williams. I didn't need Dr. Fabian to interpret my dreams. All I
needed was to put the ball in play, the one I had been carrying since
the jinni initiated me.

All those years Dr. Fabian and Dr. Friend had said only obvious
things. They had talked about sorrow and fear, anger and guilt,
depression and arousal, as if these were commissions in and of
themselves, as if my life was solely a clinical objectification. What
about the fields of snow to the horizon across which Michael, James,
and I pulled our sleds at dusk, the vastness of other worlds I looked
at in the night sky...? What was all that saying?

It had a whiff of Jimmie Rodgers singing not exactly "Honey-comb," but yes *the lord made the bee / and the bee made the honey,"* but more, much more; it was the Louisiana Territory, the *Pequod* in the whale nursery, a colony on Mars, and *"Oh Shenando'h, you rolling river.... "*

More mysterious than life itself.

I sat at my desk and without drafting began to write.

"One Friday about the middle of last March I arrived home in such a happy frame of mind it was apparent I was feeling more than the natural relief the weekend offers at the end of five long days.... " I was describing the first time Billy and I got together on the subway. I retold our entire friendship right through the trip to Grossinger's, sleigh rides with Michael and James, rotifers, my friend's arrival with his old-fashioned suitcase ...my disgust at his presence, my shameful turnabout.

It was well past midnight, as Bob stayed up watching *The Late Show.* I had summoned myself into a storytelling spell, and I kept going even after he turned out the lights. In the morning my mother complimented me on my long stint of homework. I barely heard her. I was onto something.

All through Saturday I scorched memory into narrative. I scrawled with a pen till I couldn't bear it, took a break, sat at the window, ate a snack, then came back, my capacity not only unabated but enhanced. At intervals I rewrote my draft and typed it into an accumulating stack I hid at the bottom of a desk drawer. I had no idea what I was making, but I was addicted to it. I recreated my daydreams of Joan Snyder, my fantasies of Harriet. I took the story of Karen right to our encounter and denouement at Grossinger's. I described her as a clipper ship on the Nile, trailing Egyptian scents. I thought, "I can't believe I'm doing this. I'll never be able to read it in class."

But the deed had its own giddy momentum. By Sunday I was recalling Nanny, my first sessions with Dr. Fabian, my tussles with my brother, the bus to Chipinaw, Judy on her bike. Where was all this suddenly coming from?

I arrived at Mr. Ervin's on Monday with a sheath of thirty-five typed pages. There was no possibility of presenting this material in public, no chance at all. Right up to the last moment I was reassuring myself: "I will show him the amount of work so he knows what I did, but I won't read it."

"Mr. Grossinger, look at that. I never would have thought!" Mr. Ervin was so delighted that he halted my protests with "Tsk, tsk" and summoned me to begin without delay. The class seconded him.

I balked. I had promised myself, under no circumstances.... "It isn't really writing. It's just about myself."

"Go on. It's your true maiden voyage."

"I'm not sure—"

"Read!" I pretended to be aghast, but something had changed. In my heart I had already made the leap.

I read it as one might a fairy tale to children—slowly and in wonder. This was not Dr. Friend's office. I was making a confession of a far different order, infinitely more dangerous and more powerful. And *real*—finally, finally not Pinocchio. I dropped my concern for how intimate and shocking it was, how it was stuff I would tell no one. In my reading it aloud, it seemed not to matter.

Even as I invoked events I released their humiliation and tawdriness, my oafishnesses and betrayals—and I was inexplicably vindicated. Merely by proposing my history I had changed it. Now, as I reached page ten, I didn't dread, I actually looked forward to the more provocative sections with delight. I soared. I was in the fire.

When I finished I gazed around the room at faces of people I had never seen. We had gone fifteen minutes past the period, past the end of school; still, no one said anything. Finally Mr. Ervin turned to the most accomplished writer, Mark Weiss, the one who had composed the Civil War story, and asked, "What do you think?"

"I think it's the best thing that's been done in the class all year."

I couldn't believe what I heard. My mind was tumbling. "So that's it," I thought. The path had always been there, and I had never seen.

I couldn't have known, but I may have intuited (even then) that the magic was not the clue in the embers or a confession of secrets; it was the realization that I had been a witness to my own event, that I had never completely identified with the things happening to me. The witness was there in the courtyard of 1220 when Nanny pointed to figures blown across the night. I couldn't come close to perceiving it then, for I was a mere and mute embodiment of that dark. The witness observed someone else peeing on the floor and daydreamed in my body. The witness kept me out of trouble but also kept me out of life. Compared to this, Dr. Fabian's symbols were cotton candy.

The years of dialogue with doctors had at last brought forth their antithesis—and their fruition—that my life need not be the raw material of dreamwork and therapy, need not be sustained only by symbols; it was something in and of itself.

"It seems so simple," Mr. Ervin said weeks later, "but it's not simple at all. I dare anyone else in this room to try it."

For the remaining years of high school and beyond I wrote my story. I now go back to what is left of those first raw pages, the ones my mother overlooked when she discarded my scrapbooks and the other relics of my childhood. I recover episodes I no longer remember. Here, for example, is a minor scene from a meal that winter:

> "How's the food?" Bridey asked as she dished out my share.
>
> "Okay," I managed weakly.
>
> "Okay?" Bob protested. "I think the food is spectacular when you cook it."
>
> "Yes, it is, Bridey," Debby added.
>
> "You don't sound too talkative tonight, Richie darling," my mother said after the flurry ended. I nodded and did not look up. "Did school go okay today?"
>
> "Yep."
>
> "Are your grades okay?"
>
> "Yep."
>
> "Well, Richie doesn't have anything to say tonight. How about you, Jonny dear?"
>
> "Great. We played football after school. I got an A on my history test."
>
> "That's wonderful, Jonny."

"It is," Bob said. "Richard has compiled at enviable record at
Horace Mann, and I only hope you can emulate it."

What strikes me now is how ordinary, even banal it was. At the
time I imagined exquisite subtlety in my mother's inquisitorial
misdirection; in Bob's hostility masked by flamboyant irony—that's
why I recorded it. But the real issue, the only issue, was how I was
always on the outside of a sanctum, a family, they sought to protect
against me—*my* family. Back then I assumed it was because they
hated me; now I know they didn't hate me at all—I was part of
them, though not a part they wanted to admit. I lived out a terror
they desperately—every instant in fact—struggled to conceal.

Too wide awake for her own sanity, my mother had woken us to
the darkness of the universe with a kind of Dostoyevskian majesty.
She crumbled under its epiphany, for the true cavernousness was
mind-boggling. The others didn't see it or want to see it. Now I
understood the difference: *I did. And that's what I was loyal to.*

Only in flickers of déjà vu does the person writing this memoir
come back to me now. I realize I was his only hope, his excuse
for persisting. He was writing to me as much as to anyone. I alone
could rescue him from his drab, forlorn world, and for that reason
I reinvoke him and bring my imagination and healing back to
him then, now—even as then, then, I called out to myself in some
unimaginable future, to document the desolation and ensure that
I survived.

2

ANDROGYNY

One afternoon, not long after my maiden voyage in Ervin's class, I was sitting in the Horace Mann cafeteria, doing my Latin translation, when a songful voice from the next table caught my attention. I looked up and saw a boy talking to his friends. He was acting out an episode for someone, waving his arms, stomping back and forth, making pictures in the air. He flashed a smile, then turned melodramatically grave. What happened next was mysterious. I knew it was "him." The recognition was so concise and instantaneous, the feeling of adoration so utter and primal, I felt as though he had always been there and I had never seen him.

His face was deep and elfin, a glimmer of Gil McDougald's rookie card. His voice flowed melodically over the scales.

His name was Keith, and I recognized him as a presence at Horace Mann from the class beneath mine, a regular in plays and the glee club. I had previously noticed something mercurial, almost fiendish, in him as he strode the hallways, delivering messages from offices to classrooms, a student volunteer. But I had never paid attention, he was just another kid. Now he exuded charisma and charm.

I began to obsess about him. He became the central focus and devotion of my life. Every time I saw him I was startled, as though I had encountered a famous person in the wild. What could have caused such a spontaneous metamorphosis?

Lying in bed at night I wove fantasies around Keith. I imagined him and me as roommates in a cottage by the ocean. We watched waves as they crashed in. I instructed him in playing Ocean Ball.

Then we rode surfboards together and rolled in the foam. We dried each other off with towels. Afterwards as we lay in the sun, and he teased me about my obsession with the Yankees. There was a grassy yard with wild blue flowers, a table on which a pitcher of lemonade sat. It was our home.

At my Friday concerts I crouched by the Magnavox, invoking Keith as gently and palpably as I could—his yellowness, his whimsy and irreverence, his farmboyishness along yon ancient Scottish burn, master of the lyre.

And the Platters sang "Twilight Time" and *"Oh yes, I'm the great pretender … / pretending that I'm doing well."*

Then Brook Benton: *"Go on … go on, / Until you reach … the end … of the li-ine.… "*

As music poured like honey I felt as though I could see a billion miles in my head. Through the stars, to something else … where nothing should be.

When I went to Grossinger's that Thanksgiving I brought Keith imaginarily beside me in the car, observing everything a second time through his eyes. "See," I said as trees and homes near and far swept by in the gathering darkness. "This is the route we take. It's the route we've always taken since I met my father and Aunt Bunny."

I had brought along samples from my chemistry class, so Michael and I soaked pine cones in the elixirs, then looked for the faint reds of iron and greens of copper as they caught among logs in the fireplace.

That fall my brothers and cousins had become obsessed with speed skating. They all had new long blades and looked so cool as they crouched low to the ice, whipping around like Irving the Fox. When I told Grandma, she called the pro shop and arranged for me not only to get fitted for my own but receive lessons.

The rink had been a recent no man's land for me. With its over-wrought show music, stumbling galoots and prissy ballerinas cutting backward against the traffic, I felt no incentive to go there (except occasional lassitude). It was the site too of my debacles with Karen and Billy.

Now I saw the ice in an entirely new light: it was a racetrack.

"Look at these, Keith," I mimed silently as I sat on a bench and laced the boots. Then I strode along the rubber mat, feeling the full fulcrum of my blades.

I had used figure skates for years, so I found it almost impossible to make headway on such elongated stilts. I was landlocked on the ice when my teacher, an Austrian named Kurt, arrived in a spray of ice shavings, grabbed my arms, and guided me around while I emulated his stride.

Perfecting this motion on my own became the focal point of my weekend. While my brothers whizzed about the empty rink, I worked up to a moderate pace near the side until Irv Jaffee intervened: "Wait till we close. Otherwise, you three are going to kill someone, a paying guest most likely! I know about this stuff. I won a few races in my day." Yes, two gold medals in the 1932 Winter Olympics!

Speed skates weren't allowed at the rink in Central Park, so I had to wait till Christmas to test mine again. My brothers had moved on, but I was determined to race. After breakfast, bearing my runners in mittens, I headed to the rink and immediately sought out Kurt. The morning was crisp and bitter, a deposit from the night's near blizzard still crashing down from branches at irregular moments. A frigid Catskills wind bit my skin. "Yes, I'll teach you but not today." He grinned and pointed, "I got someone better." He called over an older man in a Grossinger warm-up jacket. I didn't know who this was, but I read the name over his pocket. Long ago I had watched him pass a pack of skaters in Madison Square Garden: Ray Blum was a hero from the dawn time.

I felt as though DiMaggio himself were coaching me as we stepped onto the ice at closing time. He got me to bend my ankles more, pull in my butt, lift my feet without dragging the blade tips on the ice, whip out my strides, crouch perilously near the ice at the corners to pick up speed, his own motion silken and seamless as he swallowed the rink in great strides. "There's a trick to this," he said. "You have to trust the blades, learn the meaning of the glide, of quiet speed. You have to go slow to go fast. Save your effort till you need it."

I joked that I was a sexagintesimal behind him (the minute behind the second hand), but I experienced the old spooky transference, a magician bestowing his power. I had learned baseball, swimming, and dream interpretation that way; now I was receiving a dollop of Ray's grace.

After a few days of silent lessons, the Lone Ranger was gone without an adios. He never gave a head's up or said "See ya" or "Hiyo, Silver and away.'" But I took that as a sign of transmission and trust.

Now that I could zoom, I practiced in between sessions after helping Kurt and Irv with the resurfacing. I was cultivating an inner rhythm and velocity I had long craved in sports: in baseball, in running, in tennis. I had never thought to find it on blades.

Dating actual girls seemed impossible, yet at times, the lure of "acquiesce" would envelop me. Back in 8C I'd lock myself in my teeny study bathroom and follow some fantasy, a story of a girl spontaneously investitured, glimpsed on the subway or recalled from camp or Hotel lobbies ... barely breathing, my lips half open, my heart thumping, the inexplicable hint of a sneeze in my nose. I would go *into* it, *through* it, and out the other side, back into my familiar self eased and transformed. It was a trance of mutation I never would have thought possible had I not experienced it in the flesh. Its residue was a warm sap that in no way betrayed the blood and ecstasy behind it.

This was the same darkened privacy in which I transformed my Minolta images in a black plastic churn into strips of indelibly lucid windows—negative derivations of what I had imaged through the lens. After viewing them in the twinkle of alley light, always surprising, always exactly what they should be, I hung them on the shower pole to dry.

So, in that single small bathroom sitting on the same stall lid, I presided over two crystalline transformations, one photographic and chemical, the other made of pure ether.

Personal acts in private space were my solace then, my deliverance from household mediocrity. I invented a different series of games for the larger bathroom, including a football one using a broken corner of soap as the ball, the squares on the floor as players, the lines that formed them as yard-markers, and the circle inside the ring-handle of the hamper for finger-kicking extra points and field goals. A well-worn chip of soap would spin along grids and land perfectly in a distant square between the field markers—a forty-yard completed pass (if it touched any part of a line, it fell incomplete). Then, clonk!, a flick of two fingers whacked the extra point against the hamper.

I devised a coin game for sitting on the toilet, using the different-sized squares and rectangles of the floor as targets and bouncing a dime high off the walls. It played like a Skee-ball alley with flat boxes instead of raised rings. The smallest square counted for six; the rectangle, three; and the large square, one. I had twelve shots to get twelve points (or lose) in a series of best four-out-of-seven matches—Gil McDougald's number still the duodecimal basis of all contests in my mythology. Very little skill was involved. Despite some amazing streaks—the dime bouncing off the tub and walls and spinning or rolling crazily—the game was pure lottery and spectatorship.

Though I could reverse the outcome of the 1960 World Series a thousand times on the bathroom floor, none of them counted, none of them were recorded or remembered; but one day that would be the fate of the 1960 World Series too. No one alive anywhere in the universe would know that it happened.

Days at school were interminable. In a new obligatory body-building program I was assigned to alternate periods of weight-lifting and swimming. I felt puny and defective as though my bones might break instead of the barbells go up.

My face became so covered with acne my mother took me to her dermatologist. From then on, every other week, I'd visit him myself to have my pimples popped. There was no gentility to his process. He wrapped a hot medicated towel over me and went pimple by pimple with a pin, scrubbing with gauze to get out the goo. As he worked he lectured me on diet, skin care, and the lotion Phisohex. Not only did the treatments hurt like hell, they scraped against my ennui and irritation, abrading them into something more hostile and morose. He was touching my very mask.

At home I'd work his white liquid (with its paradoxical aroma of bubblegum) into my skin. Constant soreness around my cheeks and eyes and a mottled appearance became part of me. My acne was not just an ailment; it was how I felt about the world.

When Uncle Moe showed up as a rare dinner guest that December he presented me with an electric razor—a ritual conferred on him as an honorary kinsman. I had hoped to avoid that deed forever, but as I checked the mirror I knew it was time. A faint fuzz of black bristles marked the same unknown boy as the sores.

Afterwards the three adults took me downtown for a preview of the movie *On the Beach*. We were among a small number of people in a skyscraper office, my mother having scored comp tickets through the Fontainebleau.

After human life on Earth was annihilated by bombs and ensuing radiation, the lights in the room went on, startling us back to reality. I blinked and stretched. I had just seen the end of time. Now we had a deferment, but for how long?

The elevator got stuck on the twenty-seventh floor, and my mother became hysterical. She was always emotionally right if off-target in just about every other way. Two of the men in our group pried open the door and gate and gave us each a hoist. After we climbed out, we took an adjacent elevator down, Martha giddy and trembling.

In my review for the *Horace Mann Record* I proposed that the chance event of a Coke bottle dangling in a window shade (sending out a signal drawing the post-holocaust submarine crew to Australia) replicated the "accident" that might have set off the war in the first place—and might still.

I considered nuclear war my topic. The "bomb" was conceived when I was and cast its shadow over my life. It would lie dormant for months and then renew its grim reality with a start. God, it could happen, the end of everything, *this very minute!*

The previous summer at Chipinaw I had walked around in a daze for two whole weeks after a red-haired counselor known as "The Mad Hatter" swore in one of his wild soliloquies we would never get to be adults, any of us. Though the guy was by consensus nuts, his words couldn't be shaken off as quotidian Chipinaw blarney: "They're going to blow it all up one of these days, and all of our fat asses with it! Just by accident! There isn't a chance in hell they won't!"

How had I lost sight of that cardinal fact? This whole unhappy parade was leading to oblivion. It would be like *On the Beach,* the last straggling survivors singing "Waltzing Matilda" to revive their flagging spirits. Would I get to be even seventeen, let alone twenty?

When I argued against the bomb, my parents defended it vociferously, claiming that the attack on Hiroshima ended a horrific war and saved lives. "You didn't have brothers in the Pacific!" my mother snapped. "You don't know what war is."

So I quoted her lines from *Night of the Auk,* a blank-verse play that I had watched on TV (I had just gotten the script at Womrath's): *"We broke their back with one quick crunch / And cheered a reddened flag of sudden victory. / But on their streets, and in their houses, / In the churches, schools, and hospitals, / In the dentist office, in the playground, / The flame of our treachery to humanity / Seared the flesh, the blood, the very genes / Of four ferocious students armed with all the terrible retribution / Of their abacus, textbooks, and lead pencils. / ... What have we done in all the intervening years, / We, high moralists, hope of Earth, / With that great treachery crouched upon our conscience? / What mass confessional has absolved us?"*

As I concluded my oratory, Bob applauded, calling out, "Bravo, bravo." Yep, Arch Oboler was on a Faulkner-like roll when he pulled those stanzas out of his measured rage. His metrical beats of remorse never failed to send tingles down my spine. My stepfather got it, or at least wasn't blind to the issue; in fact, he carried around a copy of the *Record* with my review and shared it with assorted colleagues, including a professor from Grinnell he met on the plane.

But my mother sat there that night as I read from Oboler, stewing and looking pained. Then, rising promptly from her chair in a demonstration of relief that I was done, she declared, "He always has to be superior, but he can't get more than a B+ in English!" And she bumped angrily against me as she vacated the room.

On the Beach was no aberration or quirk. It was part of a general awakening. Suddenly, it seemed, everyone in my circle was hearing the sirens the way I had for years, awaking to their implications with newfound horror. That December in the auditorium the whole of Horace Mann was addressed by a visitor from a group called Moral Rearmament. I had no idea what the name meant, but a number of clued-in intellectuals were incensed, so I joined their group indignation. A sour man in a blue suit evaluated in chilling terms how vulnerable we were to an attack by the Russians. He said that they had submarines lurking offshore even as he spoke. "They mean to do it. Have no doubt about that, young men." He wanted the United States to expand its arsenal and strike first.

The fatal pronouncement having been uttered, I sank into my familiar holocaust gloom—a dull, defiant paralysis, as the speaker droned on, itemizing the type and degree of weaponry we'd need to defend ourselves. I felt sullen and defeated. For years I had been afraid of air-raid sirens and confrontations with China or Russia, but I hadn't fully grasped the sort of world we were in, that nuclear war *was taken for granted,* that everything special or important was a diversion from the inevitable clash of warheads. It was so vast and overarching that it hardly seemed worth trying anymore. What did Shakespeare or the pennant race or the Hit Parade matter? All that counted were those two-bit radioactive canisters by which all outcomes would be reduced to the same cipher, though not before—we had just read John Hersey's *Hiroshima* in English class—flesh was burned off and eyes melted. Why were we even born?

Then partway through the inventory Bob Alpert rose to interrupt: "So what you're saying is that they can wipe us out four times over and we can only wipe them out three-and-a-half times!" The auditorium erupted in a spontaneous ovation.

"Are you a Communist, sir?" asked the speaker. He was drowned by hisses and catcalls. Each time he began again the uproar resumed.

We were all secretly on the same side! We were cheering for Tinkerbell to get relit! I had never before felt so proud of my generation.

The next day Headmaster Gratwick reprimanded us about courtesy to guests, but it was unclear why this speaker, so different from anyone else Horace Mann had ever invited, should have been allowed to plague us with his misanthropy. Bob's stand was a heroic moment, not an incivility. He should have been given an award. Not only were atom bombs horrendous weapons that could incinerate our lives in an instant, the invocation of their reign of terror *was itself a lethal force,* neither exemplary nor neutral. It had the aim of browbeating us, whipping us to venom while turning us numb and helpless.

Moral Rearmament was a sales pitch fueled cynically by fear. When one of us seized back the power in all of our names, I realized that my dread of this man was greater than my dread of the bomb. I would rather not live at all than be in his thrall.

Even the holocaust had a human mask. Its terror was mutable.

The Moral Rearmament speaker faded. Life returned to its rhythms, patterns, and moods. The minutes, hours, and days resumed their spell, as the things that had occupied them became real again. The intruder, who had briefly seemed larger than reality itself, dwindled into a shrill nobody, a mouse in suit-and-tie that roared. Existence was too dense to be coopted for long by an Idea.

All that winter I was enchanted by Keith. Hardly understanding the impulse, I honored his presence as that of a mythic being: Cupid the boy. He was my amulet, his light brown hair combed in a self-conscious wave across his forehead. When I glimpsed him in stray moments I would commemorate these as omens and signs, for they changed the color of daylight. It was as if Athena suddenly revealed her true nature to a mortal, turning autonomously from a woman into a goddess. Of course, only the chosen one saw.

Keith was ostentatiously booting his schoolbag in front of him. With a heraldic flourish he was Mercury delivering a message to my class. The rest of the hour vibrated at a different frequency.

One Monday I arrived at school feeling itchy and sore, every blackhead burning, subway stench in my pores. At lunch a voice from behind the desserts said, "What do you want?" I stared, for a moment, into the eyes of Keith.

In chapel choir Keith's Latin solos filled the auditorium,

transmitting hope and consolation. In myself I found only his shadowing—flat and unlivable. In him, it was realized, vibrant.

The name I gave this event (when I described it in my writing or
talked to Dr. Friend) was borrowed from how I thought of Rodney
once: Keith was my "idol"—today I would change it only to its
Greek root: *eidolon:* "apparition."

One afternoon he starred in a Gilbert and Sullivan production. I
brought along a small battery-run recorder. That night, after everyone else had gone to bed, I took the machine into the bathroom,
ready for a numinous performance.

Most of the windows in the courtyard were dark. There was an
old man reading a newspaper, a woman in a black evening dress,
part of a body at a kitchen table with flowers—all made memorable
by the fact that Keith was about to manifest, all frozen in time by
the hissing blank at the beginning of the reel. Then, I heard him.

I have no idea what words he sang, but I made my own lyrical
gibberish out of them, then turned to the terse magnetic strip again
and again, for luck and confirmation: *"They are, they are, the quarums*
they seek. / They are, they are, and they are. / They are, they are, the
quarums they seek. / Statitimski is hidden afar, yes afar."

At Christmas I hung out at the Grossinger's Nightwatch, but there
were always cooler, quippier guys. One afternoon, in fact, the whole
rock-'n'-roll group The Tokens who sang, *"Hush my darling, don't*
fear my darling," swaggered into the room looking like a street gang
and declared themselves in their Brooklyn accents, "Where duh
girls? *The lion sleeps tonight, baby!"* The "girls" were totally snowed.

Departing the tattered social realm, I took my martyrdom to a
more pagan temple. I fetched my skates and snuck into the closed
rink. I switched on full floods, picked some pop music from the
rink's limited repertoire ("Witch Doctor" and the score from *West*
Side Story were my favorites), and raced around for a half hour or
so in the frigid black. It was my father's hotel and I could do what
I wanted, break the rules until he found out. He would have been
appalled at the electric bill and insurance liability, but no one else
dared stop me.

Stars above the golf course, the glowing crystal became a chapel, its frozen surface mine to inhabit and strafe—my track of Martian-canal ice. I was racing alongside Ray Blum, ready to make my final charge into the lead, Grossinger's written diagonally on my soul. But this wasn't any ordinary meet or trope of Silver Skates. I was at one-third terrestrial gravity, flying above the surface, igniting and outstripping my melancholy, converting it to pleasure.

The threads I cut were the grooves of my life. Almost mechanically I set before me figures of my life: my mother, Jonny, Rodney, Karen, Keith; I blended with them to enact greater swiftness, ripping the ice in quickening steps, pushing tempo beyond breath, beyond agility, beyond stamina: *"I told the witch doctor / I was in love with you / And then the witch doctor / He told me what to do."*

Zoom, clip the corner low, trust the blades, make myself one with my own velocity.

"He said that / ooo eee, ooo ah ah, ting tang / Walla walla, bing bang."

I invoked and dispelled the fog of studying, the core loneliness, so many unrequited desires—all translated into an orbital dance. Those I wanted to defeat I defeated. Those I wanted to love became part of me. Those I didn't understand my feelings for, I tested.

"Tonight, tonight / won't be just any night...." was my absolute theme song, when I could get myself up to my fastest. Turntable to loudspeaker to skates, it was Keith and me, dark sonic arcs hitching breaths of ice, hollowing my skull, blades rasping, tearing for a quickening grip at corners. They held my fury and apotheosis. It was euphoric, if a bit hyper.

I wouldn't have begun to understand the psychic proposition of chakras, but I recognized their effects in my being. I was raising the overall vibration of my aura, changing the color of my feelings from brown and black to indigo and phosphorescent violet. Plus, this was an era when athletic accomplishments were a mark of being a guy, a viable human being; I was graving an indisputable male signature.

I was north of Horace Mann, north of New York City, north of Westchester and its parties, north of the subway, beneath the Milky Way. And then, soaring to epiphany: *"Tonight there will be no morning star...."*

That was the droplet at my heart—a faraway sun that gave light to unknown worlds.

On New Year's Eve I sat at the teen table dateless. When the lights went off and "Auld Lang Syne" began, I imagined time itself evacuating through the walls. These were famous seconds, rustling by like pages of old books. I ducked through the fire door into sub-zero night. From roofs and trees, snow glistened. Icicles hung in moonlight as if on Luna itself. A sudden wind shook frozen pods like rattles on the uppermost branches, as frigid a plaint as I had ever heard. When the Earth performed such a requiem, I was a mere ember, a speck of carbon sustained by desire. I took off my jacket and tie and unbuttoned my shirt and collar. I let in the icy serpent. Then I ran, the Hotel's din fading under my escape velocity.

Through frost flowers on my bedroom window a single streetlight radiated delicate grains. I lay there, engulfing Keith in my warmth, or was it I in his?

I spent the winter trying to call Keith's attention to me. I typed up slides for Wednesday sings, putting unusual lyrics on them, which I submitted anonymously with symbolic messages (which, of course, he would never decipher). I joined the carnival publicity committee and set up an exhibit, using a battery-operated guzzling monkey with a beer can, a banana, and an expanding stomach. Keith came by, stood and watched, then said, "Isn't that sexy" to a friend. Puck the imp! A score!

Another time, I heard him mutter as he was walking down the hall, "Don't tell me he's done it again." Each syllable and cadence was precious.

But Keith was changing inside me. I tried to keep him innocent and unsexual like the kids in my old spaceship drama, but he had an implicitly androgynous quality. Four months after I transfigured a pixie-like schoolmate into an eidolon, the other shoe dropped. I imagined him driving a car and picking me up outside my apartment building on a Friday afternoon. He would laugh and look into my eyes. As I played with his hair, his smile melting mine, he became something that was neither boy nor girl and lay atop of me, swallowing my desire in his icon.

Beyond this vision a scenery formed on its own, a cornfield and haystacks, moon-yellow—the shade and fragrance of straw I associated with him. He was wanton and luminous; he arose from a leather trunk in the attic; he played the panpipes. He held me prisoner in his room, drawing me unto himself. In this fantasy he was no longer Keith my friend and guide; he was the resolution of my ungauged desire.

I wanted to lose whatever was left of myself in him. He could jump on me, beat me up, and that would be okay, for soon enough I would be burnt away and nothing more than part of him. I was a shred of steel filing, and he was a dense, raw magnet, drawing me forever unto himself. He was still elfin, but gamy and seductive too. And now he knew my reckless hunger for him.

I checked the sperm from such fantasies to see if it was bloody or dark.

I arrived five minutes late at Dr. Friend's, so the door from the waiting room was open. I walked in and placed myself on the couch, fixing my eyes on the photograph of broken pottery.

"I'm sorry I'm late. The train was incredibly slow. It just took forever getting to 168th Street."

"There's no need to be sorry." His voice as always detached.

"Of course there is. I wasted some of your time." I was parodying a tone he often took.

"If I were you I would think more carefully about whose time is being wasted."

"Okay. One point for you."

"My, aren't we angry today. Angry, sarcastic, and bitter. What's all that about?"

"Nothing."

"Nothing?"

"Nothing at all."

"Well, what are you thinking about?"

"Only about how the damn train slowed me down."

"Was it all the train's fault?" I didn't answer. "Was it really all the train's fault." I stared at the second hand sweeping away our time within the clock on the far wall. The radiator hissed, the odor of its steam musty, trite.

A few minutes passed and then I said, "I hope you didn't think I was going to sit around here and answer stupid questions about trains all afternoon."

"You were the one who brought up the train."

"Well, you always tell me what I'm thinking. You do, don't you? Well, if you're not going to talk, I don't see why I should."

I lay there quietly for a while and then unwittingly closed my eyes. A drowsiness engulfed me....

I awoke with a start—it was dark outside. I was totally disoriented, my hour almost up. I felt instantly contrite. "Hey, that's the first time I ever fell asleep here."

"There's always a first time."

"I feel better now."

"Well, you escaped. You used up the whole session without talking about the thing that's bothering you."

"I feel sad."

"Good. Maybe we can use the remaining time and accomplish something."

"What should I talk about?"

"What did you dream? Do you remember?"

"Nothing really."

"Oh come now."

"I was in the country somewhere with Keith. Late afternoon. The light is very green."

"Any perceptions."

I saw the second hand erasing my last minute. I recalled an apple tree, Keith beneath ... as if Keith were me. Then I remembered. "It just faded into a bunch of cartoon characters dancing around and jumping in and out of the back elevator shaft of our building."

"Where were you?"

"Running around the hall trying to escape from them." There

was no reply. Then the overhead light clicked on, signaling the end of the hour.

I heard him getting up. I turned and looked right at him. "I'm having fantasies about Keith. I'm thinking about him as a girl … and the fantasies are *so strong.*" I was pleading with him now. He was expressionless. I dropped my head and smiled at the wooden soldier on his desk. "I'm afraid I'm.… "

"You're afraid of what, that you're a homosexual? Nonsense. Everyone who's ever lived has had those fantasies. A boy, a girl, what does it matter in the mind? You're reaching out to something unknown, something you want and don't yet understand. And you miss the obvious—that thought and action are two separate things. You can think whatever you want, and it doesn't mean you are likely to do it or that if you did, it would be the same thing." He paused and considered. "It's really that you are so guilty—guilty of what you are, guilty of what you aren't. What you want you hate yourself for wanting. You obsess, and then there's no way out. Perhaps that's the reason for Keith. He's not real, you know. No doubt you have created him in order to share the burden of your guilt."

I froze in sheer wonder. After weeks of sterile, boring sessions the face of the master shone again, reminding me of the power of insight to heal and transform. In recent months I had become such a wise guy, a big shot—Richard the star writer, Richard the psychiatric pro, Richard the speed demon. Now I bowed to the inevitability of the unconscious, the power of the unknown.

A realization born once of a chemistry set spilled in a dream had come again. A long, entangled mystery unravelled, exposing Keith for what he was—another semblance, cast against a lifetime of mystery visitors. He was a feeling I had always had, a vagrant figure encompassing the allure in the world. No wonder I had chosen a magnificent child playing the flute to represent him. The Keith who bounded through Horace Mann and sang with the voice of the forest was my blond and wild twin in whose seductive grip, dark sparkly "I" became beautiful too. In my hunger to encompass him—and girls through him—he had become the captive side of desire, yet always driving me toward who I was.

I couldn't say that then, so I said, "There's nothing bad about these thoughts? I'm not doomed?"

"Of course not," he smiled back. As I went through the door he added, "Why do we always accuse ourselves of the worst?"

"Because we're crazy or something," I laughed.

He looked up startled, then gave out his deepest-ever sustained guffaw. "See you Friday, you funny kid."

3

MOON RIVER

It became spring. I wore light cloth suits to Horace Mann and awaited the new baseball season with the ardor of childhood. It was the year of American League expansion—there were two new teams, the Los Angeles Angels and a second Washington Senators (the first one now in Minnesota), which gave the pennant race an air of magic. Since the number of teams had always been fixed, it was as if two new planets had just been discovered in the Solar System. How would they play and look in the standings?

From the first exhibition game I was clipping Yankee box scores from papers and pasting them in a datebook with clear Magic Mending Tape, the piny smell of which still reminds me of spring 1961.

Soon after the regular season started I stumbled on a gold mine: Grossinger's shared a box at Yankee Stadium with Eddie Fisher's company, Ramrod Productions. Not only was it rarely used, but the strips of tickets were kept in a binder in the Hotel's New York office, currency for the taking. From then on, every Friday that the Yankees were home, I would ride the subway straight to 57th Street and then call a number of friends depending on how many seats I had. A lanky sports fanatic from history class named Jake had become my fungo partner and Yankee pal; he was always my first choice.

In our cubicle behind the visitors' dugout we were surrounded by hardcore season ticket-holders with their spiral-bound scoresheets and pages of stats. They would debate strategy as the game unfolded.

If I inserted an opinion they might pause in curiosity, hear me out, and, to a one, dismiss it. But they had short memories and would invite me back into their colloquium. It was a burlesque routine: they would argue, bicker, yell at each other, then turn to me for a verdict. Whatever I offered they opposed in chorus: "No! No!" "How could you…?" "What are you, crazy?"

One afternoon that spring, I predicted that Johnny Blanchard, who hadn't batted all year, would get a key pinch hit. Joe Glazer, the resident expert, was furious at the time that Ralph Houk had sent him up with the game on the line. He said, "Aw, c'mon, kid. Whadda you know?"

"Third-string catchers love third-string catchers," I jived.

When I proved right he gave me an irritated swat, not able to conceal half a smile.

My mother did not interfere with my schoolwork anymore, but junior year from either a misunderstanding on her part or hyperbolic rhetoric by Mr. McCardell on parents' visiting day, she got it into her head that my entire academic career hung on my junior "Profile."

The "Profile" was meant to be the most challenging English assignment of our tenure—a biography in the style of *New Yorker* pieces. From the get-go she and I had a disagreement about my topic. I figured that it didn't matter whom I chose, as long as I wrote well; she was adamant that I select a prominent figure. She quickly rejected my more modest ideas—pitcher Billy Stafford and adman David Ogilvy—and, through a newspaper friend of Bob's, lined up an interview with Dag Hammarskjöld. I fell months behind starting on my draft while waiting for the fabled appointment. A week beforehand, he cancelled, and I was relieved. I couldn't imagine why the secretary general of the United Nations should take time out from trying to prevent nuclear war to talk to a high-school kid, and I was glad I didn't have to be that kid.

The paper was due on the Monday after Easter. Now, with three weeks to go I didn't even have a subject. When Easter vacation came, my mother tried to keep me home to work on it. Not only was she certain I would never find someone suitable at Grossinger's, but she remembered how embarrassed she was when I wrote my practice Profile a year earlier on Lou Goldstein. "Can you imagine it, Bob," she said. "He writes about that idiot and hands it in at … Horace Mann." She said the name as though she still had a greater claim on the school than I did.

Against her remonstrances I went to the Hotel as planned and, with Aunt Bunny's help found a quick accomplice—Freddie Rosenberg, an insurance agent in Liberty who was the husband of her close friend Marcia and looked like Paul Newman. He wasn't secretary general even of his own office, but he was available.

During the next two weeks I doggedly hung around Freddie, transcribing his story in his own words, from personal interviews in his office to off-the-cuff remarks to secretaries and clients on the phone. One Sunday he took me ice-fishing "with the guys," boasting all the way that he was the only one with a biographer. I stood on the lake, barely able to grip the pen and pad in the wind to take down his jokes and off-color comments about his wife. Then I claimed one of the Hotel's office IBMs and sat among the secretaries, typing my notes into the "Freddie Rosenberg Profile." On Monday I handed in the longest paper in the class by far, over fifty pages. Freddie had written it for me.

My mother was appalled. "His classmates are doing the Mayor of New York, the Editor of the *New York Times,* and who does he come up with: Freddie Rosenberg, insurance agent from Liberty!"

Mr. McCardell all but agreed, declaring, when returning my venture with the rest, that he knew my subject better than any other profilee—far better, in fact, than he wanted to know him. Nothing else sounded quite like Freddie Rosenberg saying, "Fuck them royally and fuck them all"—that from a section he read aloud to the class. He then became the first magister to give me the grade that was to typify my subsequent academic career: A or F, inked as such, on top of the first page. Luckily it was the former that he averaged into my final grade.

Later that spring, while taking a Fontainebleau reservation on the phone, my mother got into an extended conversation with a camp owner who, upon hearing she had eligible kids, so impressed her with a song and dance about his facilities that she invited him to our apartment to show his slides. We gathered in the living room for the pitch. I was only a peripheral observer, but our visitor had been coached. After Jonny and Debby were signed up and I was headed back to my study, he said, "Wait a second, son," and made me an unexpected offer: I could live with the waiters and be paid $500 to edit Kenmont's newspaper, the *Clarion*.

I had nothing left at Chipinaw, so I said okay.

Kenmont turned out to be the spiffy "country club"–style camp that Wakonda aspired to. There were no scheduled activities for teenagers, so most of the guys spent their days at the golf course and tennis courts or on the lake in rowboats and canoes with girls. The two campuses—Kenmont and Kenwood—were contiguous without parietals. A coffee shop was open for socializing till 9 p.m.

I read my bunkmates at once as self-important jerks. Ranking each other out was their main relational activity. Even by low Chipinaw standards, I found little empathy or intimacy; that was all repressed lest we be thought homos. Life was a perpetual contest to see who could put a peer down the hardest, then how wittily the person would come back. They repeatedly said lines like, "You stupid iriot!" (imitating the comedian Buddy Hackett) and "How're they hanging?"

On the initial morning of camp we were given instructions by a short man about thirty. "Now look here, you guys. I'm kind of with you the first week to make sure you obey the rules. I don't give a damn if you smoke, drink, or fuck around, but wait till after the first week. You see, the head counselor's new and—"

"What's his name?" interrupted a fat, curly haired kid named Love, who carried an umbrella, though the sky was clear. He waved it in the air.

"His first name is Bob. He's from the U. of Florida and majoring in recreation. His second name sounds like a sweet-smelling flower, and I couldn't spell it if you gave me all the letters."

"Oh swell. Sounds like a real winner, doesn't he?" Love said, smiling at the group. "Let's give him three big cheers." And each time he yelled, "Hip, hip!" and waved his umbrella in the air, he was followed by a chorus of "Hurray!" Then he nodded sharply and sat down with a grin of satisfaction. The meeting dispersed without conclusion of the lecture.

Two of us were outsiders—campers who had never been to Kenmont. My fellow newcomer was immediately dubbed Spartacus because he acted dumb and automatically did everything Love asked of him. Love named me Lightning after the sluggish character on the *Amos 'n' Andy Show* because I was slow to respond to goads and put-downs.

I had brought along a tape of super-realistic sound-effects and, before my bunkmates knew I had a recorder, I turned it on under my bed toward midnight. One jet followed another, each one louder and closer to a sonic boom.

"Jeez, I didn't know there was an airfield around here," Asher exclaimed.

"Must be since last summer," remarked Eric.

A train sound followed ... first a remote whistle, far away ... then closer and closer until it seemed about to crash through the bunk. "Christ almighty!" Eric bellowed, jumping to his feet and yanking on the light. When they discovered the source they fired their empty beer cans at me. Then Fred drained one on my covers, and they turned over my bed and pummeled me on the floor in the blankets.

"Lightning's asleep," Asher said. "Let him be."

"What do you mean let him be!" Eric retorted, as he flipped over the mattress and jumped on top of it and me. Fred kept whacking his pillow against my head.

"It was an all-star prank," I wrote to Jake the next day, "better than their dumb rank-outs, and not one asshole congratulated me for it."

My passion that summer was the Southern novelist Robert Penn Warren, as his oratorical flights were touchstones for my own emergent prose. While aspiring to the same lyrical epiphanies, I ended up with clunkier, more ambivalent passages, so I memorized my favorite Penn Warren hits; for instance, about the moon borrowing its light from the sun in *All the King's Men* and, midway through *The Cave,* recounting the demise of a man trapped underground while giving his departing soul a radiant wellspring: "... the handsome and generally admired carnal envelope of Jasper Harrick is, even this instant, as certain chemical changes begin, entering the great anonymous economy of nature. His soul, assuming that he ever had one, has flowed back to that burning fountain whence it came." My writing hung similarly between revelation and doubt.

Meanwhile summer became a languid puzzle through which I wandered, preoccupied with novels and baseball games on the radio. It sufficed to have a catch now and then with my brother or find a meadow in which to lie and read among Queen Anne's lace and purple clover. During part of each day I prepared the *Kenmont Clarion,* sending young kids on assignment, editing and typing their articles, cranking the mimeo, and dispatching the sheets for campus-wide delivery.

Most nights I hung out in the coffee shop with a soda or shake and my book, lost in Kentucky towns amid sales of debt, secret lineages, and almost-passing octoroons, RPW's nineteenth-century tales of statutory intrigue and romance. When there was a ballgame, I brought my radio shaped like a baseball (that Milty had gotten me from the Hotel's novelty supplier that spring) and sat on the side, listening to Mel Allen and colleagues, watching other kids dance. I had no courage to "make a move," in fact no move to make. The days of summer glided by.

Then one evening Eric announced that he was breaking up with Tina, a petite, sullen-looking blonde I had been admiring from a distance. A few nights later I left my radio and novel in the bunk and showed up at the coffee shop early. I took a seat closer to the action.

Tina came in later than usual and staked out a bench in the far back with a friend; the two huddled there, whispering. I had spent the whole day working up to this deed and I couldn't drop it because of an unfavorable-looking break. I strode across the room with the eerie sensation of transecting polygons of a cubist painting. I stood at her bench and asked if she wanted to dance. With a look of resignation, she rose, stared at her friend, and then paced listlessly ahead of me to dead center on the floor. She turned to face me, eyes cast downward. I set my hands on her back and waist. She was stiff and brittle. I hadn't expected that; I had imagined her as fiery and lynx-like, the way she looked. She was cold cardboard, a cut-out of a pretty girl in a dress. It would have been presumptuous to dance close, but it wouldn't have mattered because she wasn't there.

To all the things I tried to say, she chirped intentional sarcasm, "Oh, isn't that nice!" After the dance, turning on a dime, she strutted back to her friend.

The main thing I thought, standing there for all to see—and yes, everyone was staring at Lightning's disgrace, the only handy entertainment—was that for the first time I wasn't afraid the Russians might bomb. In fact, I hoped if they did, they would do it right away. Fred came running up to me. Ever since he had heard a song called "Paco Peco," he ended all his big exclamations with an "o." "Lightning, why do you have to be such a shmucko? She's not the right type for you. She's much too fast. You make a fool out of yourself when you do stuff like that."

I departed the coffee shop, *"Michael, row your boat ashore ..."* fading as I strode through grassy fields beyond the rec hall, toward the brief forest, headed back to the bunk, the stars (as ever) a bottomless cipher. Between daydream Tina who lived in Neverland and candy-Tina with whom I shared one dance were imaginal worlds I could neither fathom nor trespass. Though I imagined myself in exile, I felt inexplicably huge and liberated, as if sorrow, dram by dram, were magically being churned into joy.

My mishap delighted me, for the courage to act and be revealed outweighed the paltry result. In awe of the universe, I commiserated silently with habitants of distant worlds. The twinkling presentation was so durable and vast it had to be real, to them too; it had to hold the meaning behind everything that was happening.

Then I intoned (along with Dion & the Belmonts) the obvious song: *"Each night I ask the stars up above .... "* Its denizen wasn't mirage-girl Tina, a fleeting stand-in. It was an aggregate eidolon: Annie Welch, Joan Snyder, Harriet, Karen, girls unnamed and forgotten, a Puerto Rican teen in a yellow dress glimpsed from the El:

"... why must I be a teenager in love?" Because that was the question, *but only in its largest sense.* Stars and melody, words and beat came together, evoking an Elizbethan elegy or *The Fairie Queene.* It may have been narcissistic melodrama, teen kitsch, but the bigness I felt was inherent and unmistakable.

I thought back to Samuel Coleridge's Ode on "Dejection," elucidated in English class a few months earlier—1802 England, addressed to an unavailable woman, Sara Hutchinson: *"May all the stars hang bright above her dwelling, / Silent as though they watched the sleeping Earth!"*—the couplet as cogent on the playing fields of Kenmont as the sheep-filled meadows of the Lake Country, nor disparate from Bobby Darin crooning, *"Somewhere beyond the sea, / She's there, waiting for me...."* Or those Everly Brothers in their pompadour mummery, *"Let it be me...."* The mystery woman, the mystery man, the mystery mission, the unknown witness, the Beloved: "A Nocturnal Upon S. Lucy's Day," "Ode on Intimations of Immortality"—all our lives our inner selves reach out for such an assignation. And it could not have been stated more clearly by that least likely garage band: *"Can't you see I came to the party / 'cause I knew that you'd be here."* Welcome to a festival universe—fast-moving clouds over an untended world.

On the radio back at the bunk pinch-hitter Johnny Blanchard swinging two bats in the on-deck circle (in my imagination, Joe Glazer hunched in his box recalling my act of heresy and divination).... Johnny Blanchard, third-string catcher, hard drinker, sacred bum, came up to the plate and ripped a grand slam in the bottom of the ninth to pull out a game against the Red Sox. And in that epiphany Joe Glazer made a blessing and sent it my way with his greeting and compliments, "You nailed it, kid!"

And from farther off in time and space: *"The voice I hear this passing night was heard / In ancient days by emperor and clown."* No kidding, John Keats.

The Yankees chased Detroit all that summer while Mickey Mantle and Roger Maris piled up unprecedented numbers of home runs, both ahead of Babe Ruth's 1927 record pace. For much of July I listened on my radio. Then I heard that George, the chubby middle-aged steward of the kitchen, was a fanatic Yankee rooter and had a TV in his room beside the dining hall, the only one in all of downtown Kenmont. George was notoriously unapproachable and surly, plus he despised the wise-ass waiters in my bunk, but *I* wasn't them. After a few weeks he must have discerned my legitimate interest (and non-asshole status), for he invited me to his "palace," as he called it. Thereafter I became a regular guest. I stretched out on the floor while he sat on the edge of the bed in his undershirt with a beer. It was barely more than a oversized closet, but at summer camp a TV was a towline into civilization, and Johnny Blanchard rewarded us with a string of unlikely hits.

George and I would keep the silence of each other's company, discussing only crucialities of the game except for his occasional commendation: "You're a real mensch; how do you stand living with those shit-faced creeps? Tell me that!" He didn't expect an answer, that was my virtue.

I remember how instantly alert we were whenever the Tigers' score was announced.

"Whitey Herzog has just homered for Baltimore in the first."

"Make it two on," George said.

"A runner on base, so Detroit's down 2–0."

"We'll take it."

One evening the older kids visited the nearby Shakespeare Theater in Stratford for a performance of *Macbeth*. In my wildest dream I would not have imagined ... there was Keith in the crowd, the real boy. I had never talked to him, but now it was simple. I mean, we were the only two HM kids there. We chatted like any schoolmates about how each of us had gotten there, then ... good luck and goodbye. Dr. Friend was right; Keith was simply another person. The eidolon had been my creation.

Summer reached its apex in mid-August. No dawn fog—at seven the sun was already a blazing ball. Lawn-mowing tractors perfumed the air, grasshoppers launching and landing in the distance. I had broken my middle right finger playing catch with Fred—we were pitching to each other and he was showing me his curve—now the splint was finally off. I hadn't held a ball in three weeks, my longest abstinence. Even in the daunting heat, I wanted to play. So I found my brother, and we collected a sack of hardballs. I ran to center field. He swung from the backstop.

I had the rhythm that day, throwing my body in the path of sinking liners, tumbling over and over with the ball.

"You're a prophet!" Jon shouted.

It was true; the day was jubilant, auspicious beyond reason.

We kept changing places, batter and fielder, until we were both soaked and exhausted and lay silently together in the grass. Then we parted. He headed toward his bunk; I veered to the coffee shop where I bought a cold orange.

"We've sold a lot of these today," the boy said as he dropped a cup over the bottle. I guzzled down a brief torrent. A fan turned ineffectually, as flies buzzed around rolls of gummed paper rich with flies. Over in the corner Asher was lying on his belly next to a tall, pretty girl I hadn't noticed before. He had his shirt off, and she scratched his back while throwing out witty asides. "What's this?" … stopping and scraping a little. As he strained to look up and around at himself she sassed, "Oh, nothing, son," and went on drawing in curlicues on him. She was so quirky and droll I couldn't keep my sideways glance from her. She had reddish brown hair, and there was something distinctly Keith-like about her—the theatricality, the playful intelligence, the melodic, showy voice.

Once again, an image of Pan had captured my wandering attention.

Through the remainder of the summer, though I never approached her, I watched Jill. She was spunky and brash, more than a match for Asher. I would overhear him talking excitedly to Eric about her: "She French-kisses! She stuck her tongue in so far I thought I was going out of my mind."

Eric could barely contain his lust and envy.

The last week of camp I was standing with George in the kitchen before lunch, poring over the day's stats. Maris had hit two more homers; we knew that, but had just discovered, to our chagrin, the

Tigers won their late game. A voice from behind me said, "Oh, don't tell me Maris hit another."

Jill moved in between us like a pro to scan the box scores. "My favorite player's Wally Moon. I want to see how he's doing. There. Not bad, not bad!"

"He's okay," I added unnecessarily.

"He's better than okay," she shot back. Her eyes were pale, transparent; she had on large earrings, and her hair was arranged in a complicated French twist. George went on studying the page as though the phenomenon wasn't there.

The next day the boys played the girls in the annual softball game in which the boys had to bat left handed (or right handed if they were lefties). Jill was the Yogi-catcher with a mask on. She fell to her knees and deftly grabbed an outside pitch on one bounce as I batted. Then I fouled one back; she threw off her mask, dove, and just missed it. Her lipstick and busty polo shirt notwithstanding, she was a player.

After Kenmont I returned to Grossinger's where storm clouds were gathering. Jay and his brothers had been absent for years, and now Jay's parents, with Barry's father as their lawyer, were suing my grandparents over abuses of management. Aunt Bunny told me that they were justified. "But what can we do?" she lamented. "Your grandfather owns all our shares, and he insists on acting on his whims without consulting his partners. When he dug the first hole for the indoor pool he was warned that he would hit reservoir pipes going into New York City. He said nobody was going to tell him where he could dig on his own property. He got one giant geyser, and it wasn't oil!" She flipped two fingers and her thumb in the air. "So then he had to fill in the hole and pay the fine too. Now he's off on some other hare-brained scheme and your father hasn't the guts to stop him."

Uncle Paul had entered a more cantankerous phase—cursing the union organizers, bawling out guests for not being dressed properly in the dining room. And everyone in the family, as usual, was choosing sides.

But Grossinger's was still my haven. I played ball on the staff field with Jerry, watched the Yankees on TV, shot rolls of Kodacolor, and wrote about the summer. As Aunt Bunny and I came dripping into the cabana one afternoon from a swim I told her about Jill and, en route through the lunch buffet, she responded with an insanely flagrant idea: "You should call her and ask her out."

"I don't even know her," I protested.

"She'd be flattered."

"Sure she would.... Anyhow, I don't have her phone number or address."

"Call the camp office, dummy. What have you got to lose? If she doesn't want to go you're back where you started."

"But what should I invite her to?"

"You know the answer to that. Invite her to a ballgame. Get tickets from the office."

When she made the suggestion I was sure there was no way I would do it. She said it too facilely, without any appreciation for the outrageousness of such an act. After all, she hadn't viewed the consequences of my mere dance with Tina.

But she had opened Pandora's box. It was a simple, gutsy plan, and it had the advantage of avoiding another unrequited fantasy. It was also vintage Grossinger's—bold, daffy, overflowing with hope.

I evaded the gadfly for days, but it wouldn't let me off the hook. Finally I phoned the Kenmont office and asked for Jill's number. That was hard enough to accomplish gracefully, without bolting and hanging up while the secretary was searching.

Until the following morning I kept it in my pocket like a stolen gem, trying to enjoy it before it was rendered void. Then at nine-thirty I dialed quickly so that I wouldn't stop myself. I listened to the line ring and ring, mesmerized, every few seconds jolting myself to cognizance of what I was doing, preparing for her voice ... and when it continued ringing I was totally relieved.

I grabbed my novel and headed to the pool. After the legendary buffet—turkey, tongue, blueberry tarts—I hiked to the staff field and joined a group of Puerto Rican staff hitting and fielding fungos while they shouted in Spanish.

I played at being the kid from Grossinger's that whole day, as I pondered my daring gambit. Observing myself in the role took nothing away. It was a great all-time ploy.

I waited until evening. The phone rang, twice, three times … suddenly a click … and her voice.

"Hello."

"Hi. This is Richard Grossinger. Do you remember me from camp?"

"Oh yes … and how are your Yankees?"

"Okay, I suppose."

"Do you go to ballgames now that you're out of camp?"

"No. I'm not in New York.…" And eventually: "How would you like to go to the Yankee-Cleveland game this Saturday?"

"Hmmm, this Saturday? Let's see … I'm busy. How about next Saturday?"

"They go on the road Monday."

"Oh, no! I'd really like to."

"There's one other chance. How about October 2nd? It's a Sunday, the last day of the season. And who knows how many home runs Maris may have by then."

"True, true.… Sunday the 2nd is fine with me."

We set a meeting place and time (her apartment at noon) and I hung up the phone. I went tearing out the front door and ran around the house twice before rolling into the tomato patch. I lay there in the leaves, thanking them for being what they were, the sun too.

"I told you it would work," Aunt Bunny said.

"It's because she likes baseball."

"I wouldn't bet on it."

I returned to the City with new hopefulness, and my final year of Horace Mann began. I had Virgil, Honors European History, Honors English, Mr. Ervin's writing seminar, and advanced algebra.

My mother and I seldom spoke beyond trifles. As the years had amassed in their unruly stack, we developed a protocol, a tacit truce. After all, I was getting A's and B's at school and acting more or less like a gentleman. It was clear that I had done something unforgivable

once—*that* could never be pardoned—but she couldn't keep lam-
basting me for the same crime, so we based our relationship on a
presumption of my guilt as we performed a masquerade of amnesty:
a stilted cordiality of house arrest. We hung on its fulcrum, two
trapeze artists, unable to look at each other, yet, while falling away,
stretching the tension between us to the boundary of our existences.

She was my mother, which Aunt Bunny, however wonderful,
could never be. There was something about this woman, her scarred,
craggy landscape, that grounded my life in hers and made her inal-
terably real. She got there through grief and pain, she was joyless
and spiteful; yet I imbued her even as I fought her. I can't remember
her ever hugging me with good will or saying a kind word without
an agenda. But she touched bottom. Through her I gauged where
my own depth and texture went, how I was put together. Without
her I had no ambit or shape.

Richard Grossinger, son of PG, was a flicker in the dusk. Richard,
son of Martha Rothkrug Towers, was the cartilage of my being.

Her interest now was in how good a college I could get into, not
because she pictured my leaving home to attend but because that
was the next stage in the hoax we were perpetrating, my imitation of the career of her brother Lionel whom we had seen all of
once. So that fall my father drove into the City with my adopted
brother to take me on a trip to look at New England schools. Aunt
Bunny had hoped that such exposure might inspire Michael to do
his homework. It turned out to be a slapstick affair. With Uncle
Paul's one good eye keeping us (mostly) on the road, we crossed
various mountain ranges, winding among Williamstown, Amherst,
Dartmouth, and Middlebury. Michael and I kissed the ground each
time on our arrivals, to PG's chagrin.

With their bucolic quads, ivy-covered masonry, and rolling fields,
these schools were on a scale as much above Horace Mann as Horace
Mann had towered over P.S. 6. I could hardly believe I would be not
only taking classes at one of them but living there. Something else
I had never contemplated: it was the single payoff for all my hard
work and high grades, the privilege to apply to elite institutions.
Otherwise, studying for A's was a dead-end game.

I knew that my grades made me a strong candidate, but my father decided to prove one of his choice maxims: "It's not *what* you know, it's *who* you know." At Amherst, which had the most majestic campus, he arranged for a prominent alumnus, a priggish shrimp of a Catskills attorney, to meet us at the Admissions Office and make his presence known. At Dartmouth, for a similar reason, we ate lunch with the football coach.

I was mortified by the Jewish lawyer and the coach, but Uncle Paul kept insisting that getting into these schools was a matter of connections. "This is America," he said, "not communist Russia."

"What about merit?"

"Lots of people have good grades. That doesn't mean they get accepted."

I wasn't an informed shopper either. I was chasing scenery and a mood more than curriculum. My unequivocal first choice was Swarthmore, in the suburbs of Philadelphia. When I visited the campus myself by train, I felt as though I had found Blueland, long rows of trees and a small-village feeling. It was also the bohemian summer camp I had never been allowed to attend. I was hell-bent to apply and made it my first choice, but Mr. Gucker, Horace Mann's Director of College Admissions, put on the brakes. He asked me to fill out the form for early decision at Amherst.

"Why? I'd rather just try Swarthmore."

"Swarthmore is a second-rate school. You should at least apply to the best college you can get into. That way everyone ends up where they belong."

So I did the paperwork, and on my seventeenth birthday I received an epistle with a dean's inked signature, congratulating me on my acceptance. "What should I do now?" I asked Mr. Gucker the next day.

He had received a carbon, so had a ready answer. "Write a letter to Dean Wilson thanking him and say you look forward to attending in the fall."

"But what about Swarthmore? I haven't even applied."

"Now you don't need to."

Everyone thought it was so great I got into Amherst that I allowed myself to feel good about it too. After all, it was a cool place to go. I imagined autumn meadows, New England farmhouses, wise girls at nearby Smith and Mount Holyoke.

Dr. Friend observed the whole process without comment. "I wanted to see what you would do," he remarked afterwards. "I assumed you would pick Columbia because I didn't think you were in any shape to leave treatment. But you never even considered that or consulted me. You never considered that applying to Amherst *was* termination. I finally decided that getting you away from your mother was more valuable than any service I could provide."

The Yankees held first place, and Maris kept hitting homers so that on October 2nd he had 60—he had caught Babe Ruth.

I put on my powder-blue shirt and a sports jacket and took the subway downtown to Jill's. She was waiting casually by the awning and approached me with her winsome Kenwood smile: "So we meet again, Yankee fan."

The October game, though meaningless in the standings, had a World Series flavor because of Maris, and we talked baseball and stats all the way to the Bronx as crowds increased stop by stop.

Jill was a dazzling blend of antitheses—a pretty girl and baseball. Those dual energies stirred different parts of me, bumping into each other without ever quite meeting. Eros and ERAs were radiating from a tall Keith-like girl with an almost jock swagger, spouting effortless baseball lingo. Pure oxymoron. Should I treat her like my baseball crony Jake or like seductress Karen? That was the easy part: after all, I could take turns and experiment, mix and match. The harder part was knowing whether to feel the self that hung out with baseball buddies, little at stake, or to feel the unabridged charge of an attractive girl. There too I vacillated, dipping in and out of energy fields.

I had sat in Eddie Fisher's box with schoolmates dozens of times; yet it was as though I had never been there before. Even Mr. Glazer kept his distance, as Jill and I chatted about Kenmont and class-work—she went to an all-girls' private school downtown. She had nothing good to say about Asher except that he was cute. "He's not someone I'll be seeing anymore." And then, mid-game, Maris came to the plate, took a ball, cleared his spikes with his bat, adjusted his uniform, took another pitch. Tracy Stallard threw again, Maris swung, and the ball sailed in a rising arc down the right-field line. As the Stadium recognized the moment, it erupted in a roar. Jill threw her arms around me, as we hugged and cheered.

In the digital era I have searched numerous videos of that moment without finding even a blur of fans and faces where we sat. Maris pulled the pitch to right and then set out toward first-base in his moment of triumph, yet at a pace and posture that showed respect and homage to the baseball gods. The camera tracked him on his circle of the bases, but the 109 seconds either follows him into a crowd of his welcoming teammates at the plate and then entering the home dugout or terminates its pan a fraction of a second before reaching our section behind the visitors' dugout. Even in a time machine I could not go back to our first date.

Jill became a faithful phone-and-letter friend after that. We wrote and called crosstown about baseball and literature. She rooted for the Reds to beat the hated American Leaguers in the Series. When the Yankees won, she sent what she called "a humble note of congratulations."

I invited her to another high-profile event—a sold-out concert by the Limeliters at Carnegie Hall for which I got tickets through Grossinger's. Wry philosophical Lou Gottlieb, high-tenored Glenn Yarbrough (years later the voice of *"Baby the rain must fall* ...), and polyglot banjo fiend Alex Hassilev were my new enthusiasm; I had been trying to interest my friends in their songs all fall without success.

That night they belted out a repertoire from "There's a Party Here Tonight" and "When I First Came to This Land" to "The Rising of the Moon" and "Morningtown Ride," an occasional Spanish or Russian ballad and novelty song thrown in. Afterwards Jill called them "an intellectual blend of the Clancy Brothers and Kingston Trio"; she wasn't going to let me know whether she approved, she was withholding judgment. We found a coffee shop and talked for two hours about the matter and Ibsen whom we were coincidentally both reading in school.

Soon I realized I didn't have to dredge up big events; I could just ask Jill out. We went to *Breakfast at Tiffany's* at a theater on Lexington and then Ibsen's *Ghosts* on a small Greenwich Village stage. Every other week we checked the movie and theater sections and made our selection, conferring by phone as Saturday approached. Each time I would take the subway to her apartment, and from there we would hail a cab. After the performance we would have dessert at a restaurant and sit around talking about what we had seen. She considered herself an accomplished literary critic and thought I was undisciplined and far too psychological, so she challenged me on just about every symbol or interpretation I offered.

Sometimes we went back to her apartment and continued our discussion in the living room. If her mother was up she joined in. The three of us jabbered away for an hour or more. Then I came home late on the subway and let myself in the back door.

The early darkness of the Solstice approached from a direction I had never known. City lights danced, and I was nearly happy. The song from the movie carried the ambiance of my life: *"Moon river, wider than a mile, / I'm crossing you in style, someday ..."*

Yes, she had been a "moon" figure from the first day I saw her with Asher. Even our initial point of contact was an outfielder named Moon.

In the shower I sang at the top of my lungs, trying to capture the precise resonance. Occasionally Bridey joined in from the hallway, trying to steer me back into tune: *" ... my huckleberry friend.... "*

I remember Jill as Audrey Hepburn in the movie, curled on the living room sofa, blowing smoke in the air, conscious of each self-conscious motion she made. Part of me would be talking to her, and part of me would be looking at the remarkable girl: her face, her eyes, the curve of her breasts, her lips, her clothes, her pocketbook, her smooth legs, her fancy gestures, her womanly movements.

I could never forget what Asher said, though I detested him for it because Jill had become my best friend and his words were always in the way, goading me, telling me I somehow wasn't as attractive or special as he was. His description was a maddening abstraction without connection to my own experience. Once, though, I took Jill's hand in mine while we were walking. At first it felt ridiculous, too silly even to believe, but when she pressed my hand back I felt as though I held her entirely and was held by her as we walked along.

When I talked to subway friends, they were full of notions as to how to get started, but it was always the same advice adding up to nothing: "You know from that guy Asher she gives, so what are you waiting for?" They seemed concerned that I not lose my "big chance." Such was teen world 1961—lingo and posturing, urban prep school notwithstanding.

One December Friday on getting home from school, I felt particularly gloomy and called my huckleberry friend. We had been out the past Saturday, so it was too soon to see each other again by our established pacing, but I wanted to hear her voice and took a chance. When I asked her how she was, she moaned, "Dreary Friday." I was delighted—a soulmate. "Yes," she said, "we should by all means go to the movies tomorrow night."

All the next day I hung around the apartment doing homework distractedly, wishing I felt easy about her. I had become obsessed with what it would be like to kiss Jill. I imagined lying on top of her and making out, her long elegant frame moving with mine, her eyes, as ever, teasing, bewitching.

As often as I forced myself to squash the daydream, to render more lines of Virgil, I came unfailingly back to its reverie. My entire being balked at Latin conundrums. It wasn't just that Jill combined all the fantasies I had ever had; it was that she was enough of a buddy I could imagine them coming true.

After the movie what had never happened happened as I had imagined it might. On her lead we went into her room instead of the living room. I sat in a chair, and she stretched out on the bed, back against the wall. I heard my hollow voice talking while my imagination was exploding. She was so exciting, smooth blouse over her breasts, thick teased red hair, adroit curl of her voice, alluring and friendly both. I tracked the growing lateness of the hour, getting later each time I glanced. In my mind all of time was draining away. I was numb with feeling; I didn't know what to do.

She began to show signs of getting up. I moved toward her, stood there. "What?" she said.

How could she not know? I made a gesture toward a simple kiss. She took a step back, looked at me bewildered, then said, "No."

"Why?"

"Because it would ruin everything."

Later—though in years—I thought that perhaps she was telling me it had always ruined everything, that she wanted this to be different. But I was raw and wild then, and I couldn't bear the thought of Asher being allowed so easily, me not at all. That night when I left her I ran ten blocks down Fifth Avenue against a whipping wind, over and over screaming Emerson's lines in my mind:

"I am the doubter and the doubt, / and I the hymn the Brahmin sings."

... ran past buildings and storefronts until I reached apotheosis in myself, and exhaustion.

I never called Jill again.

5

GRADUATION

Senior year brought its own privileges. We sat in our fabled lounge and watched *Amos 'n' Andy* and *Bullwinkle Moose* during first-period study hall.

Tim Moore playing sly George "Kingfish" Stevens with Ernestine Wade as his fiery wife Sapphire Stevens hadn't been booted off the air by the NAACP yet, so we got to appreciate African American comedy at its fifties finest. Usually Andy Brown (played by Spencer Williams) came into some unexpected scratch, so Kingfish busied himself with schemes for how to relieve him of it. For instance on one occasion he sold Andy a cut-rate tour of the world—passengers had to travel blindfolded. As they strolled through Central Park, Kingfish announced, "Ah, I see the famous obelisk of Egypt." When Andy wanted to take the blindfold off and look, Kingfish resorted to, "Ah, but I'm afraid that's the more expensive tour and youse can't afford it, son."

In my favorite episode Kingfish decided to sell the newly affluent Andy a property, but the particular real estate hoisted on his unsuspecting friend was actually a piece of cardboard deployed on an empty lot, a photograph of a house with a cutout door on it. I don't remember what gullibility led Andy to fall for such an overt deception, but he made the purchase. He then brought dim-witted Lightning to view his new domicile. The trouble was, whenever they tried the front door, they ended up in the backyard. After a number of such forays, Lightning was finally inspired to investigate further. Circumambulating the structure, he declared, "That's one mighty thin house there, Andy."

These guys were everything Horace Mann wasn't, and we loved them for it.

From a closet at home I rescued a hockey game with a marble and tin men, which Jonny and I played addictively for years before abandoning, and donated it to the lounge. Tournaments ran continuously thereafter alongside the TV. Then we voted to spend class funds on a new model with moving men in tracks and a wooden puck.

But our teachers were not going to allow a year in the tank. Mr. Clinton, whom I now had for the second time, intended his Modern European history course to be the tour de force of our Horace Mann education. Over six feet tall with a mop of white hair and the fierce countenance of Samuel Johnson, he spent weeks filling us with an appreciation for the Church and the complexities of feudalism. Inflamed by the decay of worldly things, he would bring famous lives to an end always with the same declaration: "Death, as it must to all men, came to Charlemagne, Charles the Great...." Death later came to Ferdinand and Isaebella, Cabot and Magellan, and Philip of Spain, even Martin Luther the reformer. After that we were submerged in the details of the Thirty Years War so graphically that I imagined Gustavus Adolphus riding out of the woods behind Van Cortlandt Park, leading a Swedish army, his minister Oxenstierna at his side.

We spent weeks on Erasmus and the northern Renaissance and then studied Jacob Burckhardt on the Medicis and sixteenth-century humanism in Italy. For Clinton, the Church was the single great institution of humanity—ameliorating and yet corrupting, simplistic and violent in its politics but profound in its ceremony. He enacted his Mediaeval passion so convincingly in class that Bob Alpert dropped left-wing politics and, to the horror of his parents, denounced their synagogue and began attending Mass.

There was a cult around Clinton. Rumors about his past ran the gamut from priesthood to Satanism to student seduction. Whatever the truth, he commanded our attention. I remember how, after attending the funeral of an ex-student who had died young, he spent much of the next class describing the corpse in the open casket. "The difference between life and death is infinitesimal," he preached. "He was strong, strapping, handsome, a youth, lying there, but he had already entered the country from whose bourne— Shakespeare—no traveller returns." And then he wept openly before us, took out his handkerchief and sat silently sobbing at his desk for the remainder of class.

Another eccentric arrived during my junior year. Berman was a strange-looking man, almost like a mutant: totally bald though young; flat, thin eyes with an impenetrably morose expression behind black-rimmed glasses. He ate with us in the student rather than faculty dining room where he conducted sessions on the mystic Meister Eckhart and the Russian occult philosopher G. I. Gurdjieff. Chuck Stein told me Berman was a member of an ancient Rosicrucian order.

It was through Chuck rather than Berman that I became involved in the occult. Since many of my classmate's poems were based on tarot cards, Mr. Ervin suggested that he bring a deck to class. Bright-hued vistas of "The Magician," "The Wheel of Fortune," and "The Hanged Man" were set on the table before us. Packed with symbols, the images were at once baseball cards, commercial ads, and illustrations from *Grimms' Fairytales*.

Chuck interpreted their gestalts to the creative-writing gang: "The wild red roses are our five senses." He held a palm over the Magician's garden. "You can feel their energy coming out of this card." As we each gave it a playful pass, the red and yellow surface did seem unduly hot. "The Wheel of Fortune is the Galaxy pivoting in seasons and cosmic epochs." He rotated it clockwise in midair, turning its Hebrew letters into a brief dreidel; then he set it down and picked up another. "The scaffold is the scaffold of Creation— the Hanged Man is really right-side up; he just seems upside-down from our limited perspective."

My favorites were "The Star" and "The Moon," two extraterrestrial landscapes with creatures emerging from the same pool of cosmic vibrations. Their murals featured an elemental crayfish, a pelican on a bare tree, an angel pouring water from earthen jugs, and a sky bursting with yellow and white suns. The forces portrayed here, Chuck declared, were greater than cosmic rays from all the visible and invisible stars of the universe.

I wanted to learn more, so my friend led me downtown. I was flabbergasted that the beautiful Spanish-looking girl who had ridden the subway silently with us for years greeted Chuck with a bear hug at 242nd Street. Her name was Julie Garfield and she went to Buck's Rock. Chuck lived in Yonkers, so this juxtaposition had not previously occurred.

We travelled Broadway all the way to Dr. Fabian's old neighborhood near 14th Street. There Chuck turned into a used bookstore. Its downstairs, heralded by an overhead sign, was our destination: "Basement of the Occult." There owner Donald Weiser removed hand-engraved tarots from locked glass and showed us arcane landscapes in enormous luminescent decks. Then he talked of alchemy, reincarnation, UFOs, and the coming revival of the hermetic arts.

The first item I bought was the Waite deck drawn by Pamela Colman Smith, the same set of seventy-eight cards that Chuck used. The second was a book, *The Tarot* by Paul Foster Case. When I read Case's descriptions that night I felt as though I was ascending through Robert Penn Warren's mere placeholder symbol into the fountain of souls itself:

"In contrast to the Magician, who stands upright in a garden, the High Priestess is seated within the precincts of a temple. The walls of the building are blue, and so are the vestments of this virgin priestess. Blue, the color assigned to the Moon, and to the element water, represents the primary root-substance, the cosmic mind-stuff.… "

I stared at this woman in her robes of gossamer indigo. She was seated between twin pillars, an arras of unopened pomegranates behind her. I thought: "She is unconsciousness; she represents all that is hidden inside me." What Dr. Fabian had once alluded to now had a Torah-like representation; it was still invisible, but I could hold a scrap of it in my hand. Believing that all-out panics were in my past, I was ready to become a pilgrim, to go on the quest that he had posed on my thirteenth birthday.

A week later I bought a second book, Arthur Edward Waite's *Pictorial Key to the Tarot,* mainly for its appendix on fortune-telling. At home I set the cards on the rug and used Waite's Celtic Cross formula to read my first draws—for Jonny, then Bridey, who was initially concerned that fortune cards might not be an appropriate activity for a Catholic but finally couldn't resist. Years later, she told my sister that my use of the deck proved I was in league with the Devil.

My mother would have no part of it—she hated me in this guise—meteorologist, Hiroshima critic, tarot maven; it was all the same to her. But Bob accepted a reading and complimented me on my pizzazz: "I'm not sure you're a fortune teller, or that there *are* such things, but you've got a fine sense of theater."

At Waite's direction I picked a Significator card to represent the person whose fortune was about to be told. Then Bridey or Jon shuffled the remaining cards while pondering an issue in his or her life. After being satisfied that the deck "got" it—my instruction—she or he handed it back to me. I took cards off the top in order.

In Bridey's case I first made the stern, unsentimental Queen of Swords her Significator, then covered it with the top card from her sort, showing the major influences over her, then topped that card with another showing what crossed or opposed her. At the Significator's crown the third card off the shuffle revealed what she hoped for as well as the best that could be achieved under the circumstances. Below the Significator I set the fourth, the foundation of the matter, showing (again, according to Waite) what had already passed into actuality. The fifth card, placed behind the direction from which the Queen was facing, disclosed what had recently passed and was fading. The sixth card, in the direction of the Queen's clairvoyant gaze, foretold what was coming into being and would shape the future. Then the seventh through tenth positions were taken from the top of the remaining deck and placed in a vertical row apart, indicating respectively the person herself, the tendencies at work in her environment and among family and friends, her unconscious hopes and fears regarding the matter, and—the tenth card—the outcome, the culmination of the influences of all the cards, drawn and undrawn.

When I brought the tarot to Grossinger's at Christmas, Aunt Bunny was so taken with her reading that the next afternoon she invited a group of her friends from town for tea and fortunes. I picked female Significators and read the Celtic Cross for four dressed-to-the-nines ladies. Amazingly they wanted this and had patience to see it through; in fact, they were instant zealots, swayed somehow by the combination of esoteric images, forbidden knowledge, and my patter of gypsy put-on. The issues they brought were nontrivial: domestic, romantic, and financial quandaries, confessing them in surprising detail and listening attentively in a way that they would not have otherwise. Without the cards these bourgeois matrons wouldn't have given me the time of day.

Despite the fact that I kept explaining they weren't supposed to tell me *anything,* that the cards were larger than their stories, and blind, to boot—still, they laid it on the line: wayward husbands, risky stock portfolios, intrusive relatives, troubled children. They believed in this stuff more than I did, so I became their cosmic ventriloquist.

Amid tabletop jumbles of kings, queens, knights, pages, pentacles, swords, cups, wands, and major trumps, I converted shuffles to imaginative narratives. Using Waite's and Case's thumbnail glosses, I found perfidy, felicity, adversity, riches, impediment, and allies. I evoked secret quarrels (the Seven of Swords), having rejected three things and awaiting a fourth (the Four of Cups), and loss of one identity before taking on another (Death). My favorites were the Five of Pentacles (mendicants in rags on crutches, hobbling in the snow with a stained-glass window shining above them) and the Six of Cups (children sniffing the flowers of memory). For the former I reminded my subject of her potential for happiness and salvation while she wallowed in self-imposed exile. For the latter I warned of the deadly attraction of eternal return, of living too nostalgically in the past.

I knew never to predict actual things ("abuse of the deck," Chuck had told me), even for the Ten of Swords, where the guy lies on the battlefield with ten huge blades piercing his body from head to thighs (bringing an unhappy gasp from Connie, who drew it). I spoke like Dr. Fabian, only of difficulties that could be overcome through insight and knowledge.

"You should charge for this," Marcia said.

"I can't," I told her. "I'd lose the power."

At the time, I regarded it as a game, my readings a mixture of *The Interpretation of Dreams,* Waite, Case, and dead-reckoning. I thought I was popular and got so many repeat requests because I was a writer as well as a symbol maven—and that the women were charmed by getting their fortunes told by a kid.

Perhaps—but there are actually always two levels of divination and it is hard to know where one ends and the other begins. You tell the story literally in the cards and play honest broker, and you tell *another* story that you are getting from elsewhere. It is not that it is *not* in the cards but, even if it is, you are not getting it from them in the same way. Yet paradoxically you are *only* reading it from them—they fall into place as you go.

That is what I was doing unconsciously—only I didn't take it seriously. I didn't grasp any of it then, had no context to grasp it. A natural empath, I mirrored my subjects even as I had mirrored my mother from day one. For Aunt Bunny's friends it was a passing idyll; for Martha Towers it was a horrific visitation—and by a whelp out of her own flesh. I didn't merely reflect her panics, I reflected what she was terrified of.

As an ingénue tarot reader, I was sought not because I was entertaining but because I gave *accurate information despite myself.* And that's *why* I was entertaining.

Decades later some of these women were still telling me that I had foreshadowed major events in their lives (like Freddie Rosenberg leaving Marcia for another woman). You could lay down a hundred draws without getting ones as on target as those that appeared magically in 1961. It was effortless for me to weave such draws into compelling narratives.

But how did I trick myself into some sort of confluence of time inversion and telekinesis, into scrying both cards and psychic energies?

I think it was the same as how Fabian did it: from trying to be a good storyteller and therapist while telling myself that that's *only* what I was doing. I didn't consider that I was consulting auras and picking up higher-dimensional waves: the mindstuff described in the books, the supernatural heat Chuck had demonstrated in class. I thought I was following instruction booklets in the same protocol as building model airplanes or playing Monopoly, with a dash of science-fiction theatricality cum Freudian melodrama thrown in. Then the cards flowed like Atlantean cinema, and pictures arose in a teenage fool's mind.

There is another thread here, and it will take some backtracking to capture. When I was thirteen years old, a new brand of soap called Zest debuted with a flurry of television ads that showed people bathing in waterfalls amid orchestral crescendos. A voiceover described "the Zest feeling"—a whole different kind of sudsing action that made you downright ecstatic: *"For the first time in your life, feel really clean."*

I was curious what it would be like to wash with something other than our house brand, Camay, so I convinced my parents to buy me a bar. After unwrapping its parchment, I held a marbled bluish-green amulet like a Babylonian bar imprinted with runes.

When I scrubbed myself with Zest that night in the shower, I became as exuberant as the people in the ads. The soap felt liberating, slaphappy. I couldn't identify the precise source of its energy; it wasn't the foaming action, but there *was* something rhapsodic about it—perhaps its subtle fragrance, vaguely like Queen Anne's lace and other wildflowers. (Of course, this was good old, innocent bathing, hearkening back to satyrs in waterfalls and shaving-cream sprees; it had nothing to do with my later erotic digressions.)

When my spirits needed a lift thereafter, I took Zest into a bath or a shower and, as I got the suds in under my arms and between my toes, I was transformed.

I told my Horace Mann friends about Zest, but to a one they laughed, and the few that tried it reported nothing special (as they had presumed). Although I knew it was ridiculous to ascribe joy to a bar of soap, I still suspected that they were missing something: *They are not letting themselves feel it.*

For months thereafter I looked forward to baths and showers. I used Zest to get myself happy, to bust out of melancholy. To my mind I had discovered something important that my peers were either too uptight or too snotty to admit, something major and magic about the world: the Zest feeling.

The following summer I packed a few bars in my camp trunk and showed the jade ovals to bunkmates. At Chipinaw we showered together, so I got a chance to watch the soap in action. No one in my bunk experienced the Zest feeling, or anything at all, but they mercilessly spoofed it with dances and paroxysms that left them writhing in fake ecstasy on the moth-littered stone. I blushed but was undeterred.

I continued to feel the ebullience of Zest. A shower with its lather made me less homesick. It turned the Chipinaw sky bluer, its flowers deeper yellow and orange. I flew across the outfield with uncommon grace.

A natural proselytizer, I kept touting Zest. Yet from bunkmates I continued to evince blank looks and loony cutting up. I insisted they were wrong. So they sought an outside expert, our counselor.

He took their side. "There is no Zest feeling," he said. "That's what ads are supposed to do—convince you to buy things. It's all in your imagination."

If it hadn't been the fifties, if America had privileged sacred practices over recreational meaninglessness, if we had been initiated into some sort of inner life instead of being told it didn't exist, then he might have been able to report: "The imagination is a powerful tool by itself; it can turn ordinary things into magical ones and unleash boundless love. We each have the power inside us to be happy and experience miracles every day. We have an innate quotient of generosity and the desire to serve others. *And that capacity is contagious.*"

He would have encouraged me to find the source of the Zest feeling in myself, in the native beauty and wonder of the world; to cultivate and spread Zest's compassion, even to practice a better poetry than Zest, as Wordsworth did, as Buddha did: the "visionary gleam," "splendour in the grass," "empty essence, primordially pure." Not a soap, but a measureless radiance beyond summer breezes, in a night ablaze with stars, as we sang Taps, swaying and bundled together in the void. Our counselor might have invited me to turn

Zest into art or prayer. Instead we earned little felt stripes to sew onto the arms of our Chipinaw jackets: red for arts and crafts, blue for religion, white for service, yellow for sports, green for nature cabin. Zest was *all* of these.

Our mavens thought they had better stuff than Zest, but all they offered were patches and slogans, soporifics and zest-killers, games reduced to their lowest denominators: mirth that wasn't mirth, play that was hardly playful, prayers that earned no god.

Of course, not only couldn't my counselor have said such things but, if he had, none of us would have believed them. So, the guy succeeded in setting me straight. He made me ashamed of my gullibility. The Zest feeling went away. I became cynical and modern again. After all, it *was* just soap.

I didn't buy any more Zest. Every now and then I came upon a bar at someone else's house, tried it, and, despite myself, felt a glimmer of the old Z jubilation—but I dismissed it as my impressionability.

The next year I read two books in English class that raised my consciousness about suggestibility and the relation between puffery and products. Their author, Vance Packard, a pop sociologist, scoped out seductive influences in ads—the subliminal messages behind icons that make us want to buy things. Borrowing ideas from his book *The Hidden Persuaders,* I decoded a series of Old Gold cigarette ads for my English term paper that spring, showing how the placement of objects in each still life associated the product with either pleasure or success. The particular campaign I chose ran in *Life* and *Look* and involved little cameos as if rendered by Dutch masters. Each put a pack of Old Gold among personal items like an astrolabe, an expensive watch, a bottle of brandy, pearls, a fountain pen, a denim jacket, etc.

Of course, I had hung out at Robert Towers Advertising long enough to know that my stepfather's agency didn't design subliminal art. They were into straightforward spiels—postcard landscapes and chic designs, "classics," Bob declared. He would go through the Sunday *Times,* find one of his, and crow, "Look at that layout. It's Johnny Mercer; it's Rodgers and Hammerstein; it's Hemingway."

He insisted that I was reading things into Old Gold ads, that the point of the advertising business was to show something opulent and attractive—no one hid symbols in layouts. "Richard, you don't need the Vance Packards of the world to make effective ads. Lose that bum!"

But I assumed he was too small-time and regional to do the really advanced stuff.

Being in midtown, he was able to deposit a carbon of my paper onto the desk of the Old Gold guy at a nearby agency. A week later he reported the man's response.

"He said it was a good piece of work for a high-school student. Your teacher should give you an A, and he'll have a job waiting for you when you finish college; but he also said to tell you to forget the subliminal crap. It's a load of malarkey."

A mere year after my flirtation with Vance Packard, Chuck Stein introduced the poetry of Charles Olson in our creative-writing class, then read aloud "The Moon is the Number 18," setting on the table before us the blue-and-yellow matching trump with its crayfish emerging from a stellar pool, baying wolves and twin battlements on either side of a winding mountain path, a lunar face dripping golden embers.

I felt a different joy from the intoxication of Zest: a celestial event showering worlds with hermetic particles—a lot heftier than soap suds. This was truly "old gold": a matrix of living minerals as well as a splash of primal manifestation.

The naked horned couple chained blindly to a half-cube in The Devil, trump fifteen, bat-winged beasts, became comely Lovers in a garden in the sixth trump, the Satanic figure suddenly a smiling angel, the cube now whole—but only once they realized the chains about their necks were loosely hung. Whether to be in heaven or languish in hell was their choice, just as Zest had been my choice to throw off the shackles of America, to convert my gloom into happiness—to accept a subconscious field of operation. In the seventh trump, that same male and female pair became black and white Sphinxes bowing before the Charioteer of the Earth's first temple under a curtain of stars heralding the birth of the Symbol and advent of human society.

The cards didn't go away like soap. They matured in me and gave me a sense of my own existence. Zest returned and stuck this time and, even better, I was able to transmit it to others by laying down the deck and telling its stories.

The tarot understood sadness and love, romance and destiny better than I did. It turned crises into opportunities. It showed me that I was *never not* among sacred things. It anointed me a lay Hierophant, a doyenne of Pentacles, a hero on a grail, a psychotherapist beyond portfolio, always, even when riding the subway, when playing left field or studying for a math exam. It gave an ordinary boy an esoteric alphabet and a way to glimpse the hidden universe. It made me serious and worthwhile to myself.

It is *all subliminal*—that is, latent and iconic. The world is a giant, uninterpreted tarot in which a bar of soap can also be a Star.

Of course, I am getting ahead of myself, confiding news I came to decades later. But those were its seeds. Their crucible was the dream of a chemistry set interpreted by a Village doctor. They were raised to the next exponent by a tarot deck from the Basement of the Occult in the same Village. Their true gestation is unknown, beyond my lifetime.

After so many years Horace Mann was ending. I was now an elder in the temple that First Formers were entering as mere tykes. It was hard to believe I had been recruited into the cult so young—the current denizens of Pforzheimer Hall looked like third-graders.

The reign of A's was over—their mirage no longer fooled me—and I found it impossible to work with the same dauntless spirit. In fact, I didn't understand how I had done it for six long years since dinner at Tavern on the Green.

I had changed, but the school hadn't. In English we went from *Hamlet* to the rage of Timon of Athens and his banquet of stones. In history I imagined Clinton a kind of Timon as he dragged us through the Industrial Revolution at breakneck speed, threatening and slandering us in comparison to seniors of other years. This wasn't just his standard performance; he was appalled by our uncritical enthusiasm for mysticism, our lack of respect for school tradition, our sloppiness and longish hair, the rowdiness of the Senior lounge, and what he termed our "insolence" as typified by Alpert's public outbursts and Stein's campy satires. Recently Chuck had stood blocking the way to Chapel, stomping like Rumpelstiltskin, as he tore dollar bills to pieces and threw them at astonished underclassmen, proclaiming that money was the source of all evil.

"The worst class ever, hands down," he declared. "I had hoped for better than wise-asses and smart alecks for our seventy-fifth-anniversary year."

He wasn't prescient enough to see the counterculture—almost no one was. For we were mere pikers compared to what was coming down the road just behind us.

Mr. Metcalf threw plenty of baseballs in those final months. He too thought we were an embarrassment to tradition—unrepentant slackers. I looked for some concession or relief to acknowledge our journey from Caesar to Cicero to Vergil, to ratify our tour of duty, but it seemed as though he wanted only to rush us through as many stanzas as possible before we got away for good.

I peaked at midterms, after my acceptance at Amherst. At that point I got A's in Latin and English and an A+ on the famous senior history exam, said to be the hardest test in the school. I had mastered the chronicle of the world up through the French Revolution and then written like a demon for two hours.

Mr. Clinton extolled me as one of the best he had ever had. He made out my desperate scrawl, the clock outracing my mind-splay, as I check-listed Robespierre, the Jacobins, and doomed figures through Thermidor to the guillotine, all in the last five minutes (and a stolen forty-five seconds before a ruler snapped in front of me). It was a mere list because I had budgeted my time poorly and expended too much on other questions, but Clinton had written, "Outline style excellent!" Wow, I couldn't lose.

When we returned from Christmas holiday for our last term, I hung out with a group from Westchester who played hockey on a frozen pond Fridays after school. It was my baptism in the sport, and I adored the live action with its rhythms, the aesthetics of each actual score through the busy slot (like in so many of Jonny's and my made-up games). Ice hockey captivated me in a way that soccer never had.

Each ball or quoit (with its shape and role in the sport to which it gives rise) determines the mood and tenor of its caper. Footballs, tennis balls, basketballs, ping-pong balls, even shuffleboard disks weave energy fields, and to me suddenly none were as delectable as the chaotic scrum cast by a small flat cylinder of rubber ricocheting on ice. Piles of coats formed the two sides of the goal, and missed shots rolled across the pond toward infinity.

Having played only with tin men, I was unskilled at stickhandling. I could race but I couldn't dribble or shoot. I tried to control the puck when it came my way, kicking at it with speed skates as it rolled behind me. I never managed to advance through clusters of opponents before someone parted me from my prize.

For that whole winter we tried to get hockey sanctioned as a PE sport, a difficult proposition at a school without a rink. Our hopes were based on the fact that there was a facility visible from the El, only a few blocks down Broadway. We spent months going through formal procedures ... a signed petition ... finally a faculty sponsor willing to accompany us there and ref our games—we found a young newcomer who had played in college.

Why this one victory, so paltry and late, should have obsessed not only me but thirteen other seniors is, in retrospect, baffling; yet we threw our heart and hopes into it. Finally one of the coaches suggested that if we were so gung-ho, we try flooding the tennis courts. Grateful to be let out of a day of body-building, we spent an entire gym period on this foolhardy adventure. A hose was dragged out of its frozen coat, ripping up ice as it dragged along; then liquid toppled out in sputters and sloshed over snow. Drifts filled with water and caked. Those of us with shovels pushed snow against the fence, forming barriers to keep potential ice from running out.

It was an engineering impossibility and, though we were laughing, our soaked shoes eventually froze, making for an unpleasant ride home. The next day I tried gliding on the surface we had laid, but after two strides I went through it. It recalled my dreams of skating down winter streets that became summer ponds with lily pads and turtles.

Finally we got permission to hike to the Broadway rink with our coach. From PE we marched out of Horace Mann, down the hill, along the El, through the aromatic zone of the industrial bakery, through the many lands that bordered our hermitage, unvisited these many years—factories, warehouses, groceries, hardware stores, restaurant outlets: the Bronx. Carrying skates and sticks, bubbling with enthusiasm, we came to the outer gate only to find that the rink had already been rented to a girls' school.

I peered over the wall. Half the ice was lost to warm weather anyway. On the other half, girls, so many in different colored clothes like flags of different nations, were skating there—had been, in fact, all winter.

That image became my harbinger for the dissolution of Horace Mann, a rigorous academy crumbling into something without boundaries or definition. HM of yore had held the world in place while we bumbled through adolescence. The half rink with its female flags was blithe and common, way too lenient a replacement for all that we had braved and survived.

Some of my hockey friends had access to cars, and during spring vacation a gang of them drove up to Grossinger's. Just like that, no mention to PG! I left word at the front gate and they zipped on through.

After the rink closed for the guests that afternoon, we designated colored squares along the wall for goals, then played in various combinations of four on four, using rink master Irv Jaffee to round out the teams. He whizzed in and out of us, the old fox, teasing with the puck, ritually shouting, "Keep it on the ice, boys," which was hard for kids used to zinging it. But there was plenty of expensive glass at stake.

One afternoon near the end of February I bought a *New York Post* for the subway ride home. Whereas once I would have thought only of getting as much of a head start as I could on my homework, now I combed the sports for every last morsel of baseball. There were only spring-training dregs, so I read the hockey news even though I didn't follow the sport.

I knew the basic storyline from banter among my friends: the Rangers, a perennially bad team, had been in the upper echelon through the early part of the season after picking up elite defenseman Doug Harvey from the mighty Montreal Canadians near the end of his career. He had provided heretofore absent leadership, but now they had fallen into a battle with Detroit for the fourth and final playoff spot. That night they were playing the last-place Boston Bruins at Madison Square Garden. The *Post* said they had just traded for a defenseman named Pete Goegan. His diphthonged name was the trigger: I liked the "oe" between "g's."

I had never seen a hockey game, or, for that matter, any pro sport but baseball. But I wanted to know what the game looked like, so I stayed on the IRT till 59th Street and showed up at Bob's office. Hunched over drawings with his art director, my stepfather turned and looked at me. "What's up, Rich?" he asked impatiently, understatement hiding his astonishment at this after-school visit. I showed him the *Post* and asked if he wanted to go to the Rangers game.

He scanned the article and underwent a flip of moods. "You know something—you and I have never once been to the Garden. I used to live there." Breaking all precedent, he called Bridey and told her not to expect us for dinner. We ate quickly at his account McGinnis's near the Garden, then joined the arena crowd.

The rink startled me—how large its surface, the dwarf-size nets: rope-like cages replicating how we laid our coats, not long and wide like soccer goals (as I had imagined). I was startled too by how cold the breeze off the ice. Carrying sticks like spears, the players skated around their own nets, two different-colored warm-up gyres grazing at their midpoints.

After the anthem a referee dropped the puck; suddenly there was a swarm of players in front of the Rangers goal, the goalie fell down, and a red light went on as the crowd booed. Boston scored again almost immediately. Then the Rangers got to play with an extra man, a rule I knew nothing about. Andy Bathgate, the star, shot it from way out; somehow it went through the players in front of the net and bounced in. The light behind the Boston goal flashed and the crowd exploded.

For almost two periods thereafter, the Rangers surrounded the Boston net but were unable to put the puck in. The territory was always so clogged, and the rubber bounced zanily over it, onto it, and across its opening as ooo's and aah's undulated across the arena. By now I was totally in the frenzy, poised in expectation, sighing in disappointment. I loved the speed and bumptiousness, the dragon's lairs for goals, the potential of illuminated flashes proclaiming scores. There were only a couple of desperate minutes left when Bob's adopted favorite, Irv Spencer, passed to a player whose slicked-down black hair looked like his name, Dave Balon. As I strained to see, the red light went on; the game was tied. And that's how it ended.

I blabbed about this event so much to Jonny that my enthusiasm became contagious and soon he was as involved as I was in the fate of the Rangers. That weekend we got Bob to take us to a game together.

The Rangers were beaten soundly by surging Detroit, but an announcement after the match took away some of the sting: for the first time in ten years, hockey would be on radio in New York—for the remainder of the season.

Several nights later Jon and I sat with our schoolbooks open, the radio beside us, the game beginning. I sensed trouble as my mother and Bob burst in the front door late, deep in altercation. They went straight to their room and continued shouting. I knew from the shift in cadence that their agitation had scapegoated us. Sure enough, Bob came marching down the hall as her emissary and directed his comments at me: "Just because you've stopped studying is no reason to drag this boy in too."

Obediently I took the play-by-play into my study but kept Jonny posted on the score through the door.

A week later the Rangers and Red Wings met in a showdown. Jon and I kneeled by the radio: "Ingarfield and Ullman are ready. The puck is dropped.... "

Detroit seemed to score at will and took a quick 4-2 lead. Then a Ranger defenseman slid in a long shot. We clapped. My mother shouted a warning from her room. We lowered the volume. The Rangers scored after the next face-off, then again a minute later. We cheered with clenched fists in silence. But as the last seconds were counted off, the Rangers passing the puck around from player to player in ritual keep-away, we couldn't contain ourselves. Our muffled shouts rose to squeals. "You better tell those two maniacs I've had enough of this nonsense. You started this crap with your goddamned hockey, and you'd better stop it right now." I felt an old familiar rush of guilt.

I awaited Bob's appearance. I knew well the blend of pain and anger that would be on his face, his lips pressed in bottled emotion.

"C'mon, Richard," he pleaded. "Enough of this *chazerai*. Let this boy get back to his studies. What's wrong with you? Have you quit dead on the last lap?"

I seemed to have. In lieu of homework I was playing a spinner baseball game in the bathroom, inventing a whole season between the two new National League franchises, the New York Mets and Houston Colt .45s. Using their expansion rosters to make out line-ups and keeping scorecards of every game, I brought stats from my made-up league to school, and Jake and our baseball crew perused them. Guys adopted favorite players; mine was the ex-Red Elio Chacon, now a Met. After Jake picked Merritt Ranew of the Colts, every Monday he came rushing up to me: "How'd my baby Ranew do over the weekend?" Once he even had me bring the game to his home in Yonkers. "C'mon, Merritt baby," he shouted, as I spun away.

Then the real Mets took the field in spring training. I was enchanted by the look of former Cincinnati Red, Jay Hook, in his blue-and-orange New York uniform, blue letters across the front, throwing Met curves. It was like a whole unexplored Babylonian civilization suddenly in our midst, a new game on the radio dial, emerging fresh and untarnished by prior pennant races. The Mets didn't have to win. Everything about them was novel and enthrall-ing, even their names: Herb Moford, Choo Choo Coleman, Charlie Neal, Larry Foss, Al Jackson, a menagerie of fairy-tale characters like the packs of Earthlings who replaced Flash Gordon in the days of P.S. 6. I was at the beginning of time again, among unknown legionnaires.

In the second exhibition game someone neither I nor the announcers had heard of named Rod Kanehl replaced Neal at second base and, a couple of innings later, ignited a game-tying rally with a single. All through spring training Kanehl continued to amaze, the master of 1-1 in the box score (one at-bat, one hit). Against all odds he made the team. Once in New York, he rode the subways recreationally; a fan darling, nicknamed The Mole, but I had spotted him first.

My performance at midterm now seemed contrived and pointless; I couldn't wrest my mind back on studying. The bubble separating me from the world had dissolved. I saw crocuses and dandelions everywhere. From the classrooms of Tillinghast Hall I heard crows repeating calls they had always made, children raucous at play, workmen drilling into 242nd Street, the jargon and clatter of worldly commerce—a symphony that had been playing extrinsically. Now the cacophony was deafening.

Horace Mann had become unfamiliar, spooky and hollow without my noticing when or how. It was as though the buildings had stepped back into perspective and I viewed them now from afar, objectively—interdicted castles, decorous penitentiaries surrounded by a far vaster metropolis. Their halls and fusty rooms no longer fazed me; this wasn't life and death—it was a suburban private school.

I saw the rust on lockers, each brown clump of granules defining a possible universe. Ants and flies commanded most of it even as we passed them insensibly. Now I recognized them, creatures as real and busy as me.

I noticed cobwebs in ceiling corners, spiders crawling along cracks, chips missing from moulding, sweaters and coats unclaimed for years. Why was all this suddenly so vivid and lucid? Why I did care so much when for years I simply came and went with assignments, sustained by A's and B's?

Something was happening at the very roots of perception. It wasn't

Superman's x-ray vision, but my focal plane had shifted its nodal point. I was entering an alternate kingdom of matter, one made of soot, desiccation, and decay.

My lessons, having come to their uncalculated conclusion, were regurgitating the sum of data crammed into a child's brain. Framed and ingested as innocuous facts, they had been assimilated unconsciously, transubstantiated into minotaurs and mutts, merging finally with Nanny's ghosts, the New York Highlanders, interpretation of dreams, Bill-Dave, the Hardy Boys, and Ken Holt to form something beyond recognition or ken. What I had been learning was now a world-view; whatever it sought to inculcate was my own. I no longer needed magisterial warrant to proceed; I had transcended the initiation and was *inside* the eros of corrosion, the syzygy of mere mass.

In Latin I was unprepared for the in-class translation for the first time in three years, so I got the tiniest of the punitive baseballs hurled at me. In math I couldn't solve a new category of equations and failed a spot quiz. In history the nineteenth century rushed by, a thousand details from the Industrial Revolution and ensuing skirmishes. I couldn't concentrate; I couldn't pin down or memorize more facts, let alone all the secularisms of modernity. We were suddenly in the Balkans, World War I—hundreds of new names, dates, and battles unlearned, thickets of text, the twentieth century a tangled parody of all the centenaries that preceded it, the impending final exam a nightmare beyond reckoning. I didn't care anymore; my mind had become a sieve. I had gotten into Amherst, but would I even graduate?

Forsythia sprang up like fire, bushes from Wordsworthian odes. I heard birds making rackets outside our windows, saw branches thick with leaves and blossoms. A ball of sun blazed insect wings over the field. Where had the time gone? My teachers looked gawky and sad, their authority crumbling into caricature. Underneath it all bubbled a new anxiety of not being prepared, slipping into the backs of classes, praying not to be called on ... breathing a sigh of relief when I wasn't. This was *so* unknown.

I stared out the train window at landscapes and buildings and realized how many times I had viewed this scenery and now I was looking at it for just about the last time. Part of me belonged to it, and I didn't even know what it was—black children playing in parks, old men walking like beetles, shadows of my vehicle careening down through shadows of tracks onto pedestrians and cars and cobblestones—so complicated and ineffable. I felt them like a disease, a light growing in me, a poison making me limp and thirsty. I felt much more too—solitude, impatience, longing—Dostoyevsky's infinite spaces.

I remembered how it was once okay to notice spring remotely: the glad return of warm weather. But that fell short of a mushrooming reality, the way florescence burst from wintry slumber, interstices in every dimension at every scale of vine and bud. It had so long been a dream without a landscape, without real twigs and buds, cobble or dirt. Now the wind was subtle and vast, the May clouds palpable and creamy, cumulus and beyond cumulus, reaching for another designation and class of name. An unearthly light invaded every dandelion, each stone gargoyle; the air was filled with seeds—more than I could grasp or count.

I had missed the sheer enormity of existence. Physical reality was manifesting spontaneously, and it was pulling me away from the abstraction I had honored as Horace Mann.

Kids pushed past one another in the hallways of Tillinghast Hall, mindless and rude. Seniors were still manipulating the tin men in the lounge when Chuck stopped me and read a poem about Donald Duck. Brief and silly, it was exactly right. "What's with you?" he asked.

"I'm trapped in the Six of Cups."

"Go 'way, breeze," he said. "Go back home." I knew that that was his antidote to life's malaises—avant-garde minimal, faux light-hearted—but it wasn't mine.

"Don't you like breezes?" I played along.

"Yes, but I was thinking of it at the time, and it came." He made a silly face. "What's in *your* brain?"

"How funny and insane this place that makes me come day-in, day-out, won't ever leave me alone."

We walked around the track. Aimlessly I kicked cinders. I remembered times I lay on this field studying devotedly before this or that class. In my mind I heard and still honored Mr. Metcalf's rendering of Virgil's onomatopoeia, *"Magno cum murmure monte."* Oh, to be in such fealty and wonder again! But the feeling with which the memory left me was already as ancient as my life.

I had intended once to reclaim everything by simple narrative—therapeutic confessions and autobiographical prose—but even Kingsley Ervin knew I had lost the thread (the labyrinth as well). I was telling my story from mere habit.

"Just because you were so successful with it," he proposed one afternoon, "doesn't mean the style will last forever." Our class was filled with ambitious younger kids already imitating me, and I was trapped between jealousy at their success and weariness with the whole affair. "You need to dig deeper." But what was inside me was hollow and intangible; it had neither a plot nor a name. Its feeling recalled my phobia of the dungeon stairs. In childhood when I felt this way I panicked; now I could tolerate the sensations, but they made me mournful beyond words.

I put aside what I had come to call "the novel" and wrote a science-fiction tale, about a man who unsuspectingly took an office elevator past the penthouse into higher dimensions; another about a Cheshire Cat Hunt on a distant world (and hunters who developed sympathy for their telepathic prey); then a fictional narrative through the mind of a child named Joey. I read them to the class under maples on a day so muggy we were allowed to take off our jackets and ties. Branches brushed against the stones of Tillinghast, the air a nectared sponge. I felt lethargic, brittle. Chuck's tarot cards lay in the grass, awaiting a poem. Flowers fell from sky. I was marking time.

Every Senior in Honors English was required to give a speech to the whole school, but each year a few escaped for lack of enough chapels. Four of us were yet to go when the final slot was being delegated. "Any volunteers?" Mr. Baruth asked. All year I had made myself invisible at selection time, and now there was but one small window of jeopardy. In an interlude of attempted anonymity, slinking in my chair, I suddenly recalled a feeling I had had once as I sowed my baseball cards through Central Park.

This speech was not a thing to be dreaded. It was a chance to meet my estrangement head-on, to call out the shadow life I was leading. My hand shot up, to the amazed relief of three classmates.

Most chapel speeches were topical and neutral, a historical account, an analysis of a scientific problem, summer travels in Europe, but I dug deeper, as Mr. Ervin had advised, and found exactly what I wanted. On the appointed day, I sat on stage beside Dr. Gratwick. I was going to spill the beans!

My confidence lasted until my name was called.

I rose dizzily. "Richard Grossinger" was a fiction, the thing they called me; it wasn't who I was. But then who was this whirlpool of notions?

Standing at the podium I feared at once that my resources were too shallow. I looked at a sea of faces, Rodney and Keith somewhere among them, and almost lost it. I stumbled in a false start, and then began for real.

I described the long years of work leading only to a world vast beyond comprehension. Without naming anyone I portrayed Rodney's bluster and described attitudes toward girls in an all-boys school. I alluded to my "idols" and intimated how I feared falling in love with boys.

I certainly had everyone's attention—half in empathy, half in horror of what I would say next. I spoke my final words with a calm precision:

"How did we get here? How did I come to this difficult moment at the end of Horace Mann? I think back, and I am a little boy in a noisy playground. My nurse pushes me on the swing, up and down, in sun and into shade. I am lying in bed having sneaked back from the movies one night at camp to hear some wild, long-since-gone fastballer named Bob Wiesler try to win his first game of the year against Washington. The swimming counselor heaves the lemon-line over my head. I swim after, grab it from the water, and throw.... I remember a TV show, a comic book found on the beach, men on beds of spikes, tortured in steam showers, unable to change their fate. I remember listening to Allie Reynolds pitch and Walt Dropo get a hit in the second game of a doubleheader on a car radio so long ago. I am standing by the road on the last day of camp, waiting for my father to pick me up. I am only a baby, and warm summer light shines on rotten apples beneath the trees. The world goes beyond us into things we cannot imagine. It is already too late, and I am about to become someone I don't even know. This is my moment to say goodbye, for all of us."

I ended by quoting Robert Penn Warren:

"Were we happy because we were happy or because once a long time back, we had been happy? Was our happiness tonight like the light of the moon which does not come from the moon, for the moon is cold and has no light of its own but is reflected light from far away."

A gulp of silence ... return to the velvet chair beside Gratwick, then the applause, like the gathering rustle of my first Chipinaw rain.

I had finally performed my *bar mitzvah*. I had preached the only Isaiah in my heart.

Now I was ready to face the consequences. I made an appointment with Mr. Clinton and, at the end of the next school day, climbed the twisting stairs to his citadel. As I edged to the door I saw him sitting on the master's throne, playing with his belt a notch out from his paunch, smiling and glowering intermittently.

I announced my presence. He got into character quickly, snarling, "To what do I owe?"

I confessed at once that I had fallen way behind. He sat bolt upright in the chair.

"You, my star pupil? You dare to tell me this. You whom I trusted. This is horrible, Dickie."

"I'm sorry, sir. I just don't understand what's happening to me."

"Sorry, shit! You're going to be a damn sight more than sorry." His face changed like the sun passing through clouds. "You were one of the best I ever had. Dickie, you were like silver plate. Now what I see is silver plate covered with shit!"

"I tried—"

"I thought you had some depth to you, but I was wrong. You're all surface, there's nothing inside." A pause. "You let me down." He sat there in silence, his head bowed. When he looked up at me, his voice was so soft it was almost inaudible. "What have you been doing when you haven't been working in my class?"

"I've gone to a few hockey games. I've been following baseball. I went out ... with a girl."

"Girls!" he shot back. "Are you like all those other shits that sit there in class with their erections?"

I was shocked. "No, sir. I mean—" Why would he even say such a thing?

"Shut up. I'm talking to you. Would you betray my course?"

"No sir."

"Well, then you better catch up, dickhead!"

I started to respond.

"That's it, you shallow shit. Meeting adjourned."

Clinton was more than I could handle, and the impact of our session was instantaneous. I went home, got out the history book, and fled my ogre chapter after chapter, well into the next morning. I studied continuously until I was ready to take the Advanced Placement with a clear conscience. No all-star performance like at midterm, but at least I got by.

In truth, my situation was less perilous than I imagined, for I was goofing off only by comparison to prior standards. I felt truant not because I was playing real hooky or at risk of failing classes but because I was uncomfortable with my own being. I was like a creature undergoing metamorphosis, a pupa molting and awaiting a hit of new DNA. I couldn't conduct larval activities anymore, but they were deeply enough ingrained that I carried out their injunctions autonomically. I maintained a credible grade point average, a drop-off from between A- and B+ to between B+ and B. Except for Clinton my apostasy went unnoticed. I got my "cum laude" at graduation, as our official valedictorian briefly referenced my speech, then dispatched us to the winds.

On the last day of Horace Mann, Mr. Metcalf never let up once from his fury of translation. Not a hint of requiem after five years of meetings together, not a token of fare-thee-well sorrow. When the bell rang he said, "You're all good boys," and we left. Math class ended with cheering and hoots, English with a lecture on good study habits in college. Clinton's class was the last; he greeted us with a scowl and said, "Take out a piece of paper and write about the period between the First and Second World Wars." Then he broke into a big belly laugh. He was still laughing as we scurried down the hall, dismissed without a meeting.

One week later I left the gym after the math final, my last, strode from the sawdust into the full sun of the afternoon, where it had been all day and was now decaying. The flowers were painfully yellow. They had waited six years for my first day of freedom, but I had grown old and wanton in the process. Now freedom was just a rumor of a childhood that had abandoned me. The air was sodden as mud. I felt mainly its weight. I collapsed under the subway fan. Where were my classmates? I was inexplicably alone after years of train camaraderie. I changed at 168th Street and got off at 86th. I had an hour left before my last session with Dr. Friend, so I went into the Park.

It was already summer there. Mica twinkled from pavement. My other lives were scattered about: the Hares and the Hounds, the orange-drink man with his waxed cylinders of nectar, Bob hitting fungos, long-dead squirrels and pigeons. These were severed from me by something opaque yet palpable. The world then was an agony, a terror without reconciliation, a melancholy beyond knowing, but it was simpler than it would ever be again. I thought once that growing up would help. I thought that I would find the traumatic moment, the clue in the embers. Now no such thing existed. In their place were a Hierophant and a Fool.

I studied in order to become learned, to know the hidden truth. But vastness and ambiguity stretched to each horizon, and dandelions everywhere bid me back to Oz as they locked me out of Oz forever. I wanted to somehow capture this errant intimation, to justify myself, to declare the stubborn reality.

I was writing for my life.

I could say the Horace Mann adage in Latin: *"Magna est veritas et praevalit.... "*—"v" pronounced always as "w." Our alma mater's gaining verses were *"Men come and go, / stars cease to glow, / But great is the truth and it prevails."* It was an embarrassingly overwrought refrain, but it had a stealth epiphany. "Stars" took it outdoors and made us a celestial choir addressing something larger and more abiding than schoolwork: the enigma of Creation beyond the birth and death of suns; beyond anything taught, though everything intimated, in our lesson plans—in the denouements of Donne, Keats, and Melville; in the formation of cirrus clouds, the sound of cosmic rays, the waning of the Middle Ages. We were singing for our lives too.

Wordsworth wouldn't have composed the hack lines of Bob Ackerman, Class of '53, but he would have understood the extravagance of their allusion. I could recite his more elegant phrasing by heart as Baruth had once required: *"There was a time when meadow, grove, and stream, / The earth, and every common sight, / To me did seem / Apparelled in celestial light.... "*

I had become a scholar in the Grecian temple of my dream; I had reduced its arcana to ordinary events. Now *("Though nothing can bring back the hour / Of splendour in the grass, of glory in the flower.... ")* I wanted to return to childhood and make the journey again.

I began to compose an account of the walk home out the east side of the Park to the drugstore—recalling how, after Sunday baseball with Bob and Jon, I was so thirsty then I imaged waterfalls of pink lemonade and bubbling brooks of yellow lemonade topped with white lemon foam, until the soda-man poured it onto crushed ice, and I sat there sipping, there being nothing else of me. On the way home Jonny and I ran down the block catching make-believe fly balls, leaping beneath awnings, diving at the pavement, my left hand brown with Neatsfoot oil in which we adoringly drowned our gloves.

I thought of the days at Bill-Dave when we finished playing and would sit under the cherry blossoms with Ranger and the Bully. I pictured the sweet sticks of pastel-colored chalks with which we drew our trails, and how we crossed the Park for hours in feint and counterfeint. I remembered Halloween at Pelham, when they hid the pumpkins, and I found the third and last one buried in a hole in a tree, packed in with dirt and leaves. But they wouldn't let me keep it as my prize because it was such a good hiding place they were sure I had peeked. Again and again on the way home Bert called me a cheater; yet all I had done was make a brilliant deduction. God, they were terrible—I walked among them in a daze.

I remembered the tombs of the Egyptians at the Museum and how we dashed through them, fleeing ghosts. I thought of how augural it was when the woman with absolutely white hair arrived to unlock the door of her bookshop and I stepped into its antique aroma and knew just what volume to pluck from the Hardy Boys row in the back.... And Gene Woodling's homer falling into the upper deck.

In sixth grade, I was the only one old enough to read who didn't walk to school, so on the Bill-Dave wagon I rendered the street signs aloud to the younger kids, making them laugh with my inflections: "Stellllaaa Doooro!" and "Prexy's ... the ed-uuu-cated hamburger!"

Some days at P.S. 6 the rain would drip from the top of the window to the sill, the schoolyard damp, the benches soaked. We walked in gloomy halls, mud footprints.

Each item returned to be acknowledged and counted ... an Oh Henry! candy bar ... a Superman comic ... a red plastic water rocket ... a blue and yellow metal truck ... Tarzan rescued by the animals at the Trans-Lux theater ... my mother's hand patting Vick's Vaporub on my chest. Time itself was cascading in all directions. Then I stepped into the elevator and pressed Dr. Friend's number: I had come to termination at last.

The final hour became a half hour, and then there were only fifteen minutes left. Still I lay there cold and untouched, aware that the seconds were ticking off the end of this too. I waited without sorrow or regret.

"What do you feel now?" he asked.

"I feel nothing."

"Do you feel numb?"

"No, nothing."

"Think of it," he said. "After five years this is the end and you lie there emotionless. Is that possible?"

"I don't like to admit it, but it's true." I tried inside me to feel something, to cry, but there was nothing, only an irritation and a wish to leave. "I don't even know how I was ever afraid, how I ever panicked. I remember waiting day after day for our next session just so I could tell you something important. But now it's all gone."

"Then just talk."

"About what?"

"The rules are the same, even in the last session. Talk about what you're thinking."

I thought back to when Dr. Fabian died and how I had come to Dr. Friend for the first time. Now he seemed so real, Dr. Fabian phantom and far away. Yet it was Fabian who had found and saved me and taught me like his own child. He was already a saint, but he had become a remote legend, no longer applicable. I began to say something, but I stopped. My throat hurt so much I couldn't talk. "How about that! My throat is too sore."

"Does it feel sore?"

"Can't speak."

"Describe the feeling."

"I can't."

"Where is it sore?"

I pointed. "Way back in there."

"Do you feel sick in any other way?"

"Yeah, sort of. My side feels weak, as though I'm out of breath. It's the old Saturday feeling."

"What are you thinking about?"

"I'm not thinking about it anymore." Then I realized I had to pee real badly. I told him that and began to squirm.

"You're not on a hot seat, you know."

"Isn't it sort of obvious why I'm restless? It's kind of natural when you have to go." We had become two teenagers "ranking" each other.

"You're stalling for time."

"That's not true. I have to go so badly. Can't I just go to the bathroom and then come back and finish?"

"You can end the session if you want."

"That's all?"

"Richard, don't you see? You confronted Mr. Clinton; you had a disagreement with Mr. Baruth and had to make up a test. You practically failed math. You wasted hours and hours trying to get to a skating rink that was already rented. Why? Because that was the only way you could express any feeling. Now school's over, and you're about to leave me. You want to cry, but you're unable to."

I searched inside me for the sorrow he was describing, but I didn't find it. I didn't find anything except the urge to pee. It was burning so fiercely I could barely think. The paradox of the situation fascinated me. This was a Nat Fleischer hypnotism show.

"You mean I don't have to go?"

"Nor do you have a sore throat or a pain in your side. They're created for the moment."

"How can that be true? I feel them. They're real."

"Do you think I don't remember? Your head hurt; you were dying. You had cancer. Again and again you have come here seeking relief, imagining that if this or that feeling went away, you'd be happy forever."

"I still believe that, you know."

"So, you're not perfect. No one is. Maybe you'd like to convince me that you're so sick you can't possibly leave. But you've already made that decision. Something in you wants to go on. I imagine you'll have your problems, perhaps terrible ones, but you'll make it. And I'll always be here, thinking of you, rooting for you, here for you to come back to if it gets too hard."

I knew that I would never come back. This office, with its rich smoky aura, was the past. It was no longer me. The tarot cards were the future; the writing was the future; some girl I had yet to meet was the future. I could sense the movie camera panning away. "Feel scared," I told myself. "Feel scared that this is it. You're on your own." But I didn't get scared when Dr. Fabian died, and all I could feel now was the lingering soreness in my throat and the agony of having to pee. I began visualizing the blocks along Central Park West, imagining how fast I'd run to get home in time.

I had thought the ending would be so different, something like my glorious speech at Horace Mann, but here I was, squirming on the couch, unable to get up and go to the bathroom because I didn't want that to be the last thing. I lay there watching the second hand. It was too late to recoup anything. It was done.

"Good-bye, Rich."

I got up and turned around. "I don't know what happened to all the great things I was going to say now."

"Well, have a good summer and remember not to fall into a rut in college."

"Good-bye," I said with a short nod.

I was in suspended animation, then freefall in the elevator. I marched down the long chandeliered lobby, silently and melodramatically chanting my farewell. I was prepared to dash, but when I hit the street I realized I didn't have to pee.

6

Teen Tour

Months earlier a travel agency offering a cross-country tour for teens had made reservations for the group at the Fontainebleau, and my mother impulsively signed me up. I insisted I wouldn't go, but she held the slot and, with my attention on finishing Horace Mann and getting ready for college, I made no other summer plans. My father refused to allow me at Grossinger's for that long, and I had outgrown camp.

By early June the tour began to take on fresh appeal, crazy as it was to imagine myself on a marathon of buses, trains, and boats with strange kids and chaperones. The transition occurred in my unconscious. I dreamed of being on an ocean liner, giant fish swimming around glaciers, Chipinaw's dale transported to Italy and France with torqued and Eiffel towers, boys and girls at a forest festival that fused a Robin Hood movie with my grade-school daydreams of other worlds. So on the first of July, Bob escorted me and my suitcase downtown in a cab. We were a bit late and I was nervous.

"Don't worry," he said. "These things never get started on time."

"Maybe it will be a mirage and I can go home."

"C'mon, Richard. This is a chance to see some of the great venues in the world: Niagara, Banff, San Francisco, New Orleans. I don't understand you kids. If someone had offered me such a trip at your age.… "

Not having had breakfast yet, he requested a stop at the Automat. I answered by staring at a clock through a shop window. "Ten minutes," he argued. "Give a man ten minutes."

We pumped coins from his pockets into slots, opened little doors, and took out released plates of food. I quit on my slab of ham halfway through, but he seemed to dawdle forever with coffee and eggs. Finally he closed the *Times*, and we walked across the street into Grand Central Station.

We found the meeting-place at once—a spiraling cluster of teenagers. The tour leaders introduced themselves: they were a music professor from Rutgers named Simmons and his wife.

"My husband's very interested in this line of work," offered Mrs. Simmons, "because he's as fascinated by trains as most youngsters are by spaceships these days."

"Looks like a nice bunch this year," he called out, approaching with his head half turned. He had square clumps of hair on either side of a bald pate.

"Yes, Sherman; it does."

"Excuse me," Bob interjected, commandeering Sherm's attention by name, "but your wife told me you were the expert on trains—"

"I am."

"Then could you tell me how soon this group will be departing?"

"We hope to get started in—" He paused to look at his watch. "About an hour."

"See, I told you," Bob said. "You lousy so-and-so wouldn't even let me finish my scrambled eggs." He gave me a friendly swat.

"Sorry. You were right."

"This looks like a young girl's nightmare," he commented as he scanned the group. "Any guy would give his right arm to be on this tour." In fact, when we finally all collected, it was twenty-eight girls and ten boys boarding a train to Buffalo (the 2.8 ratio, as tour members came to refer to it). "It shows how little some parents think of their kids," my stepfather concluded. "I would never send your sister on an unbalanced trip like this. She'd wind up with an inferiority complex."

With New York receding behind us, Mr. Simmons stood at the front of the car and struggled through a speech about not getting separated from the group, how to receive our food money, proper behavior with the opposite sex; then he concluded by promising us that the good experiences would outnumber the bad by two to one.

"Oh, you can give them a better prospect than that, Sherman," his wife coaxed.

"Okay. At least five to one. But only if you know how to be a good sport."

On the train to Buffalo a group of guys—total party boys—gathered with a cluster of girls from Florida and Georgia in the back of the car. They shouted and laughed, breaking into slapstick and group cheers. I heard so many choruses of *"Mi-a-mi Beach; / our boys are brave and bold and true …"* that it seemed as though I had known the song my whole life.

I joined a promising quartet up front. Harve was an immense, placid blob who had to be intelligent because he was headed to Yale. Barry was a tall, stiff, prep-school guy with dark-rimmed glasses and a gamut from diffident to snarly. Stan was a prototype of The Bug from Orenda—brusque, sarcastic, combative. He paraded his street smarts, openly contemptuous of Harve's and my Ivy League ambitions. Those were pure New Yorkers, while Alan from Baltimore was tall and handsome with a rugged face; he was amiable but with an edge, acting suaver and more worldly than the rest of us, as if the sole adult.

Lucy, Laurie, Carol, and Dorothy sat across from us. Dorothy and Carol were from Atlanta and called each other "Bean." They kept busy playing a childlike game—"I See a Barr" (meaning "Bear").

I thought Lucy was especially lively and cute with long hair, a pointed peg nose, and a wide-open doll's face. When we finally got around to telling the names of our schools, she announced dramatically, "Oh, what a school of cheaters. I go to Adelphi, and we played your school in soccer. Your coach 'reffed' and practically handed the game to them."

It seemed irrelevant, so I tried to make light of the matter, but she kept coming back to it. Each time her eyes met mine she snapped, "Remember, your school cheated." Yet I was still imagining her as a girlfriend on the trip.

After lunch Mr. Simmons stood and addressed us again, but he was continually interrupted.

"Hiya, Sherm," called out one of the party guys named Greg.

"I'll make the jokes," retorted Mr. Simmons. "You, I hope, will laugh at them. Now, first, you are Arista Co-ed Frontier Number One and will remain such throughout the summer."

"Bar mishap," inserted Mrs. Simmons, getting a laugh of her own.

He went on to describe schedules and events over the next several days, including a "Maid of the Mist Boat Ride" and "the earliest departure time of the summer—sorry—three in the morning. The operator will ring you."

"What if we refuse to get up?" Greg's friend Tony yelled back.

"Well," Mrs. Simmons interjected, "all I can say is: we'd hate to leave you at Niagara Falls, but it would be easier to lose you there before we get to like you."

Midway to Buffalo, Greg approached Harvey and me in the aisle and asked if we'd like to contribute to the ICF.

"What is it?" Harve asked.

"Never mind. Just contribute. It's a good and timely cause." Tony and Charlie stood behind him, stifling giggles, three wise guys from central casting. Tony was dark, Italian, and stringy; Greg was a dapper pudgeball; Charlie looked like the guy who called us fags for chasing leaves in First Form. They all had the same shit-eating grins, but Harve actually seemed concerned.

"Forget it," I told him. "It's a joke."

Greg turned quickly to me. "Can't you picture all those poor, sad illegitimate children you'd be leaving unfed by not contributing to their fund. You two should be ashamed of yourselves. Plus, if you don't contribute, you don't get—" he rolled his eyes—"any of the benefits."

Later in the afternoon Harve and Laurie paired up, so I sat alone talking to Lucy. She was an avowed baseball fan, Mickey Mantle her favorite player. She had even written him letters (no responses yet). I kept a conversation going, fielding her questions about Grossinger's, finally taking out my tarot and reading her fortune.

The train pulled into Buffalo at twilight. Noticing Harve carrying Laurie's suitcase with his own, I took Lucy's from her hand, saying, "Let me."

I was trudging along, balancing hers and mine, at turtle's pace when Barry came swooping in from behind and, with a clutch of a hand, ripped the bag from my grasp. "It's okay," I grumbled; "I have it."

"No, that's my job."

I let go.

"Well, at least," she declared, "you showed him how to be a gentleman."

When did he lay claim to her? They had barely spoken on the train.

At the motel in Niagara Falls I was assigned to a room with Alan, Barry, and Stan. Dropping off our luggage, we surveyed the accommodations—three beds and a cot. I agreed to take the cot, saving us having to do the odd finger out. Then we headed downstairs for dinner.

Over decades most of the tour's events have been erased or truncated in my memory. When I first read an old draft of this book, forgotten people sprang from dormancy, entire events returned. I was surprised by how faithfully I recorded our adventures, as if to exclude a single incident would be a forfeit of something precious. I had anointed myself keeper of our grail, a young Willa Cather. After all, I had been describing Wordsworthian meadows and Melvillian storms long before I got put on that runaway train.

I am struck mainly by how my journal was flooded with teen clichés and notions of romance common to the era, spun into tapestries by loneliness and the deep-rootedness of my compulsions. I seemed to return to the oracle again and again with the same question, yet never to hear its answer.

Arista Co-ed Frontier Tour camped at nightfall on the Canadian side—some of our group queuing into couples and making out in plain sight. Barry rolled in the grass with Lucy. From hidden floodlights hues faded and reappeared, a light green so subtle I tried to taste it like a wafer against my palate, a lake-top blue, a daffodil yellow.... It was as though the Falls were diluting a primal rainbow.

"Color," I wrote in the faint light of a souvenir stand, "is what the Magician spills to make the world for the Hierophant and the Hermit. Without color this is all a simmering void, realm of the Fool."

The next morning we donned black-hooded raincoats and boarded the *Maid of the Mist*. The Simmonses stood in the prow, twin George Washingtons. Soon, fine droplets tinged my face. A loudspeaker blared: "... and numerous men have tried the much-publicized feat of going over the Falls with a wooden barrel as their mere protection from its mighty waters." I felt a layer of mist over my face. As we got nearer, the spume grew thicker, and the Simmonses summoned everyone back. Lucy shrieked as Barry forced her into the spray. They were like a cigarette commercial, "the breath of springtime," slightly out of control.

I stepped forward, threw off my hood, and let the Falls blow across me in sheets until my hair and face were doused. I thought of Coleridge and his ode to dejection; I wanted to feel something too, to fend off "... *viper thoughts* ..." and "*Reality's dark dream....*" The Lake poet had nailed my mood from another century: "*Oh! that even now the gust were swelling, / And the slant night-shower driving loud and fast ... ! / Might startle this dull pain, and make it move and live!*"

On the way back to our room I bought the current *Sporting News* and, as we straggled along the street, I scanned International League stats, checking out Met and Yankee minor leaguers. Afterwards, as most kids gathered at the motel pool, I claimed the empty chaise next to Lucy. Putting on the Yankee-K.C. game, available through a Buffalo affiliate, I began writing a letter to Jake. "I wish I could send Mickey a postcard," Lucy interjected, "and tell him what a wonderful time I'm having." The line between ingenuousness and self-parody was hard to gauge. "Do you think he'll ever come to Grossinger's?"

"Maybe this winter," I lied. She was so irritating but so pretty, sitting there in four different colored squares of a bathing suit, each covering one quarter of her torso.

"You'll get me his autograph? Oh, please!"

"I'll try."

"And then maybe I'll forget your school cheated."

I slid into the pool and swam laps, game in earshot. Maris hit a homer with two on in the eighth to tie the score and spur a mood shift that became an anticlimactic letdown. "What's Mickey doing?" Lucy called as I headed back to the room. I didn't answer.

Changing into slacks and a sports shirt, I was planning to devour the *Sporting News* while tracking the tie game. There was no way I could have foreseen what happened next.

I felt a stab of disquiet, a forerunner of panic. It registered as a kind of numbness, an eerie abyss. I had no clear sense of my own being. I couldn't settle down because the sensations inside me were too restive. The mood had no premise, gave no indication of what to do, even how to address a next moment. If Lucy had miraculously knocked on the door just then and offered to be my girlfriend for the entire trip, it wouldn't have extricated me. I was too deep in a vacuum, and my ambivalence about her only added to my mounting terror and dissociation.

I never really wanted to go on this tour; now I was in big trouble. I needed to act fast because I was far from anything familiar. *Giant fish were swimming around that glacier for real.*

I clicked off the Yankees and froze all movement and thought. I stood looking at myself there. Who was this guy? What was he doing in Buffalo? I took a breath, hoping the warp would pass, into some more explicable state like homesickness. In a moment of elation that went as quickly as it came, I considered withdrawing from the tour and asking for a refund for my father. But something in me balked at the logistics: where and how to begin such a process and what its long-term consequences might be.

My mood turned precipitously. Panic and disorientation evaporated and were replaced by a demonic prankishness. First I short-sheeted the beds; then I partially unscrewed the light bulbs. I set a glass of water on top of the bathroom door, propped a chair against the

front door, dribbled after-shave on the pillows, and placed a note
on the bathroom sink: "Regards from the Unholy Four." I felt
relief as long as I acted. My mind filled hyperactively with schemes
faster than I could dispatch them. They surged ahead, substituting
pranks for terror *at the identical pitch.* That was the mechanism of
relief: antidoting an undifferentiated anxiety with activities that
engendered a parallel maniacal glee.

It was human, of course, but it felt like insect kinesis, a mindless
response to a blind stimulus. Desperate not to get caught, I installed
booby traps in frenetic succession, sure that each next was one too
many but setting it nonetheless.

When my roommates returned I feigned joining them, falling
into ambush after ambush. They assumed it was Tony, Greg, and
Charlie and vowed revenge.

The phone rang in the middle of the night. "Oh hell," Stan groaned.
"They must be kidding."

Our group filed out, past morning papers tied in wire bundles
beside the shut souvenir stand, past a dozing clerk … boarded a
bus idling with its headlights on, travelled along bumpy backroads,
then accelerated onto a highway … falling asleep, awakened, onto
a train, asleep again, awakened in Toronto to switch trains. Barely
conscious, I was stretching in the aisle when a girl named Shelby
asked me to carry her suitcase. "To where?" I asked.

"As far as we go."

Sporting a distinctive pineapple-like hairdo, she was tall and
thin with tiny Oriental eyes, a long black dress, utterly appealing, prettier than Lucy on an imponderable scale that I, like most
males, kept. I carted her bag proudly. Only later did I realize it
belonged to her grumpy overweight friend—Alan was portering
hers. Bamboozled again!

Afternoon rolled by—long rows of haystacks, children standing outside their homes to watch the train pass, cows resting in
the shadows of trees. I dialed the radio obsessively in hopes of
getting the Mets Triple A Syracuse club against Toronto—the
Sporting News said they were starting their two bonus rookies in a

doubleheader—but the dial alternated hum with static.

We were roused near dawn at Port Huron, divided into groups, and put in small cabins aboard a waiting cruise ship. Three shrill blasts of the whistle ... then the shore levitated away, black smoke pouring against blue sky. Shelby stood by Alan on the deck, chic sunglasses, orange kerchief whipping.

"It's quite a liner," he said.

"Well now it ain't the *Queen Mary*," she smirked.

As the Great Lake stretched to horizons, we were set free, denizens of a floating hotel. I attached myself to Shelby and Alan. We explored various sections of the deck, in our meanders being served tea and cookies by a travelling maid and shooting a few rounds of shuffleboard. Then we went to the piano room where Shelby played tunes and sang witty flirtations to Alan: *"Am I the one for you? For who? For you?"*

He seemed amused, nodding his fixed Bogart grin. Feeling like a third wheel, I tossed an imaginary sidearm pitch. Shelby didn't miss the gesture. "I'd play ball with you," she offered, "but I didn't bring my glove."

Alan looked askance.

"You don't believe me? I have a Marty Marion model, and I played shortstop for my camp. How about them there potatoes?"

As the tour assembled in the dining room, the god of tricks came back to me, and I was a cut-up at our table. With a spoon I fished the single very tiny strand of spaghetti out of my soup (which was nonetheless called "spaghetti soup") and stared at it with exaggerated scrutiny. The table was in an uproar. I had already loosened the tops of the shakers so that Greg got a plate full of salt.

I was out of control; the deranged blueprint just kept popping into my mind. I told "The Shaggy Dog Story" until they were literally falling off chairs onto the floor. Even as I despised this performance, I kept going: "Why that's the shaggiest, shaggiest, shaggiest, shaggiest, shaggiest dog I've ever seen.... "

"I've had enough!" Marcia screamed. "Enough!"

"No," Shelby insisted. "I don't think I've got it yet. What was it?"

"Why that's the shaggiest, shaggiest, shaggiest, shaggiest, shaggiest,

shaggiest dog I've ever seen."

"If you don't shut up," Barry said, "we're going to throw you overboard."

Then Laurie got us going on "No Soap, Radio," the non-joke ending in a false punch line.

Alan and Barry stared in confusion. "I just don't get it," Alan complained again.

"No soap.... right?" I repeated. "No soap.... radio!"

Lucy erupted in fake laughter. Shelby was holding her hand over her mouth as though she wanted to laugh but really shouldn't. Alan shook his head.

Finally Lucy told him: "Don't you get it? The joke is that there's no joke, but everyone laughs."

"Ha, ha, ha," Barry said, grabbing her by the waist and giving her a sloppy kiss.

As the meal dispersed, I went to the cabin to get my radio and journal. Alan was my lone roommate and I dislodged his bed from its moorings. Then I propped a ladder against the door to fall outwards when opened.

I hurried onto the deck. A cold wind slapped the waves. Foghorns sounded far away. I felt a mood-shift; instantaneously the shenanigans were gone.

The sky was a planetarium. As I turned the dial, ball games came from everywhere, Richmond-Jacksonville, Indians against someone, Pirates-Colts. A long, thin cloud passed across the moon. Inside the cabin, much of the Arista tour was gathered in serenade: *"The sun shines bright on my old Kentucky home...."*

I wrote: "Stephen Foster, penniless and ill at the end of his life, imagined those words, that melody, in a place far from here. We don't have a right to his prayer."

"Someone sabotaged the whole damn room," Alan announced angrily, as I pretended to check for more traps under the bed. "There's a real wise guy somewhere!"

The next morning Arista Teen Tour strolled off the boat at Port Arthur, Ontario. I was standing mesmerized in the sun when Shelby grabbed a FUNERAL PARKING ONLY sign off the street and handed it to me to conceal under my jacket for her. I was scared of getting caught but hung on in two-fold desperation. Further down the street she managed to charm an empty box from a department store clerk and then slipped the sign into it. On the customs form she filled out COMICAL SIGN, added her signature, and mailed it home.

"That's about the coolest thing," pronounced Greg, "that anybody has done so far on the trip."

She smiled proudly.

A group of us wandered past Main Street into town. We stopped at a bowling alley, but it turned out to involve tiny holeless balls and only five gigantic pins. Too bad—this wasn't my game. But it *was* Alan's. "Duckpins!" he proclaimed and proceeded to knock down more of them than the rest of us put together.

I felt sorry for the proprietor because it was a shabby old hall and we were the only customers. He seemed so pleased to have us, but we weren't real, we were dumb Americans on a teen tour. We didn't acknowledge him, just charged into action as if he were the butler. I asked him about the history of his establishment and the game. He talked enthusiastically, making me even sadder. I felt sorry for the alleys too, the lonely alleys, thinking they were being called into operation for real bowlers rather than spoiled American teens.

Outside, Shelby inexplicably turned to me. "Let's take in the sights," she proclaimed, grabbing my arm. "You and I'll hit all of Port Arthur."

We traipsed along Main Street, staring into clothing and pawnshop windows. We weren't a couple, we weren't even friends; I didn't know what we were. In the back of my mind I held a detached image of myself on a pitching mound, throwing strikes, again and again my right arm brought around, fastball down the middle, mirror image after mirror image. Shelby selected a hamburger place for lunch. The flag whipped in from left; I checked second and fired. The batter was way behind the thump in the mitt. I was a kid pitcher against blue sky, number 12 on my back, the quick feet of Al Jackson, the sudden twirl of Art Mahaffey.

We were headed in the door when Alan came up behind us from nowhere and swooped Shelby up, putting his arm around her and turning the corner—identical to what had happened leaving the train in Buffalo, only this time the whole person rather than just the suitcase.

I saw the ball bunted down third and raced over, grabbed it bare-handed, and fired to first—just in time!

From the train my mind followed silos, trees, patches of forest, farms, a stately rhythm of endless prairie into sunset. Through a core of apple-clouds a gleam of orange shot; far away on a hilltop, two windows reflected the ray. Then nightfall....

In small groups my trainmates, those still awake, began to pick up each other's songs, "Michael Row Your Boat Ashore," "They Call the Wind Mariah," and "Them Old Cotton Fields Back Home." Others stirred, lolled, idly joined the chorus. In a corner Barry and Lucy, Harve and Laurie were two inseparable heaps. Stan had his arm inside a chubby girl's blouse. Other couples nestled and kissed, the Simmonses oblivious or uninterested. This all seemed to have arisen from nowhere, my exclusion from it axiomatic. *"The rain is Tess, the fire's Joe...."* I settled into memory, figments of long ago—Pine Cove, the Knickerbocker sign blinking over the city, Jonny fighting ghosts, all past redemption now.... *"and they call the wind Mariah."*

We travelled the entire next day on the train. The girls from Florida and Georgia continually reprised a clapping song. They stood in a circle and pounded their hands in rhythm to: *"The spades* [pronounced "spides"] *go two lips together, tie them together, bring back my love to me."* Then the chorus: *"What is the me-ee-ea-ning of all these flow-ow-ers? They tell the stor-or-y of love from me to you—cha cha cha."* After that, they fell together, laughing.

We reached Winnipeg at nightfall and checked into our hotel.

I was fast asleep when Stan's voice jolted me. His breath was right up against me as he grabbed my blankets and tossed them on the floor.

"Hey!" I said.

"Shut the hell up."

"What's this all about?"

"I'm warning you. Shut up or I'll kill you." He stuck his fist under my chin.

"Maybe first you'll tell me what's wrong."

"Who said you could take the big bed and leave me with the cot?"

"Remember, it's my turn. I had the cot in Niagara Falls."

"You asked for that cot, goddamnit!"

"I'll trade if it means so much to you."

"It will solve only one problem. What's it going to do about Alan's bed? What's it going to do about our sheets and the water traps? What about the light bulbs? What if we had retaliated against Greg and Tony? I bet *that* would have been hilarious."

It was the moment of retribution I had been awaiting. I wondered how I had been found out, how long people had been mocking me behind my back. Though Horace Mann and Amherst were my calling cards, I wasn't superior to them; in fact, I was more of a dork than anyone else. After a flutter of vertigo I summoned all my rationality and candor, sat up, and said: "I *meant* to tell you. I don't know why I did it." It was the truth.

"Great. And what about your stupid jokes at supper? What about your interfering with Alan and Shelby? What's it going to do about the fact everyone thinks you're an idiot?" I stared in stunned silence. "Going for that walk with Shelby was just so stupid, so obvious; how could anyone do that. Alan's trying to score with her, and you're getting in his way. She's using you against him. Don't you understand that? She's a cock-teaser, and he's working for the honor of all men."

I didn't really. It was as though I was in a play with Alan, Shelby, and Stan. Not only hadn't I learned my lines, I didn't understand the script or roles assigned to the other characters.

"I'm sorry," I said. "I'm guess I'm acting like a jerk. I don't know why. But I'll try harder."

"Will you keep your ass away from Shelby?"

I couldn't believe I was a threat to Alan, but I promised.

Then Stan gave me a friendly shove. "You're taking this amazingly well. You make me think human beings are worth my trouble."

I thanked him and started to get up.

"Stay where you are. I'll sleep in the fucking cot."

Next morning in Winnipeg we were told not to leave the hotel pool area. We were there only one day, and the city wasn't supposed to be interesting enough for sightseeing. But I had read in the paper that the Class C Winnipeg Goldeyes were playing Grand Forks that day, so I grabbed a map and transit schedule off the front desk, figured out the route, and surreptitiously slipped onto the summery street.

The ballpark was miles from town, so I boarded a bus along Portage Avenue and took a seat in the last row, relishing my freedom as signets of an unknown city rolled by. This was my own excursion, not on the roster, not included in Arista's sales pitch to parents: Winnipeg, Manitoba, Canada.

Hiking past houses on Telfer Street, I darted in and out of lawn sprays, delighting in newly cut grass, the tall trees, the rural spaciousness—Goldeye Stadium in the distance: orbital apogee.

I arrived in the sixth inning, no admission fee. The audience was so diffuse that I could hear individual names as the fans cheered for home-team players (only one of them, pitcher Chuck Taylor, would ever play in the majors). Minutes later I grabbed a foul ball ricocheting off a nearby seat, my Northern League treasure! From there I savored my separation from Stan, Shelby, and the rest ... then gauged parallax all the way to apartment 8C in New York City. I was a needle in a haystack, beyond the naked eye. If I had known how never to return, to start my life over here, I would have.

Reversing the route, I slipped back into the group at dinner. No one knew I had gone.

From Winnipeg we boarded a train west to the Columbia icefields where we clambered aboard tractors for a ride across a glacier. We stared down through the rainbow ice of potholes and made snowballs of dinosaur crystals. All day Stan and Alan kept joking about how much that glacier and Shelby had in common. I was now their confidante and ally.

We journeyed from Jasper to Vancouver and spent an afternoon touring Stanley Park. Live penguins—little white, black, and yellow beings—inspired Shelby to do a zigzag penguin walk. She wore a tight skirt with a shiny black belt and a short-sleeved blouse with a man's jacket over it. For the first time she and Alan were apart, and she made a conspicuous effort to avoid him, hanging around with me instead. He had found another companion, an older girl named Judy, and was walking a few strides away from the group, arm around her shoulders.

At an outdoor cafe Shelby took the chair next to me and continued to play buddy-buddy. As we waited for our food she peeled back the cardboard layers of two matches to form stick figures; then she placed one atop the other and lit them. The torsos twisted and curled about one another, the limbs rising in flames. Fire crawled down the arms and legs, making a surprisingly realistic depiction of sexual intercourse. "See that," she said. A thin stream of smoke rose from the quivering ash as the figures clasped and held tight.

I nodded.

"I'll bet."

Then she peeled and lit a second pair. I was silent. "You and I are going to have a regular orgy tonight."

I flushed, part thrill, part shame.

She asked me about what the boys and girls did on raids at my summer camp. I tried to be cute and evasive, but she would have none of it. "Did they do this?" she asked, raising her eyebrows and puckering her lips, "or that?" raising them even higher. "How about some of this?" She rolled her tongue, as the whole table laughed.

Later in the meal she examined my jello and, pretending to find a contaminant in it, suggested I wash the cubes in my water glass. To please her I dropped a few lime squares in. Everyone was giggling as the jello floated about.

"Don't try to make me look stupid," I pleaded softly.

"Oh, don't mind the others," she retorted louder. "We can have fun and they don't even have to notice."

After the meal I made a beeline away from her, but she trailed close behind. We passed a stand with a sign above it: PO' BOY

SANDWICHES. "Boy sandwich," she called out to me. "Is that another way to have boy?"

She was taunting me with my interest in her, so I said nothing and increased my pace. I passed Lucy and Barry, Harve and Laurie. The sky turned dark. Shelby and the teen tour were gone. I kept walking. I came to a fountain and saw the harbor lights of Vancouver beyond, as the Platters alone might have sung them.

The port shimmered, rough vessels of human commerce at anchor, yawing with the clank of sea-weary metal. Once again I had been called to witness a miracle, a world limitless and inscrutable, bathed in tarot light.

Tony, Greg, and Charlie with their female sidekicks had been into creative disruptions and spontaneous theater from the first day, and the Simmonses did little to bring them under control. Their delinquency came to a head in San Francisco at the famous hungry i nightclub where they tried heckling and disrupting the evening's performer, stand-up comedian "Professor" Irwin Corey, master of topic-shifting double-talk.

Professor Corey abruptly stopped his routine and asked the stage-light technician to put his spot on our group. What followed was a straight-talk scold from the hobo savant, his bushy hair sprouting in all directions. The Professor somehow turned it into a lecture on the Solar System, how to make ice cream, and cockroach biology before returning to his sermon on audience decorum by making a distinction between *funny* heckling and boorish brain-dead disrespect "of which the three morons before me are as fine a specimen as you will ever see." It was not only a performance for the ages, it was vindication of my sense that our tour had run amok.

In L.A. I was able to escape again, this time with permission. Grossinger's old P.R. guru, Milton Blackstone, picked me up in the hotel lobby and drove to Eddie Fisher's house.

The evening was high comedy. The three of us got lost trying to find Dodger Stadium and, after wandering among freeways, caught only the last inning of the Angels game. "It's more exciting this way," Eddie said. He was amused that I had seen him and

Elizabeth Taylor out in a rowboat together on Grossinger Lake when he was having an affair with the actress while still married to songstress Debby Reynolds. "The press would like to have been a little birdie on your shoulder," he mused. "Well, they crucified me soon enough."

The next morning I floated on an air raft in Eddie's pool while he read some business ledgers with Milton. After corned-beef sandwiches, the singer sent his regards to the Grossinger family and then took a fifty-dollar bill from his wallet and handed it to me "to entertain the girls."

That was the most impressive adventure anyone had to report. In Hollywood, where everyone had been celebrity sighting, I alone had hung out with a real star. Lucy kept asking to shake my hand, "whichever one Eddie last touched." I stood in the lobby embellishing my account with every last detail I could think of.

In the group was a girl named Betsy, one of the identityless cheerleaders in the Florida chorus. Standing there, she suddenly seemed substantial and sprightly, like someone I had never seen. Gravitating to her, I struck up a conversation and then sat next to her on the train to San Diego and again on the bus into Mexico.

Her life, as she presented it, was beach parties, sports cars, varsity sports, and motorboats. Its key figure was her boyfriend Bob, All-City end who made the winning catch in the homecoming game. As information, it was stock and corny and should not have held my interest, but she had an odd probity, was appealingly guileless and tender.

As we passed neighborhoods of lumber scraps and Coca-Cola crates, she observed the procession with shocked concern. Mainly guys, but girls too, on this tour acted as though everything was a comedy for their benefit, an opening to trot out wit and bravado (like Shelby handing me the funeral sign); nothing was *really* real. Now everyone else was cracking up, making jokes about whose mother came from here and who was going to major in Tijuana architecture next year.

As for Betsy, her solicitude was spontaneous and heart-felt; it was as if she had never considered income distribution or deprivation.

Of course, she had; she wasn't puerile or a dummy. It was more that she looked at the world with open eyes and empathy, qualities lacking in our 1962 teen milieu.

She listened my own tales of childhood with disbelief: "I can't imagine why you had such a hard time." She shook her head. "Well, that's at an end. You'll only meet friendly people now, like me."

Lightly tanned, her hair gently flipped up in back, she had tiny black berries of eyes and a bit of an Eskimo feel about her. Plus a funny mouth, pointed out slightly at the top.

I read her tarot beneath a tree in Anaheim—telling fortunes was my most reliable means of courtship. I chose the Queen of Pentacles as her Significator—kindness and prosperity. Then I set her shuffle on the grass. She picked up the cards one by one as I offered my interpretations—the Wheel, the Hierophant, the Lovers. "Yes, these are special, quite special," she declared. "I could never understand them like you. What do I know? I'm a cheerleader wondering which of these pictures is her boyfriend. Is he a Knight? Is he a King?"

"He could also be a Queen," I said. "Men and women are combined in all the cards."

"No, that he isn't."

At Disneyland she returned to her Florida friends and, though I looked all day, I never spotted her in the crowds. I took a banana-boat through Africa, a paddle-craft down the Mississippi, then played baseball on old-fashioned pinball machines in an arcade, late afternoon into evening. As I put each silver ball-bearing in play with a lever, the goal was to push the flipper with the right timing and send it beyond the outfield into grooves for hits. Each of nine fielders guarded holes that gobbled up outs.

Suddenly fireworks erupted over Disneyland Castle. Dangling at the end of a long, thin cord, Tinkerbell soared across the sky past gingerbread peaks—one hour to curfew. I fell in with a group from our tour at Mr. Toad's Wild Ride; in fact, I found myself standing next to Shelby, half-expecting to go through it with her, our status still ambiguous. Smooching couples on line confirmed, as if we didn't know, that this was a tunnel of love.

"Are you going to protect me from the monsters?" she asked,

sidling up to me.

I nodded. I knew this wasn't happening, but my heart thumped anyway as we came to the front of the queue.

"See you later, 'gator," she snapped with a naughty grin—and was off.

I looked for an escape, but the attendant was holding open the next empty cart. I took the seat. Immediately I was swung down a track into blackness, drawn by the machinery of the ride.

A glow appeared in the far sky, dark blue from the exhibit's sun having just set. Then things got crazy. My car crashed through a wall. I careened wildly off the road. I was on a highway screeching past other cars, going the wrong way. I rammed a detour; barrels came tumbling down, about to pulverize me, but froze in midair. I burst through an old warehouse. Suddenly I was in court; a judge jabbed his finger and cried out GUILTY! Shrill, screeching cartoon characters danced and pointed my way.

Next stop for my vehicle, Hell: devils roasting people, orange-red flames, the chief diablo laughing like the deranged automaton he was.

I had dreamed of that judge my whole life, so I couldn't help but take the matter personally; his verdict was against me, always.

The tableau was beyond parody. I felt inklings of dungeon panic, tremors that were unequivocal. Satan chortled away. He knew I was trapped here, no way out, no way to stop the ride. Restoring harmless Disneyland animation took all my concentration.

Then I realized how much the diorama resembled the tarot Devil. I knew his alias all right: if only his prisoners could feel how loose the chains were about their necks ... if only they could know that elsewhere in the deck he was a winged Angel ... and they were Lovers.

I was euphoric! I had used a symbol to abate a trauma. Dr. Fabian would have been proud!

"Geez, Richard," commented a friend years later, "can't you just go to Disneyland? Well, okay, so Disneyland really is only packaged archetypes."

The next morning the air was clammy, the train station rich with steam. "Hey, Betsy," I called. She turned from ahead of me on the platform. I ran and caught up. "Let me carry that for you."

"No, thanks. You've got your own bag." I took it anyway.

I sat beside her as we pulled out of L.A. She was wearing yellow Bermuda shorts and wondered how I could stand my black slacks.

As we worked our way through swerving doors to the dining car, the train stopped in Yuma. It remained at standstill for two hours as we lingered at our table. Betsy talked about when her brother was born: "I kept saying to my mother, 'Whose little boy is he?' And my mother kept answering, 'Why, he's my little boy just like you're my little girl.' 'But who's his mother?' I kept asking. I couldn't get it, that she could be both our mothers at the same time."

Then she tried to recall how it felt when Bob kissed her for the first time, describing her moment of fear and then the rush of excitement: "'Oh my my my my,' I thought. And then I worried that I'm only me, and me isn't really very much for him to love. But he knew who I was, just like my Mommy sometimes does, and that's really great from a boy."

Betsy was not a potential girlfriend, nor would she become one, but I loved listening to her and she grew into the heroine and muse of this book. Everything I had to say, the chasm and mystery of my past, was transfigured through my feelings for her.

She was not a classically pretty girl, a Shelby or Lucy, so it had taken me a while to notice her, but her sexuality was innocent and magnetic. When I imagined being with her at one of those parties she described, kissing her, I felt a different allure, a sort of motley charm. She was a mermaid, bottomless and salt-like and blue-green as the sea, and I was undiminished beside her.

I had wasted most of the summer. We were already headed east.

When our ice cream came she said, "Yum yum," and I said, "Yuma," because the train was still there. As she laughed, my mind flashed to another dusk, at 1235 Park when I was sent to the corner drugstore to get a brick of chocolate, strawberry, and vanilla, a number-two combination, for our family dessert. I was returning with the cold package pressed against my belly when the untracked spook, the hidden familiar to my existence, caught me.

That originless throb haunted my childhood—a primal wave of terror, a sense that I wasn't who I was, always a mournful other, there again at Disneyland. It was the worst sensation in the universe because it went so deep without motive. It must have been born with me, for its power was beyond my American kid's body.

While I stood at the dungeon stairs, Betsy danced on Southern beaches, calling to me to remember that one day we would sit together at a train station in Yuma. At least I had found her. Before, there was nothing; now I had the whole of creation in tow. Or so I thought, as I stared out the window at the Dipper over Arizona.

The last ten days of my journal are mainly my record of adventures and talks with Betsy, on a Grand Canyon hike, at Six Flags Over Texas amusement park, on various trains. In New Orleans she knelt alongside the pool, drying off, dark wisps of hair stuck to her neck. I drifted by, my arms wrapped around a plastic beach animal, my legs curled up. "I'm just a barnacle," I called out.

"You *are* a barnacle," she smiled back.

After I got dressed we broke the rules by hiking downtown. We spent the afternoon wandering in New Orleans. At one point Betsy stood straight and tall on the street, doing what she called her "happy walk," half collapsing giggling, half marionette. It was contagious, as we laughed and bumped into each other.

We visited antique neighborhoods, sprawling parks, a used bookstore. We raced each other across a lawn. There was even a goodnight kiss on her cheek.

I forgot where I was—that we were part of a tour, that we hadn't been brother and sister our whole lives.

The next morning we boarded for Miami—end of the line for Betsy. With the other Florida girls she would leave and go home while the rest of us continued to Washington D.C. and New York.

I was train-weary, sick of the almondy steam, the queasy stop-and-go rhythm. When the conductor came around, I spent part of

Eddie Fisher's money on a sleeping compartment.

Dusk turned to night as we rumbled east, lurching and bumping along. I watched lights passing outside, "lights of people"—I scribbled in the glow of a tiny bulb—"whom I will never know, who will live beyond me forever. And then, someday, I will pass a light in the darkness and it will belong to one of the people in this group. Everyone, including Betsy, is about to fall into the great anonymous void."

I recalled an old trance state before sleep: visitors in the courtyard, a gift of a saucer. But from whom, really? The question dissolved before an answer, only that I existed at all—that there was this great vast density masking form without form. The saucer arrived with no precursor, yet it wasn't a chimera or illusion; it was stable and durable enough to last all of childhood.

Out of the same formlessness Betsy had come to claim me. But was she the mother tucking me in, or the mother of my child tucking him in?

At dawn, billboards indicated we had passed into Florida; the landscape was dense fog. Then a faint butter sun bled through, tinting the trees along the tracks, most of them covered with Spanish moss. It was somber but exhilarating. I had never seen such a planet, as it cast its science-fiction glow.

I had my life in front of me, and I knew a girl.

"I'm so excited I'm shaking," Betsy said from the seat beside me at breakfast. "Do you think Bob'll get off work? Do you think my car will be there? Wouldn't it be great if I get to drive my own car home? Thank you for being such a great friend." She promised she would visit me at our hotel. "You'll get to meet Bob, and then my family will throw a big party for the whole tour. You'll get to see my house!"

As the train wound into the Miami station, Bob was waiting for Betsy. She ran into his arms, and he held her against him and swung her back and forth like in a movie. In my mind I chanted ten syllables I had memorized from Shakespeare's *Corialanus* for such occasions: "The sorrow that delivers us thus changed...." The perfect voiceover.

The next time I saw Betsy was at the outdoor pool. She arrived with Bob, tall and broad-shouldered, hardly any neck, soft blue eyes and a tough mouth. Swaggering as he walked, he said that he had been looking forward to meeting me. "How are the Yanks doing?" he asked, noting the Miami pickup on my radio.

"They're losing one-nothing."

"Great," he said. "I love to see them lose. But then again, I shouldn't get my hopes up. They always win in the end."

"Who do you root for?"

"Me? I don't like baseball too much. I'm from Detroit originally, so I root for the Tigers. Most of the time I just root against the Yanks. Betsy tells me you've got a box behind third base at Yankee Stadium. That's cool."

He pulled a beach chair beside me, and Betsy set one on the other side. Then she asked me to tell him about high school.

I seemed to astonish him with even the most commonplace details, so I played the naïf. When he wondered where I went when I dated, I told him I didn't, so he kept pressing me: "What! There were no girls in the school. You studied all the time!" He turned to Betsy in disbelief, glad he wasn't involved in such. She smiled knowingly, for we had already performed this duet.

Then he questioned me on whether she had been a good girl on the trip. "Oh, yes," I proclaimed.

He smiled proudly. "See, she's turning red. She's passionately in love with me, and I don't even know that I can stand her presence. Why, she walked up to me the other day on the corner and kissed me. Now what do you think of a girl who—" She had taken a glass of ice water and poured it on him. Then he said, "You're a good girl, Bets," and grabbed her legs. She dove away from him, then underwater. He followed. As she kicked and fought, he called back to me, "She's a regular tomboy, isn't she?"

"That's my hair, Bob," she said.

"I know. I know. Truce! I'll let you go."

Later I sat with her alone by the side of the pool. "You know, Bets, someday I'm going to write a story about this trip."

"Will I be in it?"

I nodded. "You'll be one of the main characters."

"Thank you."

"You don't need to thank me. You're such a great character that there wouldn't be any story without you."

Bob had dived in the pool and was surfacing, staring back at us, waiting for her to join him.

"Why?" she asked. "What makes me a good character?"

"You're part of a theme I'm only beginning to understand."

"What kind of theme?"

"A sort of 'growing up' theme."

"C'mon," Bob called out.

"I'm just an immature little girl, and a lazy one at that."

"You're growing up in your own way."

"Bob won't even let me carry a balloon at a carnival because he thinks it makes me too young and silly. He doesn't understand that staying a little girl is part of me. Do you, Bob?"

"What?" He came climbing out and strode over with a look of mock impatience. Then he turned to me. "Betsy tells me you can get me Rocky Colavito's autograph at Grossinger's." I nodded. "Tell me, is he a decent guy? Some people say he's a wiseass and a show-off."

"My stepmother says he's one of the nicest of the players."

"You see that, Bets? Old Bob doesn't miss."

They headed to the beach, so I went upstairs and put the game on TV. I watched them out the window, throwing a football back and forth. He sent her out on a long pass. Running through surf, she muffed it but showed good form. Then they disappeared from view. Tony Kubek had just come back from the Army and was in his first game of the season at shortstop. It all seemed fake—the smell of sun-tan oil in our room, even the hallowed call of Mel Allen.

I looked out the window. On a raft some girls and boys played diving tag. "Stafford checks his runners, winds, and fires."

"Go to hell, Stafford," I said with a bashful smile. "I hate you." But I was addressing myself with faux drama, a novelist transcribing his own lines. I recalled a spring day, cerulean sky outside the windows of Horace Mann where I sat and worked from books piled beside me, no end in sight. For what?

I knew now that Miami Beach was where I clutched the primal Easter egg, the one that my real father had rehidden at the beginning of time. Then I was sent into exile, following my mother into her life. It was too late to change these antiquities now. The hook was in me too deep. I was a castaway forever in my own land. I wrote, "I look upon a sky-blue, rose-red, sun-yellow world that is perfect, that I lost and now lose again."

The day before the end of our stay in Miami Beach, Betsy invited the tour to her house. We arrived in separate cabs. Her mansion was even more palatial than I had feared—fancy iron gates all around it, grillwork shaped like sleighs, her surname. We followed a long winding driveway to a formal entrance.

For me it was just one more barrier: If I was already eight runs down, bottom of the ninth, it might as well be ten or eleven. Even Grossinger's was hoi polloi beside the lifestyle signified here.

Betsy answered the door surrounded by two large barking poodles and a smaller one. "Don't mind the dogs. They're good buddies."

"Do we have to go through customs?" Marcia asked.

"Of course not," she laughed. "Come in and you can put on your bathing suits in that little house across the driveway. Wait. My brother will show you."

It was as though we had been travelling the whole summer in a dark train to get here, where she had been all along.

Floats and balls were thrown into the pool. Servants were cooking frankfurters and hamburgers; platter upon platter of food arrived. It was pompous and syrupy, and Betsy was inaccessible in the busyness, but I enjoyed being there and watching her.

Later in the day she called me inside to meet a friend of my father. I was in the pool, so I dried myself off, put on my shirt, and walked through the living room. People were dressed in shirts and ties. My body seemed bare and tenuous in that company, but I tried to be polite.

"There was a picture in a frame on a table inside," I wrote. "It was a photograph of Betsy as a little girl. Her face was a bit awkward, with thin eyes, a half smile." Then I reached the epiphany of my book: "The wind blew gently, the tree leaves rustled slightly, the flowers dipping and rising in a ripple across the beds. It was that famous warm, humid, sleepy summer. Hers was a face like the face on the rarest baseball card, that you would see in someone else's pack and then never again because there was only one. You would open pack after pack looking for it, that face, the shade of blue in the sky behind, the home-team uniform."

I wanted to hold her, hold onto her, have her hold onto me. But I knew that I was leaving her company and returning to what I had been. I couldn't just grow here in her light like a vine for years on end. Her family would ask me to go away. She would get tired of this object trailing about her. She would want a man, a family, children.

I would have to grow up; there was no other path. Her body was real. In the end if I was to know her I would have to get down in the mud with her and fight it out. And it would be a fight, for I wanted to destroy the false aura that surrounded her, that kept me from her. In time she would have to change anyway, and her light would be different, but her Betsyness, that pathos and joy, would not break down like iron in fire; it was a part of her that would not ever be destroyed. That's what I told myself. I had to find my own identity before she would reveal hers to me. I had to stop walking the line between idiot prankster and ingenuous Amherst-bound sage.

The following evening we had a last-dinner award ceremony. After-wards Bob was pointing out Dorothy and Carol. "Now if I was on this trip and didn't have Bets, that's who'd get my attention. There's still one night left and plenty of girls," he winked.

"None," I asserted, "like Betsy."

He nodded agreement. "They don't come much better. She may not be as pretty as some of the rest, but she's pretty inside—and that's what counts. You say she was the nicest girl on the trip. Everybody says that. Everybody around here says she was the nicest girl at Beach." He shook his head in wonder. "When I first kissed Bets," he said, putting his arm around her as she joined us, "I wanted it so bad. I don't ask no questions 'cause I don't wanta hear no answers. I just leaned over and kissed her." He paused. "I love this girl here. Even with football I was never important before Betsy."

Betsy came to see us off the next morning. Stan and Larry were hugging her, saying goodbye, but I didn't want to part on their terms. I left the tour and walked five cars to the back, posting myself at the last dusty window. The train lurched sharply and then began to move. My eyes met hers, and I shouted, "Goodbye, Betsy" through the glass.

Actually I said nothing. I didn't even see her.

I watched Miami, tears pouring down my cheeks, my heart open, staring out into a void, streets sliding mechanically, surreally.

At least I had Betsy looking over me. I thought, "I am coming home with an ally. They can do me no more harm."

PART FOUR

INITIATION

SEPTEMBER, 1962–APRIL, 1964

I

AMHERST

Dressing for the final time in the bedroom Jonny and I shared, I fixed on an oblique ray of sun incising the top of the courtyard, marking the moment, setting it as a sign for eternity. Silhouettes of pigeons purred against parapets. My last breakfast in the Towers family was a quick lump in my gut.

My brother shook my hand with a shy grin. I gave Debby a kiss, hugged Bridey, and approached my mother. She held back tears; yet I had no wherewithal to comfort her. "Just get me out of here," a voice inside me screamed.

The elevator arrived with a noticeable clunk. "Hold it on eight, Jimmy," Bob said. "We've got a year's worth of Amherst College gear." It was superfluous theater, for he had already phoned ahead and Jim was arriving with a rolling cart. Downstairs I helped the doorman and my stepfather load a pair of suitcases, three cartons, and assorted loose items into the trunk of his double-parked car. I had no idea when I would be back, so I took records, record player, ice skates, baseball glove, and my favorite books. (When I next set foot in 8C, I would discover that my study had been all but fumigated, my photo albums, writing drafts, and the assorted souvenirs of my childhood long ago tossed in the trash.)

For my departure from the city of my youth the sky could not have been more robin's egg blue, the vista of the Park more eerily serene. It was just another day igniting, like all the others here, a blanket of taxis on its avenues, an orange rind of memories in my heart.

We crossed bridges onto turnpikes, up through Connecticut into Massachusetts, tinges of russet in the trees, field flowers mostly blue. I set my mind to the speed of the highway.

Eventually Bob was inspired to recall his own years at CCNY, as he invoked Amherst with reverence: "No Jewish kid from the Lower East Side would have dreamed of going to a real Ivy League school. This shows how far we have come in one generation."

So far that the issue was meaningless to me. The gap between my generation and his seemed almost a mutation of species; it was a surprise to discover that he identified with me at all. One thing we had left, however, despite harsh words over the years, was our friendship. We were both outsiders to a regime we didn't understand. Discussing my mother was taboo, but I could mention Betsy and have him know what I meant. After all, we were both guys.

He had a rational, reassuring response: "The first one is always the hardest."

We didn't need to ask directions in town; traffic was flowing into one bottleneck. As we turned uphill onto the campus, an officer directed us to my dorm, James Hall, which formed a central quad with three others like it. Across the green was Johnson Chapel. Its white clock tower had been visible above the hills for miles. Now it rang out the hour, a welcoming troll.

On either side of the quad, melees of parents and freshmen carted wardrobes, trunks, hockey sticks, crates of record albums, boxes of books, lamps, stereos, etc., item by item, indoors. After we hauled my things up the stairs of James to the fourth and uppermost floor, we arranged them on the floor of my room. Then my stepfather and I walked around the quad to the War Memorial, a raised granite slab inscribed like a compass and clock. It overlooked ballfields so vast that ten softball matches could have been played on them simultaneously without overlapping. The sun singeing grasstops in late-afternoon gold, it was a stunning vista to the mountains. This was the sort of scenery that had captivated me on my New England tour; now it filled me with awe for what I was about to undertake.

The former Ruben Turetsky took it in slowly and solemnly. I could tell he was wrestling with many overlapping mysteries: me and him, me and Jon, him and Jon, him and Martha, CCNY and Amherst … his own path to the moment. Then we hiked back to his car and, in the fading afternoon, he extended a hand. As ever I felt the ambivalence of opportunity lost. We had done the best we could, and I wished I could erase any lingering awkwardness. He could see I was apprehensive, but he didn't know why. "You'll manage," he finally said. "I'd put my money on you in the clutch." He reached for the car door. "I envy you, Richard, going to this school." A moment later he cranked open the driver's window to call out, "Be a mensch." And I was alone.

I had one of the few singles. That had been my mother's idea. When housing forms came she warned, "If you let them assign you a roommate, you could end up with a nut," and I took her advice. As usual, she was wrong; now I keenly regretted my deference. Just about everyone else was engaged in setting up doubles and triples, getting to know the blokes with whom they'd be living. I sat in a solitary space, unpacking sporadically, hanging on to my old world in a Mets doubleheader on the radio. By the end of the second game I was totally depressed. But here I was, an Amherst freshman—no turning back.

Just before dinner, I was paid a visit by two guys who shared a room down the hall. Sid was a tall, folksy kid from Portland, Oregon—talkative and cheerful. Alan was a poet, his diametric opposite—a husky, sad-looking guy with a scarred face who came from nearby Massachusetts. Our first conversation was at dinner in Valentine Hall, wherein Al confided that he planned to commit suicide someday because he didn't want to leave an event as important as his own death to circumstance. This seeming folly sent Sid into conniptions. "How could you say such a thing, roomy? I didn't put 'suicide' down on the housing form, you know."

Al just chuckled. "How do you know what *I* put down?"

When Sid failed to budge Al on ontological grounds he tried to convince him that death wasn't really an issue now, certainly not when we were at the beginning of our lives, "We're young. We shouldn't be thinking morbidly."

"Ah, but there you trick yourself," Al replied playfully. "I certainly hope it's not an issue, but the crux is—you don't know when you're going to be called on to make a decision, so you had better be ready."

Then we switched to hockey (Sid followed the minor league Buckaroos in Portland, Al the local Springfield team)—and romance (Sid wanted to marry his high school sweetie Barb as soon as he graduated, and he offered a few unrequested bars of their favorite song: *My love is higher than a mission bell (how deep?) / Deeper than a wishing well.... ";* Al was "still looking"). The next evening Al and I sat in my room, reading our writing aloud to each other—his metaphysical love poems and my narratives of the teen tour.

My room lay almost at the juncture of the two arms of the James "L." Down the opposite aisle from Sid and Al, it seemed the entire freshman football team and their cohorts were assembling a private fraternity by trading assorted roommates to other floors and dorms for like-minded jocks. On several occasions they asked me to accept a reassignment, but I had just gotten there and, anyway, changing rooms was against the rules. I could tell that my recalcitrance made me a deferred target, and I felt an all-too-familiar embattledness and isolation closing in.

Luckily another event sidetracked them. James Hall was put on quick probation because a dork on the second floor named Marshall Bloom had been caught by a maid with a girl in his room. A gang from the fourth floor retaliated, scattering his belongings, hanging his bed out the window on a rope, and generally trashing his room and filling it with toilet paper. Chipinaw had been minor league.

During orientation week, each of us students was paired with another incoming freshman. The goal was for at least two of us to get to know each other, mainly on a long hike in the woods. My partner was Ken Howard, a towering New York basketball legend who would become a Hollywood actor and portray a coach on *The*

White Shadow, a late-seventies/early-eighties sitcom. Years beyond that, I told him how intimidated I was by him.

"*You* were intimidated?" he bellowed. "I'm put with this guy who tells me he wrote a novel already, and we hadn't even been to our first class. I thought I was out of my league."

I had forgotten that exchange, but it shows how unconscious I was. I felt like a pipsqueak next to Ken, in more ways than one, but I came off as a braggart. It wasn't even *that* kind of a novel.

Going to Amherst meant being automatically enrolled in a batch of required courses, something I hadn't envisaged when applying (sort of like enlisting in the Army without considering that it was an institution for fighting wars). All my classes (except for the one elective I was allowed—Introductory Philosophy) were part of a freshman syllabus that had become a lauded benchmark of American education.

Compared to Horace Mann, the work seemed easy: modest assignments with virtually no memorization. The priority was "analysis." In history our inquiry began with interpretations of primary-source documents from ancient and Mediaeval times. We moved from the Laws of Hammurabi and Annals of Tacitus through Henry IV at Canossa, money and credit, early European cities, Cellini, Calvinism in Scotland, Machiavelli, and the Incas and Aztecs. In the process we received handouts of laws, speeches, missives, journals, even prayers, and were asked to find their subtexts and protocols—a forerunner of academic deconstruction.

Physics likewise was a course in rethinking the basic laws of nature (with correlative math in another class). We were expected to derive our own formulas as we rolled steel balls down chutes and dropped weights onto carbon paper on the floor.

English was purely a writing seminar—three times a week we turned in papers in which we considered "how one knew what they knew." The first assignment proposed, "'I can make my past anything I want simply by thinking it's so.' What is your judgment of this remark? Does it not at first sight seem to you a fatuous statement? What is fatuous about it? But is there something in it? What 'truth' do you see hinted at?" Another assignment asked, "What is a lie? Have you ever been told a lie? How did you know it was a lie?"

Years of psychoanalysis had prepared me for such riddles.

Meanwhile the New England landscape—its quaint streets, impinging woodlands, and harbingers of autumn—was far more clamant than school. Only gradually did I realize I was at a place that had no precedent in my life. It wasn't like school or sleepover camp or even the idealized college I had imagined attending. And once again, I was going through the motions in a daze.

At World Series time I took the Trailways bus through western Mass and Connecticut down to the City to watch the Yankees take on the Giants. Our family had tickets from Bill Stafford on the day he was the starting pitcher.

The first morning in New York I rode a near-empty subway car an hour behind the student rush and climbed the hill to Horace Mann. I walked its grounds like a time traveller—no trace of the Class of '62 anywhere. At lunch Mr. Clinton invited me into the faculty dining room. While I sat eating and regaling a number of my former teachers with descriptions of Amherst, Mr. Metcalf strolled by. I popped to my feet and pursued him.

"What Latin're you taking?" he snapped.

I froze. I was starting to say that we had only one elective and I had picked philosophy when he turned his back and walked away.

The next afternoon, Jerry, Aunt Bunny, my father, and I watched the Yanks squeak by the Giants, 3-2. Ex–White Sox ace Billy Pierce matched Stafford in shutout innings until Roger Maris' crowd-erupting two-run single in the seventh. Jumping to my feet, I added my jubilance to the din. Stafford carried a two-hitter into the eighth, then lost his shutout in the ninth on Ed Bailey's sudden man-on poke into the right-field seats. Following a visit to the mound from manager Ralph Houk, he got Jim Davenport to fly out to left to end the game. Afterwards we met the Billy by the clubhouse and followed his car to his house in Rye for a barbecue.

For about five minutes I got to stand beside the towering Yankee with my burger and beans. I tried to be cogent as we exchanged prognoses for the Series. After a while Billy ribbed me, "You care more than me 'bout whether we win or lose. Either way, the season's over in a week. Then it's women, not baseball—" checking to make sure his wife was safely out of earshot. Probably not, so he added, "that is, if I wasn't married to Janice."

Stafford the ballplayer and Stafford the guy were two different fellows—no surprise there. I had understood that since Uncle Paul presented a nine-year-old to his favorite player. The previous winter when Jerry and I joined Billy at the Grossinger's bar, I was astonished that he didn't know the names of half the players on the Kansas City A's. "But I can recognize them," he said, "and that's all they pay me to do."

Billy had raised an old, familiar dichotomy—girls and baseball. On the night of my senior prom Rod Kanehl got a rare start against the Giants. Without anything resembling a girlfriend to ask, I had ended up calling my Chipinaw tentmate Bud's sister Sharon. It wasn't that I felt a romantic draw to her, but the three of us had hung out together at Grossinger's the previous winter and she was charming, foxy, and sophisticated, an exquisitely etched china doll who ticked like a fine clock with a slight English accent—or something resembling it—though she was pure Long Island. She had floated the idea back in December when my lack of a date came up in idle chatter: "Just ask me. I'm available and a friend."

As I was getting dressed for the evening, I heard, "Playing first base for New York and batting second, number ten, Rod Kanehl." After a brief tug of indecision, I slipped my baseball-shaped radio into the orchid box, then transferred it to my jacket pocket once I was in the cab. From then on, two entities pulled my taffy brain in polar directions: a tall dark girl with bright red lipstick in a backless dress and Kanehl's at-bats.

The evening never got in sync: a procession of antithetical intentions, missed opportunities, stolen chairs, and a legendary class wolf I barely knew flirting and then dancing with my date. As he did, I slipped away to the bathroom to hear (at the precise click of the "on/off" dial), "Now here's Rod Kanehl, a rookie who's had himself quite a night. He has a single and his first Major League home run in four trips to the plate."

"Yes!"

But how could I return to the table from that—Sharon twisting on the dance floor, sitting down, silently regarding me? The evening was unreclaimable.

I was part of a group headed to a Basie Street club. I was sitting through a long, banal show. Then the rest of them were going to a party and I was in a limousine taking Sharon home. I had chosen the rookie over the girl, since there was apparently no having both.

It would be years before I began to decipher the baseball muddle. It was no longer a child's fetish or even a primitive attempt at individuality. In fact, I was embarrassed enough after an Amherst classmate called me "Mr. Baseball" that I tried to hide my addiction as tantamount to pornography. Baseball had become other things by then: it was a vehicle for tribal loyalties, a clan ceremony (when no others were at hand), and a container for primitive rage—gestation in a family that was mainly *against* things, who hated more than loved and wished ill on others routinely. The radiation of that had to go somewhere, be stored in a safe vessel through its half-life so as not to contaminate the rest of my life. Baseball gave me a repository for anger, envy, and greed, for revelling in another's failure, something a fan does every day. In later years, baseball was a way to cheer for the redemption of the outcast (the underdog Mets), to reclaim the waif I was. I was never truly a baseball fan; math-physics clued me it was just a convenient abacus, a quadrant of Cartesian coordinates with a moving spherical mass, totemic spacing, Topps ikons, and statistically delectable probabilities. I was a fan of energy, magic, restitution.

I watched the seventh game of the rainout-delayed Series alone in the basement of Mientka's TV repair shop in the village of Amherst, my brain a nubbin as I paced out Willie McCovey's ninth-inning at-bat, 1-0 Yankees, two outs, tying and winning runs on second and third. "I feel sorry for you," snapped a technician, "if you care so much about this." Bill Stafford had said almost the same thing a week earlier. Was my neurosis that obvious?

The game ended in a line-drive out—too fleet even to think about the consequences if it had been hit a foot higher or to Bobby Richardson's left or right—probably having to face my alienation from just about everything else a few weeks sooner. Instead I jumped with clenched fists and raced onto the street.

I was alone. There was no evidence of a climax anywhere in smalltown New England. Ringing with pride in my team, I headed back to James to write the day's English paper. But the Mientka serviceman had spoken prophecy. By the 1963 Series I no longer cared what happened to the Yanks.

Autumn came abruptly, red and blood-orange trees, squirrels burying nuts in the quad, the ground littered with a patchwork of leaves following a night rain, relics that crinkled under footsteps after days of brisk transparent cold. Dusk began in late afternoon. Then snows covered it all. I sat in my room Friday evenings, harmonizing quietly with Johnny Horton, dead in a plane crash while I was still at P.S. 6:

> *Today I'm so weary,*
> *Toda-ay I'm so blue,*
> *Sad and broken-hearted,*
> *And it's all because of you....*

I imagined Betsy leaving Bob and suddenly showing up in Amherst, running across the quad to meet me after class. She had a twinkle in her eye as we hugged, oblivious to the crowds. She'd tell me she was fleeing the lunacy of Miami Beach. We'd move into the village and make our home in one of those cottages on Pleasant Street. A classmate my age was actually married and living in town; perhaps Betsy was wealthy enough to support us both till I got my novel published. In the end I settled for mailing her an Amherst sweater with a big felt "A," unlikely as she was to wear it around Dade.

On Saturdays the dorm floor turned into a nightclub—speakers in the hallway, red bulbs in the ceiling sockets, guys carrying beer mugs, their dates in purple-and-white Amherst scarves.... I sat in my room, dialing in Ranger games from scrambled airwaves, writing this book, playing records:

Life was so sweet, dear,
Li-ife was a song.
Now you've gone and left me,
Oh whe-ere do I belong...?

I did homework mechanically and tried to grasp its deeper implications. Since there were none of the usual sorts of yardsticks, details
I could regurgitate on exams, it was hard for me to gauge how my
teachers thought I was doing. I was surprised to get C's in history
and philosophy and D's in physics and math. I did well in only two
courses: Humanities (in which we read and discussed Greek and
Roman classics), and English (in which I was awarded one of two
known A's among the freshman class). But there I was a ringer: I had
already written the narratives that served as most of my assignments.
I had long known that my present changed my past, that there was
more than one truth.

My professor, Leo Marx, a prominent faculty member who didn't
usually teach freshmen, was delighted by my insights, though he
warned me (in sharp red) that mere psychotherapeutic interpretation had the effect of freezing and oversimplifying things. He
also chided me for sentimentalizing the past. Yet he considered
my company worthy enough to invite me to dinner at his home, a
privilege for a freshman. I sat with him, his wife, and their young
son and daughter, and answered questions about life in the dorms.
Professor Marx reciprocated with disclosures of the inner workings
of Amherst College. He and some other faculty deplored the ribald
aspects of campus life, and he used my reports as ammunition at
committee meetings.

He also advised me on the correct approach to a writing career
by recounting paths of famous novelists he knew personally—
James Baldwin, Norman Mailer, Saul Bellow. He did not think
that Robert Penn Warren was of a quality I should imitate. "A poet
maybe, but he writes those damn novels just to make money." I
was deflated by this news.

Every few weeks the Marxes invited me back, as their hardwood
table and fancy silverware became an Ivy League version of Abbey's
and Dorey's cabin. I felt the caution of an iconic presence, so I ate

slowly and with what manners I had and tried to speak courteously and well.

Yet Marx loved fireworks, so he'd invariably throw out challenges. A placid round of melon before soup would turn into a rousing debate by apple pie. He was a renowned scholar and I was his unruly young disciple. Even as he routinely railed against my notions of mysticism (which he considered "ridiculous") and my associations with Grossinger's and baseball—"pure kitsch," he declared—he continued to praise every paper I wrote and went into helpful detail when he criticized me: "Mawkishness again, Grossinger! What tells you this is more than that?"

Then—after years of false alarms and reprieves—the bomb was back, center stage and at a whole new rung of peril and brinkmanship. The Russians had assembled an arsenal of rockets in Cuba; additional missile-bearing ships were headed there. American destroyers awaited them in a blockade. This was the long-feared impasse that had no diplomatic resolution.

The maniac's prophecy at Chipinaw had come of age. The moral-rearmament goon, jeered by the student body at Horace Mann, was about to have the last laugh, us wise guys shown to be fools, dead ones at that. It was *On the Beach* for real, an angry Nikita Khrushchev banging his shoe at the UN hardly the sort of cranky elder from whom to expect mercy or restraint. A night was approaching when the human race would become as extinct as the Arch Oboler's auk. Only this time it wasn't science fiction.

Though they would not target Amherst, radiation would blow in with the disturbed air. We would be dying on campus, among the *"millions who … crawl the ashened Earth,"* as Oboler's guilt-ridden scientist lamented, *"their flesh a ragged shroud around them."* Yet life at Amherst went on oblivious to the approaching holocaust. Sid was mainly obsessed with the fact that he hadn't made love to Barb or, for that matter, anyone. Al tried to convince him that it no longer mattered, but his roommate was inconsolable (though in a slapstick way that didn't seem to take the threat seriously).

As the rendezvous approached, my sense of desperation increased.

Not only was my own existence at stake but the meaning of all that
had ever been: the Middle Ages, cumulus clouds, rose quartz, cosmic
rays. I wanted to get off of Earth, but there was no spaceship, no
alternate world. My grade-school fantasies mocked me with their
facile, apocryphal escapes. The life I had mustered was forfeit, and
ultimate Color War, with its psychotic generals, was about to reign
forever. I put my anguish into a poem:

If they bomb,
I will be lost
in a frightened puff of smoke,
my head whirling
with questions about the stars,
my mind fighting off visions
of its own burning vitals,
its own roast nothingness,
lying in a heap of blackbones....

My heart is sorry
knowing that
no more will the strawberry girl
give her first kiss
to the rusty boy.

One button
will still the sound
of every mandolin,
will fry the dream of love
into pale cold vapors....

If they bomb,
your violin of brown hair
will turn to straw
and blow as ashes in the wind.
Your wee eyes will melt
into eye juice, dripping
into the random mold of the ground.

The algaed pond will
snap, crackle, and pop
for centuries.
Clouds will sparkle
with strange water.
The land will phosphor
with electric dew.
And Orion will lonely pace
the heavens.

I called my parents, and Bob Towers bargained well with Armageddon; the old pro provided the perfect lines: "Don't be ridiculous. They're politicians, not madmen." I felt momentarily reassured.

With the hour of the converging ships at hand I went dutifully to the holocaust in philosophy (as did everyone else in the class). Professor Epstein opened by asking, "What is the most important thing to do now if this is truly the end of the world?" A titter crossed the room, but he deflected it with a confident smile.

He was maddening to me. I couldn't get past his (or Charles Sanders Pierce's) semantic sophistry. At one point in the semester I had summoned up all of my nonexistent psychic powers to try to make the overhead light—still glowing though unconnected to a power source—descend from its socket to just above his head, to force him to give it one of his pat explanations.

"I know what you're all thinking. You want to run over to Smith, right? Well, I believe we should spend our last hour doing the thing that makes us most human, that allows us to experience the highest form our species has attained—the philosophical dialogue." Then he proceeded to conduct a normal class on Peirce's notion of inference, a boggle of equivocations and anomalies.

I couldn't believe this world. It was *all* misdirection and casuistry.

I kept glancing at the clock, the minute hand ... then the seconds ... five, four, three ... right through the assignation of ships. No sirens. Class ended, and the ordinary world turned ordinary again. We had been living on borrowed time since Los Alamos anyway, and the real danger was probably buried so deep we would be caught napping when it came.

Now I know (from disclosed documents) how close we came to oblivion: no more life on Earth—no *New Moon,* none of the decades of unborn folks who followed.

All autumn in physical education we lined up in rows at the outer edge of the playing fields, to be cudgelled through turns on an obstacle course—a series of ropes to climb, bars to swing along, tunnels to crawl through, hurdles to dive under, walls to catapult, broad ladders to scale and descend. Some classmates mastered the maze quickly and passed on, but most of us were left in our purple-striped sweats, waiting in queues to squirm through a tire, then dance on irregularly placed rocks and slither through a ditch, frost sticking to blades of grass pressed under our hands. This was *"we will fight our countries baa-aatles / in the air, on land, and sea"* to the hilt.

Just when I had given up hope (for the coach had said, "None of you get out of here alive!") we spazzes were set free. I signed up for ice hockey three times a week.

The Amherst version bore little resemblance to pond scrimmages in Westchester. There were real nets and refs. I wore kneepads, elbow pads, shoulder pads, a cup, and a helmet with a face guard. We tried to pass the puck from corner to corner to set up shots and use our sticks to take it away from the other team. I scored my first goal on a deflection through skates and raised my stick in astonishment.

Suddenly I adored being in college: colorful hockey garb, snacks of french fries and maple shakes (called frappes in Massachusetts) at the coffee shop, Al, Sid, and the gang at dinner, late hours of cama- raderie in the reserve reading room, carting my clothes in a sack to the coin laundry in town, friendly chatter with shop proprietors. A deeper sense of estrangement came only in the undertow.

Weekends were its heartbeat. The partying on the dorm floor seemed to get louder and wilder each week, music and drinking starting as soon as Friday classes ended. I remember a kid nicknamed Jynx twisting up and down the hallway, shot glass in hand, whooping to the beat of Buddy Greco, *"This could be the start of something big!"*

Girls arrived from Smith and Holyoke, dressed in evening

coats—and with them female laughter and perfume. I sat in my room listening to the Rangers at Chicago or Montreal, staccato rushes up and down the rink. The stridency of the sports announcer had kept me company all my life. Now I needed him like air to breathe.

One evening there was a strip show, complete with theme music and hoots, underwear and bras tossed into the hallway. I couldn't decide, as even in simpler times at Wakonda, whether the girls were the guys' victims or collaborators. When I caught glimpses of their impassive or sad faces in the hours past curfew I felt sympathy, for they were drunk and helpless as they fought off (or hung onto) guys.

I was heir to the dilemma of Jeremiah Beaumont in Robert Penn Warren's *World Enough and Time,* as he stared at a picture of a young martyr tied to a post. Sometimes he fancied he might seize her from the fire and from the crowds cheering her agony; other times he imagined jumping in and perishing beside her. But there were also moments when he imagined himself among those who bore the torches and revelled in the victim's agony. I was filled with similar reciprocal emotions—wanting to be one of the guys, hating them for who they were, identifying with elusive female energy, as Bing Crosby crooned the ancient ballad in my mind, *"Each sweet co-ed, like a rainbow trail / Fades in the afterglow ...,"* those sweethearts of Sigma Chi.

The next morning James Hall's sexual successes were scored on bathroom doors. Names of girls were listed in a vertical column alongside deeds alleged, the guys' initials or insignias. Leo Marx was aghast, as I described this ritual at our next dinner, but he applauded my solitude. Would that it had been so simple! The world around me was receding at light speed with consequences I chose to ignore.

At Christmas, Ray came to transport me to Grossinger's. There, donning the prestige of my Amherst jacket with its leather sleeves, I went back to the teen disco, the Nightwatch, where I pursued and befriended a girl from New Haven named Mackey who turned every guy's head. She had a tight, wiry body and seductive eyes, dressed in black silk ("no underclothes," boasted an older kid who had danced with her), smelled like mint and leather, and turned down my New Year's Eve offer: "Sorry. I'm gonna go to New York, find me the corner of a bar, and get drunk."

Back at Amherst I sank into Ethan Frome winter. I no longer knew what I wanted to happen. At times I pined for Betsy; at others it seemed important just to get out of this place, or at least out of James Hall, to become a full-fledged writer somewhere. Coursework had become meaningless beside the turmoil in my soul.

Horace Mann was a melting pot of intellectual passions. Now I longed for its collegium—lunch gabfests with Berman, Ervin's interludes of tarot and poetry, even Clinton's obscene zeal. Except for Professor Marx, none of my teachers showed enthusiasm for ideas. They seemed to delight in creating petty quandaries, then solving them (or not) with self-satirical egos—all so witty and clever. My rotating batch of history and humanities profs were preppy and cynical. One of them responded to any astute questions with lines like "I guess I just don't know that one" and "You've stumped me. Next?" We read Sophocles, Herodotus, Nietzsche, Peirce, Aquinas, Hume, cracked their crypts and exposed their flaws. Discussions featured rhetorical hairsplitting, my own wordy contributions either critiqued or dismissed. It felt more like a cult of wise guys than a university with professors.

Even our lab atmosphere was smug and ironical, with members of the football team constantly forwarded as models to demonstrate laws of nature to the rest of us.

Science had once been a viable alternative to writing for me—a possible career—but I didn't experience the Amherst version as old-fashioned science; it was one-upmanship in which Amherst men tried to outsmart Newton and Galileo, pretended to reinvent the laws of physics and were given grade points solely for style. My physics teacher ignited the homecoming bonfire with a Rube Goldberg-like contraption.

I stopped going to either math or physics, falling irreversibly behind. They had become another obstacle course.

Generalities are specious, the above no exception, but they approximate a tone and milieu. There was a requisite hipness to most discourse ("fine, fine, fine"—pronounced with breezy, detached enthusiasm). The default posture was to be wry and aloof or you were uncool. My classmates were preparing to be doctors proficiently, playing hockey proficiently, dating proficiently—generic good guys. Amherst even had a self-satirical slogan—"cowboy cool"—set against Harvard's pretext of highbrow scholarship. Fancy cowboy hats were a favorite campus garb (though one upperclassman went through the day in monk's robes and sash carrying a giant flag—a lion's crest—of one of the German duchies).

I had a few buddies—Marx of course, the poet Al, Marshall the guy whose room was trashed, Syed Zaidi, an Iranian upperclassman who introduced me to Hindu philosophy, and Ken Cousins, a sophomore linebacker on the varsity football team and a poet. These folks and I were united in resistance to the monolith, but I was struggling emotionally too, and at a scale Dr. Friend had presaged.

One Saturday I wrote a description of the party developing down the hall; I named the piece "Elmer the Cow" and sent it to the *Amherst Literary Magazine*. My title was a synthesis of "Elmer's Glue" and Eeyore the donkey, snow piled on his back (in *Winnie the Pooh*) because he had no home—a blend of self-pity and rebellion:

> I went to the window, opened it, grasped the fluffy cold from the sill, and squeezed it into nothing in my hand. I looked straight down at a steaming drain-pipe, up at the hurried snow falling from heaven-black, out at where I knew the mountains and stars to be.
>
> The music droned and twanged in the hall, and I opened my door. I was looking at a messy-haired girl and a smooth-haired drunk boy. He had her pinned against the wall....
>
> My friend, I hate to be bitter, but Amherst was a snowdrift doused in whiskey, beer, and perfume—smeared with lines of red lipstick and broken brown glass, melting into a river of mud—clogging the delta to the great and endless sea (where a rowboat waits for me).

To my amazement, it was published. The day it appeared I found the pages torn out and nailed to my door, obscenities scrawled on them.

In early February a maintenance crew replaced the marked-up bathroom doors with coated Formica. The only one around by chance to view the demolition, I felt a manic glee as the rune-cluttered

relics got hauled off, likely by petition of Leo Marx. I don't know
what spell came over me, but it wasn't the first time I did something
too dumb and death-wish to believe. With a bunch of felt pens I
covered the new doors with grade-school pictures: penguins with
party hats blowing horns, baby animals.

That evening a committee of about a dozen from down the hall
appeared at my door and ordered me out of my room into the
john. There they presented me with Ajax and paper towels and
ordered me not to leave until "every surface—every single one—is
unblemished."

"Can't you let the school give us nice new doors," chided Jynx,
"without polluting them with your porn." The rest laughed.

Chastened by the quick arraignment and antipathetic mob—how
did people always know it was me?—I worked assiduously for an
hour, scrubbing the drawings fainter and fainter until they finally
dwindled into pale spots. As an inspection crew approved my work,
I stood there trying to look contrite. Then I skulked away and
closed my door. The knob came off in my hand. My mind raced,
sorting options until its own tumblers dropped into place: it had
been rigged! I was locked in!

I looked hastily about, as I promised myself not to panic. A crowd
gathered and began pounding my door and jeering. These were no
amateurs; they had hung a bed out a window. Yet I felt strangely
detached. The person they were assaulting *was* an asshole; he deserved
this. I sat on the bed dazed, fascinated. Their epithets like my mother's
had no meaning; they were like the roar of a distant crowd.

Then a liquid began to flow under the door into the room. Before
I had a chance to think what it was—lighter fluid! A curtain of
flame shot up. I told myself that this was part of the prank, that I
still wasn't afraid. I opened the window to get rid of the smoke.

At windows elsewhere in James, kids were chanting for me to
jump. I felt a wild surge, like my fury at my brother during our
brawls, but there was no way to get at them, even to fight and
be beaten to a nubbin. I looked for a weapon and found only my
hockey stick. Good enough! Leaning out the window as far as I
could I swung away, whacking at those taunting me, driving them

back inside, busting windows. The feeling and sound of the glass smashing was gratifying. Then I could hear, as if far away, Al and Sid arguing with guys outside my door. There was shoving and angry words. Finally they crashed in, pulled me out, and led me down the hall to their room. I sat there insensate, in a kind of shock.

The next morning Dean Esty summoned me to his office. He had a one-sided version of the event and didn't want to hear a rebuttal. He told me that I would be billed for the broken windows and I was now on probation.

Word of the incident spread rapidly. A group from Stearns, the neighboring freshman dorm, came the next evening to express empathy and solidarity. When I recounted my penalties, to a one they said I should fight back: "Those morons do all that shit, and you get blamed." They told me that lots of other students, upperclassmen too, were on my side. They offered to circulate a petition on my behalf.

I was grateful for the fellowship, but I wanted to be left alone, to have this unearned fame evaporate at once. I was no hero, no martyr; I had no one but myself to blame. I was crazy dumb Richard Towers from the Martha and Bob Towers household, a jerk who finally got his due. I had been wandering in a stupor, playing asinine pranks and daydreaming, almost forever. It wasn't gallant or romantic; it was bullshit.

The shouts and flames, the broken glass, had woken me at last: my fantasies of Betsy and "Elmer the Cow" jeremiad were self-aggrandizing delusions.

There was *one* consequence of the mayhem I didn't hear about for twenty-one years, which is how long it took me to return to Horace Mann after the 1962 World Series.

Mr. Clinton was still there. When a student of his I thought of him as an old man. Yet, after two decades, he had turned surprisingly young again and welcomed me with tenderness and observable joy. At lunch we talked about the years gone by.

"Do you remember when you were locked in your room freshman year at Amherst and it was set on fire?" he asked.

"You knew about that?" I said, astonished.

"Knew about it? Dean Wilson from Admissions had the gall to call us up and complain about our recommending you. He said you weren't the caliber of an Amherst man. I gave him some choice words. His ears were burning."

Tears formed at the corners of my eyes. They had known? They had been my supporters? Horace Mann, in all its years of silent complicity and rigor? "I was pretty crazy then," I confessed, "and I brought it on myself, but still, locking me in the room and setting it on fire—"

"Those prep-school sadists. I know the quality of human being. I told Dean Wilson that. I shoved his piety right back up his ass."

In the spring I applied as a transfer student to both the University of California in Berkeley and Swarthmore. In April I took the bus down to Philadelphia to visit my old first choice. It was barely spring in Massachusetts, but Pennsylvania blossoms were already on the trees, as boys and girls sat studying on the many lawns. Compared to Amherst's obstacle course, this was nirvana.

The Dean of Admissions was blunt. "Your grades don't merit a transfer, and you're on probation. In any case, we consider Amherst a model of what we'd like Swarthmore to become."

In little more than a semester I had squandered my entire Horace Mann career.

On my way north I stopped in New York. I went to my mother for solace. She sat in her bedroom as I will always remember her—by the window with her reflector held taut against her throat, looking away from me into the sacred sun. She told me that I was missing classes, to go back to school. She never opened her eyes or put down the silver cardboard. She didn't want to look at me, she said, until I got myself straightened out. She had had enough of my nonsense. My performance was an embarrassment both to her and to Horace Mann.

Math and physics were a lost cause. But otherwise I did the required work and kept up my coursework. I even had the gumption to try out for freshman baseball, which meant carrying out drills in an indoor diamond called The Cage. I participated in workouts with two other shortstops (the outfield, where I wanted to be, was overcrowded). Fielding grounders and throwing across the greenhouse sod was as grueling and vacuous as ropes and tires. I was good enough to be on the field with them but not to make the team. So one afternoon I ended a career of competitive hardball going back to first grade, for good this time. "You're quitting!" the coach snapped when I told him I wanted to switch to intramural softball; he insisted on hearing those words before he would sign my release.

"Okay, I'm quitting!"

But games were fun again. I played center, made catches that had people shaking my hand at lunch, and even hit a few home runs. I finally got to come down from a higher league.

That spring Leo Marx took me to lunch at the Lord Jeff Inn with a friend of his from New York: Catherine Carver, a senior editor at Viking Press. He had advised me ahead of time that she was highly respected in her field, having worked with many famous authors, including Saul Bellow and Hannah Arendt. Her willingness to meet me on the basis of the few English papers he had sent her was an honor. A slight, dignified woman with a mannered voice, she skimmed through the high-school novel I now called *Salty and Sandy.* Continuing to peruse it during dessert and coffee, she asked for my carbon to take back to New York. A week later she wrote:

> This is just to say how very glad I am to have seen you, and read some of your manuscript, on Monday. As I told you then, I think what you've written is clear evidence that you are going to be a writer; and although I can't say until I read all of it how much work this book is going to require before it can be published, I am certain that there is a novel in those 600 pages…. Even the roughest of them has a quality of expressiveness that is very much your own; I am most hopeful about your future in this line of work—as you should be.

For the remainder of the spring term I nurtured those words. I had no intention of returning to Amherst.

I also wasn't returning to New York. My father was paying for college, and we both assumed I would live with him and Aunt Bunny, no fanfare or negotiation required. I had escaped my mother's realm by surviving it. I had molted at last.

The day before I left for Grossinger's I received Miss Carver's special-delivery packet with section-by-section instructions for turning my book into a publishable novel. This was the real deal! And I had a whole summer with my sunnier family to carry it out. The first time I would get to live at Grossinger's I could begin my career as a novelist too!

My father dashed that scheme in about thirty seconds. "You're living in my home, you work for me." As far back as my mother's attempts to valorize prep school, he had made it clear that he looked down on intellectual pursuits. I had assumed the prestige of Viking would transcend his objections and he would recognize me as an aspiring writer—but that was pure naïveté.

"You can't just study," he averred. "You've got to prepare for life."

"But writing *is* a job. It isn't school."

"It's too competitive a field. You'll never make it. You need a real career."

I had waited all my life for him, and now ... who was he? Expecting me to begin hotel training at once, he had made up his mind to place me in the bureaucracy at his own first job: assistant dead-letter clerk. Debate was pointless; he was presenting a *fait accompli*.

Michael and James were at camp and Jerry was upstate with his family for the summer, so the house was nearly empty. I inherited Jerry's small room on the third floor next door to Emma, a large elderly black woman from Carolina. She had worked for Aunt Bunny's parents for three decades and had come out of retirement to help prepare meals and cocktail parties for our family. She called hotel maids to do any serious cleaning and spent much of each day in her room watching TV—she never missed a Mets game.

Major-league baseball had receded from me that spring in the trials of college. Now I didn't care about the Yankees anymore, didn't identify with the self that had rooted for them, but I lay on the floor of Emma's room many an evening and afternoon, watching the early Mets with their procession of ne'er-do-well hopefuls—Elio Chacon running the bases like a crazy man, Jimmy Piersall traversing them backwards as a spoof on baseball, Bob Miller pitching his heart out and the bullpen blowing the lead, Marv Throneberry summoning a droplet of his minor-league power as a Yankee farmhand while missing second and third like a locomotive without a conductor, Jim Hickman evincing the clout and speed of Mickey Mantle, then evanescing back into strikeouts. Sitting up in the bed in her nightgown, almost bald without her wig, Emma moaned, hooted, clapped, and did her knitting. It was as good ballgame company as I had ever had. Plus the shifting roster of Metropolitan troops reminded me of my old armory game: Duke Carmel, Cliff Cook, Galen Cisco, Ron Hunt, Cleon Jones. I was hooked, a Mets fan henceforth.

Assigned to train me, the elderly woman who ran the mailroom spelled out my dreary parameters the first morning. I was expected to sit at a desk for eight hours logging undeliverable letters in a ledger. Since the Hotel was a transient establishment, there were dozens of these items daily: for guests who had long ago left; staff who had been fired or quit, or never came; one-night-stand entertainers; even celebrities who hadn't been there for years or never been there.

It was soon clear that the only functional part of the job was re-addressing mail to those few who had actually left forwarding information. With an alphabetical list to consult and occasionally update, that part took an hour, sometimes two. My other six hours were spent going through grubby filing cabinets trying to match names on envelopes to anything at all in the crumpled chaos. In one week I didn't find a single match; yet my supervisor thought it worthwhile to spend as much as half an hour trying to locate a staff member from ten years prior—to try to forward a card that said: "Greetings from Tennessee" (on both sides). Ultimately all this mail ended up in dead-letter boxes, the log books themselves piled in similar cartons, sealed, then stored in a dusty closet.

A fan rattled all day, and a janitor periodically passed through, sweeping scraps off the floor, cigarettes from ashtrays into a metal container on a stick. This was Grossinger's too, one of the enchanted tableaus I soldiered through in childhood. It registered quite differently now, to one trapped within. I struggled against intermittent surges of panic, scarier than the glimmers I felt during captivity in a burning room. My father had changed from hero and protector to warden—and there was no rescue squad in sight.

I itemized the organizational inefficiencies of the mailroom, expecting PG to see that the job was a waste of time, not just for me but anyone. He shook his head: "You'll learn discipline. And it's where I began."

My next ploy was to have Catherine Carver write him a sanguine letter, but that didn't move the needle either. "If she wants you to work for her, let her pay you."

By the second week I was no longer under supervision, so I took to throwing more and more of the unforwardable items into the dead-letter box without checking the files. Finally, I stopped entering *any* letters into the ledger and tossed all of them. I finished the job in less than an hour and sneaked back to the house to write.

Aunt Bunny and Emma were my lookouts. If my father came home from work to watch television (as he did at some point almost every day), they alerted me and created a diversion so I could leave by the fire escape.

At Catherine Carver's suggestion I worked only part-time on *Salty and Sandy,* while beginning a new, more traditional novel *The Moon.* My characters were based on people from Amherst and the teen tour, each chapter told from the viewpoint of a different person. Every fifth chapter (assigned to "The Moon") was conceived as the mind-flow of a cosmic being.

Living at Grossinger's was still the fulfillment of my fondest childhood dream. Although the experience wasn't what I had imagined, it was bounteous enough and, other than my sentence to the mailroom, the landscape was as convivial and beatific as ever. During weekends I hauled my typewriter, two makeshift paperweights, and a stack of paper to the family cabana and worked on sections of my books, taking occasional breaks to swim and socialize, sometimes with other authors working there. For several mornings I typed next to playwright Paddy Chayefsky at the adjacent cabana. At one point he looked over my shoulder and pointed out false lines in my dialogue.

Aunt Bunny and I had never had this much time together, so we chatted like magpies, an intimacy my father barely tolerated. Seeing the two of us together he snarled, "Richard, fix me a Coke on ice." I stomped into the kitchen, prepared it, and set it beside him. Without a "thank you" he barked out his next order: "Go to the Hotel and pick up the evening papers and my crossword puzzle book." There were countless such directives and ruses, more knee-jerk than premeditated. Males of his bent played Humphrey Bogart over Jimmy Stewart. He not only didn't like conversation, he was a proud Philistine; he didn't want any serious topic within fifty feet.

Meanwhile Aunt Bunny, like Grandma Jennie, assembled her own clan of friends, mostly male, from the bevy of journalists, movie directors, entrepreneurs, and scholars of indeterminate origin who frequented the Hotel—on the grounds as paying guests, paid lecturers, gratis celebrities, or honorary family. As these luminaries came and went all summer, I hung around with my stepmother's clique, reading fortunes and engaging in repartees of politics and literature.

Then there was Jennie G. herself. While I was passing through one of her soirées early that July, I ran into Milton Blackstone. Long rumored to be my grandmother's paramour, he had just addled the Grossinger's universe by marrying an outsider from Florida in his mid-fifties and was now chaperoning two girls my age: his stepdaughter and her friend, a blonde beauty-pageant winner from Miami Beach named Helene. In presenting her to Jennie, Milton explained that she had ambitions to be a singer and had come to Grossinger's to be discovered. He ratcheted his voice up a notch to remind all within earshot that he had discovered Eddie Fisher not far from this spot as a singing busboy.

After introductions, the two girls chatted with me and, when Milton and his family said their goodbyes, Helene and I were left standing together.

She wasn't a type I was beguiled by, though she was a striking young woman—a pin-up moll, short and curvy with an artificially vivacious personality. In conducting conversation, I was more comfortable treating her as an honorary adult, unconnected to my own adolescence, a luminary like actress Kim Novak, who was dating the Grossinger's ski instructor. I did, however, ask one unavoidable question. And, yes, of course she knew Betsy—she knew both Betsy and Bob; Bob was "a real close friend" of her own boyfriend Spike. We gabbed through dinner at the family table, where she recounted the series of unlikely events that had led her to the Hotel. Unfortunately, Milton was no longer in the talent business, and the best that he could manage was a job as the G.'s assistant teen hostess, performing occasional stints with the band.

Helene didn't seem to notice that I was a pariah with girls, for after she got a room in staff quarters she called me daily and we began to see each other in the evenings. I was surprised by our exclusive companionship, but I rationalized: she was ambitious, I was Jennie's grandson, and since she had a boyfriend back home I was a good foil to keep other men away.

Helene dressed flashily—bright lipstick; flashy, loudly colored blouses; high heels; too much perfume. She was quite sexy in her low-cut dresses, throwing rehearsed smiles, so why wasn't I more captivated?

I hadn't yet set definitive parameters for girlfriends, but I had consistent passions and predilections. I liked mysterious, shadowy, wittily coy or nuanced girls, even ghostlike wraiths, girls who seemed to have come from Oz or Atlantis. Helene wasn't magical or bewitching; there was no enigma or subtlety to her, she was just another brassy Jewish girl, ambition and fame written all over her. She equated my writing with her singing and considered us two talented teenagers waiting for our big breaks. Up in my room she sat on the bed, I on the chair, and I read her safe passages from both books, after which she sang rock 'n' roll ballads.

I stared at this amazing-looking creature on my bed belting out love songs a cappella and flashing the most fulsome looks, thinking how she would have played on fourth-floor James. A decade or two down the road, she would have been Miss Thing.

Helene loved to review the precise parameters of our relationship: we were buddies, "platonic friends," not romantic partners. All the while she encouraged me to have hope for Miss Sley; in fact, she told me one night that she was going to give me a present. She smiled coyly, then said, "Betsy and Bob are no longer going together." I knew from Betsy that she was heading off to the University of Colorado in the fall. The news of her separation from Bob was a surprise, but I had no idea what to make of it.

That evening after dinner, as Helene and I were strolling to the Lake, she stopped and kissed me forcefully on the lips before I could even think. "Don't you know what that is?" she said. "It's a pedillo."

I stared blankly.

A car wound around the crooked road and came toward us in the distance. "Only one headlight means—kiss your partner."

It was my first kiss.

Grandma Jennie bought me a bike, so I raced along Hotel paths, back and forth between the mail room and home, the ballfield and rendezvous with Helene, as the summer found its merry pace and rhythm. I was happy again. I could finally savor my emancipation from the Towers household, for I was free of the teen tour and gauntlets of freshman year at Amherst too. Helene and I enacted our non-romance night after night: in the bar, at movies in town, sitting in chaises at the cabana by the deserted pool under stars, holding hands at the Lake. I played softball on the staff team, wrote new chapters of *The Moon* and, slipping into my father's office at night, called Catherine Carver on his New York line.

"Exciting stuff," she said in praise.

I remember the evening Helene came to cheer for me at a game against Brown's Hotel. She was wearing an enormous panama hat with a pineapple on top of it and a dancer on top of the pineapple. Everyone stared, and some players whistled. Caught between secret pleasure and blushing, I dove for a grounder down the line, trapped it in the webbing, and threw from my knees with all my might to first. This *one* time (though always in my iterated fantasies) I got the out.

People were talking about the play the next morning, and a few staff tried to convince PG to come to our next game. He said he would, but it didn't happen. In his whole life he never once saw me in a game. We never threw a baseball back and forth either. We weren't that kind of father and son.

Late in July I got my grades in the mail: A's in English and humanities, which, combined with my complete failure of math and physics, pulled me barely up into the high D's. The University of California wrote that my grade point average did not allow admission as a transfer student. Meanwhile, Amherst wasn't giving up. A letter from Dean Esty indicated that I could enroll for sophomore year, as long as I made up the lost credits; I didn't have to repeat the math and physics courses. I resigned myself—even looked forward to—returning.

Aunt Bunny went to visit her parents in Atlantic City for a stretch of early August, and late one afternoon I came home to what appeared to be an empty house except for Emma watching the Mets upstairs. I was startled when my father shouted for me from the back porch, a place used mostly for storage. I opened the door to see his substantial bulk draped over a very young woman on the wicker couch. As she raised herself I noticed she was short, busty, and very made up. He had a broad guilty smile. "I just wanted you to know," he remarked disingenuously, "where I was,"

Later that week he chose to pursue the topic. He asked if I had slept with Helene. His vicarious interest repelled me, and I said that she was just a friend.

"Let me tell you something, Richard; they're always your girlfriend when they hang around you. It doesn't matter why. Maybe she thinks you'll get her a break in show business; maybe she thinks she'll marry into this Hotel. You know you're not going to marry her. So why not get some experience. Just don't get her pregnant. And if you do, tell me, and I'll pay for an abortion." It was the whole father-son service in one brusque speech. I guess he thought it was his job and, from my growing up with my mother, long overdue.

I tried to set him right:"I don't think any of that is going to happen."

He wasn't listening. He recounted how many different girls *he* had screwed in college. Then he added abruptly: "I think you need to get laid. I know some models, real high-class Rheingold girls." His mouth vacillated between a smirk and a leer as he referred to the playgirl hostesses for a brand of beer popular then. "You tell me when you're ready, and I'll make the arrangements."

"How could you think I'd want that?"

"What are you—different from everyone else?"

We stood there in mutual intransigence. He wasn't that far removed from the guys who locked me in my room. When I was a child I could look up to him and enjoy his bounty and company. Now, although he wouldn't have put it that way, he wanted my soul.

My rejection set a wall between us. His routine glances became disapproving. I wondered if he knew about my truancy from the mailroom.

Perhaps, years ago in their warnings about him, my mother and Bob had not been so wrong! Once again, I was an enemy in the native household.

In past vacations I made friends with Gene Kaye, a disc jockey at WHOL in Allentown, Pennsylvania, who hosted Grossinger's events. When he arrived to deejay a summer dance, I told him about Helene.

"So the kid wants an audition, right?"

I nodded.

"No big deal. Out of friendship for you, my man, and out of respect for your family who has done so many fine things for me, say no more."

The following weekend I sat in the back of the Terrace Room with Gene and his "buddy from the business" while Helene went through her set with a makeshift band. The guy thought she was fantastic and arranged for her to go to New York to cut a demo; he even gave her a new name: Aileen Frances. "You found me my own Catherine Carver," she declared. Then she hugged me with unabashed delight.

Late one afternoon that week I got a phone call from the highway outside the Hotel. Jay and Barry were passing through. I tore down the hill to greet them. They pummelled me in delight as I slid into the back of their car. Proud of his recent license, Jay drove us on dirt roads past Chipinaw and around Silver Lake. "You realize this is it," he warned. "Our families are at war. We probably won't see each other for a while. But I want you to know you're still my cousin and I love you."

I shifted awkwardly and said, with what dubious sincerity I could marshal, that I loved him too.

"It's terrible to have to tell you this, but your grandparents and your father and aunt are schmucks and common crooks. Do you think it's fair that they make all the decisions when we own shares?"

"No. They imagine they built the place and that your family is just taking advantage of the way the will was written."

"Do you agree?"

I shook my head.

"My grandparents were their partners; they put up the money; they always acted in good faith." After a pause, he moderated his tone, "I feel sorry for you. Your grandparents are stupid and greedy. My mother and father want to preserve the fortune; they care about their kids. And your parents, if you don't mind the expression"—he looked at me with a probing grin—"are idiots." We all burst out laughing, though mine was a contact high. They left me back at the bottom of the hill. The next time I saw Jay was fourteen years later, surrounded by "gofers" and secretaries, huddled over a Wall Street screen.

On the evening of Betsy's birthday, Helene and I dialed her on my father's speaker phone. "Hello, guess who? I'm at Grossinger's. You know me, still trying to become a star. And guess who got me the big audition?" Before Betsy could answer I said hello.

"It's so nice to hear your voice after all those great letters," she replied. Whatever else she was or wasn't, she was a paragon of empathic grace.

I told her I had decided to stay at Amherst, and she thought that was the right decision. Then she said excitedly that she had pledged a sorority at Boulder before entering. I didn't have any reference point to comment, so I told her I was sorry to hear about Bob. She said, yes, she was terribly sad and hoped someday they would get back together because they had something special. My sentiments were duplicitous, but our exchange wasn't.

Afterwards Helene, full of excitement, was telling dumb stories about Miami Beach, ostensibly because they involved Betsy in some manner. I was preoccupied and dour, which bothered her. We climbed the stairs to my room. I set myself against the backboard of the bed, and she surprised me by getting on the bed too, then leaning against me.

"I want you to hug me the way Spike does," she announced, arranging herself at an angle so that her head fell back against my chin, my arm around her belly. We sat there quietly like that for a long time. I kissed her neck and moved my arm, but she stilled me.

"I saw the way you lit up when you talked to Betsy. I'm jealous even though you're not my boyfriend. I'm used to thinking I'm the one boys chase, certainly not Betsy. But I don't want to go any further with you because of Spike."

Still from that evening our relationship was closer, almost boyfriend and girlfriend. We danced in the nightclub and kissed on her doorstep, as I shifted more into daily camaraderie. After my father noticed me dancing with her one evening, he called me into his room past midnight and asked if I had gotten anywhere.

"We're still just friends."

"You're not the only one."

"What do you mean?"

"She's double-dating you." I had never heard the term. "Don't you know? She's slipping out at night with other guys after you take her home." I shook my head defiantly. "Richard, don't be naïve. What she's not giving you she's giving to someone else. She's not the innocent you think."

The next morning I arranged a ride for Helene to cut her demo in New York in the Hotel car. Back in the evening she was still flying from the rush of it, but she indicated she had to talk to me. We moved out of anyone else's earshot. "Your father was in the car, and he said, 'Give my son a break.' What did he mean?"

"Goddamn it!"

"What?"

"It's not you. It's him. He meant what it sounds like."

"To sleep with you? Who does he think I am?"

"He's a jerk. Just forget him."

But one night that week I sneaked back to the Hotel in dungarees and a T-shirt—tie and jacket the required evening attire—to pick up milkshakes for Emma and me from the canteen as the Mets went into extra innings. As I shortcut through the back of the Terrace Room, I spotted Helene dancing with an older guy from the athletic staff. After that I avoided her until she came looking for me.

"I went dancing with a friend," she retorted. "No big deal, huh?"

That's right; no big deal. Betsy was the issue, not Helene. My friend Sandy, the portrait artist in the lobby, was creating a lifelike pastel of her from a photograph I took in New Orleans, and I went every day to check on his progress, which was sluggish because he preferred paying guests. Yet I remembered the feel of Helene's body against mine, the charge of her presence, and I was trapped. I surely couldn't wait for Betsy, but I also couldn't imagine pursuing Helene. Go an inch more one way and I saw my grotesque father grinning at me; an inch the other, and I had this abstract love for a girl I might never see again.

When Aunt Bunny returned in mid-August I meant only to tell her about my dilemma, but our conversations were never constrained. Soon the incorrigible story-teller in me was recreating the entire string of events since she left. She evinced surprisingly little concern about Paul's "escort."

"What's one more tramp with him," she sniffed. "It's my kids I care about. I won't permit him to destroy my children. What was he going to do when he took you to the whorehouse anyway, wait outside or go in with you? No, don't tell me, I already know. Well, sex with him is a crock of shit."

Spike arrived the next morning—a surprisingly timid, gawky chap—to retrieve his girl. They packed his car with her suitcases and drove off together, back to Miami Beach.

Then one afternoon, just before Labor Day, I walked into my father's room as he was emerging from his cavernous clothes closet. Out of nowhere he slapped me across the face, knocking me to the floor. Then he took a belt and began lashing me with it. I lay there, my head cradled in my arms. The pain was incredible, but the shock of it frightened me more. I couldn't believe this was happening—not Uncle Paul from the Penny Arcade, Dr. Fabian's ally! Only when he stopped did I get up. He stood there, breathing heavily, glaring at me with venom, a stranger. He was a brute of a man, barely in control. "You don't ever go to Aunt Bunny again with stories of me."

As I left the room he shouted after me: "I won't make that offer again, you fag."

Michael and James were just home from camp, and at dinner that night my father was telling silly jokes and playing riddle games with us. We were guessing fruits. He had picked an egg—no wonder no one got it. When we protested it was unfair he said, "Richard should know that one. An egg is the fruit of a hen." Then he gave me a hug as he headed for the living room. "Come watch the Mets try to win one," he said.

As we sat there silently, they did.

I made a copy of my revised *Salty and Sandy* and mailed it off to Catherine Carver. Then, my bike in the trunk, Sandy's portrait of Betsy mounted in non-glare glass on the back seat, Ray and I headed out in the Hotel car—Route 52, the Taconic, the Mass Pike, back to Amherst for sophomore year.

2

Phi Psi

In the spring, when I was intending to transfer, I went through Amherst's rushing ritual anyway. Every freshman visited and was shown around each of the thirteen fraternities; it was how the system worked, was made fair and egalitarian, at least to appearances. Amherst 1963 provided no social dorms for upperclassmen—no living quarters in which women were permitted after curfew. Sophomores, juniors, and seniors who did not live in fraternities got spartan rooms in North and South Hall under the same parietals as freshmen—and there weren't even enough of those cubicles to go around. Although independent national organizations, the fraternities served as necessary housing for much of the student body.

Construction had already begun on so-called social dorms that would transform Amherst forever but, before that, most guys disappeared into the fraternity system, essentially not to be seen again in civilian life except for classrooms and, occasionally, the dining hall—a central grouse of Leo Marx and his colleagues.

The fraternities at Amherst were ranked by status, at least in the minds of students. The top two or three had most of the campus leaders: those who were to become congressmen, astronauts, chairs of academic departments, doctors, corporate executives. Two of the fraternities were nominally "animal houses" (some of the guys from my wing of James ended up in them). The others were individualized by temperament and styles of social life.

One was different. Kicked out of its national for admitting a black in the fifties (as unlikely as that sounds today), Phi Alpha Psi had abandoned rushing. It didn't engage in pledging—selective admittance to forge a collective identity—only a voluntary sign-up sheet left on a living room table until its quota was reached. More by fortuity than design, Phi Psi became the safety valve of the system, siphoning off Amherst's rebels, progressives, and outcasts. The membership was a potpourri of rock musicians, poets, political activists, motorcyclists, early conceptual artists, and theatrical improvisers as it ran the gamut from Phi Beta Kappa physicists to the first druggies and hippies of the sixties.

A three-storey Georgian mansion directly across College Street (Route 9) from Valentine dining hall, Phi Psi included a large field along the road and a parking lot in back. Down behind the lot was "The Glen," a small patch of remaining forest in a ravine with a stream running through.

At the time Amherst was a small rural town, so there were no extra-collegiate avant-garde institutions or watering holes. Phi Psi served as a hostel, a hangout for artists, including college dropouts in the area and eccentric recent alums like Eric the Rat, a fabled renegade who lived in the woods near Belchertown. In this guise, the house appeared in short stories in *The New Yorker* and *Playboy*.

Since Phi Psi was well under its quota I joined despite my application to Berkeley. During the remainder of the spring term I spent many an evening in the manor's parlor rooms where activities ranged from discussions of Wittgensteinian philosophy and campus politics to poetry readings, string quartets, and a touring jug band and skiffle trio—their pianist and songwriter had attended Amherst as a recent member of Phi Psi. Another alumnus-led piece of performance art consisted solely of improvisations around the word "striations."

The downstairs featured two large living rooms, a library, and two student domiciles. The windowless basement was a social room with a ping-pong table and makeshift bar, complete with a Budweiser sign that was plugged in on Saturday nights concomitant with the treasurer ordering a keg (not necessarily Bud). Its darker rear had tables, chairs, and open space for dancing. A permanent stale-beer odor prevailed.

Most student billets were on the second floor, including two singles and a coveted triple with a balcony—luxury quarters compared to the dorms (after all, the building was modelled on a New England estate house). The third-floor attic had two student flats, but most of it was gigantic unfinished, unheated sleeping rooms. It was the custom to keep beds out of social space downstairs so that there would be more public territory. Each of these bed quarters was an end-to-end unfinished, unheated section of attic with rows of beds. Each bunk was covered by an electric blanket. Their tiny reddish lights dotted the nights—Massachusetts was pure Arctic by early November.

Phi Psi had space for forty residents, so when I realized I was coming back I wrote ahead and was amazed to be offered an accommodation on the second floor because someone had just dropped out. I was told I would have the room to myself and, upon arrival, I arranged it after my taste from local shops and antique stalls: a cheap coffee table, a butter churn to keep papers in, Sandy's portrait of Betsy centered on the wall above ears of decorative maize.

Then, just before classes began, a transfer student named Greg showed up out of the blue and joined the House. The verdict of the Phi Psi council was that I share my room with him. A short, husky, Shakespearean actor with a booming voice, he was appalled by my lack of taste and was in the process of relocating my belongings in the closet when I first laid eyes on him.

"What's going on here?" I demanded.

"Just accommodating my stuff, that's all. You can't take up the whole room anymore."

After we chose halves, he countered my Betsy/butter churn sector with a busty Renoir in a gilt frame over a straw hamper containing three artfully triangulated bottles of French wine. As he stood there admiring it, I pondered the incongruity of our forced domicile—we couldn't have been more opposite in style or spirit. Jointly, though, we bought used desks and a faded green couch, likely in its twelfth or fifteenth student room.

Those last days before classes I spent as many hours per day as I could bear alternating between *Salty and Sandy* and *The Moon* on my electric Smith Corona, as Greg stormed in and out in obvious irritation. "This is absurd," he finally erupted. "You think you can monopolize the space like a private studio."

"I'm finishing a book."

"I'm finishing the great American novel," he mocked in singsong. Then he proposed that we negotiate for private hours, in particular Saturday-night use of the room, because, as he put it, "I need to get my social life going."

Since I wasn't dating I conceded that option, a munificence I soon regretted, for he arrived early each Saturday with a different lady and locked me out for the remainder of the evening. I sensed the event was usually a failure, for he was in a permanent foul mood.

Next door was Phil, the president of Phi Psi, a physics major with one of the highest grade-point averages in the school. He was elegant and handsome, with a bit of the Kennedy look, engaged to a pretty senior from Smith.

Further down the hall was an intimidating character: a very tall Rasputin-looking junior with fierce eyes, bushy brows, and a long beard, one the few at Amherst. Jeff Tripp played the guitar continually, as he matched notes plunk for plunk with records of Bob Dylan and Dave Van Ronk. His favorite song was "Don't Think Twice, It's All Right," which he performed so often and with such studied care that for a long time I thought he was in the process of composing it. I tried to avoid him because he was contentious, but I had a reputation from my freshman-year antics and Greg was the younger brother of a friend of his, so he became an early inspector of our room.

At first he lampooned my "decadent" reading tastes—Robert Penn Warren; T. H. White, *The Once and Future King;* Hamilton Basso, *The View from Pompey's Head.* Though daunted by his presence, I was eager to learn adult stuff—so I didn't defend myself.

One of his amusements was to prod me to confess my escapades in pop America. As he heard about Arista Teen Tours, he wickedly satirized "the rich kids on safari." He admired my talent with tarot (bumming fortunes for himself and a train of girlfriends) and laughed aloud over my story of meeting Paddy Chayefsky. "The cat wrote one good line," he said. Then he performed it theatrically: "'I don't hate your father; your father is a *prince* of a man!'"

When, on request, I tried to summarize *The Moon,* I ended up saying it was about a town in Florida, using cosmic and unconscious forces to explore inner worlds. Tripp couldn't stop laughing.

"This is the twentieth century, man. Next time someone asks you what your book is about, say it's about sex and death, because those are the only things it could be about and the only things worth writing about. If it's not about them, then it's about avoiding them."

Within a few weeks he had me reading Samuel Beckett and Vladimir Nabokov, as he tried to teach me the difference between sappy melodrama and more radical modes of perception. "They're advertising men you're glorifying, not artists; they don't know anything about the mysteries." He intoned the word dramatically—"the missss-teries." Committed to the droll absurdities of *Molloy* and *Malone Dies,* he loved to burst into my room at odd moments quoting Beckett lines that turned the universe upside-down:

The sun shone, having no alternative, on the nothing new.

Come on, we'll soon be dead, let's make the most of it. But what matter whether I was born or not, have lived or not, am dead or merely dying, I shall go on doing as I have always done, not knowing what it is I do, nor who I am, nor where I am, nor if I am.

As Tripp's soliloquies rattled the walls, I stood in admiration. Nihilistic irony and stark minimalism were faces of the universe that I had missed entirely: the bare existential fact of our existence, without overlay or metaphor. These texts broke with my prior aesthetics and gave me a blunt, tough, philosophically charged target to shoot for in place of the metaphysical aphorisms and sentimental lyricisms I had been adulating. Beckett was wry and casual, street-wise and fierce.

"Oh, Grossinger, you're so goddamn young," Jeff sighed. "You know nothing; I have to teach you everything."

I wondered why he thought I was worth it.

> Yes, a little creature, I shall try and make a little creature, to
> hold in my arms, a creature in my image, no matter what I
> say. And seeing what a poor thing I have made, or how like
> myself, I shall eat it. Then be alone a long time, unhappy,
> not knowing what my prayer should be nor to whom.

Much of what Jeff taught me was social information: don't chatter;
don't tell dumb stories; speak with style ... just the right amount
of irony. When I participated in house meetings he accosted me
afterwards with his critique, telling me what I did that was good
and what was horseshit. "Jive, man! Don't whimper. When you jive
you're as good as anyone here. When you whimper you're fucking
Elmer the Cow." He mocked my excitement over Grossinger's, my
offhand acceptance of its aristocracy, celebrity fuss, and corny uses
of fun, and he especially despised the portrait of Betsy hanging in
my room. "You've got this two-bit American cheerleader hanging
in a virtual shrine!"

Tripp drove a black Porsche, which was a sacred car in the house
lot. He brought back splashy actresses and dancers from Smith,
Mount Holyoke, even Radcliffe. So far as I knew no one else had
ever ridden in the vehicle. When Greg asked him for a lift to Mount
Holyoke, Jeff stared him down hard: "Look here, man; this buggy
is to tote cunt. Got it?" The beginnings of a smile froze on Greg's
lips. Then as he felt the full rush of shame, he slinked away.

One night a bunch of us from the House gathered at a table in
Valentine where a senior named Dave, who was short on money
for the weekend, mused about selling his post-mortem body to a
medical school for a couple of hundred dollars. When Tripp challenged him, Dave kept saying, "What's wrong with it? Just tell me
what's wrong with it, Jeff."

I waited anxiously for his answer, but he turned to me and intoned:
"My student will respond."

I gulped, my mind raced for a second, and then I said, "Because
it's making too big a separation between life and death."

He broke into a big smile and, putting his arm around my back, said, "Exactly!"

Across the hall from Jeff, in the big triple with the balcony, was a senior named Paul Stern. He was no older than me but had gained two years by accelerating through public schools on New York's Lower East Side. A tall, ungainly, stork-like kid with glasses, Paul had *no* social poise or sense of irony; he was artless and endearing, and he grew into my best buddy.

Unlike me, Paul came of age in a politically articulate family. His parents were union folks who worked for the City and subscribed to the *Socialist Worker;* he was reading its columns back when I was learning about symbols in dreams. Once he realized I was unsophisticated on global issues, he took to selecting articles for my education. I learned about how the U.S. looted Third World nations while oppressing its own lower classes. From high-school friends like Bob Alpert I had leftward instincts, but they were vague and uninformed; I had never seen the facts so convincingly put forth. Communist propaganda had always seemed to me brutally simplistic, like a "B" movie; capitalist propaganda I had overlooked. I now realized it was even more insidious with its bribes and hoaxes, for capitalism *itself* was propaganda as it camouflaged the plunder of its underclass in deceptively benign idioms adulating "The Free World." I had not understood any of that during the Cuban crisis or beneath rote denigrations of the Soviet Union validated by Khrushchev's crude bellicosity.

"Of course the Russians fight us differently," Paul explained. "They're poor; they have a less developed social system. The proof is in the results: how many fascist dictators do we support? How much of the resources of other nations do we consume through the sham of a laissez-faire marketplace? People say, 'Well, they have only one party and no real elections,' but we have only one party too: the capitalist party. We run two candidates and offer a supposed choice, but it's smoke and mirrors, a pretext to keep folks tranquilized, imagining they are in charge of things. Communism may use thugs and armies to enforce its power, but capitalism uses the marketplace; it's far cleverer: it enslaves us in our fabricated desires." He paused for effect. "We are much shrewder propagandists than they are."

All of this was spelled out incontrovertibly in issue after issue of the *Worker*.

"What takes the cake," Paul pronounced with a whimsical shrug as we crossed Route 9 en route to dinner at Valentine, "is that even at our fair, supposedly liberal institution, most of the peons fall for the dog-and-pony show. What do you think happened to you in James? Indoctrinated zombies imitating other indoctrinated zombies!"

I was ripe for radicalization. My father had unmasked himself as a prototypical capitalist—greedy, anti-union, contemptuous of others, philandering and abusive as well. But it wasn't just him. Seemingly the whole generation of my parents was as blind to our nation's exploitation of the goods and labor of Third World countries as they were to the atrocity of Hiroshima. These items weren't even on their daily drawing board, and they would have considered anyone who gave them more than a moment's consideration a communist.

Those first months at Phi Psi changed my political as well as my aesthetic philosophy, my baseline sense of the world. I saw the James Hall harriers, the Miami Beach playboys, and the opulent teenagers at Grossinger's as oblivious agents (and dupes) of the same unspoken conspiracy. Of course I had been uncomfortable all my life. But it hadn't just been personal madness or trauma. I had been raised in decadence and corruption too. My parents, my counselors, my bunkmates, even many of my friends were bullies, mindless exploiters of the weak and disenfranchised. Meanwhile Tripp was exposing most of the thinkers and novelists I had admired as mediocre poseurs and formulaic intellects.

I was beginning to see a world beyond Grossinger's as my fallback identity, though it would be years before I gave it a form or figured out how to commit to it. Our lives mattered! They weren't just foils or riddles with clues. They mattered for themselves. Otherwise, " ... *dead or dying* ... " for sure.

Paul was a member of the House jug band, a clique that sat around his suite many evenings dialing in WWVA, Wheeling, West Virginia, a country-and-western clear channel, and joining the jamboree. Even Jeff approved of that, switching to bluegrass on his guitar: *"Will the circle be unbroken, / bye and bye, Lord, bye and bye.... "*

"It doesn't get any better than that," he said, as faraway fiddles, autoharps, and mandolins disseminated a sepulcher sound.

"They might be right-wing hillbillies," Paul guffawed, "but they've got the rebel spirit."

"Moonshine *is* politics," Jeff effused. He was right. I couldn't imagine anything more antithetical to Amherst than the hayseed preacher introducing the next song.

During Phi Psi's public meetings, with Jeff's encouragement I took to debating some of the stodgier seniors, once by prepared doggerel as he openly applauded my line about a toilet that hadn't been flushed for many moons. Then he remarked with a chortle, "You guys have been nailed by a mere whelp."

I proposed that we scrap our vestigial link to the fraternity system and go it alone as an independent enclave. "We're just a bad imitation Phi Gam," I declared. The seniors shouted me down, while Jeff strummed his guitar as a strophe between rounds.

Yet I got traction. For years on Thursday nights Phi Psi had provided free jelly and glazed doughnuts and apple cider for its members. Now we threw "coffee hour" open to the Four College community. Soon we were running poetry readings and forums for an audience of townies and non–Phi Psi students, even a few attendees from UMass on the other side of town.

Virtually every night Paul and I trooped to Valentine together, perfect company for each other on the topic of magical girls and unconscionable men. Paul had his own Betsy—a co-ed of the same name from Bennington whom he had met during the previous spring break at a work project in Springfield—they had sheet-rocked and painted the inside of a ghetto house together. Afterwards she had driven him and a friend back to Amherst. All last summer in New York they had, if not "dated," at least hung out. But now she was being pursued by a married grocery heir named Huntington

Hartford—innuendos of my father and Helene. Her latest message
to Paul was that their worlds were too different for romance.

"After all," he said, chuckling, "I'm the son of two people working in the welfare department of New York City, and I was almost
tarred and feathered out of college freshman year for distributing
Socialist Worker pamphlets at dinner. She's peerage with a social
conscience, slumming."

So I wasn't the only freshman who had brought the wrath of
jockdom on himself. In fact, Paul had heard about my "room burning" and written a letter to the campus newspaper at the time. "I
accused the college, meaning the moneyed alumni, of utilizing
students as their accomplices," he recalled, "while wielding frat
power to enforce their oligarchy." I had missed that issue because
I had been visiting Swarthmore, so he pulled it out of a drawer
for me; his column had been sardonically retitled "Wasteland of
Hypercriticism?"

During the following weeks we filled in our lives for each other.
With the attentiveness of a Psych major he heard out my accounts
of my dual family. Then, as I offered a blow-by-blow rendering
of my summer at Grossinger's, he whistled and said, "Boy, your
father sounds like a real winner. Just the type we imagine running
corporations. It's almost too good to be true."

I addressed his own vicissitudes by tarot, dream analysis, and
freelance surrealism. When he was about to call his Betsy for a
date, I suggested he go there by balloon, taking off from the Phi Psi
yard, passing over the mountains, landing, visiting, and returning
in similar fashion.

"Balloons are cool," he laughed. "I like the idea of going by
balloon. Or even better: I could charter a blimp. Take that, Huntington Hartford!"

When Bennington Betsy responded by suggesting they rejoin
the work gang in Springfield and repair some more houses, he was
deflated. "You did go by balloon," I told him. "Now you're back.
Your next move is to hire a private army to storm the grocery chain
with bows, arrows, and catapults. Phi Psi could provide water-balloon support. We could flood them out."

His roommate Toby thought this was hysterical. "I can just picture the ice-cream cartons floating down the aisles and everyone looking bewildered. That'd get rid of our turkey image on campus fast."

Paul glanced quizzically at me, then said, "You're pretty good at waking me up and making me look at myself."

"What do you expect?" I half-shouted. "I've been telling myself the same stories all my life. I'd like to send that same army down to Florida when they're done and blast all the crystal and silver on Pine Tree Drive into the sea."

Paul's motto was "the greatest good for the greatest number," and I soon adopted it as my new credo for myself. In early October I startled everyone in Phi Psi by proposing at a House meeting that the whole fraternity transfer to Cal/Berkeley en masse as a political statement. I argued so persuasively that Paul and I were put in charge of a steering committee to draft a letter of application. Most of the members signed it, though only as a symbolic gesture against Amherst College. It was doubtful that any of them would go to California in the unlikely event we were accepted.

Paul and I were intoxicated with our plan. We fantasized an article in *Time Magazine* explaining that the artists, writers, musicians, and many of the best students were fed up with Amherst's elitist social system and consumerist education, its gang rapes and book-burnings. Yes, there was a parody book-burning at one of the fraternities. The event may have been lampoonery, but the books and fire were real.

Tripp was thoroughly disgusted. "It's bullshit ... the wrong issue. You don't want to have to do with *any* college. They're all bunk. Why draw the line at Amherst?"

But I was stubborn and zealous. I even took the step of signing up to make a farewell speech in Chapel. Required morning chapels, like those at Horace Mann, were not religious services but occasions for the community to gather and hear speakers of different persuasions, much as at a New England town meeting. When my time came I stood at the podium and, drawing on my newfound pluck, attacked the "cowboy cool" world in front of President Plimpton and an array of students and faculty. I satirized Amherst's phony critical intelligence, its gentleman jocks whom I characterized as provincial, anti-intellectual, and anti-women, contributing to violence and exploitation.

In retrospect, my speech reads like liberal clichés and adolescent utopianism—a disappointment to my memory of the charge I felt running through me at the time. Its sentiments were far less heartfelt and singular than those I had expressed two years earlier at Horace Mann. Yet I thought of myself as awakened, liberated. I wanted to re-cast "Elmer the Cow" as spokesman for the masses.

I compared the local milieu to Horace Mann, where Bob Alpert stood against the war-makers and Clinton directed our attention to the veil of life and death. Then I invoked Swarthmore, where, I said, with stagey elegance, "Girls and boys sat under trees dropping flower petals into one another's philosophy books." I closed by quoting the dying Malone.

I hadn't earned the voice I spoke in. A novice politico riding borrowed enthusiasm, I must have seemed naïve and churlish to most of the audience. Yet I captured an energy, a mood that was prevalent if indeterminate and unarticulated at the time. The speech was well received in some quarters, and I picked up many new friends as well as raised Phi Psi's profile as Revolution Central.

After my freshman-year buddy Marshall Bloom asked me for a copy, without forewarning he printed it up and distributed it on campus—an imperious deed blamed on me to this day. Soon after, President Plimpton invited me into his office to discuss the matter. He said that I had raised a number of good points, ones that were being considered by the administration, and he hoped I would stay and contribute to the college's transition. He thought it would be character-building and offered his assistance.

"My door is open," he said. "Just come by."

I thanked him, but I imagined then that I had an appointment with destiny. I didn't see how transferring was as much a fantasy as interstellar travel. I never pictured what it would be like to enter a large public university on the other side of the country.

One morning a group of us stood on Paul's balcony when a row of grade-schoolers passed with their teacher. "Look at the men up there," pointed one little boy.

"Ooo," shuddered Toby as he giggled, "he called us men." But that's what we were.

With the freedom to choose most of my own courses for the first time that fall, I felt like a pilgrim in a treasure trove: the book-sized Amherst catalogue with its pages upon pages of intellectual adventures organized by department. I expected college life to improve, but the fates continued to confound me at every turn.

I signed up for creative writing and found myself in a class that so little resembled Mr. Ervin's it might just as well have been Martian cribbage. It was taught by an aged poet named Rolfe Humphries. In the early part of the century he had been Amherst's only football All-American and, unknown to me before I enrolled, he relished filling the roster with current players because, as he put it, athletes were the most disciplined writers. Much of the team was in the course to pick up a gut "A."

Humphries disliked my work as much as it was possible to dislike anything politely. "You've got a lot of succulent imagery," he jibed, "but I doubt there's any meat on the bones." Everyone snickered in solidarity against an upstart too big for his britches.

After a while I stopped reading my work aloud and simply listened to him adulate ballads of the locker room and fine-tune students' translations of French surrealists.

My Shakespeare teacher, Mr. Baird, was a grandiose replica of Mr. Metcalf. At the first class he told us that all students were ignoramuses and he hadn't heard an original idea in forty years. Then he confined our written assignments to single paragraphs cobbled in class: "The less of your idiocies I have to endure, the less cranky I'll be when grading you." He also delegated us passages from *Hamlet* to memorize and then tested us on our recall. I couldn't resist commenting, as I handed in my transcriptions: "Sorry I didn't think of anything original." He chased me out of the room with a quavering fist. Probably just high theater, but my stunt made the campus rounds.

My European literature course had a spectacular reading list (Camus, Sartre, Malraux, E. M. Forster—stuff which I had looked forward to for years), but another arrogant, self-important teacher, a younger man named Guttmann, wrote "No!" all over my papers and gave me D's on every one. My formulations of symbols and cosmic mysteries were rejected in single red slashes, as though no further explanation were necessary. Still I refused to tailor my writing to his pedant's reduction of art to sociology. Freshman year had burned grade consciousness out of me. I thought of myself as a rebel in search of greater truth. Forster's soliloquy in *Howards End* defined me to myself:

"Only connect!... Only connect the prose and the passion and both will be exalted, and human love will be seen at its height. Live in fragments no longer. Only connect, and the beast and the monk, robbed of the isolation that is life to either, will die."

"Only connect" became my adage alongside "the greatest good for the greatest number" and words of the indefatigable Beckett: "I was not made for the great light that devours, a dim lamp was all I had been given, and patience without end, to shine it on the empty shadows."

My other subjects were psychology, geology, and American Studies. Unfortunately, Introductory Psychology had nothing to do with Freud. It was mainly statistical. We read books on sensation, perception, and memory, and, for a term paper, were asked to make up our own personality tests. I devised a scale of "salty," "sandy," and "oinky" through which I proposed an evolution of consciousness based on Abraham Maslow's spectrum of self-actualization (its ninety calibers included amethyst-salty, strawberry-sandy, papoose-oinky, tobacco-saltless, cellophane-sandless, buckle-oinkless, etc.). It was the same romanticism that Tripp and Marx decried. But I couldn't thrash through my ritual coronation of Betsy to anything more cogent, so I wallowed in its preciousness. It was emotionally all I had, and it kept me going.

"On to the peaks!" was my professor's sole satirical comment. He gave me a B.

Geology provided primordial images for *The Moon*—prehistoric volcanoes, rivers born in rivulets and churning in stone for millennia to form canyons, overflowing their banks and dying into oxbows like the lake of that name in Northampton. That was the main use I made of our curriculum: metaphors. Otherwise I found the ritual of lava and diastrophism sterile and formulaic, culminating only in the science of oil. We were being trained for Esso and Standard.

At his instigation Leo Marx was my teacher again, this time for American Studies, his real specialty. There he was not nearly as receptive as in freshman English. He told me, even before the first meeting, that he wanted me to develop critical faculties this year at the expense, if necessary, of my creativity. When I handed in my poem "If They Bomb …" for an assignment to describe our political philosophy, he rejected it ("Political, maybe, maybe; philosophy, no!") and asked me to try again. He also preached vehemently against Phi Psi. Because it was a fraternity—though a renegade one—he gratuitously prejudged it, calling it "undisciplined" and "indefensibly anarchic." My pleas on its behalf convinced him only that I was being indoctrinated. "The lady doth protest too much.… Richard, the only place for a serious student is a dorm."

But Marx and I found a far more meaty bone of contention. During the fall I had begun corresponding with my former class-mate Chuck Stein, now at Columbia, because I was reading the work of his literary mentor Charles Olson. I had considered Olson "Chuck's thing" in high school. His poems were obscure riddles outside my range of intellect or interest, relevant only insofar as my friend used them to elucidate his own art. Though they had a spirit of bigness and cosmos, I preferred Robert Penn Warren, Faulkner, Nabokov, Hamilton Basso, even Stephen Crane—stuff I could get at and interpret by sublimation, displacement, and allegory, my neo-Freudian legacy. Part of me remained a pop psychoanalyst who hunted deft symbols and subterfuge meanings. Another part, like my lit-crit former girlfriend Jill, dismissed the postmodern perspective as indulgent obfuscation—gnarls of allusions cluttering in inaccessible screeds. But now, after my encounters with Tripp, discursion and open-field composition earned a free pass: gateways to a different kind of profundity. And that brought Olson back into my purview.

First I bought his small blue collection *The Distances*. Like *Malloy* and *Malone Dies,* it was published under Grove Press' Evergreen imprint, which drew the two outlier writers into cahoots. Then I used Chuck's notes to forge a path through each poem.

Olson was a plunge into the total unknown. He sounded nothing like Robert Lowell and Archibald MacLeish, the two most admired poets locally. *Their* lines were as smooth as butter, a marching band; *his* were jagged and jazzlike, alternating between the gruff vernacular and delphically esoteric. His proposition of words as things rather than symbols required a switch of focus and valuation, but it became a backdoor to the riddles of freshman English and history, as well as the mystery of the quantum hinted at in my physics course. The trick was to stop looking for lyricism, wistfulness, and evocation; Olson was more like bebop or high skiffle.

There were plenty of multidirectional metaphors and levels of code in just the first couple of pages: kingfisher birds, the glyph "E," Mao translated into French, translucent eggs and fishbones, and a large gold wheel of 3800 ounces—all arcanely strung together in rhythmic ciphers suggesting something as remote and exigent as cosmic rays.

Though I couldn't articulate it, I intuited what he was saying. It lay at the heart of Cro Magnon cave paintings, Neolithic myths, continental drift, and the voyages of Cabot and Champlain, a tapestry that was simultaneously astrophysical, etymological, Eurasian, Mediaeval, non-figurative, and avant-garde. *The Distances* was far more complex and integral than anything in the Amherst curriculum, for it approached the invisible backdrop to the whole shebang: culture, cosmos, meaning itself. That was a parley I could believe in!

To Leo Marx it was the last straw. "He's a lunatic," he shouted at me in his office after summoning me for a meeting after class. "Even his own students don't know what he's talking about. Reading iconoclasts like that, you are going nowhere fast." He was so exasperated by this fresh sacrilege he could hardly think of anything strong enough to invoke. "Ask Katey Carver what she thinks of him," he finally screamed, dramatically throwing up his arms.

I did, and my editor at Viking agreed emphatically, instructing me to seek more suitable reading material. As a start she sent me Saul Bellow's *Henderson the Rain-King,* marking a few of the passages she had written for him, a playful slip of confession. I wondered why she hadn't resorted to Bellow sooner, but I guessed that Olson was the straw that broke the camel's back. I read the novel, but it seemed fake. It didn't have to do with real Africans, real madness, or the local gods it feigned to invoke. By then I had come to accept Tripp's judgment of most American novels: advertising slogans disguised in spurious narratives. At least Olson offered rogue and mutinous recourse, the possibility of a more radical map of reality, beyond the governing mirages of Western academia. His texts as well stowed no subterfuge plans or adult agendas for me (which Marx had in spades). He held out no promises, sought no adulation. No one else could have written his words.

Olson was making me an offer, "Find me and you find yourself." That was what I had believed since my initiation by Abraham Fabian, but I had never run across a matching text or anyone since to keep me company and show the way. *The Distances* did it by saying, in effect, "Truth is just as ambiguous and evocative and dangerous as it feels, so go to it and good luck to us all, because reality's the same as a Minoan map or a Mayan zodiac and we are drawing our own figure on the world, on the universe and syntax too."

A sequence called me back to Betsy at the Yuma station but at a different frequency that had the power to pull me out of my perennial funk into true art. I posted it above my desk:

> *O love who places all where each is, as they are, for every*
> *moment,*
>   *yield*
>   *to this man*
>   *that the impossible distance*
>   *be healed.*

"Yes!" I shouted inwardly. "Yes!"

In the cusp of autumn 1963 I rode my bike along county roads, pulling into fruit stands, lugging back bundles of grapes and apples in its twin baskets. At twilight, pedalling to keep the headlight on, I glided through pumpkin and tobacco fields. Unknown spirits hung just beyond in the gloaming, providing voices for *The Moon*. At my desk among Indian maize and pumpkin gourds I wrote:

The Moon was out, faint jigsaws on a faraway slice of light, the light pale down on the trees. And jigsaws were there if one looked closely enough. They were there as faint stains on a light that has been shining long enough to be stained, proof of mountains and valleys, deep and uneven, high and rocky, black as the space that separates planets.

On Earth, when mountains rise and valleys cut into beds, vegetation grows lush and deep, and in the depths of vegetation is the dirt and mystery of the world. There in the dampness insects live their whole lives: some emerge, flutter about for a while, then return. Down in the depths of vegetation, water flows and mud rots; pollen flies up, and leaves die and disassemble, matted down into rusty sand. There are worms and bugs and moles and fish....

But the Moon is ragged and craggy and empty and cold. It hangs in the sky, a lantern of emptiness, trying to tell us, playing its sterile fire on the burning vegetation, offering eternal life, an eternal answer.

It is unheeded. It is too ghostly and full of mystery, too faraway to be understood by such as us. Its stains are too faint.

Saturday nights at Phi Psi those guys with dates drank and danced, a tape deck serving as a continuous jukebox, the reels assembled from our various collections, mine among them. Others popped in and out, bullshitting, hanging around the keg. I sat in a corner with Paul and dateless others, listening to songs, sharing conversation, stuffing myself with pretzels and peanuts, refilling cups from the tap. These were the best friends I had ever had.

Someday, when I'm awfully low,
When the world is cold,
I will feel a glow just thinking of you....

So sad, so finite our lives against the great secrets, but so warm and friendly in the Phi Psi basement ... until, weary and a bit high, I carted myself to the spaceship attic and crawled into my berth for the cold flight through the Galaxy.

Early in the year, fraternities were invited to gatherings called mixers at Smith and Mount Holyoke dorms. I joined cars full of

Phi Psi members and found myself in congested scrums in which a handful of girls were surrounded by guys from not only Amherst but more far-flung colleges like Dartmouth, Williams, and Yale. It was barely possible to cross the room, let alone find a female not already engaged in small talk. A tall, smiley Phi Psi junior named Fred was generous enough to pack his Rambler full of plebes. He attended every mixer just for the opportunity to add names to his address book. He considered an evening a victory if he garnered the phone number of one moderately good-looking girl—though who knew if he ever called them? I watched him snake his way through the landlocked masses, beaming and indomitable, like an autograph collector. I gave up after a pair of futile outings.

From friends in North Dorm I heard of another strategy. Many students had procured the last two years' freshman picture books from Smith and Holyoke. These provided hometown and high school of each girl next to her photograph. Guys had gotten dates simply by phoning dorms and asking by name for a girl selected from her mug shot, then asking her out. I tried to interest my friends in this method, but the response was a flurry of horrified looks and "Not me's."

Two years earlier I had simply picked up the phone and called Jill. Now the same inner troll would not leave me in peace until I tried this foolhardy stunt. I wanted to risk my new articulateness. I considered myself daring and radical like Tripp, but still unborn. Jeff was fully socialized, past baby fat, a glamorous man. "What's a phone call to get a date," I teased Paul, "compared to the greatest good for the greatest number!"

He chuckled and comically wagged his noggin.

I sat in the House library beside him, turning pages of the Smith Class of '67 book, girls who had entered one year behind us. I finally selected a pretty face from Music and Art in New York—someone from more or less my own background. Tripp, passing by, smiled beneficently. "Grossinger," he said, "I can remember when I took my own first puny chances."

Surrounded by muttering cohorts, I acted from an *esprit* of group heroism, playing my role to the hilt. I told them to give me space, then swallowed hard and dialed. When the phone was answered I asked for Amy. There was a torturous pause, then the clatter of her approach ... a questioning "Hello?"

I said who I was ... and would she like to go out Saturday night?

"Sure, why not."

Just like that.

When I reappeared in the hallway Paul was so excited he could hardly contain himself.

"Now," I insisted, "someone else has to try." But they all ran away.

That Saturday afternoon the first blast of hot nectar from the shower was like a shot of eternity. "God," I thought, "so much has already happened, I've been alive so long." I tended to drift numbly and hyperactively from day to day, to quell the past and its glimmerings. But a rush of anticipation and holy water sent memories flowing from my heart ... treasure hunts in Central Park, the shower room at Horace Mann, my dates with Jill. With a sudden buoyancy I began to howl: *"You're lovely, / Never never change.... "* And then Olson: *"Hail and beware the dead who will talk life until you are / blue in the face.... "*

"What a medley!" proclaimed Jenkins, our jug-band director, from the adjacent faucet.

In myself, there was something almost happy, almost enough joy and wonder, enough camaraderie, to get myself through this life.

I ran to the hitching corner at College Street and flagged a quick ride from an upperclassman.

Amy was red-haired and sprightly, a prospective painter. We kept up a lively conversation all the way to Amherst with ample ties of shared interest—subway routes and Manhattan prep schools, modes of aesthetics, disappointments in our respective colleges. We spent much of the evening in the Phi Psi basement, occasionally dancing, talking to my housemates. We went up to my room when Greg left and continued our conversation, chastely and formally; then we hitched back.

The evening had been a success, but there was no tension between us—flirtatious or intellectual—no reason to call Amy again.

The next time I switched to the Mount Holyoke '67 book. But

the moment I saw my date in person my heart sank. She was less animated and far chubbier than her picture, and she was hackneyed, politically conservative, and patrician. We had a hard time finding anything to talk about and hitched back at nine. I was so relieved to be rid of her that I didn't try the picture books again for two weeks.

On my third go-round I returned to the Smith book—and good old New York. I called a girl named Susan who had gone to Riverdale. "Since when does someone from Horace Mann ask out Riverdale?" she griped perkily. I was momentarily flustered. Then she said, "I'll go out with you. I dig Phi Psi."

Leaping out of the stairwell I shouted, "I've tied Jim Brideweser's record!" He was a Yankee utility infielder who had gone three for three on the last day of the 1953 season—his only three at-bats of the year (outside my armory game).

Susan was a field-hockey player—heavy-boned and sinewy; she was also witty and argumentative, her savvy and poise moving faster than I could dodge. To her I probably seemed tight and unfledged, wet behind the ears. She was primed for the big time.

We traded jibes with Paul and crew in the basement (Susan the clear victor), drank too many beers, and midway through the evening she took off on her own as I stumbled into the attic and went to sleep. I remembered her as a fierce, admirable girl I didn't want to be paired with again. I saw her next, fully realized, blouse and stylish pin, nineteen years later in New York at a Doubleday book party for a baseball anthology I had helped compile. She was a top-echelon publishing executive by then and had made a point of coming by after work to say hello.

"I hope you don't remember what happened that night," I said, shaking her outstretched hand.

"Only that it wasn't good, but I have followed your writing ever since and always rooted for you."

Thirty years after our date in Massachusetts, she became my daughter's publisher.

Out of the blue a writing teacher at Mount Holyoke invited me and two other Amherst authors to read from our work in a dorm lounge. I was the envy of Phi Psi, Fred above all. "What a golden opportunity!" he kept telling me. "What great odds! Share a few numbers with your old buddy, will you?"

In my fantasy I would read stirring prose, and some folksinger girl—blue eyes, long straight blonde hair—would come up and talk to me afterwards. Then we'd go to a café. She'd turn out to play guitar, compose her own songs, and perform plaintive renditions of "Puff the Magic Dragon" and "If I Had a Hammer"—a wispy, wide-eyed variant of Mary Travers of Peter, Paul, and Mary. Full of high hopes, I accepted a ride to South Hadley from one of my fellow readers.

The event itself was a comeuppance. The other two authors, both seniors, were far more brilliant and risqué than me. Their turns of phrase and plot were nuanced and hilarious. When my turn came, I felt overmatched, defeated before I began. I was embarrassed to hear myself introduced as working with Saul Bellow's editor at Viking. Neither of the more sophisticated novelists had a sponsor.

I took my place at the podium. As I began to read, my words mocked me. I sounded pious, pompous—back at the mole village. In the audience I glimpsed faces of girls—real girls, eager for the goods, an aesthetic they could admire. I knew that my whims and fancies had nothing to do with them. The whole writing conceit was bogus, a tale of hot air that I kept pumping up to keep from total despair. Even my notion of "pretty" was shallow, an unexamined artifact of the era's doctrinal propaganda—pure kitsch.

I was a fraud—or worse, a con—proclaiming innocence and lofty ideals while seeking what everyone else wanted too—fame and romance. In any case, the girls flocked to the other two readers, so I ducked out quickly and stood on the highway, hoping to hitch a quick ride back. Of all people, Jeff Tripp pulled up in his Porsche. "Hop in, man," he ordered, ignoring his own statute. I felt a bit androgynous as I took my seat.

He was drunk and barely made the curves. "Don't worry," he said. "I may be out of my head, but I drive better in that condition than most people sober." It was exciting, a quick nostrum for my still palpable lapse of un-Tripp-like bluster .

Instead of going back to Phi Psi he continued into town and

parked outside a hamburger place. A sorority-plastered car from UMass pulled up next to us. Four charismatic gals in shorts got out, or maybe it was that such a vivid quartet is always entrancing.

"Well, lordy look here," Jeff said, standing up. "I wish I had my hat on, so I could tip it to the ladies like a decent drunk." Then to my astonishment he called out, "Hey, cunt!"

I slid behind the door into my seat and stared the other way.

When I looked back, I saw that they were giggling at this tall, scraggly figure approaching with a long beard—as though they had been about to be offended but noticed a sacred fool. "You, you're the one I'm talking to. Baby, would you come home with me?" He half-sang the borrowed Dylan verse.

She was wearing a sassy T-shirt and instantly turned her back and walked away.

"Well, Grossinger, tell me if what my eyes see and my ears hear is true. The ladies will have nothing to do with me tonight. Is that so?"

"It's so," I told him.

"Well, I feel more like dining anyway. Shall we adjourn inside?"

Over a hamburger he took us back to his high-school days in Philly: debutante balls, blues and country his escape, then a totally out-of-context scene of accompanying a woman to Boston, having decided to marry her when, en route to the courthouse, his car broke down. "I stood there, weepin' in the street over my goddamn buggy. And finally she said, 'Who do you care more about, me or the car?' I had no money, so I just sat there, bawlin' behind the wheel, and she damn got up and walked out on me. I deserved it. That woman had every right."

"Did you ever see her again?"

"No, man, you mistake my point. I'd get married anytime on a whim. If something should happen to take me out of the mood, sobeit. Hey, Grossinger, why didn't you stop me there? It's not a 'mood.' I don't believe in mood. It's that there's a right time and a wrong time, always. Always! I certainly don't want to be married. It's just at that moment it's what I had to do."

"It makes sense," I offered, not having a ready retort but not wanting to miss my cue again.

He consumed huge bites, then continued in a different vein. "I don't really care about my own death. It's boredom that terrifies me. I'm going to die like Malone anyway, my eyes shot, old fucks shoved up my prick, my mind indistinguishable from my ass, trying to write it all down with a pencil stub I keep losing in the sheets."

We walked back to the Porsche. He shot onto the road in a dizzying lurch. "When I left Joanne," he began to croon but quickly changed to prose, "she was standing on the corner. I floored my vehicle and left her standing at sixty. And Grossinger, if you ever use her name in front of me, I'll never talk to you again. From this moment onward. Okay?"

"Sure thing."

Among the kids with whom I occasionally went to dinner at Valentine was a fellow sophomore named Jon who lived across the hall from me in a single. A prestigious dude who could have joined any frat but preferred the exalted bohemian life among us, he was the only one in Phi Psi who had a private bed in his room, also a refrigerator and a bar. A certain style of statuesque blonde stayed over. He subscribed to *Playboy* and collected first-edition erotic classics—a ringer among us.

Jon was not an obvious stud—he was a large, somewhat plump Jewish guy from New York with an arrhythmic body—but he had savoir faire and a wealthy pedigree, plus a new Corvette and state-of-the-art stereo. He was smooth and well-groomed, with an insistent easy-listening personality. There was something seductive, almost foppish, about him, as though, male or female, he was always softening you for the kill.

Jon liked to debate literature with me. He considered himself an aficionado of the arts and insisted that I didn't have enough experience to be writing novels. He would come by my room and initiate a conversation just before mealtime with the goal of continuing in Valentine. He took our intimacy as well as his authority for granted, as he pulled manuscripts off my desk and perused several pages before delivering his analysis. "You think you're being daring," he declared one evening, "but this is nothing; it's not even sexy."

Then he went back to his room, retrieved Henry Miller, and read me a few passages. "Now this is real fucking!" he exulted with an almost beatific smile.

The selections were carnal beyond anything I had imagined, like a man cutting a woman's pubic hairs and pasting them on his lip as a mustache.

"That has nothing to do with me," I protested. "It's vulgar. And it's sex for sex's sake."

"It be so!" Jon acclaimed, his innate amoeboid motion affirming while clashing with his sentiments.

Jon was the most obdurate version of a type I had encountered for years. In fact, I fashioned a hybrid character fusing him with Rodney (from Horace Mann) and Bud (from Chipinaw), a Miami Beach wolf pursuing the heroine Peggy in *The Moon*. During Jon's and my rituals of affinity I had my antennae attuned, for he would provide the protagonist's best lines: "We went to the movies. I took her hand and placed it on my cock, and it just so happened she didn't take it away." He chuckled. "Then we came back here and fucked."

"Fucking is pretty good," he pronounced another time, "but really only about—I'd say—a time and a half as good as masturbating."

He loved to describe incidents of girls bathing with him, sucking his cock, and so on; he recited these in thoughtful monotones as though searching in himself for their true meaning, vaguely troubled that he couldn't generate more titillation. But he was convinced he was on the right track; he had to be—after all, sex transcended any other deed or mortal meaning; the quest for it was the staple of our existence, the sole and sheer object of our desire. Oddly, Jon seemed to require another's vicarious participation to savor and get the promised mileage from his own experiences.

Early in November, he mentioned a girl he thought I'd enjoy meeting. "I dated her freshman year, but we broke up. She's a writer." His eyes met mine meaningfully. "I think she dropped me because she's looking for someone creative. Now I hear she's dating a guy from Penn, but she might like talking to you." He leaned forward in conspiracy. "I'm sort of curious to learn what she's up to. Maybe you could be my spy."

Her name was Lindy, and she was a sophomore at Smith. When I called; she appeared at the phone quickly and had an immediate negative response: "I don't know you."

It was a wonder I hadn't gotten that before.

"Jon is not the best reference you could have, you know. One of the things I worried about when I broke up with him was that his friends would start calling me." Her voice was sharp and clear, full of personality; years later I learned that my classmates regarded her as the prettiest girl in the Class of '66 freshman book, but I had stuck to '67, so hadn't bothered to look.

I explained I was no friend of Jon, just a writer who happened to live down the hall from him. I told her that I was working on a couple of novels and had a New York editor.

"I'd like to meet you; that's fine. But I'm not sure I want to troop over to Amherst. Why don't we have dinner in Northampton?"

I agreed, and we set a time on Saturday night.

I hitched to Smith on the premise of two writers getting together to talk shop. I precast Lindy as gentrified and world-wise like her one-time boyfriend, and I was mainly concerned to come off as a legitimate author.

I stood among the other males in the reception room at Laura Scales house, waiting for my date to appear. After a few minutes she came bounding down the stairs, tall and lithe with an open face, certainly attractive—dark eyeliner, long light brown hair. "Where are we going?" she said perkily. I had no idea. "How about Wiggins Tavern? I'm not against using this occasion to dine some place fancy." It was the classiest restaurant in town, old-fashioned and expensive.

We set out on the road that hugged the campus. It was just past nightfall, and street lights in Northampton were coming on. As we crossed into the town's action she dealt away our single point of connection. "Jon is an egotistical ass," she declared, "a brief freshman flirtation. He was exciting, with his wealth and social poise. He'd score theater tickets, and it was one fine restaurant after another—a real gas for a girl from Denver—though I didn't play tennis, a big demerit for that." She flashed a "poor naïve me" smile. "When he flew out to visit me at Christmastime I saw right through him. Even worse, so did my parents." I laughed at the image of animalcule Jon trying to appear like anything other than an urbane hustler. "I learned my lesson. I'm dating an architect in Philadelphia now."

We came to a curb with a puddle. "Jump," I said automatically.

"How chivalrous!" But she cleared it by a good margin. I jumped behind her.

There was a new playfulness now as we strode past darkened buildings through the lobby of the tavern into its lantern-lit restaurant. The ornate setting evoked Towers family dinners in New York, but *we* were now the adults: me and this unknown young woman being seated at a table of fine linens and sparkling goblets. We shared quick grins. After reading menus and ordering, we took turns spinning our autobiographical tales.

I told her about my childhood, Drs. Fabian and Friend, Aunt Bunny, Betsy, Mr. Ervin's writing class, Chuck's poems, Charles Olson, Leo Marx, Katey Carver, and Phi Psi. She described growing up in Colorado, her family's summer cabin in a mining town, her two older married sisters, years of ballet, her high-school romances (one on a trip with a group from her parish, St. Barnabas, to help build a church in Cuernavaca), her difficulty in her biology course ("not well prepared by my dippy prep school"), her poetry, her godfather the poet John Ciardi, her parents' troubled marriage, and her weekends with her lover Steve in Philadelphia.

We had an instant rapport that allowed us to go anywhere and confess anything without the customary awkwardness of ungauged intimacy. It was as though we were two very articulate members of an advanced species discussing the foibles of a lesser species, namely ourselves. We parleyed back and forth almost effortlessly through drinks, the meal, dessert, her coffee, and then afterwards in the bar, a beer … and another. It seemed as though we had been talking for weeks when we had to race back in time for her Smith curfew, stopping here and there to stare at shop windows while catching our breaths. She was a great discovery, even if not a possible girlfriend.

In the weeks that followed we spoke every few days on the phone. I gave her ideas for English papers, and she tried to think of girls I might go out with, though none of them seemed quite right—too academic or too stereotypically New York and Jewish. We sent writing back and forth in the mail and commented on each other's work (her poetry had a great deal of wit plus a bent for the surreal). When she got back from an unexpectedly discouraging weekend with her boyfriend, she called Sunday night, and I commiserated at length. Then, as Thanksgiving approached, it was evident she didn't want to see him again so soon and couldn't go home to Denver for just four days. I offered her a trip to Grossinger's, adding, "You could meet Aunt Bunny."

She rallied at the prospect and formalized it the next day by promising to write "your Aunt Bunny a letter at once, thanking her and accepting her invitation."

But then one afternoon, walking back from class, I saw people running with radios. President Kennedy had been shot, maybe killed....

I think now of Phil Kaufman's movie *The Wanderers,* Richie the gang-leader at the end of his reign, aimlessly scouting Bronx streets, looking for a world that no longer existed, stopping in a crowd to gaze at a bank of TV sets in a store window—news clips of Dallas.

And, on the soundtrack, words written by a young black soul singer still working at his father's luncheonette: *"Oh I won't be afraid; / no I won't be afraid.... "*

In the City in which I *didn't* grow up—an esoteric moment, peeking from behind curtains into the obscurity of a new era....

Of Amherst itself that day I recall nothing.

On the mail table the next afternoon was Lindy's letter:

> This is a special, sad time. Now I think it is best I go and be with Steve, best for me, best for you too. Our friendship is good and means a lot to me, so I know you understand. Give my regards to Aunt Bunny and tell her I'll see her the next time.

I took a bus from Amherst to Grand Central Station and lugged my suitcase onto the uptown subway. Its soot had a distinctive railroad grime, the streaming throngs familiar too, anciently so. I could no longer pretend the char and sopor had nothing to do with me. I had become another of those adult travellers I had stared at as a child without comprehension. Their trance was the base mood of existence, *Molloy* and *Malone* in action, and it subsumed me as much as it did mass commuters returning to their apartments from a day at school or work. But I knew how to stand anonymously in a car packed with strangers, stabilizing shifts of gravity, how to make my way home without thinking. I wasn't maudlin or tragic, just weary, a sense of being lost in a strange world, repining for more innocent times but not wanting to find out what was inside my mood. I was pleased just to be surviving, all the way to Central Park West.

My father had surprised and disappointed me by declaring, at the last minute, that I should spend this vacation with my mother, not out of empathy for her but because his house was allocated to other guests, my room included. My Thanksgiving had gotten downgraded in phases from a chauffeured trip to Grossinger's with Lindy to a subway return to my natal household. I grumbled, then pleaded, but the deed was done. I imagined too that, after the summer's dustups, I was not quite a welcome-home prodigal son.

I did have one small concession to look forward to. Aunt Bunny had promised to take me and my friend Paul to dinner on her way up to the mountains from the City.

Even in the short time I had been away, the Towers family had changed dramatically. After years of struggle, Robert Towers Advertising had found its metier. There were more potential clients than Bob could handle, and he plugged a host of new accounts, from local restaurants and clubs to hotels in Vermont and New Hampshire. Upgrades were everywhere: toasters, radios, lamps, drapes, cutlery. The living-room furniture had been re-covered and fitted with plastic, making it uninviting to sit on. Bridey's role had changed from nurse to housekeeper, as she worked daytimes through dinner, then took the subway home.

Jon was the big story. It seemed that, almost from the day I left, he had turned into a delinquent. The first sign was coming home late, then terrorizing his parents with tales of hopping onto the subway tracks and waiting until the train was in sight before climbing off. He was no longer doing well at Horace Mann—on probation for bizarre incidents like shooting at teachers with a water gun and throwing a rock through the auditorium window. He had been caught staging fights behind the gym. His compulsions, self-dares, and battles with ghosts had been raised to a fateful level, but no one seemed to seem to recognize the connection between a hand on a light bulb and subway chicken—their common theme of repetitive thoughts engendering self-destructive acts. Alone with my stepfather briefly in the kitchen, I encouraged him to find Jon a therapist.

"I should inform you," he replied, "that your mother refuses to hear of it."

In her Medusa stare I froze. All the strength and resilience I had gathered during the summer and at Amherst seeped out of me. She told me I didn't look well, that I had lost weight. This was her oldest portent as well as her fallback position at transitional moments like these. It felt like a punch to the gut—sapping my energy and giving me the chills. She had had my number, always.

She berated me for my grades, for time wasted goofing off at Grossinger's, for the way I was dressed. She didn't want to hear about new friends at Phi Psi. "They must not be much of an influence from your performance at school." She rattled on about such matters willy-nilly until her harangue swerved into a litany of offenses I had committed against my brother. Jon's change of character she pinned entirely on me—after all, he and I had become companions toward the end of my family residence and he had adopted *my* tarot cards, *my* magic talk, *my* poets. She accused me of corrupting him out of spite and rivalry and to get my revenge on her. Then she turned abruptly and marched into her room. No warmth or hug, not even hello—that would have been seen as compliance or capitulation.

The speech felt thoroughly rehearsed; I could tell that she had been long nursing this rhetoric, some of it probably since the day I left. It kept her own panic at bay.

At one point I inserted a tentative mention of psychoanalysis. With a fed-up look she replied, "One crazy kid is enough," as though the logic of that were obvious.

Omens and traces were everywhere. Bridey glared for no particular reason. Bob and Jonny closed doors behind us; they didn't want to be caught fraternizing with me. Debby would have nothing to do with me. Taciturn and unapproachable, she gave me a look that said, "We all know how terrible you are and, now that I've had time to think about it, I am not going to be taken in by you the way I was." This had been my mother's—and the household—story since before she was born.

In our room I regaled Jon about Amherst life: Tripp and Beckett, Phi Psi. He listened attentively; he was a more sober, taciturn kid, not interested in sports or grades anymore; he wanted wizardry and initiation. He had been going to Harlem clubs, listening to blues and gospel; his favorite singer was Sam Cooke, his favorite song, "Chain Gang."

The tarot was hardly my doing. Times they were a-changing: he and his friends carried around Waite decks and were more superstitiously into the occult than Chuck and I had ever been. They expected the sky to break open any minute, different scenery to bust through. I was amazed at how adeptly he had taken my same journey and yet gone elsewhere.

He asked for reprisals of Chuck's now legendary acts, particularly his destruction of dollar bills. He had heard of Bob Dylan but not yet encountered his actual music. Then he asked me to tell his current fortune, so I set down Waite's Celtic Cross: plenty of wands and pentacles, the Moon and Hanged Man in prominent positions. Afterwards I put on my record of Dylan singing, "And A Hard Rain's A-Gonna Fall." Bridey peeked in from the kitchen, clearly offended. "Who is that singer?"

I told her, but she had never heard of him.

"Is he an old man?"

I said I didn't think so. "He's a songwriter. That's probably him on the cover with the girl."

"He has a terrible voice. He should get someone else to sing his songs." And she returned to the kitchen, mimicking the lines in a lilting melody: *"Oh, where have you been, my blue-eyed son.... "* as if it were from *Finian's Rainbow.* "Hard Rain" is a long ballad, so she returned many times to check it out with the same baffled look.

The next morning I called my friend Paul at his parents', then Aunt Bunny at the Plaza to confirm our three-way date—it was on. All day, however, a persistent snow fell. By late afternoon a near-blizzard danced helter-skelter down streets and avenues, bringing early dusk, Central Park blanketed in oxide. My stepmother called from a gas station; she was already across the George Washington Bridge on her way home. I was unable to reach Paul before he left for the subway, so I sat by the window watching the last vestiges of the Park vanish in twilight as street lights popped on.

My stepfather was the first to return from work, and he was excited to remember that I was visiting. When he heard my predicament, he extended an invitation. "What's wrong with our having your cohort to dinner here? I'd like to meet some Amherst students, especially a Jewish kid from my own turf. Let your brother experience the Ivy League before he runs himself right out of competition."

A half hour later the doorbell rang, and there was Paul, poking his way into a setting about which he had heard so much. He betrayed a clinical curiosity, as he shook hands with Bob and Jonny. Bridey greeted him from afar.

Worlds were colliding with misleading ease.

I quickly apprised Paul of the change in plans. He said, "Fine. We'll do this instead." Then he whispered, "I actually *want* to be your guest here tonight. I promise to take thorough notes."

We sat in the living room exchanging anecdotes. Paul's tales of his aunts and uncles set Bob rocking with laughter: "I know the guy exactly," my stepfather rejoined. "No matter what you say, he's the expert, he has it all."

"Right," Paul continued. "And every day he's calling the patent office because he's got a new invention, gonna change the world."

They moved on to the *schnorrer,* the distant cousin who comes over every other night uninvited for dessert, and to make his suddenly pressing long-distance calls: "Just one more, please," and then, "Oh,

I forgot, I have another, but this one is *really* the last."

Then Bob supplied his own cast of Lower East Side characters rife with what he called *schmegegge*. After that the topic shifted to Marxism and trade unions. I expressed surprise at hearing him in such lockstep with Paul's radical politics.

"Richard," my stepfather said, "you're talking to an old labor leader, a supporter of the oppressed. I love anyone who rebels, who attacks the establishment. I'm an Allen Ginsberg fan. Now I'm a Bob Dylan fan. I'm an original Catskills rabble-rouser."

When my mother arrived she was flustered, first by my presence—had she forgotten I was there?—then by the unexpected guest. She refused to look at Paul, let alone say hello. Instead she put her evilest eye on me as she continued into the kitchen where she greeted Bridey with gratuitously elaborate overtures. From there she hurried into the bedroom, removing herself from our company until making a late reappearance at the meal so that she had to be served one course behind.

I knew from instinct that she was on the verge of either a panic attack or a rage; I had seen that bi-fold mask many times, harbinger of some of our worst pogroms.

Paul was entertaining the family with accounts of Amherst and Phi Psi and, after being introduced to my mother, a greeting she acknowledged with a terse nod, not meeting his eyes, he continued his spiel. She cut him off at once and asked me why I was still here.

"Not at the meal," Bob said. "Have your heart-to-heart later."

"Would you rather I weren't here so you could all talk behind my back?"

I felt apprehension but also a twinge of pleasure. I was watching our drama at last through an outsider's eyes, playing the most famous scene in my life, one that had been repeated with variants back to the dawn of time: I knew Hamlet's role, I knew the King's lines, I knew the Queen's responses, I knew the maid's foil. I had played every version and motif of this tragedy or farce hundreds of times. Which one would we enact tonight?

"We're not talking about you, Martha. Paul was telling us about the Lower East Side—where I just happened to grow up. And

Amherst—where he and Richard presently go to school."

It seemed that right then everything would explode, but we proceeded without incident from that soliloquy to dessert. There was no more conversation; it had been effectively doused.

It was time for Bob to drive Bridey back to the Bronx. In a burst of desperately sanguine enthusiasm, he announced that he would pick up ice cream on the way home. "What do you folks want?

"Chocolate," Debby said at once.

Bob responded with a line Paul never forgot, was still quoting twenty years later: "Chocolate? What's wrong with vanilla?"

"Now that's contrariness," he chuckled back at school. "He asked the kid what she wanted and she told him." For the rest of his time at Phi Psi Paul would smile at pertinent moments and insert, "Chocolate? What's wrong with vanilla?"

My mother then demanded that Richard's friend leave.

"He can't have dessert with us, Martha? And you might dignify him with a name."

"He wasn't even supposed to be here. He was going out with Auntie Bunny."

I couldn't check my own surge of anger before I fell into exactly the snare she had slyly baited. "You can say her name without mocking it!"

I had lit the simmering fuse. My mother's voice shot up several octaves, and she was breathing heavily. She began screaming at me for incidents going all the way back to childhood when—she proclaimed—I chose the Grossinger's over her. Anyone could see I was a troublemaker—look at what I had done to my poor brother; look at the kind of vagabonds I brought home, the so-called friends I had now. She yelled at Bob, Jonny, and Debby, even as they sat there staring dumbly. She exhorted them to come to her support. But no one spoke. Medusa had paralyzed us.

"Go, all of you! Just get out of here!" When Bridey, who was virtually her temple maiden, stuck her head in from the kitchen, my mother told her to leave too. She was planning to depart for the Bronx anyway, just not at that exact moment, so she had to run down the hall to retrieve her coat and purse.

The six of us stood in the foyer with expressions ranging from Debby's icy stare to Bob's grimly pursed lips. As we awaited the elevator my mother reappeared at the door and began shouting again. "You ingrates. You tramps. Go. Go. I don't ever want to see any of you again!"

She was loud enough to bestir Dr. Gordon, the psychiatrist who lived across the hall. We had spent years muffling our fracases so as not to arouse his attention. That taboo was now out the window too.

"Maybe I can be of assistance here," he offered.

"You no-good crook," she hollered as he proceeded into the hall and tried to calm her. She wrenched herself loose, pushing his hand off her shoulder. "Go away. And don't try to tell me I'm crazy. Just go back to your rich patients."

All our prior dealings with him had been cordial and neighborly, though no doubt he had overheard the pogroms. He held his ground and told her that she didn't have to suffer this much; she slammed the door. He shrugged majestically, seemed to wink at the rest of us, and slipped back into his nook.

Out on Central Park West we split into groups. Jonny and Debby joined Bridey and Bob, while Paul and I continued to walk downtown in the falling snow as we hatched a plan. Our Phi Psi mate Chuck Jenkins, whose home was St. Louis, was exploring New York for the first time in his VW Bug; Paul had his hotel number. "If we can reach him he might be able to rescue us."

By now, epiphany had replaced the gloom that had been ragging me all day. I had flipped energy fields and was flying. Sensing a mythic theme, even an epic crossroads, I raised the ante. "If we get him, let's drive straight up to Grossinger's. After all," I added with a sly smile, "dinner with Aunt Bunny *was* the original plan." Gleefully Paul concurred.

My true compass was setting in—my mother couldn't stop me from going to Grossinger's *whenever I wanted.*

Jenkins was holed up at his fleabag, watching the storm, bored. Glad to be enlisted in something more lively, he agreed to get himself uptown pronto. After nursing him through directions, Paul called his own parents, told them where we were headed, and asked them to pretend they hadn't heard from us. One hurdle remained—for me to fetch my belongings upstairs.

We took the service elevator in order to use the apartment's rear entrance and negate telltale noises. I slipped my key into the lock, made a quick, soft rotation followed by an equally deliberate push. As I tiptoed through the kitchen to my former study, I felt like an American spy in East Berlin, behind enemy lines, my ass at stake. Luckily my mother was occupied. I could hear her on the phone in the bedroom, still hysterical, Grandma Sally her audience now.

She was denouncing the whole Grossinger family, saying how they had cheated her out of her rightful desserts and ruined her life. Over and over she mentioned Bunny as some wanton home-wrecker. She had plenty to say about Richard: an ungrateful lunatic who was flunking out of college because he cared for no one but himself. A thoroughly intimidated Paul hid behind the garbage can next to the elevator. Only after I made my escape did I realize that I was light-headed and shaking.

Twenty minutes later Jenkins' green Bug swung around the corner and, as Paul and I cheered, Phi Psi's jug-band leader parked by a hydrant and got out. Paul patted him on the back; then we some-how fit my suitcase, slid in, whipped down 96th Street, and headed through driving snow toward the Hudson River Drive and George Washington Bridge. I was jubilant, streams of white flakes adding to my adrenalin rush. I was finally fleeing the Gorgon.

Crowded into the Bug, its wipers barely keeping the road visi-ble, we coasted up the New York State Thruway—the pavement a carpet of snow matted with tire tracks. We arrived at PG's house after midnight.

My mother's barrage of phone calls had woken my father. He guessed that I would show up there sooner or later; either that, or I had gone to my friend's house (but his parents had no idea where we were). When we arrived he was hardly welcoming; he said we looked like three deserters from the Cuban army. He put me in the basement (since the house was full) and sent Paul and Chuck to staff quarters.

As he pieced together the events of the night in his office the next morning he grew increasingly agitated at Paul's parents. After reprimanding the three of us he dialed them on his speakerphone and berated them too: "I don't believe in parents collaborating with children against other parents. That's not how it works." But they held firm, supporting our rights as Paul grinned with pride. PG ended the conversation as politely as he could, and then, to my delight, released us for the remainder of the weekend. Fittingly he saw an advantage to my presence—that, as a worker from the summer, I could cast a vote in the next day's referendum: whether or not to unionize. "But for which side?" I puckishly asked Stern and Jenkins. The union had me disqualified anyway.

All Thursday, Friday, and Saturday the three of us took a combined recreational and sociological tour of the Hotel, delighting in the scenery and food while assailing displays of decadence and bad taste. Everywhere we looked we saw blacks, Chinese, and Puerto Ricans sweeping rugs, polishing windows, wheeling carts of laundry. Overweight, overdressed New Yorkers, most of them Jewish, flaunted jewelry and performed unnecessary public dramas, barking at wives, husbands, kids. How had I missed this so completely!

But it was a turning point. I had run away from home. I had told everyone that I didn't live with my mother anymore. On the mail table at Phi Psi was her response—a carbon of her letter to my father, disowning me and turning over full responsibility to him. "That's the way Richard has always wanted it, so now I will grant him his wish."

"No one is responsible for a nineteen-year-old," he told me coolly on the phone. "I wrote her that if you can't take care of yourself, then heaven help you."

The beginning of December was dominated by tests and papers, though we made time for a literary evening at Phi Psi featuring my freshman-year buddy Al Powers, Stephen Mitchell (the best poet in Humphries' class), Jeff Tripp, and me. I invited Lindy to read too.

"Sorry, I'm off to Penn this weekend."

In fact, she said, she was overwhelmed with schoolwork during the next month and getting behind on her assignments, so she asked me not to call for a while. She was obviously a Philly guy's girl, so I left her in the past and all but forgot about her.

My best pal then was a kid named Schuyler whom I met inauspiciously during intramural hockey. While attempting to pass, I ineptly whizzed a puck by his shins—lifting was not allowed. Shaking his stick over his head, he threatened to castrate me if I did that again.

I knew him from afar as a rebel in Marx's American Studies class, but his remark had the effect of thawing the barrier between us. Walking back to our lockers we shared Marxian foibles, then continued the discussion during lunch at Valentine. Schuy considered me the professor's favorite, which he deemed a *de facto* betrayal (after all, *he* was Marx's daily whipping boy). I assured him that King Leo was now down on me too. "He doesn't like my reading material, he doesn't like Phi Psi; he only wants me to imitate him and his buddies."

"He's supposed to be one of the good-guy teachers," Schuy complained, "but he's just another authoritarian 'my-word-goes' bwana. He's all for revolution and protest, but in his own class he can't listen to someone else's opinion without losing his cool. Just because he's teaching *Growing Up Absurd* doesn't mean he's living it or on our side."

Schuy was a paradox. A virtual prep-school icon in style and appearance, he was as bright as anyone I knew, a natural athlete, and strikingly handsome—a mop of sandy hair and classic features. But he was fiercely independent, alienated from every peer group at Amherst, including Phi Psi. "Just another social club," he snarled, "a lot of ignorant guys practicing reverse snobbism." He was not trying to date girls, though he was very into them in his mind.

He was mainly on guard—resentful at being hustled all his life, determined not to be taken in again if he could help it. One Saturday night he and I hitched together to a mixer at Smith, talking up our excitement all the way. Yet in meager follow-through we hung in the crowds along the wall. Whereas I was a deer in headlights, frozen by systemic paralysis, Schuy was noble and defiant. I thought he was far and away the most attractive guy in the room, yet he never left our vicinity along the wall, offering only a volley of churlish remarks, one of them quite memorable: "They're so damn good-looking, but that's what they're playing at. I'm just not gonna go for it. Let one of them act like a normal human being and come over and ask me to dance." No one did.

Helene had invited me to stay with her at Christmastime and, after a round of family diplomacy, my father agreed to take me to Miami with him and Aunt Bunny because they were going there anyway.

I rode the Trailways bus out of Amherst to Idlewild ... and stepped off a jet in Betsy's city. She was my *dream lover until then,* more so in her absence because she had been quoined by daydreams into a full-time cohort and idol. Her alias had stayed loyal to me through the ordeals of freshman year, the betrayals of both my families, through assorted reproaches, failed dates, and other ignominies and debacles. She was the luminous Miami girl, watching over me from her other Earth, nullifying the forces opposing me. She alone could reach across the cosmos to the voice behind the dungeon stairs and charm and amuse it on my behalf; she had been its antidote. Now I had to face that she was a real person too, with her own agendas and trajectory.

Sun throbbed through listless Southern air. I kicked a broken coconut shell along the ground. Bodings were everywhere, but I had little hope.

The first two days were an unexpected throwback to Uncle Paul, hero and guardian of my childhood. He showed me his haunts: the Grossinger Pancoast he once owned (now the Algiers—"but it's on lease," he joked, "we get it back in ninety-nine years"), the restaurant in which he and Grandpa Harry were partners, even the house where he conducted the original Easter egg hunt.

I enjoyed being under court protection, as I ate dinner at a pricey French restaurant with him and Aunt Bunny, then joined them on a yacht with business associates. The next day I sat on the beach with my stepmother—jabbering magpies again, drinking rum cokes. The proximity of Betsy was a constant prod, but I put a screen around it and walked in my father's ancient shadow. On the third day, I moved to Helene's.

I expected a normal Jewish family, but I found a cartoon-like parody of my New York household: a sardonic, abusive father; a sluggish, oppressed mother; neither trying to hide long-practiced acrimonies or barbs of contempt. I wondered why Helene even stayed there; after all, she had cut her own record, "You Better Leave Him Alone," a minor hit on the Roulette label, promoted as the debut of a "hot new teenage rocker" between Lou Christie's "Shy Boy" and Dinah Washington's "A Stranger on Earth." A local star, she was performing regularly in clubs.

She had broken up with Spike and recently rejected a marriage proposal from a much older, carrot-topped lawyer (she showed me his photo) who wasn't wanting to hear no for an answer. Relieved to have me at hand, she asked point-blank if I'd be her boyfriend now. "Don't you see," she pleaded. "We're both going to make it. We should make it together."

I deflected the topic, for the anticipation of Betsy obsessed me.

It wasn't until my fourth day in Florida that she returned from college. I called. We arranged to meet at her house on Pine Tree Drive the next morning.

I got off the bus and walked for blocks under the tropical sky, manuscript under my arm, this book in its embryonic form. Coconut palms rippled eerily. It was my life in cameo. Movie cameras tracked me from across the street.

Internally I knew better. I could barely separate Betsy herself from her character in *Salty and Sandy* or Peggy in *The Moon;* she had become an illuminated being. Helene had told me she was back with Bob, and there was nothing in Betsy's and my infrequent newsy correspondence over the year to suggest that she in any way considered me a possible boyfriend. But I needed to see her, for this was the conclusion to my novel. Catherine Carver and my readers-to-be were waiting.

I was led into the mansion by a black butler. Betsy met me at the edge of the living room and reached with quaint refinement for my hand. She was the same plain but charismatic being whose pastel portrait had hung on my wall all year. Her voice was familiar and strange, it had been in my head so long. I was in the temple of the goddess whose simulacra adorned my innermost chapel.

We sat there, she on the couch, me on the adjacent chair. We had nothing in common except a vestigial rapport, and even that an eroding memento. She was already a sorority girl, while I was quoting the *Socialist Worker* and Samuel Beckett. But I had to speak for myself: "I really looked forward to seeing you. You look great." I had broken the seal with stilted lines I couldn't rescind. I could see Tripp shaking his head, laughing, "Cowed, were you, by your two-bit cheerleader?"

She knew what I was carrying, so she said simply, "May I see it?"

For the next hour or so I sat there skimming magazines while she turned through the pages. My mind raced through an inventory of what she was reading—my descriptions of her, my transcriptions of her words, my fantasies of her coming to Amherst and us going off together. It didn't matter any longer. It was a 100-percent total confession.

I stared at every last thing in that room many times, each piece of kitsch art, each item of museum-vintage furniture, the queue of *Reader's Digest* books on the shelves, the view through the sliding glass to the pool. I had come too, like a troubadour, to the castle.

She straightened the pages neatly into a pile and returned them to their box. In her eyes I could see the answer, or perhaps it was the question, searching my own piercing look in order to understand—but, in any case, it was final, and I knew it. "You should go," she said.

I got up and walked to the door, Betsy a step behind me. "I had hoped—" I started to say.

"You'll find someone right for you," she interrupted. "Thank you for letting me read it. You didn't have to."

I strode down the long driveway, out the iron gate, past the coconut palms, into my life, which was waiting in the Miami afternoon. I encountered something almost prehistoric, that had no name or meaning. I felt drained and feverish, an atavism of Bill-Dave Saturdays. I tasted a toasted almond popsicle in my mind. I walked for miles, past houses, fallen coconuts and oranges, lamp posts, stores, trying to harbor every breath of tropical flowers, to record each feeling and its echo, singing the old songs in my heart, and telling myself, with feigned drama, that it was over.

I did not see Betsy again, nor did I have any further communication with her; yet periodically I dreamed of that mansion with its iron gates and palms.

I come long distances through the South or find myself in Florida to my astonishment and decide to look her up—why not? I go to the front door and am told she doesn't live there anymore ... or that she has died. Or she appears, hopeful and shining, as she was, in some version of that living room. Or she is an old woman, sad and defeated.... And I long to recover the purity of the feeling I had for her once.

The dream has a vague background synesthesia woven from strands of Betsy's song for Bob that Arista summer, Bryan Hyland's American ghost ballad "Sealed With a Kiss." A more profound and mournful hymn than its dippy title, its resolution of minor into major chords holds a devotional tension all the way from Bach's organ music and old English lute songs to the Beatles' "And I Love Her":

> *I'll see you in the sunlight,*
> *I'll hear your voice everywhere;*
> *I'll run to tenderly hold you*
> *But baby, you won't be there.*

Such was the landscape of astral Betsyland, as the dream grew and changed with my own aging. In one version she was divorced and caring for dozens of young children in a slum; in another, she was on her way to the beach with no appreciation for how far I had come to find her. She nodded a quick hello and hurried on.

For years we never spoke in dream, but then we did and, though I don't remember what she said, it scalded new light and sensation along the perimeters of an unlived life. I experienced a Pacific wilderness, fragments of an Australian Aboriginal ceremony, a beach far older than Miami where she showed me patches of glacial ice, gullies exiting from the planet's core among ordinary sunbathers and palm trees; then she vanished into a crowd. Or she came from a room in an old Hardy Boys book and provided the resolution to a different mystery.

When I awakened I felt a tremendous loss, but also a wonder and freshness for having been there. I was never *not* regenerated by that dream.

I know that Betsy wasn't an appropriate girlfriend and that she was kept alive in me in the form she first manifested: as the anima, the mirror of my lost female self but also the presence of the Other, a naiad from a time before language. At a moment of life change— of leaving my mother's gloomy household—she appeared in the guise of a Dade County cheerleader to lead me into the care and spaciousness of the world, to insist that I fulfill her potential in me ... to open my heart ahead of time to women who *would* love me. Without her I would have been stumbling across the threshold from darkness into darkness.

Yet "anima" is a name for a symbolic transformation of many masks. Her form of appearance changes as we change, bringing latent parts of ourselves to consciousness as they are needed, discarding familiar reference points so that we become estranged to ourselves. We think we are dying, or in love. That's where the rest of our life always emerges, from the muse who leads us where we weren't able to go on our own.

But just because Betsy was the projection of a force inside me, a stand-in for a mother I didn't have (and that Aunt Bunny couldn't be) does not mean she was not an eligible girl. In truth, eros failed, and our lives twained without either of us understanding who the other was or might be. Perhaps such broken romances are absolved by the universality of the feminine and masculine (yes, we are all the same woman, the same man, acting out the same metadrama). Perhaps our losses are healed recurrently in later love. But there remain holes in the dreamtime, things ever needing mending, alternate realities floating through space-time, seeking planets and possibilities for their rendering. Through their eternal return we experience we will never be made whole. Not in this body, on this world anyway—nor in this swift-moving slick of relativity.

That night Helene and I went to a drive-in. In the car she leaned against me as I put my arm around her. She giggled at the atrocious comedy on the screen: *"It's a Mad, Mad, Mad, Mad World"* starring Milton Berle, Buddy Hackett, Ethel Merman, and a host of other comedians and vaudeville refugees. I felt apart and disinterested. A dying man kicked a bucket away—ha, ha, ha. Helene roared and grabbed and shook me as if to squeeze some humor out of a stuffed ape.

On the way home I slid back across the front seat, but she told me it was proper in Miami Beach for a date to sit flush against the driver: "Don't embarrass me!" I felt that that was silly and also made me an obstruction, so I angled myself against the door. We didn't talk. She pulled into the driveway, and stared at me. I longed to be on that jet plane going home.

"It's over for you with Betsy," she said. "Why don't you take me seriously?"

"I guess it was something special with her. It's nothing against you; it either happens or it doesn't."

"How would you know?" she said. She leaned over, put her mouth on mine, and kissed me long and hard. At first I felt like pulling away, as though from a gushy relative. But she put her tongue inside and rolled it up and down. I felt a wave of excitement begin at my roots and flower through my whole body. I held her and kissed back. I was trembling, as she sucked me further into the kiss. But instead of continuing, she pulled away and looked back at me probingly. She said, "Let's go inside. There's time for us."

Not really. Her parents were sitting up, so she went straight to her room. The next morning she rushed out early for rehearsal and she had a date with Bozo the lawyer that night. I left the following noon and didn't see her again until five years later in Detroit when she had three children by him and was no longer singing professionally.

3

THE RAINBOW

I returned to college after Christmas with a new strategy for transferring. A dissident English professor named Roger Sale had departed Amherst with a rousing farewell speech two years earlier. Decrying his students' blind obedience to authority and substitution of cults of personality around faculty for real scholarship, he admitted that he had been disruptively eccentric himself and said and done outrageous things in class, but that was only in order to wake "smug robots" from habits of "abstract servility:" their unspoken "contempt for knowledge" and "huddled scholasticism." Accusing the college of "a rather dogmatic sense of its own superiority," he proposed that its aim of excellence from its students was cultivated primarily "in order to maintain this superiority" or, more properly, its illusion. The school was "snotty, elitist, avowedly Protestant, and provincial … a box filled with agile white men like a squash court."

His concluding elegy was a quick, wry jab at Amherst's collective hubris: "So, I say goodbye. You are off, I hope, in spite of all I have said, to lead. I am off to where the dream is not of a whole man but of a whole society. Go to hell—and thank you."

Sale was memorialized as an underground hero, and people compared my chapel oration to his. He was now teaching at the University of Washington. I wrote to Professor Sale before Christmas and, when I got back from Florida, I found a letter from him on the Phi Psi table, encouraging me to apply to Seattle and offering to help if I came there. I sent at once for an application.

Between semesters my roommate Greg had left for the dorms, so

I reclaimed the whole space. In his former corner I hung an ancient horse from Lascaux alongside Paul Klee's knight in a rowboat. In the Klee a comic figure speared at three crooked fish dilating through a bent shaft of opalescence, its sourceless glow lighting a universe of more and less deeply-bathed cubes from white azure to blue-black. Alongside pranced the primordial steed of our species, fierce and cute, the spare charcoal of its mane and hooves seminal to everything. These were my insignias: vortices to the unknown.

For second semester I signed up for three new classes—only Leo Marx's American Studies section and Geology carried over. I enrolled in a seminar on D. H. Lawrence; an Abnormal Psychology course taught by Roy Heath, a visiting professor from Pittsburgh (where he was a colleague of my mother's brother Lionel); and a survey of modern European drama. The latter was inspired by Tripp, who was directing a production of Beckett's *Waiting for Godot* that he was planning to take off-Broadway.

The three magical-realist "Jeans"—Anouilh, Giradoux, and Cocteau—were a revelation, and I became an enthusiast for the theater of cosmic irony. Rehearsals of *Godot* were going on day and night in the Phi Psi living room—Jeff starring as Pozzo, with a whip, monocle, greatcoat, and breath freshener alongside my former room-mate Greg's older brother Brett as Estragon. I loved the performance of paradox, the shift into the negative space.

In these avant-garde playwrights the conventions of theater digressed into something between staged philosophy and science fiction. Men stumbled across minimal sets calling out to gods who were their own inventions, pulling characters out of parking lots in other eras. Antigone and Oedipus were reincarnated as Europeans performing Freudian myths that were themselves pre-Homeric apologues. As Anouilh put it, "I do not want to understand. I am here for something other than understanding. I am here to tell you no, and to die. To tell you no and to die."

"No" was something I had not rehearsed enough—no to my mother, no to Leo Marx, no to PG, no to the dungeon stairs, no to Betsy. I may have demurred and rebelled, fled or disobeyed, played pranks and gone amok, but I never said a confident no or defended the bastion of my existence.

My theater teacher, Stephen Coy, was an admirer of Tripp, so, for once, I had authority on my side—free rein. For my term paper I wrote sixty pages of my own Anouilh-like imitation of *Hamlet* in which the ghost of Hamlet's father cries out, "Stop in the name of Jean Cocteau!" Later, Hamlet reads a baseball magazine on his bed after delivering a key soliloquy, and America's role in Vietnam is satirized in Denmark's "Norwegian crisis." The vendors selling food and souvenirs during intermissions are actors in the play and speak key lines—there was, in effect, no intermission, though the audience wouldn't immediately know.

Passing my old Shakespearean tyrant, Professor Baird, on one of the paths that crossed the campus that winter, I let drop a "Hello, sir."

"Watcha doing?" he snapped distractedly. This of course was the man famous for his canonization of the Bard and disdain for student work. I needed to get him into my script.

"Most recently I rewrote *Hamlet*," I deadpanned.

It would be impossible to imitate the startled grunts and outraged syllables that followed. So I cast him as a second Pollonius, wandering in from the twentieth century to dismiss the play in person.

Tripp told me that in America not being able to drive was "tantamount to not having a dick." So, I immediately looked up "Driving Schools" in the *Yellow Pages* and enrolled in private lessons with a man who turned out to be the Northampton High football coach.

"That's who *should* teach you!" Jeff roared with delight, as he leaped into his own vehicle and bombed onto College Street.

For six weekly sessions I hitched to Northampton. From there the coach took me out on back roads where I performed the rite of passage to his drumbeat of commands.

At Horace Mann I had taken a month-long class, so I had already experienced the weirdness-thrill of sliding behind the torus onto the throne of Bob Towers (and numerous Grossinger's chauffeurs), then commanding a vehicle's mazy course. My first spin began as a broken line of lurches along a block of Riverdale. But once I got over my reticence, it was pure Penny Arcade. As I was propelling myself over the scenic drum, HM's driving domo, Mr. Zachary, must have detected a dangerous shift because he asked me to pull over. I presumed a mechanical error.

"Don't ever forget," he pronounced sternly, "that every moment you are behind that wheel you hold life and death in your hands. Ever!"

"I like that one," said the Northampton coach. "I'm going to steal it for myself."

I made one bad move when I confused coach's directive, turning against my own better judgment to the left, ending up in a tobacco field.

"What the fuck!" he blurted in startled horror. "'Right!' Right right right. Right means right."

It was my only miscue. A month later I got my Massachusetts license in the mail.

Jeff had nailed it: the document felt like enfranchisement, tribal permission, an irrefutable coming of age.

In Psychology we began our semester by studying the etiology of neurosis, which brought back memories of my subway concierge Neil quizzing Dr. Fabian after my sessions. Our coursebook, Norman Cameron's and Joseph Rychlak's canonical *Personality Development and Psychopathology,* might have been Neil's graduate text. Its opening pages christened the famous id, where torrents of primal libido got discharged until the nascent ego contained and bound them into a personal identity. Such was the emotional energy of our lives—cathected and transformed as "fantasies, daydreams, conflicts, object relations, the self, and social roles." No more statistics to parse—this was "inner sanctum" stuff.

Dr. Heath was a mild, reassuring professor, not unlike a psychotherapist himself. Because of my background with Fabian and Friend—a legacy I recounted at our first meeting—and his connection to my Uncle Lionel, Heath and I became out-of-class buddies, sharing meals in town, sometimes with my friend Paul joining us.

Early in the term the professor took our class on a trip to Northampton State Mental Hospital. Patients flocked around us, vying for attention. One young man cornered Paul and me and showed us a sketchpad of his inventions, page after page, meticulously drawn: men with wings, elaborate pulleys and windmills. He told us that the police had incarcerated him there to steal his work, and he asked for our help in escaping so he could apply for patents before it was too late. We promised to try.

Another guy confided to Dr. Heath that *he* was the psychiatrist and the doctors were his patients. I whispered to Paul that Anouilh would have agreed.

Then a grotesque, over-dressed elderly woman took both my wrists in her hands and told me that she knew my grandmother. Surely that couldn't be true, for she didn't even know my name. But people had tossed that line at me since I became a Grossinger, and I loathed it to the point of being uncivil. Grandma Jennie appeared on TV so often selling rye bread in a commercial that began, "Hello, I'm Jennie Grossinger" that, at Horace Mann and Chipinaw, kids nicknamed me "Jennie."

Now I felt as though a madperson had read through my paranoia and was flouting it.

"Don't let them get to you," Dr. Heath had warned, "because they will."

Back in class I questioned whether most of these inmates had real diseases—neuroses and psychoses by Cameron's definition—or whether they were simply victims of a capitalist society. What I had observed were women deemed too grotesque or unattractive to find husbands, elderly folks without homes, prodigies who couldn't adapt to cultural norms. I applied the sociological arguments of my American Studies reading to the terminology of my "Abnormal" textbook and wrote interlocking term papers.

Paul Goodman's *Growing Up Absurd* was my link between Freud's theory of neurosis and the addictions of our rat-race civilization. Goodman had connected the anguish and exile of individuals to the vapid materialism of our culture, almost gleefully assaulting the world in which my parents had spent their lives: "human beings working as clowns ... thinking like idiots ... Alternately, they are liars, confidence men, smooth talkers, obsequious, insolent.... "

No kidding! That covered the landscape, from Grossinger's and the Nevele to midtown Manhattan and the conclaves of politicians. No wonder Godot never came. No wonder Quemoy, Matsu, and the Cuban Crisis. No wonder Betsy, Helene, and the rest ... Barbie dolls, startlets in soap operas, dupes in vehicles for capitalism. Even our sexuality didn't belong to us. Schuyler was right—"Growing Up Absurd" was the least of it: "If there is nothing worthwhile, it is hard to do anything at all. When one does nothing, one is threatened by the question, is one nothing?"

The source of these proclamations, Mr. Goodman himself, visited Marx's class—he was a friend of the professor. A group of us went to lunch with our guest afterwards. I had expected a thoughtful social critic, even a compassionate elder, so I was unprepared for the gruff, belligerent curmudgeon who spat sermons at us and pushed aside our questions by saying that kids our age cared about fucking and nothing else. After he made that assertion the third time—seemingly oblivious to the fact he had already said it twice—Schuy and I stomped out.

Goodman's book remained seminal to me, but in my mind I had appropriated it from its author. The man was right, of course: we were stuck in adolescent fantasies and probably useless for more nuanced discourse. But that didn't make us libidinal beasts without discernment. It wasn't sex that drew me; it was the texture of seductive feelings. It was the way things changed and were changed into each other in the tinder and alchemy of masturbation, a vast, cryptic river flowing into *"Oh, Shenando'h, I love your daughter.... "*

I was roused at one level by the lure of girls but at another by the fathomless labyrinths of feeling in myself where guises radiated deeper guises and were entangled mysteriously, one veil over another, closer to Keats' nightingale than *Playboy* magazine.

We were all bound away somewhere, across some "wide Missouri," coming from, going to, an insoluble riddle. That's what I sought in my own erotic depth, the sense of how deep *I* went—and my desire went.

For Goodman and Beckett the magic of desire had been lost in the sludge of the world—discarded in the garbage cans of Tripp's stagesets. At finale, the prophets warned, we will find our hearts and souls empty; we will be unable to go on. But I was still brimming with hope. I honored Beckett because he was spare and pure, but I didn't want my birthright stolen by cynics and lesser muck-a-mucks.

Catherine Carver spent many months with the finished draft of *Salty and Sandy* and the polished sections of *The Moon,* and she finally wrote back that, although I was very talented, I had not yet written a book publishable by Viking. She trusted that by continuing to work with her I would get to that point. She presumed that we would talk the next time I was in New York.

I was crestfallen, though I knew all along that something wasn't right. My writing felt too childlike and iconoclastic for the world of Saul Bellow. Yet my fantasies of the future were tied to being a novelist, and this woman was my Tom Greenwade—he was the scout who found Mickey Mantle when sent to look at another Oklahoma player. She had discovered me and was my champion in the bigtime.

With no fallback life on tap I skipped a Friday of classes and took the bus into Manhattan to meet Miss Carver for lunch. She picked a distinguished literary restaurant where she told me right off that *The Moon* was going in a dangerous direction, away from reliable narrative into occultism, and she warned me again about reading Olson. "You are no longer making believable stories or creating characters who are real. Some of the writing in *The Moon* is truly inspired, but I think it belongs in essays, not novels. Even so, you are elevating the tarot to an unwarranted, almost absurd level." She wanted more Grossinger's, more irony, more satire, more sex—in general, more action and less philosophy.

She was asking me to abandon the writing that was most meaningful to me. I needed the view from Luna to transcend the banality of my own plots. I needed the scope of Olson and Beckett to yank me out of beach parties and teen gossip and get me into the greater cosmos.

My father was in the City that afternoon, so we had dinner in his hotel room. He too was interested in the career implications of my lunch with Catherine Carver and, when he heard my disheartening account, without forewarning he picked up the phone and dialed without explanation. After a few seconds I realized that he had called the popular novelist Harold Robbins.

"Harold, Paul Grossinger here ... yes, you can do something for me this time." In the course of the conversation he wrote down an address. "You meet him at his place; he'll read your work and tell you what it's worth; then you'll know whether this woman is just pulling on your chain."

It had the crudity of all his offers, but I too wanted to know what Harold Robbins would make of *Salty and Sandy*. It was such a preposterous, tantalizing notion I didn't think of passing it up. The next morning I took the bus downtown and rode an elevator to a penthouse where a middle-aged man in a silk bathrobe led me into his living room and offered me Danishes while he sat on a sofa flipping through my manuscript. After fifteen minutes he let me know he was finished by taking a deep breath. Then he said:

"You're a writer. You've got a ways to go, and this stuff isn't ready to publish, but these editors, they're frustrated college teachers; they want to latch on to some young kid and school-marm him. I don't know what kind of writing you're going to do, but keep going and it will work itself out. Don't change for her, for the promise of publication." As I left he thought to add, "When you're ready, come see me. I may have my own publishing company by then."

The next time Catherine Carver wrote me I replied candidly, telling her the gist of my exchange with the author of *The Carpetbaggers*. She had a markedly unhappy response—carbon copy to Leo Marx.

"How could you even listen to such a hack!" he berated me after our next class. "First Charles Olson, then Schuyler Pardee, now Harold Robbins. I put myself out for you. Look what I get. You taught me an important lesson: never get too close to students."

But Tripp enjoyed the Harold Robbins affair. "Serves Marx right," he chuckled. "The fatuous dictator!"

I called a girl out of the Mount Holyoke picture book. Jane was a tall pixie who discovered a scratchy, old *Alice in Wonderland* platter among my records and insisted we dance to it at once. Giggling compatibly and stomping like puppets, we acted out the "Lobster Quadrille": "'*Will you walk a little faster,*' / *said the lobster to the snail.* / '*There's a porpoise right behind us,* / *and he's treading on my tail.*'"

Despite our merriment and shared admiration for the mock turtle, she turned down subsequent invitations to revisit him or me.

Then one night in February I made a "picture book" date with a girl at Smith and, on the chosen Saturday, hitched over to Northampton to meet her. She was late coming downstairs and, while I stood in the foyer, a striking-looking blonde on desk duty asked where I was from and what I was studying. She was curious too about my choice of a date. When I told her how it had originated, she smiled and offered, without hesitation, that I was in for an unpleasant surprise. A silence followed. Then she confided, as if sharing another secret, that she herself was a writer.

She was a compelling being with a sad, demure face, the aura of an old-fashioned fairy-tale maiden.

This was who I should have been going out with, but then my date appeared.

Nancy was a small energy packet of girl who was already practicing the twist on the way to the highway. She was looking forward to an evening of partying and announced right off that Phi Psi was the pits and we should go elsewhere. I seemed incidental to the matter, a pinball that had put her into independent motion. She talked so incessantly about a new British rock group that it was years before I could listen to The Beatles without bias. All evening I looked forward only to getting back early enough to see if the girl was still there. She wasn't … and I hadn't even gotten her name.

But I was friends with a senior who dated a girl from that house, so I asked him to inquire discreetly. Her name was Ginny, and I called her the next night. "Of course I remember you," she said.

I started to explain how she had been right about—

"Do you want to go out this weekend?" she interrupted. It was like Tripp saying, "Stop chattering." As simple as that.

What I saw the second time was a lean, medium-height girl with a complicated, mature face and an inexplicably heavy heart. Amid campus weekend hoopla, her melancholy was reassuring, even beguiling. Her dress had lots of lace, and she wore a pearl necklace. We caught a ride to Amherst and, after a visit to the basement (where she was much awaited by a curious Paul and crew), we went upstairs where I sat on my desk and she settled on the couch. I read to her from *The Moon* and Olson's *Distances*. She followed from a small sheath of her own poems, concise landscapes and startlingly graphic love psalms; then she read a few favorites from my collection of D. H. Lawrence's poems.

Ginny was from Wisconsin, though she had spent lots of time in the South; she was a sophomore like me and was also thinking of transferring. She bore many of the same sorts of grievances toward Smith that I did toward Amherst, bemoaning the ritualized dating, materialistic values, and downbeat teachers. She was a kindred being, though her depth was ungaugable.

After she had finished the last Lawrence poem, there was a silence, and I asked if she wanted to dance. It was so obviously a request for contact I at once regretted it. "Maybe that's not such a good idea," I added with a bashful grin.

She said she didn't like to dance but gestured for me to come by her on the couch. I did. We looked at each other, and I saw in her a mirror of my wanting, a mouth opening, and I met it. We kissed long, repeatedly. I reached out from my heart and held her against me. This was what I had waited for, so many tangled years from the dream of Annie Welch. It wasn't just a single kiss, or a feint in a game I didn't understand. It was a time and place to do nothing else but feel someone and be kissed, and kiss. And there was so much to it—hair, a neck, a back, a backbone, a face, lips, a tongue, pausing for a breath and looking at each other, beginning again simultaneously.

As we walked silently back to the College Street hitching corner, she said, "I could feel it that first time I saw you. I knew this would happen."

During February and March we went out each Saturday night, sometimes to dinner, sometimes to a movie, but always to my room where we took up kissing and caressing. Loving was not some elusive thing in my future; it was as intrinsic as the desire that led to it, in fact more so, for not being fantasy. I was in a waking dream.

I was astonished to hear Ginny had a boyfriend in law school in Virginia whom she was thinking of marrying. I couldn't imagine what she was doing with me, but she was open about her feelings. "You're very wonderful," she said, "but I don't know who you are. You don't even know. You're the original 'ugly duckling,' and I have no idea what you'll become. I'm the first person to reach you, so I can touch only so much. But I love the part of you you let me touch. Anything else going on in my life is immaterial to that."

I wasn't nearly that articulate. I couldn't communicate or even understand my absorption in her, but I clung to it like a life raft. I wasn't infatuated the way I had been with Betsy or even Harriet at Wakonda. I didn't idolize Ginny, but I was addicted to her. She seemed dainty and fragile, opaque and ulterior, so that my passion seemed to dissipate right through her, but it didn't matter because the weekends had become their own intoxication.

My Lawrence course had built slowly, and now, in this spring of the birth of eros, *The Rainbow* and *Women in Love* imbued me with the lives of men I might yet be. Paul Goodman may have seen only adolescent lust, but Lawrence detected a spirit drawing souls together beyond discourse. It was a force lodged in our hungering cores, transforming not sublimating, giving rise to the miracles of domesticity and children: the generations of creature life on Earth. Mutual attraction was as natural and unconscious as fields of flowers and wild rabbits, and it was not discardable as mere instinct or id; it was the basis of civilization, of church, of art, of the starry heavens too. It was the mystery of existence, even as I had suspected.

Lawrence meant regular rough and scarred men and women, not just playboys and dandies; in fact, he mocked the big talkers and had his women prevail over them, their eros actual and boundless rather than an adjunct of male fantasy:

> … her limbs vibrated with anguish towards him wherever she was, the radiating force of her soul seemed to travel to him, endlessly, endlessly, and in her soul's own creation, find him.…

Desiring *was* the mystery. I felt that profoundly with Ginny. It wasn't a wish that came to an end in fulfillment; it went on forever. And then Lawrence ...

> There is only one clue to the universe ... the individual soul within the individual being. That outer universe of suns and moons and atoms is a secondary affair ... the death-result of living individuals.

A secondary affair? How incredible to think and believe that and then be able to say it! Certainly my physics and geology teachers wouldn't agree. Even my Lawrence professor considered it mere rhetoric.

Ginny said one night that she wanted to smother my pain. She hugged me and stroked my back, but I still felt untouched and wanted her hand to go to my penis. She resisted the cue. "It's too soon," she said and instead began a long kiss. I felt the magnetic flow of my attention onto her and wanted to find its resolution. I drew her thread deeper and deeper into my own being She was so luminous and evanescent I couldn't feel where I met her ostensible seduction—or joined the ragged edge of my own desire. My attraction toward this girl was sinuous and indirect, like an old, old cloth bearing some of her lace and elegance, a gap across which I could feel nothing but waves of curiosity and wonder. The thing between us was a faint, unexamined amber, a glow fluttering alive at the slightest friction.

Down the hall in another universe the Phi Psi jug band was closing out the evening, Paul on base and kazoo, Jenkins on slide guitar, Toby rapping thimbles on a washboard, Paul's new girlfriend blowing into a jug. Half of my attention wended toward them as I observed Ginny moving, eyes cast upward, in her own quiet, a rhapsodic trance beyond me, the face of a white moon.

I couldn't go there; I wouldn't find her if I went. Her essence was a mystery to me: who she was, who she *thought* she was, what sort of woman she would one day become. For all her animal propinquity, her casually lewd presence, she might as well have been a literary figure, Ursula in *The Rainbow,* a girl in the dazzling glare of her own fantasies and apotheosis.

I let go of the Delphic Oracle till another day. We hitched back to Smith.

A Saturday night later, I picked a handful of flowers in the Glen behind Phi Psi and brought them to Smith. Ginny strolled downstairs, short sleeves and a skirt for the warmer weather, a quixotic smile. Delighted with the gift, she insisted on finding a jar and taking them to her room. Then we hitched a ride to Phi Psi.

We spent an hour downstairs, talking with Paul, Phil, and Ellen ... drinking tap beer. Ginny was a saint in pale sequins, as we danced to Patti Page, the "Tennessee Waltz," so that I felt like the hero of Hamilton Basso's *View from Pompey's Head* at the crossroads of his life, dancing with his sweetheart even as the song, matching its words, stole her away *("Now I know just how much I have lost ....")*. We went upstairs. The blossoms-on-peach fabric that made up her dress swooped in and under to follow her shape, framing the line of her breasts. Without a word we fell into our tryst, our only interest each other's bodies.

I strained against prior boundaries to contact her, to come to a verdict, to know what followed. She was telling me stories of her brothers in Baltimore, her summer in France where the family she was living with broke apart before her eyes.

I reached under her blouse for the first time and felt the band of her bra in back. She continued to clench and kiss, and I moved to the front and explored the frilliness covering her breasts. Deeper waves rolled through me, and I rubbed against her with my groin and pulled her onto me. She responded effortlessly, as if she was already there. Our bodies wound in frictioned counterpoint, rhythms and chords I never knew. Something darker and older than desire was drawing me now. At odd junctures I felt flat, as though its current had stopped and nothing was happening, but the spark kept reigniting.

Her face in semi-darkness was a vague almost inhuman mask, floating in its own space, its arc of contemplative romanticism. I kept reaching out through a feeling in my penis that was spreading throughout my body, trying to hold her on it, hold me in her ambiance. I put her hand against my hardness, but she took it away. I sat upright and looked at her with questioning eyes.

"We're still not there yet," she said. "We can't force it."

"Why aren't we there?"

"I don't know. There's something missing. It's not you. There just hasn't been enough time."

I trusted her, but I was suspicious. "Is it because of your friend in Virginia?"

"I'm going to see him next weekend, and I want to be clear. Yes, I sleep with him. But he's not the problem I have with you. I'm overwhelmed by you. I care terribly for you. But you're more than I can deal with."

I turned on the light, and we sat in silence. She put a hand gently on my face. In my unslaked craving, the mercy of her gesture was too much.

I left the room. I ran up the stairs to the third floor, through the attic onto the roof. I stood in the night air. At a distance I could appreciate her again. As a fantasy, she filled me with desire. I climbed back through the hatch and lay on my bed fully dressed. I wanted to cry, but my throat and eyes were hardened against it. Instead I reached for my genitals and rubbed them. I spat on my hand, then rubbed harder. There were no tears there either, only the dull side of disappointed lust. I strained to summon the scene in my room back into my mind so that this time she took hold of my hardness. Staring blankly into her face in my mind I pulled the current up through my surging breath and shot out a bitterness into the sheets, my fingers instantly on top of its warm film, rubbing it into the surface in some meager extension of pleasure.

I returned to the room where she was reading, and we talked idly for half an hour—my evasion now a barrier between us because I couldn't tell her the truth. We left in time to hitch back before her curfew—a thoughtful goodnight kiss at the doorstep. She said she'd see me soon. There was no evident cloud on the horizon, just a deepening of the puzzle. I assumed things would go on as they had and culminate somehow. I didn't think beyond that; I barely even thought *that*. Hitching back from Smith in the rear of a car full of kids, I stared numbly at the night. In my mind, indelibly stuck, refusing to let my thoughts go blank, were the words of "Wild About my Lovin'" as plunked by Tripp on his guitar:

I ain't no iceman, no iceman's son,
But I can keep you cool till that iceman come.

Two days later I got a letter:

Dear Richard,

Thank-you, thank-you, thank-you for the flowers. They've made me so happy. My room has been warm and cheerful because every time I've looked at them I've thought of you and that wonderful part of you that I can't understand but is so important & must survive even if transplanted in Washington. I know what you mean, Rich, about losing the words & the experience—the derivatives. I suddenly realized that everything you say means something. It is all so important and I wanted to cry out to you & ask how you understand & what you understand. I wanted you to pull me out but you can't & I can't and now that my panic is passed I wonder if I want it.

The flowers are dead now. There was no fuss or anything. They just died without a whimper. I couldn't stand it—that they should die & be gone and everything would go on as usual so I write you as nearest of kin to inform you of their passing. They lived well and died bravely—not losing their dignity when their beauty faded, leaving behind a vase and a brown paper bag. More than most.

I express my—I'm overdoing this. Well Rich, thank you again. Have a good weekend. I have an exam tomorrow, then am leaving for U.Va.

'By
Ginny

I didn't realize it then, but that note was farewell. Mine, not hers. Ginny was the enchantress I had been seeking for years, so she wasn't easy to give up, but she was inscrutable and had a fiancé. Though wild horses wouldn't have kept me from her—on a conscious level anyway—I had reshuffled the tarot and was ready to deal new cards.

I came upon her letter ten years later while cleaning out files and was moved to tears. How thoughtful and eloquent she had been, how heartfelt her statement, and generous! I was a stubborn child, twisted up inside. In all my bravado of complexity and themes within themes, I couldn't hear her simple rightness and respond to her as she deserved.

So I tried to answer ten years late and say "I'm sorry." I wrote to Smith for her address and found out she had left after sophomore year; they had an address for her under a married name in Cochabamba, Bolivia, care of the Peace Corps. My letter came back "addressee unknown."

The last time I saw Ginny was a summery April Saturday a few weekends after her trip to Virginia. I hitched to Smith in high spirits and went to her house and asked for her.

"Hi, hi," she said excitedly, poking her head out of the kitchen. "I can't see you today. I've got lunch duty and then a big paper to write. But call me—we'll set another time."

I'm sure I would have, but before I could, the fortune teller laid down a different hand.

As a twelve-year-old I read lots of adult science fiction so, when asked to write a term paper in Second Form English at Horace Mann, I had a ready topic: "Themes and Symbols in the Work of Robert Sheckley and Theodore Sturgeon." That was when I incorporated the notion of alternate probabilities into my life.

Sheckley's premise was that the present is made up of infinitesimal minutiae. The movement of a single object by a careless time-traveller could alter the whole course of history. What if a rock had been seized as a weapon in a moment of battle by the chief who was to unite the American Indian tribes into a nation that discovered Europe? What if that rock were kicked out of his reach a thousand years earlier by a time-traveller from a 22nd-Century Indian Empire? If the chief were then prematurely killed for the cudgel being beyond his reach, the traveller might find not only that he had no country to return to but that he himself was impacted in time and space, unable to be born.

"Worlds without end," wrote Sheckley, "emanating from events large and small; every Alexander and every amoeba creating worlds, just as ripples will spread in a pond no matter how big or how small the stone you throw. Doesn't every object cast a shadow?"

My life was made of such shadows, a raffle of undrawn lots. Ever since reading Sheckley's story I had played a game with probabilities, tinkering with paths to alternate universes. Periodically I would take an unplanned route to check if it made a calculable difference in my life. While I could not (of course) know what I missed by my detours, I never succeeded in altering fate in any obvious way. On this morning, as promising as its blue sky, yellow buttercups, and dandelion riots, I was disappointed in not having Ginny go out into the spring with me, and I did not want to return to Amherst.

What I failed to see was that she was receding anyway at light speed, already a residue of something ineffable. Upon reaching the turnoff to the hitching post, I decided to cast my lot with the ripples ... and pivoted in the opposite direction. Then I walked three-quarters of the way around a block rather than corner to corner.

Whether by accident or subliminal design, I came to Laura Scales House and remembered Lindy. I went in and asked for her at the desk. I was in luck. Minutes later she appeared in the stairwell.

"What a surprise! I was sitting in the smoker feeling depressed and sorry for myself, not able to do a stitch of work, wishing I had some wonderful visitor ... and then you just arrive." I asked if she would like to go for a walk into town, maybe a glass of lemonade; and she nodded. "Wait, though," she added. "I want to go upstairs and change."

She came back wearing a blue and white striped polo shirt, a light sweater, and tan slacks. After a hiatus of almost six months we took our second walk into Northampton. After ordering sweet rolls and lemonades at a café, we picked up our narratives at an outdoor table.

It hadn't been working out for her in Philly; she felt used on the weekends and then cast aside—no real conversation, no emotional contact. So, she wasn't going there for a while, and Saturdays were particularly lonely. Her classes were also discouraging, her teachers uninspired, even vindictive, mainly concerned with a narrow line of critical thinking.

I could object similarly about Amherst, but at least I had a few good courses now and was surrounded by lively people at Phi Psi. I told her about Paul Goodman's visit, Schuyler, D. H. Lawrence's *Rainbow,* and a bit about Ginny. I even recounted how the ripples had led me to her doorstep. She found that remarkable and foolhardy, but she was the perfect audience, for she heard and gave back every nuance and resonance.

We returned to the campus, a charge of ideas and rhythm between us. Everywhere sun, birds, flowers filled the air, and my mind and heart. I told her a sudden inkling—that Freud had discovered only the method of symbols, but nature itself from the beginning of time had been creating clones, replicas, cues. I identified them wheeling about: the screech of blue jays, patterns of clouds and leaves, signals not needing interpretation or criticism. "The trouble with our teachers is they think they can explain things. But there's nothing to explain. There's only the breeze, the Wheel of Fortune, clover, a horse in a cave at Lascaux, billions of stars."

She shifted the conversation to *Moby Dick,* the subject of the paper she was trying to write when I arrived, and I pointed at the sun that Ahab said he would strike if it insulted him. *"That* is the White Whale," I said as we glanced briefly at the blinding disk. "The same primal force is there. Ahab wanted to strike at the heart of nature itself. Moby Dick was just his passing snare."

"I can see that," Lindy said. "So much more powerful than a symbol to be a real breathing creature, a real sun." She was lucid and sparkling, tall and strong, challenging me with a forcefulness that met my own. She spoke not of magic and literary allusions, as I was wont, but of emotions and feelings and how hard it was to reach people. "For me they always seem to skitter over my surface like bugs. Their shallowness even betrays this lovely day. Maybe only the trees and fields can be touched, and they don't speak. Certainly I couldn't touch Steve, or Jon before that, and it doesn't appear as though you could touch Ginny."

I adored her directness. Her face conveyed an Athena-like intelligence, and her eyes were filled with both sensuality and knowledge. I felt that afternoon like the Magician presiding over the First Trump, spinning out worlds without diminution. She was the Priestess of the Second Trump, deepening them, weaving them together, making the universe calm and lovely. After our snacks we found a place on the grass and held court there till late afternoon. Then we hiked back to Wiggins Tavern for dinner.

This was the beginning—we both must have known.

The following Saturday I met her again, downstairs in Laura Scales. She was more dressed up, in a blouse and dark skirt, light perfume, and we hitched to Amherst together. I felt uncertain who we were as boy and girl. To me she was as perfect as anyone could be, present and contacting, sexy by force of her intelligence but also stunning with a Circê look I could never resist. She was tall and statuesque, regal but lithe, her body a dancer's, elegantly poised, strong and nimble, large hips, full but delicate breasts. Every movement was comely and aesthetic, her own, no wasted motion. She honored a vaguely crablike scuttle as she walked, a sideways predilection, breaking up lines, casting spirals about me, her swoops and gestures as fresh and entertaining as her talk. Her mouth was large and sensuous, her pale eyes intense and focusing under heavy brows. Was this a date?

We took a table in the Phi Psi social room, drank beer, ate pretzels, talked. I felt so pleased to be with her even if she wasn't entirely a girlfriend. There was a brief predicament when Jon peeked in with his current consort, but he saw Lindy and was quickly out of there.

I asked her if she had noticed him and she nodded. "He's still chaperoning around *les* selected *femmes* like some sort of mogul. He's pretty gross."

"He's also a fake. For all of us still, it's our parents' money," I said. "We haven't done anything yet. It's so easy to pretend and lose who you are."

"For girls it's especially easy. You're taught to please men, to be what they like, and you do that so easily you don't even realize you're doing it." She paused. "This friendship is a great relief to me, like a break from the whole tyranny of dating."

My heart sank at that comment, but I didn't back off. In the first chapter of *The Rainbow* Tom Brangwen was carrying a load of seed in his cart out of Nottingham through Cossethay; that's when "she" passed him on the road—the unknown woman who corralled his mind and soul. "The load of seed" was both a cargo and a symbol, not just for the male gamete but the germinal force itself. Tiny seeds birth us blindly into being, and in their ripening bear us toward fruition. We don't have a choice, Lawrence warned. When we least expect it, nature summons men and women from obscurity to be each other's lovers.

There was a silence between us, and she said, "let's dance," and I said "okay." The Phi Psi basement was the setting, but it had become another, almost allegorical space. I held her almost fragilely as if to preserve every molecule of our contact, its different weight, scent, her blouse, the feel of her head against mine, the tightness of her bones and muscles, her sweet, gentle angularity. She was denser and springier than Ginny—*she was there.*

I didn't know what was proper—dance close, dance chastely apart—but she automatically danced close. I felt myself transported, as much by the sense of our fitting together—the solidity and definiteness of her and me—as by an erotic feeling. I was inundated by her whole presence and bearing. It was the first dance that didn't feel spurious or self-conscious.

I was the deejay. It was my own tape playing, a compilation I had made in the fall, a band from the movie *The Alamo* ... the Brothers Four. I heard it as the theme song of *The Rainbow:*

> *A time just for reaping, a time just for sowing,*
> *The green leaves of summer are calling me home....*

Oh, everything! In that moment every intimation I ever had filled me. I didn't have to know the answer or articulate the mystery. Just as I was, I was complete.

I experienced the generations of life on Earth, how single men and women each come into being, grow, find lovers, have babies, plant their crops, die. I had spent my time on dream planets. But Lindy was the grace of the whole West—and I was holding her.

> *A time to be courting*
> *A girl of your own....*

And then she did something startling. She playfully blew in my ear, not just once, but continuously, a soft, sustained breath. I had never felt anything so tender and tantalizing. My body froze in rapture, as though all my attention had to go into perceiving this before it passed. She blew harder, looked at me, smiled, then blew in my other ear. With adolescent awkwardness I felt myself become hard and extend out against her. She acknowledged that with a smile, and then shifted her head and put her tongue in my ear and rolled it there so smoothly and deeply I felt as though it were passing through my brain. I drifted in bliss trying to make that ear even more available to her. And, at last, my feeling sustained the feeling in the song:

Twas so good to be young then, to be close to the earth,
And to stand by your wife, at the moment of birth.

Now I glimpsed the pathway to the center and saw how rich and complicated the world was—not my mind but the world. Everything I had both feared and wanted had an existence, an autonomous tangibility. In my senses I tumbled through primal symbols, fragments of memories … a tulip garden at the edge of creation, the forest of my sixth-grade dream, the essence of those aromatic vines coursing through my ears. I saw a friend I had as a child named Phil, a magician Dr. Fabian, kids from Bill-Dave baseball, Chipinaw campers singing "Friends" in a chain, all combined in me, all once, all briefly, because they didn't have to be (and nothing in the universe could be) forever. I wanted to acknowledge them each and thank them for being alive, for me being alive, for sustaining me to get this far, to this large a reckoning.

The sense of doom was gone. I felt only my freedom. We left the basement and went to my room, and she lay atop and freely kissed me and laughed, and put my hands on her bare breasts. Then she jumped up like a sprite, and said, "Enough of this stuffy place." And we climbed onto the Phi Psi roof overlooking fields between lit manors, sounds of Saturday night bands drifting together. It was peaceful just to lie there and look at stars, in the breeze feel as though the planet itself were rolling in space. I hugged her more tightly and she began to breathe harder and run her hands along me, feeling the

lines of my waist, and then my chest—that secret territory, realm
of imagined diseases in childhood. Her touch opened it to feeling,
and I took my shirt off under the starlight.

"You look great, alive," she said. "Beautiful. You *are* beautiful.
Don't you know that?" she demanded, shaking me with a smile.
Lying alongside, I held her silently, feeling her shape against my
chest, thinking it was her that made me beautiful.

She rolled onto her back, and I straddled her waist gently, my
knees on the gravel, as she drew my hands once across her breasts
and along the lines of her body. She let go and I tried to feel her
without violating the dignity with which she opened to me. It *was*
like praying.

She put her hands on my nipples and felt my torso, undid my belt.
She pulled me on top of her again, and putting her tongue in my
ear, reached down with her hand and held me and gently played
with me—all the time the link between us lucid and real, the point
of contact unbroken. "Don't be afraid," she said, though I didn't
think I was. "It's a fine thing. It's a lovely full hardness."

And then we stopped and went no further. I lay there, her hand
on my chest, exposed and joyous in this place. This was the extent
of it, as much as I needed in order to feel absolved.

That night, at bedtime, I read Olson's "Moonset" poem from
Gloucester, December 1, 1957, 1:58 a.m.:

> *Not*
> *the suffering one you sold*
> *sowed me on Rise*
> *Mother from off me*
> *God damn you God damn me my*
> *misunderstanding of you*
> *I can die now I just begun to live.*

My mother, Mr. Clinton, Abbey West, Betsy Sley: I could reach
back to each of them and tell them, forget it, whatever happened,
it's okay. The kid is going to survive.

PART FIVE

THE CEREMONY
APRIL, 1964–JUNE, 1965

I

THE PANIC

Two nights after Lindy's visit to Phi Psi, Jon came into the bathroom as a few of us were brushing our teeth. Making a show of ignoring me, he turned to Dave and said, "Did you see? My former live-in whore was by here the other night."

I whipped around. "You fat bastard!"

He seemed startled more than anything, that someone dared address him so irreverently. "You're going to take that back," he insisted.

"Like hell I am!" I stared hard at him, then added, "Pretentious jerk!" and looked away.

He put his head down and charged at me like a rhinoceros and, as I swung back, he tried to pin me against the mirror. I slid out of his grasp. He lunged again. Toothpaste, shaving cream, sundries crashed to the floor. Then Dave grabbed him and, with Phil's help, pulled him out and led him back to his room: "Cool it, man; cool it."

A week later Jon moved out of Phi Psi into the dorms.

Life had followed the script of a Lawrence novel—a hermetic undertow that carried me beyond plot and character into the heart of my own text. Betsy had stood at the gateway, an unknowing guardian spirit. Then I had a date with the wrong girl ... and someone else was in the alcove, waiting.

Where Ginny led, I followed as if Lawrence's Ursula and Gudrun were my guides—until we were riven down separate paths. Lindy was waiting at the ripples of the Stream of Probability. What was elusive with Ginny was as now tangible as life itself.

We made spring into our continuous study date: alongside Paradise Pond at Smith, on the Phi Psi lawn, in Valentine between meals.

During the term Schuyler threw in with Larry and Jim, juniors from my Lawrence seminar. The four of us maintained a running satire in the dining hall as we spoofed Amherst styles, noting the passage of "cowboy cool," "big man," "jockdom," and "pseudo-intellectual popinjay." Larry and Jim were high-stepping cowboys of their own contrivance; decked out in jeans and leather, they shared a souped-up old sedan and spoke in periodic Laurentian and Keatsian mime. It was running theater—cut-up plus panache.

One Saturday Larry drove us to a swimming hole north near Vermont: Jim, Schuy, me, and our dates. I felt an ancient wistfulness, as Lindy and I lay on our backs in bathing suits in the grass ... clouds blown apart in the jetstream. I was chasing the bare eclipse of a form, itself a shadow. Beyond the hill, the land dipped precipitously into the unknown, an obliquity that masked a chimera. Something indelible was lost; something equally remote beckoned. I saw on a smoke-thin arras a Sphinx. I felt my own skeletal existence.

Then we dove into the water, smashing sky. That icy plunge resolved all muddles, a splash into the Now, as water opened my heart to gratitude beyond complication. No indecision or keepsakes allowed—shun sixes of cups, those munchkin children in their gardens of forever throwback nostalgia!

That evening Lindy, Tripp, and I took a walk along backroads—he delivering dialogue from *Godot,* she improvising with gumption and wit. Then she spat from a small bridge into headlights—a Colorado method, she said, to gauge the speed of cars. "Pretty tough girl," he confided later. And he was the ultimate judge.

Schuy's friends turned out to be more than collegiate rebels and cowboy poets; they were rogue revolutionaries. After keeping their alter egos secret for months Schuy finally confided in April that Jim (known as Axis, a near-homonym of his last name) was king of something called "guerrilla warfare," conducted on Saturdays after midnight at the Psi U fraternity house. "It's beyond description," he said. "If you could just see it you'd realize that Phi Psi is a bunch of wimps."

Later that month he extended a guarded invitation: Axis had arranged for me to witness a skirmish as a noncombatant. He couldn't a hundred percent assure my safety, but I would be under his protection. If he prevailed no one would bother me. If he were defeated it was every man for himself!

Just after midnight I met Schuy at North. From there I followed him along College Street to Psi U. He elbowed a crack in the front door, pointed the way downstairs, and then led me through catacombs to an unlit sector. I expected an empty cloister, so was startled by what I saw. The room was crammed wall to wall with bodies. A single lantern shone. Occasionally someone let out a shout, but mostly we jostled one another in a zombie-like group sway.

Suddenly—with a scream—Axis leaped onto the bar. His chest was bare, painted in blocks of color, American Indian style. He stared down at the revenants. Then he danced in place as others threw objects at him—mostly their cups of beer. He retaliated with the hose from the keg, its spray splattering the crowd, a few beads of moisture reaching Schuy and me at the fringes.

Gradually the scene became more frenzied, as Axis goaded the others with taunts. People tried to yank him off his perch, but with the help of his allies he beat them back. Clashes broke out, and Schuy whispered, "Stay close … just watch. Do you see, it's *The Plumed Serpent!*"

He meant Axis' favorite Lawrence novel, in which males transcend their mediocre social condition and enact soul-magic. But this was an Ivy League fraternity not a kiva. The ritual at the bar was more like a primitive attempt at courage, a way of striking back against the allure of women. Here in the basement, after curfew, their dates dispatched, they could be godmen and literary critics at the same time:

> Now she understood the strange unison she could always feel between Ramon and his men, and Cipriano and his men. It was the soft, quaking, deep communion of blood-oneness. Sometimes it made her feel sick. Sometimes it made her revolt. But it was the power she could not get beyond.

As some of the brethren raised hand-made torches, the room shimmered. The keg nearly empty, Axis demolished it with a hammer.
He poured kerosene on its pieces, and Larry applied a torch. Spinning before the fire, brandishing a lance and dislodging challengers
who came at him with sticks and ropes, Axis all but transmogrified
into a visage from Aztec myth. As the Psi U basement resounded
with baritone chanting, I saw a parody of late baroque Lawrence:
males in round dance, fascist and patriarchal.

Schuy and I slipped out of the communion while Axis was still
king—though we had to shove past grabbing arms and punches of
a few "enemies" to clear our way. Nowadays I smile when I read in
the *Amherst Alumni Magazine* of the "king's" appointment to boards
of psychiatric hospitals. I wonder what his colleagues would make
of his reign in the Psi U basement.

Later that spring Paul and a fair complement of Phi Psi made plans
to join Freedom Summer, a campaign to register African Americans
in the Mississippi delta. As students from various New England colleges showed up in our living room, Tripp was a scornful spectator.
"It's a waste of time. What are these jerk-off college kids going to
do against the resident rednecks? Protests don't bring change; they
just generate conflict. Only acts of radical art bring big enough shit
into the world." He struck his guitar strings a few times.

While some of our guests bristled in umbrage, Paul commented
sardonically, "Count on you, Jeff, to stand in the way of social justice."

"I certainly hope so. 'Propaganda is a soft weapon; hold it in your
hands too long, and it will flip around like a snake, and strike the
other way.' I'm quoting someone with a much deeper grasp of such
matters than Martin Luther King."

"Who's that?" Paul bit.

"Jean Anouilh."

Jeff, it turned out, had a personal stake in our loyalties. He had
invited an avant-garde film-maker he long admired to show his
work the weekend of the Mississippi-bound gathering. He wanted
Phi Psi—and especially me—at *his* event. I was ambivalent and
told him so.

"Well, get your priorities straight, guy. This is a crossroads, and what you choose, you just may become."

The filmmaker's name was Stan Brakhage; he was an official guest of the college, but he had arrived a few days ahead of time at Jeff's invitation and was staying in Phi Psi. After spotting him, Jenkins warned Paul and me to expect "a cross between a water buffalo and a Spanish revolutionary." It wasn't a bad thumbnail. Aloof and humorless, Tripp's burly gunslinger prowled the second floor, snubbing the rest of us while passing between the bathroom and the stairs.

My ambivalence came to a head on Friday night when Brakhage's showing coincided with a parley for Freedom Summer participants. Right up to the last I intended to go to the meeting, and I was angry at Jeff for pressuring me otherwise. Had he no appreciation for the Dylan of *"You better start swimming / or you'll sink like a stone"*—this self-anointed maven with his Porsche, guitar, and private acting troupe? But then I found myself walking from the dining room to the theater with Schuy, no clear reason except that this was where my heart had been all along.

On stage in front of a screen, waiting for the room to settle, Brakhage paced, hands behind his back. Schuy admired his snarl: "No one's gonna push him around. He's a tough hombre all right!"

After a flamboyant introduction from Tripp, the artist launched into a discursion of his aesthetic theory: "My work has largely been preoccupied with birth, sex, death, and the search for God. That's it, make what you want. Narrative cinema like Hollywood is a great pleasure, I grew up with it. It was my hobby and my church. People in the darkness share the same tears, the same joys. But what my film is about is totally different: the closeness of the eyeball to the brain, the literal rhythm of seeing, of existence, of survival. It's not a story or some throwaway event. It's how we live and see before we die. Each space between the sprocket holes of film is an individual picture which will, when projected, flash prisming colors in some other darkness at a fraction of a second. My inspiration for that is later Webern or Johan Sebastian Bach, but visually, 24 or 16 frames per second since the medium is light. I am a fool of light."

Then he read from his journals, punning and undercutting his own meanings, to stay free (as he put it) of the patterns of literal speech. At one point he appropriated the "ie" from "Vietnam" to a make statement about the parenthetical drift of consciousness toward mindless warfare. It was that brash and untethered.

Twittering and hissing, much of the Amherst audience left before the lights were dimmed, their catcalls echoing down the hall. But I was elated. I had been preparing for this talk unknowingly for months. Brakhage was the opposite of cowboy cool, and he certainly wasn't some water-buffalo cartoon—that was Jenkins' misread: cultural stereotyping plus a predilection to mock anyone who didn't fit. This was a guy who survived by defying conventions, by inventing his own forms and confronting the universe head on.

In concluding his riff, Brakhage described a marriage outside societal norms, a partner and artistic collaborator named Jane, the birth of their children in a cabin in the woods. Like Lawrence (whom he quoted several times) he was showing us how to live on the roller-coaster, of mind and heart.

In the first film a man in slow motion struggled up a snow-covered mountainside, his dog running beside him ... light distorted, mirrored, scratched, twinkling, eroding, reconstituting, floating disjunctively in layers that seemed to dissolve through one another into new images at different scales and perspectives. Sudden flares of the sun's corona shot through a black silhouette of a tree ... then both were gone and we saw the actual surface of the film cracking, a baby being born ... snow falling ... wild flowers ... unfinished spirals ... night traffic ... fragments of faces ... actual constellations ... waves of colored fish ... a brief moon with clouds crossing ... he and his wife naked as lovers ... nothing ... a door opening to a house ... a woman's breasts ... candlelight.

This irregular chorus rose and fell in visual harmony. *Dog Star Man* was beyond science fiction or surrealism; it was a pulsating, irreducible life montage.

The second film was only four minutes long and made from moth wings, flower petals, and blades of grass pressed between strips of splicing tape. "As a moth might see from birth to death if black were white," Brakhage explained.

It was one thing to record moths in their nocturnal flutters; it was quite another to make the translucence of their wings the basis of the glow on the screen. Here matter transcended metaphor, transcended even cinematic montage and, in casting an opalescent death frolic, educed something fundamental about nature and art.

The next film was pure night interrupted only by widely separated strokes of lightning. Suddenly a syncopated double-star appeared, as if to remind us that our life takes place in a burst of radiance on a strange world under inexplicable circumstances—then a single unearthly cry: the slowed-down recording of a child being born (this was the only sound in any of the films). *Fire of Waters,* its maker called it—fire of the light of which we are made, waters of the birth canal in which we are washed ashore.

Schuy was thoroughly won over. As Brakhage stayed in the front answering questions, my friend remained long after I got sleepy and returned to Phi Psi. The next day at lunch he summarized his take:

"We're completely enslaved by these advertising images, all the crap we're supposed to be—so that we can look like soapsuds men, so that girls will like us, so that we can get jobs. He's outside of that, so he's able to make his own things—and without the derivative academic language of Marx and his buddies."

In truth, there was no resemblance between the life Brakhage presented and that of my teachers and parents. They came from two different civilizations, two different solar systems. And his, oddly, was the more familiar to me.

Frustrated at having missed such an event, Lindy hatched a plan on the phone. Upon hearing that Brakhage lived in the mountains outside Denver, she proposed maybe I could come visit her at Christmas and we'd go find where he lived. An inventive and daring strategy, it seemed to assure a future for us too!

Later that week she and Schuy joined my Abnormal Psych class at the movie *David and Lisa.* Lisa was a mute, schizophrenic girl-child, darkly beautiful; David was an uptight compulsive teenager, obsessed with clocks and death, phobic about being touched. They were residents of the same mental hospital and, gradually through the story, drew each other out. At first she talked only in rhyme, saying things like, "Hello, kiddo" and "Today I'm low, low; so, David, go, go, go." In the culminative scene, as she unexpectedly breaks her rhymes, he approaches her, hand extended, desperate for connection, asking her to take it ... and she lays her fingers gently across his and clasps them.

Schuy was enraged at this outcome. "What's wrong with alienation?" he demanded. "He didn't want to be touched. He understood clocks were the enemy. Why couldn't they leave him alone? Why did some pretty girl come along and invade him?"

But I was all for David's submission to Lisa, letting her contact and melt his shell. Soon after the showing, a classmate who liked to play literary critic, a guy who later wrote for *Esquire* and *Playboy,* ridiculed the movie at dinner by reciting Lisa's rhymes in a dopey voice. My words never impeded his ego trips, so this time I picked up my plate of spaghetti and sauce and dumped it on his head.

On a Saturday morning in mid-May I was sitting in a patch of sun in the Phi Psi stairwell, hand-scooping breakfast from a carton of Corn Kix into which I had poured half a carton of currants. I was reading the *New York Times,* feeling mellow and content. There were Mets box scores and articles, plus seasonal averages. Lindy and I were going out that night.

I felt a sudden jolt from nowhere, a shift of texture. The ocher hue on the rug seemed to flicker, become unstable. I took a quick breath and put my attention back into the stats, but they were chaff compared to what was happening.

There was a brief hiatus before the paling came again—a wobble followed by a series of tremors, their sheer output incredible.

I bolted from the stairwell and sank to the floor of my room, squatting with my legs drawn up to my chest. I felt another upheaval materializing, the biggest one yet, dilating from my center.

I told myself that nothing was really happening. It was some sort of passing sensation like heartburn or a headache. Take an aspirin; maybe it would go away.

I knew better. I could tell how fixed and solid it was. Everywhere I turned, it was coming at me like the tentacle of an invisible octopus, looming up from the background, neither simple nor manipulable.

As if to grab its thread, I reached behind my neck and contacted a string of odd bumps. Had I developed tumors? I grabbed frantically along the top of my backbone. It was hard as stone!

I raced to the bathroom mirror, running my fingers up and down my spine. I had always had a backbone, but what was that floating lump above it?

The childhood panic was back. I had thought I had vanquished it, outgrown it like bedwetting. But it had been there all along, an eclipse of an unknown form at the lake, an immeasurable depth of sky and clouds.

There were times as a teenager at Grossinger's when I woke homesick, which made no sense given I was "home," or at least where I wanted to be. But the light was too wan, the color of sun on the walls. It made me feel that the joys of the Hotel weren't that at all.

Usually this melded into something more remote and wistful, too vague even for Dr. Friend's radar. I tried to explain it to Aunt Bunny because she had perfect psychiatric pitch, but she was stumped too. She assumed it was a form of anxiety, or that maybe I *did* miss my other family.

Flurries of Hotel activity swept away the mood.

Other times I melded with a diabolic presence, like when setting pranks at Niagara Falls.

Yet all told, till that spring morning sophomore year of Amherst, I had not had a full-fledged panic since my tutor Mr. Hilowitz charmed me out of the last one in sixth grade with tales of the French and Indian War. Occasional flutters of terror I rationalized as aftershocks of childhood, normal mood shifts in an erratic universe. I had grown up intrepid and tough, a weed through debris. I didn't turn into the mental patient everyone predicted or an irreparably damaged teen. I applied to the best colleges, got into one, and went. I was dating the prettiest girl in the Smith book and, even when I found out, I didn't back off as unqualified.

Despite asocial acts, despite psychiatry's warnings about primal trauma—its cyclical breakdowns—despite the comeuppances of freshman year, I placed no limits on myself. I could still be anything I wanted. I identified with my sanity alone.

But Dr. Friend had seen the other side of the coin. He expected me to apply to Columbia; he knew that Amherst was pure bravado. He recognized, all along, that panic had been biding, not diminishing, veiling itself in false rollbacks, tracking me through daydreams and compulsive rituals, instigating neurotic gags and numb binges to postpone the inevitable relapse.

For all my vigilance, I had failed to recognize the truth. This wasn't a stable life I was living like Stan Brakhage or even Paul Goodman. It was phases of a fugue, all the way back through Horace Mann and Chipinaw. For years I had been a centurion, keeping at bay wolves who weren't wolves and who wouldn't be held off indefinitely.

My mind had become sophisticated, articulate. I had been trained and taught by adepts. I had replaced the obscure bogeymen and augurs of a five-year-old with informed hell realms, nihilistic proxies, incarceration in a God-forsaken universe—a view validated by no less than Samuel Beckett. To think that I had exalted his lines without realizing Godot *was* the dungeon stairs. I couldn't embrace its literary form while fleeing its sober fact.

This was a life-or-death matter. If nature was warped and malevolent, existence tragic, there was nothing to be done, no bargain to be struck. Same deal always—spooks and aliens at the window, storm troopers at the door. Same as my brother punching ghosts in the dark, asserting valor against invincible, maniacal intruders.

The real threat was a million times worse than the Cuban missile crisis, for nuclear war would only incinerate life. Beingness would be blasted into nothingness. *This,* however, would go on forever, waking me up from every life and death to experience it again. The only remedy was to be totally expunged from existence—never to have been at all.

I summoned Jean-Paul Sartre and Albert Camus to my aid. *They* knew about the darkness of infinite spaces: the wasted sky, the false dawn, troubled sleep, fugitive reprieves—they understood the void left by an absent or unwilling god. They were not afraid, not like this; they had survived a World War and a Nazi puppet regime. They found dignity in resistance. They didn't freak out or devolve into berserk jigs.

We were all in this together. The universe didn't select me alone as its pawn and quarry. My plight was universal not personal. If they could sing in the darkness, I could sing in the darkness too.

Time passed. Colors restored themselves; life began to take hold again. The pangs became a weather front from which I was separating. I sensed them in the near distance, their premise absurd. The cure was *live*. Nothing special: *Just live.*

"Hurray!" I whispered to myself, thinking to charm the demons by my ingenuousness. "Hurray again!"

I rejoined the human race at lunch and spent the afternoon studying for a geology exam.

Lindy and I met for dinner in Northampton and afterwards sat on a lawn at Smith; she stroked my suspect backbone, felt nothing odd, and reassured me. The anticipation of seeing her buoyed by the logistics of hitching there had sustained the day. In her presence the world was soft and sensuous again, a mere fraction out of orbit. I thought maybe I could outrun it and live.

But panic came the next morning with the dissolution of dreams. Sleep had not dissolved the spook, it only made matters worse, *much* worse. My nightmares were not showdowns with hideous entities or plummets into an abyss; no terrifying things happened—I was not chased, threatened, drowned, pushed off a cliff, or dismembered by Hitzig. There were only pasteboard events, labels on bottles, from which I awoke dizzier and more frightened than from any "real" nightmare. It was a nightmare *only because it felt like a nightmare*—far worse for scaring me with a banal skit. It was a nightmare without amelioration because there was nothing to ameliorate, *nothing* to ameliorate it with. Everything was a foil of cracking glue.

I was drifting from any landmark, context of any known shore. Getting dressed, I heard someone's distant radio like a foghorn in another world. I saw the vernal celebration outside, guys beyond the window in T-shirts and shorts—so much lush easy-going life it was intolerable. Just two days ago I had been one of them—baseball, banter, milk shakes, spring fever. I was a bit of a rebel, a nut, but okay. Now I passed like a phantom. I ate without appetite, exchanged speech without recognition. I plodded through pretenses of classes and conversations. I couldn't meet the challenge that every "cowboy cool" dude (whom I had so cavalierly mocked) aced with each casual step across reality.

I remembered the alcove of the Y with its fruit machines, as real as yesterday, more so in its mucid gloom. Not only were the apples poisonous, they weren't apples, they were red decoys. I saw a natal sun through swamp vines from a Miami-bound train. They were dismal then, yet hauntingly beautiful and profound. Now those same vistas were neither romantic nor literary, they were cold and lethal.

I thought: I can wait this one out.

I couldn't. Every second, my heart beat … and I took another breath. This thing was bigger than the known universe!

I was back with the five-year-old, experiencing a lesion of consciousness, the insufficiency of the world to repel the greater dark,

Through the next night too, I woke terrified from sterile dreams, often with a start—jangly phenomena like a film that wouldn't stay in its projector track. I dreaded falling back to sleep.

Throughout the following day I paced the world, looking for anywhere to alight. Spates of terror came and went. I couldn't hold up my end of the bargain or contribute to the collective mirage. I searched inside me for anything mutable, capable of faith or humor. But time itself had stopped. I had moved outside to where existence stood static and still as a grandfather clock in an abandoned house, that would never tick again. The world was a fake paradise, its occasions stale and inappropriate, everything in it a cruel hoax.

I tried to study. I sat in classes in order to be somewhere, but I had to muster every ounce of concentration just to keep myself moored.

I had truly fallen down the stairs, past Nanny's grasp, into the darkness forever.

I bolted.

Lindy was studying for an exam but took time off and walked around Paradise Pond with me. We sat on its far edge. "You'll be okay. You're really a wonderful person; you've just forgotten. It's as though your mother put something inside you—a curse—and you have to find it and defeat it. Ghosts are so much harder than daylight. But you're courageous. You'll do it."

I returned to Amherst, heartened by her support.

Days passed, interminably. I wrote Dr. Friend for the first time in more than a year. He sent back three sentences of upbeat encouragement. I sensed his unwillingness to admit the obvious, that we were the blind being led by the blind. He was cheery by professional obligation and pride, in honor of Freud, who wasn't cheery at all. Standing by a bust of the master (in a film shown by Heath to our class), Freud's biographer Ernest Jones had declared, "Life is not to be enjoyed, life is to be endured."

Two weeks ago I would have opposed such cynicism on principle. Now it was my mantra.

I hitched grimly back to Laura Scales.

"You show up here looking spooked," Lindy snapped, "and what can I do that I haven't done?"

I stood by her, sheepish, agreeing. She was a scholarship student needing to keep up her grade-point average; she had too much schoolwork to squander any more time on someone else's crisis.

Her down-to-earth obligations shamed me. But I was desperate and she made an offer to study together by the pond. Beside her I was in a state of remission and grace. I finished a week's worth of overdue assignments as the sun crossed the sky.

We headed toward her dorm, late afternoon, holding hands. She grabbed my arm and wrist together, as though to snap me out of it, coaxing me with lines from David and Lisa:

"Your face is nice; not like snow, not like ice."

I laughed appreciatively.

"Haven't you been this bad and gotten out of it?"

"Never this bad. Never like this."

"Well, maybe that's just because nothing has been at stake before."

I knew that she was right. She was trying her best to help, but this was *her* life too, and she couldn't just give it to me.

I promised to let a week go before I called again. During the days at Amherst I let tremors build and disperse. I tried to defuse them by reasoning against their hysteria, tracing the semblance of their origin in me. I packed in as much mundane life as I could. I asked my panic to teach me. And it did.

I could tell Dr. Fabian now that it wasn't just the fear of something terrible happening; it was far more convoluted than that. "Okay, Fabian, how about this: a combination of horror, hopelessness, arid grief, and blind desperation? It's inconsolable because no one can help; obsessive because you can't take your mind off it; restless because, with your mind on it constantly, you flee frantically from place to place. It is paranoid because it suspects others of humoring and falsely reassuring you. It is isolate, cut off from human contact, the antipode of eros—and ineradicable.

"How was that, Fabian?" I cried out as if from Beckett's empty stage. "You thought you knew everything, but you didn't know the likes of it when you led me down the primrose path of Paul and Martha's divorce. What a red herring! What a song and dance! *You* were waiting for Godot too."

On a Saturday afternoon, a week into the fugue, I looked back through all the years and saw nothing, just thousands of meaningless ballgames on which I had wasted my life, staged psychiatric sessions bought by blood money, Towers and Grossinger melodrama, pages of nervous-energy writing rejected finally by Catherine Carver. It was a wasteland. It passed for a life because no one had looked at it closely. I wasn't the hero of my own romance. I wasn't a scion of magic and vision. I wasn't a spokesman for my generation. I didn't care about the greatest good for the greatest number. I was self-involved and ungrateful—Martha's bane, Jonny's saboteur, Dr. Fabian's traitor, a petty prankster. I had been grade-hungry at Horace Mann; now I was sloppy and negligent—same narcissistic guy.

No wonder my friendships were thin and empty. No wonder I

felt obscure and forlorn that day at the lake.

All the time telling myself, no! retreat!—I hitched back to Laura Scales.

"I can't keep doing this, Rich! You've got to solve this yourself. You're not some special case. We're each of us alone with our own ghosts."

We went out again. "Just a short walk this time," she made me promise. She loped beside, withholding comment, in warm sun then shadow. I wanted to be regular like her, to stand up and live the damn life.

Yet ordinary existence seemed like play-acting, and I couldn't fake it or carry its weight. Nothing except the fact of us interested me, its symptomatic relief. Everything else was a life sentence. I thought, "I'm destroying this, this one possible thing I have."

"I'm weak," she said. "Don't you see that? I can hardly save myself, let alone you. The world is not ugly; the world is good and beautiful."

I trudged silently as the sky proved her right, showing its last sienna-mauve hues before twilight. Why couldn't I be there too? The beauty of ordinary things had once been good enough, the flow of mundane events. I had been kept on track, as I looked forward to each next pleasure, challenge, novelty, even impasse, it didn't matter. Regular stuff, like every other gal and guy, every creature of field and sky too. In fact the gods had treated me well. Why couldn't I give up this fixation, let go of the string and float with the other balloons? Whose faith was I keeping, whose meaning pretending to impose on meaninglessness?

A cat bounded across the path and stared up. Lindy smiled and extended a palm in its direction. Everything was so studied, so flat.

We reached her house. "End of the line, kiddo."

How did anyone live?

For lack of any better option I kept going to classes, almost losing hold of Geology because I didn't have patience to sit through a lab with rocks across the floor imitating a landscape for our autopsy. I wrote my response as a Beckett-like script, with the monadnocks and mountains and rivers announcing their roles aloud. It was a wonder I found breathing room to pull it off. But I got Professor Foose's bemused C.

Abnormal Psych was my single solace, for I could pore over the textbook for symptoms that applied to me, and many of them did. I mostly feared being like Dostoyevsky's Ivan Karamazov, a specter passing through a nihility. I wanted to be a solid, diagnostic episode in nature like an oxbow lake or continental drift, an explicable fault line that Dr. Friend could cite from his years of work with me—any voucher to stop my open-ended free-fall. Even the deepest fire-spewing volcano had a cause, a thermodynamic vector and libidinal charge behind it; it could be charted and tracked. Cameron and Rychlak made that clear:

> Anxiety attacks are acute episodes of emotional decompensation usually appearing in a setting of chronic anxiety, and exhibiting to an exaggerated degree the characteristics of normal fright. The fright usually comes from within, from a sudden upsurge of unconscious material that threatens to disrupt ego integration. The anxiety attack often climaxes a long period of mounting tension to which the anxious person has been progressively adapting, but with ever-increasing difficulty. Finally the limits of tolerance are reached, he can compensate no further, and the continued stress precipitates a sudden discharge into all available channels.

"... *into all available channels!*" No kidding, guys!

> Whether or not the patient is able to verbalize what he is doing and what attracts him, the basic situation is the same. He is impelled to repeat his futile, frustrating behavior—in overt action or in fantasy or daydream—because of the relentless pressure of unconscious infantile urges, fears, temptations and conflicts.

The more the underlying anxiety increases, the greater the somatic discharge, and vice versa, until terror becomes inevitable. The attack merely relieves a contemporary build-up of cathexis and tension; then innate, self-perpetuating anxiety reasserts itself and begins recruiting toward the next attack. At least as good as a rupture in the crust of a planetary object!

But what were those infantile urges, temptations, and conflicts? How could I get a grip on them, defuse their charge, turn their torque, their flow of lava the other way? How could I apply seismic leverage to something so impalpable and fugitive?

The answer *was* the question: the outbreak of terror is how the unconscious gets the attention of the ego. Something even more unbearable is being converted to "mere" panic and given passage in its camouflage—something obviously bottomless and brutal because panics are horrific in themselves.

Was it that, without terror, there would be nothing at all, I would drift in empty space forever, no jetties or signs? William Faulkner conceded as much in *The Wild Palms:* "Between grief and nothing I will take grief."

Perhaps that's why Jon fought ghosts in the night. Better them than nothing.

The next time a wave of panic came I went straight to Heath's house. I was about to see him anyway—he was scooting down his front stairs en route to our class. I tried to explain my state, but I had no words for it. In frustration I clenched my fists, ran fingers through my hair down over my face, grabbed my arms. I dug my nails into them as deep as I could. He stopped and gave me a mystified look, a gaze both of wonder and admiration. Then he began walking again. "What affect!" he finally declared without breaking stride. His observation cast a mirror, and I saw myself absurdly, a figure in a textbook.

"There's a battle inside you," he continued, "an enemy you can't face. It has no identity, no symbolic form, no reconcilability or contingency. Everything in this so-called world must look to you like some sort pale imitation of the world inside you. Obviously no one understands; they just cite textbooks like me. Only *you* know. And that leaves you so alone. It is an existential state more than a pathology. You are teaching me something about death instinct. You are fleeing death by pursuing from it. And you are pretending to know what you are frightened of because that at least suggests there *is* a world, there is a solution."

"I deserve an A in this course for living it."

Both of us laughed, as I accompanied him to class.

That night I dreamed of an immense wind. It blew across darkness, carrying images, image fragments, scraps of paper down avenues of the City. Fierce, unformed animals—wolves and cats and curs—tore off the dream shroud, led me through its scar into a hollow, a gentler void. UFOs patrolled an outer sky of too many planets and moons.

This counted. This was an actual place.

They never spotted me as I ran through high grass and hid in vines. The wind was frantic, bracing, euphoric. Everything that needed to be changed it ripped apart, swallowed into its momentum without distraction or regard. It was as elating a spectacle as I had ever witnessed, and it was core. It cleared the stage and re-set me.

In the morning I felt both better and worse. I was woozy and hung over but, paradoxically, not as afraid. I went to geology without fully appreciating the shift. I finished the day's lab by working through half my lunch hour. Then I realized: I had a spark, I was normal again!

I ran back to Phi Psi in glee. It was over! I knew that implicitly, even as I knew when it began with currants in cereal. There was no explanation; it was just gone. In its place was something like the dream wind, carrying the most beautiful images across a spring morning—shards of a yet-unwritten ode. The world was magnificent, the clover and dandelions so exquisite they broke my heart. The sky was scrumptious, a sheer miracle.

The shadow of doom had been replaced by an ebullience so fathomless and vast, with so much rhythm and design, it was absurd. Was this ever a stunning day—such azure infinity, so many blossoms

of primary colors, such delightfully goofy insects and birds, each
of them stately and wondrous to exist at all! I didn't have enough
outright kudos for them, but I found a patch in the Glen and took
those lines that came:

> *Day of blind flies, lethargic clouds, tardy stars.*
> *Once again you have come to haunt me dead....*

Four sheets of paper later I came to a crescendo:

> *And for the first time you asked the only question*
> *That you could never stop asking*
> *Until weary with wrinkles and questions*
> *You stood by another fence,*
> *Eons apart,*
> *And knew that the sun of the tarot,*
> *That Apollo,*
> *That the golden blood of susans*
> *Were born before men*
> *And planted in men's eyes*
> *To pull men back*
> *To the honeyrod fields of time.*

The phrases and beat translated themselves from nature as lucidly
as if they were stanzas of Virgil. Nothing eluded me, nothing fooled
me; subjunctives and strings of participles were right at hand, in the
breezes, fragrances, and luminosities of spring. All I needed was to
decode the mumblings of a slightly unfamiliar dialect into words.
Correlatives arose wherever I looked: a back-up first baseman from
the old Yankees (Don Bollweg transformed into granite-gneiss pinstripes), daisies across fields of childhood, the haunted land beside a
cobblestone road, *"a tiny dead bug / drifting across a marsh moon / into
the black / forever," "the fleeting blackbirds from maple pies (four and twenty
in four and twenty speckled swarms)," "the Spaldeen rabbit bouncing home."*
The stream through the Glen uttered the oldest proverb of my life:

> *Depart this dawn-haunted house.*
> *Depart this laughing kitchen. It is*
> *A tide of the rising sun,*
> *A spooking hole*
> *For the dancing yellow heart.*

Run out beneath the long sky
Before it mellows
To the purple wine of twilight,
Comes supper comes terror!
Comes terror if you have not sweated, loved, or sung a song
On a day of the haunted dawn.

By mid-afternoon I had entered the realm of the planet Jupiter:

... a sea of Jovian pomander
of squashed gases,
of methane-smoking caterpillars,
of purple electric breezes
That come with the ozone rain
And the neon rainbows.
With spring I am launched
From the quiet frozen moon
Of Io
To the dense bosom
Of swirling clays....
The prehistoric wish,
The Cro Magnon sperm,
The weeping willow of Om,
All lost   All not lost:
The ancient baby of Tigres
The young ageless of Atlantis....

After twenty pages I dropped my pen into the grass and calmly took in the summer that had arrived in my absence. I was starving. I felt as if I hadn't eaten for days. I ran to the snack bar and ordered two cheeseburgers, a plate of fries, and a maple-walnut frappe. I sat there consuming them in bliss, each sip like the first time I ever experienced a tree's creamy caramel sap.

Years later I arrived at a cover story for my panic: I had been coasting impetuously, thinking to get by on the status quo, to ride my new identity into happiness. But I had to *earn* my freedom from my mother's whammy. The Greeks knew this: once Medusa hexes you it is no mean feat to break her stare. She doesn't yield to mere persuasion—she won't grant passage without exacting a toll equal to the gift

At some point in childhood I had walled off a paranoid terror that was unsustainable, probably unsurvivable, cocooning it inside my life, below its discharge threshold and spike potential. Cocooning isn't a usual strategy. People with traumas tend to eke them out, averaging their waves into duller, more dissociated states. But I wanted to be sane, and not just sane, I wanted to *feel* what was happening. Not only did it interest me, seemingly from the get-go, but it led to those magical, elusive layers of epiphany and gloom—the heart of meaning. And each state was too real and salient just to discard or antidote.

As long as the venom was bundled and insulated, I could coexist with it. It didn't supplant my normal existence or get deflected by the usual Freudian aberrations, inhibition or denial, into dysfunctional maladies.

After sixth grade, I panicked only fleetingly, and they were brief supernatural visitations, modes I could diffuse or turn into binges and pranks. Otherwise I became a moody, erratic boy, comforted by my own soap opera.

Lindy ended all that in a flash. She drove me out of the solipsistic trance I wrapped around my teenage years. She intuited the truth too, that nothing real had been at stake before. She wasn't "pretty." She wasn't a "girl." She was far more stringent and irreconcilable than that.

The price of being found by her, of getting the so-called "true romance" I had wanted more than anything, was having to wake up. There was no free ride there either. It wasn't just that I couldn't stay in my bubble—I would have willingly accepted *that* deal—it was that the act of being touched by another person was radical and ineluctable. Lisa's charm notwithstanding, David had it right.

Without warning, I changed personae overnight. I lost the capacity to bury myself soporifically in box scores, Corn Kix, and other artless totems. I couldn't be a child anymore and I couldn't *tell myself* I couldn't be a child, for I wasn't ready to be anything else. I had resisted becoming a man, not for the usual reasons, I believe, but because I didn't want to rouse the dungeon-keepers or give them reason to suspect hubris on my part. I didn't want them *even to know I existed*. That was the carapace of the cocoon.

Now I needed a shot of whatever was in that chrysalis, however ghastly, to claim my spirit, to grow a male backbone, to meet my plucky, no-nonsense girlfriend with some degree of style and grit.

The spring-of-'64 panic came when I was nineteen and a half. I made a hairline crack in the cocoon, and through it the entirety of my life got recapitulated in delayed terror. I could not be conscious of what was happening because there was no conscious form of it. It was beyond mediation: too complicated for ordinary intention, too elliptical for analysis, hieroglyphic and paradoxical beyond ideation. It couldn't blandish by words or insights; it had to assert itself by pure exigency. To be conscious was to be token and strategic, was not to do it at all.

There was no substitute or stand-in for the mystery of life itself.

And it said: feel this, you have always been willing to feel. It said: break asunder, you will know how to come back together. It said, meet your shadow before its separation from you becomes schizophrenic. It said, forfeit joy and solace; their concession will inoculate you against later loss.

You will awaken fresh, able to see the world in utter, meticulous depth, find words you never knew, taste maple for the first time, parry obliquities and chimeras (for they are as devious and bottomless as they seem), court your lady for real.

I had been scared to death, almost obliterated at birth, but I crawled out of that venom on a leaf floated to me by a child.

A long latency followed, for I wasn't ready to fly. Now my wings were drying off.

I panicked because, at core, I suddenly didn't know who or where I was. My conscious self thought I was eating Kix and currants, dating at last, happy as a clam, or at least happy enough. My unconscious self realized how deep the waters had gotten, felt the bends, and sent its warning signal across the interstellar-like barrier that separates unconscious and conscious space.

I thought I was in civic territory, another mundane neutral zone, but I wasn't. I had entered the chapel unawares, for the gods needed to rouse me for sacred battle.

After the incident, I came to think of panic not as an enemy but a teacher and truthsayer. What I didn't realize then was that it was also a transubstantiating shadow, a preparation by proxy for real crises that were to come. Having sparred with the ghost within, I was ready to confront forces in the world that opposed me with far more insidious gauntlets—for they could never be as dire and seminal as what I had already undergone. My family and its subculture stood against the kind of man I needed to be; they had always stood against it, and that fucked up my childhood and made my brother my foe. I had to win that ribbon on my own, have the moxie to see it through. That was what panic was teaching me. By taking the dark bath, by being immersed in the baptismal waters of Flash Gordon's horrific shower, I was awakened, prepared, tempered.

Jon had been wrong about those ghosts: you weren't supposed to defeat them by literal or lavish exertion, and you couldn't defeat them, it was a false battle. The courage required was more like Christ's: submission, obliteration, then rebirth. Faith means faith in the unbearable too.

I said "a cover story," meaning as penetrating analysis as I can do. It is more like shreds of overlapping cover stories. No one knows the big picture. Crises with deep roots come closest to spilling the beans, to disclosing who we really are—they are looking-glasses through which our personal reality forms.

Before the end of the semester Lindy went to Penn to see her old boyfriend Steve again for a weekend. I was dismayed but still exhilarated for having gotten out of the whirlpool. I figured rather than wait this one out, I'd put myself in motion too. The previous summer I had made friends with one of the hotel drivers, a kid about five years older than me named Jimmy McAndrews. He said that any time I'd like to bypass my father and phone in a trip from Amherst he'd be thrilled to come and get me, see that part of the world. So I called Jimmy at Traffic, and on Friday afternoon, like magic he was sitting in the Phi Psi parking lot in my father's black Cadillac.

"I don't think anyone really knows where the PG went," he told me. "But no one will miss it for a while. Everyone will think someone else has it."

It was great to have the Hotel come to me.

On the way home Jimmy heard my tale of woe about my new girlfriend who, sadly, was checking out her past guy in Philly—even that scenario so deliciously secular compared to the pagan oppression of panic. As he let me drive my first two hundred miles on the open road, we mustered a plan. Coming back on Sunday we'd intercept the last bus from Philadelphia in Hartford. Maybe she'd be on it; then we'd drive her back to Smith.

Sunday evening we filled the PG with sandwiches, fruit, cookies, and Heinekens and timed our departure so that three hours later we beat the bus by fifteen minutes. Astonished to spot me out the window, Lindy immediately got up and debarked. She collected her suitcase and jumped in.

By the time we reached Smith we were all three jiving and drinking beers.

The following week I received an acceptance letter from Seattle, but that seemed a pipe dream. Once again I went to the Phi Psi room committee, hat in hand. They assigned me the large double on the first floor for fall, to be shared with a wide-eyed sophomore-to-be from Boston named Marty.

The last visit with Lindy was agonizing. We were already planting a necessary distance between us and, as we strolled by the Smith boathouse holding hands, we argued about where our relationship was going. The time apart would be good, she said. Now that I was strong again I should build on my strength. "We can date new people and write each other as confidantes, wonderful intimate letters about our adventures." Her jovial mood made me sulky. I accused her of tearing down what we had.

She had brought me me a goodbye card with a quote she had hand-copied from painter Joan Miró: "Everywhere one finds the sun, a blade of grass, the spirals of the dragonfly. Courage consists in staying at home and close to Nature. Nature who takes no account of our calamities." As I read it, she added, "Remember that, dear, the next time you get stuck and I'm not around."

She said we would always be good friends but could never be more than that. I didn't want such a limit, didn't see any reason for a limit now that we were parting anyway.

Fred had loaned me his mythical Rambler for the trip to Bradley, Hartford–Springfield's airport, so I drove the forty-five minutes there. I kissed her quickly. Our goodbye passed without lingering—a girl with a suitcase merging into the crowd.

Upon my arrival at Grossinger's my father told me with a hint of sadistic fanfare, "You've been promoted to desk clerk." I flashed him a cod-liver-oil look. Playing hotel was not in my plans, plus a visible front-office role afforded no loopholes for escape. After thinking about it for a day I told him I'd rather find my own job.

He was momentarily speechless. "Okay," he responded with a series of perturbed nods. "I'll give you a week. If you don't get something by then you're washing dishes all summer."

That seemed a fair challenge. My main impasse, transportation, was quickly solved when Grandma Jennie offered to lend me her Lincoln Continental, the JG, for the summer. It was far too ostentatious a vehicle for a nineteen-year-old with radical visions and only three hundred miles under his belt, but there were no ready alternatives. I knew that my father gave her periodic grief about it; apparently she held her ground because, other than continually making me re-park it in a spot that existed only in his mind, he never interceded.

Lindy was going to intern at the *Rocky Mountain News* in Denver, and I figured a newspaper was the most promising opportunity for me too. Setting off in my oversized white sedan, I turned east out of Ferndale onto Route 52 and drove fifteen miles to Ellenville, site of the Nevele. For the next three days I tried newspaper offices from there through Monticello, Liberty, and smaller villages, filling out employment forms that were probably in files discarded when computers took over thirty-five years later.

Then I worked my way west on 52—the less populous direction out of Liberty along the Delaware River, across train tracks into Hortonville, past ramshackle farms and covered bridges. This was even less promising: no newspapers at all. On my last allotted day I came to the Pennsylvania border town of Callicoon, thirty miles from home. On its main street I saw a classic Norman Rockwell storefront: *The Sullivan County Democrat.* It seemed too mirage-like to be real, a façade I might have conjured as the state line imposed a fateful barrier. Compared to my cognitive map of Grossinger's home county, Pennsylvania was as uncharted and remote as Wyoming, and my prospects were sliding fast, dishwashing on the horizon. I poked my head in far enough to glimpse an alcove dominated by hanging galleys and stacks of metal type.

Its proprietor was a mountain of a man named Fred Stabbert. He extended a hand to the young stranger and, with a cordial bark, grilled him in the doorway, his bulk precluding further entry.

He was succinct: he'd hire me once he determined I wasn't running away from home. "The last place I need trouble from is Grossinger's." The *Democrat* was the one anti-hotel paper in a conservative Republican county, and it struck Fred as odd that the son of the owner of its largest resort should show up at his door looking for work.

I was ecstatic. The twenty-two miles from Callicoon to the G. flew by like ten. Fred no doubt took pleasure in his phone call to Paul Grossinger that afternoon. I imagined their cagey exchange. My father said nothing initially, but at dinner that night he seemed genuinely pleased—though he added quixotically, "So you don't want to go into the hotel business?"

"You know I want to be a writer."

He agreed he knew that.

I sent Lindy an account of these events and began work on Monday.

For the first week at the *Democrat,* I sat at a desk proofreading county news and writing captions for photographs of car wrecks, retiring supervisors, and high-school swimming stars. Fred kept teasing that he was working me up to bigger things.

I enjoyed the time there regardless, especially bag lunches with

him, his sister, and the rest of the crew by Callicoon Creek, luxu-
riating in sun and breeze off the water, exchanging regular chitchat
and repartees. I tried to bring everyone a dessert from the previous
night's meal at the Hotel. My boxes of cakes and cookies were much
anticipated, the politics behind them discounted, their yummies
promptly eulogized and devoured.

Finally Fred dispatched me across the Delaware into Pennsylvania
to cover a town meeting about snow removal. I mailed my front-
page article to Lindy.

Her job in Denver was comparable, except that she was an intern
at a big-city daily. She proofread too and rewrote other people's
articles. Otherwise, she was sent to cover veterans' meetings and
hundredth birthdays. Her first letter detailed all that and then stated
explicitly everything I most feared:

> You will unfortunately get to know me much better in letters.
> Unfortunately in that what I write in these always has and will be
> too truthful; whatever last trace of a gossamer mask there was is
> now off because we have started letters. They are the great disarmer;
> I'm stripped now because they are the first and last source of com-
> munication. Your letters I prize too much, perhaps even more than
> many of our conversations which were distorted by fear on both
> our parts. What will happen is that I will end up talking about you
> a lot more than you will about me in these letters, which fact is a
> fact and deserves to be wondered at. I think you're interesting but
> I also think I'm interesting—but in the last ding dong ding dong
> of the world it will be you we'll go down discussing because I
> am uncomfortable under the glare of the operating table light....
>
> I am not so secure that I don't love love when I see a little of it
> flowing in my direction. I think I am horribly idealized in both
> your and Aunt Bunny's eyes now, and probably to see me again in
> flesh and blood would wreck the beautiful image that has somehow
> been created. Connect now with the moments when you hated
> everything I said during the last times, as I do, but then always give
> the exquisite rationale that I do, that those angers were because I
> was leaving. All this makes me tiptoe and not count on a thing—
> people or you seem to be so changeable that I'll be wary and fly

back up my tree before eating out of your hand.

I'm very ordinary. I go to work every day and am a cub reporter on a Scripps-Howard tabloid. I write crap well and they like it and me.... I see Steve as often as I can which is infrequently. I was in Aspen with him when you called, and there is no sense in playing games, leading you on, or worst of all, having you build images of me (too positive or too negative). I don't want to be another Betsy; idealization is not flattering to me. Steve is the end of a long quest and search. I have perhaps found him prematurely because now no one else will ever really do in his role. You and he play different parts. I play a part to you which is not sufficient for you; you will need someone else to play the part that Steve plays in my life. The role is indefinable—it's not exactly that of a lover but perhaps that of a stronger person. I'm too weak for you in the end, and you are too weak for me. This is maybe too much honesty, but I would rather knit alone than have any sham falsity. What you are is perhaps the closest friend I have and have ever had. I can't depend on you but I can write you with this candidness and not be afraid of losing your friendship....

I dread next fall in a way (and this will hurt you, but don't let it) because we will either split or change. I dread having to face you because I will have to be freer than you let me be. If I can't be as free as I want I'll just fly from you, try to get away and out of your pocket. I'm only good when I'm free to study, grow, explore, and develop on my own and the only people who have ever held me have been those who let me fly. I'm nobody's parent, wife, lover; only friend.

Fred directed me to Ellenville to talk to a Japanese man who was saturating the Hudson and Delaware Valleys with cherry trees. I took down his tale: immigration to America, homesteading in rural New York, a vow to spread this gift from his homeland to his adopted country. I posed him in front of his orchard. My boss loved the story and decided I was more valuable hunting up human-interest features than proofreading. I was given free rein to come and go.

I drove to small socialist hotels and bungalow colonies—diametric opposites of Grossinger's—where I interviewed guests and staff. I met Kurt Shillberry, the most vocal opponent of the resorts' tax breaks. He thought that establishments like Grossinger's should pay for their share of County services at a rate in keeping with their revenue. Shifting restlessly on the couch, my father perused the published interview, then guffawed, "You're a dreamer!" But at least he smiled.

Fred heard about a community of black Jews called the Gheez living in the woods by Callicoon. He thought it might be too dangerous to investigate, but then he shouldn't have mentioned it. I edged the Lincoln to the end of the last dirt road and walked a quarter mile to their encampment. They were delighted by a press visit and took me on tour of their huts and temple, all the time spieling gospel and Biblical history. They had a gigantic queen whom they carried on a litter, but I saw only pictures of her and the throne. Fred published most of my account, removing my exotica about Egypt.

Next I picked another remotely situated institution, a boarding school called Summer Lane modelled after the radical Summer Hill schools of England. The director, a towering young minister, met me at the gate, then escorted me past clusters of suspiciously staring boys. Reverend George von Hillshimer was a Civil Rights activist who had been on the recent Freedom marches in the South. From his collar up he was a priest, but otherwise he was a charismatic gang leader, officiating over teens in leather jackets and bracelets, clusters of them dragging on cigarettes around low sheds. In the hour that followed, George proved capable of spontaneous oratory as well as bursts of startling ferocity, especially when something more untoward than tobacco caught his eye. He seemed more dangerous than the kids.

For the remainder of July and August I left the newspaper office once a week at noon and drove back roads to Summer Lane to share sandwiches with Reverend George in his grove. We talked Lawrence and James Baldwin, and he read to me from his own political and philosophical writings. "It is crucial," he admonished, "not to live a typical American adolescence, which is self-indulgent and conscienceless. Go through life as a hero. James Baldwin dreamed of 'another country' without prejudice and human-inflicted pain. Well, he knew—and we all know—it doesn't exist. Your generation has to make it from scratch."

My clippings delighted Lindy. "I am of course jealous you get to range through far-out and meaningful territory. And they support you? I'm astonished."

Well, not always. I sent her my typewritten editorial about the presidential candidates in which I compared Lyndon Johnson to a man driven by a malign unconscious force, as the tides by the moon—the moon being Barry Goldwater, whose war-mongering had purportedly stampeded LBJ into sending troops to Vietnam. I closed: "It is nightfall in America!" Fred had refused to publish it.

"You're too damn radical for me, boy," he said. "This stuff is downright depressing."

To the amusement of the staff, Fred and I engaged in ongoing ideological debates. Head of the county Civil Defense agency, he insisted that atomic bombs were no big deal. "It's just one more weapon," he informed me. "It's been the same since the caveman. You invent a weapon; then someone finds the defense for it—so you build a bigger weapon. You can't halt that parade. Atomic bomb's just a big bomb, but it's not *more* than a bomb."

I was glad it was only the Civil Defense (and the *Democrat*) that Fred oversaw; still his rhetoric frightened me. I feared instant holocaust if Goldwater were elected, and the fact that a union guy like Fred could support his position on armaments was disconcerting. Leo Marx had tried to convince us that the liberal tradition of Thomas Jefferson and Adlai Stevenson *was* America, its ascendance inevitable, but outside of Amherst and New York City I never seemed to encounter it.

Driving country roads back and forth to Callicoon and newspaper assignments I visited sleepy antique shops and, on my salary, bought old jugs and lamps, which I used, along with props left over from Hotel banquets (including a plastic potted tree), to decorate my room. I created an informal shrine in which I hung

Klee and Miró prints. I lay in my arbor, reading Olson and Nabokov and enjoying the sounds of Phi Psi: Bob Dylan, Jim Kweskin, Dave Van Ronk.

"Change or lose me," Lindy had warned. Since she had gone back to Steve I did not feel disloyal noticing a pretty waitress at a station near the family section. She was a heavy-boned girl with an Eastern European face. Casting subterfuge glances her way, I tried to discern if she was really as attractive as I thought she was. She *was*—her appeal gave no ground. A riveting actress with rolling hips and a pouty stare, she lugged trays more fully loaded than most of the men, delivering fancy chow from her platters with a sulky, imperial demeanor. She was charismatic, impossible not to look at.

We seemed to catch each other's eye more than I was willing to admit, telling myself those self-conscious smiles were part of her routine act, not for my benefit. Then one night in early July after the dining room had closed and she was cleaning her station, I approached cautiously until she looked up, a twinge (perhaps) of "Finally!" in her moue.

My role at Grossinger's had become totally ambivalent to me. Whereas once I took my identity from being the owner's son, now I was embarrassed by ruling-family privilege and tried to downplay my affiliation. Yet it was part of the courage I drew on in approaching her—that, plus pure beguilement and the reckoning in Lindy's letter.

Her name was Jean, nickname Smokey. Polish Catholic, from Pennsylvania, she was working for her college tuition and despised the Hotel and its guests (as was evident to anyone with half a brain).

"Yes," she said, she'd love to go out to dinner, "off the grounds presumably."

Through July, Smokey and I saw each other regularly, supping at local inns, going to movies, exploring backroads, listening to records in my room. After two such dates I kissed her while dancing and she kissed me back. Then we stopped dancing and lay on the bed making out.

We hiked to a meadow on the edge of the woods and wound together in the grass. Her dress was shiny over her large butt and hips, her perfume pepperminty. I was encouraged by her sighs and rough hugs, but she broke off, jumped to her feet with a hearty laugh, and brushed away the weeds.

Schuy had gone with his family to their summer home on Martha's Vineyard to race his sailboat. He was working with his Psi U buddy Larry in a restaurant as a dishwasher:

> Thanks for your two letters and I'm sorry I didn't write before. It sounds to me like the best thing about this Jean is that this all gives you a chance to get Lindy in some kind of perspective—get some of your power back, speaking 'Davidwise'—which turns out to be the same problem I have here. The first day on the job I saw this interesting and thin attractive girl—after a day made an Axis-like remark to her about how the people around seemed all to be so affected by the bureaucracy and so forth, took her out to coffee, etc. All was nice—she turned out to be a Smith grad who writes poetry, hated Smith, didn't date Amherst, is earning money to go to Europe, and anyway I really like her.
>
> Her name is Dona, and I'm kind of relieved to be going out with someone with such a derivative name, like in the song, "I Had a Girl, and Donna Was Her Name"—you know, the embarrassing mushy one. I have been dating her a lot. I can't stand her being a waitress right there and me washing dishes. I don't understand what my position with her is, and what I'm trying to do is make her change her mind about her being 22 and graduated and me being 21 and (I lied) a senior—and I really do think she is 22 (and I'm not really 21), but I don't think it should make such a difference. Anyway, I'm trying to act tough—you know, the way Axis does—to try (I guess) to shake her up. But I'm pretty weak about it. I guess I've been seeing her quite a bit. A week ago we had this big moment at a party, and it was "I do love you, but I'm not in love with you; I want you to be a friend, even though I know how ridiculous that sounds."
>
> I have been sailing every day now for three or four days, since I got the boat in the water. In the first race I did well till we got lost in the fog and had to be towed in. Larry is my crew, and we are living together in this little sort of shed-garage apartment. There's

a bunk for you if you want to come visit....

Coaxing a few days off from the *Democrat,* I drove the Thruway north past Albany to the Mass Pike, then veered south of Boston. Beach towns to my left, I caught sudden quaffs of salt air, found the Terminal, parked, and caught a ferry.

Larry met me at the dock, and we went straight to the fabled restaurant. When I saw Dona I fell in love with her too. She was a brown-haired, sun-tanned Jersey girl with a 1920s style reminiscent of a co-ed strutting the Charleston, Schuy poked his head out of the kitchen in his dishwasher's costume and greeted me clownishly.

After closing, the four of us went to hear Jim Kweskin's Jug Band. It was a small club, the performers breathtakingly close—thimbles on washboards, honking jugs: *"Washing-ton at Valley Forge, / Freezing cold and up spoke George.... "* Between sets I edged over to Kweskin and mentioned Phi Psi, where he had played before my time. "Hangin' out with Mr. Tripp!" he proclaimed with several nods. "Well, give him my best. Maybe you guys can come up with some bread and get us back to Amherst." Then he sidled away.

The next afternoon while Schuy raced, Dona and I sat on the beach trying to spot his sails. She knew I was a writer and had brought along her binder of poems. She read from it—clean lucid lines, playful and insolent—one piece of free verse suggesting to a lover that they spend their lives together scraping off the insides of Oreo cookies with their teeth. She invoked landscapes of bygone summers, toy boats, shiny pebbles.

I had only the cards with me, so I laid them in the sand and read her fortune: felicity, strife, unexpected bounty.

All the next day Schuy ignored both of us. When he wasn't washing dishes he worked on his boat. So Dona and I used his car to drive the single road to the cliffs at the end of the island. We talked Freud, Lawrence, and Sartre, as she pointed out the sights. Rapport established, she questioned me about Schuy, why he had to act like a tough guy. I tried to cast his motives in the most favorable light. "It's really quite silly," she remarked.

Yet I hardly understood my buddy anymore. He was growing a mustache and had declared that his name was now Scotty. That evening at work he pretended not to notice Dona except to snap commands her way. Later he explained: "I have to break her, like a horse."

He smashed the two 45s I brought him as a gift—Richie Valens' "Donna" and Paul Anka's "Diana," saying, "That's exactly the kind of mushiness that destroys relationships." He was not amused by my suggestion that Anka's words could be flipped from *"You're so young, and I'm so old"* to *"I'm so young ..."* Then he berated Larry for his performance on the boat, blaming it on his reading Yogananda's *Autobiography of a Yogi,* "I need sailors, not candy-ass Hindus."

"This is all bullshit, man!" Larry snapped. "Who do you think you are, Axis or something? You have no idea what you're talking about. You're running off at the mouth, acting like some spoiled cretin. Try treating your girlfriend like a human being for a start."

Then Schuy ordered him out of their shared domicile (his mother owned it, so he held that card): "Take your belongings! Go find another place to live!" When I tried to mediate, he cut me off, "Just fucking leave too. I don't want you around here either. You're both children. I've got *enough* problems."

I asked Larry if he could run me to the dock. It was perilously close to the last ferry, and I had no fallback position. I caught it by a minute. Driving the Mass Pike barely awake, I woke once with a start, the car drifting toward the guardrail. I pulled into a rest stop and fell asleep on the front seat. In the morning I covered the remainder of the 300 miles.

It had only been three days, but Grossinger's felt like somewhere I had never been. My room was someone else's too, though I welcomed its guise; I had no better offer. The Hotel always wooed me back, perhaps for its luxuries and prerogatives but mostly for the sheer spaciousness and optimism of the place. It no longer felt the way it had in childhood, but it still touched something deep and dormant in me. I had a daffier, more rhapsodic self there, one that floated up and met cumulus parades that stretched far beyond Grossinger's. I touched a calm and peace inside me and imagined endless possibilities. Of course it wasn't Grossinger's. It was creation, but I couldn't get into it any other way. Grossinger's was where I first felt it and where I had to be for it to happen.

With one day left before work I headed into New York City, the first time driving there myself: rock 'n' roll on good old "Double-U A B C," hitting the George Washington Bridge and rattling across. I shot down the Henry Hudson Parkway like the Towers Mercury of yore, crossed over at 96th Street, and parked in the basement of 300 Central Park West. Without advance notice, I stood at 8C and rang the bell. I hadn't been back since fleeing eight months ago. After my family got over the shock (and I finished distributing pastries and lox), I was welcomed by everyone, even Martha.

"How about some old times together," Bob said, finishing off the last of the salmon with an appreciative smile. "Feel like the reservoir?"

"Of course."

As we took our commemorative stroll—Debby tossing crusts over the fence to ducks, now as then—my mother unexpectedly clutched my arm and slowed her stride, causing us to straggle behind the rest. She told me how difficult my brother had become. "I can't control him anymore. You were impossible, but at least I could reach you."

"Right. I was the loyal one."

She nodded, missing the irony. "He's beyond me."

I feigned surprise, but I had always known. My duplicitous attempt at sympathy she brushed off like a fly.

In the afternoon I drove uptown to Chuck Stein's apartment near Columbia. It was our first meeting in person since Horace Mann. He had changed dramatically in two years, having become a full magus with a bushy beard and a pipe. In the hour before sunset he led me to his favorite bench along the Hudson. There I quizzed him on Olson poems. After he deciphered a few lines, he reminded me that it didn't matter whether one got all the references or not. "Like Brakhage films," he said, "the meaning is not in the literal presentation. It's in the mode of consciousness the words represent."

On the phone I had asked Chuck to teach me how to use the tarot as a meditation tool, and he offered to do so on my next trip into the New York. Now he removed my deck from its box and went through it, pulling out the major trumps: twenty-two sovereign cards without wands, swords, pentacles, or cups. Each of their landscapes, he explained, was more than just a solitary arrangement of symbols and messages. The cards had relationships among them and could be placed in a matrix representing the formation of the universe and everything in it—though it took a shift of perception to get it.

I knew the basic designations from Ervin's class and my books, but I lacked specifics and a formula. Neither Waite nor Case told his readers how to design a matrix of trumps. Chuck had learned the rudiments of tarot meditation from Case's posthumous course—biweekly lessons in the mail from Builders of the Adytum in L.A.—but then he put his own spin on the curriculum, and that was the abacus he was about to lay out.

First, my friend ordered the cards by numeral; then he sorted them on the grass in three rows of seven, the Fool on top. A daydreamy youth strolled along the mountains of card zero, carrying elemental plasma in his knapsack. "He's the source," Chuck declared, "of all substance and form. Note how he bears its atomic fuse fecklessly." He pointed to a white rose dangled between the thumb and fore-finger of the Jester's left hand. "He's oblivious to the fact that he's about to walk off a cliff, but then he's not a person as much as a ground potential. Zero is the cosmic egg that contains all the other numbers and number systems." He wagged his right hand over the 21-card alignment beneath the yellow-skied cipher.

The Fool's lemon background reminded me of my first Gene Woodling card. Yellow was the Sun, Marvin Gardens in Monopoly, my favorite Sorry! token—Revelation!

"Look at the whole as a dynamic grid with something akin to binary code or the *I Ching* hexagrams but in parallel rows of seven operating below the forcefield of the Jester." He waved a palm back and forth across the pictures in the grass as if to stroke their invisible steam. "They represent successive phases by which vibrations become molecules and cells and are translated into the world as meanings and designs, thought with form. Let's start at the beginning of the first row."

Card one was the Magician, white hydrogen garments under red robes, an infinity sign above his head. Chuck pointed to his right hand raised upward and bearing a trident. "That wand converts cosmic into worldly energy. The downward-pointing left hand conducts its current down into Nature."

"We felt its heat," I reminded him, "in Ervin's class."

He smiled. "That was a gimmick. We're moving on." I flashed him a playful pout as he proceeded. "On a wooden table before him—see, there are the four artifacts of the lesser arcana: wand, pentacle, sword, and cup. Those are the implements he uses to create phenomena."

To the left of the Magician (our right), clad in pale blue watery robes, sat the High Priestess, at her feet a crescent moon. "She is reflecting and converting the Sorcerer's magic." he remarked, drawing an invisible line from the Magician's trident to a scroll marked "Torah" in the Priestess' lap, its 'h' hidden by her robe. "The drapery of ripe pomegranates behind her represents the latency of Creation. Without her mediation the Sorcerer's field of operation would never get conducted into matter and mass."

"Or into paramecia and diatoms," I offered, for I had internalized the flow between the Magician and Priestess back at Horace Mann where it evoked Freud's unconscious latency for me.

"Into any set of values, encodings, or syntax," he rejoined.

In card three a deeply contemplative Empress reclined in her curved cathedra, in her right hand a scepter crowned by the world. "DNA at work," observed Chuck. "The twelve zodiacal diadems on her tiara represent the space-time continuum." He made a quick circular motion around her head. "It's Eden but also biological diversity, Nature itself."

"I think of it as the reflecting mirror of the chlorophyll molecule."

"Sure. She converts the Priestess' transmissions into a lush grove and garden represented by those trees behind her and the ripening corn at her feet. See how its stalks rise to meet the current of her robe. That's a continuation of the Priestess' garment."

The next vista was a stony ram-adorned bench formed by

mountainous uplift. There a grim Emperor held forth. "He has
to wrest his domain from the first three cards," Chuck explained.
"Magicians spin phantasmagoria till time immemorial, at least on a
cosmic level. Emperors issue laws and physical rubrics, apply them
to nature. The fourth trump keeps every molecule in the universe
in place. Newtonian territory."

"I suppose he can't intervene to save to save a single swallow," I
proposed, "because his equations are essential for the preservation
of matter. If he interceded unlawfully, Nature itself would collapse."

"Yep, you've got it." I was pleased; I had been nurturing that
conceit since assimilating Case's summary.

At position five was an androgynous Hierophant. "He encompasses
both prior pairs," Chuck demonstrated, lifting the card and waving
it back and forth. "Magician and Priestess, Empress and Emperor.
The Hierophant founded the first temple and organized the universe
in symbols and cycles. He's responsible for the tarot deck itself." He
thought about this for a moment, then added triumphantly, a cat
pouncing on a canary, "I get him now in a whole different way:
each card's field contains all the trumps in microcosm, so the overall
matrix is operating at 22 to the 22nd power."

"That's perfect!" I exclaimed. "Here's my take on the Hierophant.
While the Emperor is holding three dimensions in a cube and
locking the stars and planets into their courses, the Hierophant is
inventing astrology and shamanism. During the Renaissance he
turned them into religion and science. He conquered the Emperor
with a single eclipse, but they actually enveloped and transmuted
each other, sort of like your matrix of twenty-twos."

He nodded. "Can you imagine Clinton listening to this? He'd
shit a cow." Then he brought our attention to the next trump,
the Lovers. "They are Adam and Eve in most versions, but really
any man and any woman. From far off, the Magician's golden orb
illuminates their passion. They are looking at each other's souls,
but first they have to transcend their false-personality egos."

He paused for a moment to let me drop into the frame: a naked
woman looking up at a winged androgynous angel, fiery corona
for its hair, wings and hands conducting rays from a golden sun-star

onto a planet. A naked man beams at the woman as she beholds the higher being.

"Eve gets her illumination from the macrocosm," Chuck demonstrated, dabbing a line from her eyes to the angelic effluence. "Adam has to find the reflection of the macrocosm *in her*." He circled a finger around the billowing clouds between them, for they deterred the man's view. "He can't get it from inside himself; it's not there. But she is looking right at the form and transmits its essence to him. The card doesn't necessarily mean man and woman; it's also spirit and soul, anima and animus. It's saying that nothing in the universe operates on its own."

From the Lovers he switched his direction inside the matrix, electing to follow the sixth vertical column rather than complete the first row. Directly beneath the Lovers was Death, card thirteen, a skeleton in armor on a pale horse bearing a black banner with a white snowflake-like ornament—kings, princesses, and children crumbling before his prance. "Now we're following a different tier of emanation. See how the erotic energy of the card above gets translated into a wholly different form in the card below. Death is a kind of love. It creates by transforming; it preserves essence while destroying appearance. What you are calling a snowflake is actually the white rose of immortality. Here, by the way is your Scorpio card: resurrection."

He paused, then amended his take. "The Waite card is misleading. He had some sort of nonsense about concealing a few of the images' esoteric meanings. In traditional versions, there is no horse. The skeleton is standing or walking on the ground, chopping with his scythe. Hands, feet, and decapitated heads lie fall around him. In Case's version a shape like a UFO appears in the left-hand sky. I think that goes back to a mark or rune from centuries earlier, before anyone knew about flying saucers. In general, Case gives esoteric meanings, Waite provides fortune-teller's thumbnails."

From card thirteen he continued a vertical trajectory. "Below Death is its own collective manifestation, number twenty, Judgment. Don't be fooled by the traditional symbolism here. This is not the Day of Judgment but the simultaneous appearance of every creature and event on Earth. They are arising from the coffins of three-dimensional space and floating on a timeless, dimensionless ocean. Waite and Case both spell this out: the forces represented by this trump tear down the limitation of form as teeth break up food." He clenched and extended his fingers a few times over the sea of coffins, then went back to where he had left off with the Lovers.

At the end of the first horizontal row in position seven sat the Chariot, its meaning familiar. It was my favorite symbol complex, so I playfully paraphrased Case, "In his false-motion vehicle flanked by black and white sphinxes beneath a cloth sky, the Charioteer establishes the first city."

"Do you see the fusion of all six of the prior cards here?" Chuck asked.

I did.

"Why don't you summarize them so that I know you got it."

"Okay, the cyclotron of the Magician, the binary ciphers of the Priestess, the floral patio of the Empress, the algebra of the Emperor, the esoteric mudras of the Hierophant, and the galaxy-igniting passion of the Lovers, all leading up to a pre-Persian, pre-Mayan metropolis at the dawn of civilization."

"Good. Remember, the Chauffeur of the seventh trump rides along, unaware that his armor is a symbol too, that his words are not objects, that his vehicle is motionless."

"Yes, the zodiac has become a woven arras, a bonnet hanging above a stony cab travelling so fast it is stationary: the Earth, the City."

That caused him to look up at the darkening violet over Jersey and realize that our window of visibility was closing. "Let's get enough done," he urged, pointing to the second horizontal row, "so that you have a foundation to build on." He picked up at card eight, Strength. "The Waite version is wrong here too. Supposedly showing the angel holding the lion's jaw shut rather than opened conceals some important secret. Anyway, in the traditional version his jaw is opened because he is breathing the first row from the atomic table and formless mind into history: hunters, cultivators, tribes and villages. Of course, it's not really the elements or even their electrons; it is the force behind all that, which is represented by the infinity sign over the angel's head. Jaw opened or closed, the point is, such a lion cannot be mastered—he can only be charmed."

At position nine under the High Priestess, a Hermit stood on snowy mountaintops, bearing a cookie-like star in his lantern. "He has wandered through the integers," Chuck intoned, tempering his voice heraldically as if beginning a fairy tale. "He is an old man with a beard, yet younger in cosmic time than the Fool."

That was the "Stein Man" I knew, the wood-chuck-chuck-chuck from Horace Mann—whimsical and magisterial, an inscrutable blend of Donald Duck and Spinoza.

"The Hermit has no cardinal power. All his potency and wisdom come from his acceptance of prior forces that precede and make him up." Was this attribution or confession?

Night with its early stars was fast upon us, as my friend hastened through Sun and Moon and Star, assigning crabs, pelicans, and battlements, elucidating pools stirred into motion by cosmic meditation, the blue strands of our five senses poured from an angel's earthen jug onto an alien landscape, ocular jellies sucking up the wisdom of molecular sand.

There in evening's glow, Venus bright over the Hudson, the twenty-two buds of the Major Arcana seemed to radiate with not only the last dregs of sunset but their own phosphorescence as they formed a magnificent foliage in the grass. Barges travelled on the River (a form of card seven), the Palisades and Jersey lights (card four) beyond.

So did Chuck teach me the esoteric tarot.

We reentered the metropolis, the World as cosmos—the last and twenty-second trump. The City brooked no sphinxes or tridents; it spun so fast its inhabitants were unaware of its motion. As the zodiac opened and closed at the speed of light, the cube melted, and the anagram of the Wheel of Fortune ran through its permutations *(tarot, ... tora ... rota ...),* Bull and Lion faced each other no more. A new dimension arose trillions of years in the future when there would be a different universe—a different reality for consciousness, a different deck for the descendants of humanity.

We hiked back along the avenue at the Western edge, down its lamp-lit thoroughfares. Creation shimmered inscrutably. Even streetlights and billboards had become illuminated papyri, sacred flames with meanings. Then Chuck proposed that gossamer threads of our very thoughts were manifestations of the forces of gravitational fields around stars—they were cosmic mind-stuff generated by the energy in the deck.

The dancer had become the dance.

On a midsummer eve Aunt Bunny and her compatriots packed wine and towels and hiked to the Lake. The men took their clothes off and dove into chilled water. Afterwards we lay in the sand philosophizing—Johnson versus Goldwater, the bomb, bad marriages. Sam the revolutionary wished he had died there in the hills with Castro on assignment for *Time* because everything since had been downhill for him—his marriage, his career: "Total bullshit, capitalist crapola. Is that what our lives are," he mourned, struggling for articulation against the stars, "one flash of brilliance and then it's over?"

A renowned art-film director couldn't believe Bunny would stay with Paul, so he proposed to her on the spot; she turned him down.

"You'd tire of me," she said.

In late July I made friends with one of the few black guests at Grossinger's—well, not a guest but a regular named Bitty Wood. He was in residence all summer, as his wife, Damita Jo, a nightclub singer, used the Hotel for her base. They hung out there with my grandmother's consent—she still had the authority to sponsor long-term residents, or at least no one dared override her. A lanky middle-aged musician, Bitty sat in the lobby talking bop and poetry, rapping fingers in constant rhythm and laughing with easy good humor at the cluelessness and ostentation around him.

"Dump that freeloader, will you!" my father barked one evening. His threats were not idle ones. Milty Stackel, Irv Jaffee, Jack the waiter ... all had been fired. Each time I'd come back after months away someone else would be missing. Nat the hypnotist, Abe the athletic director, Kurt the ice-skater. "Crooks," he would say.

"All of them?" I would ask, disbelievingly.

"They stole from me." His eyes riveted in revenge.

When I arrived at the beginning of the summer Jimmy McAndrews was gone too. He had made the mistake of phoning some friends in California from Traffic and then joking about it. "Big deal," I said angrily, "a few West Coast calls. He was basically an honest kid."

PG couldn't get over the fact I had known and hadn't told him. "And I don't want you hanging around with you-know-who," he said, not willing to dignify Bitty with a name. "It doesn't look good."

In my letters I brought Lindy up to date on Chuck, Schuy, Diana, my job, the Hotel, even Smokey. She was sorry to be so slow in answering. Her only mention of Steve was an embarrassed aside that he had dumped her. But now there was someone else:

> I date police reporters and get depressed by their views, and for the first time in my life went out with a married man the other night. I must have been totally out of my mind to think that all he wanted was intellectual companionship, but I didn't know so found out. I don't want to do reference work in sin; there always seem to be bigger and better sins just when you think you've exhausted the list. He was interesting, as people are....

Smokey and I continued to spend evenings together, exploring our flirtation. But our making out was becoming more like a wrestling match. One night her kisses became bites; she gnawed my upper and lower lips as if she were perforating a line. It hurt more than seduced. I held her, half like a boxer trying to restrain an opponent, half like a lover. Then I let go and ran my hands lightly over her body under her dress. She sighed, returned my hug, then clawed my back, first sensually, then more like a panther—ow! Suddenly she sat up hard against the wall—thump! She put her hair back in place. I looked at her.

She said nothing.

A short, swaggering cook at the Hotel had taken a liking to her and begun to date her on alternate nights. When she and I went out to dinner, he followed the JG on his motorcycle, buzzing us left and right. One time we lost him en route to a diner but, when we came out ninety minutes later, the car wouldn't start. Then—in speechless mime—he appeared from behind a tree, threw open the hood, plugged the distributor head in, and zoomed off on his cycle. She shook her head admonishingly.

The next morning at breakfast I blabbed a version of this event to the Head of Security who was nursing his last cup of coffee as I arrived. Some guy wanted to date the girl I was going out with and had messed with the JG, I said. No big deal, just an entertaining story. That night Jean shot over from her station to confront me, eyes like guns. "You shouldn't have done that!"

I looked at her blankly, imagining something sexual. "I would have handled it," she fumed; then more quietly: "There wasn't any damage done."

The house detective had approached her courting cook and threatened his job.

"I didn't mean for that to happen," I protested.

"Sure, you didn't!" She turned and marched away. I saw myself now through *her* eyes, sitting at the head table among the bosses— the owner's son, a model of false innocence.

I went to apologize to the cook at his post in the kitchen. Before I could speak he spat out his challenge: "You can do anything you want, but it's not going to stop me. Do you know that I've given her my mother's ring? That ring is sacred to me!" He was almost hysterical. "I'm going to marry her. I just want you to know that."

"I'm not your rival," I said. "Smokey's just a friend." But, even as I tried to appease him, summoning all the earnestness I could muster, I was blarneying us both. Jean and I were *hardly* just friends We may not have gone beyond the rudiments of making out, but that was daring for its time, and a luxury and novelty *pour moi.* I had never engaged in idle erotic play before, so I wanted it to continue. Yet my sexual dalliances couldn't approach the gravity of this guy's propositions. Even with the distributor-head caper, I was profane by comparison.

I was beginning to see my heedlessness, my vain assumptions and spurious modesty. It had been a joke to try to pass myself off as an artist or Jean's peer. I was the boss's son, a ruling-class fink; I could never *not* be that.

A muddle of agendas, I tried to explain myself to her in a letter. I knew we weren't right for each other, but how to say that without risking the what was left of our tryst. I acknowledged that she had this other, more serious courter. But was she encouraging his pursuit—did she want to marry him—or was she merely angry at me?

Likely if she had been a boy (or I a girl) Smokey and I would have been enemies. I was the wiry, innocent youth; she the bruising, worldwise trucker. We necked as much out of antipathy toward each other's types as attraction. Unconsciously we were combatants from centuries of our ancestors' wars.

She wanted to pummel me as much as caress me; the more intimate the act, the less she could discriminate the two. My appeal was mainly as an object of curiosity, plus a sadomasochistic desire to touch the enemy, to seduce him and get him under her power. *But I was just as curious about her.*

I closed my letter by apologizing for what that had happened. I wanted to sound noble and pure. I oozed false innocence. Her answer was indignant and revealing: "You think just because your father owns this place you can make all the rules and push everyone around."

We parted enemies. We had indulged in a brief erotic encounter before sinking back into our ethnic stereotypes.

Lunchtime at the *Democrat,* everyone was shooting the breeze around the presses. I sat at a lone desk in the copy room, laying down the tarot as Chuck had instructed me: three rows of seven, The Fool aloft. Before me sat the upside-down Hanged Man; the Magician with his platform of sigils; the High Priestess with her rippling robes and fruited veil; the Tower with its larval sparks and toppling king and knave; the lantern-bearing Hermit; the many-rayed Sun with its row of flowers and child-bearing horse; the angel of Temperance pouring her unidentified vibration between gold cups; the legatee of Justice, bearing an ethereal sword in one hand, the scales of quantum physics in the other—he, the Charioteer, the

Devil, and the Lovers quadruple personae of the same emanation. Like Vance Packard's "hidden persuaders," these keys radiated a subliminal message; only it hadn't been loaded cynically by executives at ad agencies but was disseminated by avatars in other realms. (The admen's too of course, over the long haul.)

In the sun in the window the cards were beautiful—not great art but beautiful: their esoteric colors, the faces, the glyphs, the white pillars of temples, the stream of celestial mind-stuff deliquescing unconscious waters....

I followed the azure rivulet that materialized out of the Priestess' robes, pouring across the downed oxbow moon at her feet, bubbling behind the granite cliffs of the Emperor, between edifices of the Chariot and the City, until it drained through galaxies and civilizations into pools of Star and Moon and became an ocean of many dimensions on which ordinary boxes floated.

An actual blue seemed to trickle across the semblances as they came together—a three-dimensional deep image as alive and real as the world, only more radiant and essential for converting symbols into meanings. It was startling, hallucinogenic, not like a dream at all but an emanation from a different portal.

Then I looked up and saw the water along the rocks of Callicoon Creek. It had transferred its subliminal after-image to the shiny inked cards and turned their cartoon into a four-dimensional hologram. Matter, phenomenon, and symbol were one. I had known that intellectually; now it was lucid.

Leaves rustled against dusty windows, sunlight through them and dust breaking into thousands of coins on the table. Around me was the yellowing rag on rollers, the decay of history, of material reality. All this lived and would die, as Beckett had observed, but it wasn't empty or, more accurately, its emptiness was precisely its fullness. *Malone* and *Malloy* had roused and inspired me, but their despair and nullity were not the foundation of the universe; they were a way to feel how profound and antithetical *the forces of the universe actually are.*

Our lives posed no danger to the real Creation. Even the atomic bomb was the handiwork of the Magician; so was Fred's fallout shelter—a mere Hierophantic outpost and shack. The Death Card stood near the center with his scythe. In my mind's eye the hermetic archetype prevailed, commuting Waite's horse-borne skeleton into its more fearsome unmounted form, mowing down every living form but obliterating nothing, transforming only so that new cells, new molecules, new electrons, new views of the cosmos were born from the paring of antiquated ones: a billion insects dancing in the fields beyond.

I could hear the ripple of the Priestess' robes, Callicoon Creek rushing toward Jeffersonsville. I stared at its twinkling rocks. I looked up through the trees at a disk in the sky. Even the so-called hydrogen of its formation was a mask concealing a Magician; Ahab knew as much. I turned down to the deck and, for an instant, saw white suns exploding everywhere, in alien skies against dreamlike arrases. I saw wheels turning and currents delivering signs deeper and deeper into substance. The figures of men and women wandering through the deck became the same man and woman, not at different moments but at once.

This wasn't a fantasy. I was staring into the actual cosmos with my third eye.

The vision held for five seconds, maybe six, maybe seven; then the cards fell back into their temporal grid.

I stood in a daze. Tears crinkled the corners of my eyes. I wiped them away and poked my head into the next room. Fred, his sister, and the others were back at work. I wanted to shout, but I couldn't. They were standing in spirit fire and didn't know it.

And at night, filled to the brim, I had no doubt anymore, so I sent Lindy my joyfulness in a poem:

> *Do you listen*
> *To the burning of the stars?*
> *I am the burning of the stars:*
> *Listen to me....*
> *Do you search*
> *For the silent sandy people?*
> *I lead them:*
> *Follow me.*

Do you hear
Sometimes a distant lonely whisper?
I hold one promise:
It is there.
Do you want
The rainbow flock?
I am one of its sheep:
Want me!

"Some long overdue letter here," she wrote back a week later. "I thought your poem was beautiful and good. It sang, as they say here, and the song it sang was good. You are doing good things still, are amazingly productive and active politically and writing-wise."

We were more than halfway through the summer and still dancing, still possible—still on the brink.

2

HALLOWEEN

In August, Fred assigned me my grandmother's Senate testimony on the prospective construction of a Sullivan County Airport. "This way," he teased, "I'm sure to get the inside dope." I flew to Washington with her and Milton Blackstone. Milton had long believed that aviation was the only way to save the Catskills. Confident in his powers of persuasion, he viewed the hearing as an opportunity to address the real power brokers. We were checking into our hotel when Grandma was paged. Minutes later Milton whispered the news. While we were en route, Harry Grossinger, back in New York, had died of a heart attack.

Standing there transfixed, Grandma barely noticed us, her gaze on a remote horizon. "At last!" she whispered. "He lived too long, the bastard."

It was a woman I had never seen.

We rushed back to the airport where Milton hired a private plane. He would stay and testify; I would accompany my grandmother home.

We squeezed into a cabin with two young pilots. They taxied, took off, and headed north. We flew inland from the coast, then over the New York line, the co-pilot consulting a map (neither had been that far north) ... finally to the vicinity of Grossinger's.

Enormous thunderheads loomed over the Hotel. I saw them up ahead, floating in 3-D Ektachrome, violet, amethyst, and black, laden with moisture and ions, the G.'s familiar grid of buildings below at Monopoly-board scale. As the pilot descended to land, we floated into sudden darkness. Hail slapped against the windows. The plane rocked and jerked. My grandmother staring into empty space murmured bitterly, "It's him. I can see him. He's trying to keep me out."

The pilots ignored her as an addled old woman. They rode the bumps and howled in glee.

I trusted her vision implicitly, but I was also unafraid. If it was Grandpa indeed, I presumed he would spare me. First, though, he would make his point.

Each time we approached the Grossinger's runway, we were buffeted so hard we were forced to pull away.

"It ain't gonna work, buddy," conceded the pilot.

The storm was brief and concentrated—by newspaper accounts the worst flooding ever recorded in the county. It washed out both of Harry's current skeletal constructions and blew down trees that had stood for centuries.

The pilot searched in nearby sunshine for an alternate site, finally picking a meadow outside Monticello and radioing its position. By the time we came bouncing along the pasture the JG was waiting at the edge of the weeds.

My father retreated to his sister's house on the grounds to sit *shiva*, the required Orthodox mourning. Aunt Bunny stopped seeing her friends out of solidarity and respect. She did not realize how much she required their support to keep her sane, how long she had been out of touch with the G.'s ethnic provincialism and *shtetl* roots. In her mind she was a fledgling intellectual apprenticing with mentors, a young woman entertaining potential suitors. She had been transacting this dual identity so gracefully and incontrovertibly that she had forgotten it was on loan, dependent on her husband's willingness to live a double life too. Now the disparity of the two worlds—one inescapably intimate, the other almost, but not quite, possible—tore her apart. I watched her become more and more morose. One evening I found her sitting on her bed, arms tucked in close to herself, fists clenched.

"Jeez," she said, "this is the big one, the blue devil itself. I don't know if I can make it." She braced, back against the headboard. Earlier that month she and I had gone to see *Night of the Iguana,* the movie of Tennessee Williams' play about panic; now she was invoking Williams' figure of speech. She had the same instinct as I had had a few months earlier, wanting a name for the unnameable, an escort in the uncompassed void. I pulled up a tremulous chair. For all our discussion of panic I had never seen one of hers.

After cuffing her clenched fists into each other, head hung, eyes shut, she slowly regained composure and paraphrased Richard Burton's lines: "This is like a crucifixion without nails. I see twilight through the branches, the coming dark. Like the iguana I am one of God's creatures at the end of its rope."

"At least you are eloquent in your pain."

She laughed. "A lot of good it does me."

When my own words ran out, I combined Beckett and Keats as if a playwright were penning my lines too: "Was I sleeping, while the others suffered? Am I sleeping yet? This is the court's eternal session, the courtiers crushed by the golden weight of their robes. Tomorrow, when I wake, or think I do, what shall I say of today?"

"Thank you, Richard. You bring me the best company, the kind that recognizes who I am, what's happening to me." That was a given—I had just been there. "Your father hasn't a clue."

On the stereo I played Jimmie Rodgers—plaintive, accordionlike notes: *"...someday some old familiar rain / will come along and know my name...."* We both knew that rain; our lives were joined by it.

The next weekend, putting her hopes in a change of scenery, she arranged for a Hotel driver take herself, my brothers, and me to her parents' house in Atlantic City. The trip coincided with the Democratic Convention beginning August 24th, so instead of requesting time off I persuaded Fred to let me cover it.

In reality there was nothing to cover. It was like a stadium with no game, endless cheering for invisible home runs, and I could barely see anything from the back of the hall, just rollicking, placard-waving delegates. Only the belief that all this bedlam was a rally against the warmongers made it tenable. *Time* rover Sam Halpern, my pal from Bunny's soirées, had warned us, under a bright moon at Grossinger Lake, that prognosis was an illusion; beneath their guises Goldwater and Johnson were the same man. "People say this is a crossroads election," he announced. "I don't think so. I think it's a charade. And we are fools to allow it."

Paul Stern had proposed as much at Phi Psi. The years would prove them right.

Bitty Wood was also in town for the Big Event, and one night he picked me up and drove us to a nightclub where we sat at a table listening to jazz. The comedian Dick Gregory sneaked up and startled Bitty by embracing him from behind; then, after much laughing and riffing, accepted his offer to take the empty seat. The two men traded lyrics back and forth.

"Something big's coming down in Philly," said Gregory. "The people is angry."

"Amen, brother. Amen."

I couldn't believe that a kid from Grossinger's was privileged to be in their company. But Bitty put his arm around me and said, "He's my man."

If the heart of human existence is sheer terror on one side, the power of the Magician on the other (and real politics in the ghettos, Bitty Wood), then what are thousands of people cheering and brandishing their banners for? I sat up past midnight writing these thoughts to Lindy and sent them off—Atlantic City postmark.

Our letters crossed. There was one waiting for me at the Hotel. She was delighted I got to go to the convention and wanted more of an account. She was seeing the married man, a fellow reporter. She wrote. "He's the star of the *Rocky Mountain News* city room. I'm the only girl city-side, so this is a daring and foolhardy affair to try to hide. There's also the risk my parents will find out." She told me not to worry about her.

I went out driving at night—rural catacombs, closer and closer to Silver Lake as if drawn by Chipinaw. In droves along the roadsides were camp counselors—guys and gals my age hitching back to their jobs from an evening off. I zoomed past in my ridiculously pretentious car. Buddies waiting tables at the Hotel had told me that picking up hitchhikers was a good way to meet girls, so I summoned my courage one night and stopped alongside a female cluster. I took three of them back to their camp, five miles of small talk. The one called Diane, the prettiest, was spunky enough to ask me to invite her to Grossinger's "or better still, Amherst Homecoming weekend." I meant to get her Bronx number but lost my chance. The camp's owner was waiting at curfew by the gate. He looked at the license plate, quizzed me, then proclaimed, "No son of Paul Grossinger is going to have anything to do with my girls. [Pause.] Give my regards to your father, young man."

I did, and he loved it. He was still telling the story decades later, guffawing, "No son of Paul Grossinger.... " So the locals knew his scuzzy reputation.

I got out of there so fast that the wheels of the Lincoln spun dirt. That was mortifying too, as if I were intentionally showing off. The takeoff, plus the owner's salutation, deterred me from reconnecting with Diane. When I finally found my nerve, the camp had closed for the season.

Another night I came to a moonlit meadow where, as Chipinaw tots, we had gone for haywagon rides. I turned the car around by pulling onto the shoulder. My headlights, crashing through branches, illuminated a field. I stared into its nocturnal waterglobe, a vista as crisp as a tarot card. In front of me hung a gigantic web, the stony silhouette of its maker at the center. This was a focal rune, startling for its clarity—trumps are rarely dropped so explicitly into the world.

I had come to a warp in my own fabric. I knew that spider. His placement was a marker, as indeterminately recognizable as the crack between ceiling and wall had once been. It was an omen from a more complicated landscape or from an impersonal intelligence. I read the dichotomy of my life in him: terror or revelation, I had to choose. He made that offer neutrally, a signature at the crossroads. What preference has a spider, after all, what axe to grind except ballast in his gossamer strands? Trump eleven, sword and scales— on one side the Wheel of Fortune, on the other the Hanged Man.

Back at the house I began pouring myself glasses of straight vodka. I put the Kweskin Jug Band on the stereo, Geoff Muldaur singing

"Wild About My Loving": *"Well, sergeant, sergeant please, / women 'round here won't let me see no peace."* I was probing the depth of the blues, my right to be this askew … and suddenly I was dizzy. I called out to Emma who thundered down the stairs: "Oh, Lordy, you damn drunk."

I was glad she lingered. I could sense the periphery of an unforgiving cloud.

"You haven't watched a single ballgame with me all summer," she pouted. "You just fussing about girls. No wonder you drunk. You'll be good and drunk till you forget about them dames, mind me." I followed her back upstairs and collapsed on the floor before the Mets game. When it was over I stumbled into my room and fell into an amnesia-like sleep.

During my lunches with George von Hillshimer, he and I had talked about my brothers, in particular Michael because he was as academically marginal as many of George's kids and had already bombed out of two institutions similar to Summer Lane. A victim of Grossinger's with its vagrant lifestyle and lax parenting, Michael had little use for authority or schoolwork. By fifteen he was mired in a quirky combination of rage and slapstick, watching TV for days on end in his pajamas—cartoons to comedies to Westerns to "Little Rascals," old movies all afternoon. I began to imagine Summer Lane as his salvation, a community acknowledging alienation without trying to crush spirit—and remarkably just down the road.

George was candid about his motives: if a Grossinger kid attended his school, it would not only generate some income but might get the County off his back. When I told Aunt Bunny, she was dubious but ultimately agreed to an audience. "I trust your judgment," she said, "and we've run out of other options." A few moments later her contrary voice spoke. "Unfortunately Summer Lane sounds much too far out for your brother. And bringing your father together with a man in a collar—that won't fly. But call your friend, and we'll see."

I invited Reverend von Hillshimer to dinner.

I warned him about the deadly cocktail that would be served—Zionism and xenophobia. George pooh-poohed the matter—old hat to him. He was a professional firebrand and jangler of paradigms, seasoned anew in Mississippi. Confronted by a mere marshmallow resort he couldn't reconcile himself to less than full triumph. Discounting the true longshot, he became megalomaniacal, rehearsing speeches he planned to deliver, getting ahead of himself to the spoils of success. Folks at Summer Lane were casting spells, doing rain dances. I had set in motion a fiasco I could no longer interdict.

I gave George directions. With a predatory smile, he promised not to wear a collar.

On the eve of the event I called the front gate and left word to let Mr. von Hillshimer through. At the appointed hour I paced the top of the hill, scanning for his car. Right on time the jalopy rumbled up the main drag and literally spat three times before exhaling beside a row of Lincolns and Caddies. George patted each of them on the fins and bowed to me. I grabbed his hand in delight.

Aunt Bunny seated him on one side of the table beside Michael, James and me on the other; herself and my father at the heads. Emma served salad as George introduced himself to my brother. He quizzed him about his present school and then began to describe Summer Lane. With tentative interest, Michael met his gaze and asked: "So how much work do kids have to do at your place?" Before George could answer, my father interrupted.

"I should tell you, Reverend, I attended military academy myself in Peekskill and I don't like regimented schools." George started to respond, but PG raised his hand and asked to finish. He said that he and his wife had put together a list of schools for Michael to consider and he thought it best he stay within his own religion.

He lectured so long and imperiously that I cringed. It was clear that wasn't going to give Summer Lane a chance.

I knew that George had a lot at stake and also that he would not stand being humiliated. I watched him lose and regain composure. When my father ran out of steam, the feral priest called up his reserves of energy and, with admirable restraint, answered all PG's objections one by one. On a roll, he made extravagant promises, like that he would hire a rabbi of my father's choosing. Then without waiting for a response, he turned to Michael and asked him what he was looking for in a school.

PG jumped back in. "Reverend, the matter has nothing to do with Michael; it's Michael's parents who are making this decision. If you have anything to say, please address it to me."

I could barely keep myself from interceding. Here was a man of stature and achievement: a minister, a marcher for civil rights. He was soliciting Michael's legitimate opinion. He shouldn't have to be subjected to bullying and rudeness. I turned to Bunny for help.

"I'm afraid what happens to Michael is his father's decision."

"Do you agree?"

PG was glaring at me as she stammered, then found a tack: "I'm sure Mr. von Hillshimer's school is excellent, but I don't think it's for your brother." Ostensibly victorious, my father decided to lighten the mood with a series of jokes about his experiences with "men of the cloth." Reverend George kept any subsequent thoughts to himself. He remained unruffled and polite.

No matter how angry I had been at my father in the past I had always thought of him as a decent person at core, reliable when the chips were down, even after he beat me. Now I saw a willful, spoiled child—a smug, self-aggrandizing autocrat—ordering around a black maid and, under the thinnest sham of civility, flaunting his wealth. A part of Bunny was wed to this man, irrevocably. She was no help at all. As for what Michael might have wanted—that got lost in the shuffle; they didn't care about him having a voice.

We made it through the meal without further embarrassments. After dessert I accompanied George down the stone path through the garden toward his car. We were silent most of the way as my mind raced for something to say. "This place is a menace, my friend," he finally offered. "Leave quietly and by stealth or it will cannibalize you." Then he bent over and collapsed on the lawn. I didn't know what was happening; I thought maybe he was sick. I started to run back to the house for help. Then I realized he was actually rolling in the grass laughing. I was simultaneously startled and relieved. He pulled his body up to its full height in metameres like a giant cricket. "You'll have to pardon me," he said. "I was holding all of that in."

I smiled nervously as I assured him it was okay. I apologized for my parents and for bringing him there with false hopes. "They were worse than I ever imagined."

"So it wasn't a bad evening," he proclaimed with unpredictable cheeriness, "because you learned something." He took a few more steps and, as we reached his vehicle, turned back to me. With a hard stare he added, "Forgive me, Richard, but at my father's house in Germany your father wouldn't have been fed with the hogs."

I heard him say it, shook his hand, and waved to him as he drove off. Then it sank in. He knew, as did I, that he spoke as a German less than a generation after Hitler. He had reduced my father to a farm animal. I felt the coldness of his glance. I was a Grossinger too. Would I have been fed (or even denied service) with his father's hogs?

Yet another part of me met him in brutal assessment. My father was not just a grumpy clown; he was an irresponsible boor, even a thug—I had to know that by now. I stood, looking out over his Hotel, the glowing glass cupolas of the indoor pool and faux Tudor façades of guest buildings, an iconic skyline. For virtually my whole life I had deemed this place a paradise, a haven and sanctuary. I may have mocked it or decried its elitism and lack of social conscience, but I considered it an important locale in the universe.

Now I realized it was nothing. It was the cheap passing vanity of Jewish peasants, arrogant and graceless in their fortune, oblivious to the Wheel of Fate whose turning brought them to this perch and could crush them in a tick, even as it had crushed far greater dynasties and nations.

Bunny's panics returned big-time. She lay in bed trembling, grasping at the end table, the headboard, her pillow, anything. Then she tossed the pillows away and clutched the bottom sheet so tightly I thought it would rip. She was sobbing.

"Paul," she cried to her husband, "I'm useless. Have them put me out of my misery."

He indicated I should leave.

He wouldn't let me see her later. "Not after the damage you've done. I *told* you two to stop talking. You just upset each other. She has enough problems as it is."

A doctor came from New York and ordered her to be hospitalized. My father announced she would be "incommunicado." "Indefinitely," he snapped, as I watched her being bundled off into the Hotel car.

What did I feel then? Hard to say. Numbness, fury, relief I had escaped a similar predicament unscathed.... Transitions paralyzed me. At moments like this I turned into Martha, my mother's alienation and narcissism my default state too. That quashed any nascent sympathy or tenderness. What I felt mostly was defiance. And selfish regard for my own survival.

This wasn't my family, it never had been.

A week later I heard that Bunny's "cure" was to be shock treatment followed by two months of hospitalization. Meanwhile PG had stopped talking to me. He didn't seem to know I existed. Whenever he passed me he looked away. On one occasion, though, he stopped to acknowledge my presence with Emma and the Mets in the living room, asking, "How's my communist son?"

"Okay, I guess." I was moved to tears by this backhanded revival of his affection.

"What's the score, are they winning for a change?"

Emma took up the volley: "They'ze havin' a fine night, Mr. G."

Just before I left for college—when I was most alienated from him, and he from me—he called me into his office and told me he had a surprise. I racked my brain for what sort of riddle this was. "Go down to the front of the Main Building," he resumed with a deadpan grin. I would not have guessed in a million years. As he watched from his window, the head of Traffic handed me the keys to a small yellow car parked at the entrance. "It's yours apparently," the guy declared. "Ford Mustang."

I had never heard of the model, but it was a cool-looking, racing-car-like object.

"You won't be monopolizing the JG anymore, I guess," my father yelled down.

I packed it for Amherst with my jugs and plastic tree, cans of

twilight-blue paint, a discarded stained-glass lantern from the
Nightwatch, and a bright lemon Mexican blanket I had bought in
Greenwich Village. I loved the car's new bowling-alley smell and
the way the miles climbed into their first hundreds as I drove into
Massachusetts. This was a magnificent, unwarranted gift.

I spent the days before school painting the walls of my room indigo. I
made a temporary couch in the corner by draping my sunny coverlet
over a mattress. Then, with screwdriver and electrical tape I put in
an overhead stained-glass fixture by trial and error—my first light.
"City boy no more," I thought, picturing Mr. Borrig and Ramon
there watching.

My aesthetics startled Marty when he arrived. "But I guess it's
okay. It's, well, uh … different. I can live with it, I think. It looks
a little like an oasis at sunset."

As a junior I had to declare a major. English was the only practicable
option left. In order to catch up on credits I signed up for seminars
on Yeats, Faulkner, and Sixteenth-Century literature, plus a writing
class, this one at Smith with a visiting novelist named Stanley Elkin.

Lindy called me as soon as she was back, and I sped over to Laura
Scales. She sprang downstairs, vibrant and bubbly. We stared at each
other; then she said, warily (as Lisa), "Hello, kiddo."

We smiled, kissed quickly, and walked outside. I pointed to the
car: yellow baby with a red, white, and blue LBJ/USA bumper
sticker.

"What! They just gave that to you?"

I nodded, grinning.

"I hope it doesn't spoil you," she said.

I gave her a look of—how could you think such a thing?

"We can't repeat last spring," she interjected after a while. "I'm
in love with Jim."

He had left his wife and, in a month, would be moving to New
York to take a new job with an advertising agency. From then on
she would be seeing him regularly.

"I'm not really right for you and, by pretending, I'm making it hard for you to find an appropriate girl."

"How do I fail?"

"I have no way of making it sound nice. He's so much older. He's a man."

"What am I?"

"Not yet a man."

"Can you wait?"

"It's you who can't wait. You think you're in love with me now, but you'll find so many nymphet girls who will fall at your feet you'll forget I even existed. I don't want to be around for that."

"I won't do that," I insisted.

A cat came out from a yard and wound around her legs. "Maybe if I had a cat, I wouldn't need to get married. You want to arrange that?" Girls were so mercurial and unpredictable. To me this was dead serious stuff.

After dinner I lingered in the car outside Laura Scales, asking perversely if she had slept with him. She avoided the question ("None of your business"), but I persisted, until she said of course she had. Long after she had gone upstairs I sat there in my funk, unwilling to start the car.

I was at Smith each week for my writing class, so sometimes Lindy and I went to lunch together. Many of our exchanges were playful and low-key, but I had lapses into solipsism. One time, I berated her for her taste: Who would go out with a bourgeois reporter from a second-rate newspaper, some guy who would leave his wife and kids for a college girl—plus a job in an advertising agency of all things? She defended herself in a letter:

> Cut the shit, kiddo, about the dilettantism. Just like everyone else you go along saying great things and then just fall on your face every once in a while by saying something like that. I've thought about the journey that's ahead of me and of us. Because I am in love with a man who is more bound to the earth than I am does not mean I am a dilettante. For all my haziness, I am damn sure of what I must do to stay alive in this world by preparing for the

next (and I don't mean heaven), and if anyone or thing becomes a threat to that aim, he will fade out, as Steve did. Let me be free, and cut the "I told you so's" and the "You'll be sorryies."

For two weeks after that I kept away, not calling or visiting, trying not to think about her … until, one day, walking from the parking lot to my class, I passed her riding her bike and waved cheerily. She looked at me, burst into tears, and sped off, a kelpie on tires.

"She must care," I thought, "I must be special to her."

With the graduation of the seniors ahead of us and the entry of a new sophomore class we were upperclassmen, no longer the greenhorns of Phi Psi. Tripp was back, but not as a member. He had dropped out of school, and his family wasn't paying any bills. He had an old credit card that still seemed to work, so he would fill my car with gas and I'd give him cash. He lived in the woods east of Amherst in a cabin with that other renegade Eric the Rat. From there he was casting a new play.

His Porsche had fallen into disrepair, so, throughout that fall, I picked him up on the dirt road and drove him to his auditions with actresses. "I knew it was worth cultivating you, Grossinger," he said. "You're a man of compassion."

Schuy returned as Scotty with a full mustache. I rarely saw him. Focused on building up his grades to apply to graduate school in psychology, he worked hard all week and on weekends drove into New York to see Dona.

"I've got to make every moment count," he told me in a moment of rare volubility and candor. "I've got no more moves to spare."

I was relieved to not be there yet.

My course material seemed to corroborate the summer's vision—the alchemical metaphors of the sixteenth-century poets, the mind-flow through *As I Lay Dying* and *Absalom, Absalom!,* the lunar pulses of William Butler Yeats. Amid cricket songs and linnet's wings, I drank from the fountain of *"I will arise and go now, / and go to Innisfree"* while imbuing myself with Faulkner's rhythms and themes.

An omniscient voice spoke from beyond Miss Rosa, Quentin, and Charles Bon—perhaps Faulkner himself: *"who even at nineteen must have known that living is one constant and perpetual instant when the arras-veil before what-is-to-be hangs docile and even glad to the lightest naked touch if we had dared, were brave enough (not wise enough: no wisdom needed here) to make the rending gash ..."*

This was not only vaguely but *precisely* my life, the sort of precept I needed in order to act—brave enough, no special wisdom needed, the arras-veil hanging quite docile and even glad to my lightest naked touch, if only I dared.

Absalom's valiant lyricism struck at my heart; it bore my sense of peril, of withheld apotheosis, of dark and coiled ancestry: *"the prisoner soul, miasmal distillant, wroils ever upward sunward, tugs its prisoner arteries and veins and prisoning in its turn that spark, that dream which, as the globy and complete instant of its freedom mirrors and repeats (repeats?, creates, reduces to a fragile evanescent iridescent sphere) all of space and time and massy earth.... "*

At nineteen I too was living a constant and perpetual instant, careening before a mystery within another, striving for words where there were none, trying to give voice to a fleeting oracle, to dash my own breakwater syntax upon the fog-ridden lagoons.

Then there were higher churches sounding more ominous calls. *"And what rough beast,"* warned Yeats, *"its hour come round at last / Slouches towards Bethlehem to be born?"*

I had the tarot matrix, but I needed a personal article of faith, something to tie my acts of soothsaying to the boy on 96th Street with his gift of a saucer. I required a different dream now, a more anchorable spaceship. Like Bridey, I needed a church with a human confessional and a priest to put Fabian and the Hierophant on a common wavelengths. Otherwise I was far adrift in my own labyrinth.

For years since my Horace Mann pals had posed Jung as a less colonialist alternative to Freud, I had been eyeing the black volumes of his *Collected Works*. When I first heard the name, I thought he was Chinese and imagined his texts as Confucian or Communist. Once I got who he was—none of the above—I tried to deduce what manner of symbols might be in them, how they could be different from those in the all-encompassing *Interpretation of Dreams*. "Symbols don't have to be Western," Bob Alpert had pontificated. "They can be Egyptian, Persian, African, even American Indian. No one made European logic king of the universe." He insisted that Karl Marx and Carl Jung were reconcilable insofar as they both subverted the bourgeois belief system.

It made sense, but I was still faithful to Dr. Fabian. Wary of anti-psychoanalytic detractors. I found ample excuses not to explore a different take. After all what did Egyptian symbols have to do with my own unconscious? Now in the autumn of my awakening and discontent, an African detour was precisely what I craved.

In New York I bought two volumes, *The Archetypes and the Collective Unconscious* and *Symbols of Transformation*. I started with *Archetypes'* color plates of mandalas, a patient's representations of her inner world. In them I recognized some of Chuck's motifs of tarot divination but transposed into a psychoanalytic context. Here were the Magician, the Chariot, and the Star, operating as preconscious personal symbols, yet projected onto a mytho-historical canvas.

Beneath familiar biographical motifs were layers of primordial forms and shapes, not limited to our experiences, even to our lifetimes. Jung dubbed this "the collective unconscious" to distinguish it from the mere subliminal mind of our egos. It contained primal material given shape by archetypes—transpersonal elements of the universe, the planet, and of course the human psyche. These transmitted certain shapes, many of which were symmetrical or geometric and entrained by archaic imagery from the Earth's biological and cultural evolution. Their patterns broke through spontaneously as characters and themes in fairy tales, myths, and dreams, and were present subconsciously in the texts of early alchemists and astronomers, giving psychic as well as material form to minerals and constellations. Archetypal symbols were repeated in unbroken chains from Babylonian zodiacs and designs in Mediaeval European stained-glass windows to pictographs in Navaho sand-paintings and the integers of mathematics and particles of modern physics.

In a way I couldn't have foreseen, the symbolic system into which
Fabian had initiated me was primeval and vast in all directions.
For Jung, psychoanalysis was not just a roll call of traumas or a set
of protocols for treating neurotic symptoms; it didn't epitomize
bedwetting or other behavioral malfeasances; it was an excavation
of the soul's lost autobiography. Not only do we suppress, as Freud
assayed, our instinctual drives—forbidden wishes and desires—we
deny our genealogy in a fathomless universe, our connection to the
psychophysical reality of Nature.

Each of us attempts to restore this link, to give form to Psyche's
unconscious narrative. Through everyday acts we animate a saga Jung
called individuation—an assimilation of our ordinary experiences
into myth-like dramas with ontological, even theogonic implications.
Enhancing that process should be the *true* goal of therapy.

Had Fabian known this? And if he approved of Jung's primordial
representations, why had he not applied a complex like the Shadow
to my metastasis of the dungeon stairs or invoked a supernatural
taboo-smasher like the Trickster or Clown to embrace my chimerical
pranks? That would have been more in keeping with their augury and
scope: the god Pan waking from his nap with a start and, not knowing
where he was, giving such a startled shout that it stampeded the flocks.

Instead he aggrandized a minor social rift, my parents' divorce;
he must have been a loyal Freudian through and through.

Reading Jung was like drinking from the pebbled fountain in
Central Park, quenching an old thirst. His texts reclaimed the world
of Freudian symbolism as if I were a wide-eyed whelp back in a
magician's chamber, about to be shown the floating veil over the
world but this time at an exponential scale.

Jung projected elementary symbols through a hierarchy of *a priori*
meanings that had been dormant in them all along. The clue in the
embers was the glyph in the papyrus, the rune in mosque, the angel
in the stained-glass window, the Corn Mother in the sand-matrix.

Fabian and I never took the transformation of signs or its under-
current of profundity into what it felt like or portended. A sacred
kaleidoscope intimated throughout our five-year exegesis was never
even addressed

In *Symbols of Transformation* Jung analyzed journeys of rebirth from New Guinea to old Cambodia, from the sages of India and Rome to the Tlingit natives of Alaska. As I worked my way through "The Hymn of Creation," "The Song of the Moth," and "The Battle for Deliverance from the Mother," I began to understand my earliest panics differently. I had been involved in a primitive form of magical conversion, the same operation as shamans and alchemists, though at a level appropriate for a child.

Jackal-headed Anubis bending over a mummy, the sun pierced by the teeth of an alchemical lion and dripping blood—these were ciphers, fused layers of overarching meanings that transcended and encompassed their own images. They weren't the sort of historiographic deconstruction we did freshman year either—they were an iconography *preceding history*.

I had been drawing on such hidden archetypes, individuating through them. They had guided me into publishing the *Chirp* during Color War. They had chanted through Buddy Holly and Dion & the Belmonts. They led me to the tarot, then to Jung himself. Even baseball had been an act of individuation—the negative charge of 1960 World Series converted through Melville's *Whale* and the Kalin Twins singing "Forget Me Not" into my first pages for Mr. Ervin.

There *was* an exogenous intelligence and it was trying to provide me with a vehicle more germinal and lasting than a saucer, though it owed a boy a saucer too, to get him wending homeward via unknown stars.

The voice on the radio had posed a threat to my initial phase of consciousness. The sheer depth of the universe and our existence in it is terrifying, especially if encountered too young, if forced upon a child's unshaped psyche by a lesion in its vicinity. Consciousness cannot handle premature revelations without fissuring and coming asunder. An ego formed under these circumstances is at continual risk of obliteration from an immanent source that feels both extrinsically real and to be emerging from *its own unconscious*. That's why there seems no escape.

The unformed ghosts at my window, the custodians of the dungeon stairs were not remorseless antagonists and tormentors, they were symbols of transformation right from Jung's logos, fugitives perhaps from my mother's failed integration. And their abominations provided the precise energies needed for their transubstantiation.

The universe creates anathemas—as brutal and devious, malign and convincing, as possible—in order to fashion a pathway for angels. Without hell realms, there would be no ground for salvation, no cobble for creatures like us to tread a cosmos, no way to expiate karma. Our demons hold the seeds of transformation and metamorphosis *before any conscious transmutation has been attempted.* That is why they are so scary, so harsh and cruel—because they're as seminal as they are unadulterated.

They stalk and terrify *because they have nowhere else to go.* Where else would (or could) the universe store such ogres? Where else would it harbor its germinal source-design? How else might it cipher and camouflage its own peaceable kingdom from too many unfinished monstrosities on the prowl, each with a blind salacity to sodomize, desecrate, and ravage heartlessly from its own unexplored shadow? It had to house them somewhere, for they are part of Creation, tossed in the same initiatory wave so that we tumble in each other's goop.

We are in the diaspora, on the brink, in the wet sheets, together; we require each other to complete our missions and meanings.

I had long considered the Gorgon's stare-down absolute, an imposition of her will for which there was no reasonable response but terror. When I sensed her presence, in my mother or the voice on the radio, I ran amok like a chicken without a head. In Jung I found ambiguity, even a wink. The demons were not malefically fixed; each had bottomless potential for transmutation. Each implacable gaze, each terrible agenda had another charge, a different interpretation entirely, not just in my psyche *but in the universe at large.* Even Cerberus, the three-headed hellhound at the dungeon stairs, could become a friendly mutt. But he wasn't going to do it on his own. *I had to convert him.*

I am articulating knowledge that it took me decades to absorb, digest, and find language for, but it began that October as I rode the esoteric shock waves of my panic while absorbing the possibility that Lindy might be lost forever.

During that melancholy autumn of '64 I intuited a new fortune for myself and for Creation. It wasn't just a hungering darkness or hopeless wait for Godot that led, if not to atomic war, then a Malone-like death. We weren't doomed. We were on a more enigmatic and wilder and more abiding journey. The *entire shebang* was up for grabs. We could reclaim it, maybe even liberate it, though, from its present incomplete manifestation and the sheer depth of the archetypes, the road ahead was long and zigzag and at a scale that dwarfed all of history.

Dream interpretation and science fiction gave me a jump-start in childhood. Tarot and writing took it to the next level. Then Jung extended permission and possibility, melding Yeats, Faulkner, and Freud with the greater trumps. He provided a way to integrate my traumas and inhabit my own ragged life. He snapped my vestigial trance of outer-space melodramas with their unstated burden that I had to daydream planets to get myself into outer space. The universe does not require rockets or aliens to take us to the stars. Its cosmic realms are astral and intrinsic; they belong to us by birth.

Back at P.S. 6 I seemingly made up a spaceship and interstellar landscapes whole-cloth from nothing. But not so—the confabulations of a child contain archetypes too, symbols already in circulation. There is no *tabula rasa* in the psyche.

When I daydreamed escapades in grade school it was more than a maudlin yearning for connection and self-importance, it was an expression of an internal depth and connection that I could evince no other way. It was my attempt to stay on the road to Oz, keep faith with the Tinman and Lion, instead of bowing to the stark secular regimes offered by my family, Miss Tighe, and Bill-Dave. I maintained a child's version of ancestral spirits in the only form available at the time. I stubbornly held to it, not knowing what it was, only that I experienced its hypnotic power. These were all acts of individuation.

Jung conferred his absolute credential as a psychiatrist at a time when Freudians were still my authority figures and priests. Sixteen years later while studying dreams in San Francisco with Charles

Poncé, a renegade seer in the Jungian lineage, I brought him the dream of a chemistry set:

> I am returning to Dr. Fabian's dark brownstone in Greenwich Village. I have to pee very badly, and I stumble into a bathroom so dark I cannot see the toilet. As the urine hits the "water," I smell sulfur and hear hydrochloric acid bubbling in the bowl. I rationalize that it is not my pee but a substance in the toilet. In any case the gurgling stops. Then, as I am leaving the room, I hear the sound again, like sizzling rice soup. My upper lip is burning from having been splattered. I am wondering why there is a scalding element in my urine. I think I must tell this dream to Charles.

"You know what this is," I remarked at once, "it's a version of the first dream that Dr. Fabian interpreted for me. Now I'm going back to him not *with* a dream but *in* the dream. His office has become part of the dream. Back then it was an incident involving a chemistry set. Now it's sizzling rice soup."

Charles knew my original dream as well as Fabian's interpretation, so he sailed right into a reinterpretation:

"You dreamed once of a chemistry set that spilled. You brought that dream to a doctor who told you that the substance in the test tube was urine, that you were dreaming of wetting your pants. I think this can all be viewed another way. You brought your first harvest of symbols to a wizard. He recognized them as symbols. He said, 'What is happening in this dream stands for something else. It is not a chemistry set. It is an act of peeing.' He also said, 'Another meaning is speaking through you.' He gave you a gift and initiation of symbols, but then he limited their meaning to a representation of the asocial act of wetting, mere household sabotage. Like your mother he grasped only the aspect of your wetting associated with misbehavior. He failed to recognize the mercurial waters, which you now bring back to him thirty-five years later to remind him that his earlier analysis was lacking but that he gave you the crucible of the symbol by which to complete it. You are repaying him for what he practiced instinctively, offering him an essence he passed on unconsciously to you."

"So I am dreaming now in order to change the dream, the therapy then."

"You are dreaming the same dream in order to change *an authorized interpretation of it that you have been carrying around your whole life,* and to fulfill your half of an ancient bargain made between a rabbi and a child.

"Back then you dreamed of mercurial waters too, but Dr. Fabian, again like your mother, could see only a wet bed. He could explain your wetting only as a form of rebellion, of primitive consciousness. You really came to a magus with a primordial dream of burning waters, of consciousness stirring to be born. He told you the burning waters were urine. But you were telling him, 'No, they are the seeds of a sorcerer.' He couldn't see that. He couldn't see you as an alchemist longing to get training, to receive his baptism, to learn to transmute. He saw a child needing toilet training, symbol containment. So now you want to show him the real dream in a way that can't be missed. You participate in his *own* individuation even though he is no longer alive."

"So even then it was an alchemical dream," I exclaimed, "because Dr. Fabian's real interpretation was not that the chemical was urine but that *it was a symbol at all,* that it stood for something else— anything else. Before I brought him my dream I had dreamed unknowingly, as a child dreams, never thinking of my sleep journeys as transmissions or texts, as anything to decipher. His act of asking me to bring him a dream to interpret changed the way I thought of my dreaming and my life, it changed everything. Then my unconscious dreamed alchemically, and it came out as a toy chemistry set. We never had a chemistry set—our mother wouldn't have allowed poisons in the house—but we did have dangerous wood-burning tools that gave off a chemical smell, that we were told to keep away from moisture; you know, electricity and water. And its coils sizzled toxically one time when we disobeyed. I apparently turned them into a chemistry set, and Dr. Fabian converted the chemistry set into an alchemical one by turning its secret potion into urine, something much closer then to my heart."

"And," Charles continued, "this is what your present dream is saying: 'I was a magician then, and you didn't see it. I gave you the gift of my first dream, my first intentional magical act. And you thought I was just peeing, you thought I was dreaming Freudian symbols."

"Yet I got mercurial seeds anyway by the fact that Dr. Fabian exchanged the dream for symbols, not by his specific interpretation. After all, he was a magician who didn't know it. Then I dreamed the dream over for you in order to salvage him, and also, I guess, to reestablish the act of interpretation in the present."

"Not interpretation," Charles interrupted. "Consciousness. The problem of 'keeping dry' is an alchemical matter insofar as 'toilet training' requires bringing consciousness to the autonomic realms of the body. You were peeing not only antisocially, but in a struggle to free yourself from unconscious elements. Your new dream, by casting wetting in the mirror of Dr. Fabian's interpretation, was a step up the ladder. Now you are saying that you are finally ready to complete the act, at least in dream form."

"Fabian had reached out in the darkness and took a boy's hand, but we were both in darkness. Now I am reaching back and trying to guide him to where I am."

"Precisely," said Charles," but not just him then or you now—*you then, him now.*"

As I journeyed deeper into Jungian archetypes and symbols, I went on an errand to recover some of my old childhood favorites from the Amherst town library: *Grimms' Fairy Tales, Hans Christian Andersen, Nine Tales of Coyote, The Dragons of Blueland.* I reconsidered talking crows, winged dragons, learned spiders, and wish-granting fish. These are not just imaginary beings from fables and legends or putative visitors from other dimensions; they are our unspoken selves. Rapunzel and Sleeping Beauty, the Indian maidens courted by Coyote in human form—I had known them unconsciously long before I awoke to their representations at camp dances and on teen tours. Joan Snyder was not only a cute girl; she was as old as the moon. Night after night at Chipinaw I had to rescue and redeem her again to give birth to myself.

Revelations swept over me that Massachusetts fall as a college junior; they softened and healed me, as Jung became my solace and path.

After classes one Friday I drove into Cambridge to meet an old friend from Horace Mann, James Polachek. I knew him as a buddy of Chuck's and a member of our circle: a tall, shy kid with a large-featured but intelligent face, who played the violin and carried its shape and imprint on his personality. Now he was studying Chinese and philosophy at Harvard.

To enter his apartment I ducked through a bamboo curtain. A knee-height desk and a Japanese frame with pillows were Jim's sole furniture. Two silken hangings and a shell screen formed a room within a room. As incense tinged the air, single sequential bells sounded on his stereo. My friend had spun his own spare Oriental web.

Together we wandered through Cambridge, visiting bookstores, sharing literary and occult insights—our so-called lives—in an olden city, no longer tied to the purlieus and curfews of prep school.

After a while I told him about Lindy. I took comfort in representing my grief as a passage through the Underworld. "No way to arrive at the full moon without the dark moon behind it," I mused. "I'm a Scorpio born in the rubble of November, fighting to survive millennial darkness." He silently endorsed the spiel, so I took it to the next level. "Regenerate," I declared with a tad more cheer and vim than I had. "That's what Scorpios do best. Just when you think that they're dead and gone they awaken with almost magical powers."

I did a fair job of convincing myself, but the flood of obligatory sapience enervated me. By dinnertime I was mum and morose, as we hastened through drizzle to an Italian restaurant. Wetter than I realized, I accepted a towel from the maître d'. Then Jim and I sat, warming in pleasant surroundings, a crackling fireplace making the scene baronial. This was no Horace Mann outpost. I had no homework, no mother, no brother, no home.

Jung couldn't help me here. Thank goodness for the offer of a towel!

Finally I sank into the sheer texture of existence. It was all okay, even if it wasn't. At least I wasn't scared.

I sipped wine. Neither of us said anything for a long time.

"Look around you," Polachek offered suddenly. "We are in the material universe, but everything is magnificent beyond words. No matter how cheap and poorly made, it all has a sacred property; it's all beautiful." I followed his eyes to the ceiling candelabra. It was a multicolored electric wheel, replica of a soul. All by itself the fireplace was transmuting sacred flames.

"Even here," Jim continued, pointing to the empty Chianti bottle on which a candle dripped blue wax over the yellow and pink wax of prior candles. As I followed his gestures, timeless awe settled over me. "No surprises. Exactly the way it should be, no matter what we do to contaminate and tarnish it."

Goddamn, was this universe deep!

The plates in *Archetypes of the Collective Unconscious* showed a succession of convergent mandalas: a man and woman standing in a lotus, within another lotus, within the phases of the moon and cycles of the planets. Three rabbits chased one another's tails. These patterns were transposed sequentially onto nighttime New York, riverside church steeples, gold vestry windows. An amoeboid glow broke through stone armaments and blossomed over Fifth Avenue.

In Waite's Five of Pentacles two beggars—one lame on crutches—passed outside a chapel. As they hobbled barefoot in snow, yellow light poured through a stained-glass oriel.

This was the card of exile, of finding oneself beyond the sanctuary, unable to get in. Yet the sanctuary was right there, staring at me all along. Matthew Arnold had written as much nearly a hundred years prior: *"Set where the upper streams of Simois flow / Was the Palladium, high 'mid rock and wood; / And Hector was in Ilium, far below, / And fought, and saw it not—but there it stood!"*

The Chianti bottle was my hearth. The plate of lasagna was an offering, red and alabaster, from the belly of Ceres.

Suddenly I felt safe, totally safe, and I wanted to cry. In fact, unbidden tears were rolling down my cheeks. The world had revealed itself again, and I was home. Even the ghost child bearing a brick of ice cream back to the 96th Street apartment, even Lindy's absence were redeemed, were part of the simple fact, the privilege of being here at all.

I had lived till then as a mendicant in the Five of Pentacles. Now, in the blues of a lost girlfriend at an Italian restaurant with an old friend, I surrendered to unknown gods at last.

Nelson Richardson was one of the sophomores who hung around Phi Psi. A self-proclaimed poet who with his pale glasses and mop of blond hair looked like the artist Andy Warhol, he had recently—just that summer—been in residence with the poet-monk Thomas Merton at Gethsemani, a Trappist monastery in Kentucky. In September when we met I found Nelson conceited and arrogant. He never paid House dues, yet spent more time there than many who did. He had also—behind my back—called my literary reputation "a lot of fuss over nothing," so I assumed he was a jerk and avoided him.

People kept bringing us together, and we kept sloughing off the occasions. Then we came face to face in the Glen where we had both retreated to study. With no one around to sponsor affinity we looked clearly into each other's eyes. Neither of us spoke it, but we agreed silently, "Let's get this over with and talk."

He told me about the monastery, its regimented life and shadow sexuality, how that left him uncertain of his own feelings toward either men or women. He worried about the ease with which he could pull off an act and be a "character" at Amherst, the way other kids just bought it, as though he were a priest or some sort of oracle. "I didn't fool you, though."

I apologized for holding it against him and told him why it was a hard time for me. I described my panic of the preceding spring and how I blasted out of it with a poem. I quoted some lines I knew by heart.

He whistled acknowledgment. "I would call that a text of madness. You didn't write it, you *received* it. The beings who watch over you decided that your exile had gone on long enough and they sent you instructions on how to end it. You wrote those down, but of course they are in the language of the angels not of a psychology book." He paused for a moment. "Or, maybe the panic was the poem, and you resisted its message until you had suffered enough to be allowed to speak. Either way, the words, as you know, are approximations of another language."

I couldn't have been more wrong about Nelson.

He told me that his own revelations were more Trappist, in the form of angels. "But they're not—you know, 'angel' angels, cherubim and the like. 'Angel' is just the Greek word for messenger," he reminded me as we crossed the street toward the dining hall. "Their kind are everywhere. They are carriers of information from divine beings. This rock is an angel. That bird is an angel. Even that asshole from Beta over there is an angel. The forms of the world are merely the clothing angels adopt. Without those markings we wouldn't know they exist. We ourselves wouldn't exist." He stopped walking just before Valentine's door and looked dead-seriously at me, a gaze more sentient than either of us expected. "Don't you see—we pick our angels. Lindy is your angel. You chose her willingly. Now you are doing grateful penance." He had a melodic voice that made him a seraph singing sacred advice in scales.

"But you chose Thomas Merton," I offered. "That seems a little more intelligent."

"Even you know better than that, Grossinger!"

Chuck had loaned me a book called *Magick in Theory and Practice*. It was written by the notorious Aleister Crowley who cast spells to seduce women and defeat his rivals. But there were other, more spiritual aspects to his work, notably his theorems for a "magickal" science that included—hence transcended—physics of the Amherst freshman variety. Crowley asserted that, through our wills and desires, we conducted the primordial forces shaping earth and heavens—that mind took precedent over matter. Like Nelson, he urged me to regard all events as messages from higher masters to my soul, for nothing that happens to us is arbitrary. I carried his axioms around with me like the debris of fifties rock 'n' roll:

"Every intentional act is a Magical act."

"A man who is doing his True Will has the inertia of the Universe to assist him."

"Every force in the Universe is capable of being transformed into any other kind of force by using suitable means. There is thus an inexhaustible supply of any particular kind of force that we may need."

"Every man and every woman is a star."

On a night in mid-October, I was driving home from dropping Lindy off at Smith after a dinner out. I gazed across silver pumpkin fields and received a spontaneous transmission out of *Archetypes and the Collective Unconscious:* Lindy was Persephone, imprisoned in the underworld by a smooth-talking reporter. I was the animus-warrior, rushing to save her before she swallowed the fatal pomegranate seeds.

Though I recognized a reckless throwback to my saucer fantasy, I knew that this one had a scintilla of truth. I mainly had to balance my tendency to narcissistic aggrandizement with a newfound receptivity to messages. Angels who had once given a child a humungous vessel for his escape now offered a young man more modest and salient means.

A litany of ancient songs and coyote tales blew over the car, as I felt a wild and invulnerable joy, warm and cozy, yet spreading to the ends of space and time.

> *Done laid around and stayed around*
> *This old town too long....*

It was time to act.

Scorpio within awoke and reclaimed his dormant power. He identified himself as my erstwhile trickster self—or made it impossible that I mistake his wiles for anything less than feints of clairvoyant magic, thwarted or bungled because I was too young and unschooled. I didn't have the emotional tools or a numinous repertoire or even entrée to my own core compassion, so upsurges of anxiety made me reckless and cruel. I had been listing perilously toward my mother's paragon: a malign witch. Now the spirits were calling and I was ready.

My Coyote Self proposed an all-encompassing, transformative prank: I would hold a ceremony in the Glen on Halloween, three days before my twentieth birthday.

I was so convinced of the rightness of this event that I managed to get just about everyone in the House to blend with my exuberance. We never had to transfer en masse to Berkeley; we could make a more salient stand on local ground.

For the rest of the week Nelson and I mapped out how to pull it off—candles, mandalas, fairy-tales, slides of nature, a flute and a xylophone, bells, jugs of apple cider. I invited acquaintances from all over campus. Then I called Polachek and Stein and they both agreed to attend. Chuck said he would bring his friend Josey who, I had heard, was a witch with magic powers. The clan was gathering to make medicine: Porcupine, Thunder, and Bear.

Even Tripp accepted: "Staging a Halloween happening in the Glen demonstrates an excellent sense of theater, man."

But Persephone would be absent in the land of Pluto. Lindy told me that, ceremony or not, it was the first weekend Jim would be in New York. They would all have to do without her. She wrote:

> I can't come to Halloween with you, kiddo, as you know, because my Jim needs me and I need his closeness and love. There is a price to pay, and I pay it by missing Chuck and Polachek and the whole world of talk that I'm dying to hear, souls over Fifth Avenue, and Pegasus and Persephone myths. It seems ironic as hell to me and absurd that some other cute thing will hear the magic you have to say, but that's my price to pay, for not being clever enough to do two things at once, to fleece the gods completely....

In her last letter the week before leaving she told me to "speak softly with the spirits and respectfully, and they will know that you feel the connection with the past and them acutely. I hope that time past and time present merge, gradually, for then you will have the essence of time."

"I guess you'll just have to do your ceremony without her," Tripp said. "A worthy challenge for you."

I answered him by writing a quick jingle based on a well-known radio station's ad:

N E time
N E place
in New York,
any double you, there's
always something happening in
Neeeewww Yooorrrk.
jesus yes!

"That shows spirit, Grossinger," he affirmed. "It's a battle cry."

On Friday we began preparations in earnest. Nelson suggested we each make a personal mandala. Most participants painted theirs on slabs of plywood; I used a black discarded nightstand top. On it I rendered my own version of Jung's Fifth Avenue scene. I stained a white baseball with black stitches, colored the skyline of Central Park West, and placed symbols for Lindy and me reaching across the baseball and touching, while in the lower lefthand corner—with a nod to the Crowley—a stray voodoo figure, a city-side reporter, was banished.

That night I dreamed that Chuck's subway girlfriend Julie appeared as an editor at an occult publishing house in New York. I went to her offices with my manuscript as to Viking Press to see Catherine Carver. She led me into a deserted ballroom where mammoth tarot cards hung on arrases. It had become the Museum of Natural History at night. A priest sat on a pedestal before a buffet, like those at Grossinger's except that the carved ice figures at its center were alchemical symbols. She said, "We are the Sixth Trump, the Lovers," and embraced me. I looked up. On the ceiling was a painting of a giant smiling angel, embodying us in her deck.

On Saturday morning Polachek's VW bug sailed into the parking lot, toting two records of Chinese temple music. Jim immediately set to work painting an impeccable High Priestess on a piece of plywood fifty times the size of the Waite card, a veil of extra-radiant

maroon pomegranates behind her. The basement was soon filled
with mandala makers from all over campus.

Chuck appeared mid-afternoon, trailing not only Josey but a
short, surly kid from Bard College named Harvey Bialy. He looked
like a cartoon of a fiend and spoke in an ornery manner. The three
of them huddled together in the living room, a cameo of beatniks.

As far as Harvey was concerned, Bard was the center of the universe, at least for colleges, and he let everyone know that it was a
"bad joke" he should be dragged up to Amherst "for a Crowleyite
ceremony of all things." Although I wouldn't hear about it until
much later, three years ago he had gotten into a fight with another
kid while leaving the main branch of the New York Public Library.
His adversary was racing up the massive stone stairs with a guitar
when its suspended case bumped Harvey and almost knocked him
down all the steps. The two got to jivin' and calling out their
stuff, and Harvey did what he often did—insulted a stranger for
pleasure of it. On this occasion he apparently said something like,
"After all, Woody Guthrie's a bum." Bobby Zimmerman began
shoving him and they wrestled and punched each other on the
steps, no doubt a comic spectacle.

As Tripp surveyed the arrival of my friends, he stood by the side,
smirking at my characterization of Josey as a witch. "She's a sweet,
tubby Jewish girl from New York; that's what she is," he whispered,
but once I led them to the basement she did paint a beautiful abstract
Moon on a square slab of pine, vibration-like Hebrew letters rising
from crayfish in a pool to form the pulsating lunar node.

The outcome was totally up for grabs as we marched to the Glen.
But Nelson came through! He had arranged our mandalas amidst
ten torches, placed five long candles and two squat ones on an altar,
and set metal railroad poles pointing into the heavens. Marty had
hung speakers in the trees, so Polachek's bells and flutes filled the
universe with its music of the spheres.

I carried an extension cord and boxes of slides I had culled from
the Astronomy, Biology, and Geology Departments to the mysti-
fication of professors eager though to encourage extracurricular

appreciation of their topics. We set the projector going in a loop—galaxies, flowers, amoebas, rivers, volcanos, craters of the moon, mountains, birds, the planet Jupiter, glaciers—one after another, enormous and rippling on the bedsheets strung among the trees. On the grass, torches made our mandalas shimmer and come alive. Meanwhile the real sky above was full of constellations. From the darkness came the notes of an Oriental temple. Then Nelson read the first of *Nine Tales* of bright-eyed Coyote, his journey to the Upper World via the tallest tree in Idaho Country, whereby he met his Spider ancestors who warned him that the human race was coming.

"Now this is a real party, Grossinger," Tripp exulted, collapsing back on the grass with an appreciative sigh. I had bored him in the past by bringing Grossinger's steaks, barbecuing in the fireplace, and declaring it a banquet.

After a while I moved into the candlelight of the altar. "Why are we out here?" I asked. And I offered glimpses of archetypes, science-fiction realms, and trick-or-treat Halloweens. "We have come," I concluded, "finally to what we are. Through this ceremony we deny the false carnival colors and adolescent rituals of America, the neon and gloss that douse our lives with fake significance and blind us to our true natures." I was channeling Jung, Olson, the tarot, Robert Penn Warren, and maybe Zest soap:

> It is a belief that we are something more rather than something less, that we are being robbed of that something more, that belief, if any, that should make us listen more closely tonight. Not that we will find it, certainly not in one casual evening among friends, as hardly in one casual life among warmongers. We are merely to be reminded that it is still there, to be stirred again with the haunted fairy tales of a childhood that once seemed filled with a secret and a majesty that the world never became....

That was the overture. Then I reeled in a giant fish I had been trolling for years:

> What bothers us are the forces that pretend to know something they don't. What bothers us about the too-blue Sunoco sign or the

over-ripe can of red paint is that they are filled with energy but sourceless.... They are as bright and sparkly as anything lit before our eyes, yet directionless, lacking any sense of the ghosts that fill each of our daily existences.

And there is a source, a great pull of mind-stuff, resting in electric calm out in the bends of the universe, the stars, Orion, Sirius, Vega, Alpha Centauri, cutting loose forces that fill the forces within us....

You are the stuff that the stars are made of; all is not bleak existentialism; there is a temple, a sanctuary.... There is a second self in you like an eagle locked in the belly of a pigeon—and it is incredible if you have not noticed him kicking to be free, to be off and back to the sky....

In truth, we are all like the earth goddess Demeter, searching for the lost Persephone; she is held captive beneath the earth. Our fields; they will not flower. Man has failed where he has not realized that it takes evil as well as good to drag the soul up from the depths, it takes the black temple as well as the white one, the dead baby on the cover of the "National Enquirer" as well as the infinitely more terrible white star that can consume into dust and energy a thousand such sacks of lifeless bones....

I reached my crescendo:

And every black-eyed susan man has worshipped has grown an ugly weed he has tried to cut away, not realizing that it is the balance between the two and the tension formed by the balance that weights and sashes the scale, and the scale holds up the earth on its giant back....

Soon enough we too will be gone and others will take command, expecting from us a Bible and a Holy Grail, and still we may write a chapter of one, and still they may say our prayers before a burning Orion Sinai, and still they may quiz them as forgotten Easter Island gods....

This is our chance to be immortal, the stars overhead our legacy, our eternal to-be. We are stopping tonight to acknowledge these facts, to pause in the middle of a noisy nowhere and reflect on the everywhere all about us, to dance for a second the dance we are dancing every second anyway.

Having delivered my speech I fell silent. Then others read poems and Indian myths and offered blessings, after which we sat watching the slide loop with its billowing images while listening to temple bells. Nelson served cider and cookies.

Harvey was visibly moved. "I want a copy of that talk," he declared back in the House. "There are people at Bard who will be very interested. *Very* interested!"

On Sunday night Lindy called to find out how the "great event" had gone. I talked a blue streak … incident after incident, trying to make my speech again to her … until she told me to stop because she wanted to say something. "I had a terrible weekend. I don't know what I ever saw in him. Outside the city room and Denver he lost all his luster. It was a fantasy, I guess. Will you forgive me for all I've put you through, kiddo?"

Three days later on my twentieth birthday I received a pair of communications in the mail. They fit together magically. Aunt Bunny was out of the hospital and her friends were holding a celebration in Manhattan. I also got a packet from Harvey's teacher at Bard, the poet Robert Kelly; he enclosed a mimeographed batch of his recent work called "Weeks" while indicating that he would like to meet "the author of that wonderful Halloween prayer." Kelly was a well-known hermetic writer in the lineage of Charles Olson.

The entire universe seemed to be wheeling around me and changing course. I felt a rush of infinite possibility. I called Lindy and suggested that we could manage both events, the party and visiting Kelly, by staying at the Hotel, a perfect median point. That way she could meet Aunt Bunny, see Grossinger's, and come with me to Bard. Then I held my breath. Her response: "What a delightful idea and invitation!"

Waves of awe and gratitude spilled over me, the precise obverse of panic. The future seemed open-ended, ransomed at last.

On November 5th I drove to Smith lightheaded, an old vigilance taunting me with the dread that she wouldn't be there. But she was standing outside Laura Scales in her down jacket with her suitcase; she looked at me with her wise gray eyes, hugged me, and handed me a package and a card with a poem, saying, "Belated happy birthday, honey." The package had a cotton dress shirt, and the poem began:

> *Who is the spooked left-over wind scaring*
> *on this third day of November?*
> *It's only herding stray leaves—they keep close*
> *to one another in circling, then open out for*
> *the long stretch down the lawn....*

She started to get in the passenger side, but I handed her the keys. She splashed along the snowmelt highway, down Massachusetts into Connecticut while we talked about a hundred things—her break-up with Jim, Aunt Bunny's homecoming, Kelly's poems, Jung, Crowley, her terrible teachers at Smith.

My own class there had become a travesty. Stanley Elkin, a thickset, sarcastic man, told us at the first meeting he could never get dates with Smith girls when he was in college so he was going to take his revenge. It was a joke, of course, but it became the effective reality. The seminar consisted of little more than his thespian parodies and denigrations of our work.

He claimed that all stories were about obsessions—no exceptions—and he dared us to prove otherwise. That seemed a cheap gimmick, so I took him up on it. The first piece I wrote was in the style of Beckett, about a man walking down a hall, which was on the Earth, which was in the Solar System, which was in the Milky Way. I described the hall in great detail, but nothing happened:

"Hiya," said a man on his left.

"Good day. Bad day tomorrow, though," said a woman on his left.

"Hello," said a woman on his right.

"Pleased to see you again," said a woman on his left.

Elkin called it a fake.

"I guess the obsession is my trying to fool you," I offered.

He barked in the affirmative.

The day before in class, I told Lindy, Elkin had been tearing down a girl's story. I jumped to her defense. When he said, "You have an antiquated view of literature," I began to quote out loud from the Nobel Prize acceptance speech of William Faulkner, an author I knew he admired.

Lindy and I both knew that sermon well—an artist at the apex of public honor proclaiming that our work was a statement of undying faith against atomic holocaust. At first Elkin tried to shout me (and Faulkner) down, but when I kept going, he conceded, "So the man was a promoter. He had a fine sense of theater. Give him a platform, and he knew what to do. But don't believe a word of it. He didn't."

"Why," I declaimed, "is it such a crime in these institutions to claim that a work has meaning and touches the soul? Why is there an almost pathological denial of emotion and spirit? These things aren't the enemy. They're the source of everything that matters. Yet our teachers mock us as if they were naïve and puerile indulgences."

We were beginning to see, and tell each other, that we had been taught nihilistically. Witty progressive liberalism was the sole acceptable mode of discourse—a tyranny of fashion that Lindy, with her deep sense of humanity and associative mind, suffered more than I.

We bonded over such conversation and our spirits lifted. As we neared New York at dusk, the years rushed through me like alighting birds. Road signs proclaimed the Westchester towns from which Rodney, Jake, and Keith once commuted: Mamaroneck, Larchmont, Scarsdale, Yonkers.... Across the fields I saw a lit subway, the train I had ridden, its unknowing passengers looking out toward the highway at unknown cars. Despite everything, this was the egg in which I was hatched.

I took over driving and wove through a familiar maze of streets to a midtown apartment. We parked in an underground garage and rode the elevator up.

It was a fashionable affair: people standing around with drinks, Bunny in the center, her attention splintered a dozen ways. She seemed as I remembered her, perhaps a bit subdued. She acknowledged our arrival with a beaming smile. Later she joined us, and she and Lindy talked about her illness, then Smith. I stood beside them, delighted at bringing two great women together. When Lindy went to get her coat, Bunny used almost the words Lindy had written during the summer when talking about herself and Steve, "I hope you haven't found her too soon."

A month later she was back in the hospital. I would not see her again for more than a year.

I drove the old trail: up the Henry Hudson Parkway to the George Washington Bridge. New York drifted against the River, a galaxy of fixed and moving stars. We whizzed into the uncluttered woodlands of the Palisades, then onto the Thruway, fifteen miles to Route 17 and the Catskills. Lindy handled the final fifty miles, her breezy Colorado eighty. A familiar cluster of Tudor villas appeared over the hill at Exit 101. Suddenly the intervening years seemed an illusion, all disparagements and reproaches gone. I once again viewed the glowing gingerbread kingdom to which a child had come as a waif.

We parked in front of my father's house, beside the otherwise NO PARKING sign and walked to the indoor-pool building. It was past midnight and the coffee shop was closed, but I scaled the glass partition and opened it from inside. I made us Milty-Stackel milk shakes, mostly ice cream (six different flavors), malt, vanilla syrup. The machine beat them into froth, and we sat on the counter, drinking straight from frosted metal cups with straws, feeling foolish and delighted. Then I gave her a quick tour of the nightclub, the empty kitchens and dining room, and the lobbies.

Emma had left the house unlocked, so we went upstairs to the guest room and lay on the bed quietly kissing. Her whole being was so lovely and sweet I could not imagine stopping, but then she asked me to show her to her room. "Honey, this is not the time. We're both exhausted. We've had a wonderful glittery day; let's not force the fates."

She was right. It was only desire that held me to her body, whereas necessity bound me to her friendship and protection. I gave her my room from the summer and took the large guest room with the double closets. She returned in a nightgown, hugged me in bed, then slipped away in the dark.

3

KELLY

It was a bright autumn day, November 6, 1964. Lindy and I walked to the main building, grabbed a *Times* at the service desk, and headed down the aisle of a crowded dining room. Grossinger's regulars waved at me as though nothing were unusual. I was with a girl. I had been with a girl before. That was how it must have looked. But Lindy was a girl found elsewhere and she represented everything about me that had nothing to do with the Hotel.

After breakfast we walked the grounds in chill morning, across the golf course to the Lake, back past the skating rink and greenhouses along the ballfields, leaves ochre and burgundy on the trees of eternal return. Afterwards I led her on a tour of the kitchen, past steaming grills and lines of waiters and waitresses; in the process we collected fruit and cookies for the road. We came back to the car and filled it at the Hotel pump.

"The Big Rock Candy Mountain," I joked. "The next stop, Annandale-on-Hudson."

She zoomed out the gate and turned left on 52; it was a sixty-mile trip, picking up Route 209 at Ellenville, crossing the Hudson at Kingston. As she opened a window and lit a cigarette, I got out "Weeks" and began reading aloud:

> *Raven*   *in Chiapas....*
> *wings tensed back*
> *it has swallowed its tongue*
> *in hunger to eat*
>   *hunger to cry out loud*   *into the sky*   *I am here*

feed me unmerciful gods
who made us feed on shit
          feed me because I cry louder....
because I can crack the cheap bowl of your cry with my shriek....

"He *is* amazing," she said. "It's hard to believe we're really going to see him."

Robert Kelly lived on the Bard campus. When we inquired for his whereabouts, we were directed to a small parking lot, its driveway ending in a cluster of barracks-like apartments. As instructed, we knocked on the last door. A woman answered. Stocky, garbed in shawl and robes, she could have been a large dwarf out of Norse mythology. She stared back and forth at each of us intently enough to be rude. After taking stock of the ingénue college students, she proclaimed, "You must be Richard Grossinger and friend. Come in. Robert has been waiting for you."

Already I could hear his voice bellowing from the back rooms: "Joby, is it Richard Grossinger?"

We stepped into another reality, a den packed floor to ceiling with every imaginable size, shape, and age of book and manuscript, some lying open, others with feathers and paperweights marking places. Encyclopedia-like tomes and black binders rested on tables along with unfinished cups of coffee and overflowing ashtrays. Books and papers were scattered all over the faded Turkish carpet. Occult icons, alchemical posters, tarot cards, *tankgas,* and horoscopes were attached to the walls. It was how I would have pictured Merlin's lair: a Mediaeval flat that had been inhabited by the same two immortals for centuries.

There was no heat; the apartment was stone-cold. An ancient furnace-like unit with a pipe through the ceiling was either inoperable or, more likely, set at fifty. Across the archway leading to the entrance from which Robert Kelly was about to loom, judging by the sound, was a hand-made sign with the words: TOMORROW POSSIBLE BECAUSE IT IS.

Though we had been forewarned about his appearance, nothing

could have prepared us for a giant or his manner of entering. Well over three hundred pounds and six feet, an unkempt red mane, he transformed scale itself, inhabiting the room by gasping between breaths. He continued to alter space as he walked, like a boulder coming through water.

"Yes, yes, Richard Grossinger—wonderful speech you gave—and—" He turned to Lindy, whom I quickly introduced. Then he scurried us to chairs like a man feeding pigeons. "Is there anything happening these days at Amherst and Smith? I had thought not. And then Harvey Bialy returns with a story of an unlikely ceremony and carrying this magnificent piece of sacred oratory." He grabbed my carbon from one of the tabletops and shook the daylights out of it.

Collaborating on our response, Lindy and I explained how there was little going on at Amherst and Smith. As we enumerated the courses we were taking and what we were reading, he listened patiently, then indicated he would soon supply the remedy.

He began his discourse in the middle of nowhere, an impromptu sermon on a form of Sufi music he had recently discovered, its relation to cosmic vibrations, citing texts he presumed (quite wrongly) we knew. In fact, for the whole of the visit he seemed to gloss over the gulf between our spheres of learning as if it didn't exist or, in any case, needn't deter him from fulsome testimony. His grandiloquence recalled the high language of gospel but, like Olson, a vernacular version with shifts into hip pidgin. As he spoke, Joby interrupted constantly with emendations I didn't follow, as if everything required her exactitude and footnotes. I had to pay close attention not to lose track or slight either of them.

It was also as though we had entered a Berlitz class in which a foreign tongue was acquired simply by listening and repeating in kind. But it wasn't quite that—it was as though we were being trained for a different mode of perception and discourse, the rules of which would become evident only by our being in its midst and observing and practicing its conventions. Later I realized that Kelly was teaching in a different way from my Amherst or Horace Mann masters; he was telling us stuff all right, important facts and ideas, *but he was also changing our consciousness,* attuning it to a higher, more serious octave by mantra and melody as much as by information.

At one point he retreated to the back room and re-manifested with a pile of colorful mimeographed sheets he stapled together by virtually crushing a tiny machine as he walked. These made up a magazine he called *matter.* We each got our own copy. I turned through my pages, which were filled with poetry, notes, diagrams, and epigraphs. Right off I saw an essay on film-making by Stan Brakhage, and I told them about the screening at Amherst.

"Brakhage taught you an important lesson," he pronounced. "You see, when you are young, you think you can live on anything, like junk food, and you can, and seem to do all right—you two are testament to that. But in order to grow into men and women you need real things, real imagination, not just symbols, or the ideas of some professor who hasn't been out of the university in two hundred years."

Then Kelly asked Joby if she was hungry and, when she responded with a growl, he proposed to take us to town for lunch. In the driveway we were chaperoned to an old sedan. "Named Bloisius," Joby informed us with a maternal smile as she herded us in. She and Kelly occupied thrones in the front seat, which was decorated uncarlike with postcards and amulets on the walls. We obeyed her instructions to pile up books strewn across the back and made enough room to settle in. The smell of decay indigenous to the vehicle was a blend of oranges and bookstore parchment, not unpleasant.

Kelly hugged and rolled the wheel like an octopus with a crystal ball in his circumference as he headed for and then crossed the Rhinecliff Bridge over the Hudson into Kingston. I had driven or been driven past this town a hundred times or more en route to and from Grossinger's, including ninety minutes ago, but had never seen its interior. In my mind it was a Thruway exit, so I was eager for more of a peek.

We drifted down a lively main street and, without braking, Kelly turned into the parking lot of a Chinese restaurant, almost hitting a parked truck without the slightest acknowledgment. Inside, as we continued to talk, I had the sense of leaving the "silk route" to the Catskills and entering a parallel reality that had been operating beside it all along.

In the course of egg rolls and spare ribs, produced quickly without our ordering, by a waitress who must have known the routine, Kelly made headway through an unpredictable list of topics, quizzing us on them one by one. He began with conventional items—where we came from, what we read and wrote, what our relationship to each other was, in general who we thought we were. He certified each answer with a smile that was sometimes approving, sometimes quixotic, but never condescending, as he and Joby traded obscure asides like an examining committee. Then he made leaps of metaphor and view, dissolving beliefs we had held our whole lives. It was both exhilarating and exhausting, though we were hardly prepared for the deluge.

"What planets do you think are inhabited?" he asked at one point, picking up on my expressed interest in science fiction.

I gave a considered response, favoring Mars and Venus.

"That's the astronomer's answer; I think they are all inhabited, inhabited on other planes and by creatures indigenous to those planes. We conceive life only in three dimensions, but beings might live on worlds in other dimensions, for instance in the astral plane, while at the same time the surfaces of those worlds appear barren."

"Even Pluto?" I baited, trying to see how far he was willing to go.

"Don't be fooled by its size. It's a planet, the same as any other, and we know nothing about it, except as we have seemed to discover and name it." He drained a demitasse of green tea like a giant slurping a thimble. "You ask about Pluto. I say Pluto gives birth to the present epoch. I say that the Sun itself is inhabited. I think its core is teeming with creatures, all in an exalted state. Not necessarily higher, though. Souls exist on the Sun in their own occasion *as we do* here." He stopped to consider where to take us next.

"Souls come to worlds for specific reasons based on karma. Ours is the green planet, the realm of growth; here, uniquely, creatures transform themselves by their work. It is a precious opportunity, but it exacts a price; that is, if we squander it. Such is our desperate situation, the reason we cannot dawdle. Your professors don't see it, so they fulfill their etymology. They profess—about nothing in particular, nothing that finally matters. They go on and on as if we had time unto eternity."

He paused to order main dishes, selecting for us too, and then picked up where he had left off.

"We have very little time, almost no time at all, and the Moon is waiting to gobble us up, to trap us in habitual motion. In truth, we live our lives in an instant, effect a transmutation or not, vanish into darkness if we fail. That is the next task for you two—to live—now that you have declared yourself apart from the monster."

Then he asked us about dreams and I answered with interpretations from Jung as well as Freud. "Good basic training," he attested, "but this is still the Western dream you are talking about, the dream that stands *for* something. I am talking about a pure act of dreaming that does not have to be subservient to any system of symbols. Dreaming is no different from 'lifing'—that's an American Indian testament, though they didn't name it as such, they experienced it directly. Dream is its own mystery, its own logos, not the product of some professional establishment. Your dream tonight might be Freudian, or Jungian, but only if you interpret it as such. It could also be an utterly unknown message from an unknowable intelligence, perhaps your own, or a landscape infused from a higher dimension. Remember Blake: make your own system or be enslaved by another's." Joby started to object, but he finished the conceit himself. "Unfortunately Blake was enslaved by his own system."

"Don't dreams carry the meanings of past events?" Lindy asked. "Do you think Freud had it all wrong?"

"What about the archetypes?" I threw in. "Don't they also shape dreams at a primal level?"

"We don't even know if there is such a thing as an archetype. Jung is seductive, hence dangerous. He offers pompano so delicate they are hard to resist, but he too was enslaved by his own system. Meanings and symbols are only accouterments of a greater dreaming. But they are not the *fact* of dreaming. Dreaming is its own fact, just like lifing. What is this life a symbol for? It's not a symbol; it's a life. Now eat. Let the gods nourish you."

The arrival of dishes had interrupted our talk, as mu shu pork, broccoli beef, spare ribs, cashew prawns, and black mushrooms were tossed on the table without fanfare. Kelly praised each in turn with playfully flamboyant oblations, as he dished out generous helpings for all. We ate in relative silence.

"It is charming to be children when you are children," he opined while counting out his cash and assuring us we were his guests. "But in America they want to keep you children forever." He downed one last helping of tea. "Your professors are children—I mean, in terms of the true mages and avatars of the universe. Your parents likewise." He slowly peered around the room as if to include its diners in his indictment; then he pointed to an unlikely gray-haired gent seated by the window and said under his breath, "I know that man." After a pause during which I wondered what manner of new riddle this was, he added, "I've seen him in every Howard Johnson's in the country."

As we walked to the car, he continued the thread, "You have an opportunity to be more than parrots or pedants. Already Richard's Halloween vision speaks to that, to a deeper truth. I see it in both of you. Stop writing fiction. Stop making up things and satisfying yourself with allusions. It's not charming and inventive; it's devious and evasive. Do you want to live lives of gossip, be raconteurs for your time on Earth? Do you want to dream and breathe this fraud of a civilization? Grow up! Become citizens of the cosmos."

On the way back to Annandale he cited poetic and Gnostic masters, as he urged us to supplement our meager and modernistic educations with real texts, the titles of which he continued to compile on the back of an envelope, using the steering wheel as a writing surface while in vehicular motion.

At his apartment he offered to read to us from his work. In a hurry to get started north, we tried politely to resist, but he chided us for being Amherst and Smith drones and shooed us back into our seats. "What would your good professors think if you refused a reading from William Butler Yeats?"

I balked at being a captive audience, but he read like a jinni—Yeats was an understatement. He closed with a long poem called "The

Alchemist" with lines as good as any I had ever heard:

> *& if we do not get up and destroy all the congressmen*
> *turn them into naked men and let the sun shine on them*
> *set them down in a desert & let them find their way out,*
> *north, by whatever sexual power is left in them, if we do not*
> *seize the president and take him out in daytime and show him*
> *the fire & energy of one at least immediate star, white star....*

> *we will walk forever down the hallways into mirrors and*
> *stagger and look to our left hand for support & the sun*
> *will have set inside us & the world will be filled with Law....*

We sat in stunned humility. Each in our way, we knew that we were in a sacred space, being blessed by a priest.

In truth, it was a mystery event. If we had come in disguise, the Kellys were in disguise too, and so was the altar, camouflaged as a dingy tenement. In any *ordinary* sense the Kellys' hut was dwarfed by Grossinger's, but that tiny, rumpled apartment on the nether shore of the Hudson was a hologram of the entire cosmos. The Five of Pentacles had been drawn upside-down, the mendicants were *in* the temple.

Then Kelly told us to stick together and protect each other, as he assigned us the task of waking up Amherst and Smith. He handed Lindy the torn-off reading-list and bid us "God's speed" with a mudra of his left hand, "Until the next time.... I'm sure there will be many."

We left him copies of our work, and he promised to read them and discuss them on our return "which I hope," he added, "will be soon."

We drove into a different world from the one out of which we had trundled hours earlier, repairing like pilgrims from Plato's cave who had seen how large the universe actually was. We found the way to the Taconic and followed its gentle wooded hills up through New York to meet the Thruway just before the Mass line.

"Give me a few days to get my life together," Lindy requested at the door to Laura Scales. "It has been a radical and exhausting grail." I nodded and drove back to Phi Psi.

Several times a week over the next two months I picked her up at Smith and we set out looking for new places to dine: a tavern in Hadley, the Aqua Vitae outside Northampton, a diner in Florence, a steak house in Springfield, the local Howard Johnson's. There we ratified our emotional and artistic world. We protected the identity of our emerging twosome while enacting our apostasy within the Amherst-Smith demesne. Driven by an idealism and esoteric terminology few seemed to understand, we made appearances in our classes like double agents in collusion with a foreign polity, Kelly's Bard. Most of Amherst and Smith spoke the party line, as if there were no muses or sacred paths, offering a familiar mince of cliché pieties, half-baked assertions, existential homilies—hedged bets all.

Kelly had conferred a guidance and rectitude we had long sought. For me it was not just his exemplar; it was the tarot, the Halloween ceremony, Jung, Crowley, Nelson's angelic birds. I suddenly had numerous guides, present and transcendent. For Lindy, in her own words, "It was a breath of jarring, almost gagging cold air on the tepid waters of Smith's academic grind, which was a constant struggle for good enough grades, nothing else. It was unbidden knowledge, an alternate artistic universe of food nourishing and necessary. I didn't realize how starved I had been."

Then there was her and my relationship. We had bonded incongruously and unexpectedly, as writers and seekers, but now we had reached another, more serious phase, beyond neophyte boy and girl in a gambol or expendable tryst. Kelly wanted us to succeed as a couple too, to dodge gossipy dissuasions and normative templates. He had put down a dare, given us a high bar to shoot for, but we submitted willingly, for we wanted follow his lead and gain our personal and artistic freedom.

For Lindy it was a break with the social world of her past, its dating rituals, and the sorts of men considered admirable in that sphere. I was not the guy she had been looking for or imagining, not even close—more like his antithesis. I was not only the epitome of Jewish New York but a renegade and outcast there.

And while I may have been looking for some combination of Alice in Wonderland, Cathy Carr singing "First Anniversary," and

Emily Dickinson, I had been snagged by a combo of Simone de Beauvoir, Yvonne Rainer, and Annie Oakley.

I had no doubt found "her" too soon, but it was too late to do anything about it. We were in a trap—in my blue room with the yellow serape, not able to escape our pasts and divergent styles. We had been raised and trained differently, not only how to behave in the world but how to dress, how to witness yourself, how to be a man or a woman and how a man and a woman charm each other and expect to be charmed. Such customs ranged from the humdrum uses of social drinking and smoking to what to expect from life and love—in general how to occupy time and space and one's own desires, plus all the vestigial habits people dredge up when they try to stay close, be best friends and a romantic couple too.

Personal traits are deep-seated and loyal and do not submit to ideology or hermetic edict. My girlfriend was scrupulous about her looks, though in a playful manner, creatively attuned to the impact of clothes, makeup, and style. She was brash and a bit wild, free and easy in her gyroscope through time and space, the nuances of flirting and touch. My ways of being and moving were unconscious, or derived cluelessly from baseball and lapsed Viola Wolfe dance lessons. I was mostly *un*aware of my appearance, lost in thoughts, forgetful that I was even being seen.

She embodied a milieu more culturally sophisticated than Betsy's Miami Beach but similar in its self-assurance and sangfroid. She came from a strictly cordial family and had a fair amount of "Flower Girl" debutante glamour and Denver vogue to her. Trained in ballet from eight to sixteen and later modern dance, she was dazzling when she did the dance of her name. I was still trying to remember its sequence of steps.

I had an unexamined romantic penchant, a tendency toward literal, sentimental responses. By contrast, Lindy was cosmopolitan, experienced sexually and socially. She understood that relationship was complex, cantankerous, paradoxical, and that you usually got somewhere by going against the grain, confronting impediments and challenges rather than evading or pretending they could be finessed or overlooked. She was bored by pap and ritualized gestures and by people's knee-jerk valorizations of them, so she didn't offer any lenient routes or passes.

I had no use for ritualized gambols any more than she did. I had tarried too long with civilians: casual wayfarers, geishas and mere narcissicists. I was ready to play for keeps with a complicated partner in a game that counted. So I tried to observe and respond conscientiously.

I wasn't daunted by Lindy's fast company. I had handled my mother's onslaughts, so I didn't flinch or back off her sometimes brutal assessments—and they were doozies, as accurate and deadly as verbal arrows got. I was stoked and challenged, for I was not only Fabian's patient, I was his apprentice, a long-time psychological inquisitor, of late a literary and metaphysical reader too. I had trained a sensitivity to moods and projections, an attunement to paradoxes of intent. I didn't get bogged down. I knew how to mirror and transform. I had done it for years with sundry folks from Abbey West to Betsy Sley to Jeff Tripp.

Our inconsonant rhythms and contrary histories precluded any ease of sexuality. That part of the relationship was a struggle from the get-go. She proceeded slowly, respecting old-fashioned adolescent boundaries. She did not want us taking on more than we could handle, her own social maturity notwithstanding. Liberated sex had not made her particularly happy, and she wanted off the fast track and the sorts of yardsticks and fellow travellers it provided. "I wouldn't have blown in your ear," she told me later, "if I thought you would have misunderstood or taken advantage like most boys. I knew I could trust you." In that regard we were peers trying to change speeds and get in sync—her slowing down and me speeding up.

Life neophytes coming from opposite directions, we were training each other, trying to balance each other's excesses, reforming each other's rigidities and atavisms. That made our romance tough and diagnostic more than sexy and sweet.

We argued nightly, one more cigarette for her in the car before Smith's curfew, trying to patch it together with a conciliatory more than romantic kiss.

Lindy was clear and acerbic and embraced the confident

good-humored person when I became him, but she hectored and dismissed the perverse child. When I kneeled on the mattress looking wounded and distraught, she would say, "Enough," and go for a walk in the Glen, or sit in the living room talking with other people, waiting for me to give it up. I despised that child too, but there was no place to hide him.

"That's okay," Lindy said. "So, we hate each other. It will all come out in the wash."

Like Schuyler I was trying to scale the abyss of my failed adolescence in a single leap. Lindy was as helpful as another person, with her own destiny at stake, could be. She didn't abandon me or get scared off when I panicked, but she also didn't let my dramas take over or stampede her into compliance with desperate claims. She required that I make an ongoing, sincere attempt at normalization, to stop indulging and inflating my knee-jerk apostasies and paranoias. If I hadn't, she would have been gone in a flash.

Yet she counted on my originality and prowess for dead-reckoning, my willingness to improvise and make unconventional choices, as I pushed her to break her obedience to spurious authority and decorum and to be her quirkiest, most free-associative self.

I had to learn how to my discriminate contradictory passions on the fly: the generosity of creative imagination (good) versus tantrums of mere contrariness (bad). My pranks, fears, and epiphanies ran in overlapping synapses, so it was a challenge to sort them out and retain my dignity as well as any ease or flair. I didn't always stay on the beam of that one because I hadn't experienced, at a baseline level, that *the tracks, though parallel, weren't the same.* To my family it was *all* perverse and insane, every insight and audacity. As far as they were concerned, I had *no* visionary or aesthetic gifts. At best I was meant to become a lawyer or hotel executive. The trouble was, I had allowed myself to be minimalized and depreciated in my own mind too.

By what presumption was I purporting to court this woman? At times I would wake with a start like a man on a tightrope who had never been trained in the art; it seemed sheer overreach and bluff. I hadn't even dated yet. It was a wonder that Lindy even liked me, let alone perhaps loved me, that she saw a diamond in the rough.

When she was feeling good about our relationship, she might at random moments, even in public, let her entire weight suddenly collapse against mine like a modern dancer in an informally choreographed *pas de deux*. As I shifted with varying degrees of success to absorb her impact without losing balance, often stumbling a bit, she would pronounce with self-deprecating satire: "A man you can lean on!"

She was invoking a current fashion ad that ran regularly in the *New York Times Magazine* and *New Yorker*. A woman in a worksuit of blended polyester inclined like the Tower of Pisa against nothing but the words "A man you can lean on—that's Klopman!" The issue of whether I was solid enough to hold up her weight too (if necessary) was crucial because Klopman had been her long-time standard. Before me, there were Steve and Jim and others like them—super-confident males. When she was dubious or incensed by my failings—the absurdity of even considering me boyfriend material—she treated the clothing ad as gospel and made comments like, "I need a different kind of man, and you need someone you can lean on too. If we keep forcing the issue, we are both going to end up on the floor."

I tended to judge how we were doing by how seriously she took Klopman.

She decided to go to a friend's house outside Boston for Thanksgiving ("Remember, familiarity breeds contempt," she warned, amused that I had thought the word was "content."). I went to the Hotel and used it as a base to revisit Bard. It turned out that Kelly had guests on that day, so Harvey led me to the home of Jonathan Greene, a married student and poet. Beside the fireplace after dinner I participated in an evening of scuttlebutt during which I fielded questions about myself. Harvey sat there smoking his pipe, nodding and smirking, tossing an occasional jibe like "Don't forget, he's not only got Amherst but Grossinger's to live down."

I visited Kelly the next afternoon. He expressed concern about my "travelling without Lindy." I acknowledged his warning and promised to return together, but he was already on to the next topic.

"Why did you tell Harvey and Jonathan your story and yet never a word to me, even about Grossinger's?" I was dumbfounded that he already knew, then abashed as I pictured myself chattering away while the disciples prepared their report for the master. But was he saying that I should have told him my life tales too, or that I made an ass out of myself by telling them at all?

"It didn't seem appropriate."

"You're right. It wasn't. I caught the attention of the part of you that is awake, and you didn't think to waste my time on such nonsense. Having Lindy with you helped; you were in too serious a situation to dawdle. With those others it was just nervous energy, nothing that counts in play. That's okay. You defined them too. Nothing lost."

He had a very definite opinion about my relationship to Grossinger's. "You must have accumulated good karma in a previous lifetime. Grossinger's is the universe's way of rewarding you. Don't reject it. That would be ungracious. Try to put it to good use. Since it is a blessing to you, try to be a blessing to *it*. Not in a culturally ritualistic way, as everyone will insist at the waste of both your time and theirs, but in the true sense of magi bearing gifts. Respect the karma of your family members too. Don't deprive them of your knowledge or compassion out of second-rate political claptrap."

Then he handed my manuscript back to me.

"The speech you gave at Halloween was, in a sense, your first piece of writing. What comes before it is more gossip, social chatter of the sort you did last night." His eyes were solemn and piercing. "Confession is a trick we play on ourselves. We pretend it is personal, but it is actually the least personal act of all." I nodded, as he went on. "We were all mistreated in childhood; do we want to make that the talisman of our lives? We all have the same fantasies and daydreams; they're not of essence. It's the energy they generate that matters. Remember Crowley, turn it into the nourishment you need, make a different energy, do not let the Moon swallow you. Anyone can dance like a marionette. It is far more difficult to face our uniqueness, to speak of what is truly in our hearts."

I had waited a lifetime for Fabian and Friend—even Leo Marx—to speak with such clarity and precision.

"Your Halloween speech was personal because no one could have spoken it but you; it expressed your destiny. These Betsies and Peggies are everyone's fantasies, which means no one's." He corroborated the point by reading from a poem by Olson:

> *This, is no bare incoming*
> *of novel abstract form, this*
> *is no welter or the forms*
> *of those events, this,*
>
> *Greeks, is the stopping*
> *of the battle.*

On the afternoon of Christmas vacation I drove Lindy to the airport by Hartford. I already had my own ticket out of New York and would meet her in Denver in a four days' time. I passed through Grossinger's like a mirage. Aunt Bunny was back in the hospital by then, getting a new round of shock treatment. "How can you allow such a thing?" I demanded of my father.

"Richard, I haven't paid for your medical school yet. Leave this to the doctors."

I visited my New York family the day before my flight. I was an outsider there too, no longer privy to battles and tensions that had once been second nature. They were conducting them now without me, my mother and brother at each other's throats, my sister catatonic.

Head against an airplane window, I looked down at snowy checkerboard farms and sang on and off in my mind a silly New Christy Minstrels song that began *"I was drivin' a rig out o' Texas, / all loaded an' bound for Cheyenne...."* Then, on the other side of sky, mid-afternoon, she was standing there in a crowd in her blue puffy winter jacket with an open face that melted my heart.

"Hello, kiddo."

As I said the password back, the song's patter concluded in my brain: " *... got me a woman in Denver, Lord, / That's where I'm settlin' down.... *"

She drove us to her house in Capitol Hill near center city, though to a New Yorker it looked like countryside. Christmas lights in the windows, snow on the front lawn; this was my daydream past, my undisclosed future. Her parents, her married sisters, and their husbands were on hand. I was introduced in a flurry and offered this and that to eat and drink.

While treating me gingerly, everyone expressed enthusiasm about my visit and curiosity about my people back east. Her mother and father were older than mine, silver-haired denizens of the Old West. Since I had been briefed in advance on her father Hank's eclectic interests I sought him out for an exchange about UFOs and then Pueblo Indians.

Her oldest sister Susie was friendly if cool. Her husband was a business executive. He spoke that night with authority about profit margins.

Her next oldest sister, Polly, had Lindy's eyes and wise look, but was more slapdash and quippy, outwardly super-friendly. Her clarion of a voice dominated the clatter. After a few minutes she led me aside and whispered, "Boy, am I glad you're here. I've been hearing about some of Lindy's flings, married men and all. I always knew my good-looking kid sis was going to attract the wrong types." Then she patted me on the arm and gave me a hug. Her husband was a smooth, stocky psychiatrist who had been a flight surgeon on aircraft carriers in the South China Sea.

If the Houghs were self-conscious about my being Jewish at Christmas time, they needn't have been. We were all Americans, and I was far more committed to the teachings of Thomas Merton than to anything I had learned at Hebrew School. Angels and alchemists were Christian; the tarot was Gnostic and Qabalistic both. Christ was a rabbi who took an old prophecy to another level.

On Christmas morning I read to them from Merton's sermon on Prometheus. Its gist is that we are foolish in to try to steal things God is only too willing to give us for free. In making ourselves into heroes or thieves we deny his pure bounty and generosity. We barter away spirit for matter and goods.

The anti-materialism came across, so it was not their favorite message, but they thanked me for sharing it with them. In the days that followed, though we didn't acknowledge it, they were becoming my family too.

Denver felt a bit like my runaway in Winnipeg, only this time for real. I gradually lost myself in the adventure, touring my girlfriend's city with her—coffee shops, former schools and neighborhoods, meals and beers in Larimer Square. One afternoon I went around the house photographing vignettes of her life, collections of objects on her desk, clothes thrown over the chair.

I was in flight over the abyss, and there was no turning back. My only hope was to land on the other side.

When I called Stan Brakhage in Rollinsville I omitted mention of Phi Psi because I did not want to be implicated in Tripp's hyperboles. Happy to have unexpected visitors courtesy of Kelly, he gave us directions on finding his cabin, a couple of unmarked dirt roads in the mix. Lindy and I set out in her father's Chevvy the next afternoon: a pilgrimage into the foothills of the Rockies recalling our recent sally from the Catskills to the Hudson.

The highway to Boulder was the easy part. On subsequent mountain roads we got lost multiple times and had to turn around in perilous spots and wind back. Finally we found a hopeful lane, enough like the one Brakhage described to risk plunging into wilderness.

I stood in the snow, staring at a relic, clearing my head: a log cabin amidst drifts, piles of wood and splitting blocks, a very old car, an axe in one log.... the stageset of *Dog Star Man*.

When we came in the door I had the same giddy sensation as upon entering Kelly's—I was crossing an unmarked cosmological perimeter. "Greetings," said Brakhage, extending his hand. If the Kellys' home was a chamber of the Druid occult, this was the Orphic West out of Denver.

We followed Stan in and immediately met the real-life Jane. She was dressed in jeans and boots and had been blending batter for bread. The hearth of the cabin was spacious and sunny, filled with books, canisters, reels, and other paraphernalia of Stan's art. Small kids scampered in and out, mostly without pants.

Stan began talking, just as at Amherst, partly from the generous impulse of his thoughts and partly in resentment for the way he had been treated at the kinds of Eastern colleges we came from. As he railed about being poor and unappreciated and not having enough money even to buy film stock, our Amherst and Smith affiliations escalated, without any participation from us, into red flags of moneyed elitism.

Sitting there cluelessly representing them, we became targets for longstanding peeves and resentments we barely understood. There were moments I thought we were about to get tossed out, as when Stan thundered once he figured out my connection to Tripp, infuriated that I tried to keep it from him. Luckily he settled into a scathing commentary on my former housemate: Jeff was deluded, narcissistic, self-aggrandizing, indulged for too long by negligent parents and professors, a fatuous bombast as well. He concluded finally that he should sell his beloved Porsche, "that is, if he cares about art. And if he doesn't need the money, which he clearly doesn't, there's a film-maker in Colorado who can always use it to buy another year's groceries."

Then he asked if we were hungry. Jane disappeared for a spell and returned with a platter of a bark tea, tan goat's milk cheese, and some fresh-baked bread.

We ate as Stan took us on tour with a cast of rowdy characters: Sartre, Cocteau, Gertrude Stein, Ezra Pound. When he realized that Lindy hadn't seen his films he brought out a projector and showed a section of *Dog Star Man*. Then he told us about the death of its dog, Sirius: "Other dogs found his corpse in the snow and rubbed themselves in it. The origin of perfumes is the body's decay—you know, John Donne: the nearness of death and sex."

Day became night. Exhausted, I felt myself sliding into a quick-sand of déjà vu as well as an apathy at my core. Wind blew snow against the cabin. The meaning of everything, myself included, was evaporating. The Six of Cups had been drawn from the Greater

Deck. I felt far from anyplace and wanted to go home, if only I knew where that was.

They fed us from an iron pot of soup they were making for dinner. Afterwards, Stan posed a riddle: One night he and a friend, happy and peaceful, sitting under the moon with beers, asked each other, "Why can't it be like this all the time?"

It was a wonderful question, but we couldn't guess the answer: "Why *can't* it be like this all the time?"

"It *is* like this all the time," Stan said. "It's just that we don't know it."

They walked us back to the car and we chugged into the wintry black. As Lindy worked her way down the mountain I got dizzier and dizzier. It wasn't just carsickness; it was the whole day, the life. Though I was thrilled by our ongoing adventure, my body rejected its baptisms. I felt chilled, nauseated by unfamiliar aliments: goat's milk and Gertrude Stein and elf tea, Stan and Jane's marriage and children, now the twisting road, the intimacy of Lindy herself. I was afraid I didn't have the strength or guts to pull this off. I wanted to rest. Enough bravado. Enough radical art and transformation. Finally I was too sick to continue and had to get out.

It was the biggest display of stars I had ever seen, the Dipper and Orion outblazed. Breathing Rocky Mountain air, I shivered and improved, the bitter cold restoring a counterweight of reality. I came back into the car and put my head in her lap as she drove, her icy paw now and then on my forehead as she steered the curves. I hadn't the strength even to focus—let alone identify—constellations I saw upside-down.

I refunded my return plane fare so we could take the train east together. We tried to arrange it so that we would go to New York, reclaim the Mustang, and drive it back to school, but Lindy's mother caught on at the last minute and changed her ticket at the station.

"It's totally inappropriate to travel together," she grumbled. "Let Rich go fetch his own car."

At dawn we lay against each other half-asleep on a bench in the Chicago station ... bookends, spoons. We fit, auras and energy patterns as much as bodies. My train came first. I kissed her and boarded. I shot through the Midwest, across New York State, down Harlem, into the tunnel at Park Avenue and 96th. I took the subway up to Central Park West. It was a weekday—everyone in my family was at work or school. There in the basement garage I found my car where I had left it, all shiny yellow—Bob had had the caked mud and brine of winter washed off. In the grace of that gesture of his I drove the turnpikes back to Amherst.

Second semester I signed up for Watercolor and the History of Art. I also took History of Film, Cognitive Psychology, Hindu Philosophy, and Seventeenth-Century Literature. It was a busy schedule, for I was still gathering credits to make up courses flunked freshman year. I was also beginning to view my studies with perspective. I had arrived at Amherst dazed and confused, unprepared to use resources that made it a fabled academic destination. While most of my classmates jumped at the chance to have complex experiences and start adult life, I was deep in my own maelstrom—at war with myself and embattled with the world.

Now I felt remorse for what I had lost—more than half my college tenure. It was too late to retrieve those opportunities, so I approached the ones that remained with childlike enthusiasm. Lindy had exposed my lack of a cultural background too. Her world was infused with Monet, Klee, Satie, Prokofiev, Poulenc, Merce Cunningham. Mine had nothing at all. Both my clans had ignored the fine arts so thoroughly that I viewed them as immaterial, on the level of tightrope walking or falconry. Except for photography, my seventh-grade fling with *Danse Macabre,* and a few other token dispensations, the worlds of painting, sculpture, dance, and symphonic music were demoted subconsciously to either decorations or affectations. Since I barely even sampled them, I overlooked their unique enchantments, their range of aesthetics and knowledge—the clues they held to the nature of reality.

I continued to ignore them in college, as I marched straight into the avant-garde, admitting a few abstract expressionist painters like Klee and Miró and the atonal, cosmic-ray-like sounds of Elliott

Carter and Arnold Schoenberg—but little else.

Lindy startled me into recognition of both my hubris and deficiency. Apprised by her in a way I hadn't been by high-school and college cohorts, I was anxious to address the deficit and make myself whole. In fact, I signed up for History of Music too but failed a tone test in the first class—I didn't know the difference between one note and another—so I switched those units to a psych class that met in the same period: optical illusions and pattern formation.

Meanwhile I got a few Phi Psi classical-music buffs to tutor me on Bach, Mozart, Beethoven, *et al.* They took the initiation seriously, with listening sessions and "Name That Composer" quizzes. Holst's *Planets* and César Frank's *Symphony in D Minor* became as consummate and hermetic as the best of Bobby Darin and the Brothers Four. And the organ mystery of Franck's *Prélude, Fugue and Variation* touched something ineffable and profound that had been in me all the way back to Bridey's church. Whenever I heard those ambiguous chords repeating, overlaying, building and combining mutations at different pitches, I may not have tracked their harmonic progression, but I remembered why I was alive.

In my life after college I would try to reclaim other things I cared about but had given short shrift or missed entirely: physics, competitive ice hockey, hardball, astronomy, biology, swaths of world literature, another language, a social identity, guileless male bonds. Attempting a young man's rites of passage as a middle-aged and older civilian wasn't the same as doing them at the proper age in a sequestered setting, but it had to pass. For much of my Amherst career I had been that kid from Bill-Dave toting his baseball glove in the snow. As long as I needed to convert primal totems, I had scant time for liberal arts.

I was still on a vision quest, swapping courses and extracurricular activities for rudiments of magic, alchemy, and divination. I needed to commute demons and their corrosive imagery to breathe at all or have space inside me, one day perhaps to shoot a puck again and study the universe with equanimity.

In Watercolor we were given large sheets of cold-pressed paper and taught to moisten it and then dab or drip pigment. That was how I copied the forsythia bushes of New England spring. I had never imagined myself painting before, but my initial attempt brought back the April hill on which we read our work for Mr. Ervin, a lemon brush tinting moist white fibers with a guileless time.

I was inhabiting the oracle issued on a corollary spring day a year prior, deriving its fathomless chimera. So far had I come in a solar circuit that the cumulus-strewn azure and glacial tarn were already ancient and occult. That swimming hole held a sphinx, and its remote beckoning had become the metronome of my existence.

I felt nostalgia for things that had never happened, a bottomless depth in myself that vibrated with the mystery and poignancy of the world. And it was yellow this time, not blue: lemon and gold yellow, the basis of every deck, secular and sacred, that had been sealed or encrypted, whose bittersweet intimation girded my life.

It was there in Central Park when I sleigh-rode on Daddy's back, there as I caught the taut cowhides he lobbed.

The irrepressible joy, the desire to know, to *be* what I knew.

It was there as Uncle Paul led a child into the tabernacle of Yankee Stadium and summoned Gil McDougald across the field, and years later looking down from the subway el into unknown territories. The latency, the clue in the cinders.

A premonition of not just cosmic but soul expanse.

It was there at Chipinaw amidst whining wasps and in the tang of mown fields, and Viola Wolfe's studio where austerities of fox trot and waltz were imposed in lieu of the sacred boy-girl dance, and at the shimmering Grossinger's pool when a teenager, awash in qualms and anticipation, sought entry to a longing he couldn't catechize.

The reverie, the unaccountable premonition of sacredness and loss.

It reverberated down corridors of Horace Mann, as a novice wandered between lifetimes, past and future casting each other's cryptic veil. And esoteric forsythia sprang into fire across field and vale.

That curious twining of dread and desire that makes everything possible and indispensable.

Drawn anew, the Six of Cups proffered a turn of fate, beyond
innocence and childhood rambles. The unknowable forces of Creation, mine and the universe's, were converging on a small spiral
in the Milky Way where two of us had commenced some twenty
years prior and almost seven hundred leagues apart: Denver gal,
New York boy; now fledgling woman, fledgling man sharing a
ceremony in the Pioneer Valley of Massachusetts.

I was painting my own saffron trump.

I began dressing in the way Lindy wanted. I bought dungarees and
turtlenecks, learned to drink coffee, tried to smoke her cigarettes
and finally compromised on a pipe. It was an unfamiliar ritual,
stuffing in the tobacco and igniting it. It created a rich, fiery aroma
I associated with Dr. Friend, but it lasted only a month.

Unfamiliar rituals were what I needed. The past offered only
a sense of smallness and self-loathing. Soon enough my mother
would meet my girlfriend and thank her—with nothing short of
amazement—for going out with me. That's how they thought of
me: a weirdo, a misfit—troubled little Richie. But to myself I was
a maker of ceremonies, a radical artist, an individuating hero. No
wonder I wanted to rebuild my associations from scratch—Joan
Miró: *Women, Birds, Stars,* "Courage in a dragonfly"; Charles Ives:
polytonality, symphony in D minor; Mahler: the muffled drum;
Melville: "the apprehension of the absolute condition of present
things"; dark coffee; Brakhage: *Dog Star Man;* Gertrude Stein:
"one must dare to be happy"; John Keats: "negative capability,"
"To what green altar, O mysterious priest." Every day new. Kelly:
Tomorrow possible because it is....

Helene wrote a letter pleading for me not to drop her. Helene?
For a moment I couldn't remember who she was.

I was midway in my leap.

I stopped writing novels. I stuck my reams of confessional prose
into cartons and forgot about them.

My guides were Winnebago shamans and Celtic shape-chang-
ers, not Bellow's shamanic caricatures. I intended to blast through

Grossinger's to "The Twilight Zone" or Jack Finney's enchanted "third level" beneath New York's subway lines. For Miss Carver this had been a nonstarter—she wanted Henderson's mock sorcerers, voodoo frogs, and allegorical lions with their social-parody agenda. She preferred the *merely* ironical profundity of a literary device. But I was appalled by Bellow's spiritual shallowness and self-entitled cultural theft.

It didn't matter that I was a novice poet. I wanted to remake myself through Kelly, Brakhage, Olson, and projective verse: art as the highest activity of the mind, your relation to God and the Universe. I wanted to run as fast as I could from Catherine Carver, and I did:

> *miró*
>
>> *using brightest colors on*
>> *loops of the infinite, stars*
>>> *were made blue, gods were made*
>>> *yellow, and where*
>> *one color crossed*
>> *another, a*
> *message was born.*

> *lindy hey*
>> *lindy hey come*
>>> *to the window babe*
>> *smile babe*

> *grey sunless*
>>> *air*
>> *driven by*
> *isobars*
>>> *into*
> *sky wind.*
> *today when i was not thinking of you,*
>> *a lean bike figure*
> *drove softly by, i*
>>> *was 2fingering an acorn,*
>>>> *so I sidearmed it happily in your direction, you*

arrived
blue, your reindeer skijacket powder
  blue, your thinking notebook marble
blue, your bike scratchy with Donald Duck
  blue, its silent eye a filament of ozone
blue, i
following
  to catch you soon,
soon, kiddo.

Then I wrote my Bob Kuzava poem, throwback to a kid listening to the seventh game of the 1952 World Series, his first.

On weekends Lindy and I ranged farther. We visited an art museum in Worcester for an Australian Aborigine show. Then Boston. We collected Polachek at his apartment and went to hear Harvey Bialy read with Allen Ginsberg and some young Harvard poets. Afterwards everyone was invited to Ginsberg's apartment. A party was in progress; a dog gave birth in the corner. We stood to the side, interested but not part of it, then returned to the relative innocence of Western Mass.

The following weekend we drove to New York and stayed a night with my family. For all the angst I put into that meeting, the time was uneventful. My mother and Lindy had their tête-à-tête.

At a raunchy theater in the East Village we attended a late-night Kenneth Anger retrospective. The crowd was testy, police cars patrolling up and down the block, officers staring down those entering. The films were a blend of homosexual fantasies, motorcycle orgies, and Crowleyite rituals, but Brakhage had assigned *Inauguration of the Pleasure Dome* and *Scorpio Rising* and we were under his aegis.

During spring vacation we drove to the Hotel. My father's house was empty except for us. While puffy clouds floated above the golf course, we studied in a rowboat. The air was barely warm, a few turtles visible on rocks along the shore. Lindy was taking a course on Sixteenth Century Poetry, so read to me from Thomas Carew:

"The warm sun thaws the benumbed earth, / And makes it tender; gives a sacred birth / To the dead swallow; wakes in hollow tree / The drowsy cuckoo and the humble-bee."

It was a lush idyll—beers at the bar, dinners of matzoh ball soup, steak, and fries, capped with different flavors of sherbet and chocolate or lemon sponge cake.

We continued to Bard. Kelly had tendered an invitation to visit him while school was out, and he provided us a bare room in the empty infirmary. That night she stared down at me like a rider on a horse and said with a cheery laugh, "There, Rich, no longer a virgin." I felt oddly clinical, a post-sensual coldness and wish to get myself back. I had wanted this for so long, but it was another thing entirely, not the tantalizing forest of vines, more a combination of mythical sex and actual intimacy, a dance of man and woman bones I hadn't yet learned.

The next morning, driving across New York to Connecticut to see Brakhage show his films at Yale, the experience opened inside me. A calm, almost pleasurable nausea blossomed from my belly like a lotus, so that I had to be neither powerful nor well, just cozy as she zipped through sun-shade patches of trees and houses. I felt less as though I had become a man, more that I was a kid again, safe and whole, the heater blowing warmth, the sky an unreal robin's egg blue. I turned on the Mets opening game … an extra-inning single winning it for them.

Why can't it be like this *all the time,* Stan?

In the weeks that followed, I discovered unhappily that it can't. We lived out the prophecy that making love would become a deterrent, not a touchstone. We were stuck back in the blue room, and I didn't have the gumption or pizzazz to keep starting over, to woo her with confidence and grace. I wanted to have that closeness always, not because it was earned or even pleasurable but because it sealed the promise. I was running perhaps five years ahead of myself, hoping to skip the shoals that lay in between. I didn't want to become grim and militaristic like Schuyler, but I would have done well to heed his cautionary tale.

I made her a map of the house in which we would live: the bed-rooms of our children, the darkroom, the attic with its telescope, the garden. She began talking about how we were getting too cozy—that I was assuming the relationship rather than letting it develop. As she stomped out of the blue room one night, I lay there, drowning in my ashes. She returned, furious at my self-pity: "I hate men who drool!" It certainly would … in the wash.

The shadow of childhood crept over me like a pall, not then, once upon a time—because that was all dead and gone—but now, in the present, in the form of strictures and agonies it gave rise to. I knew deep down I couldn't just keep climbing; soon enough I would tumble back. I knew this and yet couldn't help myself.

She wanted to be free again—it happened so fast I didn't know where it came from.

She said, Whoa! Let's stop seeing each other for a while. I need to breathe. You're holding on too tight.

Familiarity had indeed bred something akin to contempt.

Earlier that spring, provoked by political satire from Phi Psi, Amherst's Fraternity Council had issued a series of punitive direc-tives, requiring our House to make more conventional uses of its tuition-sourced budget, including a regular homecoming band and a publication. At our next meeting the House jug band was deeded official status, and $100 was turned over to me to put out a literary magazine. At first I balked, but the idea of launching a four-college journal was already in the air locally.

Even before the fraternity council's directive, Kelly had urged Lindy and me to start our own magazine as a way to get ourselves affiliated in the larger 'hood—he felt that young writers should make their debut in the company of made warriors and mages. Each visit to Annandale, he gave us the newest editions of *matter.* Those goldenrod and blue-green pages were priceless, hot off the mimeo press with the recent work of avatars.

When I told Kelly about the Phi Psi edict, he suggested that the fraternity-council magistrates were the unwitting tool of my spirit guides—Crowley magick-talk of the sort we did all the time. He proposed that we subvert their intentions and use my speech as *Io*'s opening salvo: "It's channeled from your own higher self anyway, so it can herald your first serious public undertaking."

Lindy offered to handle Smith if we did it. We found co-editors at Mount Holyoke and UMass. Then, since Phi Psi's tiny allotment was hardly adequate, I enlisted house members to traipse from shop to shop in Amherst (and when the ploy proved successful, Northampton and Belchertown), begging ads from bookstores, clothiers, art galleries, optometrists, gas stations, and of course the Lord Jeff Inn and Wiggins Tavern. All of these establishments had budgets for community involvement.

After weeks of soliciting manuscripts, we laid out thirty pages of writing and artwork, including poems from Chuck Stein, Harvey Bialy, Lindy, and Dona to which we added a bonhomie sent on request by science-fiction writer Ray Bradbury, some notes on psi phenomena from a classmate, and the text of a pamphlet handed me by a stranger in Greenwich Village and blaming all mankind's woes on a comet.

But the magazine's name eluded us. Then while re-reading my poem of the previous spring, I found the moon Io circling Jupiter. The idea of such a short title—a line and a circle—delighted both Nelson and me, him as a minimalist and me as a crossword-puzzle/"moons of the solar system" buff. Using discarded window screening from the attic, he made a surface of mesh, sprinkled it with mothwings from the bowl of a lamp, added washers and nuts, smeared the whole thing with India ink, and pressed it on a piece of paper. He thought that the resulting image was perfect, but on my insistence he took a fountain pen and etched a pictograph of Jupiter in the still-wet ink. "Ever the literalist, Grossinger, making me deface my impeccable screen art with a dopey cartoon of a planet!"

With unrestrained glee I thanked him, for I couldn't myself draw a turtle. Now I wish I had let his transdimensional field stand as what it was: a gateway beyond literality.

In order to have the magazine published inexpensively Lindy and I took the work to a cut-rate typesetter in New York City and then brought her pages to the Grossinger's print shop. The keyboarder was so cut-rate that, after we gave her a list of her typos, she lit another cigarette, typed a sheet of amendments, and handed it to me. It was left to us to cut them out and paste them over her errors: "You want corrections in place," she griped, "find a fancier joint." Ninety miles away we enlisted my old friend Stanley in the Grossinger's print shop and, with a knife, pot of glue, and steady hand during a break from laying out the next day's lunch menu, he got us clean paste-ups. Then he promised to print the booklet when he had an opening in his schedule.

Lindy and I had planned to go together to fetch the cartons and drop the first copies at Bard, but by the time it was ready she was off at Williams, going out with an old friend from Denver. So, that Friday after classes, I drove the four hours to the Hotel alone.

In stacks beside rooster-clad breakfast menus sat *Io,* Nelson's image on its front. It was like an occult *Chipinaw Chirp,* artwork seamlessly tattooed among words, moth-wing-and-mesh covers vaguely suggesting Minoan tablets. I kept sniffing the fresh ink as I lugged three cartons to the car. Then I drove to Bard and presented *Io* to Kelly.

After extolling the magazine and promising to submit work to the next issue, he heard out my woes and suggested that he and I go to the Chinese restaurant for a private session. As we clanked across the bridge, his body draped over the column of Bloisius, he gave the oracle's answer: "This is life and death to you, isn't it? At least you recognize that. You were well taught by your childhood hardships. Most people in this country think it's all fun and games." His words were as startling and on target as ever. "America has teeth, you know. If you rise up and become what you are, it will try to strike you down, destroy you. All the while it will smile and pretend to be innocuous. Ah yes, that great American sense of humor that someday will surely kill us all."

I said that Lindy wanted to date other people and I wondered if maybe she was right. "Perhaps I should see other girls too."

"Those are just notions. You don't know where the gods are leading you. Simply follow. Forget the past. Be what you are now. Lindy—and you likewise—are involved in an old image of ecstasy, but 'ex' is always outside. We need to invent a new word—call it 'enstasy,' the pleasure of staying within a growing form no matter how painful. The form itself will sustain you and tell you when it is time to break off. You have only the vulnerability of your being with which to face the world. Expose yourself and be redeemed."

On a walk in the Glen the following Monday, Nelson cautioned me not to forget the angels either: "You can't write their script for them. They write for you. They write so much better than you could imagine. When you get too involved in making things happen you get in their way. Simple prayers are everywhere—like those bird sounds. Listen."

"Kywassik!kywassik!kywassik!" shot from distant trees. The primal obscurity of that code cut through me like a knife.

Then one evening in May, Lindy called and asked me to bring her more copies of *Io*. We went for a drive in the country and parked by a tobacco field. I looked at her face, no more anger in it, only a mirror of what my love for the world had become, my hope too, because I had cast it all into her. I kissed her teary cheeks as she said, "Okay, Rich, so we try again."

Years later she contended that our courtship was bumpy because she was coming of age too, going through her own process of individuation, my melodramas and mythologies notwithstanding. Human beings are complex enough creatures and the universe itself is all the more complex, so two divergent stories can occupy the same space-time *and both be true.* After all, we are operating on many different levels, psychological and psychic, simultaneously.

Now the summer faced us—and how to be together. Lindy had her own quandary with her family. There was little good feeling left at home: her sisters were elsewhere, her mother and father were not getting along—a mid-life crisis. More radical and zany than the other girls, she had grown up nonetheless a cheerful, compliant daughter in a Colorado Episcopalian setting, Mayflower Society on her father's side, Denver society on her mother's, trappings of wealth but not enough money to back appearances. In their own heedless way these parents had sabotaged her, keeping her powerless and eligible. She was supposed to marry a social prototype, a businessman or lawyer. They never considered who she really was herself or that she might contain dances and dreams not in the other two girls.

At adolescence she had been transformed from a family jester into a rebellious teenager, hanging around the circle of a friend's mom who threw weekend parties where booze, Librium, and marijuana flowed freely. On Lindy's sixteenth birthday she tossed her clothes down from the second storey and planned to slip out the window for late fireworks, but her father surprised her in the act. It was horribly dangerous—descending safely down the house would not have worked.

Her last weeks of high school were open warfare. By the time she left for college, the rifts had healed, her behavior blamed on the boys she was dating. Her family didn't shout so much as impose guilt trips on one another—obligatory confessions, apologies under duress. When Lindy talked on the phone about the shortcomings of Smith, her mother said simply, "Then you can transfer to CU." She had gone to Smith herself and didn't want it criticized.

After our visits to Kelly and the escapades of the spring, Lindy could no more return to being a compliant citizen at home—her mother dominant, her father not saying a word—than I could abide another term at Grossinger's. We planned to spend the summer together.

We toyed with the notion of working in New York—Milty Stackel had a new shop in Queens and offered to hire us—but her mother wouldn't hear of it. Her requirement was that she come back to Colorado. If that's where Lindy had to be, well then so did I. We hatched a different plan, around Aspen. "It's the most happening Colorado town," she effused. We would each go home; then she would head to the Western Slope and get a job. I would drive out, a big journey, New York all the way to the Rockies, and meet her there.

I took her to the Hartford-Springfield airport, aware of the hurdles before us. At least we were of one mind and heart and our difficulties were tactical. We kissed goodbye, and I headed to Grossinger's. My mindset was sacred warrior, "Moon River," "Gotta Travel On,"

Another Country. My book was *Lord of the Rings,* recommended
months earlier by Schuy, now critical reading material. I was setting
out from the Shire with the ring, under the shadow of Mordor.

When I told my father that I would get my own job again he
froze. "Absolutely not," he barked, "This summer you're working
for me." I nodded disarmingly, keeping my plan to myself.

The next morning I visited our old boarder Jerry thirteen miles
away in Grahamsville. It seemed sad that he and I couldn't have
another summer of playing ball, sitting in the backyard with Bunny,
but that pastoral was over. I told him what I was about to do. He
understood my wish to be free if not the irreconcilability of my
situation.

I had been under the influence of the gods for so many months
now that nothing was innocent—they were hurrying me on my
way. I was lucky to survive even that simple encounter with a friend.
A blue car speeding past me twice (going into town and then back
out at perhaps ninety) had performed a hit-and-run, seriously injur-
ing a child. A witness said it was the one that "came back through
town," which was also me because I had overshot Jerry's road. As
we sat on the porch, he got a disquieting phone call. He calculated
my degree of jeopardy—enough not to risk a constable's fishing
expedition (though my car was yellow)—and he sent me home
immediately on a back road.

I felt the malevolence of the thing on my tail. Dark forces of
undisclosed vintage opposed me. Some stranger, on a whim, could
take away my license. I could end up in jail or a mental ward like
Bunny. I could lose Lindy. And my own father was laconic, barely
conscious. I had no time to spare.

PART SIX

New Moon

June, 1965–November, 1965

I

ASPEN

At nightfall of the third day I wrote a brief note to my father, packed the Mustang: a box with a few books and records, a carton of *Io*s, and my baseball glove as well as the requisite suitcase of necessities. I set out west on Route 52. Harvey had left his Bard room unlocked for me, so I slept there, then got up at dawn and picked up the New York State Thruway at Kingston. I drove west into Pennsylvania, then across the Ohio line: virgin territory. A year ago I had borrowed Fred's clunker with Ohio plates to take Lindy to the airport. Now I was in Ohio itself, following, at a snail's pace and five days behind, the wake of her plane. Except for the teen tour and my flight to Denver, I had never been west of Scranton.

Gradually my excitement waned into a boredom of the road, its boding of the long miles ahead. The radio became tiresome. Only currents of memories held any interest. Ceaselessly they bubbled up, contacted my mind, and fell back away: punchball in the P.S. 6 yard, Dr. Friend opening his door to start a session, Callicoon Creek, June Valli singing "Applegreen."

I was driven by rage for all that had been done to me, but also by the tenderness I felt for Lindy and the immensity and mystery ahead. The morning was cool. A big sun cleared the last stars. Little by little, daytime's progression of hues permeated the landscape, gradually maturing into bright Midwestern p.m. as traffic increased. Repetitive thoughts raced, disappearing, returning, subsiding. I became quicker and more coordinated, darting in and out of lanes clogged with trucks, breaking loose again and again, into the clear.

By early evening when I pulled into the driveway of my old roommate Greg's house in Hudson, my Mustang was a racing shell. That
was the first day of my journey: 490 miles under my belt.

I arrived during an all-out locust invasion. Aliens were crawling
across the ground, flying up and buzzing in swarms, crashing against
the window as I showered and fell asleep in the back room.

Noon awakening brought Sherwood Anderson Ohio balm,
floating in zephyr-fragrant blossoms, inviting me (through Greg's
parents) to stay on a few days *("And all the world seemed applegreen....")*.
I wanted to. I saw kids lined up at an ice-cream truck, an adult
softball game in choose-up phase. There was so much unlived life
for which I felt nostalgia: things I had been thinking of and those
I hadn't, all the same now. I wished I could disappear into their
sweet opacity, stand in the village gaggle, ready to be someone's
left fielder, smash vigilance and lie exposed and anonymous, a
frog in the nameless sun. But I was in a leap and there were no
respites mid-air.

I left the next morning and set out west on the Ohio Turnpike.

I crossed the line into Indiana, then Illinois. My average speed
increased. My mind ground miles into pebbles, then loam of broken
thoughts. I began to notice police cars as I fantasized my father
collaborating with my Grahamsville accuser to bring me back—a
spell of paranoia that gradually faded. Moods came and went in a
tedium of driving; only the mileage made progress, now less than
a hundred to the Iowa line.

Habitation became sparser, landscapes more rural—farms scattered in near and far distances, corn dust in the air. Crossing the
Mississippi at Davenport, I was surprised to find Iowa Highway 80
posted for seventy-five, a new high. Wow, I could zoom!

Nightfall Iowa City, 562 miles notched on the second day. Sitting
in a restaurant with a slice of pizza I sank into *Lord of the Rings:*
"Whether the morning and evening of one day or of many days
passed Frodo could not tell. He did not feel either hungry or tired,
only filled with wonder. The stars shone through the window and
the silence of the heavens seemed to be around him.... "

Having left the Shire, Frodo was travelling through outlying districts, each of them fraught with dangers human and other, also allies he had yet to identify. He was led by a gray magician named Gandalf.

I chose a motel on a sidestreet; signed the register; then lay in fresh, stiff sheets, reading till I couldn't keep my eyes open:

"When the Elves passed westward, Tom was here already, before the seas were bent. He knew the dark under the stars when it was fearless—before the Dark Lord came from Outside."

Yes, the Dark Lord ... immanent yet so long ago.

In the morning I explored the town, the Iowa River, houses on its banks, children in their yards. I imagined Lindy and me living there someday. I even found the campus offices of the Iowa Writers' Workshop, where a British faculty member spared a half hour, let me babble about my work and, shaking my hand on parting, encouraged me to apply.

Revived by that fantasy I returned to the speedway and hurtled through cornfields. "Salt flats, salt flats," I encouraged myself as the expanse of stone whipped beneath, syncopated by blips of cars in the other direction. At sunset I came into giant Nebraska, swept past Omaha, then tapers of Lincoln at dusk. One more state to go.

Through the night, old farm teams Sam Rosenberg assigned us in Bunk 9 (Kearney and North Platte) approached at fifty miles, dwindled to digits, exited with the locals, and passed. I blended with the road's drama, an outlaw fleeing through badlands, dependent on my steed. I slept in the car at a road stop—525 miles on my third day.

I awoke at dawn. Light revealed a Western landscape: brown and sparse, occasional farms, pigs and cattle, brief azure ponds. The kid who had never driven west of the Delaware River had crossed the continent, from the Catskills to the prairie, and was headed for the Rockies. At a gas station I rapped on the car's yellow alloy fondly.

The nearness of Colorado, recalculated every few minutes, kept my brain engaged through the tedium of the western corridor of Nebraska. By the time I crossed the state line the sun was on top of me, as the miles to Denver melted into the plains. The last two hundred were nothing at all.

Mid-afternoon I came in through ranch suburbs, urban radio; found my way to Lindy's street, parked in front of her house, and emerged like a snail from my four-day shell.

Her parents regarded my arrival with suspicion. Did I plan to spend the whole summer with her? Where would I live? They didn't want a premature courtier, and certainly not me. I tried to be matter-of-fact.

Lindy was already in Aspen and, since they had the switchboard number of her lodging, I called. To my relief—she hadn't vanished over the continental divide into the anonymous Rockies like some apparition—she answered her line right away. She was both astonished and delighted: "I knew you'd try, but I told myself you might never get out of there."

She reviewed her situation. She was staying in a dormitory motel and had gotten two part-time jobs already—one writing for the *Aspen Illustrated News,* the other as a bartender-in-training at a restaurant called the Toklat. "Decorated with dogsleds and igloos," she laughed. She could begin for real on July 4th when she was 21.

I stayed overnight with her parents and left early the next morning, assuring them I would get my own place. From Denver it was a gradual ascent into the mountains, curvy roads up and down passes, occasional straight runs through high-altitude valleys. Woods became evergreen, sky spackled with cream-puff cumulus that descended tantalizingly to timberline. Finally, almost 200 miles (and five hours) west of Denver, I came out the steep chute of a Rocky Mountain pass into a small resort town, its late-afternoon main street teeming with college-age kids, a sobering glimpse of the reality for which I had traded the plushness and protection of my father's hotel. I was on my own.

I got directions to Lindy's apartment complex, found her door along a dim hallway, and knocked. The flight from Grossinger's had brought me home.

Her face and presence were famous by now, but I was surprised by her actuality. In the days since parting I had frozen her mien, forgotten her three-dimensionality: wide Modigliani brow, eyes in profile like accent marks, intelligent clear-as-a-bell voice ringing with assurance. Standing there in person, she was so real, a still picture come to life. For a moment, I found it hard to respond; then we hugged and sat together on the bed telling our tales. I relived my journey for her: imperiled escape, locusts, Iowa City. Then I heard about the exigencies of Aspen employment. After a while she pointed out the obvious: I needed a place to stay, and a job.

She knew of a ski chalet on the eastern side of town where there might be inexpensive rooms. In fact, she had thought of living there herself but couldn't without a car. We drove to look, and I snared the last room for a few dollars a night. It was a gloomy basement cubicle without a window, but I unpacked: typewriter, clothes, books, baseball glove....

For the rest of that week and Monday and Tuesday of the following one I hunted for a job, answering ads (with Lindy slipping me the classified before it was printed) and going door to door on the main drag and sidestreets. Competing with the roving horde of college students, I was routinely turned down at restaurants, the other newspaper, the bookstore, two rock-and-mineral shops, and miscellaneous storefronts. In order to get away from the throngs I offered to tutor Latin at a private school Lindy knew about in Carbondale. They thought about it for three tantalizing days before declining, "Sorry, come back in the fall." Meanwhile Lindy found a third job, cleaning house and babysitting for a postal clerk with a new baby.

I was running out of money, so I called my grandmother and started to give her an account of my situation. She didn't need testimony—she wired $200 the next morning.

From a poster on a lamp-post Lindy and I discovered that we had unexpected literary company: there was a writing program including two poets we knew of from Kelly: Paul Blackburn and John Taggart.

Aspen Writers' Workshop was located in a ski-lodge basement. After attending a reading there, we introduced ourselves and passed around copies of *Io*. Though we were not paying members, Blackburn invited us to join his seminar. That happily grounded us in a college-like scene. With Lindy working and me hunting for a job, we couldn't be daily participants but, when able, we lay in the grass of a nearby park and listened to student poems followed by Paul's playfully brilliant critiques, almost poems themselves.

We also met clusters of the Workshop crowd for lunch and dinner at an open-air restaurant in the center of town. On our meager budget we developed a passion for bowls of soup mixed with oatmeal or Wheatina—the house specialty—followed by after-dinner banter over tea.

Our best friend was Mitchell, a tall, spacy kid with curly black hair and glasses. A onetime student of George von Hillshimer at Summer Lane and a graduate of Music and Art in New York City, he presently attended funky Antioch College in Ohio, the antipode of Amherst and Smith. As intellectual as he was hip, Mitchell was a maestro of deadpan cosmic comedy. His favorite topics were Jungian synchronicity, sacred alphabets, and an avant-garde philosopher named Marshall McLuhan who had recently turned the world inside-out by placing the medium before the message. From topic to topic Mitchell had to clarify whether we were talking lineal typographic reality, phenomenological reality, tribal reality, or radio-TV electromagnetic waves. As he peppered his riffs with McLuhanesque *achtungs* and reality detours, he soon had me reading *The Gutenberg Galaxy*.

Aspen was surrounded by huge, very close mountains, an ever-present reminder that I was on a new planet, as unfamiliar in its way as Mars or Blueland. Then McLuhan fissioned the picture-postcard landscape, breaking it open its true oneiric immensity, casting four-dimensional diamonds of focus throughout the dialectics of space.

I had long sought an intellectual companion like Mitchell—a gentler, less magisterial version of Chuck Stein—someone who, like me, wandered from science fiction and alchemy through baseball history, pop songs, and New York subway stops. Mitchell and I regularly sat in the grass by the Workshop, riffing back and forth: projective verse, pre-Giotto Christian paintings, the totem poles of audio-tactile cultures, Little Anthony, the 1958 Yankees.

Chuck was far-out cuckoo too but cuckoo-sober; Mitchell let *everything* hang out.

From Kelly's original reading list I had brought along Gaston Bachelard's *The Poetics of Space,* which deepened the phenomenology of every breeze, alcove, and shadow, and Robert Graves' *White Goddess,* which tracked the origins of alphabets back to primeval tree names, not only the aspens and birches around us but the original apple trees of Wales and Breton, the "querts" whose "Q" was shaped from the enigmatic apple of Eve's first question. The rune "Q," Graves proposed (perhaps even apocryphally), came from the wild crabapple whose pome-and-stem design it replicates (hence the questions *quis?, quid?, quam?,* as well as the quest itself). "Q" was the mysterious fruit, in Celtic dialects, that Adam and Eve ate illicitly to get to the bottom of things at the beginning of time. Behind the alphabet, behind the origin of speech, lay only an atomistic chaos, not unlike the moments of sleep before dream.

This was great stuff, but I still needed a job.

Toward the end of the second week Lindy met me at lunch with a hot new listing that hadn't run—I could beat the crowd. A restaurant named Sunnie's Rendezvous was opening underneath the bookstore in the arcade—they needed a busboy. "Say you worked at Grossinger's this time," she advised. It wasn't honest, but it worked.

Sunnie was a platinum-blond ex-showgirl from Manhattan. On the magic of my surname she hired me at once, and I began the following night. It was an intimate dinner-only saloon—menu on a blackboard (trout, sirloin, fondu, etc.). The whole room was serviced by just one waiter and a busboy *(moi).*

Sunnie featured the live jazz of her boyfriend Ralph Sutton, who I would think of years later when I met the musician Randy Newman; he had recently left his wife to be with her. A serious bespectacled man, he sat at the piano all night, playing whether there were patrons or not. I imagined him equally celebrating and doing penance for his illicit romance and, in any case, he had nowhere else to go.

In addition to being the busboy I earned $25 once a week for scrubbing the kitchen floor with commercial detergent and another $20 to come in every other morning and clean the bar.

"Why pay two rents?" Lindy volunteered. "We should get a place together." It was an outrageous suggestion but I gleefully concurred. Most apartments were too expensive, yet Mitchell had heard about log cabins on a road outside town. "They're apparently really beautiful," he said, "and in the woods."

I drove west looking for some sort of Gold Rush encampment. Four miles out along the Roaring Fork River, I came upon the next best thing: Aspen Park Cabins.

The couple who owned the property were affable enough, school-teachers from Denver. For $50 a month you got a one-room cottage with a wood stove (management providing split firewood), a desk, a table, shelves, two double beds, a sink, silverware, plates, pots and pans, and a refrigerator with a freezer. All the cabins shared an outhouse. They had one unit left. "My only requirement," the educator in red-and-black plaid announced with a deadpan smile, "is that you have to be married." I swallowed hard and wrote "Mr. and Mrs. Richard Grossinger," then hurried back into town. It was my toughest white lie ever because it was jinxing what I most wanted, bringing it into surveillance way too fast. "Mr. and Mrs.?" I was still a child.

She wasn't. "You did it, Rich!" she exclaimed. Collecting our belongings in two trips, we planted our typewriters on stacks of crates, clothes on shelves, the overflow on hangers along a center pole. Books were set on small half-logs we hammered above the beds and over the sink. The cabin's second double bed served as a couch.

After arranging the dwelling, we returned to town and wheeled a cart up and down aisles picking out groceries. Felicity was to break out the cabin's plates, cups, and silverware and make our first domestic meal.

That night Mitchell was our guest. The three of us lay on the porch at sunset listening to the music of the Roaring Fork, talking Hindu illusion, tarot, and the sacred yew tree—a fire snapping inside, boiling water for noodles. As the sky darkened, our friend blessed our cabin with an epigraph from Bachelard:

"All these constellations are yours, they exist in you; outside your love they have no reality! How terrible the world seems to those who do not know themselves! When you felt alone and abandoned in the presence of the sea, imagine what solitude the waters must have felt in the night, or the night's own solitude in a universe without end!"

"Mitchell," Lindy said, "that's a beautiful, perfect prayer. I only hope we can deserve it."

After the meal we walked across the road and sat on boulders over the Roaring Fork. Shooting stars pierced the starry vault.

As I drove him back to town, Mitchell and I played with the radio, hunting for ballgames. From the High Rockies we could pull in a whole continent of them.

Dressed as a Swiss-like Alaskan maid, Lindy served drinks to a court-yard—she joked—of garnished fowls, but the Toklat traineeship never materialized into a job (she wasn't proficient at memorizing the complicated drinks), so she wrote her articles and twice a week vacuumed, dusted, and cleaned the postal clerk's house. Meanwhile Sunnie's Rendezvous was perhaps the least popular restaurant in town. I arrived nightly at 4:30 in jacket and tie. Chester, the grizzled chef, fed the waiter Bob and me scraps from his menu, odds and ends of fish, fondu, and assorted fried vegetables. Then we sat in the alcove and awaited customers.

My partner, Bob, a bespectacled cowboy freak from Wyoming with a healthy crop of hair growing out of both ears, was a career waiter and supporter of Barry Goldwater. Like Ralph, he had left another "situation" to launch Sunnie's enterprise, a mistake he now regretted, for summer tips served as his year's keep. At my level, though, the income was sufficient. After all, I was an imposter, a double agent from Grossinger's, slumming.

On most evenings it was an hour or more before the first customer appeared. Chester stared dolefully at the ceiling. Bob dropped into a stupor. And Ralph's witticisms left more and more empty space between them until he fell silent too. I spent the time on tenterhooks over the fate of Frodo the ring-bearer.

"… he looked eastward and saw all the land of Lorien running down to the pale gleam of Anduin, the Great River.…

"'There lies the fastness of Southern Mirkwood,' said Haldir.

'It is clad in a forest of dark fir, where the trees rot and wither. In the midst upon a stony height stands Dol Guldur, where long the hidden Enemy had his dwelling. We fear now it is inhabited again, and with power sevenfold.'"

"I don't care if there ain't no customers," snapped Sunnie. "I don't want you educatin' yourself on my time. At least *look* like you're ready to serve."

After reading was abolished, Bob and I stood in the alcove debating politics and our boss's incipient dementia.

No more than four of the fifteen tables were ever filled, though I found our diners a congenial constituency. I made friends with two priests from Oklahoma City to whom Bob was rude because he thought they were fags and wouldn't tip us. "Would you give the same compliments to Jesus Christ?" I asked.

My new buddies not only left a generous stack of bills but slipped me a few extras to pay for *I*os to give away at home.

During one meal I kept a discussion going with a NASA executive about the *Mariner* satellite headed towards Mars. He took down my name and Phi Psi address and promised to send early press photos (he did). Bob thought that *this* guy was a Soviet spy. Meanwhile Sunnie told me to stop pestering the clientele with "your college-boy routine."

I came in to clean around 10 a.m., pushed open saloon doors, turned floodlights onto the bar. Then I counted empty whiskey bottles by brand, hosed the walk, put in fresh ice chips, rotated the warm beers under the cold, swept away crumbs, polished tables, dumped ashtrays, checked toilet paper, and refilled bowls with pretzels and potato chips.

Sunnie had told me to amuse myself by playing records. She meant hers, but one day I brought in T. S. Eliot reciting the "Quartets":

What is late November doing?
With the disturbance of the spring....

She had forgotten to shut off the speakers by which recordings of Ralph were blasted into the arcade to lure dinner customers from the streets. I was unknowingly serenading the town of Aspen.

> *Scorpion fights against the Sun*
> *Until Sun and Moon go down*
> *Comets weep and Leonids fly....*

While I poured potato chips in the semi-darkness, unknown to me a crowd had gathered on the street.

> *Whirled in a vortex that shall bring*
> *The world to that destructive fire....*

Rumors of this performance soon roused Sunnie and, just as Eliot was intoning about *"the movement of darkness on darkness ... "* (the panorama of blue sky and aspens being stripped away), she burst in.

"Turn off the sermon, boy!" she declared. "It ain't Sunday!"

Our life in the cabin was the heart and soul of the summer. We woke into ice-cold mornings and cuddled in bed until one of us got up and put newspaper and kindling in the stove and lit a match. Black metal creaked, distributing heat, igniting our viscera like sun on two dormant reptiles. Soon smoky tree alphabets warmed the room with their sap, stirring prehistoric memories and opening another Rocky Mountain day. We hiked in bathrobes and moccasins uphill across pine needles to the outhouse to brush our teeth in glaciermelt, then take a hot-spring-like shower. Back at the hearth we cooked French toast or pancakes in the cabin's scalding black cast-iron pan.

We collected suns: the low orange sun barely tinting the morning formica; the cold white breakfast-and-coffee-on-a-log sun; the dishwashing sun in gray-water; the hot noon sun where we lay and read in high grass; the late-afternoon forest sun, aspen leaves whirring moiré patterns and susurrus; the golden sun of supper beans ... a sunset of bats and evening stars.

At night—Brakhage's moths fluttering on the screen, an owl sang alien notes. We boarded the huge bed that seemed a raft among constellations ... and sailed onto that *"river of crystal light / into a sea of dew."*

When Lindy had cramps or got a flu I brought her cups of tea and sat by her. We talked tirelessly and argued fiercely but always loved each other again. Our original passion had been replaced by an intimacy so riveting and solid, so delicate, I hardly noticed how we had become a couple.

I grew my hair long, wore blue work-shirts and dungarees, and wrote a new style of prose—clipped syntax like that of Olson but narrative, combining images from science fiction, baseball, dreams, tarot, and rock 'n' roll, framing them in Jungian archetypes, Kelly magic talk, and Blackburn-like *Brooklyn-Manhattan Transit* jazz. I gave my essays titles like "Aspect," "Syntax," "Electrons," and "Quantum." I was after a pop literary voice, something like Alyosha Karamazov crooning "Teenager in Love" to his brother Ivan, or Darl Bundren snapping his fingers Bobby Darin-like and then breaking into "Dream Lover" and "Beyond the Sea."

Many an afternoon Lindy and I sat on the front porch, glasses of ice water on the ledge, rapping on our electric keys. At five she drove me to work, came and got me at ten.

One morning I rescued Ralph's bored eight-year-old son from Sunnie's basement while his father practiced the piano and drove him to the cabin. I tossed him pitches and pop flies in a clearing—Lindy was at her newspaper job. Afterwards he looked up at the dresses and sports jackets hanging together on the pole and asked, "Does your wife live here?" Tears welled as I nodded. Male and female clothing mingled magically to make a home.

Perhaps it was not such a lie after all.

Our other close friends were Welton and Elsie, a black poet and his Jewish wife who lived otherwise on the Lower East Side. Welton was a scholarship student, star of the workshop. A smallish squat trickster with twinkling eyes and quick darting movements and lingo, he liked to tease Mitchell and me.

"I'm a street poet," he declared, "a man of the people. I'm Malcolm X and Che Guevara. I don't go for all this crazy shit about angels and alchemists and electronic higgledy-piggledy."

"Welton's a closet sorcerer," Mitchell whispered, "but we'll keep his secret."

Welton smiled in collusion. "We're at Yankee Stadium," he said, "waiting for the word. Maher-shalal-hash-baz. Will the real Martin

Luther King please sit down."

Mitchell and I could not stop laughing.

"Hey, I'm writing this poem for you guys—Dar es Salaam, Key West, Antigua, Azimuth. The number of conditions required to determine a curve is equal to the number of independent constants in the equation of the curve."

"What else, Welton?" I managed.

"What else! Sinai, Phoenix, Zajecar, Paoting, Harlem, Toulouse, Minsk. The case, the gender are irrelevant!"

In mid-July Lindy answered an ad for "kittens" and came back with a gray tabby we named Frodo. She tore around our room and pounced on our bed in the morning, chasing the covers as we shifted. Hobbit-like, she climbed on hind legs and poked her head under the curtains to track birds and rippling branches, her attention a moving bump of fabric.

On weekends we drove to lakes, wildflower meadows, and mining towns. In mid-summer, we bought tickets to an outdoor performance of Holst's *Planets* at the Aspen Music Festival. The orchestra tuned in the pavilion, then burst into melody. Mercury darted among fireflies; Mars pranced with ghosts of Indian warriors; Saturn brought fullness and old age. Uranus arrived as a magician; Neptune finally settled the revelry, a mystic and sea captain accompanied by fairy-tale sprites, nymphs, and brownies.

"If we lived on Uranus," I wrote that night, "there would be five moons: Miranda, Ariel, Umbriel, Titania, Oberon. Imagine wandering in a gaseous body in a methane breeze, Oberon setting, having nothing to do with Holst or a midsummer night, except the sound 'oberon,' pulling green spouts back and forth across a green sea."

Above timberline, meteors scraped the astrological sky.

That Sunday I imagined the thumping jollity of Jupiter in thunder and rain, washing mud and leaves, twigs and pine needles into gullies while Frodo hid under the bed. I had never suspected Earth could be this pleasurable—kitten-cat, chortle of the fire, meals together, evergreen spices in the air, a big night sky—my memories

of childhood resolving through their ancient melancholy into the joy
of bottomless presence. There *was* finally world enough and time.
I needed no other planet, no spaceship or supernal clan.

The summer is preserved in a single image: Lindy and I with
our cups of coffee on the porch or in the high grass and dew after
breakfast. Frodo runs from tree to tree, grasping the white bark
with her claws and pulling herself up like a lemur. She drops, dashes
again. I lie back against the sky.

Life had lost its narrative structure and become a timeless dance,
a waking dream.

Lindy's poems followed the path to the river, Hans Christian Andersen, the magic of children actors ... and Lindy-Rich:

> It is partly because
> he has this kind of courage that i don't have
> it is partly because
> he has this kind of courage
> that allows him
> even commands him
> to open the latch of the door and flash the
> light around on the high green weeds blowing
> and the swaying trees/ old men/
> flash the light around through the wind
> blowing out there so hard and rushing
>
> partly because of that courage
> which i don't have
> so that when he left to go into town
> i stood awhile looking around the room
> and thinking where to begin again
> and where to begin and where to pick up and begin
> to make order in my mind
> picking up i thought of what he
> had said afterwards/ that i am
> 4 people and what negotiations and wars

there are, and the same for him
well after he left as i say i played with
the kitten which was a distraction from
whatever distraction i would pick up next
the kitten curious and unafraid, bounding
finally asleep in the woodbox from which
i removed him, thinking of spiders
aware that it was so quiet picking up
threads trying to make order thinking
what kind of courage to have met him here

on this summer's night's battlefield—
the sky so porous and wind lightly through
moon shining shafts between the trees
and thinking and thinking and thinking
until finally lying again on the bed
the field opened, wind blew the flowers
gently, softly around all our feet as
four against four met, capes blowing and
standards locked in stirrups, flags unfurled
bearing signs and messages moon shining between
shafts of trees/the wind blew, ruffling
his hair and across the field mine, how
we charged
wind streaking in my ears/horse under me
swelling full with a fast thrusting of muscle
again and again we clashed/throwing each other
tossing each body into the air until
exhausted almost/we reached up past the porous sky
with one hand each, clasped a sweating hand there
each other's

after he went into town after
after that and that i stood in the room
fixated, and picked up things and lay on the bed
and finally heated up some coffee which was too bitter

i thought and thought, thinking
of that and then made some instant
which was better the kitten asleep
i put more coal on the fire, settled
down to write this about the making of
new boundaries and old wars, settled down to wait.

One mid-August day Lindy and I rose in darkness. Freezing …
no time to set a fire … stars still out. We collected Mitchell in town,
then drove backroads for miles. He pointed up a dirt lane toward
an edifice—the Snowmass monastery. Against a violet sky, shadows
pushed plows—a landscape from another century. Through stone
portals we made our way into a nave.

Resident monks, one by one, came into a stone pit, across the
ember of sun, chanted in Latin, left … until only a fly buzzed in
the patch of yellow, projecting a glyph of itself onto silence.

But we were living with ghosts too, back in my blue room,
strangers again. We stopped making love. We quarrelled incessantly.
Our pasts reclaimed us.

After dinner she left and, when I went looking, I found her at the
edge of the river. She kneeled there, crying, oblivious to words or
touch. I crouched in silence, the heavens a glittering shroud, the
Roaring Fork scraping parameters of aggregate sound. The river
would be doing that long after everyone presently alive was gone.
This universe was just too vast and difficult. But how to negotiate
my own tiny impasse in a mundane patch? The tangle inside me
felt as inextricable as the whole damn gargantuan display.

Months later, thinking back to our summer camaraderie while
drowning in nostalgia on Xenia Street, Ohio, Mitchell wrote,
"There is a honeysuckle vine which comes in our window; it makes
the air so thick and sweet it is hateful."

And that was the dilemma. Mitchell nailed it: so much feeling,
such textures of sadness, such tenderness for Frodo, the cleansing
dance of Holst's Neptune … all beyond remittance or claim.

We reached the last quadrant of August. The Workshop
disbanded. Lindy and I were going to drive straight back to

Massachusetts, but her mother insisted she come home for the three weeks before school. We packed the car at night, wound down the mountains at dawn, Frodo in a cage, Welton and Elsie in the back seat, their luggage tied to a rack. They would share the driving east with me. Frodo would stay in Denver and come to Phi Psi with Lindy on the plane.

We set her down in the sunshine of Lindy's backyard. She bounded across the grass and stopped at the fence, sniffing, considering the new setting. No aspen bark, no chipmunks, no porch. She charged through the glass door, reentering the dining room as she had our cabin hundreds of times, like a bull in the ring. It was excruciating to watch. There was nothing I could do. Summer was over.

Lindy's parents were visibly uncomfortable with our presence so, past three p.m., Welton, Elsie, and I retreated to the car. "Drive carefully," Lindy said, "and I'll see you back at school." She gave me a parting hug and kiss.

My heart sank as the bigness of the highway and flatlands east of Denver met us. It'd been so much easier to drive West with a tailwind of hope than to return East against a headwind of qualms. Something deep and hollow was sucking me in. In fact, a purplish black disturbance arose in the distance as we approached, gusting against the car. The blankets covering the luggage began to flap, the vehicle veering from their unintended sail. I pulled over onto the dirt. We stood outside, getting drenched, tightening buckles, retrieving odds and ends to inside, tying the rest back down. The moon was out by the time we began looking for a place to eat— McCook, Nebraska, 260 miles east of Denver.

"I'm not hopeful, but we'll take our chances," Welton announced, as we pulled into the first viable restaurant and ordered hamburgers. We were exhausted and disoriented, having been up since sunrise. Before we realized it, a bunch of townies had surrounded our table.

"Who are you all?" they asked. "Where're going?"

They didn't overtly threaten. In fact, they invited us into the back room for "the show." We followed, Welton remarking, "Just a little bit now 'cause we gotta get on the road."

The makeshift theater had an audience of about two dozen people, young farmer boys and their mates. On a small stage a guitar player, visibly drunk, struggled through a song.

"He used to be with the New Christy Minstrels," someone told us. "How do you like him?"

"A whole lot," Welton said.

Then he flashed Elsie and me a sign. Five minutes later he tapped my knee; I tapped hers. We stood and marched out of the room, quickly through the restaurant, the guys breathing down our necks.

"Hey, the show's just starting. You haven't seen the best part. Don't you like it?"

We scampered into the car. I turned the key at once. As we hit the highway Welton sighed, "Guess seeing a nigger's 'bout as much recreation as they've had for a while. But I didn't want to entertain 'em anymore. It could get nasty fast, I've been there."

He told me not to stop unless I got too tired. "Or you hit Iowa City," he added with a laugh. He was afraid the guy who had sublet their apartment was going to sneak off without paying, so he wanted to arrive early and unannounced. He also wanted to put a few hundred miles between himself and McCook.

I had the energy of the summer behind me, and night was friendlier than day. I drove until the sun wrote its signature over cornfields. In the rear view I caught a glimpse of the stranger I had become, how the summer had begun to shape a man who might yet exist. I had always feared looking like this—wild-eyed, unshaven—but I had waited, mostly without hope, for such a self to be born. Exiting as requested, I pulled into a parking space and announced, "Iowa City!"

"You must be kidding," Welton coughed, rubbing his eyes. I had driven for eight hours and covered 535 miles. He had a friend there, a black professor who taught "the Bard of Avon, of all things," he scoffed. We spent much of the day with the guy, took his tour of the town, then lay by the river, subletter temporarily out of mind

"It's fine, man," Welton told him as we shook hands after dinner, "but you gotta lose that cat Shakespeare."

Now Welton was driving. I collapsed on the back seat, having been up more than twenty-four hours. I didn't wake until Indiana.

We sped through Ohio into Pennsylvania. The land got greener, more familiar to East Coasters, what we had known before we dwelled near timberline. The songs were "The Eve of Destruction"; The Toys' "A Lovers' Concerto," *"How gentle is the rain.... "*; The Four Seasons: *"Let's hang on to what we've got.... "*

We were suddenly in New Jersey, approaching the City at light speed. I was wearing jeans and a work-shirt. I was still in Aspen as we pulled up to the first traffic light beyond the Lincoln Tunnel. One thousand miles covered since the Iowa River.

I saw New York from our cabin, through Frodo's eyes—Frodo the hobbit and Frodo the cat.

Stone and filth. Madness. Claustrophobia. People sitting on ledges outside brick buildings, portable radios blasting, torn billboards. My return was as miniscule as a piece of soot.

"Abandon all hope," Dante had written, "ye who enter here." So the City fused and filled my heart with dread, not of the people living there but of what I had been. No sweet nostalgia of origins, it was as anchored and sodden as lead, radiating more malignancy, almost more than I could bear. I shrank into my own tattered ghost.

This was the panic too; it always had been.

I left Welton and Elsie downtown, a day too late: the subletter had flown the coop. Then I drove to Central Park West and 90th, to the people who had once been my family. My mother approached in astonishment; she touched my face, her hand frigid. "What's happened to you?" she uttered, as though staring into my coffin.

I told her I was fine.

"Look at you. You're unshaven. You're pale and gaunt. When did you last have a check-up?"

I stayed overnight and fled a hair's breadth ahead of Mordor's shadow.

Grossinger's was in full flower, buffet tables crammed with cold meats, a Yiddish comedian on the patio prattling through his microphone, a haze of perfume and tanning oil. The same crowds moved from cabanas to coiffeurs in a lobotomized buzz. It may have been paradise once, but George von Hillshimer was right: it was a gaudy and devious hell, especially after my summer in the cabin, Lindy at her typewriter, cups of tea, Frodo bounding across the floor.

Aunt Bunny was gone, and my father wanted no part of me. I figured I'd get a lecture, but I hoped he would at least be glad to see me. He was indifferent; he reprimanded perfunctorily, then stared right through me. I knew there was no way to explain where I had been. He said he would pay my college bills for one more year; that was it. I could do what I wanted with my life. He would have no part of it. I had run away from my mother, now I had run away from him. He would not forgive that.

It was never a matter of two families fighting over me. I was orphaned by both.

All through that week, guests, executives, and assorted relatives told me I looked haggard, like a vagabond, like something that just got off the boat at Ellis Island—but I was alert, I liked the feel of myself. Their real grievance, I knew, was the fierceness with which I guarded my new shape, unshaven, blue work-shirt. I wasn't confident enough just to relax into it, so I tramped around, bristly and unyielding. I had become Schuyler (or Scotty) at last.

I drove to Woodstock to hear Kelly read and afterwards went to dinner with him and his two "wives" (he was living with a young girlfriend now as well as Joby). He was delighted with my tales of the summer, and he hoped Lindy and I would be by to visit him. As I left he called out, "You are finally beginning to look like who you are."

Lindy's first letter was dated August 30th and came to the Hotel:

> Dearest Rich,
>
> Things are okay. I miss you a hell of a lot, more than I thought I would. I am terribly aware of things. I have sat and talked with both of my parents for each night, telling them about Aspen and what's wrong with it and all the funny stories I can remember. Almost no mention of you by them, but frequent mention of you by me, of course. They are mainly wary and afraid of what they don't know about you, as they would be with anyone.
>
> I MISS YOU, BABY.

She told me her plans were to head east as soon as possible and join me, and she closed with: "I'll write again soon. I love you, honey …," the stick figure of a happy dancer sketched beneath her name.

That letter is now a torn, refolded relic: I carried it in my pocket for weeks, reading it again and again to remind myself that Aspen really happened. A second letter came a few days later. She said that she had to be frank—people who argued as much as we did were not appropriate lovers. She had found Steve again. She was going to be staying on in Denver an extra week.

I drove back to New York, but bad things were happening there too. Welton and Elsie, it turned out, weren't actually married, and Elsie's father had come to their apartment and chased Welton into the street with a gun. "A guy from Great Neck in a 1936 Volkswagen would like to murder me," he announced as he let me in and quickly re-latched the chain. "I can't feel lonely anymore."

Elsie was hiding on the upper West Side, and Welton had his TV playing nonstop upside-down. "Maybe you and Mitchell know something," he explained. "I need that McLuhan magic now." It was an old Western, horses and riders galloping off the top. He had finished his poem for us and handed it to me:

> richard feels angels battling over our heads
> discharge the froth that clouds our lives.
> the number of conditions, the case, the gender,
> are irrelevant....

He left the TV on as we went onto the street, found a beer hall, and ordered a pitcher of draft. The room was so smoky I could see particles shifting. I shared my lamentations while we drank.

> the number of conditions required for my murder
> is equal to the number of independent constants
> remaining at the end of vesper....

"What Lindy is we call 'Phat!'" he suddenly offered. "Some girls are like that; they got your soul. You don't see any other girl. You've either got to get with her or get your soul back."

"What if I don't do either?"

"Then you won't live."

The jukebox was "Eve of Destruction." Barrels of peanuts lined the walls. We ate those for dinner—like everyone else, throwing the shells onto the floor. And Barry McGuire pounded out the theme of the hour:

> *Don't you understand*
> *What I'm trying to say!*
> *Don't you feel the fears*
> *I'm feelin' today!"*

There was a cinematic beauty to my situation, its music a soundtrack of angels, an unborn tree alphabet veering by indirection toward something that could not yet be alive. The words, I thought, must mean *exactly the opposite of what they were saying.* And they gave me a grim satisfaction, pitched as they were, appropriate at every level—and at last being spoken:

> *If the button is pushed,*
> *There'll be no running away.*
> *There'll be no one to save*
> *With the world in a grave!*

Welton peered up and down the street to make sure no Elsie's fathers were following him. Then we hiked from the bar to a nearby loft where a poetry reading in progress featured Paul Blackburn and two younger writers, Ishmael Reed and Ed Sanders. We sat in the crowd along the wall, taking it in for over an hour. "Enough about the effect of the second crusade on the uses of alliteration and assonance in poetry," Welton finally snapped. "It's my turn." He waved to his friends and, on their acknowledgment, took his place at the pile of coats that passed for a podium:

> *this*
> *is a note*
> *to an old black couple*
> *in a backwood mississippi church*
> *shouting   happy   stomping*
> *sending their songs*
> *shining their light …*

I could see the fire and hope in his eyes, the desire to establish his legitimacy, to have his moment. His voice danced with jazz and

harmony. I thought he was beautiful and proud, a combination of
Sam Cooke, Bob Dylan, and Ray Charles:

in me
in the san francisco streets
in me
in the new york high glass
in me in my time.

I looked around and so wanted Lindy to see this, to hear Welton
come home to New York ... be chased out of his home by a honkie
with a gun, then appear in a loft and stop the show with his song.

in harlem in black hands
holding red roses
in the fibers
of my hair in my breath
in me   flowing
thru the world
in me to another backcountry
child that i see
on the sidewalk
shouting   black   happy ...

I called Lindy afterwards, across the time line, to tell her about
Welton and Elsie, Kelly, and the great reading that night. She gave
me her flight number and said I could pick her up if I wanted,
but—no trips to Kelly's or Grossinger's—she was going straight to
Smith. She added that Frodo would stay in Denver with her family
and have a decent home.

The next morning I drove back to Amherst and moved into Phi
Psi. My room was the same single Jon had had sophomore year.

2

ANGELS

I needed two more English courses to compete the requirement for a major, so I signed up for both Romantic and Modern Poetry. Otherwise, I followed Kelly's injunction to study real things: Biological Anthropology, African Folklore (which convened at Smith), and Attic Greek.

Embarking on a new language, I began by learning its alphabet—alpha, beta, gamma; xi and psi; mu and omega—ancient letters that put me back with the white goddess at the origin of language. Next I memorized basic words: *"Logos"*: speech; *"anthropos"*: man; *"hodos"*: road; *"angelos"*: messenger; *"thalatta, thalattes"*: sea; *"klopes, klopos"*: thief. My Greek declensions and conjugations, though comprised of new hieroglyphs, bore the templates of Latin ones which I had studied for years with Mr. Metcalf.

From Kelly's reading list I selected *The Holy Kabbalah,* which resurrected another primeval alphabet with childhood resonance. Hebrew letters, wrote Arthur Edward Waite, emanated from the Mind of God in the Creation of the Universe. Beth, gimmel, and lamed, a church, a camel, and an ox, respectively, were also the flames behind the lights Jonny and I lit on the menorah. They spelled words on one level; on another they embodied the ongoing genesis of matter and spirit into form. As primordial symbols, they continued to spill into the world moment by moment, as wavelengths of light, as molecules, as cells, as tarot keys, as archetypes, as stations on the Tree of Life. Kether, the Crown, was the Apex of Creation, the initial frequency of matter. Yesod formed the base of the autonomic nervous system. Chesed (kindness) fused God's love for His Creation with Creation's adoration of Him.

These alphabetic shapes, harbingers of subatomic particles, were originally entrusted to Adam by the angel Raziel. In Eden he probed their mystery as well as their novelty—a forbidden act. When he and Eve were banished for their crime—not the biblical cover story of a snake and an apple but the breach of Pandora's jar and release of its bottomless darkness into this world of shadows—he smuggled them into their own miasma. He lost them in its wilderness. Then the angel Raphael restored them to him, so he passed them on to his son Seth.

Meanwhile a reality of their making had grown up around his and Eve's descendants, a universe of stars and planets. A different cosmos issued from the offspring of Adam's wet dream, his assignation with the night spirit Lilith. It is uncertain whether we are Eve's posterity, Lilith's, or both.

On Mount Sinai, Moses was given two sets of commandments: The External Law and The Secret Doctrine. The first he communicated to the Hebrews. The tablets bearing the latter, in a brouhaha of mock rage at the people's idolatry of a Golden Calf, he smashed while transmitting their essence to the elders as the *Zohar*. Waite likewise bequeathed two tarots: the fortune-telling deck Chuck and I used and the more esoteric keys divulged only by Case.

Waite supplied an alternative view of my own situation too. Through the summer Lindy and I had been performing a Qabalistic act, not just as lovers but as adepts forging an angelic shape on another plane: the *Shekhinah*. Despite our bouts of estrangement and alienation and our current separation, we were still creating that form. It wasn't a matter of sex or girlfriend/boyfriend; it was whether our subtle bodies were compatible and karmically attuned to the task. If so, we were irrevocably engaged; we could quarrel, be totally at odds, be with other people, *while sustaining the sacred exercise.*

Love and sex are primordially sorcery and transmutation, rituals with astral implications like Adam's confusion (or conflation) of Eve and Lilith—that's why they feel so powerful. If we had planted real seeds, our dyad was alive and matriculating somewhere in the upper spheres. If we hadn't, the summer in Aspen would wash away and be forgotten by us anyway—a wastrel fantasy and faded dream. We would move on to other lovers and destinies.

That we were secular American kids did not absolve us of witchcraft. Kelly had made that plain: living together was an alchemical act. Any bond of real love, of Soul connection, actuated the Supernal Work, the Union of Jehovah and Elohim. It couldn't help it. The mystery of Eros reenacted the Divine Mystery of Creation, the Union with God—God the Divine Androgyne. Waite proposed as much in ecclesiastical rhetoric: "When it is said that the Blessed Vision is the sight of *Shekhinah* and the contemplation of her Divine Face, we are to understand apparently that the union of sister-souls is under her eyes and in her presence."

This one text redeemed my failed Zionist training—the Zohar allowed me to embrace being born a Jew at last, to claim a heritage ultimately so profound that it could express itself coequally in Albert Einstein, Sandy Koufax, and Bob Dylan. As fissioning yellow yods danced spark-like in the turquoise sky of the Moon card, two hermetic systems fused, revealing the sheer depth and complexity of Creation.

I realized suddenly that Eden was a state of being, a mode of perception. We were kept out of Paradise not by some Biblical illustrator's scimitar of archangelic steel but the finer blades of synapsing neurons. Our bodies incarnated our state of exile; that's how Adam and Eve got themselves kicked out, by entering the shadow play of molecules and cells. The instrument of Brakhage's cinema was likewise the sword of perception converted in the frames-per-second blink of each montage, an atonal series of such montages disclosing a secret landscape oscillating within this one. It *can* be paradise all the time, if only we would snap our coma. We'd be back in Eden in a heartbeat, we were already there.

Sister souls meant soulmates! But was this a runaway grasping-at-straws, a mere wishful indulgence—or a true-blue vision? I didn't begin to know, but I had to find out. There was nothing else in play, no other course through the darkness. If I was neurotic and self-important, that would come out in the wash too.

Elsie was back living with Welton, so when I returned to the City, she loaned me the keys to her empty apartment. I went straight there so as not to encounter my family. In my state of pilgrimage I could bide no more naysaying, no derision or sacrilege. *I* was the only allowable heretic now. Night fell on a strange city that was finally mine:

> How wild and soulless
> Is the wind,
> Driving through yonder helium towers,
> Dense metropolitan vats of subway cider,
> A pinwheeling purple sky?

All the next day I memorized Greek vocabulary and declensions, read tales of African gods, stayed true to sacred alphabets, and awaited the plane.

My sister-soul appeared down the Kennedy corridor with her handbag. I ran to intercept her. She hugged me quickly and then stared. "Babe, you look as though you've been through hell."

I nodded with a martyrish smile. Then I told her about Elsie's place. "So," she snapped "is everyone on your side?"

"They're on *our* side."

"I'm not an appendage of you."

We didn't stay in the City overnight. We drove straight up through Connecticut, wrangling about everything. I thought she was being needlessly belligerent to prove we weren't any good. She countered that we were naturally contentious.

We argued about the events of the summer and even about how much we had argued. Then we argued about the war.

"We don't even share the same opinion about Vietnam." Steve had raised salient points she now itemized: What about the Red Chinese? What about stopping them before they got the bomb? What about the spread of Communism through Laos, Indonesia, and the Philippines?

"The famous domino theory," I announced with mock surprise. "How original!"

My attitude, she said, merely demonstrated how different we were. "We don't have the same politics. I'm not a pacifist. Are you?

Would you refuse to fight in any war?"

"No, just this one."

We stopped for hamburger, fries, and frappes at our usual Howard Johnson's on the outskirts of Northampton where she made a case for remaining friends without being lovers. We could still do things together, just not as often and more low-key. On that gray evening I left her at Laura Scales with her suitcases and hastened back to Amherst.

I translated simple sentences, the mere sound of which lifted my spirits: *"hoti kai ho anemos kai he thalatta hupakooay aitoo."* I learned the names of Ice Age glaciations (Gunz, Mindel, Riss, Wurm) and sites from Olduvai to Altamira and Lascaux where bones of ancient primates and the earliest humans had been found. I imagined the long mute dream at the beginning of our species—the contrapuntal dream of grasses and animals—transformed through tree alphabets and Greek stems into the songs of Shelley: *"And the green lizard and the golden snake / Like imprisoned flames, out of their trance awake."*

Kelly had proposed P. D. Ouspensky's *In Search of the Miraculous* as the next phase in my initiation. It told of the author's meetings with the Russian mystic Georges Ivanovich Gurdjieff, identified only as G. in the book. G. adduced a scale of music-like vibrations igniting the cosmos, exploding across gaps and tonal shifts to create stars and other, cooler realms. Our world was one of these zones, a frontier tonation in a vast, multidimensional symphony wherein notes louder and brighter than a million suns were transformed by compression into stones and waters, then grasses and life forms.

I recognized the stream flowing through the tarot, linking the landscapes from card to card. Stream or ray, numerical series or vibrations—these were metaphors for a hierarchy *generating and encompassing the universe.*

In Ouspensky's version, individual molecules are products of separate small shocks, cascading across this plane as they are captured in electromagnetic configurations; hence multiple hydrogens originate at different frequencies, from hydrogen 6 to hydrogen 12,288, with 384 being water and 192 breathable air. But there was a dark side. Whatever else they are doing or telling themselves they are doing, Gurdjieff warns us, creatures are under a rudimentary edict, they must alchemize souls out of gross matter, convert the ray of Creation before it is too late. Even plants and animals are called upon to transmute material energies into finer spiritual pulsations. They do this by nourishment, breath, emotion, and larval thought. Beings that do not forge souls out of corporeal stuff meet a sorry fate at death: their overly dense charge sinks into unstable configurations, becoming subatomic neutrinos and electrons. Their identity fissions and spins apart, damning them to illuminate the cosmos for eternity. First, though, their bioelectricity, their remaining vitality, is swallowed by the Moon and spit back out at a lower octave.

The master seemed to be telling Ouspensky—and Kelly, me—that we had been born into a trap. If we failed to get ourselves out, we would be sold into fire, doomed to light the void (as stars do) at our bodies' extinction—eternal photons, never to be transmuted to spirit.

Gurdjieff's portent echoed Kelly's original warning: break with habitual action and common gossip or be consigned to oblivion, to supply the hydrogen of future universes for other souls.

There was no fallback position or escape from cosmic prerogative—become aware of the direness of our situation, and change—or be exterminated.

My visit to a frigid hut followed by a slapstick ride to a Chinese restaurant, seemingly expendable, mere diversions and borderline performances at the time—borderline whimsical, borderline crucial—were real *in the way they were designed to be.* I hadn't understood the true amusement and dead seriousness of the occasion. Now, as if by post-hypnotic command, the sequence was re-initiating me from within. Having internalized, having assimilated what Kelly was preaching, having practiced it unknowingly in Aspen, now I was *experiencing it directly.*

What was at stake had escalated almost preposterously. The game was Creation itself, the universe—but maybe it had always been. Maybe that's what the voice at the dungeon stairs was trying to tell me, why it sprang from Nanny's necromancy and gave me the fright of my early life. It was a cosmic sounding buoy, a depth gauge, saying, "This is how far down the universe goes and what will be required of you in this lifetime. Match it and you have a fighting chance. Match anything less sober and grim and you will shipwreck one way or another on some hidden reef."

Roused to untimely consciousness by my mother and Nanny, I needed to be *even more* terrified, to force myself to an amplitude of crisis I could resolve only by ego disintegration or a quantum leap.

A quantum leap it was! The dungeon stairs had awakened me to the horror of my situation but also to its possibility and hope, and in the only way I could be awakened—by gashing into a four-and-a-half-year-old's reality state deep enough to get his attention. That's what the voice behind the voice on the radio intended when it ambushed a fledgling mind. Whatever its intelligence or source, it provided rude captioning for an inchoate danger.

Sorry to say, grim and sober it had to be, given the perniciousness of the maze, the obstacles and trials ahead, the need for clarity and single-mindedness, the dazzle of so many false trails in the dark. Perhaps that was Nanny's errand all along, even if she *hadn't* left the radio on on purpose—why she was there in the first place. When the specter of dungeon stairs terrified a defenseless child, it was only trying to say, "Wake up this time around, *Frère Richard; everything* is at stake!"

The universe is operating at multiple tiers of decoy and mimicry, so caveats come in unlikely forms. A few years after the entrance of the "dungeon stairs" I heard spectral bars of "Stranger in Paradise" and I knew more or less what they meant—my rejoinder to my subway escort Neil's riddle proved that—but I didn't know what they meant *emotionally*.

The tune recalled the dungeon—the leitmotif of Hitzig with his morbid bag, a ballroom of partygoers on which a vampire-like visitation casts an eerie turquoise coma—*though the song said exactly the opposite*. It said kismet, Aphrodite, love at first sight. But a young consciousness reads the shifting winds of paradox unerringly and takes heed: *"If I stand starry-eyed / That's a danger in paradise."* The world was paradise all right, and it was "one enchanted evening" over and over. But the stranger across that fancy room was a "macabre," an alien in a woman's body—and the vision of her was the terrible depth of one's own soul.

I felt baffled and spooked then because terror and joy, persecution and revelation occurred *at a single vibration* in variant pitches. Change the modulation and one, remarkably, turned into the other.

This new paradigm was ludicrous, absurd, though it rang true, if not strictly as the thing it signified. It was the link between the phantom evanescence of a dungeon-like form and a mature trope grounded in molecular physics and Rosicrucian magic. What fused the phenomenologies was Kelly's living citation.

But can we *really* be damned to unstable helium, the debris of our lives to brighten alien homes and draw moth-like creatures to our flame? Was that the stranger in paradise? Did this make *any sense at all?*

I was bursting with new knowledge, but there was no way to use it, to share it, to give it life in the ordinary world. What could I tell my friends—that we risked being turned into electrons unless we acted at once? How could I get this news even to the core of my own being, live it, practice it, when I seemed barely to survive from moment to moment? Half the time I felt empowered and guided, the other half about to fall apart.

One night at dinner Lindy confided, almost off-handedly, that Steve had dropped her again, "I guess he didn't think I was worth altering his career plans," she said sadly. "After all, my life as an artist didn't measure up to his mentor Louis Kahn. All we did anyway was argue about Vietnam; he said I was the first person he met who was against the war." She paused to consider how much she wanted to confess. Then she decided to trust me. "When I asked him why he didn't write me all winter from Italy, he just shrugged. He's headed to an architecture firm in New York. Probably he'll find prettier and more sophisticated creatures there than me. Oh well!"

It didn't mean that she and I could pick up our romance together because she stood by her negative view of Aspen. "It took us such a long time to learn to do love, but we do hate rather easily. Can't you see? It's perverse to try to make something happen that's not there."

She called what we were lacking "love," but she meant that we didn't have the quick chemical attraction that she shared with Steve and Jim, what Kelly had called ecstasy. We were a difficult, thorny couple.

"I don't see hate," I said. "I see only anger, frustration, and the pain of transformation. Remember Kelly: enstasy."

"Rich, sometimes you are maddening."

"Always I hope."

And Shelley: *"Life, like a dome of many-coloured glass, / Stains the white radiance of Eternity.... "*

In anthropology Professor Pitkin assigned a surprisingly Gurd-jieffian book, *The Phenomenon of Man.* Its author, a Jesuit priest named Pierre Teilhard de Chardin, described an esoteric fire that imbued the hydrogen of galaxies and stars in the formation of the universe. Fecundating in the plasma of cooling stars, it crystallized on those suns' planets. Its divine embers incubated creatures on Earth at its lava phase, endowing the newly whelped orb with an incipient biosphere. Because it swirled in the same dust-cloud as its sun-star, Earth inherited the Sun's latency of Soul presence, transferred timelessly from the Tree of Life to galaxies and nebulae. Gravitational and chemical activity dispatched the letters of the Hebrew alphabet into the monadnock/oxbow zone: the uprise of continents, the filling of oceanic basins—the Spirit of God moving upon the Face of the Waters.

Here too was a Gurdjieffian posit but with an opposite conclusion. In keeping with Christian tradition, Teilhard proposed universal salvation: Christ's sacrifice had changed the cosmic rules.

Teilhard traced the evolution of *Homo sapiens* to the emergence of Divine Spirit from matter's interior, which was "the 'psychic' face of that portion of the stuff of the cosmos enclosed from the beginning of time within the narrow scope of the early Earth." In the global ocean, atoms and molecules, cooling and liquefying into myriad shapes, stirred the forerunners of DNA helices. Solar spirits came rushing into being as protists and plastids. Their bacterial lattices spread across a volcanic surface, forming a biosphere. Cooled by interstellar blackness, the planet moistened, and cells sublimated from solar particles into its hydrosphere.

As Earth transferred its molecular information into protein threads and tissue motifs, plant and animal bodies coalesced. Then the organs of larger animals deliquesced from those, as more intricate sheaths matriculated out of predecessor lattices.

So the herb yielding seed, and the fruit tree yielding fruit, and the moving creatures that hath life—the fowl that flyeth above the earth; the great whales in the deep; and every other living presence that moveth, Adam, Eve, and their progeny—were brought forth from starry embers after their kind.

This was the Ray of Creation in action. The tarot Sun—its inner star, Kether—was glimmering anew and apart as a living entity on a planet: first a worm, then a fish, then a shaggy wolf, each of them a particle of the solar body.

The Phenomenon of Man turned the universe inside-out, making the spangled night as sentient and beneficent as it appeared: "In that fragment of sidereal matter," Teilhard wrote of the primordial solar cloud, "as in every other part of the universe, the exterior world must inevitably be lined at every point with an interior one."

Now I began to view the celestial firmament as what it was: a gauze refracting a transdimensional cosmos.

Jung's archetypes and Darwin's natural selection ran together. The hominids of our physical-anthropology text, those early man-ape pre-decessors of ourselves, ancestors of the Greek *anthropos* (from whom the name "anthropology" came), were stirred to language and culture by recollections of their own antecedent lives as hydrogen inside the stellar field, not the hydrogen physicists know but Gurdjieff's pri-mordial vibrations that purled it and other elements from a higher vibration. To Australopithecus and Pithecanthropus, consciousness was a more anterior part of themselves, their innate intelligence and design principle, singing so deeply they couldn't hear it, or could *only* hear it. None of this could have happened, reasoned Teilhard, *none of it at all,* if it were not already present in the solar cloud.

The angels of Gethsemani were back ... birds delivering messages of stars. I continued to hear their cries as language, closer to Attic Greek than English, subatomic mantras that could not be translated into *any* human language. But that's why the flocks of the sky kept repeating them.

In the horn of 1965 those visions were my life-blood and consolation. As long as I believed them I was safe, so I carried them with me, reinventing my reality every hour, in fact every moment. I kept salvaging all that was lost, that threatened to lapse into unbearable memories playing *Prélude, Fugue and Variation* as a reminder and balm. Gaston Bachelard in his cottage in Dijon marked the same epitome and lived by it: "The unknown God is striving to know Himself through creatures of his making, to become through us what He has eternally desired to be." If so, what could finally go wrong? I might as well give it my best shot too.

When Stevie Wonder sang, *"There's a place in the sun,"* he meant the real Sun, that dense cocoon of hydrogen souls:

"Every branch on the tree
just reaching to be free.... "

Yes! What else would give them shape, would extend them in such a reverie of twigs and flowers?

I tried to feel this, trust it, ride it to safety. I was on a binge all right, but I needed to sustain it. I wrote my first Romantic Poetry term paper on "Blake, Gurdjieff, and Hopi Indian Verbs," citing Navaho sand-painting, alchemy, tarot, and theories of etymology. My professor, Bill Heath (no relation to Roy), gave me an A.

Then I picked up a science-fiction novel, Arthur Clarke's *Childhood's End,* in which dreaming children unlock our current evolutionary *cul de sac* and, guided by the Oversoul, cross galactic dimensions into a new universe. For Pitkin's next anthropology assignment I synthesized their quantum leap with Hopi myths of the Fourth World and my own "White Goddess"-informed theories of the origin of speech—and got another A. Not only was this state of revelation sustaining, it was backed by my teachers. Then I submitted "Religion as a Coded Language" to Professor Heath under the epigraph:

'if Barbara were an angel,' sang Coleridge
'i'd pray she'd watch over me.'
a nightingale
flew right up to John Keats   and sang
'only trouble is
gee whiz,

          i'm dreaming my life

                  away.'

Heath wrote: "You have moved from your prior papers to a more comprehensive view and closer to the burning center and point of origin. I have enjoyed reading what you have written. I cannot and will not dispute your vision. I salute you."

So far so good—but there was a long, long way to go.

Earlier that term I had reminded President Plimpton of his offer to help and he responded with swift, unexpected generosity: a grant from the Eastman Kodak fund to support both publishing a second issue of *Io* and running an arts series at Phi Psi. I immediately set to work with my housemates.

Kelly's salon provided plenty of potential poets, and Nelson and I selected films from the experimental Filmmakers' Cinematheque catalogue, home to both Brakhage and Anger. After filling three months worth of dates, we printed a calendar and posted it on campus and at nearby colleges.

Our first event was an evening of Kenneth Anger films. The Phi Psi living room was packed. As folks continued to stream in and collect in the back, I had to borrow chairs from Chi Phi next door.

After I made an announcement about upcoming films and reading, the audience quieted, and Tripp set the projector running. On the screen flashed Anger's motorcycle classic, *Scorpio Rising*, Ricky Nelson's voice backgrounding credits studded on a leather jacket:

Fools rush in
Where wise men fear to tread,
And so I come to you my love,
My heart before my head....

In New York I had been intimidated by Anger's homoerotic rites and sadistic violence, the hovering of real-life cops on the outskirts. Now, after a dose of octaves and hermetic alphabets, I saw matters differently. The cyclists of my birth-sign were not only the fascist warriors they imagined themselves—the unwitting enactors of a Crowleyite masque—they were abeyant planets of astrology, blind meteors cast through the cosmos at ungovernable speeds. *Fools rush in,* for sure ... all of us ... *my heart before my head.*

What other choice was there in a universe doomed to detonate but that had transubstantiated itself alchemically from Kether, the most hidden and sublime of all hidden and sublime things? Or—okay math-physics—from a hot, dense crumb. No difference! What other premise could sustain us in a prison formed by an illusion of time and matter at the speed of light?

Precepts from my prior term's Hindu philosophy course resonated with Claudine Clark and her backup girls on *Scorpio's* soundtrack as they doo-wopped, *"I see the lights, / I see the party lights, / red and blue / ann-nnd green."* That was the Ray of Creation crossing ethereal landscapes, springing into habitation zones as it met resistance at decisive thresholds—red, blue, and green—giving rise to unpredicated vistas. The Vedic truth-paradox chimed all the way back to my freshman-year buddy Syed Zaidi, now in India: "Somehow everything *does* exist, somehow it does *not* exist, and somehow it is indescribable. This is the seventh mode, by way of simultaneous affirmation and negation." My perennial mode too: esoteric transmission, negative capability, spontaneous regeneration.

Anger perceived our need to break out of the worldly thrall, via sex, drugs, revolution; swastikas, bikes, magic spells, finally death. That was why his Christ was led on a donkey to the sounds of Little Peggy March, *"I love him, I love, I love him, / and where he goes I'll follow...."* At our carnal tier of creation it was all the same rush to get high—the orange cocaine surge of the cyclists tinting reality, their orgy in Halloween drag; the Nazi checker game, the fatal race, Christ restoring sight to the blind man ... they were transmutations, miracles all ..., and *"I will follow him!"*

Yes, my heart shouted. Yes, Scorpio. Yes, Teilhard, Stevie Wonder, Pithecanthropus! Simultaneous affirmation and negation for sure.

At the party after the films a bearded boy named Black, a bigshot writer two classes behind me, came up to Lindy and offered to publish her poems through a small press he was starting. She drifted off, talking with him.

I had always thought of Black as a seductive devil, his writing metallic and pretentious. He was the prototypical snazzy dresser, self-proclaimed new wave—a kind of living plutonium. We had turned down his nihilistic fiction for *Io*. Now he was out to do what men in rivalry always do: steal the universe.

I heard about him next when I called Lindy to tell her that Kelly's reading was set for November 3rd, my birthday. Suddenly she had a visitor and asked me to hold on. It was Black; he had come to pick up her poems.

"Maybe they're just a ruse," she wondered aloud. "Maybe it's me he's trying to pick up."

A week later I drove to Smith to ferry her to the reading. She was waiting downstairs with a birthday present. I read the card first. It told me to be gay, not tragic, to enjoy what we had together, not to ruin it by wanting it to be more than it was. The gift was a bedspread with a brown print of ancient armies moving across it, plus a tan knit tie and a gold oval tie-clip.

Back at Amherst she insisted I put on the tie, so I did. She hugged me, gave me a quick kiss, then laughed, pulling churlishly away. "Let's not be late. I couldn't bear to miss their reaction to the first sight of Kelly."

A wall-to-wall audience had gathered upstairs in the Octagon, a small tower that overlooked the highway on the edge of campus. Almost a hundred people filled a lounge that was used to host visiting poets. This was the home field of Robert Frost and Archibald MacLeish and, though most members of the English Department condemned Kelly's visit, they were obligated, perhaps also curious, to attend.

The background purred with energy, periodic lilts of laughter. Our guest was late. He was ten minutes late … twenty-five minutes late and counting. I tried to soothe the audience by giving an extemporaneous talk on his connections to esoteric traditions, couching everything in an attempt at academic language. Their looks ranged from hauteur to bemusement. Lindy waited by the highway, hoping to flag Bloisius and save precious minutes.

After my speech, the din grew audibly more discordant, impatient. I peeked outside to check. Lindy was halfway up the stairs, pointing frantically behind her. Near the bottom the master was huffing and puffing step by step with Joby right behind him—and behind her, Button, his tall elfin girlfriend. He peered up through the spiral railing and waved as though there wasn't a care in the world. I glanced down and smiled in relief. Two minutes later, under a full head of steam, he burst into the room dangerously out of breath. While people gasped at his appearance he lit a cigarette and dragged away as if to restore his oxygen.

He looked around at the portraits of famous poets who had visited Amherst over the years, his eyes finally alighting on the one most associated with the school. "After all, Robert Frost is dead!"—his opening words. The undulation in the crowd was discernible, like a sinkhole opening up.

Kelly had introduced himself with a sacrilege, and before anyone could react he began reading:

When he was an old man
Williams spoke of the 'female principle'
& to it made
his last appeal
   still feeling its lure. wch we call
a lure
& so
degrade it
thinking it draws us
for its own ends
   but it is endless
   & without end
     & draws us.

That we may learn
              all patience to be drawn,
for there are men
who rush so rashly toward woman
all of their own hunger
all of their own need
that what womanliness
lures them
              is lost in their rage
to pursue & possess....

It was a tour de force entry, at least to my mind, a swaggering tort sweeping verse out of a fusty Frost museum into the urgency of the moment. But not everyone thought he was as wonderful as I did. It was Brakhage redux; a good portion of academia straggled out between poems.

When the reading was over, folks adjourned back at Phi Psi for cider and doughnuts with the poet. Then Kelly signaled "Finis" and drove Lindy and me and his two women into town to a restaurant in Bloisius.

We sat at a booth where he ordered dinner for three while we got dessert for ourselves. "I don't apologize for my opening remark," he said at once. "I knew you would present an overly generous version of me, and I preferred to destroy that quickly. It is useless to read to people who want to be polite." Then he took out his Camels, gave one each to Joby and Button, and offered a third to Lindy.

She shook her head. "If I'm going to smoke, I might as well stick to my filters."

"Do you believe they're less dangerous?"

"Of course."

"Who are you to allow the Surgeon General of this nation to make important decisions for you? Do you know that filter-tips have the most carcinogous tobacco?" She stared at him silently, lighting her Newport. He held up his package of Camels and gently stroked the emblem. "Does this little animal look as though he could harm you?"

She blew smoke coquettishly across the table.

On the way back to Smith she was friendly and excited. She held my hand as we walked to Laura Scales. "I enjoyed tonight. You were alive, more yourself." We stood holding each other, then a long kiss and, with a skip, she was off and in the door.

A week later Diane Wakoski arrived for our series, and I drove over to Smith to fetch Lindy again for the event. She was worried she was going to be late for a nine-thirty babysitting gig at the home of Miss Vendler, her modern-poetry teacher. In the car she let me know right off that she was coming under protest, then continued to complain all the way there.

"But this is *our* series."

"Don't kid yourself whose series it is. This is Amherst, Phi Psi, Richard Grossinger. I'm a girl along for the ride."

I tried to revive the mood with quips about Kelly's reading. But she stayed on a dour track, making like she wasn't a poet herself and my accomplice, acting as if Aspen had never happened. "I guess you're the only one who has prerogatives," she finally retorted, "the only one allowed to dispense magic."

I couldn't win, so I told myself we hadn't reached the pivotal octave. I half-believed it, half-thought I was piling cosmological license atop wishful thinking.

Schuy and Dona arrived at the last moment. They were now married and living together in Belchertown, and Diane was their favorite poet. "She rules over our marital discord," Dona joked. "She always gives me new excuses to dump this guy."

To their delight our visitor read her "Six of Cups" poem:

> I guess we want the illusion of what we want more
> than what we want
> because we think we are wise and know
> it's harder to destroy an illusion
> than what the illusion stands for:
> the star, burning the flowers in those gold cups,
> held and exchanged by the children.

Afterwards, Lindy and I rushed to the car and sped back to Northampton. Miss Vendler stood on the porch checking her watch. "I'm not amoral," Lindy said as she patted me on the knee and hurried down the driveway. She turned to add, "It's just that I'm like Diane. There's more than one of me. Remember, it's harder to destroy an illusion than what the illusion stands for."

"But also don't forget the flowers in those gold cups," I called back, "the star held and exchanged by children."

"Just because I don't tell you every second doesn't mean I've forgotten!"

Her riddle lifted my spirits, but I didn't know how to convert it. "I'm just a guy," I thought. "I can't do this without more help." Driving back to Phi Psi I wailed the finale of Welton's poem in my mind like a rock song:

> sending light
> and the fragrance of flowers
> thru me like a great
> soul coming
> from the backwood
> in me in my time
> smashing like shouts
> against the stone and glass
> of all the cities
> shouting   happy
> shining great light
> in me....

And then the last line that filled the universe with such hope:

> i believe as you believe.

The following weekend Lindy and I travelled to Cambridge for Stan Brakhage's lecture and film-showing at Harvard. We had dinner with him afterwards, causing us to drive back late. We were in our alternate reality again, as she was cold and proper, slipping defiantly from my affection as though it were a first date. There was nothing left on the surface, so I had to go deeper.

I didn't shave on Sunday or the next day. I watched myself change. I wasn't going to fake it anymore. The roughness was what I felt like. My hand reached instinctively for the stubble. I was no longer a stagehand; I could wait for Godot with the big boys too. After a week, a dark beard had begun to form.

I still carried Lindy's letter of August 30th. These were the days I reread it most often, when she seemed irretrievable. I couldn't have made it all up, I told myself. She had to be there, the person I had loved, somewhere inside.

A few nights later we met at Smith for Cocteau's *Orpheus*. "I may be quite fed up with you," she teased, "but you're still the best company I know for Cocteau."

Appearing in a brief cameo in his own film, the director set the stage by addressing the handsome Orpheus, played by actor Jean Marais, moments before a riot ensued at Café des Poets. *"Etonnez nous!"* ("Astonish us!"), Cocteau said. Orpheus was baffled, not inclined to take the offer seriously, secure in his popularity and fame. Then two motorcyclists rolled in, forerunners of the ones Kenneth Anger transposed into *Scorpio Rising*. As they felled the poet Cegeste, a sedan trailing the cyclists pulled up, and Death, a fashionably dressed woman, got out of the back. She ordered them to put Cegeste's fatally wounded body inside. "Why are you standing around, staring?" she demanded. "Get in!"

"Who me?" asked Orpheus, looking around.

"Get in!" she repeated, gesturing.

Then her chauffeur Heurtebise whisked them away.

When Orpheus awoke in Death's room, *she* was gone. All that remained were the chauffeur and the car. Now the hero madly sought this woman, Death herself. Since he did not know where to look for her, he sat in her car, obsessively transcribing message fragments that came over its radio, cosmic rays written (in truth) by Cegeste in her company.

Orpheus didn't realize that Death had also fallen in love with him.

Without permission of the authorities, Death next took Orpheus' wife Eurydice. Even so, it was Death that Orphée grieved after—as mystery, as lover—not his stolen partner. *"Etonnez nous,"* indeed!

One after another, characters in the movie wore special gloves to touch and pass through the liquid surface of mirrors into the Underworld. There, salesmen carried panes of imaginary glass through ruins.

"Out of sheer habit," Heurtebise told them, for they were no longer alive, let alone in a place where glass was used.

Finally Orpheus made it to Death's boudoir, only to learn that she was not all-powerful, that her love for him would salvage nothing, was a trite sentimental distraction in the eyes of the gods. They were two petty criminals who would be seized, separated, and punished.

Cocteau's Death was neither ruler nor goddess or effectual against the real forces of the cosmos, Gurdjieff's octave-hopping pulses. She was a face of an eternal form—one draw of Card Thirteen amid trillions of shuffles—authorized to act solely from higher-vibrational orders. When Orpheus asked her who gave these commands, expecting like John Wayne to charge in and stand up to this goon, Death shrugged and told him, "No one knows. The messages of Creation are carried from dimension to dimension, region to region of an invisible bureaucracy like so many tom-toms beating across Afrique."

The only hope was for Cocteau to run the movie backwards, against the wind of time, to undo the damage and restore Orpheus and Eurydice to their myth. The backdraft of reversed hours and days rippling their hair, the characters travelled motionlessly toward the initial incident at *Café Des Poets*—Death and Heurtebise laboring against not only gravity but a more fundamental dimensional force to achieve a nubbin of free will, Cocteau's spoof of Sartre and Camus. "We must, we must," Death shouted. "Without our wills we are nothing."

Afterwards, sparked by such magic, Lindy and I experienced a resurgence of our former spark over tea on Green Street. We chatted away excitedly until moments before curfew and then had to run back to Laura Scales. Shivering as the icy November wind cut through us, she lamented not being able to afford a good coat.

The next morning I went to a store in town and bought her the bushiest overcoat I could find. My heart beating in empathy and terror, I showed up unannounced bearing its enormous box. She was furious at my intrusion, but I impishly handed it to her.

"Think twice now," she said. "Are you sure you still want to be giving me things?"

I nodded perversely. From the outside I could see how foolish I looked, how quickly she was becoming someone else. From the inside I could only blunder on, led by angels or muses.

That evening she called me. She told me how mortified she was to open the box and find the coat.

"I can't stand you, Richard. This is the end. This is really the end."

I stood there in the stairwell holding the phone. My body rang with shock waves. "Do you realize how low it is to try to buy back someone's love when they don't want it?"

I said yes.

She described in agonizing detail how she had to take it into town on her bike, return it to the store, ask that my money be refunded. I told her that she had been freezing, that we were old and close friends, but she said I was making an ass out of myself and, additionally, that she had another date that night. I shouldn't call her again for at least three months. It hadn't worked, she added, just being friends.

I went back to my room, cried briefly; then pulled myself together. I was curious to know how much of me was left. There was something there in the center, thin and stringy, a rag perhaps, but at least I could feel it.

Sometime afterwards I heard a knock. I opened the door and was surprised to see my sophomore-year friend Paul. He was visiting from Clark in nearby Worcester where he was a graduate student in psychology. He heard my woes and said we should walk. I nodded and put on my coat. We traversed the railroad tracks, across the bridge where Lindy and I had accompanied Tripp the previous spring.

I tried to salvage the summer by a description of it, to probe it for a flaw, a clue; to rekindle its glow in my memory. Even as I entertained us I kept dragging out and postponing the conclusion of my narrative. It was as though as long as I could talk I could breathe on the summer's ember and keep it alive.

It was only a story, words, but as long as I held the stage by speaking them, I could nurse the withering play, keep the audience in their seats, extend the reality that was. I dreaded the approaching lesion of meaning and hope, for I never knew how to get past its shadow, how to find myself again.

A story, words—but a landmark in the void.

We continued to Valentine and got in line. I would have a life, I told myself. I would eventually find someone else. In fact Elsie had mentioned introducing me to her "very beautiful friend." I tried to picture who this woman might be. I had a moment of fragile elation, a chance to start over. With our trays we crossed the dining room and found a table. Then I saw in the far corner Lindy sitting with Black. I jumped to my feet. Paul glanced over his shoulder, whistled, then frowned. "Let's get out of here," he said.

We abandoned our meals and crossed the street to Phi Psi. I chose its roof as refuge. We sat there watching males stream toward dinner in the twilight. "It's not that important," I said finally. "If I could see all this differently it would be a vision; it would be beautiful and absurd."

"That's the whole of psychology you're dismissing," he protested.

"Yes, I know. It's why I'm in this state." I lay back and stared at the early bright stars, musing as though from a million miles away. "I used to think back then, when I was a kid, an infant, that my family scared me by something they did. I went through all those years of analysis trying to find the one event."

"The original trauma," he chimed in.

"Now I think it's just who they were—my mother, Bob, Bunny, Paul—each in their own way."

"It always seemed that way to me," Paul agreed. "Just as an objective observer, I didn't find anything about them you would think of as *parents*."

"The thing with Lindy is that she was the one who taught me about family. She gave me that in Aspen. And now tonight—it's like finding my family, being born, having to grow up in a summer, and then losing it, all in one year. It's hard for me to proceed with my life as it is. The road ahead is not broken apart in a simple manner. It's totally broken off in another dimension. Dead end! I don't have any place to go."

"That seems a fair picture," he acknowledged. "So what now?"

"I either jump or try to live."

He shifted half-facetiously, as though to stand in my way. We both laughed. "I don't think you're going to do that, but I'm not sure it's a good idea for you to stay around Phi Psi either. You sound dangerously like someone trying to prove he's sane and rational."

"I know. I'm speeding on the strangeness of tonight, but it's gonna run out."

"And you might not plan on killing yourself, but one way or another you're going to crash."

"I gotta walk that lonesome valley, aye Paul?"

"Yep. But the Four Seasons too: *'Walk like a man from her!'"*

We chuckled. He asked me for Schuy and Dona's number. We went downstairs and he dialed them. He wondered if I could stay there for the night. Dona said they'd come and get me.

I grabbed a toothbrush and some clothes, and we sat in the parking lot waiting. Yes, I was going to crash, but at least the world was moving in a new direction and that would hold my attention for a while. The omnipresent Andy, who had been kicked out of school for drugs, came by and, per usual, tried to convince me to take a cube of LSD with him. He said that it was all ego, illusion anyway. Why not, why not break the through the many-colored dome? He insisted his serum would cure me of whatever was troubling me, would expose the world for what it was.

"Tonight I'm just trying to be human."

"But it's all illusory anyway."

"It may be illusion, but it's also a myth, and unless we live it and make a stand, it will repeat again and again."

"Your choice!"

"That's right," Paul said grumpily. *"His* choice."

Schuy and Dona arrived, looking harried. I started to explain, but she headed me off. "It's not so good where we are either. We're talking about getting divorced."

That surprised me, but after Schuy went to bed she stayed up and explained. "Don't believe his shit about being a tough guy. He said that making love was like breaking a horse, and I'll tell you, I feel very much like a horse that was broken. We've got all of that to work through now, and I doubt we're going to make it."

"Would you rather be where I am?"

"I'm getting there." She gave me a hug and showed me the unheated back room of the cabin.

I slept on a mattress, their collection of blankets and quilts tossed on top of me. Rain gusted against window, an autumnal storm at the exact pitch of my despair. Smothered in homeyness, I drifted off to dream—only to awake with a start. The first birds were chirping. It was way too early, still dark out, the sun an exotic sapphire dissolving into the world.

The storm outside had passed, but the storm within was raging and sought any contact or recognition. Those winged songsters were too beautiful, too intelligent, too implacable, too credulous. I couldn't get them out of my head.

The world was teeming with life—with the courage of a dragon-fly, a chickadee, to face another dawn, the foolishness not to know better. I couldn't stand any of it. To exist was unbearable. I didn't want to know or think.

Then I heard Schuy and Diana arguing, their pitch rising. That gave me a fingerhold on reality and I scurried to get dressed.

Outside, edging into the woods, I tried to pick up a sign, bracing for novelty's end—the crash. But it had already happened.

It was all pain. In all directions all I could feel was pain. No clue anywhere. The natural world seemed to stretch unabated in every direction. This was the heart of Mordor.

And those foolhardy birds were saying, "This is the way you make *Shekhinah*. Did you think it was easy to make *Shekhinah*? Does this look like a world in which anything of value comes easily?" They were singing William Carlos Williams too:

"My heart rouses / thinking to bring you news / of something that concerns you / and concerns many men..., news that men die miserably every day / for lack of...."

I had no parents anymore, no girlfriend, no self, no path, no way in, no out. What was keeping me alive?

I came back. The three of us ate breakfast together while they jousted black humor about their impending separation.

I told them I thought their life was very beautiful, even their arguing was beautiful. I warned them there wouldn't be anything better. They smiled at my naïveté, and Schuy drove me back to Phi Psi on his way to class. A few months later they were divorced, and a year after that he was dead in Illinois, an apparent suicide on a motorcycle.

I packed a few things and set off in the Mustang. In my head was Lindy's lyric once for her lover Steve: *"Try to remember a time in September...."* Its haunting tune imbued me like the clarion of another world—not an ordinary other world but an alternative universe, a Europe ruled by American Indian tribes, myself someone else there *"... when life was an ember...."* I couldn't let go of the melody and the runes that appeared in it automatically like stars at twilight. Its minor chord was an epode, ringing down a corridor, illumining that other life, a different childhood: not me but Jeffrey or Rodney or Keith. I could have been one of them instead.

The notion was magnificent, and it was hollow; it was exquisite and capacious beyond knowing, but it was all somber Septembers, going back to the dawn of consciousness. The cabin in Aspen was as old as Welsh alphabet trees and Central Park autumns of my childhood. I was lost in a grim and grievous miasma. I had always been lost.

All I wanted was to get inside this damn thing—the song, the mellowness, the dreary, streaked-rain, gold/red world, to sustain even its sadness, to become its old age. And sing the words someday from within, like my stepfather when he was young and brought home our first record, *"Cruising down the river / on a Sunday afternoon...."* From there I would follow a radically different path to the present, become the mensch he wanted me to be, able to bear this life, *"a tender and callow fellow"* who could roll with the punches. But that was no longer in play, maybe never was.

I established a single plan. I would go once more to see Lindy. I would try to recover the girl from Aspen. If that failed—as surely it would—I'd continue into the City and meet Elsie's friend. I made the necessary phone calls and then set out on the mission.

Summoned by the Laura Scales switchboard, Lindy stormed downstairs. "What in the world lets you think you can browbeat me!"

But the anteroom was no place to talk, so we went outside and sat on the curb. I told myself melodramatically that at least our unborn children would want me to make one last try.

"I don't think that we're the only people for each other," I said. "But we had something special once, and if we're going to drop it I want us to drop it together." I paused to let her stop me, but she didn't. "I feel as though I haven't seen you since Denver. I've been carrying around this letter—"I held it out for her, but she shook her head as indication she didn't need to see it. "A different Lindy came back on that plane. I can say goodbye if that's what you want, but I don't want to abandon you."

Her response was a gasp of outrage followed by a haughty frown. "I don't believe that kind of stuff," she said, "and you are very unperceptive to keep trying it."

I let the resonance of the car absorb me. I accepted finally that it was over. But instead of going straight into the City I detoured via Kelly at Bard. He sat in the outer room, the sybilline Button at his side. I came as the knight to the throne and told him I was sorry to intrude, but I had two questions to ask and then would be gone. "Go ahead," he said.

The phone rang. As he reached for it he handed me a piece of paper, a poem of Chuck's.

"See if this takes care of the first one."

> *The world (or a world)*
> *is complete*
> *by that I mean*
> *there is no other*
> *world from this vantage but*
> *where the hills cut the scene off*
> *is the end of it there*
> *are no towns*
> *to the west of those mountains*

imaginable voids of darkness
black gulfs of myth where anything is....

When he finished his conversation I told him there was no need now to ask the first question.

"Why don't you rephrase it anyway. Tell me the answer you have gotten."

"Where is the other world that shadows this one? The answer is: There is no other world; everything is here."

He nodded. "Your pain is teaching you well. Your education is accelerated in this extreme state."

"What about Lindy? That's my second question. I think I have given up and am going into New York to see another girl." I was sure, in his own condition of infidelity, he would concur.

"Richard, are you going to be the troubadour all your life," he said, "singing to women on balconies? You must abandon such a role and speak to the consciousness of the woman. Tell her what you have to tell her. Right now you are wasting your dwindling energy in groups of people living dreams, sitting around coffee houses discussing irrelevancies."

His words surprised me. I imagined back at Smith that I was telling her my best truth, but now I realized I was greedy for confirmation, impatient. I was still playing games, a stupid troubadour's role.

"Listen closely," he said, "for what I am about to tell you almost everyone would miss.

"You must not make this woman into a star you cannot reach, although, God knows, you may have an easier time waking in the morning to a clear star than the rest of us having to put together a day from scratch."

I smiled, barely.

"But that is also the astrology of hell. If you can free yourself, then take her away with you and face the risks that come your way. Better those than the meaningless risks of the courtier."

"And what if she won't follow?"

"And what if we knock and the door doesn't open? And what if it won't close? What if the world is destroyed tomorrow? We all live in dread."

I nodded.

"Go to her and tell her what you have to say. That's all there is."

"Is it like breaking a horse? Is that true?"

"No. Sometimes a certain strength is necessary because of the tyranny of words. They do fail or, rather, we fail them. But I wouldn't liken it to breaking a horse. It is more like the electron seizing a positron in the heart of matter. Isn't that what lies at the creation of all things?"

"Yes."

"You have happened upon Brakhage's old riddle: everything is as we want it, if only we knew. That's what Chuck is telling you; he didn't realize he wrote it for you. But he sent it, and you and it arrived minutes apart."

"And what about the girl in the city?"

He shook his head. "Richard, don't ever try to cut your losses. Go back and tell Lindy what you have to say. You have no other course."

"This endless cycle is wearing."

"We're meant to be worn."

Then he raised himself slowly and turned toward the inner rooms. He instructed me to talk to the sybil. "I'll be back."

Button spoke in ellipses, so I told her about the ghost shadow, the *waiura,* that stays connected between people even when they are apart: "It's from Paul Radin, *World of Primitive Man.* The Maori speak of it like, 'Be of good cheer. Our *wairua* are ever with you, although we are far off.'" I wanted to make the charm work if only because it wasn't English or any known etymology.

As twilight fell, old things began to creep across the room.

"I sense a shadow," she piped, "a fright. There's a fright in the room."

"It's probably mine."

"She's not a bad girl," she continued in Delphic *non sequitur,* "just a bitch. We need bitches, though. They cut through the shit we create."

Just then Kelly returned and asked at once who had dispelled the ghost. She pointed to me. He pondered and then restated his message: "People are not interchangeable. Lindy is a girl in

Massachusetts. Go back to her."

Then he cast his usual mudra over my head and bid me farewell.

"How does he know?" I asked her.

"Because he's him."

The shadow had not been dispelled, but it was no longer the enemy. I took it with me into the car and instead of heading for either the City or Massachusetts I turned toward Grossinger's.

It was night-time now. A disorientation like carsickness came over me. In it I felt something alive, a thing with barely a mass or shape, but solid and at my center. I saw Kelly in my mind's eye—Orpheus in the room with Death—and shouted aloud, "He's right! He's right!"

I had solved the sphinx's riddle at last; Lindy was addressing me by picking the one person she knew I most abhorred: Black. She hadn't broken off our connection; she had merely changed its terms. This was the final test. She was parading before me a specter of existential nihilism in order to see if I was committed enough to break through. That was the explanation for her going from the failed relationship with Steve to an irrelevant jerk like Black. She had cast a gauntlet/grail and was waiting to see if I responded. It would prove nothing if she yielded to mere entreaties and gave it away.

A summons from the White Goddess herself! What an honor!

I warned myself that this might be more wishful thinking, a head trip, or, worse, the peak of a manic cycle. Certainly that was how I had been taught: Don't give money to blind men; don't trust strangers. But I had no choice; Kelly had left me none: I had to commend myself to angels and act.

The lights of traffic suddenly fizzed and bloomed into melody, a supernatural order of particles of which I was the core and ordering principle. I turned on the radio just in time to hear the confirming song:

Hello darkness my old friend,
I've come to talk to you again....

The Hotel loomed on the hill ahead, welcoming me always, its wayward son.

Because a vision softly creeping
Took my mind while I was sleeping....

I was aswirl with messages. The doom I had felt was merely the veil, always had been, all my life. I was at the heart of a myth, and there was nothing except these lights and suds exploding all around me. This was the seventh mode, by way of simultaneous affirmation and negation

"She is my moon," I whispered, "and he is the Blackness of my moon."

At the Hotel I stayed for a night and a day, asking nothing more than the thing it was. I walked the golf course at dawn, sat by the dancing glitter lake ... ate in the dining room, greeting everyone with warmth. There was no point in hiding or skulking anymore; I had to act with humility and honor every sentient creature.

In my heart I was back in Aspen, at last with Frodo, unafraid.

I found my father by the ice rink. I told him I might quit school. He stared at me vacantly, his bearded son—stared without recognition: "Do whatever you want. It doesn't matter to me." Then he turned and walked away. That was closure, but he stopped and, looking back at me, got in one more shot: "Go let those phony father figures Borkage and Kelly take care of you now."

He was different from my mother, but it had come down to the same: apathy, disinterest, myopia. I was alone at a scope I hadn't comprehended during all my prior AWOLs, rebellions, and apostasies. I had been alone since I left for college, in truth well before. It was a joke to think that they supported my matriculation, as anything. It was all image and rhetoric. So trapped were they in their own imbroglios they had no interest in or concern for another being. My friend Paul was right; they weren't parents. I had none.

I felt a bone-deep shudder. The prospect ahead was terrifying, if I looked, but I didn't regard the shattered past or project myself into a future. I was in the sacred fire.

I drove back to Amherst the next morning, telling myself to be true, to stay conscious, to finish the leap. I was near the edge of the abyss and would make it or fall.

I called Lindy several times that afternoon, and the next day, but she was never in ("And what if the door does not open...?").

In the evening I went to hear a lecture by Timothy Leary, the messiah of redemption through drugs. I sat upstairs in Johnson Chapel and saw her down in front with Black.

"Maps," Leary announced. "Someone must go out into the wilderness beyond the Mississippis of the mind, like Lewis and Clark, and tell us where the Indian priests are and what lands are inhabitable, what sorts of plants grow and what wisdom animals dwell there." He was talking about the world of LSD, but I imagined other interior worlds our courage might find for us. The medicine herb by itself was forfeit; in naked flesh, fantastic realms lay unexplored.

He reminded us that while our elders were worried about the Russians and Sputnik we had ignored equally vast interior hemispheres. I thought, "Yes, all the years wasted on fizzled *Vanguard* rockets and visionless accelerated science courses, no care at all to real science—that any force in the Universe can be made into any other—which is the singular truth of existence." I imagined our whole troubadour civilization paying homage to a goddess of masks and rings.

Then I took the magic of Leary under the moon and ran across the vast playing fields. I was part of them. I tumbled in the grass and dared the obstacle course to stop me. I climbed the rope, dove through the tire. I called out to Welton: *"I believe as you believe."*

I awoke the next morning on the cusp. I could see my beginning clearly from here. Nothing at all separated me from Dr. Fabian's office or 1220 Park Avenue. I had no images, just the terminus of a line with two ends. I had to keep it that way, there was no margin or leeway left. That span became the locus of points between two towns, Amherst and Northampton—no extraneous scenery, no impedance. I set the stream of matter flowing from one point to another. The whole cosmos rushed by me in a sutra of trees and houses and people. A fluvial loom swallowed landscape and led me to the next node.

I parked near the library and went loping across the campus, seeing everything in flashes and blobs, feeling the air as a force, respecting the presence of gravity. I imagined myself a leopard, with no mentality. I went to the magazine room, linguistics row, the letter "L." I took down a journal, and opened to a page in the Xhosa language. I intoned its unutterable letters, trying to imagine what the spoken flow might sound like.

"Hello, kiddo." She was standing beside me, smiling. She had come to the library too in response to the lecture, but she was looking in the parapsychology section, "P," for a journal of psychedelics.

I told her I was at Leary's talk also. I thought the answer was not drugs but prayer. She nodded.

I suggested we get some coffee and we walked onto Green Street, into a cafeteria. I had been through the rite of eight moons, the last one Black, and now a fine delicate crescent lit not the night but the astral sky.

The jukebox played, *"Sloopy, hang on"* from my quarter. *"Hang on, hang on."* We ordered coffee and pie. She sat there looking at me, "Honey, I don't know where I've been, but I missed you. I'm just glad you came back."

Notes and Acknowledgments

This 2016 paperback of *New Moon* differs from the 1996 hardcover in restoring the text's original shape. To get there I removed the last ninety-eight pages with their twenty-two years' worth of events—all of "The Alchemical Wedding" and "Epilogue." Then I rewrote the book's core, fixing its internal chronology and filling in gaps. Without altering the basic story, cast, or skein of events, I added 170 pages to a shorter timeline (1944-1965). The result is, I hope, finer detail and deeper internalization: certainly more tarot, baseball, and psychoanalysis.

The hardcover had two main problems, not evident to me when I published it. First, its real narrative ended in 1965 (as this version does); the extension brought a shift in tone and voice and lost any real closure. Second, I was too cursory the first time, left too much unsaid. The stories were so melded to me that I didn't realize how much context I needed to tell them. I spent more than twice as much time (about 1400 hours) rewriting them as I spent composing them in the first place.

What is *New Moon's* origin?

In 1987 I began working on my all-but-forgotten high-school novel *Salty and Sandy*. A shapeless spool initiated in 1960 and abandoned in 1964, its status by then was a rubber-banded bundle of pages scotch-taped shut in a box that once held typing paper. I sliced the tape with a utility knife and pulled apart the snug fit. So much time had passed that the rubber bands had dried out, cracked, and melded in Braille-like characters to the title page.

As I encountered the manuscript through fresh eyes, two things jumped out at me. First, I was shocked by how overblown and cumbersome the writing was, especially given the praise it had garnered from teachers and editors of high degree. I wondered how CC thought she and I could turn it into a volume publishable by Viking. It was indulgent and primitive, embarrassingly wussy and asshole in spots.

Yet the text was also guileless and profound, and conveyed the mystery of its times. It captured the imponderable depth and texture of the fifties and early sixties, an era usually disparaged as simplistic and banal in shows like *Leave it to Beaver* and *The Honeymooners.*

The manuscript also lacked any sort of arc, ending abruptly after the teen tour (August 1962). I had endowed the tour with with undue significance, in part to memorialize Betsy, the "salty, sandy" girl, in part to fabricate a novel for Catherine Carver, my "hello-goodbye" editor at Viking who saw a gold mine in adolescent gossip. The two motives converged so that even I couldn't tell the difference. My career goal depended on my romantic proposition, and vice versa.

I worked on *Salty and Sandy* for the next several years, trying to preserve its authenticity and sense of wonder while weeding out pretentiousness and unexamined teen obsessions. I made a new template by shrinking some sections and augmenting others. For instance, I cut an entire chapter, "The Prom and Rod Kanehl" (restoring it in this edition by a page of flashback), and I abridged the teen travelogue. I bolstered other items like my experiences with Dr. Fabian, Color War, and the end of Horace Mann. Then I added writings from college years (1962–1966), extending the timeline to November 1965. I concluded with my 1966 short story "New Moon," adopting its title for the whole book because the manuscript was no longer *Salty and Sandy,* albeit raised from its chrysalis.

Through the process of revision I gave dramatic structure to a coming-of-age journey from my earliest memories to just before my twenty-first birthday.

Then in the early nineties I impulsively expanded *New Moon* by another five years, taking it to 1970 with the three-chapter section entitled "The Alchemical Wedding." On top of that, I added the Epilogue, bringing it to 1987. The material was taken from my other two memoir books, which I had no plans at the time to publish, and from experimental prose works, mainly *Solar Journal, The Continents, Book of the Cranberry Islands, The Provinces,* and *The Long*

Body of the Dream. In 1996 *New Moon* was published in cloth with a dust jacket, Though it looked like the real thing, it was actually a prefiguring of this book (and the other memoirs in the trilogy).

I put so much work into trying to excavate my raw testimony—what novelist Jonathan Lethem in his blurb called a "defenseless consciousness uncovering itself and the world simultaneously"—from the snarled morass of teen artifice and inflation that I thought that that was *all I* needed to do. Once I accomplished the basics of that, I went ahead with publication. I overlooked the potential for writing a far richer and more textured book.

Years later when I read the e-book proof, I was disappointed that my more current insights and portrayals were missing. I kept looking for passages I knew I had written but couldn't find there. I had subliminally nursed a fantasy that the pages of every copy of the book were being updated by magic as my insights in other books got subtler.

Of course, the text was right where I left it. This new version has most of the later passages, as I have spliced in and adapted snippets from *The Bardo of Waking Life; 2013: Raising the Earth to the Next Vibration; Dark Pool of Light (Volume Three): The Crisis and Future of Consciousness; The Night Sky: Soul and Cosmos; The New York Mets: Myth, Ethnography, and Subtext);* and an essay "A Phenomenology of Panic" in *(Panic: Origins, Insight, and Treatment)*.

At the time of publication in 1996, I dubbed it a nonfiction novel. It was (and still is) halfway between a memoir and a novel. All my key decisions were novelistic and honored the genre. Like a memoir, though, the book is scrupulously true, or meant to be, but not always 100 percent *factual*. I didn't make up events or characters, but occasionally combined them or shifted a timeline or chronology to achieve novelistic ellipsis and tension.

For my psychoanalytic overview, I chose the veridicality of a "case history" over faithfulness to my understanding at the time.

The characters in this book are just that: characters. They are my own fictionalized versions of people, personifications based on some of their traits as I experienced them, occasionally composited with features and words of other people, even prochronistically. In that way it *is* a novel.

Ask any of the folks who pass through this narrative to provide his or her account of what happened and it will likely digress from mine, in some cases radically so. If you recognize anyone from life, it is the figure on whom I am basing my character, not the person himself or herself. I am telling no one's truth but my own.

New Moon is the first book in a triptych. Its story continues in my two other memoirs: *Episodes in Disguise of a Marriage* and *Out of Babylon*.

The 1996 edition of *New Moon* is a record of the enchantments through which one passes in a life; in my case a fifties American childhood (board games, candy bars, cherished toys, etc.) followed by school daze, baseball, summer camp; then the watershed of adolescence, dating, romance—initiation, apprenticeship, marriage, kids, career. Each enchantment breaks a prior trance while imposing another.

That *precis* is still accurate, though this 2016 edition tracks only through the beginnings of apprenticeship.

Out of Babylon weaves tales from five generations of my family, beginning with the imagined lives of my great-grandparents and concluding with the adolescent years of my children. It tells my brother Jonathan's story in his own voice, borrowing from his writings and letters, and relates the rise and fall of Grossinger's. Its central theme is "Why do people in families treat each other so badly while claiming to love them?" Its title is taken from a reggae song that Jon invoked ("One Step Forward," Max Romeo and the Upsetters) as a canticle to our growing up on upper Park Avenue.

Episodes in Disguise of a Marriage recounts the forging a marriage out of a mythologized courtship while exploring the deeper relationship between sexuality and spirituality. It maintains the frankness of *New Moon,* but tackles adult problems and crises, falling somewhere among such chronicles as Robert Creeley's *The Island,* D. H. Lawrence's *Women in Love,* and perhaps a less vulgar and less narcissistic—I hope—version of the popular confessional novel of the era, Erica

Jong's *Fear of Flying*. I was espousing Robert Kelly's mytho-erotic themes, the radical truth-telling of fellow poets like Charlie Vermont and Bill Pearlman (notably the latter's *Inzorbital Freak*), and the free-wheeling aesthetics of some of my loonier Goddard College students, Rob Brezsny, Art Cole, and Sheppard Powell.

Episodes picked up nuances from movies of the time too like *The Graduate, Annie Hall,* and *Blume in Love,* but with Creeley's gravitas and narrative diaphonousness replacing comedy and shtick, also with the nascent metaphysical awe that inspired *New Moon*.

If you were to imagine *New Moon* continuing through the hippie era with the same degree of frankness and romantic-magical inquiry, that would be *Episodes in Disguise of a Marriage,* not the 1996 appendage.

My thanks to Lindy Hough for her thorough line and content editing of the revised text, to Kathy Glass for her meticulous editing of the first edition, to Lauren Harrison for her meticulous summary edit, to Louis Swaim for his wise editorial shepherding, to Jasmine Hromjak for her lovely redesign, to my one-time Goddard student Jamie Rauchman for his spot-on cover art, to Susan Quasha for painstakingly re-laying the mosaics from my last pass after galleys, to Douglas Reil and Janet Levin for supporting my many triturations through ever finer sieves, to Julia Kent for introducing the book to the world, to Lydia Schwartz-Salant and Tim McKee for their editorial suggestions, and to Fred Kuriger for his generous fact check.

See www.richardgrossinger.com/2015/11/new-moon-afterword/ for an enhanced version of these notes.

ABOUT THE AUTHOR

A native of New York City, Richard Grossinger attended Amherst College and the University of Michigan, receiving a BA in English (1966) and a PhD in anthropology (1975).

He wrote his doctoral thesis on his fieldwork with fishermen in Eastern Maine, after which he taught for two years at the University of Maine at Portland-Gorham and five years at Goddard College in Vermont.

With his wife, Lindy Hough, he is cofounding publisher of North Atlantic Books and its forerunner, the journal *Io*. His works include early books of experimental prose; a series of titles on holistic medicine, cosmology, and embryology; two memoirs; and recent books re-exploring these themes, related topics, and aspects of contemporary politics and pop culture.

After living in Berkeley, California, from 1976 for thirty-eight years, Grossinger and Hough moved back to Portland, Maine, in 2014. They have also lived part-time in Manset, Maine, since 2001. Their children are Robin Grossinger, a historical geographer at San Francisco Estuary Institute, and Miranda July, a writer, film director, and conceptual artist.

For more information, see www.richardgrossinger.com.

OTHER BOOKS BY RICHARD GROSSINGER

EARLY EXPERIMENTAL PROSE

Solar Journal: Oecological Sections
Spaces Wild and Tame
Book of the Earth and Sky
The Continents
Book of the Cranberry Islands
The Provinces
The Long Body of the Dream
The Book of Being Born Again into the World
The Windy Passage from Nostalgia
The Slag of Creation
Mars: A Science Fiction Vision
Early Field Notes from the All-American Revival Church
Martian Homecoming at the All-American Revival Church
The Unfinished Business of Doctor Hermes

BOOKS ON MEDICINE, COSMOLOGY, EMBRYOLOGY, AND CONSCIOUSNESS

Planet Medicine: Origins
Planet Medicine: Modalities
Homeopathy: The Great Riddle
The Night Sky: Soul and Cosmos
Embryogenesis: Species, Gender, and Identity
Embryos, Galaxies, and Sentient Beings: How the Universe Makes Life
Migraine Auras: When the Visual World Fails
Dark Pool of Light, Vol 1, The Neuroscience, Evolution, and Ontology of Consciousness
Dark Pool of Light, Vol 2, Consciousness in Psychospiritual and Psychic Ranges
Dark Pool of Light, Vol 3, The Crisis and Future of Consciousness
Bottoming Out the Universe: Karma, Reincarnation, and Personal Identity (in process)

CURRENT TRILOGY

New Moon: A Coming-of-Age Tale
Episodes in Disguise of a Marriage (in process)
Out of Babylon (new edition in process)

OTHER ESSAY COLLECTIONS

Waiting for the Martian Express: Cosmic Visitors, Earth Warriors,
    Luminous Dreams
The New York Mets: Ethnography, Myth, and Subtext

EARLY AUGHTS TRILOGY OF SHORT ESSAYS AND LITERARY PIECES

On the Integration of Nature: Post-9/11 Biopolitical Notes
The Bardo of Waking Life
2013: Raising the Earth to the Next Vibration

AS EDITOR OR COEDITOR

The Alchemical Tradition in the Late Twentieth Century
Baseball I Gave You All the Best Years of My Life
Ecology and Consciousness
The Temple of Baseball
The Dreamlife of Johnny Baseball
Into the Temple of Baseball
Nuclear Strategy and the Code of the Warrior
Olson-Melville Sourcebook: The Mediterranean
Olson-Melville Sourcebook: The New Found Land
Pluto: New Horizon for a Lost Horizon—Astronomy, Astrology,
    Mythology